D1286562

The Blackwell Dictionary of Eastern Christianity

The Blackwell Dictionary of Eastern Christianity

Edited by

Ken Parry, David J. Melling
Dimitri Brady, Sidney H. Griffith &
John F. Healey

Editorial consultant
John R. Hinnells

Foreword by Rt Revd Kallistos Ware

B BLACKWELL
Publishers

Copyright © Blackwell Publishers 1999

Editorial matter and arrangement copyright © Ken Parry, David J. Melling, Dimitri Brady, Sidney H. Griffith and John F. Healey 1999

First published 1999

2 4 6 8 10 9 7 5 3 1

Blackwell Publishers Ltd
108 Cowley Road
Oxford OX4 1JF
UK

Blackwell Publishers Inc.
350 Main Street
Malden, Massachusetts 02148
USA

British Library Cataloguing in Publication Data

A CIP catalogue record for this book is available from the British Library.

Library of Congress Cataloging-in-Publication Data

The Blackwell dictionary of Eastern Christianity / edited by Ken Parry
    ...[et al.]; editorial consultant, John R. Hinnells : foreword by Kallistos Ware.
        p.   cm.
        Includes bibliographical references and index.
        ISBN 0–631–18966–1 (hardcover : alk. paper)
        1. Eastern churches–Dictionaries. I. Parry, Kenneth, 1945–
II. Hinnells, John R.
BX100.7.B53 1999   93–33150
281'.5'03–dc21   CIP

Typeset in 10.5 on 12.5 pt Ehrhardt by Kolam Information Services, Pvt. Ltd, Pondicherry, India

Printed in Great Britain by TJ International, Trecerus Industrial Estate, Padstow, Cornwall.

This book is printed on acid-free paper.

◆ Contents ◆

◆ The Contributors ◆

AHA	A. H. Armstrong	Formerly Classical Studies, University of Liverpool
AK	Agalaia Kasdagli	History, University of Crete
AL	Andrew Louth	Theological Studies, University of Durham
AW	Alan Walker	Vicar in Hampstead Garden Suburb, London
BM	Bohdan Matwijczuk	Ukrainian Autocephalic Church, Rochdale
BS	Bryan D. Spinks	Yale Divinity School, New Haven
D	Igumen Deiniol	Church of the Pokrov, Bleinau-Ffestiniog, Wales
DB	Dimitri Brady	Chaplain to International Students in Higher Education, Manchester
DC	David Collins	Russian and Slavonic Studies, University of Leeds
DM	David J. Melling	Senior Research Fellow, Manchester Metropolitan University
DT	David Turner	Byzantinist, Athens
E	Archimandrite Ephrem	Middle Eastern Studies, University of Manchester
EB-S	Elisabeth Behr-Segal	Writer on Orthodoxy, France
ES	Egor S. Shishigin	Yakutsk State University, Yakutia
FB	Fani Balamoti	Archaeology, University of Birmingham
FC	Felix Corley	Writer on Eastern Europe, England
GB	George Bebawi	St John's College, Nottingham
GJ	George G. Joseph	Econometrics, University of Manchester
GS	Graham Speake	Writer on Orthodoxy, England
GW	Gabriele Winkler	Comparative Liturgiology, University of Tübingen
JF	John Fenwick	Rector of Chorley, England
JFC	J. F. Coakley	Near Eastern Languages and Civilizations, Harvard University

◆ The Contributors ◆

JH	John F. Healey	Middle Eastern Studies, University of Manchester
JM	John A. McGuckin	Union Theological Seminary, New York
JP	Jaroslav Pelikan	History, Yale University
JS	John Stuart	Sotheby's, London
JnS	Jonathan Sutton	Russian and Slavonic Studies, University of Leeds
JCS	James C. Skedros	Graduate Theological Union, Berkeley
KL	Konstantin Lerner	Institute of Asian and African Studies, Hebrew University of Jerusalem
KP	Ken Parry	Centre for Continuing Education, University of Manchester
LjK	Lj. Kojic	Serbian art historian, Belgrade
LR	Lyn Rodley	Society for the Promotion of Hellenic Studies, London
MH	Muriel Heppell	Writer on Orthodoxy, England
MJB	Monica J. Blanchard	Institute of Christian Oriental Research, Catholic University of America
MK	Manfred Kropp	Johannes Gutenberg University, Mainz
MS	Mark Sheridan	College of St Anselm, Rome
MV	Maria Vorozhishcheva	Sociology, University of Manchester
NK	Nana Kiladze	Georgian scholar, London
RT	Robert Taft	Pontifical Institute of Oriental Studies, Rome
RWT	Robert W. Thomson	Oriental Institute, University of Oxford
S	Abba Seraphim	Metropolitan of Glastonbury, London
SA	Shafiq Abouzayd	Oriental Institute, University of Oxford
SB	Sebastian Brock	Oriental Institute, University of Oxford
SH	Sergei Hackel	Writer on Orthodoxy, England
SHG	Sidney H. Griffith	Institute of Christian Oriental Research, Catholic University of America
SK	Serge Keleher	Greek Catholic priest, Dublin
SL	S. N. C. Lieu	History, Macquarrie University, Sydney
SM	S. A. Mousalimas	Pembroke College, University of Oxford
TS	Tomaš Špidlik	Pontifical Institute of Oriental Studies, Rome
TW	Tom Winnifrith	English and Comparative Literary Studies, University of Warwick
VM	Vladimir Moss	Writer on Orthodoxy, England
ZG	Zaga Gavrilović	Institute for Advanced Research in the Humanities, University of Birmingham

◆ Foreword ◆

Rt Revd Kallistos Ware

'How varied is the appearance of human faces!' said Prince Vladimir Monomakh of Kiev. 'Though we should gather together all human beings throughout the world, yet there is none with the same appearance, but by God's wisdom each one of them is different.' Every human person possesses free choice, and so each is unique. This is true, moreover, not only of individuals but of communities; they display an inexhaustible variety.

Here, within the covers of a single volume, the communities of Eastern Christendom are presented in their full variety. *The Blackwell Dictionary of Eastern Christianity* attempts to do justice to the many-sided complexity of the Christian East, whether Chalcedonian or non-Chalcedonian, whether Catholic or Orthodox. At the same time it seeks to identify what the different groups share in common – 'Only connect!' as E. M. Forster said – and thus to reveal the one root under the many branches.

The editors have included within their purview all the main aspects of the Eastern churches: doctrine, worship, history, art, music and hagiography. They attempt to convey the communal and family spirit of Eastern Christianity, its popular ethos, its involvement with the daily life of the people. And they do not neglect the ever-expanding presence of Eastern Christians in the contemporary West.

This is a book that describes not only the past but the present. The editors underline the deep importance of tradition in the outlook of Eastern Christians, but they show also how this tradition is alive and dynamic. 'Tradition represents the critical spirit of the Church,' states the Russian theologian Vladimir Lossky; and the great Romanian professor of dogmatics Archpriest Dumitru Staniloae calls tradition 'not a sum of propositions learnt by heart but a lived experience'. Such also is the standpoint of the *Dictionary*. It makes clear the loyalty of Eastern Christians to the past, their sense of unbroken continuity with the church of the apostles and the early martyrs, but it emphasizes also that this is a *living* continuity.

In that mysterious work *The Shepherd*, written in Greek by a certain Hermas perhaps a hundred years after the death of Christ, the author describes how he received a double vision of the church. He sees her first as an old woman and then as a tower. He is impressed by the venerable age of the woman: 'She was created before all things,' he is told, 'and because of her the world was made.' But in the second part of his vision the church appears to him as a tower that is still unfinished, to which fresh stones are continually being added. Thus for Hermas the church is old yet young, unchanging yet immersed in the flow of time and history. The editors of the *Dictionary* have sought to do justice to both aspects of Hermas's vision, to both the old woman and the unfinished tower.

It is my hope that this *Dictionary* will convey to its readers a sense not so much of the remoteness of Eastern Christianity but rather of its immediacy and its relevance. In the modern world the terms 'Eastern' and 'Western' have in large measure lost their meaning. It is true that Eastern Christians are keenly, indeed at times excessively, devoted to their local traditions and their national distinctiveness. But what matters far more about the Christian East is its universality, its catholic and ecumenical significance; and it is precisely this that gives to the present *Dictionary* its special value.

Over the past fifty years there has been a truly remarkable growth of interest in the Christian East, and a comprehensive work of reference such as the *Blackwell Dictionary of Eastern Christianity* has long been needed. Here is a book written with clarity, accessible to the non-specialist and the beginner; yet here also is a book in which those already familiar with the Eastern churches may discover much to surprise them and to evoke their sense of wonder.

◆ Preface ◆

The editors would like to thank Professor John Hinnells, formerly of the School of Oriental and African Studies, London, and now research professor in the University of Derby, for his help and advice during the early stages of planning this volume. Thanks for help and advice are also due to Professor John Elsworth of the Department of Russian Studies, University of Manchester. We would also like to thank Mr Constantine Leventis for his generous donation towards the cost of Father Aidan's line drawings. We trust that the inclusion of these line drawings will enhance the usefulness of this reference work to our readers.

Sadly, as the *Blackwell Dictionary of Eastern Christianity* was on its way to press, a distinguished contributor, Professor Hilary Armstrong, died. He was a fine scholar and teacher and a remarkable man whose contribution to the study of later Platonism was of seminal importance, especially to students of Eastern Christianity. His work invites a new approach to the relation between philosophy and Christian thought in late antiquity and the early medieval period, and will long remain a milestone.

ΑΙωνΙα σου ΖμνΖ, ΑξιομακΑριστε καΙ ΑεΙμνηστε Αδελφὲ Ζμων.

We offer sincere thanks to all the contributors and to Blackwell's editorial staff for their stalwart support.

THE EDITORS

♦ This Book and How to Use It ♦

The *Blackwell Dictionary of Eastern Christianity* contains nearly seven hundred articles written by an international team of fifty contributors, many of whom are the leading authorities in their fields. It is a book for scholars and students, but equally and importantly it is a book for Eastern Christians and for anyone interested in learning more about Eastern Christianity.

♦ The coverage of the *Dictionary* ♦

The *Dictionary* is about some of the major living traditions of Christianity and some which are very little known. Its articles cover Eastern Orthodox, Eastern Catholic, Oriental and Oriental Orthodox churches, and Eastern churches whose roots lie partly in the Reformation, as well as dissident Eastern churches and sects. The *Dictionary* presents the Eastern traditions of Christianity in terms Eastern Christians will recognize and can own, not simply in terms of Western Christian interests and a Western view of Christian history. The Christian East is not a variant or a derivative of the Christian West.

The articles in the *Dictionary* are written by historians, theologians, scholars of liturgy and iconography, art historians, linguists, philosophers, patrologists, and musicians. They represent many different approaches to the study of Eastern Christianity. No attempt has been made in this *Dictionary* to impose uniformity on the work of the contributors. This is most noticeable in the spelling of names of people and places. Where an established English version of a person's name is in common use, it has normally been used in the *Dictionary*. Where a Greek name is often Latinized, a decision has had to be made whether to retain the Latinized form or to restore the Greek. Many contributors have used conventional English versions of names; some, and for serious reasons, have used, for example, Arabic, Ge'ez, Greek, Russian, Syriac or Ukrainian versions of names. Respect for cultural and linguistic diversity demands respect for diversity of linguistic usage. Indeed, exactly how a particular person or place is named can be a significant way in which speakers and writers assert their ethnic or religious identity. It is for this reason that biblical names are generally given in their Septuagint or Vulgate forms, not in the forms familiar in the English-speaking world from the Authorized Version. The Septuagint, the Greek translation of the Old Testament traditionally attributed to seventy-two Jewish scholars working in Alexandria in the reign of Ptolemy Philadelphus (284–246 BC), and certainly complete by the early second century BC, has always been the Old Testament of the Eastern Orthodox world; it contains a number of books recognized in the East as deutero-canonical, most, but not all, of which are included in the Roman Catholic Bible, but are regarded by Protestants as Apocrypha. Where biblical references might be confusing, both Septuagint and Authorized Version names of books are given.

The great majority of Eastern Christians belong to the Eastern Orthodox tradition. Reflecting this, the worship, iconography and hagiography of the Eastern Orthodox are represented by a particularly wide range of articles. The lives of the saints have an important role in Eastern Christian lay spirituality. The pages of the *Dictionary* offer an introduction to many categories of saint, some unfamiliar to the West. Some of the famous saints of the East are discussed, but many figures little known in the West have also been included, among them recent models of sanctity.

Inevitably, the *Dictionary* covers only a selection of possible topics. A serious attempt has been made to present that information which will be of the greatest use to the greatest number of users, while at the same time ensuring the articles cover those topics the reader would have particular difficulty finding treated in an accessible form elsewhere.

♦ The articles and the cross-references ♦

The articles are there to read, to browse and to use as a basic source of information about the different Eastern Christian churches. The longer articles put many terms, concepts, people and events into context. They offer a way of relating things to each other, of tracing their historical background, of making useful comparisons and exploring unfamiliar connections. The system of cross-references leads to related topics, filling out the background of an issue, offering further information, raising new questions.

♦ The index ♦

The index is the key to the *Dictionary*. The index lists every important name and topic that appears in the *Dictionary*. It lists many important terms and concepts that do not have specific entries of their own but are dealt with at different places in the text. It shows the full range of articles where a particular topic is mentioned. It helps you find the word you are looking for when it occurs in a different spelling or a different language. The index is the place to begin a search; it will send you to all the articles that discuss the topic you are looking for, and the cross-references in the articles will help you explore further.

♦ Bibliography ♦

Many articles contain suggestions for further reading. Each list of suggested reading begins with the most recent book or article suggested.

Bibliographical references vary in the amount of detail provided. Some small publications, for example, do not give their publisher, but are important as rare or even unique sources of information.

Writers referring to this *Dictionary* are advised to abbreviate its title as *DEC*.

♦ Introduction ♦

The need for a *Dictionary of Eastern Christianity* has long been felt; and yet problems arise as soon as we use the adjective 'Eastern'. Neither 'Eastern' nor 'Western' has a constant meaning. To Eastern Christians, 'Eastern' is a term expressing their identity and heavily laden with positive value. East is the direction of prayer, the biblical location of the earthly paradise, the source of the dawn and of the world's enlightening, the quarter from which the Magi came, the first gentiles to seek out Christ. To Western Christians, the term 'Eastern' can carry a sense of the exotic, the remote, the 'other', that which is outside the normal and normative. The issues raised by 'Orientalism' have until now been confined mainly to discussions concerning non-Christian religions and cultures, but Orientalism can affect the perception and study of Eastern Christianity. When Westerners come to look at their fellow Christians in the East, they often exhibit attitudes similar to those they show towards Eastern non-Christian cultures and religions: a fascination with the exotic or a presumption of superiority, condescending to an alien reality approached with a notable lack of empathy.

As Christianity spread throughout the Roman empire from its birthplace in Syria, it also spread into the Persian empire, to Ethiopia and as far as India. Significantly, the population of Syria included both speakers of Greek, mainly in areas close to the coast, and speakers of Syriac or Aramaic. Initially Greek, the common language of the Roman East, was the main vehicle for the transmission of Christianity; but by the fourth century, as the new religion moved eastwards, it was joined in this role by Syriac, in effect a dialect of the Aramaic that was for a long period the language of administration in the Persian empire. It was, however, the Roman empire, once it had adopted Christianity as the state religion, that became for centuries the heartland of Christianity.

Even in that early period, there was for the Romans at first an exotic element in Christianity. Romans of the imperial period were often attracted by Eastern cults, many of which were happy to initiate Roman adherents and to receive their patronage; even Judaism opened its synagogue doors both to converts and to associates who shared something of Jews' beliefs and ethical standards as 'god-fearers'. Thus early Christian evangelists like the Apostle Paul had a ready-made audience.

♦ Introduction ♦

Before Constantine the Great began to rebuild the city of Byzantium in 324, the main centres of Christianity were at Rome, Alexandria, Antioch and Ephesus. With the establishment of an eastern capital in Nicomedia the political and cultural fulcrum of the empire had already shifted to the east. The foundation of Constantinople, the New Rome, on the site of the former Byzantium gave the empire a new centre on the acropolis of which the Christian emperor and the bishop of his capital both had their residences. Constantinople became the seat of imperial Christianity, and this status was recognized in the council held there in 381, which gave its bishop precedence immediately after the pope of Old Rome.

Christianity rapidly became the state religion, with all the privileges and hazards associated with closeness to the centre of power. In effect, the church sacralized the Roman empire. When Julian the Apostate became emperor in 361 he tried to reverse the process of Christianization by reasserting pagan values. He forbade Christian professors to teach the classics, arguing that they had renounced that inheritance. Christian theologians such as Basil the Great were outraged by this imperial policy. Basil argued forcefully that Hellenic culture belonged as much to Christians as to pagans, and in doing so laid claim on behalf of the church to the ancient world's entire heritage of art, literature, science, medicine and philosophy. The efforts of Basil and the other Cappadocians saw the establishment on firm foundations of Christian Hellenism, a Christianity confident in the exploitation of the cultural and intellectual resources of its pre-Christian past.

The Christianization of Hellenism and the Hellenization of Christianity have sometimes been criticized as a corruption of the original gospel. Such criticisms are inevitably based on a Christianity which repudiates the canonicity of the Septuagint and has scant respect for the Jewish Hellenism of the deutero-canonical books of the Old Testament, which were excluded from the inspired scriptures and designated 'Apocrypha'. This Jewish Hellenism produced its finest flowering in the philosophical and exegetical works of Philo of Alexandria, himself a major influence on Christian thought. For Eastern Christians, familiar with the Septuagint and honouring it as an inspired translation, Christian Hellenism has clear biblical roots.

By the early sixth century Latin and Greek had become languages of diverging cultures. In the West, invasions of the Arian Goths caused political and social turmoil, while in the East the church was embroiled in theological controversies. Although Rome and Constantinople were normally united in defence of the same doctrines through the fifth and sixth centuries, their actions to preserve what they saw as orthodoxy contributed to the establishment of separated churches in Egypt, Syria and Armenia. All sides in the theological controversies of the period sought to invoke imperial support against their opponents.

Syrian Christianity had early adopted Syriac as the vehicle for its distinctive, austere and strongly literary religious culture. In many ways the poem became for the Syrians what the icon was to become for the Greeks. Branches of Syrian Christianity were firmly established in Persia, Arabia and India, and a related tradition, though hierarchically linked with the Coptic church, in Ethiopia. The widespread missionary outreach of the Church of the East spread Syrian Christianity throughout central Asia and as far as China by the mid-seventh century.

The loss of imperial patronage and communion with the Byzantine church did not inhibit the vitality of either tradition of Oriental Christianity, the Church of the East or the family of Oriental Orthodox churches, Armenian, Coptic, Ethiopian and Syrian Orthodox. Indeed, it may well have had a liberating effect in promoting vernacular literature and independent missionary work outside the boundaries of the empire, though church divisions were to be exploited, first by the Persians and later by the Muslims and the Mongols. Under Persian rule, the continued symphony of the Byzantine church with the Byzantine empire sometimes raised questions as to the loyalty of Christian subjects.

The rise of Islam from the seventh century radically changed the political and religious character of the eastern Mediterranean. Christians were now officially ranked as 'people of the book', protected subjects of the Muslim power, but were bound by social and legal restrictions. In the first centuries of Muslim rule Christians remained prominent in state administration, cultural and intellectual life, and Christian ministers, civil servants, scholars, teachers and doctors played a significant role in shaping Islamic civilization. Syrian Christianity became the culture of transmission, bringing the literature, philosophy, science and medicine of the ancient world to the Muslims, who in turn, via the Jews of Spain, handed it on to the Latin West.

During the same period the Church of the East continued to spread with remarkable success throughout Central Asia and into China; under Islam, it was able for the first time to establish bishoprics in former Byzantine territory, though these did not survive. The Syrian Orthodox also engaged in substantial missionary work under the first centuries of Muslim rule, directly rivalling the Church of the East. The Copts had already been active in the evangelization of Nubia, had strongly supported the christianization of Ethiopia and may well have travelled to the western edges of the Roman empire.

The theological battles of the fifth century had ended hopes for a united Christian commonwealth. Constantine's vision of one empire united by one religion never became a reality. Religious divisions were exacerbated by the punitive actions of the state. In the Near East, monotheism and theocracy triumphed not with Christianity but with Islam.

The consequences of vast territorial loss to Islam were somewhat mitigated by the remarkable success of Byzantine missions to the north, culminating in the conversion of Rus in the tenth century. The Slavs in particular were wooed through diplomatic and missionary activity alike, with the result that in the ninth century whole nations officially converted to Byzantine Christianity. Cyril and Methodius, two brothers from Thessaloniki, worked among the Khazars and in Greater Moravia. They were the most important in a succession of missionaries who worked to bring the South Slavs and then the Eastern Slavs into the Christian church. Rome and Constantinople were often rivals in this enterprise; Byzantine missionaries were pushed out of Greater Moravia but successfully established Bulgaria as a base for further evangelism.

The conflict between Latin and Byzantine missionaries was the context of a bizarre dispute over liturgical language. In an attempt to discredit the enterprise begun by Cyril and Methodius in response to the Moravian request for a Slavonic liturgy, some Latin clergy protested at the Byzantine missionaries' use of the vernacular, arguing that only Latin, Greek and Hebrew should be used in the liturgy. This was denounced in the East as the heresy of trilingualism. In an earlier period the coming of Christianity to Armenia and Georgia had led to the creation of new alphabets to serve the translation of Christian texts, so that the church had brought literacy to the Caucasus. The creation of a Slavonic alphabet repeated this process for a large area of Eastern Europe: like the Armenians and Georgians, the Slavs rapidly developed their own written Christian literature.

From 731 the Roman papacy increasingly repudiated Byzantine tutelage. The creation of the Holy Roman Empire by the popes represented adherence to a view of church and imperial authority utterly alien to that of the East. The First Crusade, launched by Pope Urban II in 1095, ostensibly to bolster Byzantine power and wrest the Holy Land from the Muslims, succeeded in occupying the Holy Land and setting up Frankish states, but was marked by the contempt the crusaders showed towards Eastern Christians, Muslims and Jews alike. The violence and brutality of the Fourth Crusade, culminating in the sack of Constantinople in 1204, poisoned relations between Rome and the Orthodox East. For fifty-seven years thereafter a Latin patriarch presided over the church of Constantinople, while the Byzantine church established alternative centres at Nicea and Arta. Paradoxically, the emperor who recaptured Constantinople, Michael VIII Palaiologos (1258–82), attempted to reunite the Byzantine church with Rome at the Second Council of Lyons by submitting a profession of faith that owed nothing to Eastern tradition and everything to papal diplomacy. He won little support and made many martyrs. The Council of Florence in 1439 was another imperially sponsored attempt to reunite the Roman and Byzantine churches. It failed. The rift was not to be healed by concessions on matters of doctrine. The emperor had deceived himself into believing that the pope could deliver military and material support from the West to stave off the Ottoman threat. The pope proved generous and did what he could, but it was very little. Rome had sought to bring the Greeks under papal obedience; the Byzantine emperor Constantine XI (1448–53) and his last patriarch, Gregory II Mamas, died in communion with Rome, but the Greek church as a whole remained sternly opposed to union. The Russian church was even more obdurately opposed.

The fall of Constantinople to the Ottomans in 1453 and the flight of Greek scholars to Italy accelerated the progress of the Renaissance. Italian humanists were captivated by classical civilization and by the learning of the Byzantine Greeks. One of the first Greek texts to be translated into Latin in the Renaissance period (*c.* 1410), and one of the earliest to be printed (1470), was Basil the Great's *Discourse to Young Christians on Studying the Greek Classics*. Here was a Greek father with impeccable theological credentials advocating, albeit with qualifications, the study of pagan literature. This was an ideal choice to start the printing presses of Western humanism rolling.

After the fall of Constantinople in 1453 the Ottomans gradually reunited the ancient Christian East under their rule until only the Orthodox north remained free from Ottoman domination. Here the hegemony of the Tatars and Mongols was broken in the sixteenth century by Ivan IV, the Terrible, of Moscow, enabling Great Russia progressively to claim the patronage of all the Christian East. The establishment of the patriarchate of Moscow in 1589 gave formal recognition to the new status and role of the Orthodox north. The sense of the religious destiny of Holy Russia was strong enough to bring about a major and permanent schism, when Patriarch Nikon attempted in the 1650s to reform the liturgical life of the church to conform to what he believed were the best Greek norms. In spite of the consequent Old Believer schism and the rise of the dissident Russian sects, from the sixteenth century onwards many Eastern Christians of the Ottoman empire increasingly looked to Russia for financial and spiritual support. However, Western culture was exercising a growing influence on Russia, culminating in the reforms of Peter the Great which included the abolition of the patriarchate in 1721, the effective incorporation of the church hierarchy into the state apparatus and the introduction of French as the language of the court. This movement was paralleled by a distancing of the intelligentsia of the Orthodox world from the Eastern church.

The pattern of administration of the Ottoman empire, where the Christians were ruled as *dhimmi* communities, virtually subordinate, non-territorial nations under their own chief hierarchs, had a lasting effect on Eastern Christian identity and on relations among Eastern Christian communities. The so-called *milet* system totalized the identity of each community, making it at once a religious, a legal, a social and a cultural entity: in effect, a nation defined by religion, not geography. This system gave enormous power over the Eastern Orthodox of the Ottoman empire to the patriarchate of Constantinople, which now ruled over once independent churches. Rival communities sought external links, some primarily with Russia, others with the West. Groups of Eastern Christians under Muslim and under Catholic rule sought security and support through union with Rome, and in the seventeenth and eighteenth centuries a number of Eastern rite Catholic churches came into existence, their relations with the papacy and the Latin church modelled on those established by the Maronites in the crusading period.

One outcome of this shift of allegiance was the founding of an Orthodox theological academy at Kiev in 1615 under Peter Mogila. The academy's use of adapted Counter-Reformation theological textbooks, intended to arm the Orthodox against Catholic and Protestant propaganda, produced generations of Orthodox clergy familiar with Latin and sharing the theological sophistication of their Roman Catholic counterparts. Protestant theology, too, had an impact on the Orthodox East, most famously in the case of the Calvinistic writings of Ecumenical Patriarch Cyril Lucaris.

With few exceptions, the observations of eighteenth- and nineteenth-century Western travellers to the Balkans and the Near East make sad reading. They saw the clergy of the region as uneducated and out of touch with events in the West. The Western travellers themselves come across as haughty and unsympathetic to the plight of the Christian communities they write about. Their jaundiced view of the Christian East is part and parcel of an emerging 'Orientalism' which refused – and refuses – to acknowledge the possibility of there existing equally valid but different systems of values.

Even at the start of the twentieth century we find Western travellers to Eastern Europe indulging their interest in the quaint and curious, and publishing books with such titles as: *Through Savage Europe, Being the Narrative of a Journey throughout the Balkan States and European Russia* (1907), and *Macedonia, A Plea for the Primitive* (1921). Nor was the application of such epithets as 'savage' and 'primitive' by any means restricted to the peoples of the Balkans; they were applied to any society or culture which did not conform to Western ideals. Even today the Western imagination still finds plenty in Eastern Europe to satisfy its pursuit of the 'primitive'.

The church historian Adolf Harnack, writing in the nineteenth century, claimed that from the seventh century onwards 'independent theology had been extinguished in the churches of the East' and that 'the history of dogma came to an end in the Greek Church a thousand years ago'. Harnack and his followers saw Hellenization as a corruption of Christianity. Even Protestant readings of church history less vehemently opposed to Hellenization than Harnack generally looked to the first centuries of Christianity as representing some kind of norm, with the consequence that everything Eastern after the Council of Chalcedon (451) is viewed as a slow slide into decadence. It is still possible to hear Protestant theologians express the opinion that dialogue with the Orthodox is impossible till they have undergone (a) a Reformation and (b) an Enlightenment.

Today the term 'Byzantine' remains synonymous with 'convoluted' and 'labyrinthine', redolent of intrigue, decadence, cruelty, despotism, duplicity. The interest of Byzantinists focuses on a historical period that ends with the fall of Constantinople on Tuesday, 29 May 1453. Of course they recognize that Byzantine culture, Byzantine art and literature, and Byzantine Christianity did not suddenly end on that day. None the less, intellectual territorial boundaries affect how evidence is received and processed. 'Byzantine', in academic discourse, is an adjective in the past tense. Yet there is a living Byzantine identity that is part of the cultural being of Eastern Christians from Alaska to Greece, from Finland to Australia. It is a strong thread among the many interwoven strands that structure Eastern Christian identity lived, in different modulations, by Copts, Syrian Orthodox, Ukrainian Catholics, Russian Old Believers, the Saint Thomas Christians of India and the Greek Old Calendarists.

In Western Europe and throughout the English-speaking world, church history was until very recently heavily biased in the first instance towards the study of the early church and then towards the religious tradition of the Western Roman Empire and its derivatives. It was a history of Latin Catholicism and the churches of the Reformation. If the net was cast wider, then the official religion of the Eastern Roman empire might come into focus. A vivid sense of the reality of churches which were never part of the *Pax Romana* or the Byzantine *Oikoumene*, or even of churches which separated from the imperial tradition of Orthodoxy, was something very rare. Yet the Eastern Orthodox are second in numbers only to the Roman Catholic church, and the Oriental Orthodox are a communion comparable in size to the Anglican or Lutheran. Eastern Catholic history is even more neglected than Eastern Orthodox. The neglect of Eastern Christianity even affects the content, the accuracy and the approach of media treatment of issues such as the generally unexamined complexities of conflicts in Lebanon, in the Caucasus and in the former Yugoslavia, or of the situation of Christian minorities in Iraq or Iran.

Since the Armenian massacres of 1915–22, the Russian Revolution of 1917, the expulsion of the Anatolian Greeks of 1922 and other upheavals, extensive migration has occurred to Western Europe, America and Australia, and to some extent that migration continues. In many places the migrants of the twentieth century found existing Eastern Christian communities in what for some was their new homeland, for others a place of exile. The diaspora raised the profile of Eastern Christianity worldwide.

After the Second World War the majority of the world's Eastern Orthodox, the largest group of Eastern Catholics and the Armenian Apostolic church in its homeland all lived for half a century under atheistic communist rule. Many Oriental Christian communities live today in countries – Egypt, Ethiopia, Iran, Iraq, Syria – which Western governments and media have for long periods treated as hostile. Eastern Christianity, along with Islam, was for centuries regarded as a dangerous adversary and treated with enmity, then as something backward to be ignored or treated with contempt or at best condescension. On occasion, entire Eastern Christian communities have been demonized in the Western mind: the Russians during the Crimean War, the Serbians and Montenegrins in the conflict following the collapse of the Yugoslav Federation.

The experience of Eastern Christians living under Islam has yet to be properly addressed by Western Christians – despite the important lessons to be learned from this situation – as has the experience of Eastern Christian communities under communist rule. Under these conditions, Eastern Christians were deprived of state patronage, of a public voice, of equality under the law, of the right to proclaim their message, and under communism of any role in social welfare. None the less, the churches survive.

Today the division between Eastern and Western Christianity is less geographical than cultural and theological. The twentieth century has seen a major shift of Eastern Christian populations. The Greek, Armenian and Syrian Christian communities of Turkey have declined drastically in numbers. What were flourishing centres of Eastern Christianity at the turn of the century are now in some cases home to no more than a fragment of their former Christian populations. At the same time, new centres of Eastern Christianity have come into existence in the traditional homelands of Western Christianity. Communities have been scattered by war, persecution, oppression and by the hope of economic betterment. It would, however, be dangerous to see this diffusion as exclusively tragic. The Church of the East, now reduced to a tiny fragment of its former splendour, has emerged in the late twentieth century as a full partner in ecumenical dialogue. The Syrian Orthodox communities of America and Western Europe have revived Syriac as a spoken language. Even a number of Copts are learning to speak Coptic. The Pontic Greeks have resisted fragmentation, despite their expulsion from Pontus, and a vibrant renascence of language, music and poetry characterizes their contemporary life. Ethnic identity, cultural identity and religious identity are being renegotiated, and often with an astonishing confidence.

Eastern Christianity in all its varied forms has, for those who belong to it, a tangible unity, a family resemblance which unites communities separated by centuries of broken communion and mutual accusations of heresy and schism. Eastern Christianity is traditionalist. It is handed on in the family and the group; it is communal rather than individual. The whole community shares a strong sense of being the church, of 'ownership' of its rites and its dogma. The community's religion is as much a matter of liturgical experience as of doctrine; celebration of Pascha (Easter) is a more powerful binding force than shared belief. The family is a crucially important part of Eastern Christian life, and the family table especially so. And an Eastern Christian family has ever-extending boundaries; marriages establish a new relation between two families, not merely two persons. The *koumbaros* (best man) too establishes a permanent relation with the married couple, godparents with godchildren, and godchildren of the same godparents with each other.

Monasticism and asceticism are important elements in most Eastern Christian communities; in many churches all the senior hierarchs are, formally at least, monks. Parochial clergy, however, are normally married men, and the priest's wife has her own important and distinctive role.

Eastern Christianity is mysteric, the liturgy and the mysteries lying at the heart of its life. There is a shared and vivid sense of the reality and power of the sacraments and a stern sense of sacramental discipline, particularly surrounding reception of Holy Communion. Many other rites – celebration of feasts, memorial services for the dead, for example – are shared with the community, and very often involve the blessing of bread, *kollyva*, or wine that is then shared with all those present.

Historical experience both fundamentally unites and then divides Eastern Christians. They look back to the Greek heritage of the first centuries. The Rome of their history is New Rome, Constantinople, for some as the Mother Church, for others as the betrayer and oppressor. Invasion and subjection by Muslim powers and by the Tatars and Mongols is a shared historical reference point, though in very different ways. The impact of the Crusades and later of Western imperialism upset the relations Christian communities had established with the Muslim society of which they were part, and in both cases the Western Christian world showed little sign of interest in the outcome. The Reformation, a crucial defining moment in the history of Western Christianity, certainly had an impact on Eastern Christians, and continues to do so, but the Eastern Churches were not part of the Reformation movement and it was not formative of their religious identity.

The impact of Roman Catholic and Protestant missionaries, however, has been felt by all Eastern Christian churches; and it is not safe to assume that churches which became part of the Roman Catholic or of Protestant communions are united in uncritical enthusiasm for the attitudes and policies of their Western co-religionists. The Church of England has a remarkable, but among Western churches very unusual, record of friendship and support for Eastern Christians, not dominated by an urge to proselytize. Western missionaries generally faced Eastern Christians with Western questions. The attempt to respond to them has often involved deploying the answers of an opposed Western tradition, or entering into discourse that distorts the message of Eastern Christianity. Some Eastern Christians find ecumenism as problematic in this respect as proselytism.

In the twentieth century vast numbers of Eastern Christians have shared with Buddhists, Jews and Muslims the problems of life under an anti-religious communist state. Emergence from the condition of oppression has given some Eastern Christians a healthy suspicion of the state's embrace; others have an apparently incurable nostalgia for life as a state church. Communist rule weighed down on the intellectual life of the Eastern churches; now there are already signs of a major resurgence in scholarly and theological activity. Negotiating the role of diaspora communities in this evolution is sometimes a painful process. At the turn of the millennium, however, it is evident that the exploration, negotiation and assertion of Eastern Christian identity is occurring in quite new ways. The sense of shared history, of the Council of Nicea as a crucial moment of unity and self-definition, of the shared heritage of the earliest Greek fathers has come into the foreground and there is a readiness to renegotiate traditional hostile readings of the events and issues that resulted in the separation of the churches.

Theological dialogue among the Eastern traditions has already proved fruitful in greatly enhanced mutual understanding. Encounter with each other in a forum such as the World Council of Churches has offered Eastern Christians a vivid experience of the unity they still possess despite the ancient divisions holding them from full communion.

After long centuries of separation the worship of Eastern Orthodox, Oriental, Oriental Orthodox and Eastern Catholics remains similar. The pattern of services, the role of ministers, the way scripture is read, the way the Book of Psalms is used, the role of preaching, the role of the mysteries in Christian life, the way spiritual relatives are part of one's life, the role of marriage in family and community, the memorial services for the dead, the respect for monastic tradition, the intimate involvement of the parochial clergy in the community: all are part of a common life-pattern. The form of church buildings, the role of clergy and the use of the church fathers (despite considerable differences of view as to who they are after Nicea) are all common elements.

If we are prepared to recognize a Buddhist civilization and an Islamic civilization, we must be prepared to recognize the existence and the importance of Eastern Christian civilization. Its metropolitan style – and Oriental Christians would not deny this – is to be found in Byzantine Christianity, but it is a civilization with many dialects: Armenian, Coptic, Ethiopic, Syrian, and even within the Byzantine family Bulgarian, Georgian, Romanian, Russian, Ukrainian. The *Dictionary of Eastern Christianity* offers a way of exploring that civilization, its range, its complexity and something of its cultural and religious riches.

· A ·

Abbā Salāmā   Abbā Salāmā Kaśātē berhān, 'Abbā Salāmā the Illuminator', is honoured by Ethiopian Christians as first bishop of Axum. Traditionally Abbā Salāmā is identified with FRUMENTIUS (Abuna Frēmenāṭos), consecrated bishop by the COPTIC patriarch ATHANASIUS and sent to Christianize Axum in the early fourth century. This identification has been a matter of some scholarly debate. Two Semitic words, probably of Syriac origin, make up the name Abbā Salāmā: *abbā* (father) *and salāmā* (peace).

   See also ETHIOPIAN ORTHODOX CHURCH.

Tedeschi, S. (1991), 'Ethiopian Prelates. Salāmā I (*c.* 300–*c.* 380)', *Coptic Encyclopedia* 3, pp. 999–1000.
Dombrowski, B. W. W. and Dombrowski, F. A. (1984), 'Frumentius/Abbā Salāmā: Zu den Nachrichten über die Anfänge des Christentums in Äthiopien', *Oriens Christianus* 68, pp. 114–69.
Haile, G. (1979), 'The Homily in Honour of St Frumentius Bishop of Axum' (EMML' 1763 fos 84ᵛ–86ʳ), *Analecta Bollandiana* 97, pp. 309–13.

MJB/SHG

Abbā Salāmā Matargwem   Abbā Salāmā II, metropolitan of the Ethiopian Orthodox Church *c*.1348–88, named *matargwem* (translator) for his leadership in promoting the translation of Coptic religious literature extant in Arabic into classical Ethiopic or GEʿEZ. (*See also* ARAB CHRISTIANITY; COPTIC CHRISTIANITY.) Although much is known about the literary activities of Abbā Salāmā II, relatively little information survives about his early life as a Coptic monk in Egypt or his long tenure as metropolitan in Ethiopia.

Tedeschi, S. (1991), 'Salāmā II (d. 1388)', *Coptic Encyclopedia* 4, pp. 1011–12.
Van Lantschoot, A. (1960), 'Abbā Salāmā, métropolite d'Éthiopie (1348–88), et son rôle de traducteur', *Atti del Convegno internationale di studi etiopici (Roma 2–4 aprile 1959)*, pp. 397–401. Rome: Accademia Nazionale dei Lincei.

SHG

'Abd al-Masīḥ al-Isrā'īlī 'Abd al-Masīḥ al-Isrā'īlī ar-Raqqī, a native of Raqqah, Syria, moved to Egypt and was converted from Judaism to Christianity by the Christian physician Manṣūr ibn Sahlān ibn Muqashshir (d. 1004?). 'Abd al-Masīḥ al-Isrā'īlī's active period seems to have bridged the late tenth and the early eleventh centuries. Information about his life and works comes mainly from Vatican Arabic MS 145, a late thirteenth-century Egyptian manuscript which preserves a *mukhtaṣar* (summary) of 'Abd al-Masīḥ al-Isrā'īlī's *Kitāb al-Istidlāl* (Book of Dialectic), a theological and apologetic treatise extant only in this abridged format. Other treatises in MS 145 once ascribed to 'Abd al-Masīḥ al-Isrā'īlī are now considered by scholars to have been written by members of the Coptic AL-'ASSĀL FAMILY. An Aleppo manuscript described by Paul Sbath which is the other known source for 'Abd al-Masīḥ al-Isrā'īlī's works no longer survives.

Samir, Kh. (1991), ''Abd al-Masīḥ al-Isrā'īli al-Raqqī', *Coptic Encyclopedia* 1, pp. 5–6.
Graf, G. (1947), *Geschichte der christlichen arabischen Literatur*, 5 vols (Studi e Testi, 118, 133, 146–7, 172, vol. 2, pp. 319–20). Città del Vaticano: Biblioteca Apostolica Vaticana, 1944–53.
Sbath, P. (1938–40), *Al-Fihris (Catalogue de manuscrits arabes)*, 3 vols, vol.1, p. 53. Cairo: Imprimerie Al-Chark.

MJB/SHG

Abgar Name, probably of Arab origin, used by several kings of the royal dynasty of EDESSA from *c*.132 BC to *c*. AD 242. The Abgar connected by the ADDAI legend with the evangelization of Edessa is Abgar V Ukkāmā, 'the Black', who reigned 4 BC–AD 7 and AD 13–50. According to legend, he heard of Jesus' troubles and invited him to escape to Edessa, confessing faith without seeing the Messiah. Historically, a more likely king at the time of the evangelization is the better-known Abgar VIII, 'the Great' (177–212).

JH

Abkhazia By tradition the apostles ANDREW and Simon first brought Christianity to Abasgia or Abkhazia. In the reign of Justinian I (sixth century) Abkhazia was evangelized from Byzantium. In this period the capital was Pityous-Soteriopolis, where the cathedral of the THEOTOKOS was constructed in 551. The metropolitan-CATHOLICOS presided over an independent church. Under the fourteenth-century Shervashidze dynasty, Abkhazia enjoyed a final spell of independence before OTTO-MAN Turks dominated the entire Black Sea region; most of the native Abkhaz had embraced Islam by 1864 when the Russian protectorate was established. The Russians revived ancient shrines and in 1875 founded New ATHOS, by the reputed tomb of Simon the Canaanite. In 1909 this monastery had over 700 monks. With the collapse of the Soviet Union the Abkhazians seceded from GEORGIA, supported by both Russia and Turkey during a brief but bloody war.

See also ADZHARIA; LAZICA; OSSETIA; ZICHIA.

Suny, R. G. (1994), *The Making of the Georgian Nation*. Bloomington: Indiana University Press.
Ioseliani, P. (1983), *A Short History of the Georgian Church*. Jordanville: St Job of Pochaev.

DB

Abouna   Also Abuna, Abun: 'Our father', a title of the head of the ETHIOPIAN ORTHODOX CHURCH. From the fourth century until the mid-twentieth century the Abouna, usually an Egyptian COPTIC monk, was chosen by the Coptic Orthodox patriarch of Alexandria. The first Abouna, FRUMENTIUS (*c*. 300–*c*. 380), was sent to Ethiopia by Patriarch Athanasius I (326–73). The duties of the Abouna were primarily ceremonial; church administration and management are largely handled by the ECHAGE. Abouna is also the title by which priests and monks are generally addressed in the Coptic church.

Bairu Tafla (1991), 'Abun', *Coptic Encyclopedia* 1, pp. 30–1.

MJB/SHG

Abraham Ecchellensis   Ibrāhīm al-Ḥāqilāni (1605–64), a MARONITE scholar. Born at al-Ḥāqil, Lebanon, Ecchellensis studied at the Maronite College in ROME, later teaching Arabic and SYRIAC at the University of Pisa and the College of the Propaganda in ROME. In 1635 he was named Interpreter for the Propagation of Faith, in which role he purused a continuing Maronite project of revising the Arabic version of the BIBLE. In 1645 he went to Paris to teach Syriac and Arabic at the Collège de France. His many contributions to Christian Oriental studies include a Syriac grammar (1628), collaboration on the Syriac and Arabic portions of the Paris Polyglot Bible (1629–45) and, in 1645, a Latin translation of Arabic documentary sources for the Council of Nicea. He was appointed a scriptor for Syriac and Arabic at the Vatican Library in 1660. Sixty-four Oriental manuscripts from his personal library were eventually deposited in the Vatican Library. Ecchellensis is representative of a distinguished group of Maronite scholars resident at Rome in the seventeenth and eighteenth centuries who were instrumental in introducing European scholars to the languages and literatures of the Christian Orient. Included in this group are, among others, GABRIEL SIONITA and the ASSEMANI family.

Breydy, M. (1983), 'Abraham Ecchellensis et la collection dite (Kitab) al Ḥuda', *Oriens C'hristianus* 67, pp. 123–43.
El-Hayek, E. (1967), 'Abraham Ecchellensis', *New Catholic Encyclopedia* 1, pp. 34–5.
Raphael, P. (1950), Le Rôle du College Maronite romain dans l'orientalisme aux XVIIe et XVIIIe siècles. Beyrouth: Université Saint Joseph.

MJB/SHG

Abū al-Makārim   Sa'dallāh Ibn Ǧirǧis Ibn Mas'ūd is the name of a thirteenth-century Coptic priest in a position of some authority, as indicated by his title *qummus* or *hēgoumenos*, now considered the author or compiler of *Tārīkh al-Kanā'is wa-al-Adyirah* (The History of Churches and Monasteries). In 1984 Samuil al-Suryani published a new edition of this treatise, which contains information about thirteenth-century Coptic churches and monasteries, and the geography and topography of medieval Egypt and neighbouring regions. In 1895 B. T. A. Evetts had identified its author as ABŪ ṢĀLIḤ THE ARMENIAN, an otherwise unknown figure whose name appears on the cover of a manuscript containing the text. Manuscript evidence collected since then enabled al-Suryani to disprove Evetts' attribution, and to identify Abū al-Makārim as the probable author or compiler.

See also COPTIC CHRISTIANITY.

den Heijer, J. (1993), 'The Composition of the History of the Churches and Monasteries of Egypt: Some Preliminary Remarks', in T. Orlandi and D. Johnson, eds, *Acts of the Fifth International Congress of Coptic Studies, Washington, 12–15 August 1992*. vol. 2, pt 1, pp. 209–19. Rome: Centro Italiano Microfiches.
Atiya, A. S. (1991), 'Abū al-Makārim', *Coptic Encyclopedia* 1, p. 23.
al-Suryani, S., ed. (1984), *Tārīkh al-Kanā' is wa-al-Adyirah fi al-Qarn al-Thāni 'Ashar al-Mīlādi; li-Abi al-Makārim, alladhi nusiba khataan ila Abi Ṣāliḥ al-A[r]mani*. Cairo.
Evetts, B. T. A., ed. and trans. (1895), *The Churches and Monasteries of Egypt and some Neighbouring Countries Attributed to Abû Sâlih the Armenian*. Anecdota Oxoniensia, Semitic Series, 7, Oxford.

MJB/SHG

Abū Ṣāliḥ the Armenian   The name of a person mentioned on the cover of one manuscript of a Christian Arabic treatise describing Coptic churches and monasteries during the late twelfth and early thirteenth centuries, *Tārīkh al-Kanā'is wa-al-Adyirah*. The English scholar B. T. A. Evetts, who knew only the manuscript containing Abū Ṣāliḥ al-Armanī's name, assumed that this otherwise unknown person was the author of the work. Later scholarship has disproved Evetts' assumption. ABŪ AL-MAKĀRIM, Saʿdallāh Ibn Ǧirǧis Ibn Masʿūd, a thirteenth-century Coptic priest, is a more likely author or compiler. Abū Ṣāliḥ al-Armanī may have owned the manuscript on which his name appears. His name, however, has become synonymous with the text.

den Heijer, J. (1993), 'The Composition of the History of the Churches and Monasteries of Egypt: Some Preliminary Remarks', in T. Orlandi and D. Johnson, eds, *Acts of the Fifth International Congress of Coptic Studies, Washington, 12–15 August 1992*. vol. 2, pt 1, pp. 209–19. Rome: CIM.
Atiya, A. S. (1991), 'Abū al-Makārim', *Coptic Encyclopedia* 1, p. 23.
al-Suryani, S., ed. (1984), *Tarikh al-Kana' is wa-al-Adyirah fi al-Qarn al-Thani 'Ashar al-Miladi; li-Abi al-Makarim, alladhi nusiba khataan ila Abi Salih al-A[r]mani*. Cairo.
Evetts, B. T. A., ed. and trans. (1895), *The Churches and Monasteries of Egypt and some Neighbouring Countries Attributed to Abû Sâlih the Armenian*. Anecdota Oxoniensia, Semitic Series, 7, Oxford.

MJB/SHG

accidie   Latin; Greek: *akedia*, literally fatigue or exhaustion. 'Accidie' became a technical term for the spiritual and often physical lethargy or torpor which is a particular danger for those pursuing the solitary life. It is frequently referred to as the 'noonday devil' (Psalm 90/91). Accidie can take different forms: listless inertia; vagueness of thought and purposeless activity; pointless immersion in tasks which are little more than acted-out distractions.
See also PHILOKALIA.

DM

Adam and Eve   The first created humans, according to Genesis. In the Septuagint (*see* BIBLE), but not in liturgical texts, Adam's wife is named as Zoe, life (Genesis 3: 21).

God makes the human being (Septuagint: *anthropon*) 'according to our image, according to our likeness' (Genesis 1: 26), the fathers reading this as an intimation of the TRINITY. 'He made him according to the image of God, he made them male and female. And God blessed them saying, grow and multiply and fill the earth and dominate it' (Genesis 1: 28). Fish, birds, cattle and reptiles are placed under the dominion of humankind, and the plants are given as food. Significantly, this account speaks of the human being as created 'male and female' without any suggestion of subordination.

Genesis 2 represents the Lord God as forming the human being from the dust of the earth and breathing 'into his face the breath of life', so that 'the human being became a living soul', and God 'planted a paradise in Eden,' placing the human being there to tend it. The woman is created from the human being's rib as companion. God forbids them to eat the fruit 'of the tree of knowing good and evil . . . In whatsoever day you eat from it, by death you shall die.' Tempted by the serpent, whom the fathers identify with the Devil, Eve eats the forbidden fruit and herself persuades Adam to do the same.

Eastern theology sees humanity as constituted in relation to God. Adam and Eve are living images of God called to grow into full DEIFICATION. ORIGEN argues in *On First Principles* that all rational beings were created in unity with God, but all save the soul of Christ and possibly the highest angels fell in various degrees from contemplation of the Godhead; their rank as angelic spirits, celestial intelligences, human beings or demonic powers reflected the degree of each one's fall. The 'garments of skin' with which the fallen Adam and Eve were clothed by God he interprets as referring to their embodiment in flesh. His assertion of the pre-existence of human souls before the creation of the material world and his assimilation of human beings and angels to a single original kind was rejected by the church. None the less, elements of Origen's thought survived. Gregory of Nyssa, for example, sees gender differentiation not as belonging to the divine image in human nature, which resides entirely in the rational soul, but rather as the result of God's foreknowledge of the Fall, and as a means of ensuring a kind of reproduction appropriate to the fallen state.

Humanity, in Eastern Christian theology, is created as the living point of union between the invisible and visible realms, called to govern the earthly creation as vicegerent of God. Indeed, Gregory of Nyssa sees the material world as created for the sake of humanity; SYMEON THE NEW THEOLOGIAN in the *Discourses* describes Adam as king of all that exists 'beneath the vault of heaven' (*Discourse* 5) and, like Gregory, sees the 'sun, moon and stars' as created for humankind. The Fall is, therefore, a cosmic catastrophe, sundering anew the unity of creation already damaged by the rebellion of the fallen angels.

The unity of the created order, the open and intimate relation between God and humanity, the equal companionship between men and women, the original gift of immortality and the harmonious relation of humankind with the animals are all damaged or lost as a result of the primal sin. Human beings are born damaged in a damaged world. Eastern dogmatic tradition did not, however, receive the doctrine of Augustine of Hippo that we inherit Adam's guilt and are born damned. The influence of Roman Catholic and Protestant theology has led to the Augustinian doctrine becoming relatively widespread among Eastern Christians, but it is alien to Eastern tradition, which emphasizes the personal nature of sin. Indeed, Eastern theology has generally seen death as that aspect of our heritage that leads most directly to the near-inevitability of sin. (Not an absolute inevitability, since Jesus is sinless in his humanity, and the THEOTOKOS is held to be sinless.)

The fallen Adam is commemorated liturgically in the TRIODION on the Sunday of Forgiveness, the Sunday that immediately precedes Great Lent.

DM

Addai Known to Eusebius as Thaddaeus; supposedly one of the SEVENTY disciples of Jesus and the evangelizer of EDESSA. The SYRIAC version of the story is the *Teaching of Addai* or *Doctrina Addai* (fourth or fifth century), the historicity of which cannot be upheld. The Addai story (Eusebius' 'Thaddaeus' produced by his difficulty in identifying the apostle) may be dated to *c*. 300, possibly as a polemic against the preaching of the MANICHAEAN apostle Addai. The Syriac Liturgy of Addai and Mari, originating *c*. 200 and used by the CHURCH OF THE EAST, claims a connection with the legendary evangelizer of Edessa.

Drijvers, H. J. W. (1983), 'Addai und Mani. Christentum und Manichäismus im dritten Jahrhundert in Syrien', *Orientalia Christiana Analecta* 221, pp. 171–85.
Howard, G., trans. (1981), *The Teaching of Addai*. Chico: Scholars Press.

JH

Adiabene Syriac *Ḥadyaḇ*, with its main city Irbil, lies east of the River Tigris between the Great Zab and Little Zab rivers. Irbil's history goes back to the third millennium BC, but the region became a vassal kingdom of the Parthians until it was overrun by Trajan in AD 116 and Caracalla in 216, eventually being absorbed into the Sasanian empire. According to Josephus (*Antiquities*, xx: 17–48), in the first century AD its queen Helena and her son Izates were converted to Judaism.

Tradition and the *Chronicle of* ARBELA (of doubtful authenticity) place the evangelization of Adiabene in apostolic times (by ADDAI) or soon afterwards (by Mari). It names Pqīdā as first bishop. Sozomen, writing *c*. 440, believed that Adiabene was mostly Christian by then, though adherents of Magianism are still prominent in the seventh century. Persecution of Christians occurred under Shapur II from 340 onwards and continued in Adiabene until 376. Several early Adiabenian martyrs are known, including two bishops of Irbil, John (d. 343) and Abraham (d. 345). Later martyrs include Mahanuš, a convert from Magianism, killed in 620 or 621.

We do not know when Adiabene had its first bishop, but *c*. 310–17 the bishop of Adiabene became a metropolitan, fourth in rank after the PATRIARCH. This status is reflected at the council of Seleucia-Ctesiphon of 410 and the list of dioceses under the authority of Irbil covers most of northern Iraq. Bishops of Adiabene attended early Eastern church synods, including the council of Seleucia-Ctesiphon of 484–6, though BARHEBRAEUS tells us that the metropolitan of Irbil had been driven out by Barṣawmā of Nisibis, who was active against MONOPHYSITES. Irbil had a well-known theological school, perhaps founded *c*. 540 by Paul, later bishop of Nisibis, which produced some distinguished figures of the CHURCH OF THE EAST.

Defence against monophysitism, which made considerable inroads into the area north of Adiabene, became a major concern, especially of the early seventh-century bishop Yōnādāb. In 628 Īšōʿyab of Kuplānā, later CATHOLICOS ISHOYAB III, became incumbent of the see. During the seventh and eighth centuries the city declined in importance as a Christian centre and the see was linked with Mosul, a city which had become important during the early Islamic centuries. It revived politically and religiously in the twelfth century under local dynasties and regained its independent metropolitanate. Denḥā, a friend of BARHEBRAEUS, became metropolitan of Irbil in 1256 and subsequently Catholicos (1265–81), though most of the time in exile in Irbil. He adopted a new open-door policy towards JACOBITE refugees from the Mosul region. Thereafter the Christian history of the city is hard to trace, and by the eighteenth century Christianity had disappeared from it.

Fiey, J. M. (1965), *Assyrie Chrétienne I*, Beirut: Imprimerie Catholique.

JH

Adzharia   Autonomous region in south-western GEORGIA by the Black Sea, adjoining Turkey. The Adzhars are related to the Tzanoi of the Byzantine period, who migrated westwards to Asia Minor and other Byzantine provinces and served in the imperial armies, guarding the frontiers of the empire of Trebizond until 1461. The modern Adzhar language is close to Georgian, but most Adzhars embraced Islam in the OTTOMAN period. Adzharia, like LAZICA and ABKHAZIA, is still home to a substantial Pontic Greek minority.
   See also PONTUS.

Suny, R. G. (1994), *The Making of the Georgian Nation*. Bloomington: Indiana University Press.
Ioseliani, P. (1983), *A Short History of the Georgian Orthodox Church*. Jordanville: St Job of Pochaev.

DB

Africa   Tradition links the origins of Christianity in Africa with the preaching of the evangelist Mark in ALEXANDRIA, and with the story in Acts 8 of the baptism of Candace's eunuch by the apostle Philip. From an early period the church of Alexandria rose to great prominence and played a leading role in theological controversy. Egypt was home to organized Christian MONASTICISM in both eremitical and cenobitic forms. By the fifth century EASTERN CHRISTIANITY was spreading from Egypt to NUBIA and had already been firmly established in Ethiopia. Despite the seventh-century Muslim conquest of Egypt, the slow but eventually total Islamicization of Nubia and the millennial isolation of Ethiopia, today the COPTIC CHRISTIANITY of Egypt together with the ETHIOPIAN ORTHODOX CHURCH, the ERITREAN ORTHODOX CHURCH and the EASTERN ORTHODOX patriarchate of Alexandria survive as living representatives of ancient African Christianity.
   Since the fifth-century controversies, MONOPHYSITE Christianity has been the dominant form of Eastern Christianity in Africa. By the twentieth century the Eastern Orthodox patriarchate of Alexandria had been reduced to a scattering of Greek and Arab communities and a small number of Eastern Orthodox Copts. EASTERN CATHOLICS are represented by the Coptic Catholic patriarchate of Alexandria and the small Ethiopian Catholic church, together with the communities belonging to the MELKITE Catholic church.

The twentieth century has seen both the Coptic and the Eastern Orthodox patriarchates of Alexandria take increasingly seriously the responsibilities implied in the title both patriarchs use, 'Patriarch of Alexandria . . . and All Africa'. The Coptic patriarch has a bishop with responsibility to maintain and develop good relations with Christian communities throughout Africa, whose work has resulted in several African communities entering the Coptic communion. The Eastern Orthodox patriarchate has found its numbers significantly increased by the adherence of about a third of a million African Christians in East Africa, and as this volume is published there is a real prospect of nearly half a million African Christians from South Africa uniting with the patriarchate.

The development of Eastern Orthodox communities among the African peoples of East and South Africa was based on the rejection of the paternalism of colonial missionaries, the education they offered and the cultural influence they attempted to exercise, coupled with an upsurge of independence movements as the colonial empires began to crumble after the First World War, and the spreading knowledge among African Christians of the ancient history of Eastern Christianity in Africa.

Already in the 1920s William Daniel Alexander, a black Anglican clergyman from South Africa, had become a bishop of the African Orthodox church, a church established in America and headed by the black nationalist cleric Patriarch George Alexander McGuire. McGuire was consecrated by René Vilatte, who also consecrated bishops for several other independent churches, and himself consecrated Alexander to head the African Orthodox church in South Africa. As well as establishing the African Orthodox church in South Africa, Archbishop Alexander was to play a crucial role in the development of Orthodoxy among the African Christians of Kenya and Uganda.

In both Kenya and Uganda, Christians resolved both to escape the colonial yoke and to adhere to the most pure form of Christianity invited Archbishop Alexander for prolonged visits and a small number of men were ordained by him, among them Reuben Spartas, already a leader of a group seeking Orthodoxy, who was ordained in Uganda in 1931. However, when Archbishop Alexander baptized the child of a GREEK ORTHODOX family, it was drawn to Fr Spartas's attention that the rite used was unfamiliar to the Orthodox present, which led him to suspect that Alexander was not really Orthodox and to seek entry into the Eastern Orthodox church. From 1933 approaches were made to the Greek Orthodox patriarch of Alexandria to receive the African Orthodox of Uganda into communion. The response was slow, hesitant and inhibited by the opposition of the local Anglican hierarchs. Local Greek Orthodox, however, supported the request of the Spartas community. In the event, it was 1946 before his determined community was finally accepted into the patriarchate of Alexandria.

The progress of the Orthodox movement in Kenya was repressed under colonial rule because of the overt identification of the African Orthodox with the struggle for independence. Under the regime of President Kenyatta after independence the Orthodox community flourished, not least because of the fraternal affection between Kenyatta and Archbishop Makarios III of Cyprus, as fellow leaders in the struggle for independence. Makarios III offered encouragement and practical support to Orthodox

Africans of East Africa, the Church of Cyprus founding a seminary in 1971 and soon after a technical school, though the 1974 Turkish invasion of Cyprus meant that the seminary only began full operation in 1981, being redesignated in 1998 as the Orthodox Patriarchal School. Archbishop Makarios also personally baptized thousands of Orthodox Africans.

In 1958–9 the patriarchate of Alexandria created the diocese of Irenoupolis (Dar-es-Salaam) with jurisdiction over the Orthodox of Kenya, Tanzania and Uganda. There are now well over 100 priests with metropolitans in Uganda and Kenya.

In 1997 Pope Peter VII, Eastern Orthodox patriarch of Alexandria, established an Orthodox mission centre in South Africa. Links are also being established with other African groups espousing an Orthodox identity and seeking to enter the patriarchate of Alexandria.

Baur, J. (1994), *2000 Years of Christianity in Africa*. Nairobi: Pauline Publications Africa.
Grierson, R., ed. (1993), *African Zion: The Sacred Art of Ethiopia*. New Haven and London: Yale University Press.
Munro-Hay, S. (1991), *Axum: An African Civilisation of Late Antiquity*. Edinburgh: Edinburgh University Press.
Atiya, A. S., ed. (1991), *The Coptic Encyclopedia*, 7 vols. New York: Macmillan.
Cannuyer, C. (1990), *Les Coptes*. Turnhout: Brepols.
Vantini, G. (1981), *Christianity in the Sudan*. Bologna: EMI.

DM

Aghtamar Ruined fortified palace on Lake Van in eastern Turkey, from 1113 seat of the senior Catholicos of ARMENIA. The quatrefoil Holy Cross church (915–21) has fine bas-reliefs on all facades, including one of the donor King Gagik I holding a model of the church. Saul appears wearing a turban and a king is depicted in a Persian cross-legged posture. Among the surviving frescoes is an Old Testament narrative cycle. Architecturally, Aghtamar recalls the seventh-century church of St Hrip'sime at Vagharshapat, and its sculptures anticipate reliefs on the eleventh-century Dmitrii cathedral at VLADIMIR.

KP

Agnoetai Greek, 'ignoranceists': followers of the sixth-century Alexandrian teacher Themistios, condemned by Eulogios, patriarch of ALEXANDRIA, for teaching that Christ suffered from ignorance. That condemnation was confirmed by Pope Gregory the Great in his letter *Sicut aqua* to Eulogios (August 600): 'Anyone who is not a Nestorian cannot in any way be an Agnoete. For whoever confesses that the very Wisdom of God became incarnate, in what sense can he say there is anything that the Divine Wisdom does not know?'

DM

ahl al-kitāb In Islamic tradition *ahl al-kitāb*, people of the book (i.e. peoples adhering to a sacred scripture of their own), were accepted within Muslim society

9

provided they paid a special poll-tax (*jizyah*). The Qur'ān contains a number of statements which justify this tolerant attitude (2: 63; 5: 69–70; 22: 17 and 9: 29 referring specifically to the *jizyah*, though perhaps not in the technical sense). This brought the Jews and Christians under protection (*dhimmah*) and the category of *ahl al-dhimmah*, people of/under protection, was extended to include Zoroastrians and Mandaeans (identified with Qur'ānic 'Ṣābians'). Even the pagans of Harran managed to qualify (by claiming to be Ṣābians).

JH

ainoi   Greek, 'praises': the Byzantine service equivalent to Western Lauds, the *ainoi* form a distinct part of the morning office, the ORTHROS. The title *ainoi* derives from the repeated praise verses of Psalms 148, 149 and 150 which form the body of the service. On weekdays the psalms are read without STICHERA. On Sundays and major feasts the concluding verses are interleaved with stichera, but in parish use only the opening verses 'Let everything that has breath praise the Lord . . .' and the final verses with their interleaved stichera are actually sung. The *ainoi* follow the EXAPOSTEI-LARIA and end with the DOXOLOGY.

DM

Akathist   Greek, 'not sitting': in full, Akathistos Hymnos, hymn during which all stand. The original sixth-century Akathist in honour of the THEOTOKOS, possibly by ROMANOS THE MELODIST, though this is hotly debated, forms an alphabetical acrostic, and consists of twelve long and twelve short *oikoi* ('houses': a term probably derived from Syriac terminology). In the long *oikoi* a seven-line stanza is followed by six couplets, which employ rhyme, alliteration and assonance; each begins with *Chaire*, ('Hail!', or 'Rejoice!') and ends with the refrain, 'Hail, Bride without bridegroom!'. In the short *oikoi* the seven-line stanza is followed by the refrain, 'ALLELOUIA!' There are four sections of six *oikoi*, on the Annunciation, the Nativity, on Christ and on the Mother of God. The Akathist forms part of Matins on the fifth Saturday of Lent. In Greek a section with the Matins CANON of Akathist Saturday is sung at Small Compline on the first four Fridays of Lent, and the whole Akathist on the fifth. In Athonite monasteries and elsewhere the whole Akathist is recited nightly at APODEIP-NON. The Akathist provided the model for other hymns called by the same name, some of which are in various editions of the HOROLOGION, e.g. the Akathists to the Precious Cross and the Most Sweet Jesus. A new AKOLOUTHIA for a saint will usually include an Akathist; most of these are mere pastiche.
   See also KONTAKION.

E

akolouthia   Greek term for (a) the order of a service (Slavonic: *chinoposledovanie*), or (b) the service itself (Slavonic: *sluzhba*). When a new saint is canonized a complete *akolouthia* for that saint is written, including all necessary texts for HESPERINOS, ORTHROS and the Divine Liturgy, and normally an AKATHIST and PARAKLESIS of the saint. Full *akolouthiai* exist for many saints never formally canonized.

DM

Al-'Assāl family *Awlād al-'Assāl*, 'sons of the honey producer': wealthy Coptic family of learned and prolific scholars, influential at the Ayyubid court in early thirteenth-century Cairo, their writings a high point of medieval Coptic literature in Arabic. Many of their works survive. Little is known about the family itself. The *awlād al-'Assāl* included Abū'l-Faḍl ibn Abī Isḥāq Ibrāhim ibn Abī Sahl Ǧirǧis ibn Abī al-Yusr Yūḥannā ibn al-'Assal, nicknamed al-Kātib al-Miṣrī, the Egyptian secretary or scribe; his two sons, al-Ṣafī Abū'l-Faḍa'il ibn al-'Assāl and al-As'ad Abū'l-Faraǧ Hibat-Allāh ibn al-'Assāl; and their two stepbrothers, al-Mu'taman Abū Isḥāq Ibrāhim ibn al-'Assāl and al-Amǧad Abū'l-Maǧd ibn al-'Assāl. Al-Ṣafi, al-As'ad and al-Mu'taman were the major writers. They wrote in Arabic, but also read Coptic, Greek, and SYRIAC. They contributed in the areas of theology, biblical studies, philosophy, law, Copto-Arabic philology and poetry. Al-Ṣafi participated in the Coptic Synod of 1238, occasioned by the abuses of Patriarch Cyril III ibn Laqlaq (1235–43). Al-Ṣafi made major contributions in canon law, theology and philosophy. The great Coptic nomo-canon that bears his name, *al-Majmū' al-Ṣafawī*, is still used. Al-As'ad's edition of the gospels in Arabic and his work on the Coptic calendar should be noted. Al-As'ad and al-Mu'taman prepared Copto-Arabic grammars and dictionaries (*scalae*). Their philo-logical work marks the transition of Coptic from spoken language to one increasingly reserved for liturgical use. Al-Mu'taman, a Coptic priest, wrote many theological and homiletic works. The three brothers also prepared summaries and revisions of other Christian texts. Many works of the 'Assāl await editing and translation. They remain largely inaccessible to scholars who cannot read Arabic.

See also COPTIC CHRISTIANITY.

Samir, K. (1992), 'Les confessions chrétiennes d'après al-Mu'taman ibn al-'Assāl (vers 1263)' (Arabic), *Al-Machriq* 66, pp. 481–91.
Samir, K. (1991), 'Ṣafī ibn al-'Assāl, al-', *Coptic Encyclopedia* 7, pp. 2075–9.
Atiya, A. (1991), 'Awlād al-'Assāl', *Coptic Encyclopedia* 1, pp. 309–11.
Abullif, W. (1988), 'L'unione ipostatica di Cristo negli scritti del Teologo copto al-Ṣafi Ibn-'Assāl (Sec. XIII)', *Studia Orientalia Christiana, Collectanea* 21, pp. 7–28.
Samir, K. (1985), *Al-Ṣafī Ibn al-'Assāl, brefs chapitres sur la Trinité et l'Incarnation*, Patrologia Orientalis vol. 42, fasc. 3, no. 192. Turnhout: Brepols.
Abullif, W. (1985), 'Bibliografia commentata sugli Aulād al-'Assāl; Tre fratelli scrittori del sec. XIII', *Studia Orientalia Christiana, Collectanea* 18, pp. 31–79.
Samir, K. (1985), 'Le traité sur la necessité de l'Incarnation de Yaḥyā Ibn 'Adī, résumé et glosé par al-Ṣafī Ibn al-'Assāl', *Studia Orientalia Christiana, Collectanea* 18, pp. 1–11.
Atiya, A. (1971), 'Ibn al-'Assāl', *Encyclopedia of Islam*, new edn, vol. 3, pp. 721–2.
Graf, G. (1932), 'Die koptische Gelehrtenfamilie der Aulād al-'Assāl und ihr Schrift-tum', *Orientalia* 1, pp. 34–56, 129–48, 193–204.

MJB/SHG

Alania Regions in the North Caucasus extending as far as the steppes. The Alans and Roxalanoi, Iranian peoples related to the Sarmatians, displaced the Scythians in the first century BC. Alan groups migrated westwards with the Goths, settling in Western Europe and North Africa. Other Alan tribes remained in their homeland; groups entered Byzantine service and were granted land for military service.

CONSTANTINOPLE worked to Christianize Alania, particularly under PATRIARCH Nicolas I Mystikos (tenth century). A bishopric was established for Alania and remains of Byzantine-style churches have been found in the region. The Ossetians, most of whom only reverted to Orthodox Christianity in the nineteenth century, are descendants of the ancient Alans.

See also OSSETIA; PONTUS; ZICHIA.

Avtorkhanov, A. (1992), *The North Caucasus Barrier*. London: Hurst.

DB

Alaska   Eastern Orthodox Christianity is the primary religion, and a characteristic of ethnic identity, among the following Native Alaskan peoples in their entirety: the Aleut, Alutiiq (Koniag), Dena'ina Athapascan, Ingalik Athapascan and Kol'chan Athapascan. It is the primary religion among significant social segments of Yup'ik Eskimo, Ingalik Athapascan and Tlingit. These peoples are located from the Aleutian Islands (Aleuts) and Bering Sea coast (Yup'ik Eskimos), across the breadth of the southern mainland and archipelagos (Athapascans and Alutiiqs) into the Alexander Archipelago (Tlingits).

Some settlers adhere to the same religion. There is a Greek Orthodox parish with a pan-Orthodox constituency in Anchorage, the major urban centre. An Antiochian Orthodox parish, mainly of Euro-American converts, is located in Eagle River. Russian OLD BELIEVERS, having come through the USA, have settled on the Kenai Peninsula and Afognak Island. The historical Russian settlement in Alaska was sparse and mostly assimilated. This article will concentrate on Orthodoxy among the Native Alaskans.

Aleuts began converting before the imperial Russian colonial era, through interactions with lay Orthodox sea hunters, themselves mainly north-east Asians and northern Eurasians. They began frequenting the Aleutian Islands to hunt in 1745, after the Bering–Chirikov voyage of discovery in 1741. The first known baptism of an Aleut was recorded in 1747.

A commercial enterprise established a permanent colony on Kodiak Island in 1784. When an ecclesiastical mission arrived at Kodiak in September 1794, conversions began in earnest among the Alutiiq (Koniag) people of the Kodiak archipelago and Chugach Bay area (Prince William Sound region). Small ecclesiastical missions were opened in 1840, among the Athapascan, Yup'ik Eskimo and Tlingit peoples in (respectively) the Kenai, Nushagak, Yukon–Kuskokwim and Sitka regions. Conversions had already begun in these regions through interpersonal relationships with lay Orthodox before that date. After the Russian era ended with the transfer of Alaska to Washington, DC, in 1867, conversions continued through the US possession and territory periods, particularly in the 1880s and 1890s among the Tlingits outside Sitka in south-eastern Alaska, and into the 1920s among the Yup'ik Eskimos of the south-west mainland.

Episcopal structures have waxed and waned in Alaska. Archimandrite Ioasaf Bolotov, leader of the 1794 mission, was designated bishop of Kodiak, travelling to Irkutsk for consecration, but drowned in a shipwreck in 1799 and never assumed the position. Innokentii Veniaminov, bishop of the new diocese of Kamchatka, the Kurile Islands and the Aleutian Islands, arrived in September 1840 at Novo Arkhangel'sk (Sitka), the colonial administrative centre, approximately 1,000 miles east of the

Aleutians and his seat. He ministered, however, mainly on the Kamchatka Peninsula, while also opening the missions mentioned above in 1840 and making pastoral visits in Alaska. In 1850 he was elevated to archbishop with his seat in Aian (north-east Asia); and after the archdiocese was extended, *c.* 1853, he assumed residency in Yakutsk (*see* YAKUTIA).

In 1858 an auxiliary bishop, Peter, was sent from Irkutsk and based in Novo Arkhangel'sk to serve the Alaskan portion of this massive archdiocese, Alaska having been without episcopal presence since Veniaminov's departure. In 1867, before Alaska was sold to Washington, DC that year, Peter departed to assume a position in Yakutsk. A further auxiliary bishop, Paul (Popov), was eventually assigned from Yakutsk to Novo Arkhangel'sk and remained until 1870. There was no diocese designated in this US possession at this time; parish properties had been entrusted to the Alaskan faithful (Treaty of 1867, Paragraph 2).

The Russian Orthodox church created a diocese of the Aleutians and Alaska in 1870. Bishop Ioann (Mitropolskii) was assigned. He moved the diocesan seat from Alaska to San Francisco in 1872. In 1903, the Russian church created an archdiocese of the Aleutians and North America, with an auxiliary bishopric of Alaska. For a century from 1872 all the bishops except one resided outside Alaska, while retaining 'Alaska' in their titles. The exception was Bishop Nestor (Sakkis), who resided at Unalaska from 1879 until 1882. The see became vacant again in 1917 and jurisdiction subsequently became confused owing to the divisions caused by the Bolshevik Revolution.

After the territory became the forty-ninth state of the Union in 1959, new episcopal structures emerged in Alaska. In 1972 a resident bishop, Gregory (Afonsky), was appointed by the ORTHODOX CHURCH OF AMERICA (OCA). His replacement in 1995 by the OCA became a matter of dispute in Alaska.

Native Alaskans have been the mainstay of their parishes, with their own leadership, labour and finances. Wherever a priest is not resident, a local church reader normally conducts weekly and festive services, as well as the rites of baptism and burial. A visiting priest provides those MYSTERIES which require a priest. Liturgical skills are traditionally taught by the church readers from generation to generation.

Forms of worship are canonical, conservative in rubrics and liturgical language alike. Slavonic was maintained in liturgy as a heritage, the native languages being incorporated to varying degrees: more among the Aleuts, among whom substantial translations were accomplished, and less among the Tlingits and Athapascans, among whom translations were scant. Translated gospels and/or catechisms were published in Aleut translation from 1840 until 1903, in Alutiiq in 1847 and 1848, and in Tlingit and Central Yup'ik in the 1890s, achieved mainly in co-operation with the native parish leadership and under the direction of Veniaminov; the actual translations were done by himself, his contemporaries or his pupils. Veniaminov wrote a long sermon, *Indication of the Way into the Kingdom of Heaven*, in the Aleut language. Published in 1840, it was translated into many European and north Asian languages. Since the 1970s, because of the church authorities' emphasis on the use of English, the Alaskan languages and liturgical Slavonic have been mostly displaced by English, except perhaps in the Yup'ik Eskimo heartland where Euro-American impact occurred relatively late and where some translations in the Yup'ik language have more recently been accomplished.

From the beginning of this history most parish priests have been Native Alaskans and north-east Asians. On the Aleutian Islands the first resident priests were Fr Iakov Netsvetov for the extensive Atka parish (1829–44) and Fr Ioann Veniaminov for the equally extensive Unalaska parish (1824–34). Netsvetov was Native Alaskan, specifically 'Creole', a formal social estate within Alaska at that time. Veniaminov was Siberiak, from the rural Irkutsk region. Netsvetov became the head of the Yukon–Kuskokwim mission in Alaska (1845–63); Veniaminov became Bishop Innokentii. On the Aleutian Islands, both were succeeded by Creole clergymen.

Priests have always been remarkably few in proportion to the number of churches and chapels maintained by the laity. In 1858, nine priests were recorded as serving forty-four churches and chapels; in 1972, the same number were recorded as serving eighty-four. Currently, twenty-seven priests serve eighty-six churches and chapels. Today approximately 30,000 Native Alaskans are Orthodox Christians (according to Black): approximately 37.5 per cent of the whole native population, which also includes other native ethnic groups.

With regard to the initial infusion from north-east Asia as well as the Native Alaskan mainstay throughout this history, the Orthodox church in Alaska is, and has always been, native.

Mousalimas, S. A. (1993), Introduction to *Journals of Ioann Veniaminov in Alaska, 1823–1833*. Fairbanks: University of Alaska.

Gideon (1989), *Round the World Voyage of Hieromonk Gideon, 1803–1809*. Fairbanks and Kingston, Ont.: Limestone Press.

Black, T. (1980–89). Introductions, Appendices and Notes, in I. Netsvetov (1980), *Journals: Atkha Years, 1828–1844*. Kingston, Ont.: Limestone Press.

Netsvetov, I. (1984), *Journals: Yukon Years, 1845–1863*. Kingston, Ont.: Limestone Press.

Veniaminov, I. (1984 [1840]), *Notes on the Islands of the Unalashka District*. Fairbanks and Kingston, Ont.: Limestone Press.

Valaam Monastery (1978 [1894]), *The Russian Orthodox Religious Mission in America, 1794–1837*. Kingston, Ont.: Limestone Press.

Afonsky, G. (1977), *A History of the Orthodox Church in Alaska (1794–1917)*. Kodiak: St Herman's Theological Seminary.

Oleksa, M. J. (n.d.), ed., *Alaskan Missionary Spirituality*. New York: Paulist Press.

SM

Alaverdi   Site in the Kakhetia region of GEORGIA of a church of St George in a fortified enclosure. Founded in the sixth century, the present church of the eleventh century, on a Latin cross plan, is dominated by a tall central drum with a pointed dome. Exterior blind arcading adds to the building's vertical thrust: the interior is light and spacious. Of the ambulatory around three sides, only the west range remains. The church was rebuilt in brick in the late fifteenth century, though some eleventh-century wall-paintings survive. The enclosure once contained an episcopal palace. There is also a mosque on the site.

Mepisashvili, R., and Tsintsadze, V. (1979), *The Arts of Ancient Georgia*. London: Thames & Hudson.

KP

Albania   At the Roman empire's division in the fourth century, Albania became part of the Eastern Roman empire, though exposed to Western influences. After Slav invasions in the sixth century, Byzantine authority was restored only in the eleventh century. In the northern mountains this authority was nominal, but was reasserted earlier and lasted longer in the south and along the coast. Most early Byzantine churches are found in the south, where more bishoprics seem to have existed.

The Norman invasions and the Fourth CRUSADE introduced Roman Catholicism, although the southern part of the country was generally ruled by Greeks from Epirus or CONSTANTINOPLE; indeed, many Orthodox churches were built in the turbulent thirteenth and fourteenth centuries. Many conversions to ISLAM followed the Turkish invasions at the end of the fourteenth century. The heroic resistance of Scanderbeg (Iskender Beg or George Kastriota, *c.* 1405–68), who returned to Christianity from Islam in 1443 and until his death repelled Ottoman attempts to invade Albania, took place with Catholic help from Italy, and he himself was a Catholic of the Byzantine rite. In the south there was less resistance to the OTTOMANS and fewer converts to Islam. Crypto-Christianity was widespread. By the beginning of the nineteenth century the religious composition of Albania was more or less settled along present lines, with a solid body of Muslims in the centre of the country, a bloc of nearly 20 per cent Orthodox in the south and just over 10 per cent Catholics in the north. There were many Albanian speakers of all religions outside present-day Albania, especially in KOSOVO and northern GREECE, and much of the momentum for Albanian independence came from as far away as ROMANIA and AMERICA.

Independence came slowly. The Muslim majority was reluctant to shake off Turkish rule; the beys in charge of this majority were natural conservatives; the country had three different religions, two varieties of Albanian – Gheg in the north, Tosk in the south – and no common alphabet. At one stage it seemed likely that Albania would be parcelled out among other Balkan states. In the north, Catholics and Muslims were united in not wishing to join Orthodox Montenegro, SERBIA or BULGARIA, but the Orthodox inhabitants of the south faced a problem in choosing between Greece and independence. Even today Orthodox Greek-speakers live at a considerable distance north of the present frontier, and until 1939 Muslim Albanian-speakers could be found well inside Greece. Inhabitants of the south were more progressive and well educated, but the leadership of the Orthodox church tended to direct them towards Greece: it was left to Muslims from the south like the Frasheri and Konitza families to make the running for Albanian national identity.

Midhat Frasheri was chairman of the committee which eventually decided on the alphabet in 1903. His brother Samni urged the setting up of an autocephalous Albanian Orthodox church. This was impossible in Albania because of opposition both from the Ottoman authorities and from the Patriarch of CONSTANTINOPLE. Attempts to set up a church in Bucharest failed. But on 8 March 1908 the Russian archbishop of New York ordained Fan Noli as a priest, and on 22 March 1908 the first liturgy in Albanian was celebrated in Boston. Noli had been educated and taught in Greek schools, but in Egypt had met members of the Albanian community who had persuaded him to emigrate to America. An Albanian jurisdiction was established in America in 1918–19, by which time Albania was independent.

Fan Noli did much for Albania, as a poet and as a politician, but perhaps his greatest achievement was to establish with his autocephalous church that it was possible to be both an Albanian and a member of the Orthodox church. It is true that many Greeks still regard him as a traitor and that his period as prime minister was short and unsuccessful. Nor was the establishment of an Albanian church in Albania a simple matter. An initial meeting in 1908 at Korçe had wanted services in Albanian without losing the connection with Constantinople. A congress at Berat in 1922 demanded independence, and this seemed to be granted in 1923; but relations with Greece were strained, and in 1924 Noli turned to the Serbian patriarch at PEĆ to consecrate the first Albanian bishop. Relations with the patriarchate at Constantinople were not finally regularized until 1937.

Noli's successor as prime minister, the Muslim Ahmed Zogu, later King Zog, treated all religions fairly. By this time, however, Albania's political independence was threatened. Mussolini invaded the country in 1939, and the Greeks briefly occupied southern Albania from 1940 to 1941. Many guerrilla campaigns were fought in the south, and churches suffered as a result. Voskopoje in particular, a famous centre of Orthodoxy in the eighteenth century, when it was partially ruined by Ali Pasha, suffered further terrible damage. Now only a few of the region's beautiful churches survive. The Orthodox church was caught up in the conflict between various factions. The Catholics might have found comfort in the religion of the invading forces and the northern Muslims with the old Zogist regime. The Orthodox might have felt relieved that it was the communist partisans led by Enver Hoxha from Gjirokastër in the south who triumphed. But the Greek villages tended to suffer from communists and nationalists alike, and victory for communism was a victory against religion. For the first thirty years after the war religion was tolerated, and Orthodoxy prospered a little more than its rivals. In 1968 Hoxha, alleging that different faiths led to disunity, declared Albania an atheist state, and so it remained for twenty years. Foreign visitors, of whom there were few, were forbidden to bring in any religious material, while churches and mosques were converted to secular use or abandoned. Some villagers nevertheless managed to hide icons and vestments.

The collapse of communism has led to a remarkable revival of religion, beset, however, by political complications. Albania's tradition of tolerance and the fact that Hoxha was against all religions are sources of stability. But relations with Greece are not good. There was a shortage of priests and material aid for rebuilding the churches. The Greeks responded generously. In some cases, however, Greek assistance and influence have been seen as political interference and ethnic propaganda, and as a result Greek priests have been expelled and their churches attacked. Massive emigration to Greece has led to depopulation of the villages, many of whose churches are neglected and vandalized. The largely Muslim Albanian nation has many economic problems on its hands, and public services tend to be neglected in favour of private enterprise. Thus the future of Christianity in Albania is uncertain, though its survival at all is already an achievement.

See also KOSOVO; MACEDONIA; MONTENEGRO.

Hall, D. (1994), *Albania and Albanians*. London: Pinter.

Pollo, S. and Puto, A. (1981), *The History of Albania from its Origins to the Present Day*. London: Routledge & Kegan Paul.

Skendi, S. (1967), *The Albanian National Awakening*. Princeton: Princeton University Press.

Swire, J. (n.d.), *Albania: The Rise of a Kingdom*. London: Williams & Norgate.

TW

Albania, Al'uank   Also Arran or Aghovan: regions of eastern Caucasia, approximately corresponding to modern Azerbaijan and Daghestan. Caucasian Albania enjoyed independence from the first to the sixth century. The Albanians were evangelized from ARMENIA in the fourth century and adopted a modified form of the Armenian alphabet. From 510 Albania was dominated by the Sasanid Persians; nevertheless, the local Mihranid dynasty ruled the country as an Arab protectorate up to 821. The Muslim Tats of Azerbaijan are held to be descendants of the Iranian Albanians of Caucasia.

See also NAGORNO KARABAKH.

Walker, C. (1991), *Armenia and Karabagh*. London: Minority Rights Publications.

DB

Alexandria   Hellenistic Egyptian harbour city founded by Alexander the Great about 332 BC incorporating the ancient town Rakote ('built by Ra'). Its lighthouse, the Pharos, was one of the wonders of the ancient world. Alexandria, capital of Egypt until superseded by Cairo at the Arab invasion by Al-Fustat, was a centre of Greek and Jewish culture. Under the Ptolemies, Alexandrian Jewish scholars translated the BIBLE into Greek, producing the Septuagint, later the Old Testament of Hellenophone Christians. The museum and library of Alexandria made it a famous centre of learning, notable for its philosophy, philology, textual scholarship and historical study, all important to pagan, Jewish, Christian and eventually Muslim scholars.

The relics of St Mark, traditionally the evangelist of Egypt, were interred in splendour in Alexandria. His titular successors, who held the rank of pope and PATRIARCH of Alexandria, the senior hierarch of Egypt and all Africa, ranked immediately after the pope of ROME until the elevation of CONSTANTINOPLE to second place. Alexandria's prestige was enhanced by the reputation of its Catechetical School, where Pantaenus (d. *c*. 195), Clement (*c*. 150–215), ORIGEN (*c*. 185–254), Dionysios the Great (later patriarch: d. 264) and DIDYMUS THE BLIND (*c*. 310–98) all taught.

Arius (*c*.250–336), an Alexandrian priest, was excommunicated as a heretic by Patriarch Alexander (d. 328) and condemned at the Council of NICEA (325). Patriarch ATHANASIUS (*c*.296–373) refused imperial commands to reinstate him. Patriarch CYRIL OF ALEXANDRIA (d. 444) orchestrated the condemnation of Nestorius, his Twelve Anathemas of 430 forming the basis for the definition of orthodox doctrine at the Council of Ephesus in 431.

The major part of the Egyptian church followed Patriarch Dioscorus I (d. 454) in rejecting the Council of Chalcedon (451), and imperial intervention failed to heal the division. From that time the Coptic patriarchate has headed the non-Chalcedonian church and a Greek patriarchate the much smaller CHALCEDONIAN community. From the thirteenth century to the twentieth there existed a titular Latin patriarch of Alexandria. The MELKITE Catholic patriarch Maximos III Mazlum (1833–55) acquired the titles of JERUSALEM and Alexandria together with his inherited title of

17

patriarch of ANTIOCH. A fourth line was established when Pope Leo XIII established a patriarchate for the small Coptic Catholic church in 1895. The Catholic patriarchate was vacant from 1908 to 1947, but was then restored.

Bowman, A. (1990), *Egypt after the Pharaohs*. Oxford: Oxford University Press.
Frend, W. H. C. (1972), *The Rise of the Monophysite Movement*. Cambridge: Cambridge University Press.

DM

Allatius, Leo Catholic scholar theologian and patrologist; b. *c.* 1588 on Chios, d.1669; Vatican librarian from 1661. An important early ecumenist, his three-volume *De ecclesia occidentalis atque orientalis perpetua consensione* asserted the fundamental agreement of the Greek and Roman churches, denied they were truly separated, and rejected the view that the Greek church as such had fallen into heresy.

DM

Allelouia Greek version of Hebrew *hallelu-yah*, 'praise the Lord!' one of the Hebrew acclamations, which, like 'hosannah' and 'amen', survives in Christian liturgical use. In Greek the word is pronounced with five syllables. Allelouia, a joyful acclamation, concludes many hymns and antiphons, each KATHISMA of the psalter and every verse of the ANOIXANTARIA and the POLYELEOS.

In Western use, Alleluia is identified with celebration and especially the Paschal season. In Byzantine use, Allelouia is also sung on penitential days and in periods of mourning. Where on Sundays and feast days the APOLYTIKIA of Matins are preceded by the refrain 'The Lord is God and has appeared to us; blessed is he who comes in the name of the Lord,' with verses from the same psalm, on the weekdays of Lent, and correctly on solemn fasts, a threefold Allelouia is used with verses from Isaias. Hence, the rubrics often say 'if it is Allelouia . . .', meaning 'if it is a solemn fast . . .'. During GREAT WEEK the *allelouiarion* is sung to a slow, sombre melody.

As in Western use, allelouia verses are sung after the APOSTLE reading in the Byzantine liturgy, while censing takes place. In practice, Greek clergy usually cense during the Apostle itself, and verses of the allelouia are omitted. The Resurrection Gospel at the Prote Anastasis on Holy Saturday is the one gospel sung at the Divine Liturgy not preceded by an Allelouia.

DM/E

alousia Greek; 'abstinence from washing' undertaken as a form of ASCETICISM.

DM

Altai mission The first mission among the Altaic tribes was made as early as the sixth century by the CHURCH OF THE EAST. The mission of the RUSSIAN ORTHO-DOX CHURCH was established in the Altai mountains of south-west Siberia in 1830 and closed by the Bolsheviks *c.* 1918. Success was slow. The pioneer missionary Archimandrite Makarii (Mikhail GLUKHAREV) had baptized 675 people by his departure in 1844, fewer than fifty per year. His successor as director, a secular priest, Stepan Landyshev, established seven new departments in his twenty-two years. By

1864 there were 3,200 adult Altaian converts and 1,800 children, 29 staff, 11 churches, 10 schools and 22 settlements for converts. Vladimir, a monk, led the mission from 1866 to 1883. A convent and monastery were founded, and the work spread to the borders of Mongolia. By 1883 there were 108 settlements containing 13,000 Altaians, 4,550 Russians, 32 churches and chapels and 20 schools. Two-fifths of the Altaians had become Orthodox. The 61 staff included a bishop, Makarii (Nevskii) in Biisk, 16 priests, 2 deacons, 12 native lower clergy (*prichetniki*), 26 teachers, 4 interpreters and one medical orderly.

By 1904 there were 17 departments with 83 churches and 55 schools spread through the mountains. The 213 settlements contained 25,868 Altaians and 14,657 Russians. There were 1,430 pupils at school, 440 of them girls, more than half the pupils being Altaians. The mission's Secondary Catechists' School, established in 1860 to educate native teachers, catechists and translators and now located at Biisk, had 166 students in 1904, 45 of whom were Altaians. There was one school for every 750 inhabitants. Three orphanages and ten parish charity committees helped the poor. Old people were cared for in the convents. By 1913 there were at least 25 departments, divided into three deaneries (*blagochiniya*), containing 74 schools, 2 monasteries and 4 nunneries. The flock of Altaians and Russians numbered 69,357. As the missionary areas were thoroughly evangelized they became conventional parishes, resources released being diverted to evangelizing new territory.

Mission policy stressed extensive preparatory evangelistic work and consistent post-baptismal instruction. To protect converts from attack by irate relatives, special villages were established. Neophytes were taught to live in the Russian manner and to adopt agricultural pursuits, regarded as superior to the uncertainties of their forebears' nomadism. Acculturation was strongest in the north and east, regions with most Russian settlers. By the early twentieth century mixed marriages appeared frequently in parish registers. The missionaries devised a Cyrillic alphabet, translating and publishing scriptures, liturgical texts and devotional works.

In the mission settlements all human needs, spiritual, economic, medical, moral, social and educational, were provided for as far as possible. Healing miracles were recorded, but in general medical aid involved inculcation of basic hygiene and application of current Russian remedies. Trained smallpox inoculators travelled round the villages. Small hospitals were set up; the staff were few and not highly trained, but state medical provision was virtually non-existent. Philanthropic works included providing clothes, tools, seed, food and money for the poor, sheltering widows and orphans, trying to overcome family quarrels and attempting to limit alcohol sales.

The missionaries saw their work as a God-given duty: Russians were to spread the light of the gospel among a people oppressed by superstition, disease, ignorance and poverty. Sometimes this became confused with Russia's imperial designs, but overall, among the missionaries, spiritual and pastoral concerns dominated the colonial impulse.

Collins, D. N. (1989), 'Colonialism and Siberian Development: A Case Study of the Orthodox Mission to the Altay, 1830–1913', in A. Wood and R. A. French, eds, *The Development of Siberia: People and Resources*. London: Macmillan.
Bolshakoff, S. (1943), *The Foreign Missions of the Russian Orthodox Church*. London: SPCK.

Smirnoff, E. (1903), *A Short Account of the Historical Development and Present Position of Russian Orthodox Missions*. London: Rivingtons; repr. 1986, Welshpool: Stylite Publishing.

SM

altar The holy table; alternatively, the whole area behind the *haikal*-screen or ICONOSTASIS. The holy table symbolizes (a) the table of the Mystical Supper; (b) the Heavenly Altar; (c) the Throne of the Holy Trinity; (d) the Tomb of Christ; (e) the Earth. The table is often a cube or double cube, frequently covered by a canopy. The altar-table is consecrated by relics being sealed inside it or its pillars, by washing and by anointing with oil. The ANTIMENSION is consecrated by being used to wipe the oil of consecration from the altar. The Byzantine altar-table is draped with three cloths, the first usually of simple white linen, the outermost of rich material.

DM

Al-Waḍiḥ ibn Rağāh Al-Wāḍiḥ ibn Rağā, *fl. c.* 1000. We know about this Coptic writer from the account of his life preserved in *The Coptic History of the Patriarchs of Alexandria*, a series of historical and biographical texts in Coptic and later in Arabic which constitute the official history of the Coptic church. A convert to Christianity from Islam, he took the name Paul (Būlus) and became a monk and priest in one of the monasteries of the Egyptian Wadi Natrun, the ancient 'desert of Scetis'. The biography describes his friendship with SEVERUS IBN AL-MUQAFFA', and their mutual interest in apologetic literature. Perhaps the best-known of al-Wadih ibn Rağah's extant Arabic works is the *Kitāb al-Wāḍiḥ* (Book of Evidence), a refutation of Islam.

See also COPTIC CHRISTIANITY.

Frederick, V. (1991), 'Wādih ibn Rajā, Al-,' *Coptic Encyclopedia* 7, p. 2311.
Graf, G. (1947), *Geschichte der christlichen arabischen Literatur*, 5 vols (Studi e Testi, 118, 133, 146–7, 172), vol. 2, pp. 318–19. Città del Vaticano: Biblioteca Apostolica Vaticana, 1944–53.
'Abd al-Masīh, Y. and Burmester, O. H. E., eds and trans. (1943), *History of the Patriarchs of the Egyptian Church, Known as the History of the Holy Church by Sawīrus ibn al-Muḳaffa', Bishop of Al-Ašmūnīn*, vol. 2, pt 2: *Textes et Documents*. Cairo: Publications de la Société d'Archéologie Copte.

MJB/SHG

ambo Greek: *ambon, ambonas*; in ancient times an elevated platform in the middle of the church from which scriptural texts were read, and on which officiating clergy sometimes stood. An ambo in ancient style is still used in the church of Kavalla at the foot of the METEORON. The Byzantine Liturgy of St James presumes the use of an ambo of this kind. In modern use, the *ambonas* is the pulpit, from which the DEACON reads the gospel.

In most Byzantine churches, the bema from which readings are given is raised above the floor level of the nave, and the solea, once a walkway connecting ambo and bema, is a narrow, raised area before the ICONOSTASIS, widening to a platform before the holy doors, and from which the priest reads the gospel if he is celebrating in the absence of a bishop. The bema of monastic churches on ATHOS is normally level with the floor of the nave.

The 'Prayer behind the Ambo', originally the concluding prayer of the Divine Liturgy, is now generally recited in Greek churches on the solea, facing the icon of Christ. In stricter use it is recited from the middle of the nave towards the place where the ancient ambo would have stood.

DM

'Āmda Ṣeyōn I   'Āmda Ṣeyōn, also called Gabra Maskal, emperor of Ethiopia 1314–44. The early part of his reign was marked by confrontations with the Ethiopian clergy and monks. Amda Ṣeyon I did much to consolidate and expand the state of Ethiopia. His concerns about Islamic persecution of Christians are recorded. He fought a series of military battles against border states in the south and south-east, and successfully pushed back Islamic incursions.

See also ETHIOPIAN CHRISTIANITY.

Tamrat, T. (1972), *Church and State in Ethiopia, 1250–1527*. Oxford Studies in African Affairs. Oxford: Clarendon.
Huntingford, G. W. B., ed. and trans. (1965), *The Glorious Victories of Amda Seyon, King of Ethiopia*. Oxford: Clarendon.

MJB/SHG

America   Two events during the eighteenth century mark the beginnings of EASTERN ORTHODOX Christianity on the American continent. The first is the 'discovery' of ALASKA by Captain Bering of the Russian imperial navy in 1741. In the following decades, Russian fur trading in the eastern Aleutian Islands and Alaska was accompanied by the conversion of natives to Orthodoxy. The arrival of ten missionaries from the Valaam monastery near St Petersburg on Kodiak Island on 24 September 1794 is taken by some commentators as the beginning of Orthodoxy in America, though some native Alaskans had been Orthodox for two generations before this.

During the second half of the eighteenth century Orthodox Christians could also be found in the newly acquired British possession of Florida. In 1767 a few hundred Greeks, many from ASIA MINOR, arrived at New Smyrna, Florida as part of an experimental plantation financed from Britain. The promised services of an Orthodox clergyman never materialized. The colony was dissolved after a few years, many of the Greeks resettling in St Augustine, Florida.

It was in Russian-held Alaska that the first ecclesiastical organization for Orthodox Christians in North America was established with the consecration in 1840 of Bishop INNOKENTII VENIAMINOV of the new diocese of Kamchatka, the Kurile Islands and the Aleutian Islands, with its seat at Novo Arkhangel'sk (Sitka), Alaska. In the 1850s the diocese was incorporated into an immense archdiocese encompassing the easternmost regions of the Russian empire, with an auxiliary bishop at Sitka. Three years after the sale of Alaska to the United States in 1867, a new Russian diocese of Alaska and the Aleutian Islands was created, and in 1872 the seat of this diocese was transferred from Sitka to San Francisco, reflecting the new political reality of the Russian diocese.

The second half of the nineteenth century marks a new period for Orthodoxy in America. Greek merchants, Russian sailors, and other Orthodox businessmen and labourers began settling in large coastal cities in North and South America. For their spiritual needs, these Orthodox Christians would organize themselves into a benevolent society, assess membership dues and locate a place to hold liturgical services. The first Orthodox parish founded in this manner, and the first parish outside of Alaska, was that of SS Constantine and Helen, Galveston, Texas, established in 1862. The parish consisted of Greek, Russian, Serb and Syrian Eastern Orthodox. Other early multi-ethnic parishes were New Orleans (1864), San Francisco (1868), New York (1870), Chicago (1885), Buenos Aires (1889) and Seattle (1890). Worship was often conducted in Church Slavonic, Greek and English. The most immediate need of these parishes was for an Orthodox priest. Some early multi-ethnic parishes petitioned the Russian diocese or the Holy Synod of the Russian church for clergy. Other parishes sought clergy by alternative means. The parish in New Orleans received its first priests both through the Greek consul in that city and directly from GREECE. However a priest was obtained, the initial impetus in the establishment of these nineteenth-century communities came from Orthodox lay Christians. Affiliation with the Russian diocese was fluid: some parishes came directly under diocesan control, others remained essentially independent of episcopal influence.

During the 1890s larger numbers of Greeks, Serbs, Syrians, Russians and others began emigrating to the USA, Canada and South America, establishing their own parishes. The first entirely Greek immigrant parish was that of Holy Trinity, founded in New York City in 1892. In 1895 the first Eastern Orthodox Syrian parish, St Nicholas, was established also in New York City, receiving its first priest through the Russian diocese. Holy Trinity, which obtained its priests directly from the Holy Synod of the Church of Greece, remained essentially a self-governing parish independent of direct episcopal control. This is reflected in events after Good Friday 1904, when Bishop TIKHON of the Russian diocese visited Holy Trinity. Considering himself the ruling Orthodox hierarch in America, Tikhon assumed Holy Trinity belonged under his care. Tikhon's visit prompted a Greek fear of Russian ecclesiastical hegemony. To secure its independence, Holy Trinity became privately incorporated under the State of New York a year later. The Russian diocese's claims to jurisdiction over all parishes in America had been rejected.

Mass immigration from Eastern Europe, the Balkans and the Middle East between the 1890s and the 1920s marks the largest period of growth for Orthodoxy in America. These Orthodox Christian immigrants brought with them a faith cultivated for centuries in historic Orthodox lands. Settling in an alien country, the Orthodox found refuge in their parish communities. In the parish, at times an extension of the homeland, Orthodox immigrants sought to preserve the unity of faith and culture which was a part of their heritage. This was partly accomplished through the creation of independent ecclesiastical jurisdictions.

Many early immigrant communities initially placed themselves under the jurisdiction of the Russian diocese. Albanians, Serbians and Syrians formed separate missions under the Russian diocese. However, the majority of non-Russian parishes remained independent of the Russian diocese or any other episcopal authority, being privately incorporated in the state or province in which they resided. Priests were obtained

directly from the homeland, their salaries paid by the community. While clergy sometimes found themselves at the mercy of parish boards which hired and fired priests free
from any episcopal control, lay involvement within parish life flourished and a strongly
democratic parish administration, fostered among the Orthodox in America, continues
to the present.

As the number of their parishes increased, Greeks, Serbians, Syrians and others began
to organize themselves into separate dioceses under the spiritual care of the mother
churches from whom they now received their bishops. Arabic-speaking parishes
organized themselves within two independent archdioceses under the patriarchate of
ANTIOCH, eventually merging in 1975. A Greek archdiocese, established in 1921, came
within a year under the jurisdiction of CONSTANTINOPLE. Like most other jurisdictions, the Greek archdiocese was plagued by schisms related to political divisions in the
homeland. Through the efforts of Athenagoras, archbishop from 1931 to 1948 and later
ECUMENICAL PATRIARCH, the Greek archdiocese regained its unity, and continues
to be the largest Orthodox jurisdiction. The BULGARIANS created an autonomous
diocese in 1938 and came under the Bulgarian patriarchate in 1963, though ten parishes
remained under the Russian diocese. For decades ROMANIAN parishes remained free
of episcopal control. Today there are two separate Romanian dioceses in America.
SERBIANS eventually left the Russian diocese and schism led to the creation of two
separate dioceses in 1963. ALBANIANS established their own jurisdiction in 1918–19,
the majority of these parishes placing themselves under the ORTHODOX CHURCH IN
AMERICA in 1971. Three different UKRAINIAN jurisdictions under the Ecumenical
Patriarchate were united in 1997 under the omophorion of the newly appointed
Archbishop Vsevolod of Chicago.

Several smaller Orthodox jurisdictions exist, notable among these the OLD CALEN-
DARIST churches. Most Old Calendarist parishes in America fall under one of three
Old Calendarist jurisdictions in Greece, and retain a Greek identity. Though small in
numbers, they have challenged the more mainstream Orthodox jurisdictions' involve-
ment in the ecumenical movement and what is perceived as a gradual Westernization of
Orthodoxy in America.

The ORIENTAL ORTHODOX presence in America is also due to immigration.
ARMENIANS emigrated to the USA and Canada in large numbers from the 1890s.
The first Armenian parish was organized in 1889 in Worcester, Massachusetts. In 1933
the newly appointed Archbishop Tourian was murdered during Divine Liturgy in New
York City by a faction which rejected the spiritual authority of the Soviet-backed see
of Ejmiacin. This incident split the Armenian American community, those opposed to
Ejmiacin placing themselves eventually under the see of Cilicia. The Armenian
Apostolic Church remains the largest group of Oriental Orthodox in America.

SYRIAN ORTHODOX (JACOBITE) communities were first established in the USA
and Canada during the 1920s, eventually organizing into an archdiocese in 1952.
ETHIOPIAN and COPTIC Orthodox Christians are among the most recent immigrants
of Oriental Orthodox to America. The first Ethiopian parish was founded in 1959 in
New York City, the first Coptic parish in Toronto in 1965.

EASTERN CATHOLICS began arriving in America from the Carpathian Mountains
of the Austro-Hungarian empire in the late 1870s, their spiritual needs initially met by
local Latin rite churches serving immigrant Polish and Slovak communities. The first

Eastern rite parish was established in Shenandoah, Pennsylvania in 1884. The arrival of married Eastern Catholic clergy shortly thereafter led to confrontations with Latin episcopal authorities. Mounting pressure from Catholic bishops resulted in the conversion of several Eastern rite parishes to the Orthodox Church. On 25 March 1891 Fr Alexander Toth and 361 members of the St Mary's parish in Minneapolis were received into the Orthodox Church by the bishop of the Russian diocese. Other parishes soon followed. In Canada, large numbers of Ukrainian Catholics who had arrived from Galicia in the 1890s were also received into the Russian diocese, later forming their own independent jurisdiction. The 1930s drew two more groups of Eastern Catholics (Ukrainians and Carpatho-Russians) into Orthodoxy under the Ecumenical Patriarchate. By 1964 an estimated 400,000 Eastern rite Catholics in the USA and Canada had become Orthodox.

The Catholic church responded to the loss of the first Eastern rite parishes by creating separate dioceses for Ukrainian and Ruthenian Catholics in 1924. Today, these groups comprise the two largest bodies of Eastern Catholics in the United States and Canada. Other Eastern rite churches in America, though in much smaller numbers, are Armenian, MELKITE, Romanian, MARONITE and CHALDEAN. The growth of Eastern rite Catholic parishes is hindered by a lack of clerical vocations, due in part to the enforcement of clerical celibacy, and the loss of members to Latin rite Catholic churches. The Russian diocese faced serious challenges in the wake of the Bolshevik Revolution of 1917. Loss of financial support from the Russian state (which had amounted to $550,000 in 1916) left the diocese in economic chaos. Loyalty to imperial Russia clashed with Socialist ideology. Rallies in support of the Revolution were held in local churches and Russian clergy challenged to debate openly the existence of God. Yet it was jurisdictional confusion that was the most tragic legacy for the Russian Orthodox faithful in America.

The Russian diocese initially supported the gathering of Russian bishops at Sremski-Karlovtzy in Yugoslavia (see RUSSIAN ORTHODOX CHURCH ABROAD). However, by 1926 the Russian diocese, having severed ties with Moscow two years earlier, broke relations with the church in exile. Now known as the Russian Orthodox Greek Catholic Church in America or the Metropolia, it proclaimed itself 'temporarily self-governing'. Bishops remaining loyal to ROCA moved their headquarters to New York City in 1950. Further jurisdictional confusion was fostered by John Kedrovsky, a priest associated with the Living Church movement in the Soviet Union, who in 1923 led a campaign to gain the loyalties of parishes in the USA and despite little success secured property rights to a few Russian parishes including the Cathedral of St Nicholas in New York City, the seat of the Russian diocese since 1905. The Living Church movement faltered, and in 1933 Moscow established a patriarchal exarch in New York City with residence at St Nicholas.

In 1970 the Metropolia, the largest of the three Russian jurisdictions in America, was granted AUTOCEPHALY by the Moscow patriarchate as the ORTHODOX CHURCH IN AMERICA (OCA). This unilateral declaration of autocephaly has not been recognized by Constantinople, ALEXANDRIA or Antioch, or by other autocephalous Orthodox churches.

MONASTICISM in America dates back to the arrival of the Valaam mission of 1794. Immigrant parishes, striving to survive in a new environment, had little interest in what they saw as flight from the world. Small monastic houses have been established by most jurisdictions, yet it is under ROCA and the Greek Old Calendarists that monasticism has been most emphasized.

The need to provide educated clergy, often bilingual, for parish ministry has occupied a large part of the resources of most jurisdictions. A missionary seminary was first established by Bishop Innokentii at Sitka in 1841, later transferred to San Francisco and relocated to Tenafly, New Jersey, before closing in 1923 for financial reasons. The Greek archdiocese established a seminary in Astoria, New York in 1921, but it too closed two years later for lack of funds. In 1937 the Greek archdiocese opened Holy Cross seminary in Pomfret, Connecticut, moving it ten years later to Brookline, Massachusetts. The Metropolia established two seminaries in 1938, St Tikhon's and St Vladimir's. Among the latter's faculty was Fr Georges FLOROVSKY, who served as dean of the school from 1949 to 1955, before joining the faculties of Holy Cross and Harvard University.

The Orthodox jurisdictions have essentially remained faithful to the Orthodox liturgical ethos, though over the decades pews, organs and mixed-voice choirs have become common in most Orthodox parishes. Some parishes include congregational singing. The use of English as a liturgical language has increased. The OCA uses English almost exclusively while other jurisdictions maintain the use of traditional languages, such as Greek, Church Slavonic and Arabic, to varying degrees.

Orthodox lay men and women have played a significant role in the development of Orthodox Christianity in America. Lay brotherhoods, popular especially among Slavic immigrants, were instrumental in the organization and building of parishes throughout North America. The fact that the majority of parishes were conceived, built and financed without ecclesiastical or state assistance, when coupled with the democratic ideals of the United States and Canada, fostered a strong lay commitment within Orthodox communities. Today, most Orthodox jurisdictions hold annual or biennial administrative meetings of both clergy and laity.

In 1960 several Orthodox jurisdictions, seeking a more unified voice for Orthodoxy in America, established the Standing Conference of Canonical Orthodox Bishops in the Americas (SCOBA), which co-ordinates pan-Orthodox co-operation in campus ministry, ecumenical dialogue, catechetical education, military chaplaincy, missionary and charitable work.

Orthodoxy has recently begun to appeal to a larger American audience. Along with individual and familial conversions to Orthodoxy, several groups have joined the Orthodox Church during the late twentieth century. In 1987 2,000 evangelical Christians were received into the Antiochian Orthodox Christian Archdiocese. Parishes of the Episcopal Church in America have also made wholesale conversions to Orthodoxy, some retaining the Western rite.

Eastern Christianity in America will continue to attract Christians from other backgrounds. Further, the rise in inter-Christian marriages and inevitable generational assimilation have hastened Orthodoxy's absorption into Western patterns of life and culture. The challenge for Orthodoxy and for other Eastern Christian traditions is how to preserve the symbiosis of faith and culture which occurred over centuries in their homelands and was brought to America by Eastern Christian immigrants.

Mousalimas, S. A. (1994), *The Transition from Shamanism to Russian Orthodoxy in Alaska*. Oxford: Berghahn.

Pappaioannou, G. (1985), *The Odessey of Hellenism in America*. Thessaloniki: Patristic Institute of Theological Studies.

Efthimiou, M. B. and Christopoulos, G. A., eds (1984), *History of the Greek Orthodox Church in America*. New York: Greek Orthodox Archdiocese of North and South America.

Yuzyk, P. (1981), *The Ukranian Greek Orthodox Church of Canada, 1918–1951*. Ottowa: University of Ottowa Press.

Bobango, G. J. (1979), *The Romanian Orthodox Episcopate of America: The First Half Century, 1929–1979*. Jackson, Mich.: Romanian-American Heritage Center.

Pappaioannou, G. (1976), *From Mars Hill to Manhattan: The Greek Orthodox in America under Athenagoras I*. Minneapolis: Light and Life Publishing.

Kishkovsky, L. (1975), 'Archbishop Tikhon in America', *St Vladimir's Theological Quarterly* 19, pp. 9–31.

Tarasar, C., ed. (1975), *Orthodox America, 1794–1976*. New York: OCA.

Doumouras, A. (1967), 'Greek Orthodox Communities in America before World War I', *St Vladimir's Seminary Quarterly* 11, pp. 172–92.

Saloutos, T. (1965 [repr. 1975]), *The Greeks in the United States*. Harvard: Harvard University Press.

JCS

Amharic   One of the Semitic Ethiopian languages spoken today; the official language of Ethiopia, and the language of the majority of Ethiopian Christians. The pre-eminence of GEʿEZ as a classical literary and ecclesiastical language means that very little Amharic literature exists from before the late seventeenth century. Today Amharic is the major literary language of Ethiopia, with a large and varied secular and religious literature.

See also ETHIOPIAN ORTHODOX CHURCH.

Ullendorff, E. (1955), *The Semitic Languages of Ethiopia: A Comparative Phonology*. London: Taylor's (Foreign) Press.

MJB/SHG

ʿAmmār al-Baṣrī   (d. *c*.845) Theological controversialist of the CHURCH OF THE EAST. Only two Arabic treatises by him are known from a single manuscript. ʿAmmār al-Baṣrī , along with members of other Christian confessions such as the MELKITE theologian THEODORE ABŪ QURRAH (*c*.750–*c*.825) and the SYRIAN ORTHODOX apologist ḤABĪB IBN ḤIDMAH ABŪ RĀʾIṬAH (*fl*. first half ninth century), represents the first generation of Syriac-speaking Christians to answer the challenge of Islam in Arabic. The common aim of these apologists, active during the first century of the Abbasid caliphate, was to commend the tenets of Christianity to their co-religionists and to interested Muslims, in an Arabic language that reflected the intellectual concerns of contemporary Muslim religious dialecticians. They helped lay the foundations of Christian theology in Arabic.

Griffith, S. H. (1993), '`ʿAmmār al-Baṣrī's *Kitāb al-Burhān*: Christian *Kalām* in the First Abbasid Century', *Le Muséon* 96, pp. 145–81.

Griffith, S. H. (1982), 'The Concept of *al-Uqnum* in 'Ammār al-Baṣrī 's Apology for the Doctrine of the Trinity', *Orientalia Christiana Analecta* 218, pp. 169–91.
Hayek, M. (1976), ''Ammār el-Baṣrī , La première somme de théologie chrétienne en langue arabe, ou deux apologies du christianisme', *Islamochristiana* 2, pp. 69–133.

MJB/SHG

amnos   Greek, 'lamb'. The lamb, especially the sacrificial lamb, is a symbol of Christ. In Byzantine use, the portion of the PROSPHORA, the loaf of pure wheat bread prepared for liturgical use, cut out for consecration is called *amnos*.
   See also BREAD STAMP.

DM

anabathmi   Greek: *anabathmoi*, short hymns composed by THEODORE THE STU-DITE, based on the Septuagint Psalms of Ascents, numbers 119–33, sung at Byzantine Matins on Sundays, and on feasts with a gospel. On Sundays they are divided into three antiphons, except for tone eight, which has four. They are sung immediately before the PROKEIMENON. On feasts the first antiphon of tone four is always used, hence the Prokeimenon on feasts is sung in that tone.

E

analogion   Greek: stand on which icons are placed for worship, or a lectern used by singers.

DM

Anargyroi   Greek, 'unmercenary' saints in EASTERN CHRISTIAN tradition: healers or Christian physicians who, in conscious opposition to medical practice of the day,

refused payment for work with the sick. Some were famous for healing animals. They were noted for miraculous cures both during their lives and after death. The martyred Anargyros Mokios (d. 295) was the original patron saint of CONSTANTINOPLE. The Syrians Cosmas and Damian (third century) and Panteleimon (d. 305) are the best known. The Anargyroi are commemorated together, as a group of twelve or twenty-two, on 17 October and also separately. Sampson the Hospitaller (sixth century), Cyrus and John (third century) and Hermolaos (fourth century) are invoked in services alongside Panteleimon, Cosmas and Damian. Some, like TRYPHON (d. 250), practised folk medicine while others were conventionally trained doctors. Sophia of Egypt (third century) is the only woman to whom this title is sometimes given.

Kontaxopoulos, K. (1990), *Hagioi Iatroi Tes Orthodoxias*. Athens: Kardia.
Demetrios of Rostov (1995), *The Great Collection of the Lives of the Saints*. House Springs, Miss.: Chrysostom Press.

DB

Anastasimatarion Greek, 'resurrectional': Byzantine liturgical book containing text (and sometimes music) for Sunday offices, especially ORTHROS and HESPER-INOS, all of which are rich in resurrection hymns, since Sunday celebrates the resurrection. The texts for the offices of the whole week are contained in the PARA-KLETIKE or OKTOECHOS.

DM

Anastasis Greek, 'resurrection'. The image *par excellence* of the Resurrection is the ICON 'The Descent into Hades'. Christ appears carrying the Cross as symbol of his

victory over death, the stigmata on his hands and feet. Hades is shown as a dark fissure from which the first created humans (the protoplasts) and the Old Testament patriarchs have been plucked. ADAM AND EVE appear with JOHN THE BAPTIST. Christ, the New Adam, pulls up the Old Adam and in doing so saves the human race. The robed and crowned figures of David and Solomon appear near to the priest Zacharias, father of John the Baptist, holding a horn, a reference to Luke 1: 68ff. Superimposed upon Christ's MANDORLA is a geo-metrical diagram of light symbolizing the Resurrection. This is reflected in the rays of light issuing from the open heavens above. Christ tramples down the broken gates of Hades while the keys, locks and chains of Satan's power fall into oblivion. A related description of the descent into Hades appears in the fifth- or sixth-century Gospel of Nicodemus.

Kartsonis, A. (1986), *Anastasis: The Making of an Image*. Princeton: Princeton University Press.

KP

anatolika Byzantine Sunday Resurrection STICHERA, possibly by Patriarch Anato-lios of Constantinople (449–58). There are four anatolika in each of the eight tones at Vespers and Lauds as stichera to the last four verses of the Kekragenarion and of the AINOI psalms, unless replaced by stichera in honour of the saint whose feast is celebrated. *See also* CALENDAR.

DM/E

Andrew of Cret (*c*.660–740) Saint, hymnographer and theologian. Andrew was born in Damascus. After 690 he became archbishop of Gortyna in Crete. He was a prolific author and poet, reputed to have invented the CANON. His Great Canon, a lengthy penitential poem, is sung in Byzantine rite churches on the fifth Thursday of Great Lent. Andrew was a noted preacher and many of his homilies are extant. He is commemorated in the Byzantine calendar on 4 July.

DM

Andrew the Apostle   The Protoclete (First-Called). Andrew, closely associated with his brother Peter, is venerated as patron of the entire Eastern church, because it is believed he brought the gospel to the cities and peoples of GREECE and the Black Sea regions before being crucified at Patras. By tradition Andrew consecrated the first bishop of Byzantium, Stachys, penetrated Scythia and raised a CROSS near KIEV. His relics were translated from Patras to CONSTANTINOPLE and later scattered across Europe. Andrew is patron saint of many Orthodox countries including Greece and Russia, and also of Scotland, where it is believed that the monk Regulus took some of his relics to St Andrews.

Lamont, S. (1997), *Saint Andrew*. London: Hodder & Stoughton.
Turnbull, M. (1997), *Saint Andrew*. Edinburgh: St Andrews Press.
Dvornik, F. (1958), *The Idea of Apostolicity in Byzantium and the Legend of the Apostle Andrew*. Cambridge, Mass.: Harvard University Press.

DB

Andrew the Scythian   HOLY FOOL of CONSTANTINOPLE, commemorated on 28 May with his disciple Epiphanios and on 2 October, after the feast of the Holy Protection (POKROV; in Greek, Hagia Skepe). By tradition Andrew died *c*.475; his Life records his ascetic feats, first as slave in the household of Theognostos, later among the homeless on the streets of Constantinople. Andrew feigned madness after a series of visionary experiences. His vision of the THEOTOKOS holding aloft her mantle amid a host of ANGELS, GREAT MARTYRS and other saints in the Blachernai church gave rise to the Byzantine Feast of the Protection celebrated on 1 or 28 October. Believed to be from Scythia, Andrew was also venerated as one of the earliest Russian saints. The Blachernai vision is depicted on numerous icons titled Holy Protection and popularized by icons of Our Lady BLACHERNITISSA.

DB

anestenaria   The custom of dancing barefoot on live coals, holding an icon or the gospel book. In certain villages in Thrace and Macedonia on 21 May, feast of CONSTANTINE and Helen, icon-bearing dancers perform on hot coals to music played on traditional instruments. The Anestenarides keep their portable icons in a special shrine or *konaki*. The icons are hung with bells, and red shawls (*simadia*) are draped across them when they are held aloft for dancing. Most Anestenarides are descended from the Kostilides, refugees from eastern Thrace, who settled in Macedonia in the 1920s. Many are women. The ceremony is repudiated by the Greek Orthodox Church.

Danforth, L. M. (1989), *Firewalking and Religious Healing: The Anestenaria of Greece and the American Firewalking Movement*. Princeton: Princeton University Press.

KP

angels   Greek: *angelos*; Hebrew: *mal'ak*, 'messenger'. Christianity inherited from the Jewish BIBLE the vision of the Heavenly Court (3 Kingdoms 22: 19; 1 Kings 22: 19) where angels praise God, singing (Isaias 6: 3) 'Holy, holy, holy, Lord Sabaoth, all the earth is full of his glory' (*see* TRISAGION), belief in angel messengers (Judges 6: 14), ministering and protecting angels (Exodus 22: 20) and in angels as servants of God's wrath (2 Kingdoms 24: 16; 2 Samuel 24: 16). The New Testament also presents angels as witnesses to the birth, resurrection and ascension of Christ, a theme widely developed in the iconographic tradition, where angels are also depicted, for example, at the baptism of Christ, at the Crucifixion and at his burial.

Three angels are individually named in the Old Testament: Michael (Daniel 10: 21), Gabriel (Daniel 8: 16) and Raphael (Tobias 3: 17); a fourth, Uriel, is named in the *Sibylline Oracles*, 2: 214–15, which may date from the second century. These four are venerated as the principal archangels in EASTERN CHRISTIAN tradition but churches are dedicated only to the first two, MICHAEL AND GABRIEL, the Taxiarchs or Strategoi (commanders or generals) of the heavenly hosts. They and all the heavenly host are commemorated on 8 November. The four archangels are sometimes depicted as a group; sometimes seven (Tobias 12: 15) or eight archangels are shown. EASTERN ORTHODOX tradition also honours Salathiel, Jegudiel (Jekuthiel), Barachiel and Jeremiel (Remiel) as archangels. Copts commemorate Surael, Sakakael, Sarathael and Ananael. Angels representing virtues are also represented in Byzantine miniatures and elsewhere.

The Asomatoi or Bodiless Powers, called the 'first created' (in, for example, the second-century *Shepherd of Hermas*, Vision III, 4: 1), are sometimes thought of as pure spirits, sometimes as possessing ethereal bodies or bodies of celestial fire. There exists a tradition that creation took place in March and the nine orders of angels preside over the nine months up to November.

Visionary texts of the second century offer accounts of the heavenly hierarchy, usually based on an angelically guided ascent through seven heavens, prefigured to some extent in Paul's ascent to the 'third heaven'. An everlasting liturgy of praise is offered by the angels of the Heavenly Court (Ascension of Isaiah; 2 Enoch). These accounts develop themes common in Jewish apocalypticism and mysticism.

The fourth-century Apostolic Constitutions contain a number of prayers which may well have originated in the liturgy of the Greek-speaking Jews. In three of these prayers categories of angels are listed which correspond closely to the three triads of choirs described by DIONYSIOS THE AREOPAGITE (sixth century), who lists Seraphim, Cherubim, Thrones; Dominions, Virtues, Powers; Principalities, Archangels and Angels, the names drawn from various biblical texts. The nine choirs may be symbolized by the nine ranks of bread particles placed on the paten in the Byzantine preparation rite, the PROTHESIS; each particle represents a category of saint, but their number may refer to the angels. In present Greek use the first particle represents the Bodiless Powers, but the older use preserved in Slav tradition has the first particle represent the Forerunner, the second the other prophets. In the liturgy the congregation represent the angels of the Heavenly Court; this is made explicit in the CHERUBIKON. Deacons specifically represent the ministering angels.

Guardian angels watch over people, nations, places and churches. The association between the angels and the nations is supported by the Septuagint text of Deuteronomy 32: 8: 'When the Most High divided the nations…he set the bounds of the nations according to the number of the angels of God.' References to the 'Prince of Tyre' in Ezechiel 28 are traditionally read in the light of this passage to refer to the guardian angel of that city. Michael appears in the Old Testament as the guardian angel of Israel. The Byzantine Horologion includes a canon to the guardian angel; Russian icons of guardian angels are common.

Gabriel, in Daniel 8 and 9 the interpreter of visions and prophecies, is the angel of the ANNUNCIATION, herald of the incarnation, God's messenger proclaiming and interpreting to Mary the message that she is to bear 'the Son of the Most High'.

Highest among the angels in the original order of creation was Eosphoros, the Dawnbearer, who, according to Isaias 14: 12, 'sent out to all the nations'. (In Latin Eosphoros was translated as Lucifer, the Lightbearer. Unfortunately Lucifer also translates the Greek Phosphoros, which is a title of Christ.) The same verse in Isaias describes his fall: 'How the Dawnbearer has fallen from Heaven, he that rose with the dawn'. Tradition identifies the Dawnbearer with the *diabolos*, the Adversary, Satan. In Job the Adversary appears before God as tempter of humankind, but with no sign he is a fallen angel. Christian tradition sees the Adversary as the Devil, the leader of angel rebels who defy God and are cast out by the Hosts of Heaven led by Michael, the 'Archistrategos', who replaces the Dawnbearer as the Prince of Angels. Often the War in Heaven is thought of as taking place at the beginning of creation. In the Apocalypse of John it seems rather an eschatological event: 'Then war broke out in heaven. Michael and his angels made war on the dragon. The dragon and his angels fought back, but were overcome, and had no place in heaven. The great dragon was cast down, the ancient serpent that deceived the whole world, he whose name is Satan or the Devil, cast down to earth and his angels with him' (Apocalypse 12: 7–9). The fallen angels or demons are under the power of Christ (Ephesians 1: 20ff.), but his final victory is completed only at the Second Coming. Ascetic and spiritual writers frequently see the spiritual life against the backcloth of and as a moment in this cosmic war.

The Apocalypse image of the Heavenly Liturgy (Apocalypse 4–5) focused on the worship of 'the Lamb that was slaughtered'. The mystical unity of the Heavenly Liturgy and the Divine Liturgy of the Christian eucharistic assembly, and the unity of both with the Mystical Supper, the Passion, death and Resurrection of Christ, is an abiding theme in Eastern liturgical thought, HYMNOGRAPHY (e.g. the CHERUBI-KON) and iconography. Under ICONOCLASM representation of angels was questioned partly because their bodiless nature meant they could not be portrayed. In iconography angels were generally represented as beautiful, anthropomorphic, but winged beings. Winged spirits already existed in Assyrian and Persian iconography as well as in Greek and Roman. The angels are masculine, but beardless; the eunuchs of the imperial court were thought of as representing the angels of the Divine Court and may have provided a source for the iconographic image of the angels in Byzantine tradition. It is rare for an image of an angel to bear a personal name; normally the angel is named simply *angelos kyriou*, 'angel of the Lord', or known as 'Dynamis' or a Christian virtue. Christ himself is sometimes depicted as an angel, as in the icon of The Angel of Great Counsel. Hagia Sophia, the DIVINE WISDOM, is sometimes represented as a female angel, often enthroned in a DEESIS, clearly showing her identity with the Logos. JOHN THE BAPTIST is regularly shown winged, emphasizing both his angelic, ascetic life and his role as God's messenger proclaiming the coming of his Kingdom. Other ascetics are occasionally shown as winged. Angels are not always represented anthropomorphically; other images, especially of the Cherubim, Seraphim and Ophanim, draw on Ezekiel's vision in Ezekiel 1.

Gabriel is commemorated also on 26 March and Michael on 6 September with the hermit Archippos of CHONAI, whose church he miraculously saved from a flood.

Chonai in Phrygia was a major Byzantine pilgrimage centre until destroyed by the Seljuk Turks. Michael was also honoured at Sosthenion monastery near CONSTANTI-NOPLE, but mainly viewed as guardian of the Byzantine frontiers. To this day there are popular shrines of the Archangel, like Mantamados on Lesbos, PANORMITIS on Symi and Thari on Rhodes, in the Akritika or border regions of Greece. The Mantamados monastery has replaced Chonai as the centre for pilgrimages in honour of Michael.

Angels have an important role in traditional accounts of what happens after death. The soul is led by angels before the Judgement Seat, then led through all the scenes of its life, and on its return journey faces the toll-houses of the demons who exact penalties for wrongs done.

Burke, G. (1991), *Saint Michael the Archangel*. Geneva: St George Press.

Danielou, J. (1988), *The Angels and their Mission: According to the Fathers of the Church*. Dublin: Four Courts Press.

Mother Alexandra (1981), *The Holy Angels*. Minneapolis: Light and Life Publishing.

Peterson, E. (1964), *The Angels and the Liturgy*. London: Darton Longman & Todd.

DB/DM

Ani   The ruined churches of Ani in eastern Turkey, once the capital of the Bagratids, are reminders of the golden age of Armenian church architecture. The Armenian architect Trdat built the cathedral at Ani (989–1001) and travelled to CONSTANTI-NOPLE to rebuild the dome of Hagia Sophia which collapsed during an earthquake in 989. The five-domed church of St Gregory the Enlightener, known as Gagkashen, built by Gagik, was designed by Trdat in imitation of the seventh-century church of ZUART'NOC'.

Khatchatrian, A. (1972), *Monuments of Armenian Architecture*. Beirut: Hamazkaine.

KP

Annunciation icon   The archangel Gabriel, carrying a herald's staff, stretches out his right hand, greeting Mary and announcing she will bear a son (Luke 1: 31–5). Mary

THE ANNUNCIATION

sits wearing a *maphorion*, a veil or large head-shawl, and slippers, her head turned towards the archangel. She has been spinning for the high priest in the Temple. We read in the Protevangelium of James that one of her duties in the Temple was to make priestly vestments. The story of the Annunciation by Gabriel is drawn from scripture, much of the additional detail supplied by the Protevangelium, but the Virgin's attire and throne-like seat are supplied by iconographic tradition to make the theological point that she is the THEOTOKOS. The Annunciation icon often appears on the holy doors of the ICONOSTASIS. The Feast of the Annunciation is cele-brated on 25 March.

Ouspensky, L. and Lossky, V. (1982), *The Meaning of Icons*. Crestwood, NY: St Vladimir's Seminary Press.

KP

Anoixantaria   In solemn offices, verses of the opening psalm of Byzantine Vespers are often sung to a solemn 'slow' melody. The verses are interspersed with short hymns of praise, such as 'Glory to you, Holy One. Glory to you, Lord. Glory to you, heavenly King. Glory to you, O God. Allelouia.' The singers take up the psalm from the reader at the verse which begins 'When you open your hand', in Greek *'Anoixantos sou'* – hence the name Anoixantaria.

E

Anthimos the Georgian   (d. 1716) Metropolitan of Wallachia, commemorated on 27 September. A Georgian enslaved by the Turks in his youth, he remained a Christian and studied languages in CONSTANTINOPLE. Around 1690 Anthimos accompanied Prince Constantine Brancoveanu (martyred in 1714) to Romania and became director of the printing house in Bucharest, later founding another printing house at Snagov monastery, where he became abbot in 1696. Anthimos became bishop of Rimnicu-Vilcea in 1705 and Metropolitan of Wallachia in 1708. Ottoman soldiers murdered him after he had been sentenced to exile.

DB

antidoron   Greek, 'instead of the gift'. The antidoron is cut from the PROSPHORA left after the Prothesis. It is blessed during the liturgy and distributed or offered after the APOLYSIS. Antidoron is received and eaten with reverence. Some worshippers take antidoron to their homes and eat a little, with a sip of blessed water, as the first food of the day. It is the custom for communicants to take antidoron and, in some churches, wine mixed with warm water as an ablution. It is the practice in many places, especially in the DIASPORA, for antidoron to be offered to visitors as a sign of Christian fellowship.

DM

antimension   Greek, from Latin *mensa*, 'table'. The modern Byzantine antimension is a lined oblong cloth imprinted with the image of Christ laid out for burial. The antimension should contain relics, and is usually consecrated by being used to wipe the oil with which an ALTAR is anointed when it is consecrated. The bishop signs the antimension and issues it to a priest as his authority to celebrate the Divine Liturgy. In current use the chalice and paten are always placed on an antimension during the liturgy; in earlier centuries the sacred vessels were placed on the EILETON.

Essentially the antimension is a substitute altar, which allows celebration of the liturgy where no consecrated altar exists. In periods of war and persecution the antimension has been of great pastoral importance. Roman Catholic authorities have granted antimensia to Latin rite priests in cases of great need. It is the functional equivalent of the Syrian TABLITHO and the Ethiopian TABOT.

Izzo, J. M. (1975), *The Antimension in the Liturgical and Canonical Tradition of the Byzantine and Latin Churches: An Inter-Ritual Inter-Confessional Study*. Rome: Pontificium Athenaeum Antonianum.

DM

Antioch Modern Antakya (*see* HATAY). City founded *c*.300 BC by Seleucus the Great on the Orontes to honour his father Antiochus, and serve as city of the newly established Seleucid realm. Antioch became the third city of the Roman empire, after ROME itself and ALEXANDRIA. By tradition Peter established his seat in Antioch before going to Rome, and in Antioch the followers of Jesus were first called Christians. Bishop and martyr Ignatius Theophoros, the God-bearer (d. *c*.107), was one of the most important of the apostolic fathers. Under the Christian empire, the PATRIARCH of its well-organized church ranked immediately after the pope of Alexandria.

Like Alexandria, and often in opposition to it, Antioch became a centre of Christian learning with strong emphasis on grammatically and philologically sound historical interpretation of the BIBLE. It produced leaders and thinkers as diverse as JOHN CHRYSOSTOM, Theodore of Mopsuestia, Nestorius, SEVERUS and PETER THE FULLER.

Antioch was sacked by the Persians under Khosroe I in 540, restored under Justinian, taken by the Arabs in 636, returned to Byzantine rule in 969, taken by Seljuk Turks in 1084 and by the CRUSADERS in 1098, becoming the capital of an independent principality until Muslim forces overthrew it in 1268. The Christological controversies tore the Antiochian church apart: supporters of Nestorius found a safer home further east in Persian territory where the CHURCH OF THE EAST had already declared its independence, while the city itself was disputed between two patriarchs, one CHAL-CEDONIAN, the other non-Chalcedonian.

The rise of Constantinople, the loss of territory to the new patriarchate of JERU-SALEM, and the arrival of Islam and of the crusaders all weakened the authority of the EASTERN ORTHODOX patriarch. The crusaders established a Latin patriarchate which lasted to the twentieth century, though from the fourteenth century it was a merely titular office.

The Eastern Orthodox patriarchate of Antioch often maintained friendly relations with ROME, despite the breach between Rome and CONSTANTINOPLE symbolized by the excommunications of 1054. Many Antiochian clergy maintained communion with Rome. In 1724 a pro-Roman, Seraphim Tanas, was elected patriarch as Cyril VI. One week later an Athonite monk, Silvester, was installed by Constantinople. From that time the MELKITE Catholic and Greek Orthodox churches of Antioch have existed side by side as separate entities, the Melkite Catholics being recognized by the OTTO-MAN court as a separate *milet* in 1838. Under OTTOMAN rule the city faded to a minor township.

At present the title patriarch of Antioch is held by (a) the SYRIAN ORTHODOX patriarch of Antioch, (b) the Greek Orthodox patriarch of Antioch, (c) the Melkite Catholic patriarch of Antioch, Alexandria, Jerusalem and all the East, (d) the SYRIAN CATHOLIC patriarch of Antioch and (e) the patriarch of Antioch of the MARONITES. A Latin patriarch of Antioch used also to hold the title.

Dick, I. (1994), *Les Melkites*. Belgium: Brepols.
Atiya, A. S. (1991), *A History of Eastern Christianity*. Millwood, NY: Kraus Reprints.
Wallace-Hadrill, D. S. (1982), *Christian Antioch: A Study of Early Christian Thought in the East*. Cambridge: Cambridge University Press.

DM

apatheia (1) Impassibility as divine attribute, an attribute of Christ in his divinity. (2) Freedom from dominance by the passions. In this sense, but not in the sense of impassibility, *apatheia* is an attribute of Christ in his humanity. EASTERN CHRISTIAN liturgical texts are rich with references to the *apatheia* Christ's passion grants. (3) As a technical term of spiritual psychology, *apatheia* designates a state of habitual self-control and tranquillity undisturbed by the onslaught of the passions: the passions are not dead, but as prayer and ASCETICISM promote progressive DEIFICATION, resistance to temptation and to disturbance by the passions grows. *Apatheia* is not a state of unfeeling insensibility but rather a firm rooting in God attained as the culminating point of repentance.

DM

Aphrahaṭ Aphrahaṭ or Aphraates, born in Persia *c*.260–70 and commonly called the 'Persian Sage'; author of a series of twenty-three homilies or *Demonstrations* written *c*.336–7 and 343–5. He was an ascetic, probably a bishop, and later tradition makes him abbot of Mar Mattai, though little is certain and our only real source is the *Demonstrations* themselves. Aphrahaṭ probably suffered under the persecutions of Shapur II (309–79). The *Demonstrations* survive in SYRIAC and were variously translated into Armenian, Georgian and Ethiopic. Aphrahaṭ's Christianity is biblically based and shows no awareness of the contemporary theological controversy associated with the Council of Nicea. Indeed, his works are marked by a general lack of Western (i.e. Greek) influence and by an exegetical method which is reminiscent of Jewish tradition. Many of his themes are also Jewish (circumcision, Passover, Sabbath, etc.) and there are specific points of contact with Rabbinic exegesis of particular texts. Some have thought he might have had a Jewish background. Otherwise his emphasis is on simplicity in faith and prayer.

Parisot, J. (1894–7), 'Aphraatis Sapientis Persae Demonstrationes', *Patrologia Syriaca* I, 1–2.

JH

apokrisarios Greek, 'respondent': title of Byzantine imperial ambassador, or of the representative of a hierarch to a higher authority; now used as the title of the legate of a PATRIARCH. For example, the Greek Orthodox archbishop of Thyateira and Great Britain is apokrisarios of the ECUMENICAL PATRIARCH to the Archbishop of Canterbury.

DM

Apodeipnon Greek, 'after supper'. Byzantine rite office corresponding to Latin rite Compline.

DM

apodosis Greek: solemn leave-taking of a feast of the Lord or the THEOTOKOS. Major festivals of the Byzantine CALENDAR last for days – usually eight days, twelve for the Nativity of Christ, shorter periods when calendrical complexities demand it. Intermediate days of the festival usually have hymns of their own, the feast day's AKOLOUTHIA being repeated almost in full on the *apodosis*.

DM

apokatastasis In Hellenistic philosophy, the restoration of the constellations at the end of a cosmic cycle. The term is found in Justin Martyr and Irenaeus and developed into a doctrine of universal salvation by ORIGEN. Origen was condemned by a synod in Constantinople in 543 on the basis of a series of anathemas published by Emperor Justinian. The ninth anathema reads: 'If anyone says or holds that the punishment of the demons and of impious human beings is temporary and will have an end at a certain time, or that there will be an *apokatastasis* of the demons or of impious human beings, let him be anathema.' The general concept of a final *apokatastasis* is, however, found in Gregory of Nyssa and persists in a modified form in Byzantine theology, notably in MAXIMUS THE CONFESSOR. It recurs in modern Russian thinkers such as SOLOV-YOV, BULGAKOV and BERDIAEV.

See also THEOLOGY, EASTERN CHRISTIAN.

KP

apolysis Greek, 'dismissal': sequence of prayers and blessings that formally concludes a service, and consequently conveys permission to leave the church.

DM

apolytikion The TROPARION which, together with its corresponding THEO-TOKION, is the concluding hymn of Byzantine rite HESPERINOS. The *apolytikion* of Sunday vespers, sung on Saturday evening, is normally that of the appropriate tone; on a feast day it is that of the saint(s) celebrated. The *apolytikion* of the day is also sung after Theos Kyrios in ORTHROS, at the hours of the office, and at and/or more correctly after the little entrance in the Divine Liturgy.

DM

apophatic theology Negative terminology acquired importance in Eastern Christian theological discourse from the fourth century. It was already part of Greek philosophical tradition, highly developed in the *Enneads* of Plotinus (third century). The CAPPADOCIANS used apophaticism to combat EUNOMIOS' claim that it is possible to know the essence of God. Apophatic theology is a method of theologizing which safeguards the absolute transcendence of God against misrepresentations based upon human analogies. It reminds theologians not to overreach themselves in what they claim to know about God, and prepares the ground for a proper appropriation of our relationship to the creator. In the writings of EVAGRIUS PONTICUS in the fourth century and DIONYSIOS THE AREOPAGITE in the sixth century, the apophatic way becomes the pre-eminent path along which the contemplative may travel in order to reach the state of pure prayer.

Apophatic theology is to be understood in relation to the doctrine of DEIFICATION. While we cannot comprehend God in his essence, we can experience his power and love. What the intellect cannot grasp, grace gives to the saints blessed with his divine glory.

Pelikan, J. (1993), *Christianity and Classical Culture: The Metamorphosis of Natural Theology in the Christian Encounter with Hellenism.* New Haven: Yale University Press.
Mortley, R. (1986), *From Word to Silence*, 2 vols. Bonn: Peter Hanstein Verlag.

Lossky, V. (1975), *The Mystical Theology of the Eastern Church*. Crestwood, NY: St Vladimir's Seminary Press.

KP

aposticha   A series of hymns and alternating Psalm verses sung towards the end of Byzantine rite HESPERINOS and daily ORTHROS. The first troparion is sung without a verse. On Sundays there is one troparion more than on weekdays. It the custom for the second choir to begin the *aposticha* and the same choir then sing the DOXASTIKON.

E

Apostle   Byzantine liturgical book containing readings from the epistles and Acts of the Apostles for the Divine Liturgy. The passages are organized according to the liturgical CALENDAR, each preceded by the appropriate PROKEIMENON and followed by the corresponding ALLELOUIA verse. The reader normally reads the Apostle from the middle of the nave facing east, sometimes from the PSALTERION.

DM

Arab Christianity   The phrase 'Arab Christianity' refers to those Middle Eastern EASTERN CHRISTIAN communities who profess their faith in the Arabic language. It also designates the expression of Christian life in the Arab world, where Arabic is both the language of daily life and the *lingua sacra* of its dominant Islamic culture. Discussion of 'Arab Christianity' falls neatly under two headings: 'Before the Rise of Islam' and 'The World of Islam'. In both categories, the Arab Christians received the basic formulations of their faith from other languages, principally Greek, SYRIAC and Coptic. Arab Christianity is, initially, a Christianity in translation. Having over the centuries found its own distinctive voice, it has a major contribution to make to the wider Christian world, especially wherever Christians live in harmony with Muslims.

◆ Before the rise of Islam ◆

The earliest mention of a Christian presence in Arab territory occurs in the New Testament. In Galatians Paul refers to his own sojourn in Arabia following his conversion (Galatians 1: 15–17). Subsequently, EUSEBIUS OF CAESAREA mentions a bishop Beryllus in the see of Bostra in Hauran (*Ecclesiastical History* 6: 20), where a synod was held *c*.240. Between 246 and 250, another synod gathered in Arabia Petraea to condemn, with the notable help of ORIGEN, the 'Arabian heresy'. Eusebius says the heretics taught that both soul and body expire at the death of a person, to await the resurrection at the end of time (*Ecclesiastical History* 6: 37). So from the third century onwards there is a documented presence of Christians in the Arabic-speaking territories. Some modern scholars think Philip the Arab (244–59) was the first Christian Roman emperor. By the fourth century the Sinai peninsula, the South Arabian coast, and the eastern tribal regions of the desert Arabs, reaching into Mesopotamia, had significant numbers of Christians, mainly concentrated in the Roman province of Arabia (from AD 105) and in Sinai (Palaestina III Salutaris, after *c*.358).

◆ Arab Christianity ◆

At one time more than twenty episcopal sees existed in the Roman province of Arabia, while in the ecclesiastical province of ANTIOCH surviving records mention a 'bishop of the Arabs' in the environs of Damascus and in the district of Euphratensis. From 451, the year of the Council of Chalcedon, until the mid-sixth century there is little mention of bishops of Arabia in the ecclesiastical sources, but the archaeological record, particularly in southern Syria and Jordan, eloquently testifies to the continuing evangelization of the area. In Palestine and neighbouring Transjordan, as Cyril of Scythopolis testifies in the sixth-century *Lives of the Monks of Palestine* (24–6), a bishopric was established under monastic auspices for the Arab tribes in 427. Among the signatories to the acts of Constantinople II in 553 (*see* ECUMENICAL COUNCILS) are the metropolitan of Boṣrā and the bishop of 'Adra'a. Already, however, schisms had brought about the conditions which ultimately produced the three denominations which embrace most Christians in the Arab world: the MELKITES, the JACOBITES and Copts (both MONOPHYSITE), and the CHURCH OF THE EAST, the so-called NES-TORIANS. (*See* SYRIAN CHRISTIANITY; COPTIC CHRISTIANITY.)

Beyond the borders of the Roman province, in Arabia more properly so-called, Christianity spread gradually in the Arab tribes from the fourth century onwards, particularly among the tribal confederations of the Tanūkhids, the Salīhids and the Ghassānids, *foederati* of Rome on the south-eastern frontier in the fifth and sixth centuries. The monophysite Ghassānids were a powerful Christian presence among the Arabs on the eve of the rise of Islam. Similarly, the Lakhmids, with their centre at Hīra in Iraq, who fought for the Persians for almost three centuries, were influenced by Syriac-speaking Christians; at the rise of Islam they belonged to the Church of the East. Meanwhile, Christianity had come along the trade routes into southern Arabia; a monophysite bishop in Najran is recorded in the early sixth century. In Mārib, Hadramawt and the southern Hijāz the Christian presence was strengthened by the sixth-century invasion of the Ethiopians whose presence is evidenced by several surviving inscriptions. Earlier, in 356, Emperor Constantius II reportedly sent an embassy to Himyar under the 'Arian' bishop Theophilos the Indian, said to have built three churches there. In the fourth century, Ethiopians from Axum had also preached the faith in Himyar. There is little evidence of sustained Christian presence before the time of Islam in northern Hijāz or in most of western Arabia, even in caravan cities like Mecca and Yathrib (Medina), although there are numerous reports of Christians among some Arab tribes in the region, and indications of the occasional presence of monks and missionaries, largely from Syriac-speaking communities. One Islamic tradition even speaks of an icon of the Virgin and child in the Ka'ba in Mecca in the time of Muḥammad (d. 632).

◆ The world of Islam ◆

The Qur'ān is in dialogue with Christians and Jews throughout much of its text, thereby testifying to a certain currency of Christian lore in the Hijāz in Muḥammad's day. But to date, no sure evidence exists to support the not unreasonable assumption that Arabic versions of Christian biblical and liturgical texts existed prior to the rise of Islam. For the most part the ecclesiastical languages of Christianity remained Greek,

Syriac and Ethiopic, and their traces can readily be discerned in early Islamic texts which reflect the Christian presence in the Arab world. Some modern scholars even find traces of Christian modes of expression in works of pre-Islamic Arabic poets, but their claims are controversial and unsure.

Although there were numerous Arab Christians on the frontiers of Arabia before the Islamic conquest in the seventh century and even among the Arab tribes of the peninsula, they left little or no trace of themselves in surviving Arabic texts. Presumably theirs was mostly an oral Christian culture, based on a biblical, patristic and liturgical heritage expressed principally in Greek, Christian Palestinian Aramaic, and Syriac. Along the fringes of Arabia many Arabs were bilingual. Arabic became an ecclesiastical language only after the Islamic conquest, and it happened not in Arabia, from which most non-Muslims soon emigrated, but in the conquered territories of the oriental Christian patriarchates outside Arabia.

The reign of the Umayyad caliph 'Abd al-Malik (685–705) marks the beginning of the Islamicization and Arabicization of conquered territories. By the tenth century, from the borders of Iran to Spain, a new commonwealth appeared on the eastern and southern shores of the Mediterranean, including most of the Iberian peninsula, its common culture primarily expressed in the social and artistic usages of Islam, and the widespread adoption of the Arabic language. Christians were full participants in this culture, despite their civic disabilities as a subject, protected *dhimmi* people, required by the Qur'ān's prescription (*at-Tawbah*, 9: 29) to pay a special poll tax (*al-jizyah*) and obliged to maintain a low social profile, theoretically governed by the so-called Covenant of 'Umar. It was under these conditions, in the period from the 'Abbasid revolution (759) to the CRUSADES, while Christians still made up a significant percentage of the Islamic world's population, that Arabic became an ecclesiastical language.

It happened first in the Melkite community, with its spiritual and intellectual centre in the monasteries of Jerusalem's Judean desert. There, from the mid-eighth century onwards, monks produced Arabic translations of the scriptures, Lives of the Saints and classics of patristic thought. Some even wrote original theological tracts in Arabic to present Christian doctrine in response to the challenges posed by the proclamation of Islam. By the ninth century, writers in the 'Jacobite' and 'Nestorian' communities in the Syriac-speaking areas of the patriarchate of ANTIOCH were also composing apologetic treatises in Arabic. In the tenth century they were joined by the Copts of Egypt, whose traditional language of piety and worship, Coptic, was fast giving way to Arabic. Writers and scholars in the Christian communities of the Arab world have gone on to produce a substantial archive of church books and original theological compositions in Arabic which have helped mightily to keep the faith alive in the world of Islam, although Western scholars have been slow to learn about it, and even slower to study this important expression of the Christian faith. These texts offer evidence of a theological development in Christian self-understanding in the Arab world which takes its cue from the structures and typical formulations of Islamic faith, as they have evolved over the centuries from the medieval period to the present day. Christian writers in Arabic have also made major contributions in grammar, lexicography, medicine, philosophy, science and even folklore.

It has become customary to consider the language and literature of the Arab Christians under the headings of the names of the several denominations into which they are divided: Melkites, MARONITES, West Syrians, East Syrians and Copts, as well as, in modern times, Catholics, Protestants, and Orthodox. While this usage has a certain classificatory value in the systematic organization and presentation of a vast amount of textual material, it masks the markedly similar character of much Arab Christian thought across denominational boundaries. Indeed, in medieval times certain texts, regardless of their origins, were transmitted in several different communities.

After the Crusades, Christian numbers in the Arab world steadily declined. Under the OTTOMANS they were well in the minority. By the twentieth century many communities had already forged a relationship with one or more of the great colonial powers, who afforded them a measure of protection and often a certain economic advantage, offering greater access to the burgeoning culture of the West than most Muslims enjoyed. Catholics and Protestants from the West, however, made inroads into the Arab Christian communities under the aegis of the colonial powers, their missionary activities bringing further divisions to an already splintered Christian population. Nevertheless, it was largely Christian thinkers and writers in the first half of the twentieth century who launched the Arab nationalist movement which has dominated the politics of much of the Middle East in the late twentieth century. Similarly, Christians were prominent in the arts, in education and in business enterprises in the Arab world. But by the last third of the century, with the rise of what the West calls 'Islamic fundamentalism', Christian populations in the Middle East and North Africa were on the wane again. (*See* COPTS AND ISLAMIC FUNDAMENTALISM SINCE 1952.) Emigration to the West has greatly depleted their ranks in areas of former strength. In Europe and North America, immigrant Arab Christians readily accommodated themselves to the cultures of their host countries. For many, Arabic is lost by the second generation, surviving only in church services, and the Arab Christian identity is lost in favour of the old denominational loyalties, always modified in Arab lands by membership in the larger Arab culture.

Those Christian groups which have survived in the Arab world in the later twentieth century have joined together in the Middle East Council of Churches, which since the 1980s includes the Catholic family of churches, along with Protestants and almost all indigenous Christian communities. There is among many a new and exciting effort to articulate a modern Christian theology in Arabic, well attuned to the challenging world of Islam in which their churches live.

Shahid, I. (1995–), *Byzantium and the Arabs in the Sixth Century*, vol. 1, pts 1–2 to date. Washington, DC: Dumbarton Oaks.

Coquin, R. G. (1993), 'Langue et littérature arabes chrétiennes', in M. Albert et al., eds, *Christianismes Orientaux: Introduction a l'étude des langues et des littératures*. Initiations au christianisme ancien, pp. 35–106. Paris: Editions du Cerf.

Griffith, S. H. (1992), *Arabic Christianity in the Monasteries of Ninth-century Palestine*. Collected Studies, CS380. Aldershot: Variorum.

Coakley, J. F. (1992), *The Church of the East and the Church of England: A History of the Archbishop of Canterbury's Assyrian Mission*. Oxford: Clarendon Press; New York: Oxford University Press.

Cragg, K. (1991), *The Arab Christian: A History in the Middle East*. Louisville, Ky: Westminster/John Knox Press.

Shahid, I. (1989), *Byzantium and the Arabs in the Fifth Century*. Washington, DC: Dumbarton Oaks.

Shahid, I. (1988), *Byzantium and the Semitic Orient before the Rise of Islam*. Collected Studies, CS270. London: Variorum.

Haddad, R. (1985), *La Trinité divine chez les théologiens arabes (750–1050)*. Beauchesne Religions, 15. Paris: Beauchesne.

Shahid, I. (1984), *Rome and the Arabs: A Prolegomenon to the Study of Byzantium and the Arabs*. Washington, DC: Dumbarton Oaks.

Shahid, I. (1984), *Byzantium and the Arabs in the Fourth Century*. Washington, DC: Dumbarton Oaks.

Joseph, J. (1983), *Muslim–Christian Relations and Inter-Christian Rivalries in the Middle East: The Case of the Jacobites in an Age of Transition*. Albany, NY: SUNY Press.

Trimingham, J. S. (1979), *Christianity among the Arabs in Pre-Islamic Times*. London and New York: Longman.

Betts, R. B. (1978), *Christians in the Arab East: A Political Study*, rev. edn. Atlanta: John Knox Press.

Corbon, J. (1977), *L'Église des Arabes*. Paris: Editions du Cerf.

Hechaïmé, C. (1967), *Louis Cheikho et son livre. Le Christianisme et la littérature chrétienne en Arabie avant l'Islam. Etude critique*. Récherches publiées sous la direction de l'Institut de Lettres Orientales de Beyrouth. Serie II: Langue et littérature arabes, vol. 38. Beyrouth: Dar El-Machreq.

Joseph, J. (1961), *The Nestorians and their Muslim Neighbors: A Study of Western Influence on their Relations*. Princeton Oriental Studies, 20. Princeton, NJ: Princeton University Press.

Graf, G. (1944–53), *Geschichte der christlichen arabischen Literatur*, 5 vols. Studi e Testi, 118, 133, 146, 147, 172. Vatican City: Biblioteca Apostolica Vaticana.

SHG

Arabonismos   Byzantine rite service of betrothal in which rings are exchanged by the betrothed and God's blessing sought on their pledge; now frequently combined with the service of Crowning, the actual Marriage Service.

DM

Arbanassi   Village near Trnovo in BULGARIA, first mentioned in a *firman* (edict) of the OTTOMAN sultan Suleiman in 1538. It became an important entrepôt on the trade route from northern Europe to Asia during the seventeenth and eighteenth centuries. Arbanassi possesses fine examples of Balkan domestic architecture and several important churches, mainly of the sixteenth and seventeenth centuries, stone-built with pitched roofs and small windows. The post-Byzantine frescoes in the Nativity Church are very fine, as are the carved wooden ICONOSTASES of the churches.

Bossilkov, S. (1988), *Arbanassi: Iconostases and Religious Easel Art (15th–19th Centuries)*. Sofia: SVYAT Publishers.

KP

Arbela, Chronicle of   This chronicle, giving an account of the history of the church in ADIABENE to the sixth century, was published in 1907 by A. Mingana as a work by the sixth-century historian Mšīhā Zkā (whose writings are otherwise lost). The authenticity of the work was soon questioned (P. Peeters: 1925) and tests on the MS proved it to be modern. The question of whether Mingana forged the manuscript (without using any ancient source) is still disputed. J.-M. Fiey regards the work as a fake; S. P. Brock and others are unconvinced, but take the view that the chronicle is in any case historically unreliable.

Peeters, P. (1925), 'Le Passionaire d'Adiabene', *Analecta Bollandiana* 43, pp. 261–304.
Kawerau, P. (1985), *Die Chronik von Arbela*, CSCO 467–8, Scr. syr. 199–200. Louvain: Sécretariat du CSCO.
Brock, S. P. (1979–80), 'Syria Historical Writing: A Survey of the Main Sources', *Journal of the Iraqi Academy Syriac Convention* 5, pp. 1–30.
Fiey, J.-M. (1970), *Jalons pour une histoire de l'église en Iraq*, CSCO Subsidia 36. Louvain: Sécretariat du CSCO.

JH

archdeacon   The bishop's principal deacon (not, as in the West, a priest); the principal deacon of an individual Byzantine church is usually a protodeacon.

DM

archimandrite   Alternative title of an abbot (Greek, *hegoumenos*), which came to be used by abbots of particularly important monasteries, then a rank to which senior celibate priests might be appointed. In Slav but not Greek use, the rank of *igumen* is given to celibate priests as a lower rank than archimandrite. Exceptionally, the historic parish of Manchester in England had a married archimandrite from Corfu as parish priest in the mid-nineteenth century.

DM

architecture, church   The earliest Christian worship must have taken place in buildings not designed for the purpose, but achieved by adaptation of domestic and other premises. Remnants of a third-century house church were excavated in the Roman garrison town of DURA EUROPOS on the Euphrates. Documentary evidence indicates that purpose-built churches existed by the third century, but the first substantial remains belong to the fourth century, when church building increased following adoption of Christianity as the Roman Empire's religion by CONSTANTINE THE GREAT. The standard type was the timber-roofed basilica, a form derived from Roman architecture, where it was used for a variety of purposes, mainly secular. The basilical church is a rectangular structure on an east/west axis, its central nave flanked by one or more aisles each side (*see* figure 1 a, b). The aisles are roofed at a lower level than the nave, permitting windows to be placed in the upper nave walls (clerestory) to illuminate the interior. The ALTAR is in a projection at the east end, usually an apse, sometimes flanked by lateral apses or small rooms terminating the aisles. To the west the narthex may open to an atrium. There may be galleries above the aisles and narthex. Many specific aspects of worship, e.g. veneration of relics or icons or celebration of

(a)

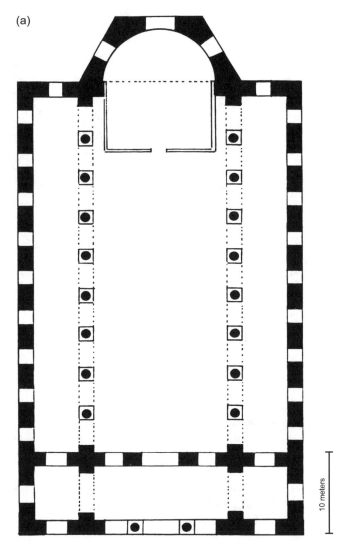

10 meters

Figure 1 Generalized basilica: (a) plan

particular feasts, were served by the chapel, often of simple rectangular form, barrel-vaulted, with an apse at the eastern end; the chapel could open from an aisle of the basilica or be alongside it, having a separate entrance. Baptistries, mausolea and *skeuophylakia* (treasuries) were usually separate structures, often centralized (octagonal, square or free-cross) to the side of the basilica and connected by a passage entering an aisle.

A mid-fourth-century programme of building by Constantine I produced great basilicas, notably at the holy places of Palestine, such as the Church of the Nativity in Bethlehem (*see* figure 2) and the Holy Sepulchre in JERUSALEM. Basilicas in this group had a pair of aisles on each side of the nave and appended structures to house the shrine site itself (in Bethlehem an octagonal building beyond the east end of the basilica sheltered the cave of the Nativity). Similar large basilicas were built in

(b)

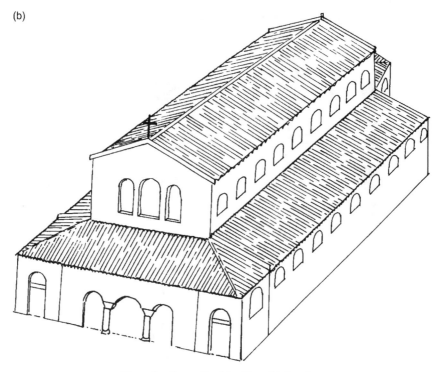

Figure 1 Generalized basilica: (b) drawing

CONSTANTINOPLE and Rome. The standard basilica was on a more modest scale, with two aisles, rather than four, as the norm. By the fifth century, from which many more examples survive, this type was in use throughout the Christian world. Regional variations in proportions, fabric and ornament reflect the development of local building traditions. The basilicas of Constantinople were squat rectangles, of brick or brick and stone; those of central Anatolia and north Syria were of ashlar; in north Italy long rectangular plans were used, with graceful nave arcades on slender columns. Carved decoration on capitals, cornices and entablatures, generally following the Corinthian order, was common to basilicas of all regions. Carving decorated the screen partly closing the sanctuary, a low wall, often of marble slabs, with at least one opening between nave and sanctuary. Set against the apse wall might be concentric stone seating for clergy (*synthronon*) and/or an episcopal throne. A stone AMBO might be found in the eastern or central part of the nave.

Roman building tradition also supplied centralized schemes based on the circle, square, equal-armed cross or other regular polygon. The shrine-church of St Babylas near ANTIOCH was cruciform. Some centralized churches were *martyria*, burial places or shrines of martyrs, a Christian development of the ancient association of the centralized form with mausolea. There is, however, no rigid correlation of architectural form and function in the Byzantine context.

Significant change appears in the early sixth century, with experiments in domed vaulting in Constantinople and Anatolia. Eastern church architecture now diverges from that of the West, which retains the basilica as its basis. In Constantinople several

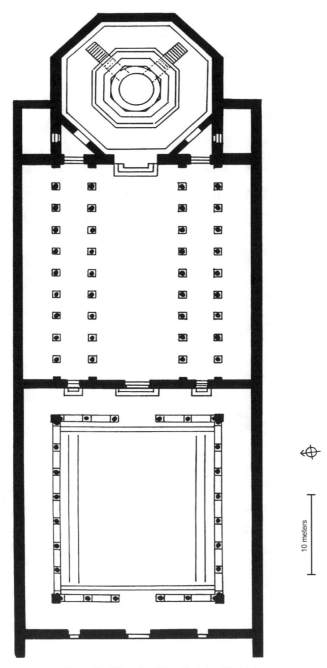

Figure 2　Church of the Nativity, Bethlehem

sixth-century basilicas had one or more domes covering parts of the nave (St Polyeuktos; Holy Apostles). The most extraordinary achievement of this trend was Hagia Sophia (*see* DIVINE WISDOM) in Constantinople, built by Justinian between 532 and 537 on the site of an earlier building destroyed during city riots. In Hagia Sophia

45

the basilical plan is modified to support an enormous dome over the central nave area, flanked by an ingenious sequence of half-domes and apsed niches (*see* figure 3). The church has inner and outer narthexes and possesses an atrium; galleries above aisles and inner narthex form a U-shape around the nave space. Interior walls are clad with coloured marble panels; capitals and cornices are of intricately carved white marble;

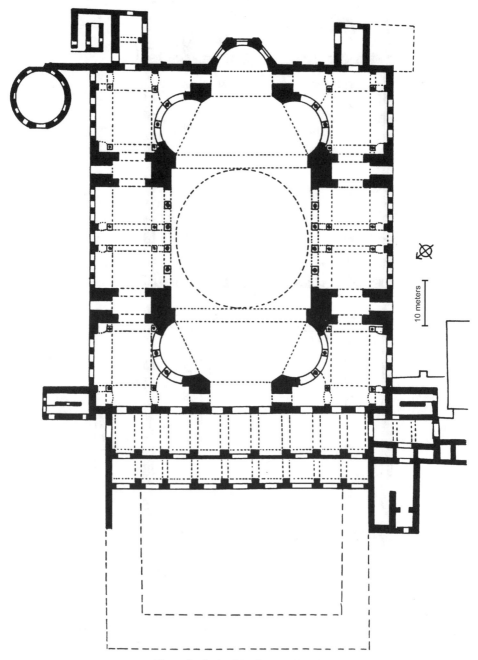

10 meters

Figure 3　St Sophia, Constantinople

and the whole vault was once covered with gold mosaic. At about the same time, much smaller domed churches were produced using the centralized double-shell formula. In these, an octagonal central space has a dome carried on eight piers or columns; it is enclosed by an ambulatory with a gallery. The overall plan may be square (SS Sergius and Bacchus in Constantinople) or octagonal (San Vitale in Ravenna). Such buildings probably had more influence on subsequent architectural development than Hagia Sophia, which was too complex to be seminal in building tradition. (Its ideas were taken up in the fifteenth century, however, by the architects of the OTTOMAN imperial mosques of Istanbul.)

The next stages of architectural development are lost in the more than two centuries when Arab encroachment removed much of the empire from Byzantine control. A handful of seventh- and eighth-century churches indicate that the dome became a standard feature of the Byzantine church (Hagia Sophia in Thessaloniki, for example, where the nave is vaulted by a dome set on huge arches, a type known as cross-domed; *see* figure 4). The basilica thus gives way to fully centralized plans more suited to domed vaulting, a process probably complete by the end of the ninth century.

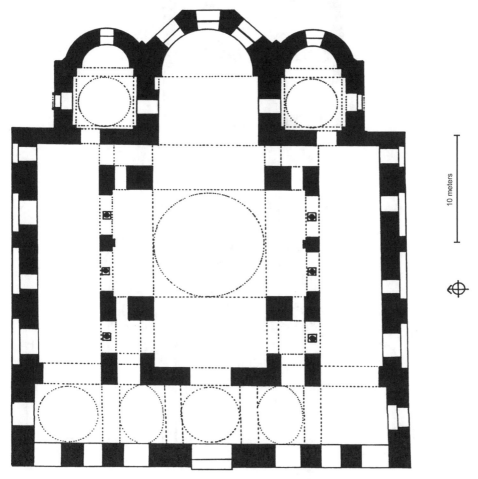

10 meters

Figure 4 St Sophia, Thessaloniki

The commonest middle-Byzantine church type is the inscribed-cross, also known as cross-in-square, or quincunx, a scheme still seen in the Eastern Christian world today (*see* figure 5). A main dome is carried on four piers or columns above a square central

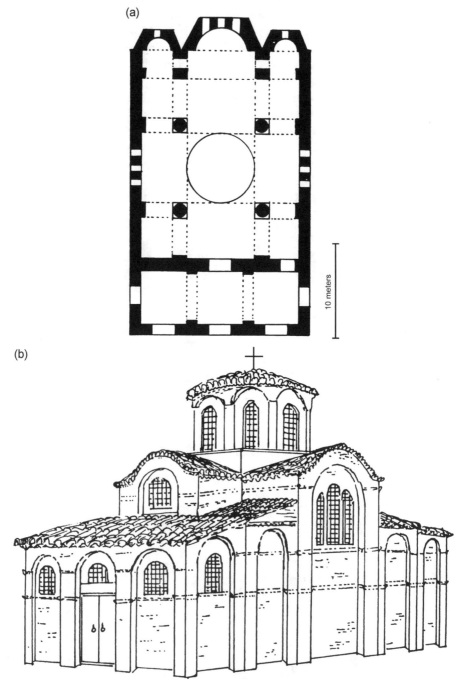

Figure 5 Generalized inscribed-cross: (a) plan; (b) drawing

bay, and around this four main subsidiary vaults (often barrel vaults) form an equal-armed Greek cross; four small corner bays then complete a square outline. To the west is a narthex, and three apses open from the eastern bays, the central one housing the sanctuary. The sanctuary is closed by a taller screen than in the early church, the ICONOSTASIS, which completely obscures the sanctuary from the congregation, except when its central doors are opened at certain points in the liturgy.

Architectural types other than the inscribed cross are occasionally found, but they too are generally centralized, domed structures. Thus the Greek-cross-octagon has its dome set on an octagon formed by small niches (squinches) spanning the corners of the square central bay; four bays form a Greek cross around this domed core and L-shaped elements complete a square plan; there is a narthex to the west and three apses to the east, and there may be galleries in a U-shape around the domed centre. An example is the early eleventh-century church of Hosios Loukas, Stiris (*see* figure 6). A regular cross-domed scheme is a relation of an earlier type (e.g. Gül Camii, in Constantinople) and the domed Greek-cross type resembles an inscribed-cross without columns, the barrel-vaulted cross arms rising from the corner bays (e.g. Kalenderhane Camii, in Constantinople). On ATHOS the inscribed-cross plan is modified by the addition of apses to the ends of the north and south cross-arms, creating a triconch *naos*, as in the tenth-century church of Iviron (*see* figure 7). Other regional variations chiefly concern the proportions of elements and the fabric used. Chapels associated with centralized churches are usually of simple rectangular form, often barrel-vaulted, built against the lateral walls of the church or, occasionally, opening from the narthex or narthex gallery.

Churches without domes are rare, but small basilicas still appear, particularly in the Black Sea region and in northern Greece. The even simpler barrel-vaulted single-nave was probably widely used, but fewer of these have survived than of the domed churches, many of which were either monastic and/or the commissions of important patrons.

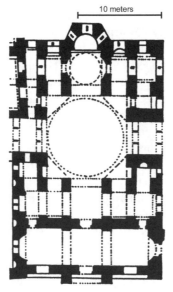

Figure 6   Hosios Loukas, Stiris

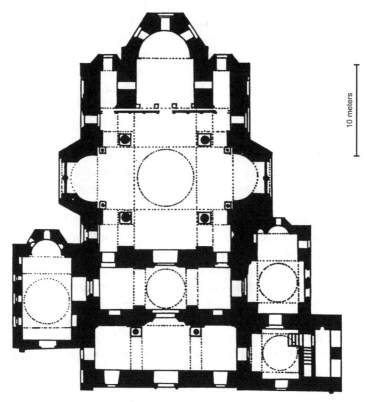

Figure 7 Church of Iviron monastery, Mount Athos

In churches of all types, the fabric is often used decoratively, in dog-tooth arrangements, as borders for stone blocks (*cloisonné*) or in 'Kufic' patterns based upon an ornate style of Arabic script. Such ornament enhances the highly textured nature of the exterior already established by the structure, with a drum enclosing the central dome, the cross-arms rising well above the corner bays and each section independently roofed.

Church architecture changes very little from the middle-Byzantine period to the end of the empire in 1453. Fourteenth-century churches in Constantinople and Thessaloniki use middle-Byzantine plans, the chief development consisting of the enlargement or doubling of narthexes and the greater prominence of side-chapels, some of them funerary (e.g. St Saviour in Chora, in Constantinople, 1321). The most striking feature of this late Byzantine architecture is its exuberant exterior decoration, using traditional features such as niches, recessed arches and bands of brick arranged in rosettes, meanders and herringbone patterns, in some cases supplemented by tile-work.

The architecture of non-Byzantine and post-Byzantine Eastern Christianity manifests various degrees of dependence upon Byzantine models. This is very slight in the scattered Christian communities of the Middle East and Mesopotamia, where church building tends to follow the local building vernacular. It is much greater in the Balkans and Russia, where Christianity was taken by middle-Byzantine missionaries. In the post-Byzantine world, there is little change in the styles of church building in Greece, but the regions to the north, free of Ottoman domination, saw innovation and development, producing distinctive local traditions. As part of the early Christian world, COPTIC Egypt took the basilica as its standard church type, and examples built in the sixth and seventh centuries still function in Old Cairo (e.g. al-'Adhrā, also known as al-Mu'allaqah). Since it never returned to Christian rule after the Islamic conquest, Egypt did not share the middle-Byzantine development of the centralized domed church. Domes that appear in Coptic churches are generally a borrowing from Islamic architecture.

A sequence parallel to that seen in the Byzantine empire is evident in the church architecture of ARMENIA and GEORGIA, early basilicas giving way by the ninth century to centralized, domed types, including the inscribed-cross and its variants. From the late sixth century there is rich development of the domed tetraconch, in which four apses surround a square central bay, the corners of which open to niches and then to small bays flanking the apses. An example is the Church of the Holy Cross in Jvari (*see* figure 8). Domes are carried on high drums, and finished with conical roofs. The fabric of all types is ashlar, often decorated with mouldings and sometimes relief ornament, including figures, as at the Church of the Holy Cross at AGHTAMAR, on Lake Van (915–21).

Archaeological remains of early Christian basilicas and some centralized buildings exist in the Balkans, but there is a gap of centuries between these and the important later phases of church building following the middle-Byzantine evangelization of the area. The inscribed-cross and other middle-Byzantine types were introduced to BULGARIA after the conversion of Tsar Boris in 865, and the return of Byzantine control in the tenth century ensured that Bulgarian church building thereafter remained close to Byzantine types. Even the unusual Round Church in Preslav (*c*.900), a rotunda with radiating niches behind the circle of columns supporting its dome, probably depends upon a Constantinopolitan model, and, four centuries later, churches in Nessebur (Mesembria) have the strong exterior ornament of the last phase of Byzantine architecture.

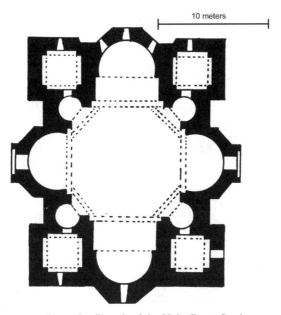

Figure 8 Church of the Holy Cross, Jvari

Many Serbian churches are distinctive hybrids of Eastern and Western medieval traditions. A type associated with Stephen Nemanja (1168–95) and his successors has a Byzantine domed square as its main element, but bays to east and west of it give a longitudinal emphasis, usually enhanced by a deep narthex at the west end. The eastern bay is divided into three by piers carrying arches, each section opening to an apse. The central domed bay may be extended by north and south arms, giving the appearance of a transept, as in the Church of the Virgin at STUDENICA (*c*.1190, outer narthex *c*.1230; *see* figure 9). Exterior decoration with shallow pilasters and arcades, and sometimes figure sculpture, indicates even stronger influence of the western Romanesque, coming from areas on the east coast of the Adriatic. In the fourteenth century there occurred alongside this Serbian development a return to Byzantine models under Uroš II Milutin, whose monastery at GRAČANICA (1321) depends upon ingenious elaboration of the inscribed-cross formula.

Middle-Byzantine church architecture reached Russia in the tenth century, largely displacing a local tradition of wooden church building. St Sophia in KIEV (by 1043) is the best-preserved of several churches known to have been built with the direct involvement of Byzantine craftsmen (*see* figure 10). Its basis is the inscribed-cross

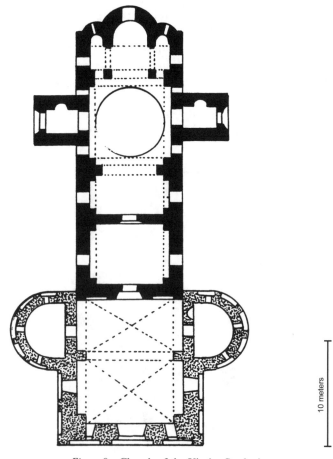

10 meters

Figure 9   Church of the Virgin, Studenica

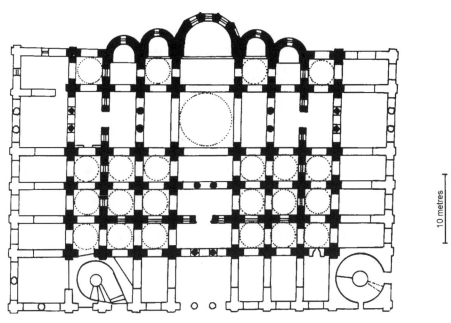

Figure 10   St Sophia, Kiev

plan, augmented with extra aisles to provide the space needed in Kiev's cathedral. Later development of this scheme is seen chiefly in proportions, as churches and their dome drums grow taller, and in the use of shallow pilasters and blind arcading to decorate exterior facades; St Dmitrii, VLADIMIR (1194) also has exuberant carved figure reliefs. The thirteenth-century Church of St Nicholas in Lipna near NOV-GOROD introduces the trefoil roof line, a pattern of three lobes at the top of each of the facades, and in the sixteenth century there appear the 'tent-churches' with very tall central spires, possibly modelled on wooden architecture. Russian church architecture clings to its Byzantine origins to the present day, in spite of an attempt by Peter the Great in the early eighteenth century to introduce the basilica along with extensive importation of Western architecture.

Church building in brick or stone came late to Romania, with the rise of Wallachia and Moldavia in the thirteenth and fourteenth centuries. The inscribed-cross appears at St Nicholas at Arges (*c*.1350), but Romanian churches have their closest relatives in the longitudinal schemes of Serbia, based on the domed square with bays to east and west. Apses often open from north and south of the domed square, producing a triconch interior. Elegant exteriors are produced by tall dome-drums topped with steep conical roofs, and facades decorated with pilaster strips and shallow blind arcading. This is sometimes embellished with paintings sheltered by deeply overhanging roofing, as in the monastery church at Voronet (1488).

Mainstone, R. (1988), *Hagia Sophia*. London: Thames & Hudson.
Der Nersessian, S. (1978), *Armenian Art*. London: Thames & Hudson.
Mepisashvili, R. and Tsintsadze, V. (1977), *The Arts of Ancient Georgia*. London: Thames & Hudson.

Mathews, T. (1976), *The Byzantine Churches of Istanbul: A Photographic Survey*. Philadelphia: Pennsylvania University Press.

Mango, C. (1976), *Byzantine Architecture*. New York: Harry N. Abrams.

Krautheimer, R. (1975), *Early Christian and Byzantine Architecture*, 2nd edn. Pelican History of Art. Harmondsworth: Penguin.

Grabar, A. (1968), *L'Art du Moyen age en Europe Orientale*. L'Art dans le Monde. Paris: Editions Albin Michel.

van der Meer, F. and Mohrmann, C. (1966), *Atlas of the Early Christian World*. London: Nelson.

Hamilton, G. H. (1954), *The Art and Architecture of Russia*. Pelican History of Art. Harmondsworth: Penguin.

LR

Armenian Christianity   Christian origins in Armenia are obscure. Sources in the Armenian language begin with the invention of the script *c*.400; the information they offer about earlier events is tendentious. Outside sources give only scattered hints. It is clear, however, from Christian vocabulary in Armenian and from liturgical and literary traditions, that Christianity was introduced into Armenia both from Greek ASIA MINOR to the west and from Syria to the south.

Eusebius (*Ecclesiastical History*, 6: 46, 2) mentions bishop Meruzanes of the Armenians, to whom Dionysius of ALEXANDRIA addressed a letter *c*.260. Whether this otherwise unknown prelate was in Greater Armenia, or in Armenia Minor west of the Euphrates, is unclear. Eusebius also notes (*Ecclesiastical History*, IX, 8: 2) that 'the Armenians' were Christian at the time of Maximin's persecution in 312–13. The beginning of an organized church can be dated to 314, when Gregory the Enlightener was consecrated bishop for Armenia at Caesarea in Cappadocia, following the conversion of King Trdat (Tiridates IV, 298–330). The titular authority of Caesarea was respected for the consecration of successive Armenian prelates. Known as CATHOLICOS, these were normally chosen from Gregory's family up to the division of Armenia into a Roman–Byzantine sector and a much larger Iranian sector *c*.387, when the see, first established at an old pagan site, Astisat, near Lake Van, was moved to Ejmiacin, near modern Erevan, in Iranian Armenia, and the authority of Caesarea rejected.

The conversion of Trdat and the missionary activity of Gregory are described, with legendary accretions, by the historian known as Agathangelos, who provides divine validation for the Ejmiacin site and information about the earlier pagan centres of worship. Resistance of nobles to the Christian orientation of the court, the anti-Arian stance of Nerses the Great (Catholicos 353–73?), and the efforts of ascetics and holy men to spread Christianity in Armenia are described by P'awstos Buzand, writing in the later fifth century.

After the division of *c*.387 Iranian Armenia became paramount, not only as containing 80 per cent of historic Armenia and the patriarchal see, but especially because Armenian literature developed here after the invention of a national script. Maštoc', a former state official who had become an ascetic missionary and attracted disciples, was sent by Sahak the Great (last descendent of Gregory to be Catholicos, 397–438) to EDESSA in the fifth year of King Vramsapuh (401?). At Samosata, he fashioned a thirty-six-letter alphabet based on the order of Greek, rendering the full range of vowels and consonants. Young assistants accompanying him had studied SYRIAC and Greek; earlier bilingual strands in Armenian Christianity were now reinforced by translations of texts from Greek and Syriac. These events are described in the biography of Maštoc' by his pupil Koriun, the first original work in Armenian.

Although Greek learned traditions eventually predominated, and biblical versions made from Syriac were revised on the basis of the Greek, the importance of Syrian influence is clear from the Armenian adaptation of the story of ABGAR of Edessa, which claims that ADDAI came to Armenia after King Abgar's conversion, although this first Christian community did not survive. Hence P'awstos calls the patriarchate 'the throne of Thaddaeus', and later Moses Xorenac'i claimed that Abgar was Armenian. By the eighth century a theory of apostolic origin via Bartholomew was in circulation.

The journeys of Maštoc' and his pupils to Edessa and Greek territory, the translation of numerous works of theology and the beginnings of an original literature involved Armenia in the theological controversies of the time. Works of Theodore of Mopsuestia came to Armenia from Edessa. Since Theodore had been condemned at the Council of Ephesus in 431, Acacius of Melitene (where Maštoc''s disciples had studied Greek) protested to Catholicos Sahak. The *Tome to the Armenians*, a letter from Proclus, patriarch of CONSTANTINOPLE 434–46, was accepted as an authoritative statement of the faith, frequently cited later in opposition to Chalcedon.

In 451 Persian Armenia was in rebellion; this is dramatically described by Elise, whose *History of Vardan and the Armenian War* (sixth century) is a classic of Armenian literature. Although no representative from Greater Armenia attended the Council of Chalcedon, the proceedings were not unknown since many bishops from neighbouring provinces attended. Zeno's HENOTIKON attracted support, and was approved at the First Council of Dvin in 506, where Armenian, Georgian and Caucasian Albanian bishops were joined by Syrian clerics opposed to the recognized church of Iran, including the famous Simeon of Beit-Arsham, a dedicated anti-Chalcedonian. The Syrians were recognized as orthodox, and the Armenians specifically rejected Nestorius and Chalcedon, reaffirming allegiance to the first three ECUMENICAL COUNCILS. The official correspondence with the Greeks, Syrians and Georgians concerning these disputes is preserved in the *Book of Letters*, which also includes many later documents. (*See also* GEORGIA; ALBANIA-AL´UANK; SYRIAN ORTHODOX CHURCH.)

Byzantine abrogation of the Henotikon in 518 does not seem to have caused a stir in Armenia. Not until the Second Council of Dvin in 555 was the imperial church explicitly condemned. Another Syrian delegation, this time of Julianist persuasion, was present, and SEVERUS OF ANTIOCH was condemned along with Eutyches, Nestorius, Theodore and the Council of Chalcedon. (*See* MONOPHYSITE.) Julianist ideas had some impact in Armenia until at least the twelfth century, but the Armenian church at large did not accept his views.

The Armenian church's general theological position reflects these early debates: recognition of the first three ecumenical councils, but rejection of Chalcedon; acceptance of Cyril of Alexandria's Christological formula, 'One nature of the Word incarnate'; and opposition to the Antiochene tradition. After 555 communion with the Greeks was condemned. The Georgians, present at Dvin in 506 but not in 555, eventually remained loyal to Chalcedon, and in 608–9 the rupture with Armenia became final. Seventh-century Byzantine emperors attempted to impose reunion of the Armenian and Greek churches. Despite partial successes, once Muslim control extended over all Armenia the Armenian church went its own way. These efforts are described in a rare pro-Chalcedonian document, surviving only in Greek translation, the *Narratio de rebus Armeniae*.

The first three centuries of writing provided Armenia with the framework for future learning and literature. Scholarship was primarily an ecclesiastical concern; but texts on rhetoric, grammar, geography and philosophy read in the schools of late antiquity were adapted for Armenian use. A tradition of historical writing rapidly developed, showing the influence of Eusebius and Josephus. The figure most influential on later generations, Moses Xorenac'i, combined oral Armenian traditions with Eusebius' *Ecclesiastical History* and many other Greek sources to produce a *History of Armenia* from its earliest settlement down to the death of Maštoc'. The mathematical and astronomical interests of Anania of Širak in the seventh century were harnessed to provide a new, independent calendar for the church. Armenians were no longer concerned with attacking pagan or Iranian religion (as in the treatise on the problem of evil by Eznik, a pupil of Maštoc'); apologetic works defended Armenian Christology. The *Seal of Faith*, a catena from the time of Catholicos Komitas (611–28), used the Armenian version of Timothy Ailouros' *Refutation of the Council of Chalcedon* as a model. Also noteworthy is a treatise in defence of images attributed to Vrt'anes, locum tenens of the catholicate 604–7. Although frescoes were common in Armenian churches and manuscript illumination was to remain a notable artistic achievement, the cult of icons was not as extensive as in Byzantium. The Cross, however, received particular veneration.

Consolidation of Armenian ecclesiastical tradition continued in the eighth century with the first codification of canon law under Catholicos John III Ojnec'i (717–28). At the Council of Dvin in 719 he attacked the PAULICIANS, who were active in Armenia for several centuries to come; he also effected a rapprochement with the Syrians at the Council of Manazkert in 726. Conflicts erupted again later, as witnessed by the Syriac anti-Armenian treatise by Dionysius bar Ṣalībī in the twelfth century.

Contacts with Byzantium were not entirely broken. Armenians continued to visit Constantinople to translate texts not yet available in Armenian. Between 715 and 718 Stephen, later metropolitan of Siunik', translated the Pseudo-Dionysian corpus and works by Nemesius and Gregory of Nyssa. He was assisted by an Armenian court official – an unusual collaboration between a CHALCEDONIAN and a non-Chalcedonian. Patriarch Photios corresponded with the Armenians, and in 862 the council of Širakavan was convened to receive his envoy to Catholicos Zak'aria. No change in the Armenian position resulted. But as the Muslims were pushed back from their earlier conquests in Asia Minor, the empire played an important role in the development of the independent Armenian kingdoms in the tenth century. Pro-Greek sentiment was never extinguished in Armenia; Catholicos Anania I (943–67) is noted for efforts to suppress Chalcedonian sympathizers, especially in the north-east. Anti-Islamic polemic also developed in the tenth century.

As Byzantium began to incorporate Armenian territory, beginning with the province of Taron in 966, Xač'ik I, Catholicos 972–91, began to consecrate bishops for Armenian communities outside the country, including ANTIOCH and Tarsus. After the collapse of the small Armenian kingdoms, the Byzantines consecrated Chalcedonian bishops in Armenia, as they had done in the seventh century, but with even less success in bringing about reunion. Nor was pressure on exiled Armenian princes generally productive. The catholicos was expelled from the Bagratid capital ANI on its capture in 1045. Not until 1146 was the see settled again, in Hromkla on the Euphrates. Byzantine control in Greater Armenia was short-lived because of the Turkish advance, and ended at Manazkert (Manzikert) in 1072. By that time numerous Armenian colonies had developed in Asia Minor and Cilicia, where the arrival of the crusaders was to bring about a dramatic change in Armenian political fortunes and ecclesiastical orientation.

Serious discussions with Byzantium were started in 1165 when the scholar and poet Nerses Šnorhali (catholicos 1167–73), met Alexis, son-in-law of emperor Manuel II, in Cilicia. An extended correspondence dealt with liturgical practice and Christological issues. Nerses' successor Gregory IV (catholicos 1173–93) summoned a council at Hromkla in 1179, where Armenian bishops from Greater Armenia, Cilicia, Syria and Asia Minor responded favourably. The positive attitude towards Byzantium is also reflected in the scholarly writings of Nerses of Lambron, archbishop of Tarsus 1180–98. But Prince Leo was more concerned with Western contacts, hoping for recognition and support in order to enhance his position among the crusader states. Emperor Frederick promised a royal crown, but died in 1190 in Cilicia heading the Third CRUSADE. After embassies to the emperor Henry VI and Pope Celestine III, Leo was crowned on 6 January 1198. Leo and the Catholicos wrote submissively to Innocent III following a council after the coronation, but they did not carry all their compatriots with them, either in introducing Western liturgical traditions or in accepting papal authority. The more the kings of Armenian Cilicia made advances to ROME, the more opposition they met at home and in Greater Armenia. Western influence increased, and intermarriage became common. Lands granted to the Templars and the Teutonic Order indicate Armenian need for military aid against the Muslims. Advances were also made to the Mongols; but after the Mamluk victory at Ain-Jalut in 1260 such support proved illusory. Catholic influence grew: by the end of the century the Franciscans had several convents in Cilicia; and when King Het'um was deposed in 1292 he took the Franciscan habit.

Hromkla was captured by the Mamluks in 1292, and Catholicos Stephen IV died in Egypt. Gregory VII moved the see to Sis. He summoned a council which met in 1307; here Roman demands were accepted at the cost of schism within the Armenian church. The bishop of JERUSALEM withdrew; the independent patriarchate there dates from this break. In Armenia the pro-Roman movement gained momentum with the organization of the Armenian Catholic order known as the Fratres Unitores. Monks at Krnay in Naxicevan accepted union in 1330, and in 1356 this group was approved by Pope John XXII under the jurisdiction of the Dominicans. Their missionary acitivities and the translation of Western scholastic works from Latin sparked the final flowering of medieval Armenian philosophy and theology in the work of John Orotnec'i (1315–86) and Grigor Tat'evac'i (1346–1409). The latter's *Book of Questions* provides the great summing-up of the Armenian theological tradition.

Although Cilician Armenia was not saved from the Mamluks by Western aid, finally expiring in 1375, pro-Roman sentiment was still strong. An Armenian delegation was present in 1439 at the COUNCIL OF FLORENCE, though the union there proclaimed was not ratified by any Armenian council. In Greater Armenia, however, resistance to

Westernizing tendencies led to the re-establishment of the patriarchal see at Ejmiacin in 1441, the see at Sis becoming increasingly insignificant until modern times. After the ARMENIAN GENOCIDE of 1915 it moved to Syria, and is now at Antelias outside Beirut.

Roman Catholic missionary activity continued in Armenia, enhanced by the development of printing. The first printed Armenian books appeared in VENICE in 1511–13. The first presses, although numerous, were generally short-lived; but momentum increased in the seventeenth century. The most significant and long-lasting result of Catholic schooling provided by the missionaries was their influence on Mxit'ar of Sebaste, who in 1701 established a religious order devoted to education; it was recognized by the Vatican in 1712. Unable to work in Constantinople because of opposition from the Armenian authorities, Mxit'ar and his followers took refuge with the Venetians in the MOREA. When the OTTOMANS took the Morea in 1715, Mxit'ar and his followers moved to Venice. This order not only profoundly affected the scholarly study of Armenian and the development of a modern literature, it also established a network of Catholic Armenian schools in Armenia and areas of the Armenian DIASPORA. The most significant of the Armenian colonies to unite with Rome was that of Poland, where the church became Catholic in the seventeenth century.

After the fall of Constantinople to the Turks in 1453 its Armenian bishop gained in importance; by the eighteenth century he was recognized as patriarch and leader of all Armenians in the Ottoman empire. The Catholic Armenians were recognized as a *milet* in 1835. The activity of Protestant missionaries (primarily American) led to the formation of a Protestant *milet* in 1850.

These Armenian churches have now spread with the diaspora across the world. The traditional Armenian church, sometimes known as Gregorian (from St Gregory the Enlightener), is split at the present time between allegiance to the catholicos of Ejmiacin and to the catholicos of Sis (Antelias) in matters of jurisdiction, but not in matters of faith. The patriarchate of Constantinople is much reduced in significance, while Jerusalem retains importance as a centre of pilgrimage. The Catholic and Protestant Armenian churches represent only a small fraction of the Armenian Christian population.

Nersessian, V., ed. (1996), *Archbishop Tiran Nersoyan: Armenian Church Historical Studies*. New York: St Vartan Press.

Thomson, R. W. (1994), *Studies in Armenian Literature and Christianity*. Aldershot: Variorum.

Valognes, J.-P. (1994), *Vie et mort des chrétiens d'Orient*, pp. 450–501. Paris: Fayard.

Mahé, J.-P. (1993), 'L'église arménienne de 611 à 1066', in J. M. Mayeur, ed., *Histoire du Christianisme*, vol. 4, pp. 457–547. Paris: Desclée.

Renoux, Ch. (1993), 'Langue et littérature arméniennes', in M. Albert, ed., *Christianismes orientaux*, pp. 107–66. Paris: Editions du Cerf.

Bardakjian, K. B. (1982), 'The Rise of the Armenian Patriarchate of Constantinople', in B. Braude and B. Lewis, eds, *Christians and Jews in the Ottoman Empire*, pp. 89–100. New York: Holmes & Meier.

Dédéyan, G., ed. (1982), *Histoire des Arméniens*. Toulouse: Privat.

Garsoïan, N. G. et al., eds (1982), *East of Byzantium: Syria and Armenia in the Formative Period*. Washington, DC: Dumbarton Oaks.

Sarkissian, K. (1975), *The Council of Chalcedon and the Armenian Church*, 2nd edn. New York: Armenian Prelacy.

Der Nersessian, S. (1973), *Byzantine and Armenian Studies*, 2 vols. Louvain: Peeters.

Spuler, B. (1964), 'Die Armenische Kirche', in B. Spuler, ed., *Die morgenländischen Kirchen*, Handbuch der Orientalistik, Part I, vol. 8.2, pp. 240–68. Leiden: Brill.

Garitte, G. (1952), *La Narratio de Rebus Armeniae*, CSCO, Subsidia 4. Louvain: Peeters.

Tekeyan, P. (1939), *Controverses christologiques en Arméno-Cilicie dans la seconde moitié du XIIᵉ siècle (1165–1198)*. *Orientalia Christiana Analecta*, vol. 124. Rome: Pontifical Institute of Oriental Studies.

RWT

Armenian genocide   From the late nineteenth century the OTTOMAN Turkish authorities feared that the Armenians, like the Balkan nations, would establish an independent state with Russian backing. Ignoring Russian hostility towards any Armenian independence movement (Russia held eastern Armenia), the Ottomans incited Muslim Turks, KURDS and Laz against their Armenian neighbours. Massacres of Armenians were organized at Samsun (1894), Trebizond (1895) and then across the Ottoman empire. By the beginning of the First World War the 'Young Turk' regime viewed the Armenians as the greatest internal threat, and in 1915 Muslim irregulars were unleashed against all centres of Armenian population and the military employed to deport all Christians from areas where they constituted a sizeable minority. This measure impacted on Greek, Syrian and ASSYRIAN Christians, but in the case of the Armenians was implemented with single-minded brutality.

In western Armenia 600,000 were massacred between April and November 1915; 500,000 Armenians were deported to Mesopotamia, of whom only 90,000 survived. In August 1918 over 400,000 Armenians were killed by Turkish soldiers advancing through the Russian Caucasus, demonstrating clearly that the Young Turks were targeting Armenians in general, not just supposed fifth columnists within the Ottoman empire. In February 1920 30,000 Armenians were massacred in Cilicia and Cappadocia; 80,000 sought refuge in Syria and Lebanon. Finally, in September 1922, with the occupation of Smyrna, the remaining 100,000 Armenians were driven out of ASIA MINOR alongside their Greek neighbours, with much loss of life in both communities. The new Kemalist leadership in Turkey sought to distance itself from the excesses of its Ottoman and Young Turk predecessors but none the less confiscated all Armenian property in 1931.

No Turkish government has ever acknowledged the scale of the 1915–22 genocide of Armenians, Assyrians, Pontic Greeks and other communities. Turkish historians claim that the loss of life was the result of isolated pogroms and the general hardship experienced by all, including the Turks, during this period. It is argued that the conflict was basically between Kurds and Armenians, or Greeks and Laz, and so forth: quarrels between minorities and fanatical religious groups in which the Turks, then waging a war on many fronts, were unable to intervene. Yet since the First World War Kurds and Armenians have generally expressed solidarity against perceived Turkish aggression, and even at the height of the massacres Muslim Arabs welcomed

Armenian and other Christian refugees in Syria and Iraq. Turkish politicians and media tend to dismiss this as a product of the anti-Turkish sentiment which they view as animating all their immediate neighbours.

See also NAGORNO-KARABAKH; PONTUS.

Dadrian, V. N. (1997), *The History of the Armenian Genocide*. Providence, RI: Berghahn.
Graber, G. S. (1996), *Caravans to Oblivion*. New York: Wiley.
Walker, C. J. (1990), *Armenia*. London: Routledge.

DB

Armenian liturgy   The Armenian rite has in many respects preserved the oldest layers of Christian worship, mirroring in its earliest stratum close affinities with the oldest Syrian liturgical material. The first missionaries to enter Armenian territory probably came from the south-west and thus Syrian influence manifested itself first and foremost in the origins and the earliest development of Armenian worship. Cappadocia and Jerusalem also contributed to the evolution of Armenia's liturgical tradition. Thus, from the beginning the Armenians had close ties first with the Syrian communities in and around EDESSA, then also with the Greek church in Cappadocia. In the *Agathangeli historia* the process of Christianization is tendentiously associated with Gregory the Enlightener who was not only educated in Cappadocia but also became the central figure in the narrative of the conversion of King Trdat and his baptism in the Euphrates. These efforts of the Armenians to associate themselves with the missionary activities of the fourth-century Greeks rather than earlier Syrian missionaries possibly originates in the fact that Armenia tried to veil its earliest contacts with groups in and around Edessa which later came under suspicion of heresy.

Despite these efforts in Agathangelos to link the conversion of Armenia with Cappadocia, the description of King Trdat's baptism betrays features which clearly point to a Syrian origin. Thus Syrian influence prevailed above all in the rites of initiation. The oldest witness is found in the description of the king's baptism in the *Agathangeli historia*, and the oldest manuscripts of the order of the baptismal rite of the ninth and tenth centuries have to be compared with the patristic evidence of the third to fifth centuries. Characteristic of the Armenian baptismal ordo is the absence of verbal exorcisms and the preservation of the Johannine baptismal theology following the old Syrian model. Likewise the hymnodic material (*Šarakan*) of the rites of initiation shows the closest affinity with the Syrian understanding of baptism. The Armenians preserved the original character of the rites of initiation, reflecting the earliest Syrian baptismal theology of John 3 with its pneumatic orientation, whereas the Greco-Latin type of baptism is inspired by the Christocentric death-mysticism of Paul in Romans 6.

The earliest formulations of the Armenian credal statements follow the early Syriac wording, and when the Syrians altered some verbs in the fifth and sixth centuries, following thus more closely the Greek terms *sarkōthenta* (incarnate) and *enanthrōpē-santa* (became man), the Armenians also coined neologisms to render more accurately the Greek verbs.

The Armenian anaphoras (attributed to Gregory the Enlightener, Sahak, Basil, Gregory of Nazianzus, Cyril and Athanasius) mirror the Antiochene, and more pre-cisely the Byzantine, structure of the eucharistic prayer; some, however, mirror the pre-

Byzantine shape of the anaphora, as for example the first Armenian redaction of the anaphora of Basil (in the manuscripts attributed to Gregory the Enlightener) which represents, with the Egyptian anaphora of Basil, the oldest redaction of the liturgy of Basil. Besides this important Armenian witness the *Buzandaran Patmut'iwnk'* (v: 28) also offers primitive layers of the anaphora of Basil. The liturgy of Basil was again rendered into Armenian after the tenth century; in the twelfth and thirteenth centuries the liturgy of Chrysostom was translated, as were two Syrian anaphoras during the eleventh to fourteenth centuries. Of far greater importance, however, was the Latin influence during this period. With the establishment of the Armenian kingdom of Cilicia the Armenian rite became Latinized because of political pressure and internal strife. Even the highest-ranking church officials favoured closer ties with Rome, and noteworthy figures like Nerses Lambronac'i (1153/4–98) translated the Latin mass into Armenian.

The oldest manuscripts of the Athanasius liturgy, now the only anaphora used by the Armenians, stem from the high middle ages and thus the tenth-century commentary of Xosrov Anjewac'i gains particular importance since it allows insights into the earlier stage of the anaphora as it was celebrated in the Armenian province of Vaspurakan in the middle of the tenth century.

The Liturgy of the Hours was decisively shaped by the so-called 'cathedral office' of fourth-century JERUSALEM. The Armenian Sunday Vigil which commemorates the Resurrection has preserved more closely than any other rite the hagiopolite structure of the cathedral Sunday office with its three canticles and three psalms, followed by the gospel reading of the burial and Resurrection, as described by Egeria who visited Jerusalem during 381–4. This Sunday vigil commemorated the three women who came to Jesus' tomb early in the morning; the Armenians named their vigil after these spice-bearing women (*Myrophoroi*): 'Ordo of public prayer of the morning time which is celebrated for the Son of God who appeared to the spice-bearing women', and the core of the office carries the heading: 'Chant of the Gospel of the spice-bearing women'. Other features in the Armenian HOROLOGION also deserve closer attention.

The Armenians preserve the recitation of the psalms in their numerical order, a characteristic of the monastic office, exclusively for the night office (*gišerayin žam*). Neither the morning office (*aṙawōtean žam*) nor Vespers (*erekoyean žam*) has or had a monastic psalmody placed before the so-called cathedral elements of the morning and evening office, in contrast to the Byzantine ORTHROS and HESPERINOS. Thus the Armenian rite reflects older layers in its office than its Greek counterpart, having preserved the archaic structure of the cathedral morning and evening office.

In addition, the Armenians, like the East Syrians, do not have Psalm 62/63 in their morning office. This is because the Syriac text of Psalm 62 differs from that of the Septuagint. Psalm 62 according to the Septuagint reads: 'My God, my God, I rise for you at dawn ... at dawn I meditated on you', whereas the Syriac text does not refer to the morning, but to the night: 'in the nights ...'. This psalm is the morning psalm *par excellence* in the Greek-speaking regions of Antioch, Palestine (in its Sabaite tradition), and perhaps also Cappadocia. The central morning psalm of the morning office of Armenia and East Syria is Psalm 50/51. Most surprising is the fact that even the old Constantinopolitan Orthros has Psalm 50: Psalm 62 is recited not in the Orthros, but rather in the preceding nocturne. The structural outline of the Liturgy of the Hours of the seventh and eighth centuries can be gleaned from references in the writings of CATHOLICOS John III of Ōjun and Stephen Siwnecʻi, and its further development is shown in Xosrov Anjewacʻiʼs commentary of the tenth century.

The liturgical year originally began, as in Jerusalem, with the feast of Epiphany (now in the Armenian rite the feast of Jesus' birth in Bethlehem and the descent of the Spirit upon him in the River Jordan), as the Armenian lectionary with its hagiopolite origins indicates. Besides the oldest Armenian manuscripts of the *Čašocʻ* (lectionary) this is also true for the earliest witnessses of the *Tōnakan* (TYPIKON) and the *Šaraknocʻ* (tropologion). It may well be that the *Yaysmawurkʻ* (synaxarion) also once began with 6 January, the feast of Epiphany, since the oldest witness of the *Yaysmawurkʻ* of Tēr Isra(y)ēl of *c.*1240 begins with 1 January, which mirrors the next stage in the development of the beginning of the liturgical year. The *Yaysmawurkʻ* of Kirakos (Ganjakecʻi) of 1269 no longer begins with 1 January but with 1 Nawasard (11 August). It is this synaxarion (not that of Tēr Isra(y)ēl) that forms the basis of Bayan's edition, and the publication of Pēštimaljean from 1834 reflects the reworking of the synaxarion by Grigor Anawarzecʻi despite its claims to present Tēr Isra(y)ēl's synaxarion. The last redaction by Grigor Cerencʻ (1353–1425) forms the basis of the *Editio princeps* of 1706.

Winkler, G. (1994), *Der armenische Ritus. Bestandsaufnahme und neue Erkenntnisse.* Rome: Pontifical Institute of Oriental Studies
Winkler, G. (1982), *Das armenische Initiationsrituale.* Rome: Pontifical Institute of Oriental Studies.
Renoux, A. (1969–71), *Le codex arménian Jérusalem 121.* Turnhout: Brepols.

GW

Arsenios Autoreianos (d. 1273) The 'Zealot': patriarch of CONSTANTINOPLE 1254–60 and 1261–5. Born in Constantinople before the Fourth CRUSADE (1204), Arsenios joined a monastery at Oxeia in the Princes' Islands, later living in various monasteries of ASIA MINOR. He was embroiled in the politics of the court of Nicea and, later, of liberated Constantinople, where he recrowned Michael VIII Palaiologos (1261). Outspoken on moral issues, Arsenios repeatedly incurred imperial disapproval. When Michael blinded his ward, the legitimate heir, John IV Laskaris, Arsenios excommunicated him; he was thereupon deposed and exiled to Prokonessos in Propontis (1265). A prolonged schism ensued, the 'Arsenite Schism', which continued after Arsenios's death in exile and even after the translation of his relics to Hagia Sophia (1284). The schism was formally ended in 1310. Arsenios is commemorated on 30 September.

Hackel, S., ed. (1981), *The Byzantine Saint.* London: Fellowship of SS Alban & Sergius.

DB

Arta Metropolitan town in Thessaly notable for its Byzantine churches, especially the Panagia Parigoritissa, Our Lady the Comforter, built between 1286 and 1296. Reminiscent of an Italian *palazzo*, the Parigoritissa is a large square structure of three stories and five domes, with a fine mosaic of the PANTOCRATOR in the central cupola. This distinctive building was once katholikon of a large monastery. The exterior of Arta's St Basil Church (thirteenth century) is decorated with red and green glazed ceramics and herringbone brick patterns. The church of St Theodora (also thirteenth century), originally dedicated to St George, houses the tomb of St Theodora, wife of the despot of Epirus, Michael II (1231–71). Nearby are other remarkable thirteenth-century churches, including the two monastery churches of Kato Panagia and of Blachernai, the latter notable for its sculptured reliefs and carved ornament on the sanctuary screen.

Rodley, L. (1994), *Byzantine Art and Architecture: An Introduction.* Cambridge: Cambridge University Press.
Hetherington, P. (1991), *Byzantine and Medieval Greece: Churches, Castles and Art.* London: John Murray.

KP

Artoklasia Byzantine rite, 'Blessing of Loaves', or 'Breaking [Greek *klasis*] of Bread [Greek *artos*]', performed before the APOLYTIKION at Vespers when there is a vigil. Wheat, wine and oil are blessed together with five loaves of bread. In Athonite use, the bread, impregnated with the wine, is eaten with ANTIDORON after the liturgy. In the monastery of Patmos the bread is distributed with a beaker of wine after Vespers at the vigil. In Russian use the bread, soaked in the wine, is distributed during the veneration of the icon of the feast during the reading of the CANON at Matins of the vigil. Many Greek parishes celebrate the Artoklasia on important feasts even when there is no vigil, at Vespers or Matins or even after the liturgy.

E

artophorion Greek: container, frequently in the form of a miniature church, usually on the holy table, in which the sacrament is reserved. Hanging pyxes are sometimes used.

DM

Ascension icon The image of the Ascension or Assumption (Greek: *Analypsis*) of Christ shown here is based on an illumination in the RABBULA GOSPELS (sixth century). The ascension took place on the Mount of Olives (Acts 1: 12); hence the rocky background. The standing figure of Christ, making a gesture of blessing with his right hand and holding a scroll in his left, is encompassed in a MANDORLA supported by two ANGELS. It is supported underneath by seraphic wings and fiery wheels as described in Ezekiel's vision. In the midst of this motif are a hand reaching down and a tetramorph, that is, the head of a man, a lion, an ox, and an eagle (Ezekiel 1: 10). In Christian tradition these heads correspond to the four evangelists, Matthew, Mark, Luke and John. Two more angels fly in bearing crowns, one for Christ and one for the Mother of God. The splendour of Christ's departure from this life anticipates his Second Coming in glory.

The Mother of God is shown with hands outstretched and uplifted, a gesture of prayer. On either side of her angels address groups of apostles who gaze up at the

ascending Christ. The New Testament does not record Mary as witnessing the Ascension: her presence points to her role in his mission. The two zones of the icon, the celestial and the terrestrial, are significantly evenly matched.

The Byzantine texts of the feast, celebrated on the Thursday forty days after Pascha, emphasize that Christ is taken up into heaven in order to send the Paraclete into the world. Angels are represented as astonished at the sight of 'our nature' entering heaven. The Ascension of Christ is also mentioned in the hymns as prefiguring his return in glory as judge of all.

Ouspensky, L. and Lossky, V. (1982), *The Meaning of Icons*. Crestwood, NY: St Vladimir's Seminary Press.

KP

asceticism The Roman empire was already familiar with the ascetic lifestyles of Cynic and Stoic philosophers, of the Egyptian priesthoods, and at least by repute of the Indian sages before the Christian church was founded. For Greeks and Romans alike, moral severity and austerity were respected as signs of self-control and excellence of character. Christianity proclaimed values already admired.

Ascetic practices such as poverty, fasting, sleep-fasting, multiple prostrations, avoidance of bathing, wearing rough and ragged clothes, and homelessness were adopted as a means of training in control of the appetites and passions and in detachment; awakening awareness of mortality and the fragility of life; awareness of divine providence; as expiation for sins and offences; as purifying the soul from the effects of sin; as a means of driving out demons; and as a way of sharing in sufferings and death of Christ. Above all, asceticism is a preparation for death.

The MONASTICISM of the desert fathers was strongly ascetic. Stylites and dendrites fasting and praying on pillars or in trees and HOLY FOOLS feigning lunacy witnessed publicly to the value of Christian asceticism.

Asceticism remains an important aspect of Eastern Christian life. Weekly and seasonal fasts (*see* CALENDAR) are widely observed, and monastic life still finds recruits. The Reformation rejection of asceticism (as tainted with notions of meriting salvation) is unfamiliar and astonishing to most Eastern Christians, for whom asceticism is a normal and integral part of the Christian life.

See also SPIRITUAL THEOLOGY.

Brown, P. R. L. (1989), *The Body and Society: Men, Women and Sexual Renunciation in Early Christian Society*. New York: Columbia University Press.
Špidlik, T. (1986), *The Spirituality of the Christian East*. Kalamazoo: Cistercian Publications.
McGinn, B. and Meyendorff, J. eds (1985), *Christian Spirituality*, vol. 1: *Origins to the Twelfth Century*. New York: Crossroads.

Colliander, T. (1985), *Way of the Ascetics*. Crestwood, NY: St Vladimir's Seminary Press.

DM

Ashtarak   The town of Ashtarak in Armenia has a fifth-century church and a seventh-century martyrium, a small central domed mausoleum built to a cruciform ground-plan which seems to have undergone some rebuilding in the tenth century.

KP

Asia Minor   *Mikra Asia* or Anatolia; originally this referred to the Pergamene empire, bequeathed to Rome by Attalos III (133 BC) and thereafter forming the province of Asia. Later, Asia Minor designated Bithynia, Paphlagonia, Galatia, Lycaonia, Pisidia, Lycia, Pamphylia, Cilicia, Cappadocia, Kommagene and PONTUS alongside the original Pergamene territories of Troad, Aiolia, Mysia, Phrygia, IONIA, Lydia, Karia and Doris towards the Aegean Sea. The Romans and Byzantines viewed Armenia (Greater and Lesser) as a separate entity, although changing provincial boundaries and Armenian migrations westwards resulted in Armenian encroachment on lands once thought to be part of Pontus, Cappadocia, Cilicia, etc.

Asia Minor's peoples were open to Christianity from the early period. By the fourth century Christianity was the majority religion. The Hellenization of the interior, in process since the conquests of Alexander the Great (d. 323 BC) also continued and was virtually complete by the sixth century, even the unruly Isaurians of Lycaonia and Pisidia being no longer distinguished as a separate group. Incursion of Caucasian tribes and the organized resettlement of Vandals, Slavs, MARDAITES, etc. ensured a degree of ethnic diversity. The Huns invaded Asia Minor in the fifth and sixth centuries and the Persians in the seventh, followed by successive Arab campaigns towards CONSTANTINOPLE, culminating in the sack of Amorion in 838. Byzantine expansion eastwards in the mid-ninth century stimulated immigration from Armenia, Syria and elsewhere. The Seljuk Turks dominated Asia Minor after the battle of Mantzikert in 1071, but the CRUSADES enabled the Byzantines to recover much lost territory in the west and along the Euxine and Mediterranean coasts. The battle of Myriokephalon in 1176 inaugurated a new era of Seljuk and Turkoman expansion at the expense of the Byzantines.

By 1300 the Byzantines held only the coastal areas to the north-west and isolated interior forts. Military campaigns failed to prolong Byzantine control of even these or establish a presence elsewhere. The regions towards the Aegean were lost by 1315 and Bithynia was in OTTOMAN hands by 1337; Philadelphia, the sole Byzantine stronghold in Asia Minor, was taken by the Turks in 1390.

Greeks and Armenians remained a significant component in the population of Asia Minor into the twentieth century. Greeks predominated in many seaward regions, including Ionia and Pontus, and inland enclaves, particularly in Cappadocia. Smyrna (Izmir), Trebizond (Trabzon) and other urban centres provided a focus for the Anatolian Greeks and attracted Orthodox Christian migrants from the Balkans and Syria.

After the First World War Greece responded to the Italian occupation of Attaleia (Antalya) by occupying Smyrna on 15 May 1919. Turkey fought back. The Treaty of Sèvres in August 1920 confirmed the Greek presence in Ionia, provoking further Turkish resistance. Continued irregular warfare led to a Greek campaign in 1921 that was defeated only at the Sangarios (Sakarya) river near Ankara. The ensuing debacle led to a disorganized Greek withdrawal and the evacuation of Smyrna on 8 September 1922. It is claimed that in Smyrna alone the victorious Turks massacred up to 50,000 Greeks and Armenians, including metropolitan CHRYSOSTOM OF SMYRNA. By 1924 the entire Greek population of Asia Minor had been exterminated or expelled, either in the immediate aftermath of the Greek defeat or in the later population exchanges.

See also ARMENIAN GENOCIDE; KURDS.

Llewellyn-Smith, M. (1998), *Ionian Vision: Greece in Asia Minor, 1919–22*. London: Allen Lane.
Housepian, M. (1972), *Smyrna 1922: The Destruction of a City*. London: Faber.

DB

Asinou   The church of the Panagia Phorbiotissa, Our Lady of the Pastures, of Asinou in the foothills of the Troodos mountains in CYPRUS, was built and frescoed in 1105–6. A narthex was added around 1200 and the entire structure is covered with a wooden pitched roof. The donor panel shows the church with this roof, which must therefore belong to the original building. About two-thirds of the early twelfth-century programme survives, mostly in the sanctuary and the west end, including images of the DORMITION, the Forty Martyrs, Apostle Barnabas and the church father EPIPHANIOS OF SALAMIS. There are later wall paintings from the fourteenth century in the NAOS and narthex.

Stylianou, A. and Stylianou, J. A. (1985), *The Painted Churches of Cyprus: Treasures of Byzantine Art*. London: Trigraph.

KP

Asmatike Akolouthia   Greek, 'sung order of service': the Byzantine cathedral office consisting mainly of ORTHROS and HESPERINOS. It was gradually displaced by the monastic office, though Simeon of Thessaloniki records it as still in use in the fifteenth century.

DM

Assemani family   MARONITE scholars of the seventeenth and eighteenth centuries prepared many of the *instrumenta studiorum*, text editions, translations, compilations, encyclopedias, manuscript catalogues, and other finding aids that are still indispensable for the study of the languages, literatures and history of Christian communities of the Near East. Members of the Assemani (*as-Sim'ānī*) family deserve special recognition for their landmark contributions in introducing the literary heritage of the Near Eastern churches, especially the Syriac- and Arabic-speaking churches, to the West.

Joseph Simon Assemani (1687–1768) was born in Tripoli, Lebanon. In 1703 he entered the Maronite College founded in 1584 in ROME by Pope Gregory XIII (1572–85). After ordination he worked in the Vatican Library and was responsible for the *Bibliotheca Orientalis Clementino-Vaticana* (3 vols in 4, Rome, 1719–28), the first and best encyclopaedia for the study of early Syriac Christian literature. At the National

Maronite Synod of 1736, in the monastery of Our Lady of Luwayza, Lebanon, he played a prominent pro-Roman role. Joseph became titular archbishop of Tyre and prefect of the Vatican Library. His cousin Elias collected manuscripts from Egyptian monasteries for the Vatican Library in 1707.

Stephen Evodius (*c*.1710–82), nephew of Joseph Simon, collaborated with him on the great Roman edition of the works of EPHREM THE SYRIAN, which appeared in six volumes between 1732 and 1746, bringing the Syriac works of Ephrem to the attention of European readers for the first time. He also published catalogues of oriental manuscripts, notably those of the Vatican Library (1756–9).

The liturgical scholar Joseph Aloysius (1710–82), another nephew of Joseph Simon and cousin of Stephen Evodius, compiled the thirteen-volume *Codex liturgicus ecclesiae universae* (Rome, 1740–56). He also taught Syriac in Rome. The orientalist Simon (1749/1752–1821), a nephew of Joseph Aloysius, taught at Padua and made his contributions in Arabic and Islamic studies.

Raphael, P. (1950), *Le Rôle du Collège Maronite Romain dans l'orientalisme aux XVIIe et XVIIIe siècles*. Beyrouth: Université Saint Joseph de Beyrouth.

MJB/SHG/JH

assist   Russian term for gold hatching in icon painting.

KP

Assyrians   A name used in English since the nineteenth century for the CHURCH OF THE EAST. It became popular especially among Anglicans, who sponsored a mission to the church and wished to avoid the pejorative term 'NESTORIAN'. The church itself now uses the style 'Assyrian Church of the East'. By itself, the term 'Assyrian' (Syriac: *Āthōrāyā*) came into use *c*.1900 to denote the ethnic group historically represented by the Church of the East. It is now a common belief among Assyrians that they are descendants of the ancient Assyrians of Nineveh. Some SYRIAN ORTHODOX, whether to ally themselves with other Assyrian nationalists or only to avoid the word 'Syrian' (with its misleading reference to the modern state of Syria), also call themselves 'Assyrian'. This usage is not officially sanctioned by that church.

JFC

Athanasius   (*c*.295–373) Athanasius was born and educated in ALEXANDRIA. Ordained deacon in 319, he attended the ECUMENICAL COUNCIL of Nicea in 325 as secretary to his bishop Alexander and in 328 succeeded him. The most learned and theologically acute opponent of Arianism, he refused to readmit Arius to communion even at the orders of Emperor CONSTANTINE THE GREAT. Between 335 and 366 Athanasius was five times exiled, being restored to office for the last time in 366. He died seven years later. Despite his opposition to heresy, Athanasius was patient with those who out of genuine misunderstanding opposed the Nicene use of the technical term *homoousios* (consubstantial).

Athanasius was a prolific writer. His biography of Antony the Great, father of Eastern MONASTICISM, aroused popular interest in ASCETICISM and the monastic life. He is commemorated in the Byzantine calendar on 18 January.

Pettersen, A. (1995), *Athanasius*. London: Chapman.
Pettersen, A. (1990), *Athanasius and the Human Body*. Bristol: Bristol Press.
Kannengiesser, C. (1983), *Athanase d'Alexandrie: Evêque et Ecrivain*. Paris.
Quasten, J. (1960), *Patrology*, vol. 3. Utrecht: Spectrum.
Cross, F. L. (1945), *The Study of St Athanasius*. Oxford: Oxford University Press.

DM

Athanasius Yeshue Samuel   SYRIAN ORTHODOX archbishop of the United States and Canada, 1957–95. (*See* AMERICA.) Yeshue Samuel was born near Nisibin, Turkey in 1907. In 1923 he went to the Syrian Orthodox Monastery of St Mark in JERU-SALEM, eventually spending some twenty-five years there as a student, librarian, monk and priest, and then as metropolitan of Palestine and Transjordan (1946). Mar Athanasius Yeshue Samuel made many important contributions to the Syrian Orthodox Church, to biblical studies, and to SYRIAC scholarship in general. He is perhaps best known for the significant role he played in the 1947 discovery of the Dead Sea scrolls. He told the story himself in his memoir, *Treasure of Qumran*. In 1948 he was appointed apostolic delegate to the United States and Canada, and in 1957 was proclaimed archbishop of the Syrian Orthodox archdiocese of the United States. As archbishop he oversaw an extensive building programme and was responsible for publishing many Syriac and English prayer books, liturgical texts and catechetical works, most notably English translations of the *Ma'de'dono* (1984) and *Anafuras* (1991). Mar Athanasius Yeshue Samuel died on 16 April 1995.

Thomas, R. M., Jr (1995), 'Samuel, Athanasius Yeshue, Abp. d.1995' (obituary and portrait), *New York Times*, 24 April, 144 B11.
Archbishop Athanasius Yeshue Samuel (1966, 1968), *Treasure of Qumran: My Story of the Dead Sea Scrolls*. Philadelphia: Westminster Press.

MJB/SHG

Athenagoras I   Ecumenical Patriarch, 1948–72. Born Aristokles Spyrou in 1886 and educated in the Patriarchal Theological School on Halki in the Sea of Marmara, he became DEACON in 1910 and in 1918 archdeacon to MELETIOS METAXAKIS, then primate of Greece. From 1922 to 1931 he served as bishop in Corfu, and in 1931 was elected archbishop of North and South America. He gave the archdiocese a structural basis for the future. In 1948 he was elected to the throne of CONSTANTINOPLE. His reign as Ecumenical Patriarch was focused on the promotion of inter-Orthodox unity and on improved ecumenical relations with the West, especially with Roman Catholics and Anglicans (*see* ECUMENISM). When he met with Pope Paul VI (1963–78) in JERUSALEM and when in 1965 they jointly lifted the anathemas of 1054, Athenagoras was severely criticized by Orthodox ZEALOTS. The lifting of the anathemas had profound symbolic meaning, but little theological or canonical significance, since the original anathemas were essentially personal, and directly affected relations between ROME and Constantinople rather than the entire Catholic and Orthodox communions. Athenagoras I died in 1972.

DM

Athonitissa   Icon type of the THEOTOKOS. Legends claim that the Mother of God visited ATHOS in her lifetime and list numerous occasions when she miraculously saved monks and pilgrims, monasteries and the entire mountain from calamity. The Athonitissa icon represents her as protector of the whole mountain: she is depicted wearing the abbatial robes standing above Mount Athos. The icon is commemorated on 28 August.

Gerasimos Mikrayiannanitis (1986), *Eniausios Stephanos*. Athens: n.p.

DB

Athos   For more than a thousand years Athos, the holy mountain, has been the principal centre of MONASTICISM in the EASTERN ORTHODOX church. The first monasteries were founded as cenobitic communities in the tenth century, though groups of monks and hermits were living on the Mount for centuries before this; by the early eleventh century Athos had acquired its characteristic attributes, its autonomy, its supranational representation, its exclusion of women and its democratic institutions.

  Athos, a rocky and superficially inhospitable peninsula in northern GREECE, the most easterly of the three fingers of Chalkidiki, is about 45 km long and no more than 10 km wide. To the north it connects with the mainland via a narrow, low-lying isthmus. To the south the land gradually rises to increasingly barren heights culminating at the tip in a spectacular peak (2,033 m). Vegetation varies, allowing cultivation of crops in the vicinity of most monasteries and dense forestation. Exclusion of females extends to domestic animals, and the absence of flocks means that the hillsides are ungrazed and of great botanical interest.

  As a result of imperial patronage the monasteries acquired land, mostly in MACEDONIA and THRACE, and treasures. Wealth attracted predators, and despite defences many monasteries were attacked and looted. After the fall of the empire, OTTOMAN authorities imposed an increasing burden of taxation on the monks and many of their mainland properties were confiscated. Otherwise they left the monasteries relatively undisturbed.

  It seems that the monasteries of Athos played a role in Greek education, and until the late seventeenth century their libraries were still acquiring manuscripts and printed books on secular as well as religious subjects. In the eighteenth century there was a decline in literacy which PATRIARCH CYRIL V tried to halt by founding in 1749 an academy at Vatopedi monastery. The curriculum, taught by leading scholars such as Evgenios Bulgaris, embraced philosophy and mathematics as well as theology and grammar, and students included laymen. Bulgaris' departure in 1759 signalled the end of the educational project. Subsequent attempts to revive the academy as a university were unsuccessful, and when William Martin Leake visited the site in 1806 he found it deserted. 'The friends of learning among the Greeks', he wrote, 'have been compelled to apply their exertions elsewhere.' Nineteenth-century western visitors to the Mount were shocked by the low intellectual standard among the monks and the neglect into which most monastic libraries had fallen.

  The traditions of HESYCHASM, closely identified with Athos since the days of Gregory PALAMAS (1296–1359), were however maintained, and in the later eighteenth century enjoyed revival at the hands of the KOLLYVADES. One result of this revival was the publication in 1782 of the PHILOKALIA. The beginning of nationalism on Athos manifested itself in the same period in hostility between the Greek monasteries and others. Orthodox monasticism was reviving in Russia, stimulated by the missionary work of PAISSI VELICHKOVSKII (1722–94), founder of the Russian SKETE of Prophet Elias. During the nineteenth century the numbers of Russian monks on Athos increased until by 1902 they outnumbered the Greeks. Attempts to upgrade their houses to monasteries were unsuccessful. It seems the tsar's hidden agenda was the conversion of Athos into a sort of Balkan Gibraltar from which he would be able to dominate the approaches to the Bosphorus and himself ascend the throne of Constantinople. Any such ambitions were frustrated by the other great powers. After the Russian Revolution the state permitted no more monks to go to Athos and their numbers dwindled naturally. But the Greeks none the less guard against the recurrence of any such build-up.

In 1902 there were 7,432 monks on Athos. There followed seventy years of attrition, not only at the Russian monastery of St Panteleimon but at nearly all the monasteries. By 1971 numbers had fallen to 1,145, but the seeds of revival had already been sown. In the remote kellia and hermitages clustering around the southern tip of the peninsula, called Eremos, 'the Desert', a number of ascetic spiritual teachers lived, each with a circle of young disciples. As the monasteries weakened the kellia strengthened, until eventually there was a redistribution of the population. Stavronikita monastery was near to closure when it decided in 1970 to revert to the cenobitic way of life and invite the learned hermit Fr Vasilios to become abbot and bring his disciples with him. Similar influxes occurred at Philotheou and Simonopetra, though in the latter case the new blood came from Meteora led by Fr Aimilianos. Soon the revival had spread to all but the few remaining idiorrhythmic monasteries and the non-Greek houses. By 1992 all the monasteries had become cenobitic.

By 1995 there were about 1,500 monks on Athos. More important than their number is their relative youth. No longer is the Mount populated mainly by old men from the land, many poorly educated; most Athonite monks of the 1990s are highly educated, energetic and devout. They work enthusiastically at the restoration of their buildings and the conservation of their treasures; intellectual and spiritual standards have risen and Athos is once again the spiritual heart of the Greek Orthodox world. The non-Greek houses, however, continue to suffer discrimination from the Greek authorities and do not exhibit the same degree of renewal. But as the new order in Eastern Europe grows stronger, and the Greeks realize that its consequences are to be welcomed rather than feared, there is hope that Athos will once again fulfil a genuinely pan-Orthodox role.

Bryer, A. and Cunningham, M., eds (1996), *Mount Athos and Byzantine Monasticism.* Aldershot: Variorum.

Alexander, Hieromonk (1994), *The Living Witness of the Holy Mountain.* South Canaan, Pa.: St Tikhon's Seminary Press.

Gothóni, R. (1993), *Paradise within Reach: Monasticism and Pilgrimage on Mt Athos.* Helsinki: Helsinki University Press.

Sherrard, P. (1982), *Athos, the Holy Mountain.* London: Alexandria Press.

Runciman, S. (1968), *The Great Church in Captivity*. Cambridge: Cambridge University Press.

GS

Australia and New Zealand   Australia covers an area of over 7 million sq km with a population over 18 million, more than 90 per cent of whom are of European ancestry. Roman Catholics are the largest religious group in Australia, followed by Anglicans. EASTERN CHRISTIANS make up probably under 5 per cent, and within that figure the GREEK ORTHODOX are the largest community.

In 1820 a Russian Orthodox monastic priest, Father Dionysii, accompanying a Russian Antarctic expedition, celebrated the Divine Liturgy in Sydney. Before the end of the nineteenth century the first Greek Orthodox church was established. Lay initiative was crucial to the development of Eastern Orthodoxy in Australia. Until 1902 the patriarchate of Jerusalem looked after the Greek Orthodox of Australia; the Church of Greece took over this responsibility in 1903, and the Ecumenical Patriarchate in 1924.

As the Greek population grew the Ecumenical Patriarchate established the metropolis of Australia and New Zealand in 1924, under Metropolitan Christophoros. The second metropolitan, Timotheos Evangelinides, came to Australia in 1932 and on his election to Rhodes in 1947 was succeeded by Metropolitan Theophylactos, who was succeeded in 1950 by Ezekiel of Nazianzos. Six months later the Greek Orthodox metropolis of Australia and New Zealand was made an archdiocese. In 1970 the Ecumenical Patriarchate established a separate metropolis of New Zealand. In 1974 Archbishop Ezekiel, elected metropolitan of Pisidia, was succeeded by the metropolitan of Miletoupolis, Stylianos Harkianakis, of the University of Thessaloniki, who was enthroned in 1975.

The Greek Orthodox church in Australia has grown rapidly. Links have been established with Mount ATHOS and with spiritual institutions in Greece. Emphasis has been laid on the encouraging of local clerical vocations and on embedding the church in Australian life. To that end St Andrew's Theological College has been established in Sydney. Numerous Antiochian, Russian, Serbian, Slav Macedonian, Ukrainian and Romanian immigrants have settled. To meet their spiritual and cultural needs, clergy of several Orthodox jurisdictions have established themselves in Australia. The RUSSIAN ORTHODOX CHURCH ABROAD has an archdiocese with churches throughout Australia and in New Zealand. A national Standing Conference of Canonical Orthodox Churches of Australia was set up in 1979 to facilitate co-operation.

The Greek Orthodox archbishop exercises his pastoral role with the assistance of his auxiliary bishops and an archdiocesan council of twelve priests and twenty-four lay people elected by the Clergy–Laity Congresses. A monthly periodical, *Voice of Orthodoxy*, is published and there is a weekly ecclesiastical radio programme. Annually, two Athonite monks and other leading figures in Greek church life are invited to enhance the spiritual and intellectual life of the community. Pilgrimages are organized each year to the Holy Land, to religious sites in Greece and to the Phanar. The Clergy–Laity Congress of 1981 instituted a Biennial National Youth Conference and in alternate years State Youth Conferences.

The development of the Oriental Orthodox in Australia is more recent than that of the Eastern Orthodox. From 1960 on, SYRIAN ORTHODOX Christians settled in the area around Melbourne; later, communities emerged in Western Australia also. In 1970 the St Ephrem the Syrian Association was founded as a focal point for the Syrian Orthodox community in the Sydney area, and in 1972 a second association, also under the patronage of St Ephrem, was founded in Melbourne. In 1978 Fr Zakaria Zeytoun arrived in Sydney to serve the Syrian Orthodox community there. Since 1978 new parishes have been established in Sydney, Melbourne, Woolongong, Perth and Victoria, where patriarch of Antioch Ignatius Zakka has personally dedicated the extensive site of the new church development named for St JACOB BARADAEUS.

In 1978–9 Patriarch Ignatius Yacoub III (1957–80) gave responsibility for the Syrian church in Australia to Archbishop Severius Zakka of Baghdad and Bosra, who conducted important pastoral visitations of his flock in Australia in 1979 and 1980. In the same year he himself succeeded Patriarch Ignatius Yacoub III, taking the name Ignatius Zakka. The Syrian Orthodox of Australia now found themselves under the governance of a learned and energetic patriarch with intimate knowledge of their local church and a commitment to its welfare. Patriarch Ignatius Zakka visited Australia in 1983, in 1987 and again in 1994, when hierarchs from his entourage visited communities in New Zealand.

In 1990 Bishop Timotheus Afram Aboudi was appointed as patriarchal vicar for Australia, in which capacity he served until his translation to Canada in 1996.

The development of the COPTIC Orthodox Church in Australia has in many ways paralleled that of the Syrians. In a period of twenty-five years Coptic churches and communities have been established throughout Australia and in New Zealand, monasteries have been established in Sydney and Melbourne, and the Coptic community has rapidly put down roots in Australian society. As elsewhere in the Coptic world, the DEACONS play an important role in maintaining the tradition of liturgical music and in supporting education and welfare projects, to which the women of the community make a crucial contribution. The emphasis Pope Shenouda III always places on the importance of the translation of services and the use in worship of local languages as well as Coptic, Greek and Arabic helps give clear direction to the work of communities. There are also small numbers of anglophone Coptic Orthodox Christians under the pastoral care of Metropolitan Seraphim of the BRITISH ORTHODOX CHURCH.

The CHURCH OF THE EAST has established itself in Australia and New Zealand. Bishop Meelis Zaia presides over an ASSYRIAN diocese based in New South Wales, where St Hormizd's cathedral is located, and with churches in New South Wales and Victoria in Australia, and in Wellington and Auckland in New Zealand.

Eastern Catholics are represented by three main communities. The territory of the MARONITE diocese of St Maroun extends throughout Australia. The eparchy of Sydney for Melkite Greek Catholics and the eparchy of Melbourne for Ukrainian rite Catholics also have nationwide responsibility for those rites. In 1998 the Roman Catholic hierarchy of Australia formally accepted the presence of married Eastern rite Catholic clergy. Eastern Christianity in Australia and New Zealand shows a diversity, vitality and confidence that speak well for the future. In any immigrant community tensions can arise between national and ethnic identity, between a sharp focus on the religious dimensions of church life and a broader sense of the church's role in the cultural and educational life of a community, between a DIASPORA identity and a local identity. These problems have manifested themselves in various ways among the Eastern Christian communities of Australia and New Zealand, but there are no signs of their being insuperable.

DM

autocephalous   An autocephalous church is one which is independent of the authority of any other. The ancient patriarchates represent the autocephalous churches which emerged in the major dioceses of the Roman empire; later autocephalous churches have tended to be national rather than regional. An autonomous church is one which is independent in the conduct of its internal affairs, but requires the approval of its mother church for the appointment of its chief hierarch, and sometimes in other matters. The status of some churches is controverted, recognized by some as autocephalous but by other churches as only autonomous.

   An older use designates an archbishop with no suffragans and himself holding authority directly under his PATRIARCH as an autocephalous archbishop.

DM

automelon   Greek; a TROPARION to whose melody are sung other troparia known as prosomia. The heirmos of each ode of a CANON is the automelon to whose melody the troparia of the ode are sung as prosomia. A prosomion has the same metrical structure as its automelon. Paradoxically, automela are often listed as prosomia in musical texts such as the HEIRMOLOGION.

DM

Auxentios the Persian   (*c*.420–70) A resolute CHALCEDONIAN, Auxentios, originally a senior administrator under Emperor Theodosios the Younger (d. 450), became a monk and left CONSTANTINOPLE for a mountain in Bithynia, where he founded one of the Byzantine empire's most influential monastic communities, which, like Mount St Auxentios, bore his name (*see* HOLY MOUNTAINS). Auxentios is commemorated on 14 February; in some modern Orthodox communities his feast is promoted in opposition to the imported cult of St Valentine.

DB

avoidance rituals   Term used by sociologists of religion for practices of conservative OLD BELIEVERS intended to preserve them from contamination by the realm of the Antichrist they believe to have been instituted by the liturgical reforms of Patriarch NIKON (d. 1681). Physical contact with his followers is avoided as polluting, as is use of things introduced after the schism (1666–7) including potatoes and tobacco. Some Old Believers, as also conservative traditionalist Orthodox (TRUE ORTHODOX), saw the atheistic communist regime as a sign of Antichrist's rule, and maintained a policy of avoidance in relation to all state institutions, some retiring from all contact with the world outside the house – a self-sacrificing intermediary transacting external business, accepting the burden of pollution to relieve others of it. Old Believers value hospitality. To that end, 'worldly' cups and plates are reserved in some households for use by visitors from without the community.

DM

Avvakum (1620–82) Chaplain to the tsar, then leader of the OLD BELIEVERS who opposed the liturgical reforms of Russian Patriarch NIKON. *The Life of Archpriest Avvakum by Himself* (1673), the first autobiography written in Russian, describes the hardships and sufferings he and his family endured. He was exiled to Siberia from 1653 to 1663, followed by fifteen years' imprisonment in north Russia. His wife was equally indomitable in her faith. Avvakum wrote some fifty works, including his autobiography, during his fifteen years in prison at Pustozersk and died a martyr, burned at the stake in 1682.

Robson, R. R. (1995), *Old Believers in Modern Russia*. Illinois: Illinois University Press.
Zernov, N. (1978), *The Russians and their Church*. London: SPCK.
Fedotov, G. P., ed. (1950), *A Treasury of Russian Spirituality*. London: Sheed & Ward.

KP

azymite Greek: a user or defender of the unleavened. A term of abuse used to condemn Latin Christians, who use unleavened bread in the eucharist. While doctrinal issues predominate in modern accounts of the schism between East and West, in the medieval period differences of custom over the use of leavened or unleavened bread, Saturday fasting, clerical beards and the acceptability of fourth marriages played an important role. This is evidenced by Cardinal Humbert's often quoted condemnation of Patriarch Michael Kaeroularios and his supporters as 'pro-zymite heretics'.

DM

· B ·

Babai In addition to the early legendary martyr Babai or Babay (*Acts of Sharbil, Babai and Barsamya*: early fifth century?), several persons important in the history of the CHURCH OF THE EAST are known by this name:

(1) The CATHOLICOS Babai (or Baboway), originally a Zoroastrian, martyred by the Sasanian King Pērōz in 484 after a letter he wrote to the Roman Emperor Zeno was intercepted. A surviving letter addressed to a Zoroastrian convert to Christianity was later ascribed to Babai. According to later tradition the Metropolitan of Nisibis, Barṣawmā, intrigued against him because of his 'MONOPHYSITE' views.

(2) The Catholicos Babai II (497–502), the first to assume the title 'patriarch of the East'. He summoned a synod of his church in 497 which, among other decisions, explicitly allowed all clergy to marry.

(3) Babai the Great, head *c*.620–8 of the monastic community founded by Abraham of Kashkar on Mount Izla and effective leader of the Church of the East during an interregnum, but refusing the office of catholicos when an election was allowed. He wrote many theological works, according to 'Abdīšō' of Nisibis' *Catalogue of Books*, including a systematic account of the Church of the East's view of Christology.

(4) Babai bar Nṣībnāyē, an active eighth-century reformer of the chant of the Church of the East.

JH

Bachkovo Monastery in southern Bulgaria founded in 1083 by the Georgian Gregory Bakouriani, a general under Byzantine Emperor Alexis Komnenos (1081–18), who died fighting Pechenegs near Plovdiv in 1086. Known as Theotokos Petritsoni, the monastery remained independent, populated largely by Georgian monks, until the reign of Tsar Ivan Alexander (1331–71), who made it a centre of Bulgarian culture. Bulgarian Patriarch Euthymios of Trnovo was exiled there in 1393. The ossuary church has eleventh-century murals painted by Yoan Iveropoulos, a Georgian by name. The church of the DORMITION (1604), one of the few large churches built in

Bulgaria under the OTTOMANS, has a depiction of the Dormition of St EPHREM, and of the Seventh ECUMENICAL COUNCIL in the refectory, both from 1643.

KP

Balsamon   Theodore Balsamon, born in CONSTANTINOPLE *c*.1135, held high office in the PATRIARCHATE of Constantinople, serving for a time as patriarch of Antioch, though the presence of the crusaders and a Latin patriarch kept him at a distance. Balsamon was an outstanding Orthodox canonist: his commentary on the *Nomocanon in Fourteen Titles* is of major importance. Balsamon promoted the symphony of ecclesiastical and imperial law and jurisdiction, and the rights and authority of the Ecumenical Patriarch. He died some time after 1195.

DM

Bardaiṣān (Bardesanes) of Edessa   (154–222) A shadowy figure known principally through *The Book of the Laws of Countries*, the oldest surviving literary work composed in SYRIAC, in which a disciple, Philip, reports a dialogue between Bardaiṣān and another disciple, 'Awīdā. His education appears to have been Hellenistic–Stoic. He held a high position in the court of ABGAR VIII the Great, but may have gone into exile in Armenia when Caracalla took over Edessa in 216. He had clearly become a Christian, but his teachings reflect a somewhat (though not purely) gnostic version of Christianity in which Christ is apparently the Word of Thought attempting to redeem chaos. Later accused of docetism (the interpretation of Christ's sufferings as apparent rather than real), he and his followers came to be regarded as heretics, an almost inevitable consequence of the growth of orthodoxy in the subsequent centuries. It is reported that Bardaiṣān used poetry and song (150 songs modelled on the Psalms) to promulgate his views. There are some quotations in the works of EPHREM THE SYRIAN, who derided Bardaiṣān's heresies. *The Book of the Laws of Countries* has as its theme the question of the moral freedom (outside the influence of the planets) which men, specifically the Christians, can exercise, whatever their location under the heavens.

Drijvers, H. J. W. (1966), *Bardaisan of Edessa*. Assen: Van Gorcum.
Drijvers, H. J. W. (1965), *The Book of the Laws of Countries: Dialogue on Fate of Bardaisan of Edessa*. Assen: Van Gorcum.

JH

Barhebraeus   Syriac: Grīgōr bar 'Ebrāyā; Arabic: Grīgōrī abū'l-Faraj ibn al-'Ibrī. Syrian Orthodox MAPHRIAN, born in Malatya 1225/6, son of Aaron, a physician of Jewish descent, hence the name Bar 'Ebrāyā, 'Son of the Hebrew'. His original personal name was Yōḥannān (John); it is not known how or why he adopted the name Grīgōr (Gregory). He moved to ANTIOCH and became a monk, subsequently studying in Tripoli. In 1246 he was consecrated bishop of Gubos near Malatya. In a succession dispute following the death of the PATRIARCH in 1252, Barhebraeus supported Dionysius of Malatya, who appointed him bishop of Aleppo. This was the period of the Mongol invasions; Patriarch Dionysius was unable to satisfy all his political masters and was murdered, his rival, John, becoming sole patriarch. Barhebraeus at some stage became reconciled to John, who died in 1263. Joshua became patriarch with the support of Barhebraeus, who became maphrian of the eastern SYRIAN ORTHODOX church in 1264 (the post having been vacant for several years). His residence was Mar Mattai monastery near Mosul. He made a dramatic pastoral visit to Baghdad in 1265, greeted even by the CATHOLICOS of the CHURCH OF THE EAST, and was again in Baghdad in 1277. Meanwhile he had visited Mar Barṣawmā to settle a dispute about the headship of the monastery. In 1282 Barhebraeus was in Tabriz in Azerbaijan and, after returning to Mosul, died at Marāga in Azerbaijan on 30 July 1286. (*See* ALBANIA-AL´UANK.) His funeral was attended by members of the Church of the East, Armenians and Greeks. His body was later removed to Mar Mattai where his tomb is still venerated.

Barhebraeus' literary output was enormous, ranging across Aristotelian logic, Christian theology, Islamic studies, philosophy, medicine, law, biblical scholia and works on SYRIAC grammar. He wrote poetry and collected amusing anecdotes. His *Chronicle* depends heavily on Michael the Syrian, but has its own value. It is in two parts, a secular history and a church history. The secular history starts from Creation and reaches the year 1193. Barhebraeus also wrote a distinct Arabic chronicle, which uses additional Islamic sources. The second part of the Syriac chronicle focuses on ecclesiastical affairs, particularly the MONOPHYSITE tradition, but also including material on the Church of the East and uses 'NESTORIAN' sources, particularly the twelfth-century Mari bin Sulaiman's history of the 'Nestorian' catholicoi.

Baumstark, A. (1922), *Geschichte der syrischen Literatur*. Bonn: A. Marcus and E. Weber.
Barhebraeus (1932), *The Chronography of Gregory Abu 'l-Faraj*, ed. and trans. E. A. W. Budge. London: Oxford University Press.

JH

Barlaam and Ioasaph   Edifying tale traditionally attributed to JOHN OF DAMAS-CUS. The main characters, the converted Prince Ioasaph or Josaphat and the learned monk Barlaam, entered the calendar of saints; Ioasaph is celebrated in the Byzantine MENAION on 26 August and in the Roman rite on 27 November. The story has affinities with the life of the Buddha and with the famous Indian Buddhist work known as *Questions of King Milinda* (Menander). It seems the story may have begun life among the Manichean communities of Central Asia.

Kazhdan, A. (1988), 'Where, When and by Whom was the Greek Barlaam and Ioasaph not Written?', in J. Heirrichs et al., eds, *Zu Alexander dem Grosse. Festschrift G. Wirth zum 60*. Amsterdam: Hakkert.

KP

Barsanouphios and John   lived the ascetic life together near Gaza in sixth-century Palestine. They were held to be gifted with healing and clairvoyance; John is often called 'the Prophet'. They were responsible for an enormous number of letters of spiritual guidance, over 850 of which survive. An edition of their letters was published by NIKODEMOS THE HAGIORITE. Their letters, which preserve much of the spiritual teaching of EVAGRIUS PONTICUS, have always been held in high regard especially among EASTERN ORTHODOX monastics. They are commemorated on 6 February.

See also HESYCHASM; MONASTICISM.

Neyt, F. and de Angelis, P. (1997–), *Barsanuphe et Jean de Gaza, Correspondence*. Sources Chrétiennes. Paris: Editions du Cerf.
Chitty, D. J. (1966), *The Desert a City*. Oxford: Blackwell.

DB

Barṣawmā The church in Persia was riven by disputes at the end of the fifth century, with Barṣawmā, bishop of Nisibis (d. *c*.491–6), who had studied at the Persian School in EDESSA prior to the death of Ibas in 457 and its closure in 489, the focus of much of the difficulty. He intrigued against the catholicos BABAI (457–84) who was eventually executed by the Sasanian king, Pērōz. In 484 Barṣawmā summoned a synod of dubious status at Beth Lapaṭ (Jundishapur) which criticized the CATHOLICOS. It also endorsed the work of Theodore of Mopsuestia and condemned Syrian MONO-PHYSITISM.

Acacius, Babai's successor, was, like Barṣawmā, a product of the Persian School at Edessa and the synod he called in 486 in Seleucia adopted an anti-monophysite stance (though there is some scholarly dispute about this). It also forbade bishops to prevent clergy marrying and indeed advocated marriage, even for bishops.

In 497 Babai II (497–502) called another synod in Seleucia in the aftermath of a further dispute between Barṣawmā and Acacius over the primacy of the see of Seleucia and other matters. The Sasanian king, Zamasp, also took an interest, particularly in the question of marriage of the clergy. The synod confirmed the permission granted to all clergy in 486 to marry. It also established the primacy of Seleucia and attempted to settle the various disputes which had been fomented by Barṣawmā.

Gero, S. (1981), *Barsauma of Nisibis and Persian Christianity in the Fifth Century*, CSCO 426, Subsidia 63. Louvain: Peeters.

JH

Basil of Ancyra Moderate Arian, defender at a number of synods of the *homoiousios* doctrine that asserted Christ is 'similar in essence' to or 'of like substance' with the Father (as opposed to *homoousios*, 'co-essential' with). Appointed bishop in 336, he was deposed in 343, reinstated in 350 and again deposed in 360, dying in exile about 364.

DM

Basil of Seleucia Supporter of the MONOPHYSITE party at the Brigandage of Ephesus, 449, but an opponent at Chalcedon in 451. Basil, archbishop of Seleucia for over a quarter of the fifth century, is known as a writer of exegetical homilies and of a Life of St Thecla. Not all the writings attributed to him are genuine.

DM

Basil Preobrazhenskii (d. 1945) Born 1875 in Kineshma, the son of a priest, Basil studied theology, then taught at Voronezh Theological Academy from 1901. He worked as a missionary preacher throughout Kostroma region and became a church cantor in 1918. During the Bolshevik anti-church campaigns Basil continued to preach, secretly teaching children the catechism after this was banned. He was ordained priest in 1920 and consecrated bishop of Kineshma in 1921. He lived in a hut on the outskirts of the town. From 1923 Basil and his helpers were continuously imprisoned and exiled. Briefly released in 1940, Basil was rearrested for refusing to subscribe to Metropolitan Sergii Starogordskii's declaration of loyalty to the Soviet regime, and died in internal exile. Basil is commemorated on 29 July.

Laur of Syracuse (1988), *Saint Basil*. Redding: Nikodemos Orthodox Publication Society.

DB

Basil the Bogomil   The *Alexiad* of Anna Komnena describes the meeting between Basil, ascetic leader of the Constantinople BOGOMILS, and her father, Emperor Alexios I Komnenos (1081–18), who tried by argument and intimidation to bring Basil to orthodoxy. Basil's defiant belief that God would deliver him angered the emperor, who ordered him to be burnt.

DM

baskania   The evil eye, traditionally believed to cause ill fortune, lethargy, listlessness and confusion. The word *baskania* literally means 'envy', as in Ecclesiasticus 14: 8: 'The envious [*ho baskainon*] is malign of eye.' The EUCHOLOGION contains prayers to remove the effects of *baskania*. Beads of blue glass are a traditional folk prophylactic against the effects of the evil eye.

DM

Bedjan, Paul   (1838–20) Born in Khosrowa, Bedjan became a Lazarist missionary in Iran (1861–80), then lived in Cologne, where he prepared for publication editions of dozens of major works in SYRIAC, including the seven volumes of *Acta martyrum et sanctorum* (1890–7) and the five volumes of *Homiliae selectae Mar Jacobi sarugensis* (1905–10).

JH

Belarusian Orthodox church   Christianity probably first spread to Belarus in the late tenth century, and a bishopric was established at Polotsk, in the lands of the Krivichi, soon after. Turov, in the lands of the Dregovichi, was a bishopric by the twelfth century. Over the next century the number of Belarusian saints, including Bishop Cyril of Turov, EUPHROSYNE OF POLOTSK and Abraham of Smolensk, indicates the strength of the emerging Orthodox culture.

This remained a vibrant tradition even after the expansion of pagan Lithuania at the expense of the Belarus principalities. Indeed, many high-ranking Lithuanians embraced Orthodoxy; some, like Nezhila/Antony, Krumiec/John and Krugliec/Eustathios, became martyrs. An autonomous metropolitanate existed at Novogrudok. However, Roman Catholicism dominated Lithuanians after the accession of Jagiello to the Polish throne in 1386.

Metropolitan Gregory Tsamblak, a Bulgarian, attended a Roman Catholic Council in 1418 but upheld EASTERN ORTHODOX tradition. At his death he was not replaced. The situation worsened for the Orthodox throughout Belarus. In 1458 another Bulgarian Gregory, a GREEK CATHOLIC, was appointed metropolitan for all Eastern rite Christians in Lithuania. Local opinion persuaded him to transfer to the jurisdiction of CONSTANTINOPLE ten years later.

Discrimination against the Orthodox population increased after the Great Lithuanian Principality was joined to Poland in 1569. After the Union of Brest-Litovsk in 1596 the Orthodox church was virtually outlawed. Orthodox reaction was manifested in the formation during the 1580s of numerous brotherhoods that sought to counter the Greek Catholic movement. It was only in 1620 that Patriarch Theophanes of Jerusalem re-established an Orthodox hierarchy in Poland–Lithuania.

In 1633, perhaps in response to Cossack pressure, a new edict promised greater tolerance for the Orthodox; but in Belarus, Moghilev was the sole Orthodox see and widespread discrimination continued. Following the partitions of Poland in the late eighteenth century and the incorporation of Belarus into the Russian empire, the balance tipped the other way.

By the early twentieth century four Orthodox dioceses existed in Belarus. Under the Riga Treaty of 1921 the country was divided between Poland and Soviet Russia. At this time Melkhisedek headed the metropolitanate of Belarus and remained in the Soviet half. He was arrested and exiled in 1925, his vicar bishops all ending their days in concentration camps (John of Mozyr in 1927, Filaret of Bobruisk in 1939 and Nicolas of Slutsk in 1931). In Polish areas over half the Orthodox churches were closed down.

After ferocious persecution, the Orthodox Church of Belarus experienced a brief revival after the retreat of the Red Army. The Council of Minsk (1942) declared the church AUTOCEPHALOUS and elected Filofei Narko as its head. Reincorporated in the Soviet Union at the end of the Second World War and again subjected to the patriarchate of Moscow, Christians of Belarus had to weather further waves of persecution and the constant pressure exerted by the militantly atheistic state.

The era of glasnost (from 1988) changed all this and in 1990 the Orthodox church of an independent Belarus was recognized as autonomous.

'Orthodoxy in Belarus', *Journal of the Moscow Patriarchate*, 1992, no. 5.

DB

Berdiaev, Nikolai (1874–1948) Russian Orthodox intellectual and writer. As a young man he was arrested for socialist activities and for criticism of existing social and political institutions. He became professor of philosophy at Moscow University in 1920, but was forced out by the Bolsheviks in 1922. He spent most of the next quarter-century in exile in France. At least twenty of his books have been translated into English. At one time his writings were influential among Western intellectuals; he caused many to reconsider the validity of the Christian religion. His Orthodox perspective on history, particularly Russian history, gave Westerners an alternative way of seeing the development of European civilization. This perspective is apparent in his critique of communism, in e.g. *The Russian Revolution* (1935) and *The Origin of Russian Communism* (1937). He came early under the influence of SOLOVYOV, and his interest in SOPHIOLOGY is apparent in his essay on Jakob Boehme, *Unground and Freedom*. As an Orthodox Christian philosopher Berdiaev gives priority to human freedom and to the concept of the person as a spiritual category.

Copleston, F. C. (1986), *Philosophy in Russia: From Herzen to Lenin and Berdyaev*. Indiana: University of Notre Dame Press.
Davy, M.-M. (1967), *Nicolas Berdyaev: Man of the Eighth Day*. London: Geoffrey Bles.

KP

Bessarion   Bessarion was born about 1400 in Trebizond and named John. In 1423 he entered monastic life and was ordained. In 1437 he was appointed archbishop of Nicea and in that capacity worked to promote union with ROME at the Council of Ferrara–FLORENCE (1438–45). Bessarion formally entered the Roman Catholic church. He was made cardinal (1439) and twice received significant support as a candidate for the papacy. In 1463 he became Latin patriarch of Constantinople. Bessarion served as a senior papal diplomat, presided over a scholarly academy devoted especially to the translation of Greek classics, collected manuscripts and was a prolific writer. Greeks fleeing OTTO-MAN power found him a generous patron. He left his collection of texts to the Republic of VENICE, where it remains the heart of the Marciana Library. He died in 1472.

DM

Bible   The bible of the Eastern churches is, with small but significant variants, that of ALEXANDRIA, as found in the great uncial codices like Vaticanus, Sinaiticus and Alexandrinus of the fourth and fifth centuries, probably written in Alexandria and of Christian provenance. Manuscripts of the whole bible, Old Testament and New Testament, are rare, as is the complete Old Testament.

◆ The Old Testament ◆

Order   The Hebrew Bible consists traditionally of three sections: Torah, Prophets and Writings. The first section consists of the five books of Moses, the second of the 'Former Prophets' (Joshua to Kings) and the 'Latter Prophets' (Isaiah to Malachiah, but omitting Daniel), and the third of Psalms, Job, Proverbs, the Five Scrolls (Ruth, Song of Songs, Ecclesiastes, Lamentations and Esther), Daniel, Chronicles, Ezra and Nehemiah. This threefold division is reflected in the preface to Ecclesiasticus, Philo's account of the Therapeutae (*De Vita Contemplativa* 25) and Luke 24: 44. The first two of these would suggest that the arrangement of the Greek translation of the Bible used by the Alexandrian Jews, the Septuagint, was the same as that of the Palestinian Hebrew. Sinaiticus and Alexandrinus have more or less the Hebrew divisions, with the Latter Prophets before the poetical books. The detailed arrangement, however, with the non-poetical Writings divided between the 'historical' and 'prophetic' books, may well be due, as Swete says, 'to the characteristically Alexandrian desire to arrange the books according to their literary character or contents, or their supposed authorship'.

The order followed in the Codex Vaticanus is different. The five books of Moses stand at the head of the 'historical books', Genesis to 4 Maccabees. Next, however,

81

come the poetic and sapiential books, Job to Ecclesiasticus, and finally the Prophets, beginning with the twelve Minor Prophets and ending with Daniel. This suggests division into past, present and future, with the prophetic writings immediately preceding their fulfilment in the New Testament. Early fathers, such as Melito of Sardis, ORIGEN, ATHANASIUS, EPIPHANIOS and Gregory of Nazianzus (*see* CAPPADOCIANS) follow the same arrangement, as do the canons of the Council of Laodicea, an early local synod, and the Apostolic Canons (attributed to the apostles but in fact later). This arrangement appears distinctly Christian and was retained by the Western Reformers, though they rejected the Greek Bible in favour of the Hebrew.

Contents of the Alexandrian canon The Alexandrian Bible contains books not included in the Hebrew canon, some originally written in Hebrew or Aramaic, others in Greek. Among the historical books, additional ones are 1 Esdras, Judith, Tobit and 1–4 Maccabees, together with a number of lengthy additions to Esther; among the poetic and sapiential books, Ecclesiasticus, the Wisdom of Solomon and Psalm 151; among the prophetical books, Baruch and the Epistle of Jeremias and a number of important additions to Daniel, notably the stories of Susanna and Bel and the Dragon and the Song of the Three Youths. Many manuscripts include the nine biblical odes or canticles, which form part of the morning office in many of the Eastern churches, and extra pieces, including the Prayer of Manasses and the Great Doxology, most of which are still used liturgically. A few manuscripts of the poetical and sapiential books include a Pharisaic work of the first century BC, the Psalms of Solomon. The Ethiopic Bible contains the books of the Alexandrian canon (except Maccabees) plus several elsewhere regarded as apocrypha, such as Jubilees and Enoch. Since the latter is quoted in Jude 14, some early writers inclined to give it canonical status, but Origen gives the general verdict that it is not accepted as 'divine' (*theia*), the fathers' usual epithet for scripture.

As early as Josephus a tradition held that the number of biblical books is twenty-two, like the letters of the Hebrew alphabet. This involves counting together certain related books, e.g. 1 and 2 Samuel, Ezra and Nehemiah and all twelve Minor Prophets. Early Christians seem to have adopted this figure: the earliest lists of 'canonical' Old Testament books treat those of the Hebrew canon as canonical, including the extra books as 'outside', but accepted and read. Thus Athanasius, in his thirty-ninth *Festal Letter* (367), has the books in the same order as Codex Vaticanus, almost certainly written in Alexandria during his episcopate, but removes five books (Wisdom, Sirach, Esther, Judith and Tobit) from their place and appends them as 'outside' the canonical ones, but traditionally given to new converts to read. He thus arrives at a total of twenty-two books, which he specifically links to the number of Hebrew letters. He includes, however, Baruch and the Epistle of Jeremias as part of Jeremias, though neither is in the Hebrew canon. It is not clear whether his Daniel is the Hebrew/Aramaic or the Greek, which includes the Song of the Three Youths, and the stories of Susanna and Bel and the Dragon. In the mid-eighth century JOHN OF DAMASCUS, in his *On the Orthodox Faith*, also lists twenty-two books of the Hebrew canon, referring to the Hebrew alphabet, and places Wisdom and Sirach outside, though he quotes the former as 'divine scripture' in the same work in order to make a doctrinal point. Similarly, he quotes Baruch as 'divine scripture' when citing 3: 38, a verse frequent in Byzantine liturgical texts, for purposes of Christological argument. Many of the fathers, from the third century onwards, also treat the extra books of the Greek Old Testament as 'holy scripture', even when they distinguish the twenty-two from those 'outside'. It seems that, though symbolic significance was given to the Hebrew canon, for the Eastern churches 'divine scripture' was, and still is, the full Alexandrian canon. The full canon is implied in the acceptance by the QUINISEXT COUNCIL (692) of the canons of the Council of Carthage (397).

The Western Reformers' doubts about the additional books influenced Patriarch Cyril LUCARIS, but his views were repudiated by the Confession of Patriarch Dositheos at a council in Jerusalem in 1672 when Tobit, Judith, Ecclesiasticus and Wisdom were expressly declared canonical. Lucaris' Questions declared those listed by the Council of Laodicea canonical and rejected those 'that we call Apocrypha' as not having the same authority from the Holy Spirit. The Synod of Jerusalem rejected Cyril's view, stating that the 'Catholic Church calls Sacred Scripture' both the books listed by the Council of Laodicea, 'adding to them those which Cyril foolishly and ignorantly, or rather maliciously called Apocrypha; namely, Wisdom, Judith, Tobias, the story of the Dragon, the Story of Susanna, Maccabees and Sirach. For we judge these also to be with the other genuine books of divine Scripture genuine parts of Scripture.' Protestant ideas infiltrated Russian theology in the eighteenth century, whence they spread to parts of the Greek-speaking churches. Modern Orthodox bibles contain all the so-called Apocrypha, including 1 Esdras, Psalm 151, the Prayer of Manasses and 3 Maccabees. Greek bibles, issued with the approval of the Holy Synod, also include 4 Maccabees, but in an appendix, while those issued by the Russian Orthodox Church include 4 Esdras. The significance of the liturgical use of these books, or citations from and allusions to them in the compositions of the hymnographers, should not be underestimated.

◆ The New Testament ◆

The Eastern churches accept the traditional list of New Testament books. In the fourth century there were doubts in ASIA MINOR concerning the authenticity of the Apocalypse of St John the Divine. Gregory of Nazianzus, in one of his poems, lists the four Gospels, Acts, fourteen Pauline Epistles and seven Catholic Epistles. He continues, 'You have them all. Any outside of these is not authentic.' His contemporary Amphilochios of Iconium, a friend of Basil the Great, writes in another poem, 'Again, some count John's Apocalypse, but the majority say it is spurious.' CYRIL OF JERUSALEM and Cosmas of Maiuma both exclude the Apocalypse, though John of Damascus accepts it. The early Syriac-speaking churches did not accept the four minor Catholic Epistles and the Apocalypse, which did not, therefore, form part of the PESHITTA, but these were included in the sixth-century version commissioned by one of the leading opponents of Chalcedon, PHILOXENUS OF MABBUG. (*See also* BIBLE, SYRIAC.)

◆ Liturgical use ◆

The Byzantine lectionary In the present Byzantine rite there are only two readings at the eucharist, both taken from the New Testament, which, except for the

Apocalypse, is read throughout the year in a modified *lectio continua*, beginning on Easter Day with the Acts of the Apostles and the Gospel According to John. From the Monday after PENTECOST until mid-September Matthew is read, followed by Luke, until the beginning of GREAT LENT, when Mark is used. Since the liturgy is only celebrated on Saturdays and Sundays in Great Lent, the rest of Mark is used on weekdays during the final weeks of Matthew and Luke. In this way the four Gospels are read in their entirety each year.

From the Monday after Pentecost the Epistles are read in their New Testament order, starting with Romans and ending with Jude in the week before Great Lent. The readings for Saturdays and Sundays follow the same pattern, but run independently of those for the rest of the week. Hebrews is also read on the Saturdays and Sundays of Great Lent.

Holy Week, the major feasts and many saints' days have their own readings, sometimes two, or even three, sets of readings, but this is not always observed in practice. Epistles and Gospels are also assigned to baptism, matrimony and the anointing of the sick, as well as other services, including funerals, monastic profession, the blessing of holy water and the offices of supplication to the Mother of God.

In the daily offices the psalter is, in theory, read each week, beginning at Vespers on Saturday. In addition there are many 'fixed' psalms in the offices: around 300 psalms are used each week. In Great Lent the psalter is read twice each week. Canon 2 of the second Council of Nicea (*see* ECUMENICAL COUNCILS) prescribes that a candidate for the episcopate must have the psalter by heart. The order of daily Matins includes the nine biblical Odes, though the second is only used in Great Lent, but today (apart from the Magnificat) they are omitted everywhere except in monasteries.

Old Testament lectionary readings are effectively confined to Great Lent, Holy Week and Vespers on certain feasts. In Great Lent Genesis, Proverbs and Isaias are read in a modified *lectio continua*, at Sext and Vespers. For the first days of Holy Week Exodus, Job and Ezekiel replace them. This pattern, a reading from each of the three divisions of the Old Testament, is also found in the readings for Vespers on certain feasts. Vespers of the great vigils of Christmas, THEOPHANY and Pascha have a series of readings from the Old Testament: eight at Christmas, thirteen at Theophany, fifteen at Easter. The royal hours on the eves of these feasts have a Prophecy, Epistle and Gospel assigned to each hour.

The liturgical texts If the use of Old Testament readings appears fairly restricted in Byzantine liturgical tradition compared with lectionaries of bodies issuing from the Reformation, it must not be forgotten that Byzantine liturgical texts, both prayers and hymnody, are shot through with quotations and allusions to the scriptures. The eucharistic prayer of the Liturgy of St Basil contains over one hundred direct quotations from and clear allusions to scripture and in places is little more than a mosaic of scriptural citations. The 250 *troparia* of the Great Canon of ANDREW OF CRETE (*c.*660–740) are obscure for anyone lacking a fairly detailed knowledge of the scriptures. For example, the verse, 'My soul, having rivalled Ozias, you have acquired his leprosy in double form. For you think foul thoughts while you do what is unlawful. Leave what you have and hurry to repentance' presupposes knowledge of 2 Chronicles 26: 19.

The use of scripture in the liturgical texts is based on the belief that the Old Testament looks forward typologically to the New Testament. If the divine Word made his dwelling in Mary, then the Temple, in which God had made his dwelling, with all its furnishings, is a type of the Mother of God. The wooden Cross, with outstretched arms like a great tree, is typified by the Tree of Life in Paradise, by Jacob crossing his arms as he blessed Joseph's sons, the outstretched arms of Moses at the battle with Amalek, Aaron's rod that flowered and the brazen serpent on its wooden pole. This last example, which is first found in John 3: 14, is evidence that typological use of the Old Testament is itself scriptural and part of a living tradition, which over the centuries the theologians and poets of the Christian East have continued and enriched.

E

Bible, Syriac The principal version of the Bible in SYRIAC became known as the *pšīṭtā*, 'Simple', an abbreviation for 'Simple Version'. This title is first used in the ninth century. The origins of the Old Testament and New Testament in the PESHITTA are quite different.

The Pšīṭtā Old Testament came into existence book by book; in the case of some books there is a link with the Targums, while some may have a northern Mesopotamian Jewish source, originally in a Jewish dialect of Aramaic closely related to Syriac. The individual books were translated from the Hebrew or, in the case of most of the Apocrypha, from the Septuagint, which appears also to have been known to the translators of some Hebrew books.

The Old Testament Peshitta manuscript tradition is largely unvarying, but until the appearance of the Leiden Peshitta (book by book from 1966) there was no scientific edition listing variants. The Leiden is based on a sixth- or seventh-century manuscript preserved in the Ambrosian Library, Milan. Other widely used Peshitta printed editions include one produced in Mosul (1887–92) and the United Bible Society text (1979, based on S. Lee's edition of 1823).

Other translations also existed, including the Syro-Hexapla, a seventh-century Syriac version of the Greek of Origen's *Hexapla* by Paul of Tella, and Christian Palestinian Aramaic translations of the Greek.

The NT situation is quite different: a number of Syriac translations were in use until the Peshitta version became standard. Certain books were excluded from the early Syriac New Testament: Revelation, 2–3 John, 2 Peter and Jude.

In the early centuries of the spread of Christianity in Syria–Mesopotamia, the Gospels circulated in the DIATESSARON of TATIAN *c*.160. The earliest direct evidence of this work is a Greek fragment from DURA EUROPOS dated before 256. This text, based largely on Matthew's Gospel, remained dominant in the Syriac-speaking church until the fifth century. A little earlier there appears to have been a growing awareness (perhaps in the context of doctrinal dispute) of the four separate gospels of the Greek tradition: under THEODORET OF CYRRHUS and RABBŪLĀ of Edessa the Diatessaron was effectively suppressed.

Already in circulation were separate gospels in Syriac, the so-called Old Syriac texts or *Vetus Syra*, which do not survive complete. These probably originated *c*.AD 200. The translations are fairly free and some have argued that the signs of harmonization found in the Old Syriac gospels are the result of Diatessaron influence.

85

The Peshitta New Testament is a revision of the Old Syriac, bringing it into line with the Greek. This appears to have been a lengthy process culminating in the early fifth century, at which point the new version was promoted by Rabbūlā as a replacement for the Diatessaron. Some have claimed Rabbūlā produced the whole Peshitta translation, but this is improbable: the Old Syriac was already being revised earlier.

As with the Peshitta Old Testament, there is little variation of text in the different surviving early manuscripts, but there is no modern critical edition apart from G. H. Gwilliam's gospels text (published 1901) used by the British and Foreign Bible Society (1920). The United Bible Society text (1979) taken from Lee (1832) is widely used, and note may be made of an edition produced by The Way International (1983). There is a recently published *Concordance to the Syriac New Testament* prepared by G. A. Kiraz (1993).

The process of revision did not cease completely. PHILOXENUS OF MABBUG (d. 523) had the Peshitta revised by his CHOREPISCOPUS, Polycarp, in 507–8. This Philoxenian version can only be identified with security in Philoxenus' quotations from it. In 616 a further stage of revision was reached with the the the Harklean version of Thomas of Ḥarkel. This attempted even closer approximations to the Greek and was written at the same monastery as Paul of Tella's Syro-Hexapla.

Dirksen, P. B. (1989), *An Annotated Bibliography of the Peshitta of the Old Testament*. Monographs of the Peshitta Institute. Leiden: Brill.
Brock, S. P. (1992), 'Syriac Versions', *Anchor Bible Dictionary*, vol. 6, pp. 794–9. New York: Doubleday.
Vööbus, A. (1951, 1987), *Studies in the History of the Gospel Text in Syriac*, CSCO 128 and 496, Subsidia 3 and 79. Louvain: Peeters.

JH

Blachernitissa Our Lady of the church at Blachernai in CONSTANTINOPLE, an iconographic type of the same family as the Virgin of the Sign and the PLATYTERA. The Blachernitissa is shown as the Virgin *orans*, with Christ Emmanuel depicted in a roundel encompassed by her bodily form, or with her hands held in front of her, the palms facing outwards. This icon type presenting the THEOTOKOS as intercessor is now also known as the Episkepsis.

See also ANDREW THE SCYTHIAN.

KP

Bogomils Bogomils appeared in the Skopje region about the time of Bulgarian King Peter (927–63). Bogomilism probably spread from the Balkans to Ionia in the eleventh century and was entrenched in Bosnia by the late twelfth century. Bosnian Bogomils survived crusades against them, including one by Duke Koloman of Croatia in 1235, but were eclipsed by the mid-fifteenth century. There is some evidence for links between the Bogomils and the Cathars.

As with other forms of dualist heresy, the theological basis of Bogomilism was the belief that two creative forces were operative in the universe, one good and one evil, all material aspects of the world issuing from the evil creative force (*see* MANICHEAN-ISM). This involved repudiation of all aspects of Christianity thought to have a human or material origin: the incarnation, all sacraments and symbols, the veneration of the CROSS and ICONS, and most of the BIBLE, apart from the psalms and the 'spiritual' teaching of the gospels. To quote the words of an opponent of Bogomilism, a Bulgarian priest named Cosmas, 'they blasphemed creation... denying that God was the creator of all things visible and invisible.' Consistently, they opposed all forms of political and ecclesiastical authority.

See also BULGARIA.

Hamilton, J. and B. (1998), *Christian Dualist Heresies in the Byzantine World c.650–c.1405*. Manchester: Manchester University Press.
Obolensky, D. (1948), *The Bogomils*. Cambridge: Cambridge University Press.

KP/DB

Bosnia-Herzegovina   Settled by Slav tribes in the seventh century. Ban Kulin (d. 1204) established the first Bosnian state. Originally a BOGOMIL, he embraced Roman Catholicism in 1203. From 1254 Bosnia was a Hungarian protectorate, but achieved independence from 1322. In 1325 Ban Stephen Kotromanić united Hum (Zachlumia, later Herzegovina) with Bosnia. In 1340 he too became a Roman Catholic. Under Stephen Tvrtko (d. 1391) the Bosnian state expanded at the expense of its neighbours, occupying Dalmatia and Trabunja. The OTTOMAN Turks first invaded Bosnia-Herzegovina in 1398 and occupied the country in 1463. The last king, Stephen Tomašević, surrendered and was beheaded. Under the Ottomans many Bosnians embraced Islam; at the same time EASTERN ORTHODOX increased in numbers and significance. VLACHS and others were resettled in Bosnia-Herzegovina. The Austrians invaded Bosnia in 1688, 1690, 1693 and 1697; the Sava region was attached to Austria between 1718 and 1737 and in 1787 the Austrian armies briefly occupied most of Bosnia. The Muslims of Bosnia-Herzegovina revolted against the Ottomans in 1821, 1828, 1831, 1837 and 1839. Only in 1850 were the Ottomans able to re-establish their authority in the region. A series of Christian revolts and general unrest preceded the establishment of an Austro-Hungarian protectorate in 1878, following the Treaty of Berlin in that year, and annexation in 1908. The assassination of Archduke Ferdinand by Serbian nationalists in Sarajevo led to the outbreak of the First World War. Intercommunal strife in Bosnia-Herzegovina during both world wars set a bloody precedent for the civil war and accompanying outside interventions in the aftermath of the collapse of Yugoslavia in the 1990s.

See also SERBIAN CHRISTIANITY.

Friedman, F. (1996), *The Bosnian Muslims*. Boulder, Colo.: Westview.
Bennett, C. (1995), *Yugoslavia's Bloody Collapse*. London: Hurst.
Cviic, C. (1995). *Remaking the Balkans*. London: Royal Institute of International Affairs.
Malcolm, N. (1994), *Bosnia: A Short History*. London: Macmillan.

DB

Bostra   Semitic: Buṣrā. Earlier an important Nabataean centre linked to Arabian trade via Wādi al-Sirḥān, Bostra became capital of Provincia Arabia (AD 105–6 onwards) and was made a colony by Emperor Severus. It became the seat of an archbishop; a magnificent cathedral was built by archbishop Julian, dedicated in 512/

13. Although Bostra was largely MONOPHYSITE (with the Ghassānids dominating the region), under SEVERUS OF ANTIOCH Julian refused to condemn Chalcedon and was forced out. He returned on the death of Emperor Anastasius in 518. According to tradition Muḥammad met the 'NESTORIAN' monk Bahira while visiting the city.

Sartre, M. (1985), *Bostra des origines à l'Islam*. Paris: Geuthner.

JH

bread stamp   Earliest surviving stamps date from the fourth century. They are round or square with a variety of indentations. Byzantine rite stamps for prosphora include IC.XC.NI-KA, 'Jesus Christ conquers'; Oriental seals are less elaborate. Patriarch NIKON altered the traditional Russian seal, something OLD BELIEVERS rejected as heretical. Other stamps, marked with sacred images, symbols and inscriptions, are used in celebrating feasts.

   See also ARTOKLASIA; PROTHESIS.

Galavaris, G. (1970), *Bread and the Liturgy: The Symbolism of Early Christian and Byzantine Bread Stamps*. Madison: University of Wisconsin Press.
Drower, E. S. (1956), *Water into Wine: A Study of Ritual Idiom in the Middle East*. London: John Murray.

KP

British Isles   Tradition attributes the evangelization of Britain variously to Joseph of Arimathea and to the apostle Aristoboulos of the SEVENTY, brother of Barnabas, apostle of CYPRUS. A separate tradition asserts the presence of Coptic missionaries in Ireland in an early period. The monastic tradition of the Celtic churches had a decidedly austere Oriental character. The proclamation of CONSTANTINE THE GREAT as Roman emperor took place in York in 306, linking Roman rule in Britain with the foundation of the Christian empire.

   A concrete personal link with the East is provided by Theodore of Tarsus, archbishop of Canterbury 669–90. Theodore was appointed by Pope Vitalian when the elected candidate, Wighard, died in ROME before his consecration. Together with the African abbot Adrian, whom the pope sent to assist him and whom Theodore appointed abbot of St Augustine's Abbey in Canterbury, he established a major school where Greek as well as Latin was taught together with a wide range of ecclesiastically important disciplines.

   The ninth-century Irish scholar and philosopher John Scotus Erigena played a unique role in bringing Eastern SPIRITUAL THEOLOGY to the West by his Latin translations of Gregory of Nyssa, DIONYSIOS THE AREOPAGITE and MAXIMUS THE CONFESSOR. *Denys Hid Divinity*, a fine English translation of the *Mystical Theology* of Dionysios, is often attributed to the anonymous fourteenth-century author of the *Cloud of Unknowing*, itself one of the most Eastern in spirit and doctrine of Western mystical texts. The eccentric but scholarly hermit and devotional writer Richard Rolle (*c*.1300–49) and the early fifteenth-century pilgrim and visionary Margery Kempe provide relatively unusual examples of HOLY FOOLS, a type of sanctity more common in the East.

   From the seventeenth century onwards individual Greeks are recorded in various places in the British Isles and some contact with EASTERN ORTHODOXY occurred. In

1628, for example, PATRIARCH Cyril LUCARIS gave the Codex Alexandrinus to King Charles I. The churchyard of Landulph in Cornwall houses the grave of Theodore Palaeologus (d. 1636), who may well have been a descendant of the Byzantine imperial house. Oxford attracted several GREEK ORTHODOX during the reigns of Kings James I and Charles I, including Christopher Angelos who wrote the first account of the Greek church for English readers, Metrophanes KRITOPOULOS, who later became patriarch of ALEXANDRIA, and the priest Nathaniel Canopius, who is reputed to have introduced coffee-drinking to Britain. Following requests by refugees from Greece led by the priest Daniel Boulgaris, Archbishop Joseph of Samos was permitted to establish the first Orthodox church in London in 1677 on a site in what is now Greek Street, Soho, donated by the bishop of London. In 1684, however, this church was taken from the Greeks and handed over to French Protestants.

Chetham's Library in Manchester, Britain's oldest free library, founded in 1670 by Humphrey Chetham and housed in what had been the house of the warden and priests of the Collegiate Church, possesses a remarkable collection of seventeenth- and eighteenth-century editions of the Greek liturgical books published in VENICE and acquired soon after publication, which are evidence of an interest in Orthodox worship in that period. In the same period the Cambridge Platonists were reawakening interest in the Greek patristic tradition and in the spiritual content of PLATONISM and the doctrine of DEIFICATION.

On the accession of William III and Mary (1688) nine Anglican bishops, including the archbishop of Canterbury, Bancroft (1677–93) and the saintly Thomas Ken (1684–1711), broke away from the Church of England since they refused to break their oaths of allegiance to the deposed James II. After the deposition of their clergy by Parliament in 1690, though with no canonical process, the Non-jurors formed in effect a separate Anglican church that survived into the nineteenth century. Their high doctrine of church and sacrament led them to engage in correspondence with the Eastern Orthodox churches in the hope of establishing communion with them. The tone of this correspondence was fraternal and eirenic, but nothing came of their overtures, as their proposals for mutual recognition and intercommunion included establishing the primacy of JERUSALEM and abolishing the worship of images, and they were unable to accept the full Orthodox teaching on the eucharist and the cult of the THEOTOKOS. In 1763 John Wesley, failing to find any Anglican bishop willing to ordain Methodist preachers, won the agreement of the exiled Greek bishop of Arcadia, then in Amsterdam, to do so. Apparently the bishop ordained several Methodist clergy, some without Wesley's knowledge. Later in the eighteenth century Frederick North, son of the former prime minister Lord North, was received into the Orthodox church in Corfu: he was later elected a member of Parliament, served as governor-general of Ceylon and became the fifth earl of Guilford. The chaplain of the Russian Embassy chapel gave him communion on his deathbed in 1827.

The Greek revolution of 1821 brought increasing numbers of Greek merchants to Britain. At first, they and the other Greeks already settled in London were granted the hospitality of the Russian Embassy chapel. The Greek Orthodox community in Manchester, consisting mainly of wealthy merchants from Chios and Asia Minor, formally adopted a constitution in 1831. Annunciation Church in Manchester, built in classical style in 1861, is the community's third or fourth church; it preserves four life-size icons of the evangelists painted for its predecessor. The community's wealth meant that in the nineteenth century its parish priests lived in style, with a carriage and horses, a coachman, a paid English choir and a handsome salary of £1,500 per year. The reforming church composer Chaviara (whose music was later condemned by the Ecumenical Throne) visited the community and for a fee of £400 provided it with harmonized music in Western notation for the Divine Liturgy and for Holy Week. He then sold the same music for the same price to the new community in Liverpool. Among the parish priests of Manchester in the twentieth century were the theologian Konstantinos Kallinikos and the future Metropolitan Meliton of Chalcedon.

The Greeks of London established a chapel in 1837–8 and in 1850 built a new church in the City. In 1879 the first services were held in the new Cathedral of Hagia Sophia in Bayswater. The community of St Nicholas in Liverpool built a fine Byzantine-style church in 1870 and the community of St Nicholas in Cardiff opened its church in 1906. The zealous convert Stephen HATHERLY opened a converted Methodist chapel as an Orthodox church in Wolverhampton in 1869, and when Hatherly was ordained in 1871 there was for a short time a growing Orthodox community of English believers; but an instruction from the patriarch brought his mission to an end and the church was closed. In the same period Joseph Julian OVERBECK was also working in Britain. After converting to Orthodoxy in 1864 he fought for decades for the establishment of an Orthodox Western rite.

The four parishes in London, Manchester, Liverpool and Cardiff were virtually autocephalous until in 1922 the ECUMENICAL PATRIARCH appointed the then rector of the Halki Theological School as Metropolitan Germanos of Thyateira, his titular see, now allocated to the chief hierarch of Great Britain, originally extending over Western and Central Europe. Germanos served until his death in 1951. He was succeeded by Metropolitan Athenagoras I Kavadas (1951–62), Metropolitan, later Archbishop Athenagoras II Kokkinakis (d. 1979), Archbishop Methodios Fouyas (1979–88) and Archbishop Gregorios (1988–). In addition to the four original Greek parishes, a Russian parish, mainly of émigrés from the civil war, had use from 1921 of an Anglican church on Buckingham Palace Road. The parish divided under two different jurisdictions in 1926 but the two communities continued to share the church building until it was demolished in 1956. Many Anglicans made contact with Orthodoxy through the Fellowship of SS Alban and Sergius, meeting leading figures of the Russian emigration such as Nicholas Zernov and Sergius BULGAKOV. The creation of the Spalding lectureship in Oxford University, initially held by Nicolas Zernov and then by Kallistos Ware, provided a focus for the academic study of Eastern Orthodoxy.

In 1947 a new mainly Cypriot parish was established in Camden Town. This was the forerunner of a massive expansion in the Greek Cypriot population of Great Britain, from both migrants around the mid-century and refugees from the Turkish invasion after 1974. On the enthronement of Athenagoras II in 1964 his archdiocese had eleven parishes; by 1970 there were over fifty and in 1998 there were sixty-six parishes with resident clergy and another forty places of worship with visiting priests. The clergy of the archdiocese of Thyateira included, by 1988, seven bishops, among them the internationally celebrated spiritual theologian and translator Bishop Kallistos (Timothy Ware), eighty-five priests and nine deacons serving about 250,000 Greek Orthodox.

In 1945 one of the two Russian parishes in London passed under the jurisdiction of the Moscow patriarchate. In the aftermath of the Second World War a substantial number of Orthodox and Eastern Catholics arrived in Britain from Eastern Europe and soon Russian, Serb, Ukrainian and Belarusian Orthodox communities, as well as Ukrainian and Belarusian Catholic communities, existed in several towns. The Serbian community of Birmingham under the leadership of Archpriest Stavrophore Milenko Zebic has built a fully frescoed church in traditional Serbian style, together with a parish centre in the style of a Serbian hunting lodge. By 1988 the Moscow patriarchate's diocese of Sourozh, led for many years by the charismatic spiritual teacher Metropolitan Anthony Bloom, had three bishops in Great Britain and twenty-seven other clergy, serving twenty-eight places of worship.

The decision of the Church of England to ordain women to the priesthood resulted in a significant exodus of clergy and people, one fruit of which was the increase of the Antiochian presence in Britain from a single cathedral in London to thirteen places of worship served by eleven clergy. In all there were in 1998 209 Eastern Orthodox places of worship in Britain served by almost 200 clergy.

The stavropegiac monastery of St John the Baptist at Tolleshunt Knights in Essex, founded by the late Abbot Sofrony, disciple of St Silouan of Athos and attached since 1967 to the Ecumenical Patriarchate, is an internationally famous centre of Orthodox monasticism and spirituality.

The Armenian Apostolic church has long-standing communities in London and Manchester, and recent years have seen a significant growth in the presence of other Oriental and Oriental Orthodox communities, most notably the Coptic Orthodox who now have three diocesan bishops as well as the metropolitan of the BRITISH ORTHO-DOX CHURCH.

The Ukrainian Catholic church has a well-established exarchate in Britain, but like the Ukrainian Orthodox has suffered from the problem of re-emigration, often to Canada. Some communities have lost 80–90 per cent of their numbers in this way.

Common to the longer-established Eastern Christian parishes, and typical of DIA-SPORA communities, are the problems of population dispersal; a community settles in an area and sets up a church, but then families move further away, often to places with no church of their own communion and ethnic group. Intermarriage has led some into other churches, and the close relation between church and ethnic community can mean some second-generation and later members drift away. Many communities rely on volunteer clergy, who often need to work in other jobs to support themselves and their families. First-generation immigrants and émigrés often assumed their residence in Britain would be temporary: for some this has proved true, but very many families have settled permanently, remaining even after return has become a political and economic possibility. The sense of identity, the culture and the language of communities have undergone corresponding change.

In recent years increasing numbers of Western Christians and others have been drawn to Eastern Christianity: of the almost 200 Eastern Orthodox clergy serving in Britain in 1998, no fewer than sixty-one were converts. Numbers of small communities now exist whose membership is mainly drawn from the native population. Awareness is increasing of the history, thought, worship, saints and sites of the Celtic and English churches of the period before the schism, and of the importance of such figures as the eighth-century archbishop of Canterbury, Theodore of Tarsus. The use of English in worship is increasingly common, and a translation of the Divine Liturgy into dignified modern English was published in 1995 by the archdiocese of Thyateira with the blessing of the Ecumenical Patriarchate. This follows in the tradition of Thyateira, whose metropolitan approved a translation as early as 1932.

DM

British Orthodox church   On 2 June 1866 a former French Dominican priest, Jules Ferrette (1828–1904), was consecrated bishop of Iona and its dependencies by the MAPHRIAN of the SYRIAN ORTHODOX church, Boutros ibn Salmo Mesko (1799–1894). Opponents in the established church of England to what they considered invasion by a foreign jurisdiction questioned the authenticity of the new bishop, despite the British consul in Damascus having witnessed the instrument of consecration. The maphrian became Syrian Orthodox PATRIARCH of ANTIOCH in 1872 as Mar Ignatius Boutros III. In 1889 he also authorized the consecration of a metropolitan to minister to converts from Catholicism in Ceylon, Goa and INDIA, and in 1891 of another metropolitan for Old Catholics in AMERICA.

From the consecration of Ferrette a succession of bishops was maintained, though the church remained very small. Contacts with the Syrian Orthodox church were not sustained and it was regarded an uncanonical by other Orthodox churches. From 1944 to 1979 it was directed by Mar Georgius, metropolitan of Glastonbury (Hugh George de Willmott Newman, 1905–79), who revitalized its mission by emphasizing the importance of British church history prior to 597 and looking to the Celtic church and its saints as indigenous Orthodox.

After 128 years of independent existence the British Orthodox Church was reunited with the Oriental Orthodox churches by its reception into the COPTIC Orthodox patriarchate of ALEXANDRIA. On 6 April 1994 a joint protocol was signed determining the relationship. In this the British Orthodox church was recognized as 'a local church, holding to the historic faith and order of the Apostolic Church, committed to the restoration of Orthodoxy among the indigenous population and desiring to provide a powerful witness to the Orthodox Faith and Tradition in an increasingly secular society'.

On 19 June, Pentecost Sunday, in St Mark's Cathedral in Cairo, Abba Seraphim (William Henry Hugo Newman-Norton), since 1979 successor to his cousin, Mar Georgius, was consecrated metropolitan of Glastonbury by Pope Shenouda III, assisted by some sixty-three metropolitans and bishops. Abba Seraphim is a full member of the Coptic Holy Synod. The protocol permits the British Orthodox church to follow the Gregorian CALENDAR for solar festivals and appoints the metropolitan of Glastonbury as chairman of a permanent liturgical commission to 'consider appropriate translations of the Coptic Orthodox service books and the use of alternative forms of services drawn from ancient Western Orthodox sources which may be adapted to the local situation' and make recommendations directly to the pope. Pope Shenouda III authorized use of the Liturgy of Saint James for the British Orthodox church, although for all other services the Coptic rite is used.

The jurisdiction of the British Orthodox church extends over the United Kingdom, the Republic of Ireland, the Isle of Man and the Channel Islands. In the British Isles the British Orthodox and Coptic communities exist as parallel jurisdictions and co-operate closely on a number of pastoral and educational issues.

S

Bucovina   Region north of Moldavia and Bessarabia, historically part of Greater Moldavia, with an EASTERN ORTHODOX majority. Bucovina was united with ROMA-NIA after the First World War but is now divided between Romania, Moldova and UKRAINE. Important monasteries flourished here in the OTTOMAN period. PAISSII VELICHKOVSKII (d. 1794) and his disciples moved to Dragomirna in 1763 but moved south to Secul and Neamt, when Bucovina was ceded to Austria by the Turks in 1774–5.

Bolshakoff, S. (1976), *Russian Mystics*. Kalamazoo: Cistercian Publications.
Metrophan (1976), *Paissy Velichkovsky*. Platina, Cal.: St Herman of Alaska Press.

DB

Bulgakov, Sergius   (1871–1944) Disillusioned with Marxism after the 1905 revolution in Russia, Bulgakov rediscovered his Orthodox roots: he came from a priestly family. In 1909 he co-operated with BERDIAEV and others in the journal *Vekhi* (Signposts). Removed in 1918 from his professorship in political economy at Moscow University, and in this period ordained priest, he was exiled in 1923, eventually settling in France where he became dean of the Orthodox Theological Academy in Paris. In England, as part of his resolute commitment to ECUMENISM in 1927 he was one of the founders of the Fellowship of SS Alban and Sergius. His essay *Karl Marx as a Religious Type* (1929) argued that communist political philosophy is incompatible with the spiritual freedom and responsibility of Christianity. He identified in the millenarianism of Marxism an inversion of the Judeo-Christian apocalyptic tradition. His exposition of SOPHIOLOGY caused controversy in some Orthodox circles and his teaching was condemned by the Holy Synod of the Russian Church in 1935. He was accused of turning DIVINE WISDOM into a fourth divine hypostasis, while he himself used sophiology to justify anthropomorphic images of God the Father.

Jakim, B., trans. (1997), *Fr Sergius Bulgakov: The Holy Grail and The Eucharist*. New York: Lindisfarne Books.
Jakim, B. trans. (1995), *Sergius Bulgakov: Apocatastasis and Transfiguration*. New Haven: Variable Press.
Crum, W. (1983), 'Sergius N. Bulgakov: From Marx to Sophiology', *St Vladimir's Theological Quarterly*, 27.
Pain, J., and Zernov, N. (1976), *Sergius Bulgakov: A Bulgakov Anthology*. London: SPCK.

KP

Bulgaria   In 1981 Bulgaria celebrated the 1,300th anniversary of its origin in 681, when the Byzantine emperor Constantine IV ceded to the Bulgar chieftain Asparuch from Central Asia the territory between the Danube and the Balkan mountains, the territorial nucleus of what became a powerful medieval state. The territory ceded was then inhabited mainly by Slav tribes who had migrated from their homeland in northeast Europe during the sixth and seventh centuries.

Both the Slavs and the Bulgars were pagans at the time of Asparuch's conquest; nearly 200 years elapsed before Bulgaria (as it came to be called) became a Christian state. This process began with the baptism of Khan Boris, who became ruler of Bulgaria in 852. By this time the territory of Bulgaria had increased considerably, particularly after successful wars against the Byzantines by Boris's grandfather, Khan Krum, bringing Bulgaria many Christian subjects, their number increased by returning Slav and Bulgar prisoners of war converted during their captivity. The immediate circumstance leading to the baptism of Boris was a treaty with Byzantium, concluded under the threat of war, which stipulated that Boris should become Christian. He was baptized, probably in Pliska, the capital, in 864 or 865, Emperor Michael III acting as godfather by proxy.

Boris was probably a willing convert; his subsequent behaviour indicates a sincere desire to rule as a good Christian prince. Baptism strengthened his position as ruler of a state which included a number of Christian subjects, and paved the way for Bulgaria's acceptance as one of the civilized nations of Christendom. However, Boris was determined that his baptism by the PATRIARCH of CONSTANTINOPLE, with its implied acceptance of Byzantine ecclesiastical jurisdiction, would not involve political subservience to the Byzantine emperor. He therefore sought to maximize the Bulgarian church's autonomy, symbolized by the appointment of a high-ranking prelate as its head. He pursued this objective with considerable political acumen and diplomatic skill. Since Bulgaria was a missionary area, Boris realized he was unlikely to gain his wish by an approach to Constantinople; at best it would be considered premature, and he could expect little support from Patriarch PHOTIOS. He therefore made overtures to Pope Nicholas I, sending him a list of questions concerning his conduct as a Christian ruler and asking for a bishop to become head of the Bulgarian church. The pope reacted promptly: his replies to Boris's questions, the *Responsa*, throw light on the spiritual and practical problems confronting a newly converted ruler. The *Responsa* were partly based on Pope Gregory the Great's instructions to Augustine on his mission to the Angles and Saxons. The pope sent two bishops, Paul and Formosus, but made it clear they came as missionaries, with no mandate for jurisdiction over the Bulgarian church. Boris soon realized that neither Nicholas I nor his successor Pope Hadrian II would help him to secure an autonomous head for the Bulgarian church. He decided to expel the Roman missionaries and return to the Byzantine fold; his formal acceptance of Byzantine jurisdiction was finalized at a council in Constantinople (October 869–February 870), later regarded by ROME as the Eighth ECUMENICAL COUNCIL. It was agreed the Bulgarian church should have a separate bishop as its head, with the title of archbishop. His exact status and degree of administrative independence are unclear, but it seems Boris had achieved some measure of autonomy for Bulgaria and, as Robert Browning says, 'he had won a partial victory in his struggle to bring his country into the Christian world without becoming a puppet of the emperor in Constantinople'.

The evangelization of Bulgaria, and Boris's hopes of establishing a truly national church there, were greatly helped by the expulsion from Moravia in 886 of the surviving leaders of the mission of CYRIL AND METHODIUS. Four of these – Clement, Naum, Lawrence and Angelarius – arrived at Belgrade, then a Bulgarian frontier town, later that year. They were welcomed on Boris's behalf by the local governor, and invited to work in Bulgaria. After two and a half decades of missionary work in Moravia, they had considerable experience of Old Church Slavonic (OCS), in which some basic Christian texts were already available. Most of Boris's subjects were by now Slav-speakers, and he realized that hearing the liturgy and scriptures in their own language would help to build up the Bulgarian church. Lawrence and Angelarius died soon after their arrival in Bulgaria, but Clement and Naum proved energetic and capable missionary leaders. The number of texts in OCS was increased, with both new translations and more copies of existing translations. Clement, whose work was concentrated in what is now the Republic of MACEDONIA, is said to have trained 3,500 native Slav-speaking priests within seven years. Naum worked first in or near Preslav, the new capital built by Boris, later joining Clement in OHRID, and there are churches dedicated to them on the shores of Lake Ohrid.

By 889 Boris felt that the foundations of the Christian church were sufficiently secure for him to abdicate and enter a monastery he had founded in Preslav. His eldest son Vladimir, his successor, reversed his father's religious and political policies, aligning himself with an anti-Byzantine, possibly anti-Christian, faction of the Bulgarian aristocracy. At first Boris took no action, but in 893 he left his monastery, deposed Vladimir with the help of his younger son Symeon, who replaced him, and then returned to the monastery, where he died in 907. Shortly after his death he was canonized by the Bulgarian church, becoming one of its first native saints.

The council of magnates and boyars at which Symeon was proclaimed ruler of Bulgaria declared Slavonic the official language of church and state; not, however, in its original form based on the so-called Glagolitic alphabet invented by Cyril and Methodius, but the revised Cyrillic form, with an alphabet much closer to Greek, a language already familiar to the small number of literate Bulgarians. This alphabet was later adopted by other Slav states who accepted Eastern Orthodoxy, notably SERBIA and Rus, and also by ROMANIA, which used OCS as its liturgical and literary language until the seventeenth century.

Boris's son Symeon, who was educated in Constantinople, was probably intended to become the patriarch of an independent Bulgarian church and was still nominally a monk at his accession. Although most of his reign (893–927) was spent in wars against Byzantium, it was also a time of cultural flowering which owed much to his patronage and encouragement. Many churches and monasteries were built; the range and quantity of literature translated from Greek into OCS increased, and some original works were written. In Bulgaria at this time the foundations of Slavonic literature were established on which the Slav nations have built to the present.

Symeon's long reign was dominated by his ambition to rule not only Bulgaria, but also the Byzantine empire. He hoped to marry his daughter to the young Constantine VII Porphyrogennetos, thus making himself the emperor's father-in-law, and co-emperor. To this end he waged constant wars against the empire, leaving Bulgaria economically exhausted and politically weakened. During the reign of his son Peter (927–69), who achieved the imperial marriage which his father had so desired, Bulgaria became in effect a political satellite of Byzantium; its church, though now headed by a patriarch, had little real autonomy.

Bogomilism, a dualist heresy called after the priest Bogomil, one of its leaders, now began to spread in Bulgaria. Little precise information is available about the number of BOGOMILS in Bulgaria, but there has been much speculation about the sources of its infiltration and the reasons for its persistence. It seems reasonable to assume that an important contributory factor was the presence of PAULICIAN Armenian troops in the imperial province of Thrace; others have attached more importance to possible deficiencies in the understanding of Christian doctrine resulting from the rapid training of native Christian priests. What is clear is that the heresy proved remarkably persistent despite the efforts of secular and ecclesiastical authorities to eradicate it. In 1211 a special synod was convened to discuss measures against the heresy; but these can have had only limited success, since Bogomilism remained a problem in fourteenth-century Bulgaria. Only after the OTTOMAN conquest of Bulgaria at the end of that century do we find no further reference to the Bogomils.

In 1018, after a series of relentless campaigns led by Byzantine emperor Basil II (976–1025), Bulgaria ceased to exist as an independent state, and became part of the empire, as the themes of Bulgaria and Paristrion; Basil II had decided that Bulgaria was too dangerous a neighbour to be tolerated, and must be destroyed. The Bulgarian patriarchate was abolished, and Bulgaria was placed under the ecclesiastical jurisdiction of the archbishop of Ohrid.

Towards the end of the twelfth century two powerful landowners, Peter and Asen, organized a successful revolt against Isaac II Angelos, and revived the Bulgarian state. Although their descendants enlarged their territory by war, and one, Kaloyan (1197–1207), obtained a royal title from the pope, they failed to establish a stable dynasty, and the so-called Second Bulgarian Kingdom suffered from chronic social and political unrest.

However, under the enlightened rule of Tsar John Alexander (1331–71) Bulgaria experienced a remarkable cultural and spiritual renaissance. At this time, the mid-to-late fourteenth century, HESYCHASM flourished in Bulgaria, its rigorous ascetical discipline including precise patterns of breathing and posture, and the use of the JESUS PRAYER. These practices were introduced into the Byzantine church by Gregory of Sinai, who spent his last years in Bulgaria; and under the influence of his disciple Teodosi (Theodosius), last patriarch of Bulgaria, combined the practice of hesychast ascetic discipline with strenuous literary and administrative activity.

By 1396 Bulgaria had been completely subjugated by the Ottomans, and remained under Turkish rule for nearly 500 years. Once again the Bulgarian patriarchate was abolished, and Bulgaria, like the other Eastern Orthodox in the Ottoman empire, fell under the jurisdiction of the ECUMENICAL PATRIARCH. Christianity was tolerated under Ottoman rule, but Christians were economically penalized and effectively deprived of leadership, and the monasteries, formerly the cultural and spiritual powerhouse of the Bulgarian church, were themselves impoverished. Christianity could do little more than survive. When Bulgaria regained political independence in the late nineteenth century, the Bulgarian Orthodox church declared itself independent under its own exarch. The Ecumenical Patriarchate's refusal to recognize the AUTOCEPHA-LOUS status of the Bulgarian church resulted in a schism that was formally ended only in 1945. In 1953 the Bulgarian church elected its own patriarch, and in 1961 the church's patriarchal dignity was formally recognized by Constantinople. The twentieth century faced the Bulgarian church with many difficulties: while still in the early stages of revival it found itself in the midst of war, political turmoil and a long period under oppressive communist rule.

Although the Orthodox church has always been the national church of Bulgaria, to which most Bulgarians have belonged, other forms of Christianity have also been represented there, notably the Roman Catholic church. Its earliest adherents were mostly the descendants of German and other Western European immigrants; their number was substantially increased by the missionary activity of the Franciscans, especially in the seventeenth century. This resulted in the creation of two metropolitan sees (Sofia and Marcianopolis) and three bishoprics. One of the first Bulgarians to challenge Ottoman political domination in the seventeenth century was the Catholic archbishop of Sofia, Peter Parcevic.

It remains to consider briefly the characteristics of Christianity in Bulgaria, especially within the Orthodox tradition. An overall survey of the long history of the Bulgarian Orthodox church shows an institution in which periods of quiescence and conformity alternated with spells of restless vitality, especially during the later medieval period; at this time Bulgaria seems to have been in a state of chronic religious ferment, when any religious teacher, orthodox or heretic, could attract some following. We find in Bulgaria both a virulent manifestation of dualist heresy and a strong commitment to the mystical ideals of hesychasm. Even in the post-communist era schisms afflicting the Bulgarian church seem to express a similar powerful but sometimes unfocused vitality. There are grounds for hope of a better future, but spiritual recovery of the Bulgarian church may be slow and arduous.

Browning, R. (1975), *Byzantium and Bulgaria*. London: Temple Smith.
Heppell, M. (1975), 'The Hesychast Movement in Bulgaria: The Turnovo School and its Relations with Constantinople', *Eastern Churches Review* 7, pp. 9–20.
Obolensky, D. (1971), *The Byzantine Commonwealth*. London: Weidenfeld & Nicholson.
Vlasto, A. P. (1970), *The Entry of the Slavs into Christendom*. Cambridge: Cambridge University Press.
Dvornik, F. (1962), *The Slavs in European History and Civilisation*. New Brunswick: Rutgers University Press.

MH

Byzantine Christianity and Greek Orthodoxy   Although Jesus and his disciples spoke Aramaic, it was in Greek that the Christian gospel was proclaimed throughout the Mediterranean world, in Greek that the early Christian communities we know of worshipped, and in Greek that the earliest Christian writings – those that came to form the New Testament – are written. Even in the western parts of the Roman Empire, such as ROME, Gaul and North Africa, most early Christian communities seem to have been Greek-speaking (though if the Rotas-Sator square in Pompeii is Christian it is evidence for first-century Latin Christianity). In the second century Christianity in general took the institutional form that remains the pattern of GREEK ORTHODOX

Christianity: communities led by a bishop, elected by the local church (though this is now quite theoretical), consecrated by neighbouring bishops, and thus standing in a tradition of authority going back to the apostles. In early centuries the local community was the community of the city (*polis*) and its economic hinterland (*chora*): each community had one bishop, however big the city, and the church, the Body of Christ, came into being in the local community, and gathered with its bishop to celebrate the eucharist. To these early centuries can be traced other distinguishing features of Byzantine Christianity: the enormous authority conceded to ascetics, and an ambivalent attitude to the intellectual heritage of the Greeks, especially the philosophy of Plato (*see* PLATONISM).

Etymologically, 'Byzantine' Christianity should mean Christianity that looks to the city CONSTANTINE THE GREAT established on the site of ancient Byzantium and which eventually became capital of the imperial empire. But it was many years before CONSTANTINOPLE acquired such prestige in Christian eyes. There were already cities with a long tradition of importance in the world of Greek Christianity by the fourth century: notably ANTIOCH and ALEXANDRIA, not to mention ROME and JERUSALEM, which sought to capitalize on its importance as the city of the Holy Places and a centre of PILGRIMAGE. The importance of Constantinople was bound up with its position as capital of the empire, and therefore bound up with the claims and fortunes of the Byzantine empire itself.

From the beginning, the Christian emperors sought to use the Christian church for their own ends, and Byzantine Christianity tended to concede a great deal to the emperor. A political theology emerged very quickly that saw the Christian emperor as ruling the inhabited world (*oikoumene*) in imitation of God's rule of the cosmos. The emperor had an important hand in the appointing of bishops to important sees, not least that of the imperial city, and any PATRIARCH of Constantinople who could not accept his religious policy customarily resigned. The emperor had a special place in the liturgy: he alone entered by the ROYAL DOORS, and he received communion in the sanctuary with the celebrants. The liturgy itself took on the trappings of court ceremonial. In contrast, the patriarch's privilege of crowning the emperor was never regarded as having any constitutional significance (anointing did not become the practice in Byzantium until the last centuries). The importance of the emperor in Byzantine Christianity remained even when political reality fell far short of the ideal: Patriarch Antony affirmed only a few decades before the fall of Constantinople to the OTTOMANS that it was wrong to say 'that we have the church without an emperor, for it is impossible for Christians to have a church and no empire'.

However, there were limits on the emperor's position in relation to the church: he had no right to define Orthodoxy, but had rather to accept it; he was not a priest, but – as MAXIMUS THE CONFESSOR pointed out – was prayed for in the liturgy as one of the laity; he might rule the empire by edicts, but the church was to be governed by CANON (as ATHANASIUS affirmed and JOHN OF DAMASCUS repeated during the period of ICONOCLASM). The authority to interpret scripture (*see* BIBLE) and tradition was not conceded to the emperor – Byzantine Christianity was never 'caesaro-papist' – but resided in the fathers, in the councils and in the living witness of the saints, of which the most fertile seedbed was MONASTICISM.

'Following then the holy fathers': these words preface the Christological definition of CHALCEDON and define the relationship of the councils to the fathers, those teachers in the history of the church (mainly, but not necessarily, bishops or monks) whose interpretation of the gospel has been accepted as authoritative by later generations of Christians. At the councils, the assembled bishops, claiming the inspiration of the Holy Spirit, recognized and acclaimed the apostolic faith in the changing conditions of the church's history. Byzantine Christianity lays great store by those councils regarded as ecumenical, that is, representative of the *oikoumene* governed by the Roman sovereign or *basileus*. This recognition is given in Eastern Orthodox tradition to seven ECUME-NICAL COUNCILS, which defined and refined Christian belief in the nature of the incarnate Son of God. As well as defining dogmatic issues, including some subsidiary matters in addition to the fundamental Christological faith, these councils produced a body of canon law. These canons, those of the so-called QUINISEXT COUNCIL in Trullo (691), are the basis of the canon law of Byzantine Christianity. The Byzantines, however, were well aware of the dangers of any code of law attempting to impose a uniformity greater than life will bear, and have always recognized the right of bishops to exercise economy (*oikonomia*) and thus tune justice to realities of the individual case.

The importance for Byzantine Christianity of councils as the touchstone of ortho-doxy, and the canons as governing the life of the church, lay behind Byzantine resistance to developments in the church in the West. There councils came to be seen as subordinate to the authority of the bishop of Rome, to need ratification by the pope, even to be called by the pope as organs of papal authority, though in the West too the traditional conviction of the superiority of conciliar authority to that of any bishop, including the pope, was slow to die. Against the notion of papal supremacy, the conviction that Rome was 'mother of the churches' and the gradual development of the idea of the pope's universal jurisdiction, the Byzantine churches asserted the notion of the PENTARCHY, the authority of the five patriarchal sees of Rome, Constantinople (granted status immediately after Rome at the councils of Constantinople I and Chalcedon), Alexandria, Antioch and Jerusalem, exercised formally through councils. Bound up with the question of conciliar authority was the doctrinal issue that came to be at issue between Byzantine and Roman Christianity, the FILIOQUE. This addition to the creed of Nicea I and Constantinople I was opposed by the Byzantines as a derogation of conciliar authority. Sometimes the Byzantines went further and opposed it as a doctrinal error.

The canons of the Ecumenical Councils, which had all taken place in the East, made rules for the conduct of church life according to the norms that had developed in the East. So, for instance, clerical celibacy, long a desideratum in the West, though by no means a universal practice, was not required by the Quinisext Council, which envisaged a married lower clergy. Many other customs regarded by the East as in conformity with the canons, but either abandoned or never known in the West – such as use of leavened bread in the eucharist, or the wearing of beards by the clergy – contributed to the growing estrangement of the Byzantine and Roman churches. The exchange of excommunications in 1054 between Cardinal Humbert, the legate of the (by then deceased) Pope Leo IX, and the Ecumenical Patriarch Michael Keroularios – although limited to the persons involved – have conventionally been regarded as marking the schism between East and West (they were lifted by Pope Paul VI and Athenagoras, the

TRINITY LAW SCHOOL

Ecumenical Patriarch, in 1965). But the real cause of the final break was the CRU-SADES, and the sack of Constantinople in 1204. A series of councils in the succeeding centuries, culminating in Ferrara/FLORENCE (1438–45), made notable steps towards mutual understanding, but could not repair the mistrust of the Latins felt by the betrayed Byzantines.

Canons and definitions regulate, but do not constitute, the life of the church. That consists of praising God in everything, both corporately, in the liturgical and sacramental life of the church and its care for society's needy and dispossessed, and individually, in a life of prayer and ascetic struggle, issuing in a life of love for the whole of creation. Byzantine Christianity sets great store by the liturgy – the church building, its arrangement and decorations, especially the ICONS, the dramatic structure of the services: all this is held to reflect the beauty of the heavenly court and the cosmic significance of the Christian celebration. The beauty of the liturgy is carried over into the devotion of families and individuals in the use of icons. One of the most distinctive features of Byzantine and Slav Christianity is not just the use of religious imagery, but a conviction that veneration of icons is integral to the acknowledgement that in the incarnation and for our salvation God made part of the material creation his own. Burning lamps before the icons, honouring them with incense and kissing them are ways in which, through them, Christ, the Mother of God and the saints are reverenced as present sources of inspiration and consolation. This recognition of the image as making reality present carries over into the attempt to see in all human beings the image of God in which they are created and to honour Him there, and into striving to purify God's image in ourselves, so that the radiance of God's love is felt by those with whom we have to do. Delight in beauty, in the liturgy, in the icons, is not something merely aesthetic, but something tested in ascetic struggle. This beauty purifies and draws out a passionate love for God and his whole creation.

This emphasis on ascetic struggle underlies the importance attached within Byzantine Christianity to the saints and the monastic tradition. The essence of monasticism is the opportunity it provides for undistracted commitment to ascetic struggle. The importance of the saints is that in them this ascetic struggle, in response to the love of God who became incarnate for our sake, has led to a transparency to the glory of God, which the Byzantines call DEIFICATION, such that they have experienced the reality that the dogmatic tradition seeks to protect. This experiential understanding of the saints was called 'inner wisdom' to distinguish it from the 'outer wisdom', the learning of the Hellenes, that of the pagan past. In fact, the distinction between inner and outer wisdom was less clear-cut than many thought: the language in which the inner wisdom was expressed drew on classical philosophy, especially PLATONISM. Nevertheless the distinction between outer wisdom, acquired by learning and intellectual prowess, and inner wisdom, the fruit of the life of prayer and asceticism, was valid enough. The claims of the inner wisdom were challenged in the fourteenth century in the HESYCHAST controversy. The hesychasts claimed to experience, to 'see', the uncreated light of the Godhead. This claim was dismissed as blasphemous by representatives of the outer wisdom, who mocked their physical techniques and repetitive use of the JESUS PRAYER in the search for *hesychia*, the quiet of the heart. The hesychasts were defended by GREGORY PALAMAS, archbishop of Thessaloniki, who developed the distinction between the ineffable essence of God and His energies, in which He makes Himself known, and which include the 'uncreated light' that the hesychasts claimed to see. The energies are distinct from God's essence, but none the less identical with God. The Palamite defence of hesychasm was endorsed by councils held in Constantinople between 1341 and 1351. The centre of hesychasm was Mount ATHOS, where the Great LAVRA had been founded by Athanasios the Athonite in 963.

With the fall of Constantinople in 1453, the Christian empire of Byzantium finally vanished, and the empire's Christians became subject to the OTTOMAN imperial authorities. The Ecumenical Patriarch became both civil and religious head of the *Rum milet*, the 'Roman nation', the Eastern Orthodox. His authority extended to the Orthodox churches of Slav and other nations incorporated in the Ottoman empire, although from the eighteenth century the patriarch came under the influence of the Greeks of the Phanar, the Greek quarter of Istanbul, and became increasingly a focus for Greek concerns. The eighteenth century also saw a revival on Mount Athos of hesychasm, associated especially with NIKODEMOS THE HAGIORITE (Nikodemos of the Holy Mountain) and Makarios of Corinth, who together published in 1782 the PHILOKALIA, an anthology of spiritual treatises that they felt belonged to the hesychast tradition. This has, perhaps, had even greater influence in the Slav countries than in the Greek Orthodox world.

The nineteenth and twentieth centuries witnessed the progressive liberation of Greek Orthodoxy from the Ottoman yoke, and also the expansion of Greek Orthodox Christianity, initially as a result of emigration, into Western Europe, AMERICA, AUSTRALIA, and also parts of Africa. In the Greek Orthodox DIASPORA, now under the ultimate authority of the Ecumenical Patriarch, Greek emigrants have experienced assimilation to the cultures they have adopted, and the Orthodox church has become a home for Western Christians attracted to the tradition of Byzantine Christianity. All this poses problems for the now world-wide jurisdiction of the Ecumenical Patriarch, not least problems of overlapping Orthodox jurisdictions, that have yet to be resolved. The latter half of the twentieth century has witnessed a revival of monasticism in Greek Orthodoxy, especially on Mount ATHOS, where some monastic communities from the mainland have migrated. All the ruling monasteries there are now once again cenobitic. Greek Orthodox theology, for instance, in the writings of Christos Yannaras, John Romanides and Metropolitan John Zizioulas, has also begun to show signs both of addressing itself to, and learning from, modern intellectual concerns and of escaping from an undue reliance on approaches to theology of German and Latin provenance by rediscovering its roots in theology of the fathers. This rediscovery of the roots of Orthodoxy in the authentic patristic tradition is not limited to theology, however, but has affected Greek Orthodox church life more generally, not least in matters of lay ministry, music and iconography.

Clément, O. (1993), *The Roots of Christian Mysticism*. London: New City.
Ware, T. (1993), *The Orthodox Church*, new edn. Harmondsworth: Penguin.
Yannaras, C. (1991), *Elements of Faith: An Introduction to Orthodox Theology*. Edinburgh: T. & T. Clark.
Meyendorff, J. (1989), *Imperial Unity and Christian Divisions: The Church 450–680 AD*. Crestwood, NY: St Vladimir's Seminary Press.
Hussey, J. (1986), *The Orthodox Church in the Byzantine Empire*. Oxford: Clarendon Press.

Meyendorff, J. (1982), *The Byzantine Legacy in the Orthodox Church*. Crestwood, NY: St Vladimir's Seminary Press.

Meyendorff, J. (1974), *Byzantine Theology: Historical Trends and Doctrinal Themes*. Oxford: Mowbrays.

Runciman, S. (1968), *The Great Church in Captivity*. Cambridge: Cambridge University Press.

Lossky, V. (1957), *The Mystical Theology of the Eastern Church*. London: James Clarke.

AL

Byzantine liturgy   The Byzantine rite is a family of Christian liturgical usages that evolved in the Byzantine Orthodox PATRIARCHATE of CONSTANTINOPLE. Its history went through five phases. (1) During the palaeo-Byzantine or pre-Constantinian era, the liturgy of Byzantium was a typical late antique, Antiochene-type rite with no especially 'Byzantine' distinguishing traits. But in the last two decades of the fourth century it began to acquire the stational character and theological lineaments that were to mark its later history. (2) In its 'imperial phase' of development, especially from the reign of Justinian I (527–65), the Akolouthia Asmatike (Sung Office) evolved, a system of cathedral liturgy that lasted until some time after the Latin conquest (1204–61). (3) Meanwhile, the 'Dark Ages' from 610 to *c*.850, and especially the struggle against ICONOCLASM (726–843), had culminated in the Studite reform. (4) The Studite era (*c*.800–1204) is dominated, liturgically, by the progress of the Studite synthesis, a monastic rite of quite different dimensions from the cathedral rite of the Great Church. This monastic rite, basically a synthesis of Byzantine monastic usages with those of the LAVRA of St Sabas in Palestine, was codified in a new type of monastic rule, the Studite Typika, which would supplant the cathedral rite of the TYPIKON of the Great Church in the restoration following the Latin occupation of 1204–61. (5) In the final phase, the Neo-Sabaite synthesis – actually no more than a second wave of Palestinian Sabaitic monastic influence – gradually modifed and ultimately supplanted the Studite rite (itself an earlier generation Sabaitic rite) everywhere except southern Italy during the HESYCHAST ascendancy on ATHOS, whence it spread to ROMANIA and the Slavic Orthodox world.

Phases (2) and (3), especially, were seminal for the evolution not only of the Byzantine liturgical usages, but of the Byzantine liturgical vision, when the basis of its structure and symbolism emerged. This was a time of formation, climax, breakdown, realignment and new synthesis, an era of ferment in which changes in the shape and perception of the liturgy would, in phase (4), be mirrored by accompanying shifts in its architectural and iconographic setting. It is from this symbiosis that the final Byzantine liturgical synthesis, noted for the singular unity of the liturgy with its architectural/iconographic setting, derives. (*See* ARCHITECTURE; ICONS.)

♦ Stational liturgy: the city a church ♦

This synthesis of ceremonial and ambience became a significant reality in the rite of Constantinople only with the dedication of Justinian's Hagia Sophia in 537. There was nothing distinctively 'Byzantine' about pre-Justinianic churches in the capital, and little of symbolic or theological import was attached to the Byzantine church building before Hagia Sophia. Indeed, most Byzantine liturgical description in the entire period anterior to iconoclasm (726–843) deals not with the church building but with what took place outside, in the stational processions and services along the principal streets of Constantine's city. Along these porticoed thoroughfares and in the large, open squares through which they threaded took place much of the liturgical activity which the Byzantines of the time thought important enough to record. Anniversaries of deliverance from natural disasters or heresy, church dedications, the transfer of relics, funerals (especially imperial ones) and the developing cycle of synaxis celebrations to be held in a determined church on pre-established days provided abundant occasions for these outdoor services.

These stations would leave an indelible stamp on the Divine Liturgy and other rites of the Great Church. Entrances, processions, accessions come to characterize all Byzantine liturgy. They occupy a major portion of the space and symbolism of the classic liturgical commentators from MAXIMUS THE CONFESSOR onwards. They were also directly responsible for the characteristic shape of the early Constantinopolitan church arrangement. Since the people did not enter the church beforehand to welcome the arrival of the introit procession, there had to be an outbuilding where the people could offer their gifts before the basilica was 'opened liturgically' with the solemn entrance of the clergy and the imperial party: hence the skeuophylakion or sacristy, located in a separate rotunda outside the church. Since the clergy and people entered the church together, rapid access to the nave and galleries from outside was imperative: hence the multiple outside entrances to the gallery stairwells, and the numerous monumental doorways on all four sides of the church. The major entrances in the west facade were preceded by an atrium or courtyard enclosed by a square portico where processions could gather to await the completion of the introit courtesies of the hierarchs and dignitaries in the narthex, and the recitation of the Introit Prayer before the ROYAL DOORS leading into the nave, before flooding into the church. Inside, the longitudinal axis between entrance and apse was emphasized, and the processions were guided to the sanctuary by floor markings and the walled pathway of the solea, which funnelled the clergy and imperial entourage around the AMBO and up to the gates of the templon or chancel that enclosed the sanctuary (*see* ICONOSTASIS).

◆ A cosmos-church for a cosmic liturgy ◆

With the development of a typically Byzantine liturgical church disposition, liturgical commentary focuses more and more on what takes place inside the church, on the church itself, and on its symbolic meaning. In this cosmic symbolism, already expressed in the liturgical texts of the epoch, the earthly church is seen to image forth the heavenly sanctuary where the God of heaven dwells, and the earthly liturgy is a 'concelebration' in the worship which the Heavenly Lamb and the angelic choirs offer before the throne of God. This is the first level of Byzantine liturgical interpretation, reflected in such fifth- and sixth-century liturgical additions as the Introit Prayer and the CHERUBIKON (573–4), and systematized in the *Mystagogy* of MAXIMUS THE CONFESSOR (*c.*630).

◆ Iconoclasm, and the 'Middle Byzantine synthesis' ◆

With Justinian and his immediate successors the rite of the Great Church can be said to have reached its apogee. This Constantinopolitan cathedral rite continued in use throughout the following centuries, even as it was being reinterpreted, even superseded, by later developments. For significant changes in liturgical understanding and practice soon rend the fabric of this 'imperial' liturgical system. The evolution of Byzantine liturgical interpretation in the century from Maximus (*c*.630) to Patriarch GERMANOS I (*c*.730) betrays this clearly. By the eighth century, on the eve of the iconoclastic crisis, the traditional Maximian 'cosmic' liturgical interpretation had begun to give way before a more literal and representational narrative vision of the liturgical *historia*. While not abandoning the cosmic, heavenly-liturgy typology inherited from Maximus' *Mystagogy*, Germanos integrates into Byzantine liturgical understanding another level of interpretation also found, though far less prominently, in Maximus and other earlier Byzantine liturgical writings: that of the eucharist not only as the anamnesis of, but as actual figure of, salvation history in Jesus, a view first synthesized at the end of the fourth century by Theodore of Mopsuestia (d. 428) in his *Catechetical Homilies*, 15–16.

This encroachment of a more literal tradition upon an earlier, mystical level of Byzantine interpretation coincides with the beginnings of the struggle against iconoclasm (726–843), when shifts in Byzantine piety led to such growth in the cult of images that Orthodoxy found itself locked in mortal combat to defend this new expression of radical incarnational realism against a more symbolic and, ultimately, inconoclastic spiritualism. Symbolism and portrayal are not the same thing either in art or in liturgy, and the effect of the new mentality can be seen at once in the representational mystagogy integrated into the earlier Maximian tradition by Germanos *c*.730; in the condemnation by the Seventh ECUMENICAL COUNCIL in 787 of the teaching of the iconoclastic council of 754 that the eucharist is the only valid symbol of Christ; and, ultimately, in the iconographic programme of the Middle Byzantine church.

The same theology is at the basis of Byzantine mystagogy and icon worship, and in post-iconoclastic Byzantium both dimensions of this theology (church building and liturgy as a mirror of the mysteries of salvation; church building and liturgy as cosmic and eschatological images of the heavenly realm and its worship) emerge already in Germanos' interpretation of the church cited below. But if theological interpretation of the new spirituality was canonized in liturgical commentaries, it could be communicated to the masses only through the ritual celebration and its setting, the liturgical disposition and decoration of the church building, as these evolved in Byzantine churches at the turn of the tenth and eleventh centuries.

Previously, witnesses could assign symbolic meaning to various parts of the Constantinopolitan church building, and there was some representational art in Hagia Sophia. But the use of extensive representational art programmes began in Constantinople only in the Middle Byzantine period, following the final defeat of iconoclasm in 843, when an iconographic programme was elaborated to express this vision to those unreached by the literary commentaries. These programmes reflect the two-tiered symbolism of the new mystagogy of Germanos: (1) the cosmic, 'heavenly-liturgy' vision inherited from Maximus; (2) the 'economic' or anamnetic *historia*, with its explicit, representational depiction of salvation history. (*See* THEOLOGY.)

In the cosmic or hierarchical scheme, church and ritual are an image of the present age of the church, in which divine grace is mediated to those in the world (nave) from the divine abode (sanctuary) and its heavenly worship (the liturgy enacted there), which in turn images forth its future consummation (eschatology), when we shall enter that abode in glory. In the economic or anamnetic scheme, which in Byzantine mystagogy first receives prominence in Germanos, the sanctuary with its ALTAR is at once the Holy of Holies of the tabernacle decreed by Moses, Cenacle of the Last Supper, Golgotha of the Crucifixion, and Holy Sepulchre of the Resurrection, from which the sacred gifts of the Risen Lord, his Word and his body and blood, issue forth to illumine the sin-darkened world.

In the iconography and liturgy of the church, this twofold vision assumes visible and dynamic form. From the central dome the image of the PANTOCRATOR dominates the whole scheme, giving unity to the hierarchical and economic themes. The movement of the hierarchical theme is vertical, ascending from the present, worshipping community assembled in the nave, up through the ranks of the saints, prophets, patriarchs and apostles depicted in frescoes, to the Lord in the heavens attended by the angelic choirs. The economic or 'salvation-history' system, extending outwards and upwards from the sanctuary, is united both artistically and theologically with the hierarchical. Within this setting the liturgical community commemorates the mystery of its redemption in union with the worship of the Heavenly Church, offering the mystery of Christ's covenant through the outstretched hands of his Mother, all made present to the unlettered in the sacrament of the iconographic scheme.

Indeed, it is only in the actual liturgical celebration that the symbolism of the church comes alive, and appears as more than a static embodiment of the cosmos as seen through Christian eyes. The iconostasis enclosing the sanctuary wherein the mysteries of the covenant are celebrated is conceived as the link between heaven and earth. Beyond and above the altar, on the wall of the central sanctuary apse, is depicted 'The Communion of the Apostles': not the historic Last Supper, but Christ the heavenly High Priest, attended by the angels, giving the eucharist to the apostles. Basil the Great and John Chrysostom, whose liturgical formularies express the same mystery, may be found there too, holding liturgical scrolls, as if concelebrating the rites being performed before them on the heavenly/earthly altar. Over the altar, in the conch of the sanctuary apse, is the Mother of God, arms outstretched in the orant position, as if interceding and hastening through her hands the liturgical offering to the Pantocrator above her in the dome. With her, in the nimbus of her womb, is the Christ child, figure of the incarnation that made this sacrificial intercession possible, figure of Mary/church as womb of God, bringing forth Jesus again and again in human hearts. Above this, at the summit of the sanctuary arch, is depicted 'The Throne of Divine Judgement', where the sacrificial mediation must intercede before God. Out from the sanctuary, frescoes of liturgical feasts depicting the Christian economy of salvation in Jesus extend around the walls of the church clockwise, in lateral bands, binding the saving *historia* of the past into the salvific renewal of the present.

◆ A reduced ritual – an increased symbolism ◆

Of course, such decorative programmes were feasible only in the much smaller post-Justinianic church, whose whole interior was a single decorative unit encompassed at a single glance. Such a radical change of venue and scale came about partly because of the socio-political and economic situation of the period. As a consequence of the 'Dark Ages', the monumental architecture of the Justinianic period was succeeded by middle and late Byzantine churches often miniature by comparison. As churches became smaller, liturgical life became more compressed, more private. The splendours of the urban stational and basilical rites of late antiquity, destined for a liturgical space that encompassed the city and tailored to the majestic dimensions of a Hagia Sophia, are henceforth played out in a greatly reduced arena.

This compression of liturgical activity to within the walls of ever smaller church buildings is accompanied, inevitably, by a shift towards greater symbolization. When rites once of practical import outlive their original purpose, their continued survival demands reintegration into a new system. In the process, such relics often acquire new symbolic interpretations unrelated to their genesis or original scope. The classic example is, again, the introit procession at the beginning of the eucharistic liturgy, originally a solemn entrance into the church. The new ritual, though still imposing, is confined within the much smaller, centrally planned churches, and the once great public introit processions, reduced to ritual turns within the interior of a now tiny nave, become a truncated, clerical remnant of the original entrance of the entire congregation.

In the new system the Little and Great Entrance processions, abbreviated to ritual appearances of the sacred ministers from behind the sanctuary barrier, perdure on a reduced scale, reinterpreted as epiphanies of Christ. In the first procession or Lesser Introit, which opens the Liturgy of the Word, the Gospel book is borne out from the altar through the nave and back again. It is said to signify Christ's coming to us as Word. The Great Entrance or Major Introit at the beginning of the eucharistic half of the service was once, too, a functional entrance into church from the outside skeuophylakion with the bread and wine prepared there before the liturgy. Reduced to a solemn transfer of the bread and wine from the PROTHESIS credence in the sanctuary, out through the nave, then back again to the sanctuary to be deposited on the altar, it is said to show Christ being led to his sacrifice, and to prefigure his coming to us in the sacrament of his body and blood. These foreshadowings are fulfilled in two later ritual appearances from behind the sanctuary chancel: the procession of the DEACON with the Gospel lectionary for the reading, and the procession of the presiding celebrant to distribute in communion the consecrated gifts.

This move towards a smaller scale also entailed a greater privatization of the liturgy. Not only are processions reduced to ritualized remnants of no practical import, which end where they began; within the church itself the ritual action withdraws to the ever more completely enclosed sanctuary. The results of all this in the liturgical disposition of the church are multiple. The atrium vanishes and the number of doorways is greatly reduced. The outside skeuophylakion is abandoned, replaced by pastophoria. The elevated synthronon disappears from the apse. The great ambo is displaced from the middle of the nave, greatly reduced in size and moved off-centre, or even removed entirely, as the proclamation of the Word becomes a ritualized formality, with even preaching, usually, reduced to the reading of a ready text from some homiliary.

♦ Retroinfluence of the new interpretation on the text ♦

With these developments the final 'Byzantine synthesis' is already in place, and a retroinfluence sets in, one in which the new symbolic system affects not only the church building, iconography and ritual but the liturgical texts themselves. By the time of Germanos this new, Antiochene-style view of liturgy had begun to spin its web of allegory not only at the entrances, but backwards and forwards into the rites that precede and follow them. One sees this verified above all in the 'economic' interpretation of the Great Entrance as the funeral cortège of Jesus. It initiates a process whereby the whole liturgical action before and after the transfer of gifts is interpreted in function of the view that the gifts at the entrance represent the body of the already crucified Lord. The development of the Prothesis or rite of preparation of the gifts at the beginning of the eucharist, especially the introduction of the prophetic 'Suffering Servant' verses at the preparation of the eucharistic bread, thereby interpreting it as the sacrificial Lamb of God; the solemnizing of the Great Entrance ritual itself and its symbolism; the resulting multiplication of burial-motif *troparia* at the deposition, incensing and covering of the gifts on the altar, henceforth interpreted as representing the deposition of Jesus' crucified body in the sepulchre, its embalming with aromatic spices and its wrapping in the winding sheet or sindon (shroud): all this is indicative not only of the inevitable ritual elaboration of all medieval liturgies, but also of developments in piety and understanding. Here they not only interpret existing text and ritual, but retroactively contribute to textual and ritual change. This is a process which the historical evolution of the Byzantine rite, the development and decorative programmes of the churches built to house it, and the way its commentators would interpret both, all illustrate to a remarkable degree.

Taft, R. F. (1992), *The Byzantine Rite: A Short History*. Collegeville, Minn.: Liturgical Press.

Taft, R. F. (1991), *History of the Liturgy of St John Chrysostom*, vol. 4: *The Diptychs*. OCA 238. Rome: Pontifical Institute of Oriental Studies.

Wybrew, H. (1989), *The Orthodox Liturgy: The Development of the Eucharistic Liturgy in the Byzantine Rite*. London: SPCK.

Taft, R. F. (1988), 'Mount Athos: A Late Chapter in the History of the "Byzantine Rite"', *Dumbarton Oaks Papers* 42, pp. 179–94.

Baldovin, J. F. (1987), *The Urban Character of Christian Worship: The Origins, Development, and Meaning of Stational Liturgy*. OCA 228. Rome: Pontifical Institute of Oriental Studies.

Schulz, H.-J. (1986), *The Byzantine Liturgy: Symbolic Structure and Faith Expression*. New York: Pueblo.

Taft, R. F. (1984), *Beyond East and West: Problems in Liturgical Understanding*. NPM Studies in Church Music and Liturgy. Washington, DC: Pastoral Press.

Taft, R. F. (1980–1), 'The Liturgy of the Great Church: An Initial Synthesis of Structure and Interpretation on the Eve of Iconoclasm', *Dumbarton Oaks Papers* 34/5, pp. 45–75.

Taft, R. F. (1978), *A History of the Liturgy of St John Chrysostom*, vol. 2: *The Great Entrance: A History of the Transfer of Gifts and Other Preanaphoral Rites of the Liturgy of St John Chrysostom*. OCA 200, 2nd edn. Rome: Pontifical Institute of Oriental Studies.

RT

ᐧC ᐧ

Cabasilas, Nicolas   Nicolas Chamaetos Cabasilas, born 1322 and probably brought up in the charge of his uncle Nilus Cabasilas, future archbishop of Thessaloniki, whose surname he took. Nicolas became close to Emperor John VI Kantakouzenos (1347–54). In the hesychast controversy, like the emperor, he supported GREGORY PALAMAS and in 1354 wrote a pamphlet defending HESYCHASM. His commentary on the Divine Liturgy represents a return from the mapping of the detail of the liturgy on to events in the life of Christ which Patriarch GERMANOS I (715–30) had instituted as the norm, and both presents the liturgical action as an earthly image of the eternal heavenly liturgy and interprets it in terms of the ways in which participants are transformed by Christ's action in and through the liturgy. The mystery of the Incarnation and the intimacy it establishes between God and humanity stand at the centre of Cabasilas's theology. His sacramental theology is realistic; he sees the MYSTERIES as changing their participants. An eirenic spirit pervades Nicolas' writings. Cabasilas may have remained a layman, but this is not certain. Nicolas is commemorated on 20 June.

deCatanzaro, J., trans. (1974), *The Life in Christ*. Crestwood, NY: St Vladimir's Seminary Press.
Hussey, J. M. and McNulty, P. A. (1960), *Commentary on the Divine Liturgy*. London: SPCK.

DM

calendar, Byzantine rite   The Byzantine ecclesiastical year begins on 1 September: for those EASTERN CHRISTIANS using the Julian calendar this date falls thirteen days later than for the minority who use the Gregorian calendar or the New Julian Calendar.

The liturgical calendar has five main elements: the daily cycle, the weekly cycle, the cycle of eight tones, the Paschal cycle, and the cycle of fixed feasts. Most EASTERN ORTHODOX churches, including New Calendarists, use the Old Paschalion to date Pascha; state law makes the Church of Finland an exception. Some EASTERN CATHOLICS, however, use both New Calendar and New Paschalion. The Old

Paschalion date of Pascha is often later than Western Easter, not only because of the Julian calendar but also since the last days of Great Week must not fall on or before the Jewish Passover. The Paschal cycle begins on the Sunday of the Pharisee and the Publican, four weeks before Lent; Lent itself begins on Pure Monday and ends on Lazarus Saturday, the eve of Palm Sunday. The cycle ends with the Pentecost Sunday, the feast of the Holy Trinity, and the Sunday of All Saints.

The opening of the ecclesiastical year on 1 September, feast of Symeon Stylites, date of the INDICTION, and now in the Ecumenical Patriarchate the Day of the Environment, is often seen as emphasizing the role of the THEOTOKOS in the salvation of the world: the Nativity of the Mother of God on 8 September, and her Dormition on 15 August, come at the opposite ends of the year. Other Marian feasts include 21 November, the Entrance of the Virgin into the Temple, and 9 December, the Conception of the Virgin by St Anne.

The Annunciation, 25 March, is a major feast of the Theotokos, but it is also the feast of the Conception of Christ, and opens the sequence of Dominical feasts. The Nativity of the Lord (and in the Eastern tradition also the Visit of the Magi) is celebrated on 25 December, and the Circumcision of Jesus on 1 January, the feast of Saint Basil the Great. Epiphany or THEOPHANY, 6 January, commemorates Christ's baptism. The feast of the TRANSFIGURATION is held on 6 August. The Passion, the Mystical Supper, the Agony, Betrayal, Trial, Sufferings, Death, Burial and Glorious Resurrection, the Assumption into Heaven of the Lord, and the Sending of His Holy Spirit upon the Apostles are all celebrated in the feasts of the Paschal cycle.

Every day the Eastern calendars commemorate saints venerated by the whole church; local, 'topical', saints; some Western saints from early centuries; and the Righteous (see DIKAIOS) of the Old Law. Paradoxically, the Maccabees and their mother are commemorated as though they were Christian martyrs. Eastern Catholics sometimes commemorate Western saints from the period of the schism and observe Western feasts such as Corpus Christi.

Starting on St Thomas Sunday, the first after Easter, each successive week uses the texts and music of the next of the eight tones for its offices. Each day of the week has its distinctive hymns and verses for each tone; they are collected in the PARAKLETIKE or OKTOECHOS. (*See also* MUSIC.)

DM

canon In Byzantine rite hymnography a canon is a series of hymns divided into nine ODES, each linked to one of the nine biblical canticles, the last of which consists of the Magnificat and Benedictus. Outside monasteries the canticles, apart from the Magnificat, are normally omitted. Most canons actually contain eight odes, since Ode 2 is used only on Tuesdays in Lent, though acrostics often show that there were originally nine. Normally three (on Sundays four) canons are prescribed, so that each ode, including the Heirmos, consists of fourteen troparia. ANDREW OF CRETE is often accounted the originator of the canon. JOHN OF DAMASCUS wrote the famous Resurrection canon of Pascha. Three notable centres of canon composition were Mar Saba (John of Damascus and his adopted brother Cosmas of Maiuma), the Studios monastery of CONSTANTINOPLE (THEODORE THE STUDITE and his brother Joseph) and Magna Graecia (Joseph the Hymnographer, d. 886, the most prolific author of canons). The Athonite monk Gerasimos, Hymnographer of the Great Church, was a major twentieth-century author, his output rivalling that of any of the early writers. Among his last works is a canon for the new feast of the environment on 1 September.

Some canons were translated as English hymns by J. M. Neale (d. 1866), who seems not to have understood the stress accent verse in which the canons are written.

E

canonarch   In Greek monasteries, the monk designated to see that the singers sing the correct texts in the correct tone. He also reads the verses of the PROKEIMENON and similar texts, duties taken over by the DEACON in Slav use.

E

canonization   Process of approving the cult of a saint, normally the act of the holy synod and chief hierarch of an autocephalous church. The process involves investigation of the candidate's life, writings and influence, of miracles worked before or after death, and of evidence for an existing cult. An AKOLOUTHIA is written for the feast day of a new saint and an ICON prepared. The actual ritual of canonization varies; the Russian ritual is particularly splendid. The oldest known formal canonizations were acts of the tenth-century papacy. Roman canonizations also involve creating an office, producing an image of the saint and the saint's miracles. Local informal cults are common in EASTERN CHRISTIAN communities.

DM

Cappadocians   Gregory of Nazianzus (c.329–90), Basil of Caesarea (330–79) and Gregory of Nyssa (331/40– c.395), all from Cappadocia in ASIA MINOR.

Gregory of Nazianzus, bishop of Constantinople (379–81), shares with JOHN THE THEOLOGIAN and the Byzantine mystic SYMEON THE NEW THEOLOGIAN (949–1022) the title 'The Theologian'. Together with JOHN CHRYSOSTOM and Basil of Caesarea he is celebrated on the feast of the THREE HIERARCHS. His Christian faith expresses itself in a variety of forms, notably his numerous poems and his correspondence. His series of *Orations*, especially his five *Theological Orations*, which argue his theological position against contemporary heresies, were influential throughout later periods. MAXIMUS THE CONFESSOR in the seventh century discusses difficult passages from Gregory's writings in his *Ambigua*.

Basil, bishop of Caesarea (370–9), is known as 'the Great'. His *On the Holy Spirit* deals with trinitarian theology and much else besides, particularly the question of patristic authority and the place of unwritten tradition. His interest in contemporary science is reflected in his *Hexaemeron*, a series of homilies on the six days of creation. He collaborated with Gregory of Nazianzus to produce the PHILOKALIA, a florilegium of extracts from ORIGEN. Basil greatly influenced the development of MONASTICISM through his so-called *Rules*. The adoption of the Liturgy of Saint Basil by the patriarchate of CONSTANTINOPLE led to its widespread use throughout the Orthodox world.

Gregory of Nyssa, brother of Basil the Great, for a time bishop of Sebaste, was the most speculative and mystical writer of the group. Melding his understanding of PLATONISM with Christian theology, he developed the idea that human participation in the grace of the infinite God must be progressive and never-ending. The influence of their sister Macrina (*c*.327–79) can be seen in his dialogue *On the Soul and the Resurrection*, in which she is his teacher and guide. Gregory also wrote the *Life of Macrina* (*see* WOMEN).

See also THEOLOGY, EASTERN CHRISTIAN.

Meredith, A. (1995), *The Cappadocians*. London: Geoffrey Chapman.
Pelikan, J. (1993), *Christianity and Classical Culture: The Metamorphosis of Natural Theology in the Christian Encounter with Hellenism*. New Haven: Yale University Press.
Barrois, G. (1986), *The Fathers Speak: St Basil the Great, St Gregory Nazianzus, St Gregory of Nyssa. Selected Letters*. Crestwood, NY: St Vladimir's Seminary Press.
Otis, B. (1958), 'Cappadocian Thought as a Coherent System', *Dumbarton Oaks Papers* 12, pp. 95–124.

KP

catholicos   Title used in several churches for the chief hierarch of that church or of a significant division of it. Though different in meaning, it is often equivalent in use to the title PATRIARCH. In the case of the catholicos patriarch of GEORGIA and the catholicos patriarch of the ETHIOPIAN church, the two titles are combined. Sometimes both are used as distinct elements of a single title, as with the catholicos of Ejmiacin and patriarch of All Armenians.

DM

Caucasus: Christianity since the collapse of the USSR   Ethnicity and faith have always been strongly linked in the Caucasus, despite decades of secularization under Soviet rule. By the time of the Soviet Union's collapse in December 1991, the revival of aggressive nationalism had thrown the Caucasus region into turmoil. Conflict had already broken out in the mainly Armenian-populated enclave of NAGORNO-KARABAKH in Azerbaijan (*see* ALBANIA, AL'UANK) and GEORGIA was heading for chaos with incipient conflicts over South OSSETIA and ABKHAZIA. All three conflicts (partly the revival of historic conflicts) soon turned into full-scale war and ethnic cleansing, leaving many people in the region both longing for the stability of the Soviet era and determined that the new state they lived in should be ethnically 'pure'. The three Transcaucasian republics which re-emerged on the break-up of the Soviet Union, Georgia, Azerbaijan and ARMENIA, were impoverished by the conflicts and the rupture in trading relations with each other and the rest of the former Soviet Union. They were also close to conflicts on the northern side of the Caucasus in many of the seven North Caucasian ethnic republics within Russia, notably Chechnya and North Ossetia.

The nationalist former dissident Zviad Gamsakhurdia came to power in Georgia amid heightened national feeling in October 1990, and was elected president in a national poll in May 1991. Although personally close to the anthroposophy of Rudolf Steiner, Gamsakhurdia had a track record as a dissident of strong support for the Georgian Orthodox church, having played a key role in the 1970s campaign to purge the church of what the dissidents believed was lethargy, corruption and subservience to the state. Another dissident complaint was the homosexuality allegedly widespread among the clergy.

In his new political role as parliamentary leader and later as president, Gamsakhurdia constantly evoked the nexus of nation and religion in determining the country's destiny, even expounding a mystical messianic role for Georgia as a beacon to the rest of the world. Such sentiments chimed with many Georgians' view of the nation as an embattled Christian bastion at the edge of the Christian world. But Georgians made up only some 70 per cent of the republic's population (1989 census), and the upsurge in national feeling caused unease among Georgia's minorities, especially the Abkhaz, the Ossetians and the Azeris. Of these, only the Azeris are completely Muslim. The Abkhaz and Ossetians are of mixed Orthodox Christian and Muslim background, although the faith of the Ossetians (both Christian and Muslim) remains heavily tinged with survivals of their pagan past. As Georgian nationalism mounted at the end of the Soviet era, Orthodox Christians among the Abkhaz and Ossetians increasingly demanded Russian rather than Georgian jurisdiction over churches in their area. Gamsakhurdia's claims that Eastern rite Armenian Catholics in south Georgia were really Armenianized Georgians added to Armenian concern. Meskhetian Turks – long-standing converts to Islam or Turkish immigrants over the centuries, deported en masse from Georgia to Central Asia in 1944 – feared that in the face of such popular sentiment they would never be allowed to return home. Church publications backed campaigns to proselytize among Georgia's Muslim minorities. There were renewed protests about the lack of Georgian schools and churches for Georgians in the Kakhi district of Azerbaijan, where the first Georgian church was not registered until 1989. Arguments over Armenian Apostolic and Roman Catholic churches in Georgia seized by the Orthodox church remain unresolved.

Gamsakhurdia became increasingly erratic and dictatorial as president and, after civil war erupted, was ousted in late 1991. Former Georgian Communist Party leader and later Soviet foreign minister Eduard Shevardnadze was brought in by the victors in 1992, subsequently being elected head of state. War against Abkhaz and Ossetian separatists revived and the two regions effectively broke away from Georgia, with Russian 'peacekeeping' forces enforcing the separation.

The Georgian church has generally backed or sought to take advantage of conditions under both the Gamsakhurdia and Shevardnadze regimes. After decades of enforced atheism and persecution, active participation by the population was low. By the beginning of Gorbachev's reign as party general secretary in 1985, the republic had just fifty-one registered churches. The loosening of the controls on religion saw this figure jump dramatically to nearly 300 by the end of 1990, and today there are more than a thousand. While Georgians retained some loyalty to the church – especially for rites of passage – during the Soviet era, the freeing of religion allowed the church and its leader, CATHOLICOS-PATRIARCH Ilya II (elected as 146th catholicos-patriarch in 1977), a greater profile in public life. In November 1992, soon after becoming head of state, Shevardnadze was baptized in a public ceremony. The Shevardnadze government generally took a back seat on religious matters, however, doing little either to encourage or to discourage the Georgian church in its ambition to dominate the religious life of the country. The church has backed the government's attempts to reassert control over Abkhazia and South Ossetia.

The Georgian Orthodox Church finally achieved international Orthodox recognition as autocephalous in 1990. (Under Soviet government pressure the Russian Orthodox church had accepted its autocephaly in 1943.)

Armenia had a far more cohesive society than Georgia, as much of the non-Armenian population had been moved out earlier in the Soviet era, especially in the post-war resettlement of entire Azeri villages from Armenia into Azerbaijan. According to the 1989 census, Armenians made up nearly 94 per cent of the population. The rise to power of the national movement led by Levon Ter-Petrosyan, elected president in October 1991, which had grown out of the movement in support of the Armenians of Nagorno-Karabakh, was backed almost unanimously in a way never achieved in Georgia. The homogeneity of the population was reinforced with the expulsion of the entire Azeri population (together with the Muslim Kurds) in 1989–90, in the wake of the outbreak of hostilities over Karabakh. Just as the Georgian Orthodox church presented itself as the national church of an independent state, so the Armenian Apostolic church viewed itself as occupying a similar position in neighbouring Armenia. As in Georgia, the church had suffered greatly during the Soviet era and actual religious practice was low, despite the fierce attachment of the Armenian nation to its historic Christian identity. In 1985 there were just thirty-three Armenian churches in the entire Soviet Union, and only fifty by 1990. However, Catholicos Vazgen I (elected 1955) enjoyed a degree of national respect even greater than that of Ilya in Georgia, despite his initial reluctance to back Armenian independence. Catholicos Vazgen, the longest-serving religious leader in the Soviet Union, died in 1994 and, in accordance with church custom, an assembly of clerical and lay delegates from Armenian dioceses all over the world gathered in Ejmiacin in April 1995 to elect his successor. With presidential approval, the head of the church in Lebanon, Karekin Sarkissian, was chosen as 131st catholicos.

The Armenian government saw it as its duty to protect the Armenian church from what it saw as unfair competition from Protestant and non-Christian groups which gained a foothold towards the end of the Soviet era. The June 1991 legislation granted the Armenian church certain privileges, despite the state's claim to neutrality in religious matters. The Armenian church remained unhappy about continued activities in Armenia by other religious groups and, after intensive lobbying of the government by the church, President Ter-Petrosyan passed a decree in December 1993 further restricting the rights of religious groups other than the Armenian church.

The general hostility of the Armenian church to rival religious groups did not extend to the Armenian Catholic church, the traditional faith of many in the Panik region of northern Armenia, and did not oppose the Vatican's nomination in 1991 of a bishop to oversee this community – which had survived most of the communist era with no clerics at all. Nor did it obstruct the revival of the tiny ASSYRIAN church in a number of mainly Assyrian-populated villages (according to the 1989 census there were almost six thousand Assyrians in Armenia, with a similar number in Georgia).

The Nagorno-Karabakh enclave in Azerbaijan, with its majority Armenian population, had no registered places of worship, either Christian or Muslim, by the mid-1930s. Only in 1988 was the Armenian church able to appoint a bishop to the newly revived Karabakh diocese and send priests to minister there. As conflict engulfed the

114

enclave the church affirmed that the region must be under Armenian jurisdiction, while urging a negotiated solution to the conflict. Catholicos Vazgen and other senior Armenian clerics took part in a number of inconclusive reconciliation meetings with the senior Azeri Muslim cleric, Sheikh-ul-Islam Allahshukur Pasha Zade.

With the exception of Nagorno-Karabakh, Azerbaijan is now almost exclusively Muslim, the only significant group of Christians remaining after 1990 being Russians and other Slavs of Eastern Orthodox or Protestant background. A Russian Orthodox diocese of Baku was established in 1994, but the bishop did not take up residence there. The Udin ethnic group, numbering just over six thousand in the 1989 census, was the only other traditionally Christian ethnic group in Azerbaijan. Since independence, the number of Christians has declined with the emigration of many Russians and other Slavs. The tiny Assyrian community (numbering a few thousand) were expelled from Azerbaijan at the same time as the Armenians, and mostly settled with their co-religionists in Georgia.

Small Russian communities of Molokans, Dukhobors and other RUSSIAN SECTS – descended from those banished to the Transcaucasus by the Tsars – remain in Georgia, Azerbaijan and Armenia, although many of Georgia's Dukhobors left the country for Russia in the early 1990s complaining of discrimination.

See also ABKHAZIA; ADZHARIA; OSSETIA; PONTUS; ZICHIA.

Boyle, K., ed. (1996), *Freedom of Religion and Belief: A World Report*. London: Routledge.
Corley, F. (1995–6), 'The Armenian Church under the Soviet Regime', *Religion, State and Society* 4.
Crego, P. (1994), 'Religion and Nationalism in Georgia', *Religion in Eastern Europe*. n.p.
Corley, F. (1992), *Armenia and Karabakh: Ancient Faith, Modern War*. London: Catholic Truth Society.
Jones, S. (1989), 'Religious Policy in Georgia', *Religion in Communist Lands* 4.
Ramet, P., ed. (1988), *Eastern Christianity and Politics in the Twentieth Century*. North Carolina: Duke University Press.

FC

Chalcedonian   One who accepts the dogmatic Christological definition of the Council of Chalcedon, 451: 'one and the same Christ, son, lord, only-begotten, in two natures, without confusion, without change, without division, without separation, the distinctiveness of the two natures not having been removed in any way by the union, rather the characteristic of each nature having been preserved, concurring into one person or hypostasis, not parted or divided into two persons, but one and the same son, only-begotten God the word, Lord Jesus Christ...' and also accepts the authority of Chalcedon as an ECUMENICAL COUNCIL.

The Chalcedonian definition, with its elaborate array of negative terms, was directed against both those who held that Christ was one by the moral union of two *prosopa* or hypostases, and those who followed Eutyches in asserting that Christ possesses a single divine nature. The definition, however, was rejected by moderate MONOPHYSITE theologians such as PETER THE FULLER and PETER MONGOS, who none the less taught that Christ is one with us in his humanity and one with the Father in his divinity. The status of Chalcedon as an ecumenical council proved a stumbling-block to

115

the sequence of imperially sponsored attempts to reunite Chalcedonians and Monophysites.

See also HENOTIKON; THEOLOGY.

DM

Chaldean church   One of the SYRIAN churches in communion with the Roman Catholic church. The claim, sometimes heard from members of the church, that they are the descendants of the ancient Chaldeans (mentioned in the Old Testament, Isaiah 23: 13 etc.) cannot be sustained. Pope Eugenius IV first used the name 'Chaldean' (a term then equivalent to 'Syriac speaker') in 1445 to designate a body which seceded from the CHURCH OF THE EAST and united with Rome at that time. That union was short-lived, but the existence of the church has been more or less continuous since the consecration of John Sulaqa as 'Chaldean patriarch of Babylon' (this is still the official style of the PATRIARCH) in ROME in 1551. The church's membership was recorded as 315,320 in 1994. There are nineteen archdioceses and dioceses, in Iraq, Iran, Lebanon, Egypt, Syria, Turkey and the USA. The patriarchal see is in Baghdad. The American eparchy with its headquarters in Detroit, Michigan has eleven parishes and 55,800 members. The present patriarch, Mar Rophael Bidawid, was elected in 1989. The Chaldean church is one of two Catholic churches belonging to the Chaldean rite, the other being the Syro-Malabar church of INDIA. Compared to the Church of the East, the Chaldeans are more Arabized, both liturgically and in their political consciousness.

J.-M. Fiey, (1996), 'Comment l'occident en vint à parler de "Chaldeåens"', *Bulletin of the John Rylands University Library of Manchester* 78, 3, pp. 163–70.

JFC

Charalampos   (d. *c*.202) Bishop of Magnesia executed under Emperor Septimius Severus. Tradition says his fellow martyrs included Porphyrios, Baptos and three women, but that a noble disciple, Galena, survived. This group is commemorated on 10 February. Charalampos is the patron of Thessaly, and protector from epidemics. During the Second World War the deliverance of the people of Philiatra in the Peloponnese was attributed to him. He is one of the few saints whose feast, when it falls in Lent, is marked by the Liturgy of the Presanctified; the other feasts marked in such a manner are the Finding of the Head of John the Forerunner and the Forty Martyrs of Sebasteia.

DB

Cheese Week   Also called Butter Week: the week immediately preceding Great Lent in the Byzantine rite CALENDAR. During Cheese Week there is no fasting save from meat. At the end of Cheese Week is the Sunday of Forgiveness, Cheese Sunday, commemorating the expulsion of ADAM AND EVE from Paradise, when a ceremony of mutual forgiveness takes place in preparation for the Lent fast.

DM

cheirothesia   Greek: 'imposition of hands'. The word *cheirothesia* has acquired a technical use to designate the minor ordination granted in the Byzantine rite to a sub-deacon, READER or PSALTES, not regarded as part of the MYSTERY of ordination. In modern use sacramental *cheirotonia* of a presbyter or bishop is performed during the Divine Liturgy, and of a deacon during the Divine Liturgy or the Liturgy of the Presanctified, whereas *cheirothesia* can be performed outside the liturgy, except for a sub-deacon who is ordained at the holy doors before the start of the liturgy. The ancient liturgical texts show that when WOMEN were ordained to the female diaconate they were ordained within the sanctuary with the same rite as male candidates and at the same point in the liturgy. *Cheirothesia* is normally performed outside the ICONOSTASIS. An abbot who is a priest can give *cheirothesia* to his monks as readers or psaltai.

Confusingly, this lower form of ordination is sometimes called *cheirotonia*, as in the description of the rite in the printed *Mega Euchologion*.

DM/E

cheirotonia   Greek, ordination: literally, voting by raising the hand, therefore, by extension, election or appointment to office. In Christian use, *cheirotonia* designates sacramental ordination in which a person is made DEACON, priest or bishop by episcopal laying-on of hands. It is contrasted with CHEIROTHESIA, though the technical distinction emerged over time. Indeed, since *cheirotonia* takes place by imposition of hands, it too is literally an act of *cheirothesia* and is sometimes called so.

DM/E

Cherubikon   Troparion sung at the Great Entrance in the BYZANTINE LITURGY: 'We, who in a mystery represent the Cherubim and sing the thrice holy hymn to the life-giving Trinity, let us now lay aside every care of this life, for we are about to receive the King of all, invisibly escorted by the angelic hosts. ALLELOUIA, allelouia, allelouia.' The hymn is interrupted after the words 'care of this life', or in Greek use 'King of all', and the Great Entrance takes place.

The Cherubikon symbolically assimilates those present in the eucharistic assembly to the ANGELS of the presence about God's throne, marking out this earthly liturgy as the mysteric image of the liturgy of the heavenly court.

On Holy Thursday the troparion 'At your mystical supper' replaces the Cherubikon, and at the Liturgy of the PROTE ANASTASIS the troparion used in the Liturgy of St James occurs, 'Let all mortal flesh keep silent'. According to Symeon of Thessaloniki this same troparion is to be used at the consecration of a church and on the anniversary of it. In the Liturgy of the Presanctified the troparion 'Now the Powers of the Heavens' accompanies the entrance of the presanctified gifts.

In the procession of the Great Entrance at a concelebrated liturgy it is customary for each concelebrating priest to carry one of the SACRED UTENSILS used in the liturgy. An ancient custom exists in the monastery of Patmos and now in the monastery of Docheiariou on Mount ATHOS whereby each priest in the procession carries a veiled chalice.

DM/E

Chevetogne   Catholic Benedictine monastery, with communities of the Byzantine and Roman rites, founded in 1925 at Amay-sur-Meuse and moved to Chevetogne in 1939. The monastery publishes *Irénikon*. The Chevetogne community has played throughout its life an eirenic and fraternal role in Catholic–Orthodox relations. It has issued important recordings of liturgical chant.

DM

Chinese Orthodox church   A mission from the CHURCH OF THE EAST is recorded on the SIAN-FU STELE as having reached China in 635; EASTERN ORTHODOXY reached China through SIBERIA in the seventeenth century. Facing Cossack encroachment, in 1685 emperor K'ang Hsi (d. 1723) sacked Albazin, a Russian stronghold on the Amur, resettling the inhabitants in China. Priest Maksim Leontiev (d. 1712), who accompanied them, dedicated an Eastern Orthodox church in Beijing. In 1695 Metropolitan Ignatii of Tobolsk sent another priest to serve Cossacks in China and recommended organizing a mission. Filofei Leshchynski (d. 1727) of Tobolsk sent clergy in 1714. Bishop Innokentii Kulchitskii reached China in 1722 but was turned away.

Some missionary work continued from the church of the Russian Embassy. The 1858 Sino-Russian Treaty brought recognition of the Orthodox Mission which separated from the legation. Isaias Polikin organized parishes south of Beijing in 1860–70, initiating translation of liturgical texts into Chinese. Churches were established in Manchuria and Chihli provinces.

Innokentii Figurovskii's arrival in 1897 transformed missionary activity. He founded a press, schools and new churches, and rallied the community during the Boxer Uprising in 1900. During the rebellion his press and all Orthodox churches except one in Hankow were destroyed. Russian missionaries found refuge in Shanghai, but priest Mitrophan Chi and over two hundred Chinese Orthodox were martyred. Innokenty returned to Beijing in 1902, was elected bishop of China and revived the mission over a wider area. By 1914 sixteen churches, two monasteries and a theological academy existed, and over five thousand Chinese had embraced Orthodox Christianity.

Since the early 1900s over eighty thousand Russian expatriates were working in Manchuria. After the 1917 Russian Revolution thousands of refugees arrived. Harbin in Manchuria became the centre of émigré life and in 1922 was made an archdiocese. Bishop JONAS POKROVSKY sponsored missionary activity among the host community of Harbin, as did Bishop JOHN MAXIMOVITCH from Shanghai. The Japanese, having established a protectorate over Manchuria or Manchu-Kuo in 1931, permitted the establishment of the Orthodox University of Saint Vladimir in Harbin in 1934. By 1941 the Harbin archdiocese had sixty churches and three monasteries.

Innokentii Figurovskii remained metropolitan of China until 1931. Simeon Vinogradov (d. 1933) succeeded him. In the inter-war period there were probably over two hundred thousand Orthodox Christians in China. All belonged to the RUSSIAN ORTHODOX CHURCH ABROAD until 1945 when, except for Bishop John Maximovitch and the Shanghai community, the church was united with the Moscow patriarchate. From 1949 all Russians were expelled from the People's Republic of China.

In 1957 the Orthodox Church of China was reorganized as an autocephalous body under Metropolitan Basil Yo-Fou-An (d. 1962). Before the Cultural Revolution there were over twenty thousand practising Chinese Orthodox Christians.

Mastroyiannopoulos, I. (1970), *Orthodoxy in the World*. Athens: Zoe.

DB

Chionadites A school of folk icon painters operating from Chionadi village in Epiros. Their icons are often naïve and frequently depict new martyrs or illustrate unusual incidents from scripture and the lives of the saints. They flourished in the later OTTOMAN period, supplying icons for communities across the Empire.

Makris, K. (1990), *Chionadites Zographoi*. Athens: n.p.

DB

Chonai Mountain citadel of Phrygia, replacing Colossai in the eighth century (now Honaz). By tradition the Archangel Michael saved a local hermit, Archippos, from demonic assaults that included inspiring pagans to flood the area. This Archippos and the first-century miracle are commemorated on 6 September; in the Byzantine period the shrine became a major centre of PILGRIMAGE and the cult of the ANGELS. Chonai was sacked by the Seljuks in 1070 and lost to the Turks after 1204. Mantamados on Lesbos, which replaced Chonai as a centre of pilgrimage honouring Michael, commemorates another miracle that saved the monk Gabriel when other monks of the monastery were killed by Muslim raiders in the tenth century. PANORMITIS on Symi also honours Michael.

Dissou, E. (1988), *Mantamados*, vols 1 and 2. Mytilene: Mantamados Press.

DB

chorepiscopus 'Country bishop': ancient term for the cleric overseeing rural areas outside a town. Canon XIII of Ancyra (314) forbade chorepiscopi to ordain priests or deacons except with written permission from the bishop. A similar prohibition in Canon X of the Dedication Synod of Antioch (341) makes it clear that the local city bishop has jurisdiction over a chorepiscopus. It is unclear whether a chorepiscopus was always in episcopal orders or a senior presbyter, like a Western rural dean.

DM

Christology The preaching of the good news of the crucified and risen Saviour did not initially entail the transmission of a complete theological understanding of the person and nature of Christ. As the gospel spread, the message was received and interpreted against a variety of conceptual backcloths derived from different religious and philosophical traditions. From the earliest days of the church, Christ was regularly proclaimed and worshipped as God. The attempt, however, to clarify in exactly what sense Christ is God and precisely how he, as Son and Logos, is related to the Father and the Spirit, rapidly led to controversy which was to divide the Christian community for centuries.

In the mid-second century Marcion (d. *c*.160), apart from cutting down the New Testament to Luke's Gospel and a selection of the Pauline Epistles, taught that the 'Good God', the Father of Jesus Christ, was not to be identified with the creator of the universe, the God proclaimed by the Law and the prophets. Gnostic teachers frequently presented Jesus as only apparently human, and as one among many divine beings; he was regularly seen as opposing the God of the Old Testament. Docetist views which presented Jesus as human in appearance only, adoptionist theories that made him the adopted son of God and psilanthropist doctrines that made him a mere man were to have an abiding influence despite their rejection as heretical.

The teaching of the Alexandrian presbyter Arius (d. *c*.336) that 'there was when he was not', and that the Son was created, raised a major controversy that the emperor, Constantine I, attempted to put to rest by means of an ECUMENICAL COUNCIL of the Christian church. The council of Nicea in 325 adopted a creed which carefully excluded the Arian doctrine: 'Those indeed who say "there was when he was not" and "before being born he was not", and "that he came to be from non-existence", or from another reality [*hypostasis*] or being [*ousia*], declaring the Son of God to be either [created] or mutable or changeable, the catholic church anathematizes.' Arianism survived the council, persisting in several different forms for centuries, sometimes winning imperial support. A separate Arian church came into existence that showed significant missionary potential, especially among the barbarian nations of the West, where it survived long after its demise in the East.

The First Council of Constantinople in 381 also condemned an opponent of Arius, Apollinarios (*c*.310– *c*.390), bishop of Laodicea, who taught that though Christ had a human body and soul, his *nous* (intellect, spirit) was divine. This was seen as sundering the full identity of Christ's humanity from that of the rest of the human race, undermining the doctrine of salvation.

The Arian heresy had raised the issue of the relation of the Son to the Father. The major Christological controversies of succeeding centuries concerned the unity of the person of Christ and the relation between his divinity and his humanity. The different styles of scriptural exegesis associated with the scholars and teachers of ANTIOCH and ALEXANDRIA and the political rivalries of ROME and CONSTANTINOPLE and of Constantinople and Alexandria all influenced the nature and the progress of the controversies. In 431 the Council of Ephesus deposed Nestorius, bishop of Constantinople, a representative of the Antiochene tradition, and proclaimed the Virgin Mary THEOTOKOS. CYRIL OF ALEXANDRIA had taken the leading role in refuting and condemning Nestorius' theology. In 451 the Council of Chalcedon condemned the archimandrite EUTYCHES, already excommunicated by Flavian of Constantinople, together with Dioscoros of Alexandria who had supported him, and condemned outright the MONOPHYSITE doctrine of the one nature of Christ. Paradoxically, both CHALCEDONIANS and monophysites appealed to the authority of Cyril in defending their positions.

Imperial disquiet at the emergence of separated monophysite churches in Egypt and Syria led to a sequence of attempts to reunite Chalcedonians with their opponents. The condemnation of the 'Three Chapters' at the Second Council of Constantinople in 553 outraged those who were horrified at the posthumous anathematization of men who had died in the peace of the church and offered further offence to followers of Nestorius without resolving the schism between Chalcedonians and monophysites. The attempt to impose monoenergism or MONOTHELETISM failed equally, and the Third Council of Constantinople (680–1) finally condemned as heresy the doctrine that Christ has but a single will.

The controversy over ICONOCLASM also took on a Christological aspect with the proclamation of the worship of the sacred images as a witness to the Incarnation. The iconoclast controversy made explicit the intimate and necessary link between doctrine

120

and worship that is an important, if not always fully acknowledged, aspect of all stages of the Christological controversies.

The outcome of the Christological controversies of the fourth to seventh centuries was the emergence of four distinct families of churches: the Orthodox Catholic church of the seven councils; the Oriental Orthodox or monophysite churches, with which ARMENIAN CHRISTIANITY associated itself; the CHURCH OF THE EAST, widely known as NESTORIAN; and the Arian churches, which eventually passed from existence. With the demise of the Arian churches, the Orthodox Catholic tradition was the only church significantly represented in the West, though the unity between Catholic West and Orthodox East was soon under threat.

The official Christology of the Church of the East was systematically presented by BABAI the Great in the seventh century. It has sometimes been misunderstood as a simplistic assertion that in Christ there are two persons, the Son of God and the Son of Mary: the Christology of the Church of the East is in fact more subtle, asserting that there is in Christ a duality of natures (*qyānē*) and a duality of hypostases (*qnūmē*) but a single person (*parṣufā*). (*See* SYRIAN CHRISTIANITY.)

Central to Christology is the need to safeguard the reality of salvation in the account offered of the nature and person of the Saviour. The wide range of Christological theories propounded by individual thinkers and schools within the different families of churches have included many that ultimately call in question the true humanity or the full divinity of Christ, or the unity of the person of the incarnate Logos. The Christological disputes were not simply about doctrine; they were also and equally importantly about the nature and form of the worship, *proskynesis*, due to the TRINITY and to Christ as *theanthropos*, namely adoration, *latreia*, and of the relative worship due to the THEOTOKOS and the saints, and the derivative form of worship offered to the sacred ICONS and relics.

The affirmation that Christ is one person, *homoousios* (of same substance/essence) to the rest of humanity and *homoousios* to the Father and the Holy Spirit, is the kernel of Christological orthodoxy. In recent years irenic dialogue among the churches has resulted in an improved mutual understanding of their different Christological doctrines, and of the degree to which, in the main, they can be seen as diverse strategies for defending the double *homoousios* while attempting to construct a coherent metaphysical account of the person and nature of Christ in terms of the PHILOSOPHICAL VOCABULARY that was at hand.

The emergence of Christian dualist movements such as the PAULICIANS and the BOGOMILS, and much later the rise of the RUSSIAN SECTS, revived Christological positions canvassed in the gnosticism, MANICHEANISM and psilanthropism of earlier centuries, but had no significant influence on the theological thought of the major Eastern churches.

Zizioulas, J. D. (1985), *Being as Communion*. Crestwood, NY: St Vladimir's Seminary Press.
Young, F. (1983), *From Nicea to Chalcedon*. London: SCM Press.
Meyendorff, J. (1978), *Byzantine Theology*. Crestwood, NY: St Vladimir's Seminary Press.
Pelikan, J. (1977), *The Spirit of Eastern Christendom (600–1700)*. Chicago: University of Chicago Press.

Chesnut, R. C. (1976), *Three Monophysite Christologies*. Oxford: Oxford University Press.

Meyendorff, J. (1975), *Christ in Eastern Christian Thought*. Crestwood, NY: St Vladimir's Seminary Press.

Pelikan, J. (1971), *The Emergence of the Catholic Tradition*. Chicago. University of Chicago Press.

DM/KP

chrysography   Greek, 'writing in gold': the linear hatching in gold leaf in icon painting on Christ's garment, and to indicate the divine energies at the TRANSFIG-URATION. Gold generally indicates the presence of divinity, as in, for example, the halo or aureole of a saint.

See also ASSIST.

KP

Chrysostom of Smyrna (1867–1922)   Chrysostomos Kalaphatis. A modern NEW MARTYR or ETHNOMARTYR from Triglia on the Propontis shores of Bithynia. Chrysostom was sent to MACEDONIA in 1902 by the ECUMENICAL PATRIARCHATE. As metropolitan of Drama and Pyrsopolis, he opposed the expansion of the Bulgarian exarchate and championed the cause of reform within the OTTOMAN empire. His political stance led the Ottoman authorities to have him recalled to Istanbul in 1907, but they later sanctioned his transferral to Smyrna in 1910. Chrysostom angered the regime again by working to help Christian refugees made homeless by the turmoil in ASIA MINOR caused by the Balkan wars and the onset of the First World War. Condemned to internal exile, he returned to Smyrna to welcome the Greek troops in 1919. When the Turkish army retook Smyrna, Chrysostom was handed over to a mob and lynched as a collaborator. He had refused to leave his flock when he could, or to support the Kemalist cause. Chrysostom is commemorated on 10 September.

See also ASIA MINOR; PONTUS.

DB

Church of the East   One of the SYRIAN churches, most commonly known in the West as the NESTORIAN or ASSYRIAN church. The former name is now repudiated by the church itself. The Apostolic Catholic Assyrian Church of the East numbers its membership at *c*.350,000, of whom 110,000 live in Iraq, 40,000 elsewhere in the Middle East and 100,000 in the USA (*see* AMERICA). There are smaller communities in INDIA, Europe, RUSSIA, ARMENIA, GEORGIA, Canada and AUSTRALIA. This DIASPORA has for the most part come into being since the First World War when the Assyrians were displaced from their former lands in Turkey and Persia. Patriarch Mar Shimun XXIII, consecrated at age eleven in 1920, was deported from Iraq in 1933 and settled in the USA in 1940. The patriarchate has remained there ever since. Mar Shimun's successor Mar Dinkha IV (consecrated 1976) lives in Chicago. The old hereditary succession of PATRIARCH and bishops – the episcopate generally moving from uncle to nephew – has now been given up. After decades of isolation (marked by, for example, exclusion from the MIDDLE EAST COUNCIL OF CHURCHES), the church has now become an active participant in ecumenical affairs.

A smaller body, now known officially as the Ancient Church of the East, seceded from the patriarchate of Mar Shimun in 1968 and consecrated its own patriarch Mar Thoma Darmo, who rebelled against the system of hereditary succession and against the adoption in 1964 of the Gregorian CALENDAR and other modernizing measures, but his cause was joined by various other groups opposed to Mar Shimun. The church has c.75,000 members, of whom 45,000 are in Iraq and 20,000 in India. The present patriarch, Mar Addai II (1969–) has his see in Baghdad.

Coakley, J. F. and Parry, K., eds (1996), *The Church of the East: Life and Thought. Bulletin of the John Rylands University Library of Manchester* 78, 3.

JFC

classical names Many early saints bore names in common use from the classical period. Their names, like those of many biblical figures, became common Christian names. The calendar of saints includes, among many others, Achilles, Ares, Bakchos, Demetrios, Diogenes, Helen, Iphigenia, Jason, Olympias, Plato, Socrates, Sophocles, TELEMACHOS and Xenophon. The prestige of Hellenic association alongside attempts to capture and transform the classical heritage can be detected in Lives like those of Galaktion and Episteme which mirror pagan romances. Interestingly, some of the saints bear the names of deities of ancient mythology rather than derivatives, although this would have probably been unthinkable to communities worshipping those deities.

Classical names have been used throughout Christian history, becoming common in later centuries. Classical names then came to be attributed to relatively anonymous groups of martyrs. A group of forty martyrs commemorated on 10 April include classical Greek male names such as Homer, Pindar, Perikles and Epaminondas. A group of forty women martyrs commemorated on 1 September bear names such as Antigone, Theano and Sappho. Ancient Greek names are attributed to the 20,000 martyrs of Nicomedia (commemorated 28 December), including Odysseus, Hippokrates and Kybele. From such lists and from plundering the Western martyrology for saints with classical names, e.g. Paris (5 August), Patrocles (21 January), Priam (28 May), an attempt to underline Christian links with the ancient world is discernible. The lists also provide a Christian pedigree for names still popular among the Greeks in particular, and helped subvert the fashion prevalent since the Enlightenment for Balkan Christians to look for inspiration to antiquity rather than Byzantium. The older practice was for Christians not holding the name of a known saint to observe the Feast of All Saints as their nameday.
See also NAMES.

Platanitou, K. (1979), *Heortologion tes Orthodoxou Ekklesias*. Athens: n.p.

DB

Clement of Alexandria Lived in the later second century and was head of the catechetical school of ALEXANDRIA before ORIGEN. His *Paidagogos* or *Instructor* provides a manual of Christian life and behaviour. His *Stromateis* or *Miscellanies* discuss a diverse array of theological and disciplinary topics. Clement was a convert, and had studied Greek philosophy and especially PLATONISM. His writings show both considerable knowledge of and contempt for the Greek mystery religions, while he sees a parallel between the providential role of the divinely inspired Hebrew prophets and that of Greek philosophers and the Indian gymnosophists.

Ferguson, J., trans. (1991), *Clement of Alexandria: Stromateis, Books 1–3*. Washington, DC: Catholic University of America Press.
Lilla, S. R. C. (1971), *Clement of Alexandria: A Study in Christian Platonism and Gnosticism*. Oxford Theological Monographs. Oxford: Oxford University Press.
Chadwick, H. (1966), *Early Christian Thought and the Classical Tradition: Studies in Justin, Clement and Origen*. Oxford: Oxford University Press.
Osborn, E. F. (1957), *The Philosophy of Clement of Alexandria*. Texts and Studies, n.s., 3.

E/DM

communicatio idiomatum Latin; Greek: *antidosis idiomaton*, 'exchange of properties'. If Christ is of two natures united hypostatically in one person, a single person, the God-man, Jesus Christ, is the subject and possessor of both divine and human attributes. He can be designated by terms that refer to him in virtue of divinity – Word, Son of God, Logos – and by terms that refer to him in virtue of humanity – Son of Mary, Nazarene: all these terms none the less designate the same person, whose divine attributes can be predicated of the Nazarene and whose human attributes can be predicated of the Word of God. The Son of Mary is eternal; the Word died on Calvary.

Mary was affirmed at the Council of Ephesus (431) to be THEOTOKOS, one who gave birth to God. CYRIL OF ALEXANDRIA, in a letter sent early in 430 and approved at Ephesus, reminded Nestorius, generally an opponent of the *communicatio idiomatum*, of this, pointing out to him that the holy fathers did not hesitate 'to call the holy Virgin Theotokos, not that the nature of the Word or of his deity took its origin from the holy Virgin'. In a parallel way, Cyril declared in his Twelfth Anathema that 'if any does not confess that the Word of God suffered in the flesh and was crucified in the flesh and tasted death in the flesh, becoming the firstborn from the dead, according as he is life and the giver of life as God, let him be anathema'. The BIBLE uses similar language: 1 Corinthians 2: 8 speaks of the Lord of Glory being crucified.

Some writers of the Alexandrian tradition speak of the transfer of properties between the natures. More generally this is denied, especially clearly by JOHN OF DAMASCUS. A reason for this apparent contradiction is to be found in a subtle different of PHILOSO-PHICAL VOCABULARY: many Alexandrian writers follow Cyril in using the term *physis* to refer to the concretized, individuated nature, the living person who bears all the attributes of both divinity and humanity, whereas John of Damascus means by *physis* deity as such, humanity as such, and in the Incarnation these remain unchanged.

See also PERICHORESIS.

McGuckin, J. A. (1994), *St Cyril of Alexandria: The Christological Controversy*. Leiden: Brill.
Meyendorff, J. (1975), *Christ in Eastern Christian Thought*. Crestwood, NY: St Vladimir's Seminary Press.

KP/DM

Communion of the Apostles An icon showing the twelve apostles waiting to receive communion from the hands of Christ, who is shown twice, giving himself as bread to one group, as wine to the other. Two ANGELS serve as deacons and holding

RHIPIDIA. The depiction shown here is based on a thirteenth-century wall painting from the Church of Saint Clement, OHRID.

KP

Constantine the Great Roman emperor and saint. Constantine, the son of Constantius Chlorus (r. 305–6) and Helena, was proclaimed emperor (Augustus) in York in Britain on 25 July 306, sole emperor in the West after the battle of the Milvian Bridge (312) and sole emperor of the entire Roman empire in 324. Constantine was an able general and an imaginative administrator, active in the reorganization of the structure and government of the empire.

Constantine favoured the Christian church, having, according to accounts left by EUSEBIUS OF CAESAREA, who knew him well, and by Lactantius (240–320), who wrote within six years of the event, received a divine revelation before the battle of the Milvian Bridge that led him to victory under a sign derived from the CROSS. In 325 he presided over the ECUMENICAL COUNCIL of Nicea, using his imperial office to attempt to enforce the unity of the church. He restored to the church property it had lost in the period of persecution and exempted clergy from the financial burdens of public office, though heretics and schismatics were denied this and other privileges. Sunday was given a special status. On his deathbed in 337 Constantine was finally baptized by EUSEBIUS OF NICOMEDIA.

Constantine founded a new city for himself based on ancient Byzantium. CONSTANTINOPLE was ornamented with new and splendid secular buildings and with three major churches. When the city was dedicated on 11 May 330 it was not unambiguously a Christian city, but it was already the emperor's chosen residence, where he gave the Christian church his patronage and favour. Constantine and his mother Helena are honoured on 21 May.

Barnes, T. D. (1981), *Constantine and Eusebius*. Cambridge, Mass.: Harvard University Press.

Ostrogorsky, G. (1968), *History of the Byzantine State*, 2nd edn. Oxford: Blackwell.

DM

Constantinople In the seventh century BC Greek colonists from Megara established 'Byzantion' at the opening of the the Bosphorus into the Sea of Marmara, where the

Golden Horn provides a superb, easily defended harbour. Byzantium soon found itself embroiled in conflict between Persia and the Greek states, then between Athens and Sparta. Philip of Macedon saw the strategic importance of Byzantium and in 340–339 BC besieged the city and attempted unsuccessfully to storm it by night. The Byzantines attributed his failure to Hecate, their tutelar goddess, whose lunar crescent was one of the city's principal symbols. From about 150 BC Byzantium was allied to Rome, but supported the losing side in the conflict between Caesar and Pompey, and then supported Pescennius Niger in the civil war of AD 193–7, with the result that Septimius Severus (193–211) laid siege to the city for three years, took it, and degraded it to a mere village, though he later rebuilt it as the city Antonia.

In the civil wars following the reign of Diocletian (241–305) the city was held by Maximian and then Licinius, until Constantine the Great (307–37) expelled Licinius in 324. Constantine refounded the city, rededicating it as Constantinople in 330. Since the city was to share the dignity of Rome as capital, appropriate public buildings were erected, including a senate house and a basilica. Constantine retained the great hippodrome of Severus' city and built his own imperial palace nearby, with a direct link to the imperial box. The palace grew over the centuries into a rambling complex of buildings. Like the hippodrome, the baths of Zeuxippus survived from the city of Severus. The walls defending the city from the Sea of Marmara, probably raised in the second century, were improved in the eighth and ninth centuries. Sea walls along the Golden Horn and the land walls extending across the north of the city date from the fifth century and are associated with Theodosius II (408–50).

The main street of Constantine's city, the Mese (now Divan Yolu) still survives, as does the foundation column of the city, a porphyry pillar once surmounted by an image of the Sun god and hallowed by both Christian and pagan sacred objects. Constantine beautified his city with statues and artworks gathered from across his empire, and established a number of churches, most notably Holy Apostles and, on the site of the temple of Aphrodite, Hagia Eirene, Holy Peace, celebrating Christ, the Peace of God, as divine protector of the *Pax Romana*.

Constantine legalized Christianity. He had presided over the ECUMENICAL COUN-CIL of Nicea in 325, five years before the dedication of the city. Christians like EUSEBIUS OF CAESAREA were in favour at court. Before his death Constantine was baptized. Under his successors Christianity became the religion of the empire, pagan cults were prohibited and Christian bishops were given high rank and grave legal responsibilities. At the Council of Constantinople of 381 in the reign of Theodosius I, the bishop of the Eastern capital was given primacy of honour after the bishop of ROME, a decision confirmed at Chalcedon in 451 and at FLORENCE in 1439.

Imperial and aristocratic patronage gave the city a wealth of churches, shrines and monasteries. The great cathedral of Hagia Sophia, DIVINE WISDOM, was dedicated in 360 under Constantine's son Constantius II (337–61), burnt in 404, restored and rededicated in 415 under Theodosius II (408–50) and burnt again in the Nika riots of 532, though a fragment of its porch survives. Justinian I (527–65) had the architects Isidore of Miletus and Anthemius of Tralles build a new church, the beauty and majesty of which proclaim the glory of Christ, the incarnate Wisdom of God, and of the Emperor, his vicegerent.

The civic manifestation of the Divine Wisdom was represented by public works such as the great aqueduct of Valens (364–78), in use into the nineteenth century, the underground cisterns, the public squares, the free rations of bread, wine, oil and even meat offered to citizens, the hospitals, hostels, baths, soup-kitchens and *diakoniai* (charitable institutions) that were a feature of Constantinopolitan life through the centuries. The emperor in his sacred palace lived by rigid ceremonial befitting the living icon of the PANTOCRATOR.

Many aspects of civic life were influenced or even organized by the circus factions, the 'blues' and 'greens'. Professional guilds, religious brotherhoods, charitable associations, and the monasteries and convents in the city exercised an important influence.

In the medieval period Constantinople was the largest and the richest city known to Europeans; it was the city *par excellence*, ten times more populous than any Western rival, a cosmopolitan city, a centre of commerce and trade, its coinage the most trusted and valued. Mercenaries, many from northern Europe, served in Byzantine defence forces and in the imperial guard. The splendour of public buildings was matched by the wealth of public art in the city, the magnificence of the rites, the mosaic, the paintings, the MUSIC of its many churches and the multitude of sacred relics preserved and venerated in them. The city was a famous centre of learning and culture. Classical literature was read and studied, Greek medicine and mathematics flourished, theology used the PHILOSOPHICAL VOCABULARY of the Greek philosophers to present Christian doctrine and explore its significance. Literacy was common, and Homer its vehicle, often taught in the family, though elementary education was also provided by schools and monasteries. More advanced education was provided by schools of grammar and rhetoric, and higher education in a variety of disciplines was offered, in some periods at the university, founded or refounded by Theodosius II in 425, with no fewer than thirty-one professors, and by Constantine IX in 1047, in other periods by a range of specialized private schools, and at the Patriarchal Academy. Under Heraclius (610–41) Latin ceased to be an official language of the empire, and it soon faded as an object of study. Greek medicine was taught in hospitals and privately. Law held a special place in higher education, since legislation and codification of law was a major task under several emperors, not least Justinian I (527–65), whose *Corpus juris civilis* systematized Roman jurisprudence, and Leo VI (886–912) and Basil II (976–1025), who updated the legal code. Canon law too was important, since the church courts played a greater role than in the West, and in some cases of overlapping jurisdiction received appeals from the civil court.

The sack of Constantinople in 1204 during the Fourth CRUSADE inflicted terrible damage. Treasures were destroyed or stolen. When the Palaiologos Emperor Michael VIII reclaimed the city in 1261, large areas of it were virtually abandoned. It was now a drain on the state's purse rather than a source of wealth. None the less the Palaiologan period (1261–1453) saw a cultural renascence in Constantinople. The mosaics and paintings of the Chora monastic church, Kariye Camii, restored by Theodore Metochites (1270–1332), and the exquisite mosaics and delicate architecture of the fourteenth-century parecclesion which the widow of Michael Glabas added after 1304 to the Pammakaristos church, present vivid evidence of the period's artistic attainments.

The OTTOMAN conquest of 1453 ended an empire which had become virtually co-extensive with the city. Sultan Mehmet II Fatih at once took steps to repopulate the city, and imported many new Greek immigrants. Greeks, Armenians and other

Christian communities of the city now lived as members of communities defined by religion. Access to the ruling class depended on conversion to Islam.

Under Islamic rule the Christians of Constantinople shared in Ottoman cultural life to varying degrees. Many were bilingual; some, of KARAMANLI origin, spoke Turkish. Christian musicians, including the psaltai, the cantors of the patriarchal church, became court musicians to the sultans, and some, like Peter Lampadarios in the eighteenth century, were expert in Ottoman Perso-Arabic classical music: Peter was even an expert on Islamic prayer chant and dervish music.

The Christians retained many of their churches, though some, including Hagia Sophia, became mosques or were put to other uses; Hagia Eirene eventually became an arsenal. The Greek patriarchate was moved to Holy Apostles, then to Pammakaristos in the Phanar quarter, until 1591, when Sultan Murat III (1574–95) converted that church into a mosque to celebrate victories in Georgia and Azerbaijan. For a while the little church of St Demetrius Kanavou housed the patriarchate, which in 1720 was relocated to the newly rebuilt basilica of St George, where it remains.

Over the years the Christians lost all save one of their pre-conquest churches. St Mary of the Mongols, a little trefoil church with a dome supported on four slender pillars, was safe since it possessed its own title deeds. One other, the Peribleptos, was in Armenian hands for many years. New churches were built, but they were low, unassuming buildings. In the nineteenth century, however, impressive churches were constructed in Galata and Pera, the areas dominated by Western European embassies, culminating in the tall, decidedly Western Hagia Triada (1880), towering high over Taksim Square. There are many Western churches in the area. In the traditionally Jewish area of Balat is the Bulgarian church of St Stephen, imported from Vienna in prefabricated iron sections and erected in 1871. The Armenian patriarchate is located in Kumkapı with its church of the Blessed Virgin (1820).

A wealthy Christian class grew up under Ottoman rule; the Greek Phanariot families – aristocrats, great merchants, senior professionals – kept alive the MEGALE IDEA, the dream of the imperial destiny of the Greeks. A more concrete project of at least establishing an independent state became the focus of political planning in the Greek and other Christian communities. When the independence movements took up arms in the revolutions of the early nineteenth century, the ETHNOMARTYR Patriarch Gregory V and many of his bishops were executed; the patriarch was hanged at the patriarchate's gates on 10 April 1821, still vested from the celebration of Pascha. The slow crumbling of the Ottoman empire placed the Christian communities of the city in a difficult position which the final collapse of the sultanate and the rise of a secular Turkish state did little to alleviate.

By 1923, when Constantinople officially became Istanbul and Ankara became the capital, the future of the Christian communities was unclear. In the event, the Greek community was to be reduced to a tiny fragment: many fled in the aftermath of the Greek invasion of 1921, many as a result of the violence and the destruction of Greek property that occurred in the mid-twentieth century, especially the riots which accompanied several stages in the evolving ethnic problems of CYPRUS. By the late 1990s the Christian Greeks in the city probably numbered under two thousand. The number of Arab Christians coming from the patriarchate of Antioch has, however, increased.

Despite all the changes the city has undergone, many ancient church buildings remain. The fifth-century Studios monastery became a mosque under Beyezit II (1481–1512), but fires in the eighteenth century and an earthquake in the nineteenth reduced it to a ruin. The early sixth-century church of SS Sergius and Bacchus, a charming but oddly irregular octagon, is now a mosque, but the entablature with an inscription in honour of Justinian I and Theodora is are still visible. Hagia Sophia was made a museum by Atatürk, though there is constant pressure to return it to use as a mosque.

The Bodrum Cami, formerly the church of the Myrelaion monastery founded by Romanos I Lecapenus (co-emperor 919–44), is in poor condition, having been damaged by fire in the thirteenth century and again in 1911. Its odd substructure suggests that it may have been intended as an imperial crypt. Feneri Isa Camii, also in a partly ruinous state, is formed from two adjacent Byzantine churches, the tenth-century THEOTOKOS church of Constantine Lips and the later church of JOHN THE BAPTIST. Gül Camii was originally the church of Saint Theodora (possibly eleventh century), converted to a mosque by Selim II (1566–74). Kalenderhane Camii is a domed cross-shaped church. Under Latin rule it was used by Roman Catholic friars, and it contains the remains of a remarkable thirteenth-century fresco cycle of the life of St Francis. Investigation has uncovered other mosaics and paintings, including a mosaic of the Archangel Michael.

The Greek Orthodox patriarch of Constantinople, the ECUMENICAL PATRIARCH, remains the senior hierarch of the EASTERN ORTHODOX churches. His flock in Istanbul and even in the whole of Turkey is now tiny, but outside of the traditional territories of the Orthodox it is growing. There are substantial churches under his authority in AMERICA, AUSTRALIA, the BRITISH ISLES and Western Europe. New hierarchies have been established in Italy and Hong Kong. His role in the development of ECUMENISM has been particularly significant.

See also SEPTEMBER EVENTS; THRACE.

Nicol, D. M. (1993), *The Last Centuries of Byzantium, 1261–1451*. Cambridge: Cambridge University Press.
Imber, C. (1990), *The Ottoman Empire, 1300–1481*. Istanbul: Isis.
Mainstone, R. J. (1988), *Hagia Sophia*. London: Thames & Hudson.
Bryer, A. A. M. and Lowry, H., eds (1986), *Continuity and Change in Late Byzantine and Early Ottoman Society*. Birmingham: Birmingham University.
Mango, C. (1986), *Byzantine Architecture*. London: Faber.
Belting, H. et al. (1978), *The Mosaics and Frescoes of S. Mary Pammakaristos (Fethiye Camii) at Istanbul*. Washington, DC: Dumbarton Oaks.
Runciman, S. (1968), *The Great Church in Captivity*. Cambridge: Cambridge University Press.
Sherrard, P. (1965), *Constantinople, Iconography of a Sacred City*. London: Oxford University Press.
Janin, R. (1950), *Constantinople Byzantine: développement urbain et répertoire topographique*, Paris: Archives de l'orient Chrétien, 4.
Hearsey, J. (1963), *The City of Constantine 324–1453*. London: John Murray.

                                                                                    DM

Coptic Christianity   The words 'Copt' and 'Coptic', derived from the Arabic *qibṭ*, which is in turn derived from the Greek word for Egypt (*Aigyptos*), have been used in

Latin and modern European languages since the sixteenth century to designate the modern Christian inhabitants of Egypt and the language used by them in their liturgy. The Arabs used the word of the native Christian inhabitants of Egypt and it was also used in late medieval Egypt, especially in the Mamluk period (1249–1517), to denote Muslims of Coptic (as distinguished from Arabic) descent. Westerners have used it, inaccurately, to mean the church in ETHIOPIA, which, prior to 1959, was dependent on the church in Egypt. The Arabic word *qibṭ* is used by the Coptic (Egyptian) Christians as the equivalent of the Coptic word for Egypt (*cheme*). With the increased flow of Coptic manuscripts into Europe in the eighteenth and nineteenth centuries and the more scientific study of the language, the word 'Coptic' came to be applied to the Egyptian language in all its dialects as spoken and written from the third century of the present era onwards, independently of the religious association.

According to the church historian Eusebius (*Ecclesiastical History* 2: 16, 24), reflecting the traditions of his day (early fourth century), the evangelist Mark first preached the gospel in ALEXANDRIA, and the Coptic church claims an unbroken succession of PATRIARCHS from that time to the present. Although manuscript evidence reveals that Christianity was firmly established in Egypt in the early second century, it is only in the last quarter of that century that it emerges into the full light of history with the figures of the catechists Pantaenus, CLEMENT OF ALEXANDRIA and ORIGEN, and the bishop Demetrius I (188–230), as well as heretics such as Basileides. By the time of the peace of the church under CONSTANTINE and the Council of Nicea (325) the number of bishops in Egypt had notably increased. (*See* ECUMENICAL COUNCILS.) Under ATHANASIUS another diocese was established at Philae in southern Egypt. The Egyptian church was unique among the Oriental churches in the monarchical structure that it developed under the bishop of Alexandria. From the third century onwards it was the custom of the bishops of Alexandria to send a circular letter to all the bishops of Egypt announcing the date of Easter and dealing with other doctrinal and disciplinary matters. Tension caused by this structure may have contributed to the Meletian schism that began during the reign of Alexander I (312–26) when the bishop of Lycopolis, Meletius, ordained other bishops. By long-established tradition all the bishops in Egypt are ordained by the bishop of Alexandria. Since the fourth century the church in Egypt has dated events from the accession of Diocletian as emperor in 284, heralding a period later referred to as the age of the martyrs because of the numerous victims of persecution, including the patriarch Peter (d. 311), at the beginning of the fourth century. (*See* CALENDAR.)

Greek had been spoken in Egypt since the conquest of the country by Alexander the Great in 332 BC and the foundation the following year of the city of Alexandria, which soon became one of the principal cities of the Hellenistic world. Greek-speaking communities were to be found in towns throughout the Nile valley and Christianity seems to have spread first among the Greek-speaking population in these towns. There is reason to believe that, at least by the second and third centuries, there was a fairly large and prosperous bilingual population of native Egyptian origin. The older forms of writing the Egyptian language, hieroglyphic and hieratic, had long since given way to the demotic script for practical purposes, but it too had given way to Greek for most administrative purposes. The creation of the Coptic script in the middle or second half of the third century seems to have been a deliberate attempt on the part of a bilingual educated elite to revive the Egyptian language as a literary medium. This script made use of the Greek alphabet together with several letters borrowed from the demotic tongue to represent sounds not found in the Greek alphabet. Documents using this script exist from the fourth century in a variety of Coptic dialects including Fayumic, Achmimic and Sahidic. The last of these quickly became the standard literary dialect, and the first major literary work to have been produced in this language appears to have been the translation of the Christian scriptures. This form of writing was also employed by others besides orthodox Christians, as MANICHAEAN, gnostic and other documents testify. Most of the early Coptic literature consists in translations from Greek works, but some early Christian apocryphal writings may have been composed in Coptic. Original Christian literature in Sahidic dating from the fourth to seventh centuries includes many lives of saints, encomiums, homilies, catecheses, monastic rules and letters.

From at least the early fourth century the monastic movement became an important feature of the life of the Egyptian church and has remained such throughout its history. The monastic movement assumed a variety of external forms ranging from the solitary hermit to highly organized cenobitic communities, and this variety is found throughout the Nile valley as well as in the delta from the beginning of this period. Two names in particular are associated with the rise of MONASTICISM: those of Antony (d. 356) and Pachomius (d. 346), who became the patrons of the eremitical and cenobitical forms of monasticism respectively. Letters attributed to them and to the successors of Pachomius, Theodore and Horsiesius are among the earliest items of Coptic literature. By the middle of the fourth century many thousands had taken up the monastic life and the fame of the monks spread beyond Egypt, attracting many recruits from other parts of the Roman empire. Soon after the death of Antony, Athanasius wrote his Life, which became the first great classic of monastic literature and was quickly translated into many other languages. The monks of Scetis and Cellia became particularly famous outside Egypt because of the accounts of foreigners such as Palladius, but the most important Coptic monastic writer was undoubtedly Shenute of Atripe, who, however, remained unknown outside of Egypt until modern times.

Due partly to the strategic importance of the city of Alexandria but also to the vigour of the literary tradition of the Egyptian church, the patriarchs of Alexandria played an important role during the fourth and fifth centuries in the affairs of the church outside as well as inside Egypt. This is particularly true of Athanasius, whose long reign (326–73) established him as the champion of the orthodox faith of Nicea against the Arian heresy. Theophilus (385–412) is known chiefly for his role in the Origenist controversy and in the deposition of JOHN CHRYSOSTOM, the archbishop of Constantinople. His nephew CYRIL OF ALEXANDRIA (412–44) became a principal protagonist in the conflict over Nestorius and a dominant figure at the Council of Ephesus (431), which he attended with an entourage of fifty bishops. His theological writings were an important factor in the refusal of the Egyptian church under Patriarch Dioscoros (451–4) to accept the innovative language of the Council of Chalcedon and the Tome of Leo. Athanasius, Cyril and Dioscoros are all revered as saints by the Coptic church.

The Council of Chalcedon (451) proved to be a turning point in the relationship of the Egyptian church with the other churches. From the point of view of the Alexandrian Christology loyal to Cyril's formulation, the definition of the two natures of

Christ by Chalcedon was essentially the adoption of the Nestorian heresy and therefore a denial of the full reality of the Incarnation. From the point of view of the defenders of Chalcedon, the Alexandrian–Egyptian theology was MONOPHYSITE, that is, it did not distinguish the two natures of Christ, divine and human, but recognized only a single nature (*mia physis* in Cyril's terminology). The dispute revolved around the sense of the word *physis* (nature), and neither side was able to recognize that the other was using the term in a different sense. In the course of the century and more that followed, various attempts were made to preserve the unity of the church (and the empire), by devising compromise formulas, by controlling the appointment of the patriarch of Alexandria or by force. The Egyptian church was not alone in refusing to accept Chalcedon, and the long exile of the most important literary exponent of the monophysite theology, the patriarch SEVERUS OF ANTIOCH, spent in Egypt (518–38), helped to reinforce the resistance of the Egyptian church. Severus is revered as a saint by the Coptic church and is mentioned in the liturgy together with Athanasius, Cyril and Dioscurus, among others.

The patriarchate of Theodosius I (536–67) was particularly decisive for the formation of the Coptic church. When he refused to subscribe to the formula of Chalcedon, Theodosius was brought to Constantinople by the emperor Justinian and kept under house arrest for over thirty years. The Egyptian church did not recognize the validity of sacraments administered by those who subscribed to the formula of Chalcedon, whom they regarded as heretics. Therefore they would not accept ordination from the patriarch imposed by Constantinople. This caused the gradual depletion of the hierarchy, and the resulting crisis led to establishment of a separate hierarchy and patriarch through the intervention of JACOB BARADAEUS, consecrated bishop by Theodosius in 543 with a roving commission. So successful was Jacob in establishing a monophysite clergy during his constant journeys throughout the Middle East that these churches became known as Jacobite. From the time of Patriarch Peter IV (576–78) there existed in Egypt two competing patriarchs and hierarchies, the CHALCEDONIAN (or MELK-ITE) and the non-Chalcedonian or Jacobite. The vast majority of the people in the Egyptian church recognized only the latter and the former was maintained in power only in the city of Alexandria with the aid of the civil and military authority. The non-Chalcedonian patriarch had to take refuge in one of the monasteries outside Alexandria. The long patriarchate of Damian (578–605), a Syrian by birth, was particularly important for consolidating the non-Chalcedonian hierarchy. A last but futile attempt to force the Egyptian church to accept Chalcedon was made with the appointment of the Melkite patriarch Cyrus al-Muqawqas ('the Caucasian', 631–41) with full civil and military as well as religious power. The Arab conquest of Egypt in 641–2 finally put an end to the Byzantine efforts to control the church and opened a new era in the history of the Egyptian church. There has continued to be a Melkite (Greek Orthodox) patriarch of Alexandria, although during the Ottoman period he was obliged to live in Constantinople. It is important to emphasize that the original division was not along lines of Greek *v.* Copt: all of the original champions of the monophysite cause, for example, were speakers and writers of Greek.

It is estimated that at the time of the Arab invasion at least two-thirds of the Egyptian population was Christian, but the pressure exerted to convert to Islam in the subsequent centuries resulted in the church being reduced to a minority status in the country. It also resulted in the gradual disappearance of Greek as a spoken and even as a liturgical language, and the substitution of the Bohairic dialect of Coptic as the liturgical language and eventually of Arabic as the spoken language of the Christian population.

At the beginning of Islamic rule, despite the imposition of the poll tax (*jizyah*) levied on non-Muslims ('people of the book'; *see* AHL AL-KITAB), the Christians enjoyed religious freedom and the Patriarch Benjamin was received with honour by the conqueror 'Amr ibn al-'Āṣ. However, in 706 a series of laws was introduced to encourage Arabization and Islamization of the population, including a law requiring the use of Arabic in public documents and a decree ordering the destruction of Christian ICONS. The latter led to revolt, which was repressed with bloodshed. In 750 Egypt passed from Umayyad rule (Damascus) to that of the Abbasids (Baghdad). A series of Coptic revolts led to waves of repression which in turn led to numerous conversions to Islam, with the result that by the middle of the ninth century the Coptic Christians had become a minority. Although the rule of the Fatimids (969–1171) as such was not hostile towards the Copts, one of the most serious persecutions took place under Caliph al-Ḥākim (996–1021), who ordered the destruction of the churches and the confiscation of their property. The Coptic population continued to decrease and the language itself began to die out.

In this situation the monasteries, particularly those of the Wādī-al-Naṭrūn, the Red Sea monasteries of Antony and Paul, and the White Monastery near Sohag, played an important role in the preservation of the Coptic heritage. Here the earlier literature was collected and copied for preservation. From the ninth to the eleventh century the majority of the patriarchs came from the monastery of Abu-Makar in the Wādī al-Naṭrūn; it was this predominance which led to the adoption, noted above, of the Bohairic dialect of the region as the liturgical language of the Coptic church. This period also saw the beginning of Arabic Coptic literature, of which one of the earliest and most important works is the *History of the Patriarchs* associated with the name of SEVERUS IBN AL MUQAFFA', which represents a tradition of historical writing continued by later authors that is our main source for Coptic history. Another important monument of Coptic literature in Arabic is the work on *The Churches and Monasteries of Egypt* by ABU AL-MAKARIM (but attributed erroneously in the English translation to ABU SALIH THE ARMENIAN). In this period also Arabic was introduced into the liturgy and from the late medieval period onwards the liturgical manuscripts tend to be in both Arabic and Coptic (Bohairic). The situation of the Copts in Egypt did not change significantly in the subsequent periods of Muslim rule (under the Ayyubids, Mamluks and Ottomans), throughout which, despite sporadic waves of persecution, Copts often held important administrative posts.

The modern era for the Copts began with the French invasion under Bonaparte in 1798, and the rule of Mohammed Ali permitted them to be reintegrated into the national life of the country and eventually to receive equal recognition before the law. The patriarchate of CYRIL IV (1854–61) marked an important step in the revival of Coptic institutions and the promotion of education. More recently, the revival in the Coptic monasteries during the last thirty years has had important effects throughout the life of the Coptic church. In recent years the rise of Islamic fundamentalism has caused tensions and even led to the house arrest of the patriarch,

Pope SHENOUDA III, from 1981 to 1985. (*See* COPTS AND ISLAMIC FUNDAMENT-ALISM SINCE 1952.)

The history of the COPTIC LITURGY (especially the surviving manuscripts) is insufficiently studied for a clear account to be given of the stages of its development. The liturgical language of the Egyptian church had been Greek from the beginning and Greek continued to be used in the liturgy, at least in part, long after the Arab invasion. In the eighth century the patriarchs were still sending their festal letters in Greek to other parts of Egypt. But there is also evidence that Coptic (Sahidic) was being introduced into the liturgy in the seventh century. It is not clear that there was ever a completely Sahidic liturgy or that there was uniform liturgical practice in the Coptic church before the time of the patriarch Gabriel II (1130–44), who made Bohairic the liturgical language and forbade the use of anaphoras other than those transmitted under the names of Basil, Gregory and Mark/Cyril. By this time Arabic was already entering into the celebration of the liturgy. The decree of Gabriel V in 1411 seems to have given a definitive form to the liturgy; by this time it had already undergone certain SYRIAN and even Byzantine influences despite the separation from Constantinople. In addition to the eucharist, the Coptic church knows the sacraments of baptism, chrism, penance, marriage, orders and anointing of the sick. The liturgical books include the EUCHOLOGION, the lectionary (*katameros*), the synaxary (lives of the saints), HOROLOGION (canonical hours), the Difnar (antiphonal), the sacramentary and the pontifical, among others.

The Coptic calendar is punctuated by a number of periods of fasting. The church celebrates fourteen feasts of the Lord, seven major and seven minor, and five major feasts of the Virgin Mary, as well as feasts of the saints and angels.

From ancient times PILGRIMAGES, often lasting as long as a week and connected with a fair, have been an important feature of popular religious culture in the Coptic church. In ancient times the most important pilgrimage centre was that of St Menas at Maryut near Alexandria. More than sixty pilgrimage centres exist, including that of St Menas, that of the Virgin Mary at Musturud, Mar Jirjis at Mit Damsis, Sitt Dimyanah near Bilgas and Deir el-Muharraq. Some sites are identified with the sojourn of the Holy Family in Egypt, a source of popular devotion already in antiquity.

Estimates of the number of members of the the Coptic Orthodox church vary considerably (from 4 million to 8 million) because of the lack of exact population figures for Egypt. It is undoubtedly the largest Christian community in the Middle East. The church organization includes some twenty dioceses in Egypt as well as dioceses outside Egypt in North AMERICA, East AFRICA, France, JERUSALEM, NUBIA and Khartoum because of the large number of Copts who have emigrated since the 1970s. By 1995 there were over forty Coptic communities in the USA, nine in Canada, fourteen in AUSTRALIA and nine in Great Britain. There are also Coptic communities with resident priests in other European countries including Austria, Italy and Switzerland. There are about 1,500 married priests in the church in Egypt. The bishops by ancient tradition are not married and are usually drawn from the monks. In addition to the diocesan bishops and their auxiliaries, there are a number of bishops with special responsibilities such as ecumenical affairs, youth and higher education. The church maintains schools and seminaries in Egypt and conducts an extensive Sunday school programme. The patriarch is chosen from one of three candidates selected by an assembly composed of the bishops, representatives of the clergy, the monks and laymen. The final selection is made by a child who draws the name of one of the three candidates. The present patriarch is Shenouda III, elected in 1973, under whose leadership ecumenical dialogue has been carried on with the Roman Catholic church, the EASTERN ORTHODOX church, the Anglican communion, and the Evangelical and Reformed churches.

In addition to the Coptic Orthodox church there is a relatively small body that follows the Coptic rite but is united with the Roman Catholic church. Although Franciscans are known to have been in Egypt earlier, the continuous presence of the Catholics in Egypt in modern times dates to the Franciscan mission in Cairo in 1630, followed by the Jesuits in 1697. Vicars-apostolic have been appointed since 1741 for Catholics of the Coptic rite which at that time numbered about 2,000. Pope Leo XII erected a Coptic patriarchate in 1824 but did not name a patriarch. Leo XIII named the first Catholic patriarch, Cyril Makarios, in 1899; he was deposed in 1910, but a second was not named until 1947. Today the church has six dioceses and about 200 priests, with 100 Coptic parishes and a total membership of about 150,000 members.

Although numerous Protestant bodies are represented in Egypt, the only one that defines itself as Coptic is the COPTIC EVANGELICAL CHURCH, founded by the United Presbyterian Church in North America in 1854 and completely independent since 1957. The church has about 250 churches and 200 prayer centres, serving a community of about 250,000 with about 340 pastors, and maintains the Evangelical Theological Seminary in Cairo and a large publishing house.

Gerhards, A. and Brakmann, H., eds (1994), *Die koptische Kirche: Einführung in das ägyptische Christentum*. Stuttgart: Kohlhammer.

Atiya, A. S., ed. (1991), *The Coptic Encyclopedia*, 7 vols. New York: Macmillan.

Cannuyer, C. (1990), *Les Coptes*. Turnhout: Brepols.

Heijer, J. den (1989), *Mawhub ibn Mansur ibn Mufarrig et l'historiographie copto-arabe. Etude sur la composition de l'Histoire des Patriarches d'Alexandrie*. CSCO. Louvain.

Bourguet, P. du (1988), *Les Coptes*, 2nd edn. Paris: Presses Universitaires de France.

Müller, C. D. G. (1979), 'La position de l'Egypt chrétienne dans l'orient ancien', *Le Muséon* 92, pp. 105–25.

Meinardus, O. (1977), *Christian Egypt Ancient and Modern*, 2nd edn. Cairo: American University in Cairo Press.

Burmester, O. H. E. (1967), *The Egyptian or Coptic Church: A Detailed Description of her Liturgical Services and the Rites and Ceremonies Observed in the Administration of her Sacraments*. Cairo: Societé d'Archéologie Copte.

Severus of Ashmunein (1910), *History of the Patriarchs of Alexandria*, ed. B. Evetts. Patrologia Orientalis 1. Paris: Firmin-Didot.

Evetts, B. T. A. and Butler, A. J. (1895), *The Churches and Monasteries of Egypt and some Neighboring Countries Attributed to Abu Salih, the Armenian*. Oxford: Clarendon Press.

MS

Coptic Congress of Assyut, 1911   Muslim–Christian tensions in Egypt, exacerbated by the assassination in 1910 of Butros Ghali, Coptic prime minister of Egypt, along with a perceived lack of unity within the Egyptian Coptic community, were the catalysts for the Coptic Congress of Assyut. Convened on 6–8 March 1911 with reluctant permission from Coptic Patriarch CYRIL V and the Egyptian government, this congress brought Copts together not only as members of a religious community, but also as Egyptians. Issues raised included a call for an end to religious discrimination in state employment and education; proportionate representation in parliament; and a Sunday holiday for Copts.

See also COPTIC CHRISTIANITY.

Bahr, S. (1991), 'Coptic Congress of Asyut', *Coptic Encyclopedia* 3, pp. 602–3.
Carter, B. L. (1986), *The Copts in Egyptian Politics*, pp. 9–15. London and Sydney: Croom Helm.

MJB/SHG

Coptic Evangelical church A member of the World Council of Churches (since 1963) and the MIDDLE EAST COUNCIL OF CHURCHES (since 1974), the Coptic Evangelical church was established as a Presbyterian national church in Egypt by the United Presbyterian Church in North America in 1854. The Synod of the Nile of the Evangelical Church in Egypt includes some eight presbyteries. It is difficult to establish accurate membership statistics for Christian churches in the Middle East; but the Coptic Evangelical church certainly is one of the largest Protestant churches in the region today; it is also a major Christian publisher there.

See also EASTERN CHRISTIAN.

Habib, S. (1991), 'Coptic Evangelical Church', *Coptic Encyclopedia* 2, pp. 603–4.
Skreslet, S. H., II (1986), 'The American Presbyterian Mission in Egypt: Significant Factors in its Establishment', *Journal of Presbyterian History* 64, pp. 83–95.

MJB/SHG

Coptic liturgy The relationship between Coptic, Syrian and Byzantine liturgies has long been debated. Only from the dates of texts of the Syrian and Byzantine liturgies have historians and liturgists been able to point to their influence on the Egyptian. The Alexandrian fathers do not provide enough material to write even an outline history of early Egyptian liturgy. The earliest complete text of an Egyptian liturgy is that of Serapion of Thmuis, dated to the fourth century.

Coptic liturgies were originally in Greek, an important liturgical language in Egypt both before and after Chalcedon (451). Evidence such as the copying of the Egyptian Liturgy of St Basil in Greek even in the nineteenth century is difficult to explain unless we accept that Greek remained so important to the Copts as the language of the Alexandrian fathers that even after the CHALCEDONIAN schism it was not totally supplanted by Coptic in the life of the Egyptian church.

The development of the Coptic liturgy remains shrouded in silence. We possess many early papyri of prayers, but the absence of rubrics and commentaries until the writers of the tenth to thirteenth centuries, who wrote in Arabic, makes it difficult to construct the history of the Coptic liturgy before 900. After that time the Coptic writers Abu al-Barakat and Zakaria Ibn Sabba' give us more information than was ever available previously on the way the eucharist was celebrated in the Coptic church of their time.

The gap between the early days of Christianity and the tenth to thirteenth centuries is so wide that some historians have believed the Coptic church came into existence as a result of the schism of 451, but several factors militate against this. The Coptic church has remained faithful to its identity, celebrated in the liturgy in a unique section called the 'Absolution of the Ministers', in which celebrants and the people are absolved of their sins 'by the mouth of the Trinity and the mouth of the holy father Saint Mark the Evangelist, Saint Athanasius, Saint Cyril of Alexandria and the fathers of the catholic church' (Brightman, p. 149). This unique prayer, which does not appear in other Eastern liturgies, confirms the apostolic succession and the faith of the fathers of the three ECUMENICAL COUNCILS of Nicea, Constantinople and Ephesus. Apostolic succession is not just a claim, it is an identity always celebrated in the liturgy. This prayer, like the Coptic calendar, confirms the place of the Coptic church in the universal church. The Coptic historian SEVERUS IBN AL-MUQAFFA' (tenth century) traced the origin of the Coptic church to St Mark in a deliberate attempt to link the origin of the church to an apostle and to the fathers of the Church of Alexandria. MONASTICISM, which has supplied the Coptic church with all its leaders, has always remained faithful to the early founders, fathers of the catholic church, the presence of whose names in the diptychs emphasizes a conscious insistence on belonging to the catholic church.

◆ The Liturgy of St Basil ◆

Of the many differences between the Coptic and Greek liturgies of St Basil, one is important. This is the PROTHESIS, complete in the Arabic but not surviving in either Coptic or Greek. This prothesis has been added to all three liturgies, of Basil, Mark and Gregory. The Arabic word for this rite is ḥamal, 'lamb' or 'offertory'. It is loaded with symbolism and has some similarity with its Syrian counterpart, but the prayers which accompany it contain, unusually, an old form of epiclesis. Abbot Matta al-Maskeen, in a study published in 1977, tried to prove that this is in fact the oldest form of the oldest eucharistic prayer and contains the most primitive prayers of the Coptic church. His thesis has not received the attention it merits, not least since it was written in Arabic, but the idea is new and fascinating; if we look carefully we can see that a whole form of consecration is buried among other prayers taken from a later liturgy of the catechumens. This does not, however, constitute a liturgy since it does not contain the words of institution and makes no reference to the Lord's Supper. The text of this unique part of the service raises other questions about whether there existed a specific office for the catechumens, who were supposed to be present to hear the word of God and the sermon. If we remove the lessons and the offering of incense, we can see the following: (1) a prayer of thanksgiving for the gift of the heavenly bread; (2) an invocation which seems to indicate that the bread and the wine have been changed into the body and blood of Christ; (3) an absolution which prepares the whole congregation for communion. All these occur before the reading of the New Testament lessons.

◆ The Liturgy of St Gregory ◆

The date of this liturgy, as with other Egyptian liturgies, is shrouded in silence. The most recent discovery is a fragment in Greek found in the keep of the Monastery of St

Macarius in Wādī al-Naṭrūn which may be from the late tenth century. The relationship between this liturgy and the writings of Gregory Nazianzus cannot be discovered by looking for exact words and expressions in his writings. One striking element, however, is the repetition in Gregory's *Theological Orations* of the phrase 'for my sake' or 'for me' when speaking of the work of the incarnate Son. This same phrase suffuses the Coptic prayers of this liturgy, which speak of everything being made and redeemed for the human race by the Son who is now praying in the name of one person, Adam, but is at the same time the celebrant, and the believers who are attending the liturgy. Creation, the Law of God and all other gifts are 'for my sake', as are the redeeming work of Christ, his death and Resurrection. In the prayers, Jesus himself is celebrant doing what he did in the upper room. No liturgy in the whole collection of the ancient church presents us with this concept of Christ as the priest of the eucharist as clearly as the Coptic Liturgy of St Gregory. It is Christ himself who by his voice changes the bread and the wine into his body and blood. This must not be used as an argument for a different theology of the epiclesis, since this was never discussed in Egypt and it is Jesus himself who is breaking and dividing bread and giving it to the church. According to Abu al-Barakat, this liturgy was used on major feasts and during Eastertide, but this not strictly observed today.

♦ The Liturgy of St Mark ♦

This liturgy, traditionally named after St Cyril of Alexandria, is the only surviving Alexandrian liturgy. Differences between the Coptic and Greek texts are due to translation from Greek to Coptic and to increasing variations which must have happened in the period after the Chalcedonian schism. This liturgy, like the others, has lost its proper beginning and follows the same order as the liturgies of Basil and Gregory up to the anaphora. The prayer clearly declaring that the offering is made to the Trinity was used as evidence against the teaching that Christ offered his sacrifice to the Father alone in the local council of Constaninople in 1156 (*see* SOTERICHOS). The epiclesis reflects Cyril of Alexandria's highly developed theology of the Holy Spirit. It is rarely used except during Lent, and in some modern editions of the Coptic EUCHOLOGION is rearranged to follow the order of Basil and Gregory.

♦ The modern Coptic liturgy ♦

We are certain that the present order of the whole Coptic liturgy has existed since 1411, when the 88th Coptic Patriarch Gabriel V edited and arranged it. Older forms have not survived and this attempt at unification has left unanswered questions such as those raised above. As a result of Patriarch Gabriel's unification the monastic offices of the hours formally became part of the liturgy, which thus came to incorporate the daily office with its midnight and morning prayers. The distinction between the parish and monastic liturgy was removed, and the monastic style of long prayers became a feature of the Coptic liturgy. The Greek Egyptian Liturgy of St Basil corresponds to the Coptic Liturgy of St Basil; its existence in Greek throughout the history of the Coptic church could be due to attempts to unify the MELKITE and Coptic Orthodox churches during the tenth-century patriarchate of Michael I. The Liturgy of St Basil has a strong Alexandrian, post-Nicene, anti-Arian theology of the Son as the Mediator, Redeemer and Co-Creator with the Father. It emphasizes the divinity of the Son, the Revealer of the Father. The eucharist, too, is a revelation to believers of the Son incarnate, crucified and risen. The epiclesis says clearly that the Holy Spirit reveals the body and the blood of Christ as 'the most holy for the holy ones'. In recently discovered Greek manuscripts, not yet edited or published, the diptychs vary and reflect local practice, omitting names of important figures such as Dioscorus of Alexandria and SEVERUS OF ANTIOCH. The famous metropolitan JACOB BARADAEUS is absent despite the fact that more than one Syrian was elected patriarch of the Coptic church.

The fraction is of importance; the unique Coptic way of dividing the consecrated bread is deeply symbolic and not adequately explained. An obvious Syrian element in the fraction, recorded only in the fifth-century Syrian writings of Theodore of Mopsuestia, is the signing of the consecrated elements and their mixing together. The circular stamp used to mark the Coptic eucharistic bread contains many crosses (*see* BREAD STAMPS). The central cross represents Christ; this is unknown in the Syrian church. This particle is taken after the consecration and the fraction and put into the chalice. The only reasonable explanation for this practice is provided by Theodore of Mopsuestia and other Syrian writers, but there is no reference to its meaning in Coptic and Arabic sources. This particle is reserved for the celebrant. The section which deals with the fraction is entirely absent from the Greek texts of the Coptic liturgy.

The Greek text of the Coptic liturgy was published by E. Renaudot (2nd edn 1847); repr. 1970, *Liturgiarum Orientalium Collectio*. Farnborough: Gregg International Publishers. For the Boharic and Arabic texts printed before 1961, see H. Malak (1964), *Studi e Testi* 233, pp. 6–8, 27. Vatican City: Biblioteca Vaticana.
The incomplete Sahidic text has been published by J. Doresse and E. Lane (1960), 'Un Temoin archaique de la liturgie Copte de St Basile,' *Bibliothèque du Muséon* 47. Louvain: Institute Orientaliste.
Early fragments were published by P. E. Khale (1954), *Balayzah*, vol. 1, p. 404 (London); H. Quecke (1979), *Orientalia* 48, pp. 68–81 (Rome: Pontifical Institute of Oriental Studies).
For English translations, see F. E. Brightman (1896), *Liturgies Eastern and Western*, vol. 1: *Eastern Liturgies*. Oxford: Clarendon Press; John Marquis of Bute (1908), *The Coptic Morning Service for the Lord's Day*, 3rd edn. London: Cope & Fenwick.

GB

Copts and Islamic fundamentalism since 1952 The Copts are the largest Christian community in the Arab world (*see* COPTIC CHRISTIANITY), numbering at least four times as many as the Christians in Lebanon, and make up about 15 per cent of the Egyptian population. Coptic involvement in the political and social life of Egypt goes back to the establishment of modern Egypt in the nineteenth century by Mohammed Ali, before the British occupation in 1882.

Religious tensions in Egypt between Christians and Muslims have often been marked by the burning of churches, executions of Christians, confiscation of private property and forced conversions to Islam. These phenomena are not new and have been part of the history of the Coptic church since the Arab conquest of Egypt in the seventh century. But it is equally true to say that there have also been periods of tolerance.

July 1952 witnessed the coup by the 'Free Officers', none of whom was a Christian and some of whom were followers of the ideology of the Muslim Brotherhood established by Hassan al-Banna in 1928. President Nasser of Egypt (d. 1970) was a secularized Muslim. Nasser, like all military leaders, did not trust secret organizations, especially those with an underground paramilitary wing. The Muslim Brotherhood was responsible for the assassination of the Egyptian minister al-Noqrashy and others; an unsuccessful attempt on Nasser's life in 1954 was attributed to them. Use of Islam in Egyptian political power struggles is not a new element in the life of modern Egypt. King Faruq saw alliance with the Muslim Brotherhood against the nationalist party, Al-Wafd, which had considerable Coptic participation, as a means to a greater role.

A similar attempt to 'domesticate' Islam – and the Muslim Brotherhood – occurred in 1970–81 when President Sadat tried to dislodge Marxists, leftists and Nasserites from the media, the army, the police, and government offices. From 1970 Islam became the tool used by seekers of political power, including the newly created parties which replaced the one-party system created by Nasser in 1954. Sadat, whom Nasser had appointed vice-president only few weeks before his death, had been a sympathizer of the Muslim Brotherhood. He revived it, permitting publication of the monthly magazine *Al-Da'wa* that had been banned since 1954. Sadat was responsible for the revival of the Islamic Movement in Egypt from 1971 till his death on 6 October 1981 at the hands of those to whom he had given political and financial support. Sadat used to give major political addresses not on 23 July, the anniversary of the 1952 revolution, but on the Birthday of the Prophet Muhammad. In 1972 Sadat initiated the creation of 'Gamaat Islamiyya' Islamic groups in the Egyptian universities to gain control of the student political voice and create an alternative Islamic leadership.

Sadat created a new alliance incorporating those who had lost their property in 1963 in Nasser's socialization of Egypt, Muslim activists, former political prisoners now released, and the remnant of the political leadership of the pre-July 1952 political parties. The alliance aimed to dismantle and replace Nasser's entire political system: Islam was to be their tool. Sadat, under the pretext of creating a new permanent constitution in 1971, encouraged those who wanted the Islamic law code, the Sharia, to become the sole source of legislation. A constitutional referendum contained an article making Sadat president for life, thus linking his presidency with the return to Sharia law. Developments following this referendum tended towards the Islamization of Egypt. Volunteers were sent with Sadat's blessing to fight the Soviet forces in Afghanistan; these men, now called *mujāhidīn* or the Afghan Arabs, were among the military groups fighting security forces in Egypt and Algeria in the mid-1990s.

Copts were members of every political party, even the Egyptian Communist Party. Their lay leadership was in constant conflict with the ecclesiastical authorities from 1882, when the laity succeeded in creating the Lay Council, 'Al-Maǧlis al-Milli', whose authority was sufficient to send Patriarch CYRIL V into internal exile. Its members were members of Egyptian political parties or public figures in Egyptian social and economic life. Their Christian life might be called nominal and some had no obvious interest in church life; but their social position was crucial, since they were the best peaceful means the Coptic community had at its disposal when religious problems approached. Few Coptic clergy were involved in social and political life, and the same can be said of Muslim clergy. The secular system of modern Egypt offered little place for either Christianity or Islam. At the beginning of the twentieth century the educated were reared in their families' religious atmosphere, but experienced no link between their religion and their education or training. The wars with Israel, particularly that of 1967, shook the foundations of secularism, especially Nasser's establishment in 1963 of Arab socialism. The 1967 defeat did not revive the national identity of Egypt which had played a major part in ending the seventy-five years of British rule in Egypt. After the Suez war in 1956 Nasser emphasized instead the new identity, Arab nationalism, which was also known, but made little progress, in the Fertile Crescent (Syria, Iraq and Lebanon). Nasser wanted to be leader of the Arab world, but lost that battle in 1967. Nasser's socialism and Arab nationalism collapsed, but Egyptian patriotism was not restored. Egypt was ripe for an Islamic revival.

In 1963 Nasser dissolved the Coptic Lay Council, whose members had for more than a century been elected by the upper-class Copts and had succeeded through their Muslim connections in gaining certain civil rights for Copts, such as the right to build churches, as well as securing jobs in the private sector. The one-party system established in 1954 deprived the Copts of their best lay political leadership. When Nasser died in 1970 the Copts had no political leaders to turn to. The twenty-five years of Nasser's reign had been a peaceful time for the Copts, witnessing a monastic revival and a flourishing youth movement; religious education had spread. New generations of Copts entered the monasteries, university graduates were seeking ordination and the rediscovery of patristic writings by the newly created Coptic middle class brought confidence in the ecclesiastical leadership. The church was growing and Western missionary activities, a means of converting Copts to other Christian denominations, were subsiding.

Two generations of Copts under Nasser were deprived of political education and participation in the political life of Egypt. The old upper-class leadership was disappearing, both through natural wastage and because of the change in the political climate. When SHENOUDA III was elected pope of Alexandria in 1971 there were hardly any leaders to act as his political counsellors, but the church had nevertheless to fill the political vacuum. Newly ordained bishops and priests, some recent graduates less than thirty years old with little practical experience, became church leaders. Pope Shenouda discovered his charismatic talents in the public gatherings he led every Friday, presenting new ways of explaining the Christian faith. The Islamic tide met this Coptic Christian revival by domesticating Islam for political gain. A collision could have been avoided had the Egyptian political leadership perceived the danger of using religious symbols, language and concepts to deal with national problems.

Judges used Qur'anic verses and Islamic tradition to pass sentence and to judge between Christians and Muslims. Constant appeal to the Islamic law on apostasy, which had not been applied in Egypt for at least two hundred years, provoked the Synod of the Coptic church to declare in a letter to Sadat that it was every bishop's duty to win back Christian converts to Islam and that they would do everything possible to bring them back to their original religion (Christianity). The riot in Al-Zawiya al-Hamra in 1979, the repeated arson attacks on churches, including the

141

historic church of the Virgin Mary in Old Cairo, Qasriyyat al-Rihan, the kidnapping of Christians girls and their forcible conversion to Islam and the great difficulties experienced in obtaining the requisite presidential decree to build or renovate a church led the Coptic synod to cancel public celebration of Easter in May 1979, declaring it a period of mourning, to challenge the government to deal with Christian grievances.

The Copts were adopting a religious approach to their problems. Sadat, having visited Israel and signed a peace treaty, was under attack from his Arab and Muslim allies. Copts and Muslim fundamentalists alike were lined up against their president, who had no immediate solution to defuse the tension.

Pope Shenouda was put under house arrest in his monastery in Wādī al-Naṭrūn. Coptic clergy were arrested and imprisoned along with hundreds of Islamic religious leaders and alleged activists. Sadat wanted to appear an innocent party in the religious strife in Egypt. On 5 September 1981, a month which opposition newspapers called 'Black September', security forces raided the homes of 'suspects', some of whom had been dead for years; many others were arrested. The peace Sadat had established with his new alliance was broken; this led to his assassination at the 6 October military parade.

Political alliances were reshaped. Muslim fundamentalists tried to overrun Assyut, and members of the security forces were killed. The mask was off; and violence continues to be committed by paramilitary groups claiming to be heralds of Islam bringing a divine solution to modern Egypt's huge and diverse problems.

The tension in Egypt between Christians and Muslim fundamentalists is a by-product of over twenty-five years of a political system fluctuating between the secular and the religious, between Egyptian patriotism, Arab nationalism and Islam. Christians were excluded from Egypt's political leadership not as part of a plan, but because of Nasser's military style of dictatorship. They lost a lay leadership with strong economic ties and social relationships with the Muslims. These nominal lay leaders lost their property in 1963, and their political role when parties were dissolved in 1954. Pope CYRIL VI, consecrated in 1959, was a charismatic healer, a hermit not interested in politics, who understood that his personal relationship with Nasser was the key to the church getting fair treatment. Pope Shenouda III, by contrast, brought up and trained by the leaders of the Coptic revival which dominated church life in the 1920s, believed in political strategies more than in close friendship and in public demonstration rather than in quiet talks with the president of Egypt.

It is difficult as yet to see whether Egypt will emerge as a secular state where both Christian and Muslim clergy have a limited leadership role, or whether religion will continue to play a key role in the Egyptian state.

Ramadan Abdel Azim (1993), 'Fundamentalist Influence in Egypt: The Strategies of the Muslim Brotherhood and the Takfir Groups', in *Fundamentalisms and the State*, vol. 3. Chicago: University of Chicago Press.
Olivier, R. (1992), *L'Echec de l'Islam politique*. Paris: Editions du Seuil.
Zubaida, S. (1989), *Islam, the People and the State*. London: Routledge.
Ibrahim, S. E. (1988), 'Egypt's Islamic Militancy', *Third World Quarterly*. London: Third World Foundation for Social and Economic Studies.
Vatikiotis, P. J. (1981), *The History of Egypt*, 3rd edn. Baltimore: John Hopkins University Press.

Berger, M. (1970), *Islam in Egypt Today*. Cambridge: Cambridge University Press.
Wakin, E. (1963), *The Lonely Minority: The Modern Story of Egypt's Copts*. New York: William Morrow.

GB

Cross From the reign of CONSTANTINE THE GREAT and the spread of belief that his mother Helena had discovered the True Cross during a pilgrimage to JERUSALEM, an important cult of the relics of the Precious Cross spread rapidly as fragments of the sacred wood were distributed throughout the Christian world. Cruciform jewels became a common part of lay and clerical attire, often functioning as marks of ecclesiastical rank; crosses surmounted Christian buildings and the crowns of Christian rulers. The cross was woven into or embroidered on cloth used for vestments. Eventually, church buildings were regularly designed to a cruciform plan (*see* ARCHITECTURE).

ICONS of the Crucifixion represent the death of Jesus, icons of the empty Cross symbolize the Resurrection. The Cross is often represented as the tree of life with burgeoning leaves or flowers: both the life-giving Cross itself and Christ, symbolized by the burgeoning cross, are thought of as the tree of life. Complex carved crosses known as KHATCHKAR are typical of Armenian Christian art. Carved metal crosses of great intricacy are found in Ethiopia. In COPTIC CHRISTIANITY use is made of the *crux ansata*, the hieroglyphic sign *ankh*, meaning life, as a symbol of the Cross.

Priestly blessings are usually given by tracing a cross in the air or over the person or thing to be blessed; in Byzantine and several other traditions the priest's fingers form the first and last letters of *iesous* and *christos*. Christians bless themselves with the sign of the cross. EASTERN ORTHODOX Christians make the sign of the cross from right to left, three fingers of the right hand held together to symbolize the Holy Trinity, two folded down to represent the deity and humanity of Jesus. OLD BELIEVERS retain a more ancient custom of making the sign of the Cross with two fingers, rejecting thereby any suggestion of patripassian heresy. Armenians, like Latin Christians, make the sign with the open hand.

A cross normally stands on or behind the holy table, and hand crosses, often of precious metal, are used to bless. Many Oriental Orthodox bishops carry a blessing cross at all times.

The major relic of the True Cross in Jerusalem, lost to Persian invaders in 614, was restored under Emperor Heraclius, in part, perhaps, to please the Persian king's Christian queen, Shirin. ISHOYAB II (628–46), catholicos of the CHURCH OF THE EAST, who acted as an emissary between the Persians and the Byzantines, may have returned the relic to the emperor. The Feast of the Finding of the Cross, 14 September, already including by the early seventh century the rite of the Exaltation of the Cross, came, under this latter name, to celebrate the return of the Cross and its public veneration in Jerusalem (631). The related mid-Lent feast of Stavroproskynesis (Worship of the Cross) prepares for the celebration of the Passion and Crucifixion. Even in the iconoclastic periods the cross remained an important visual symbol of the Christian faith; it is significant that the Stavroproskynesis first rose to prominence between the two periods of ICONOCLASM.

Canon 73 of the QUINISEXT COUNCIL forbids the marking of a cross on the floor and orders such marks to be effaced to avoid sacrilege, excommunicating any who place crosses where they may be trodden underfoot.

The apocryphal but early Gospel of Peter presents the Cross as buried with Jesus and resurrected with him.

An upside-down cross is a symbol of the apostle Peter, who by tradition was crucified upside down, having declared himself unworthy to die in the same way as his Lord. In later iconography the apostle Andrew is often shown with a saltire cross, though many icons show him with an upright one.

The common Greek name Stavros means 'Cross', but is accented on the first syllable.

DM

Crusades In March 1095 envoys of Byzantine Emperor Alexios I Komnenos (1081–1118) appealed to Pope Urban II for assistance against the OTTOMAN Turks. The envoys, who met the pope at the Council of Piacenza, arrived when Rome itself was in the hands of Antipope Clement III, who had been installed with the support of the Holy Roman Emperor as rival to Gregory VII. At Clermont in November of the same year Urban urged Western Christendom to come to the aid of the beleaguered Eastern emperor and to deliver the Holy Sepulchre from Muslim hands. He offered great spiritual benefits to those who put on the cross and joined his crusade.

The idea of a holy war to liberate the Tomb of Christ provided a fractured Western Christendom with a unifying dream, a focus for energies, an opportunity to conquer new lands and titles, and all under the blessing of God. It offered the pope a chance to consolidate his leadership in the West and extend his influence in the East, providing a means of diverting the bellicose energies of vassals, younger sons with a chance to acquire land, zealots with an opportunity to gain converts, penitents with a means to expiate their sins.

In 1096 a fanatical preacher, Peter the Hermit, arrived at CONSTANTINOPLE's walls with an army of volunteers. More arrived under Walter the Penniless, while others were crossing Western Europe, slaughtering Jewish communities on the way. The emperor quickly conveyed the disorderly volunteers to Anatolia, where, after fighting with local Greeks, most were slaughtered by the Turks.

The noble leadership of the First Crusade arrived later in the same year. Alexios treated them courteously, persuading them to swear loyalty and to return conquered lands to imperial rule. Soon Nicea was taken, and surrendered to the emperor. Edessa was treacherously taken from its Armenian prince by Baldwin of Boulogne, who proclaimed himself count of Edessa. Antioch was besieged, though the Byzantines withdrew before Bohemond of Taranto took the city on 3 June 1098 and held it in his own right. The apparently miraculous discovery of the lance that had pierced Christ's side helped him defend it.

On 15 July 1099 the crusaders, having acquired a justified reputation for cannibalism after capturing Ma'arra, took Jerusalem amid scenes of appalling slaughter. The EASTERN CHRISTIAN clergy of the Holy Sepulchre were tortured to extract from them details of where the church's relics and treasures were kept. The nobility of the crusade settled into their new principalities, Godfrey de Bouillon, Defender of the Holy Sepulchre (1099–1100) ruling Jerusalem under papal suzerainty. A Latin patriarchate in JERUSALEM asserted its authority over all the Christians of the area.

In 1125 Mosul and Aleppo were united under the authority of the Seljuk sultan. In 1144 Edessa fell. Hearing this, Pope Eugene III (1145–53) had Bernard of Clairvaux preach a new crusade, with the result that in 1147 two great forces set off, one under Louis VII of France (1137–80), the other led by the German King Conrad III (1138–52). This Second Crusade was a failure, and the Franks' unsuccessful attack on Damascus broke an understanding with the crusader princes that had endured since the reign of Baldwin I, King of Jerusalem (1100–18). In 1154 Damascus united with Mosul and Aleppo. With the rise of the Kurdish general Saladin a unified Muslim empire soon encompassed the Kingdom of Jerusalem. At Hattin, King Guy (1186–92) led a united Latin army against Saladin into overwhelming and bloody defeat. On 2 October 1187 Jerusalem surrendered, finding Saladin generous in defeat.

In 1189 the ageing Western Emperor Frederick Barbarossa (1152–90) led a great army by the overland route, despite hostility from the Eastern Emperor Isaac Angelos (1185–95). He eventually came to an agreement with Isaac who transported his men into Asia Minor, where he took Iconium, but was drowned in Cilicia.

Armies led by Philip Augustus of France (1180–1223) and Richard I of England (1189–99) set out a year after Frederick, Richard pausing to take CYPRUS from its Byzantine ruler. Initial success at Acre was followed by quarrels between rival candidates for the Jerusalem throne that divided the leadership. Philip Augustus returned home sick, leaving Richard to defeat Saladin and sign a treaty that gained the coastal area from Ascalon to Acre and guaranteed pilgrims access to Jerusalem.

On 8 January 1198 Innocent III became pope. The new pontiff, a lawyer and administrator of high intelligence and formidable energy, soon began to consider a new crusade. In summer 1197 Emperor Henry VI (1190–7), widely thought to favour conquest of the Byzantine empire, had arrived in the Holy Land, but had died suddenly, with the result that his crusade fell apart. The pope was determined that any new crusade would be under his own authority. He sent out preachers as recruiters and taxed clerical incomes to finance it. By 1201 VENICE agreed to transport the crusaders in return for a handsome payment, the Venetians providing fifty galleys in return for a half share of all conquests. Most of the crusade's leaders intended heading for Egypt, unaware that Venice might at that moment have been finalizing a commercial agreement with that country which included a guarantee of non–aggression. When the army could not pay for its transport the doge, Enrico Dandolo, old and blind but sharp-minded, himself among the crusaders, negotiated an undertaking to capture the Dalmatian port of Zara from the Hungarians. Innocent tried to veto this, but the crusade's leaders ignored his objections. When his army sacked Zara, the pope excommunicated them, but was persuaded to rescind the excommunication, except in the case of the Venetians.

The crusaders now needed money and provisions. The corrupt Isaac Angelos (1185–95 and 1203–4) had been deposed and blinded by his brother, now Alexios III. In 1197 Philip of Swabia, younger brother of Henry VI, married Isaac's daughter Irene and the following year became king (1198–1208). Irene's brother, another Alexios, had escaped imprisonment and arrived at Philip's court seeking help. He now offered the crusaders a deal: if they restored his father he would guarantee military and financial support for the crusade and end the schism between the churches. The empty offer tempted the devious doge; it provided an ideal excuse for interference in the affairs of a state he hated.

In June 1203 the crusader fleet arrived at Constantinople and in July the army attacked Galata tower, dropping the chain guarding the Golden Horn, allowing their fleet to sweep into the harbour. The city's fortifications held the crusaders for another fortnight, but on 17 July the blind doge himself led a Venetian attack that put Emperor Alexios III to flight. Isaac Angelos was reinstated and agreed to honour his son's undertakings. He became co-emperor as Alexios IV. The money, however, was not there; the army was unreliable and the church uncooperative. By the winter of 1203 it was evident Alexios could not meet his commitments.

Early in 1204 Isaac and Alexios IV were deposed and Alexios Doukas Mourzouphlos was crowned as Alexios V. At once he set about restoring and strengthening the city's defences, both Alexios IV and Isaac meanwhile perishing in custody.

Now possessing a perfect *casus belli*, on 9 April 1204 the crusade's leadership launched an all-out attack. Within four days the defences were breached, and, as Alexios V fled together with the wife and daughter of Alexios III to seek refuge with the ex-emperor, the crusaders stormed and sacked the city. Amid wholesale slaughter, works of art and literature, libraries and archives went up in flames; churches and monasteries were desecrated. A huge fire consumed a vast area of the city. An eerie debt of gratitude is owed to Doge Dandolo: his Venetians ransacked the city's treasures with a collector's eye, and to this day Venice remains the reliquary of Constantinople's art.

A Venetian monk, Tommasso Morosini, became Latin patriarch of Constantinople, the legitimate patriarch, John X Kamateros (1198–1206) fleeing to Didymoteichon, and on 16 May 1204 Count Baldwin of Flanders, with Venetian support, was crowned emperor in Hagia Sophia. Innocent III reacted ambivalently. He wrote a fierce denunciation of the sack, but decided that the establishment of the Latin empire and church showed divine intervention re-establishing the unity of the church. His support for the Latin empire and patriarchate has never been forgotten in the Christian East.

The Latins soon faced Theodore I Laskaris (1204–22), established as emperor in Nicea, as well as a second emperor (set up as rival to the Angeli, not the crusaders), in Trebizond, and a third in Thessaloniki. The Latin empire fell in 1261, and Michael VIII Palaiologos (1259–82) restored Byzantine rule, though Latin influence remained in several areas of formerly Byzantine territory.

The Fourth Crusade was not the last. The pathetic Children's Crusade of 1212 was followed by the futile operation led by Cardinal Pelagius in which Damietta was taken, an offer to exchange it for Jerusalem haughtily refused, and his army led onwards to total humiliation. Emperor Frederick II (1212–50) used diplomatic rather than military tactics to win a treaty, signed on 18 February 1229 with the ambassador of the sultan of Egypt, that returned Jerusalem to Western control; but the Muslims retook it ten years later. In 1248 Louis IX of France (1226–70) mounted an attack on Egypt that ended with his defeat and imprisonment. In 1270 he died while unsuccessfully invading Tunis.

The Mongols now posed a graver threat than the crusaders to the Muslim rulers of the Middle East. The rise of the Mamluk sultans of Egypt and their defeat of the Mongols at Ain Jalut (1260) tolled the knell of crusading hopes. In 1268 Antioch fell and in 1291 Acre, the last crusader outpost, followed.

The crusades definitively changed the relationship between the churches of East and West. The crusaders' contemptuous treatment of Eastern and Oriental clergy, the sacrileges perpetrated during the sack of Constantinople, the establishment of the Latin patriarchates: all led to lasting resentment. EASTERN ORTHODOX came to see the pope as an enemy and the Western church as a predatory adversary. The Greek East was decisively weakened, Christian minorities under Muslim rule permanently compromised. The social position of COPTS and JACOBITES deteriorated, their loyalty frequently suspected. The incentive to convert to Islam to seek social advancement grew. The MARONITES, on the other hand, and a part of the ARMENIAN church in Lesser Armenia, allied themselves with the Western church.

Norwich, J. J. (1991), *Byzantium, The Decline and Fall*. London and New York: Viking.
Maalouf, A. (1984), *The Crusades through Arab Eyes*. London: Al Saqi Books.
Godfrey, J. (1980), *The Unholy Crusade*. Oxford: Oxford University Press.
Runciman, S. (1954), *A History of the Crusades*, 3 vols. Cambridge: Cambridge University Press.

DM

Cyprus, Church of   Barnabas, companion of Paul, is revered as apostle of Cyprus. Acts 11–13 records that Barnabas, a Cypriot Jew, arrived with Paul and converted the proconsul Sergius Paulus. Discovery in 488 of the apostle's tomb, his relics and an ancient copy of Matthew's Gospel led Emperor Zeno (474–91) to support the Cypriot church's claim to independence from ANTIOCH, capital of the diocese of Oriens. Canon 8 of the Council of Ephesus (431) had supported Cyprus, but Antioch had continued to press its claims. Zeno's decree granted Anthemios, metropolitan of Cyprus, who had presented him with the Matthew manuscript, a sceptre and the right to sign documents in cinnabar and to wear a purple *mandyas* on ceremonial occasions, privileges enjoyed by the archbishop of Cyprus to this day. Justinian I confirmed Cyprus's autocephaly. Major ecclesiastical sites dating from the fourth century onwards confirm the importance of the church in that period.

Spyridon of Trimethous took part in the first ECUMENICAL COUNCIL together with his fellow bishops from Salamis and Paphos, and Cypriot bishops were present at all subsequent ecumenical synods. EPIPHANIOS OF SALAMIS, a biblical scholar of Jewish origin and metropolitan of Cyprus 367–403, fought all heresy, especially the teachings of ORIGEN. His *Panarion*, a handbook of heresies, influenced JOHN OF DAMASCUS.

From the mid-seventh century Arab sea-raids devastated the island; towns were sacked, crops destroyed and trade disrupted. Emperor Justinian II (685–95 and 705–11) evacuated a large part of the population to a region of Kyzikos that was renamed Nea Justiniana. Canon 39 of the QUINISEXT COUNCIL (692) placed the bishop of Kyzikos under the Cypriot Archbishop John, giving him primacy over Hellespontine Phrygia. When the Cypriots returned home in 698 the archbishop of Cyprus retained his new title, becoming archbishop of Nea Justiniana and All Cyprus.

In the eighth and ninth centuries Cyprus gave refuge to ICONOPHILES, especially monastics, fleeing persecution in CONSTANTINOPLE.

Justinian II established a curious fiscal condominium with Caliph 'Abd al-Malik in 688: Cyprus became a base for both Byzantine and Muslim forces, and was taxed by both powers until 965, when, under Emperor Nikephoros II Phokas, the island was reintegrated into the Byzantine empire. Economic and cultural life began to flourish; new towns were built, sometimes on abandoned ancient sites. Nicosia became the capital. Monasteries were founded. Onerous taxation and heavy-handed administration resulted in rebellion in 1043, and again in 1092.

The CRUSADES opened a grim period in Cypriot history. Ill-advised action by Manuel I Komnenos (1143–80) led crusader Prince Reginald of Antioch to launch a vicious raid on Cyprus in 1155. Other raids occurred, an especially violent one in 1161. In 1184 Isaac Komnenos, Byzantine governor of Cilicia, proclaimed himself emperor in Cyprus, but in 1191 Richard I of England, who felt insulted by Isaac, took the island; he then sold it to the Templars, who, however, handed it back. Richard then sold it to Guy de Lusignan, who from 1186 to 1192 had been king of Jerusalem. His brother Amaury succeeded Guy in 1194 and in 1197, on marrying the widowed Queen Isabel, became King of Jerusalem. Cyprus became an important military base for the crusaders.

Frankish rule led to dominance by the Latin church. Until 1260 the Cypriot Greeks were allowed their own archbishop and thirteen bishops, but lost wealth, power and land. In 1260 ROME imposed a new constitution on the Cypriot church, reducing the Greek bishops to four, and placing them under the authority of the Roman Catholic hierarchy. Attempts to resist were severely punished, and many Orthodox died as martyrs, most famously the thirteen monks of Kantara executed in 1231.

Venetian rule (1489–1570) left the religious settlement of 1260 intact. The Cypriot Greek Orthodox remained in humiliating subjection until the Ottomans took Cyprus in 1570. OTTOMAN government in Cyprus, established in 1573, meant that on the economic, political and social levels the Greeks simply exchanged one harsh and indifferent master for another. The church, however, benefited. The Orthodox hierarchy was restored, its privileges were recognized, its places of worship returned. From 1660 the Sublime Porte acknowledged the archbishop of Cyprus as ethnarch of the Cypriot Greeks. The church became custodian of religion, language and culture.

Under Ottoman rule the hierarchy were accountable for the behaviour of the people, and any sign of resistance put them at risk. Money could buy high clerical office; money could buy deposition, or worse. The Christians had rights, but as *dhimmi*, AHL AL-KITAB; protected by the Sultan, but subordinate in status to Muslims. Muslim privileges were a constant incentive to apostasy, but the vast majority of Orthodox remained loyal. Crypto-Christians, outwardly Muslim, existed; these *Linobambakoi* returned publicly to Orthodoxy in 1878, when the island came under British rule.

Greek Cypriots did not bow passively under the Ottoman yoke. Uprisings took place, but met with harsh repression. The Greek War of Independence in 1821 brought a terrible massacre; thousands of the Greeks were killed, including all four bishops.

In 1878 Great Britain signed a convention with the Sublime Porte by which it gained the administration of Cyprus, undertaking to pay the Sultan an annual tribute of £92,800. On the outbreak of the First World War Britain annexed the island, King Constantine of Greece rejecting an offer in 1915 to cede it to Greece for aid for Serbia.

At first many Greek Cypriots saw British rule as a deliverance from oppression and a step to true freedom. Schools were built; social and religious life acquired a new energy. A new style of law and administration gave greater personal security. It was soon clear, however, that the British intended to control the island's political and social life, while providing little support for its economic development. Detailed regulations encompassed every aspect of public life, circumscribing the liberty of the church.

When, in 1925, Britain made Cyprus a colony, dashing any hopes that the administrator would offer the Cypriot nation its independence, a fierce struggle began against what now appeared an alien and repressive regime. The church played a leading role in fostering the spirit of independence and in promoting the movement for national liberty. A popular uprising in 1931 was harshly suppressed. Metropolitans Nikodemos of Kition and Makarios of Kyrenia were exiled with many other leading figures. Nikodemos died in exile in 1937. Severe constraints limited the freedom of movement and action of Archbishop Kyrillos III (1915–33) and of Metropolitan Leontios of Paphos. In 1933 the archbishop died, and no election was permitted until 1946. Metropolitan Leontios, the sole bishop actually resident and active in Cyprus, became *locum tenens* of the archiepiscopate.

In 1946 the British permitted the metropolitan of Kyrenia to return, and allowed an archiepiscopal election to take place. Since the Cypriot church had only two metropolitans, a metropolitan from the Ecumenical Patriarchate also attended the electoral synod. Leontios was elected archbishop and on 20 June 1947 he was enthroned, but died thirty-seven days later. Cyprus invited two more hierarchs of the Ecumenical Throne to help inaugurate a new electoral synod. It was decided to fill the vacant thrones. The metropolitan of Kyrenia became archbishop as Makarios II (1947–50), and on his death the then metropolitan of Kition was elected as Makarios III (1950–77).

The re-established hierarchy promoted the renewal of church life, as well as enhanced levels of cultural, educational and pastoral activity. A seminary was established, as were catechetical schools, new religious associations and undertakings. Under Makarios III the role of ethnarch took on a new political importance. Representatives of the people took a significant role in the council of the ethnarchy, and from 1950 pressure grew for a plebiscite on union with Greece. Archbishop Makarios promoted charitable works, developed the organization and activity of the church, and was a leader in the struggle for independence, becoming an important figure in international politics. When Cyprus finally became independent from Britain in 1960 Archbishop Makarios was elected president.

Very soon the president-archbishop faced political problems on both the secular and the religious front. The communalistic constitution rapidly proved unworkable, and the Turkish Cypriots reacted vehemently to thirteen amendments proposed by the president in 1963. The metropolitans of Paphos, Kition and Kyrenia meanwhile were emerging as opponents of Makarios, and in 1973 they were deposed on a charge of conspiracy against the primatial throne. Two new dioceses were created by dividing those of Kitium and Kyrenia.

All other problems were overshadowed by the July 1974 coup overthrowing the president, who denounced it as an invasion by the then Greek junta; the coup was followed on 20 July by the arrival of Turkish troops and a bitter military conflict which left 37 per cent of Cypriot territory under Turkish domination and displaced about 200,000 Greek Cypriots from the north of the island. The Turkish military presence continues and the declaration in February 1975 of an independent state in the Turkish-occupied area of the island left a major problem awaiting resolution.

Archbishop Makarios returned to Cyprus in December 1974. The massive refugee problem and the political conflict with Turkey spurred the Greek Cypriot community into action; rapid economic development was the result. In 1977 Makarios III died and on 13 November of the same year, his own name-day, Chrysostomos, metropolitan of Paphos, was enthroned as archbishop of Nea Ioustiniani and All Cyprus.

Englezakis, B. (1995), *Studies on the History of the Church of Cyprus, 4th to 20th Centuries*. Aldershot: Variorum.
Hill, G. (1940–52), *A History of Cyprus*, 4 vols. Cambridge: Cambridge University Press.
Hackett, J. (1901), *A History of the Orthodox Church of Cyprus from the Coming of the Apostles Paul and Barnabas to the Commencement of the British Occupation (AD 45–AD 1878) &c*. London: Methuen & Co.

DM

Cyril and Methodius   Apostles to the Slavs, brothers from Thessaloniki. Constantine, named Cyril as a monk, was part of a Byzantine embassy to the Arab caliphate (855) and to the Khazar kingdom (860) prior to the mission to Moravia at the request of ROSTISLAV. Constantine and Methodius appear to have been working on a Slav alphabet before their departure for Moravia in 863. The alphabet they produced was

given the name Glagolitic, from a Slavonic word meaning 'verb'. The Cyrillic alphabet was developed by Cyril's disciples. Among the first books translated was the liturgical Gospel book. In 867, while in VENICE on their way to ROME, they debated with Latin clerics who argued that only three languages were suitable in the liturgy, Latin, Greek and Hebrew, a claim known in the Byzantine world as the trilingual heresy. Pope Hadrian II issued a bull endorsing the use of Slavonic in the liturgy. Cyril died in Rome in 869 and his tomb in San Clemente remains a pilgrimage site for Eastern Christians. The pope appointed Methodius as archbishop to the Slavonic nations. The political situation in Moravia, however, shifted in favour of the West and papal endorsement of the Cyril-Methodian tradition did not survive the ninth century, though the Roman rite continued to be celebrated in Slavonic. Methodius died in Moravia in 885. His exiled disciples Clement and Naum continued his missionary and translation work in OHRID.

Tachiaos, A.-E. N. (1989), *Cyril and Methodius of Thessalonica: The Acculturation of the Slavs*. Thessaloniki: Rekos.
Obolensky, D. (1971), *The Byzantine Commonwealth: Eastern Europe, 500–1453*. Crestwood, NY: St Vladimir's Seminary Press.

KP

Cyril of Alexandria   Bishop of Alexandria 412–44: one of the greatest theologians of the early church, prolific writer and preacher, and the main opponent of Nestorius at the Council of Ephesus in 431. At the Council of Chalcedon in 451 his doctrine of the Incarnation was the touchstone against which that contained in the *Tome* of Pope Leo the Great (d. 444) was measured. His writings include commentaries on Luke and John. Cyril's theology is of contemporary importance to discussions between Oriental Orthodox and EASTERN ORTHODOX or Catholics, since his formula of 'the one incarnate physis of the Logos' (Epistle 46) is accepted by CHALCEDONIANS and anti-Chalcedonians alike as orthodox.

The hostile portrait of Cyril in Gibbon's *Decline and Fall* and the equally negative fictional portrait of Cyril in Charles Kingsley's *Hypatia* have clouded his reputation in the English-speaking world. Cyril is commemorated in the Byzantine calendar on 18 January.

McGuckin, J. A. (1994), *St Cyril of Alexandria: The Christological Controversy*. Leiden: Brill.

E/DM

Cyril of Jerusalem   Cyril was deposed as bishop of Jerusalem three times: in 357 by a local council in JERUSALEM, but restored at the Council of Seleucia just over a year later; by Emperor Acacius in 360; and by Emperor Valens in 367, this time until 378. He took part in the Council of Constantinople in 381. A collection of catecheses exists under his name, which were taken down in shorthand. One manuscript attributes the five best-known of these, the *Mystagogical Catecheses*, to his successor, John II; others to both. These lectures offer fourth-century witness to the doctrine of eucharistic sacrifice, and to the discipline of the secret, the traditional reticence about the inner mysteries of the faith. Cyril's catecheses vividly depict many aspects of the sacramental and liturgical life of the church in his period. He is celebrated on 18 March.

Telfer, W. (1955), *Cyril of Jerusalem and Nemesius of Emesa*. Library of Christian Classics 4. London: n.p.
Cross, F. L. (1951), *St Cyril of Jerusalem's Lectures on the Christian Sacraments*. London: S.P.C.K; repr. 1977, New York, St Vladimir's Seminary Press.

DM

Cyril IV   Coptic Patriarch (1854–61). Dāwūd Tūmās Bāshūt, born 1816 near Akhmim in Upper Egypt, became a monk and then abbot of Saint Antony's monastery at a young age. In 1851 the Coptic patriarch sent Dawud to Ethiopia to deal with problems between the Ethiopian clergy and their Coptic metropolitan or ABOUNA. Dawud was recalled to Cairo in 1852, soon after the patriarch's death, having been recommended as successor by the patriarch himself. In 1854 he was elected pope of Alexandria and 110th patriarch of the see of St Mark, taking the name Cyril IV. Although his reign was relatively brief, it was marked by educational reforms and by efforts to strengthen relations with other Orthodox churches. In 1856 Cyril IV returned to Ethiopia at the request of the Egyptian government to assist in border negotiations. He was imprisoned by the Ethiopian emperor, but cleared of charges; he returned to Egypt in 1858, where he died in 1861.

See also COPTIC CHRISTIANITY.

Shoucri, M. (1991), 'Cyril IV', *Coptic Encyclopedia* 3, pp. 677–9.
'Sa sainteté Cyrille IV (1854–1861)', *Le Monde Copte* 9 (1980), pp. 31–2.

MJB/SHG

Cyril V (1)   Patriarch of Constantinople (1748–51 and 1752–7). In 1755 Cyril V issued an encyclical ruling that Roman Catholic and Armenian converts to Eastern Orthodoxy should be rebaptized. His ruling, which in effect applied to anyone not baptized by triple immersion in the name of the TRINITY, was motivated by arguments against the validity of sacraments administered outside the Orthodox church and in favour of triple immersion as the only legitimate form of baptism, except in case of emergency, which had been canvassed by the distinguished Chiot physician and lay theologian Eustratios Argenti.

Runciman, S. (1968), *The Great Church in Captivity*. Cambridge: Cambridge University Press.
Ware, T. (1964), *Eustratios Argenti*. Oxford: Clarendon Press.

DM

Cyril V (2)   Coptic patriarch (1874–1927). Yūḥannā al-Nāsikh, monk of al-Barāmūs monastery in the Wādī al-Naṭrūn, was elected Cyril V, pope of Alexandria and 112th patriarch of the see of St Mark, in 1874. His reign was marked by tensions with the Egyptian government, and within the Coptic community itself. The Coptic Community Council *(maǧlis al-milli)*, elected in 1874, provided for lay involvement in church matters. Disagreements between the council and the patriarch led to the council's dissolution or reorganization several times between 1874 and 1927. These disagreements also led to Cyril's exile for five months at al-Barāmūs monastery in 1892–3. The 1911 COPTIC CONGRESS OF ASSYUT was convened only with the reluctant permission of the patriarch. During the reign of Cyril V the scriptural canon of the Coptic Orthodox church was revised. Cyril V earned his monastic name 'John the Scribe' because of his love for books and learning. He endorsed the establishment of the Coptic Clerical College in Cairo in 1894, along with other Coptic educational and vocational schools. He died in 1927 at the age of 103.

Shoucri, M. (1991), 'Cyril V', *Coptic Encyclopedia* 3, p. 679.
Iris Habib el Masri (1987), *The Story of the Copts: The True Story of Christianity in Egypt*, vol. 2, pp. 302–28. Nairobi: Coptic Bishopric for African Affairs.
Meinardus, O. F. A. (1970), *Christian Egypt: Faith and Life*. Cairo: American University in Cairo Press.

SHG

Cyril VI (1)   (d. 1821) ECUMENICAL PATRIARCH and ETHNOMARTYR. Cyril was raised in Adrianople in eastern THRACE. His family were migrants from Cappadocia. Kyrillos, a scholar and preacher devoted to education, became metropolitan of Ikonion in Lykaonia (1803), then of Adrianople (1810), and from 1813 to 1818 Ecumenical Patriarch. The OTTOMAN authorities had him deposed and exiled to Adrianople. On the outbreak of the Greek Revolution the local governor intervened in his favour but Kyrillos, a noted public figure, was executed with the priests

152

Theokletos and Jacob. He is patron of Pythion in western Thrace and is commemorated on 18 April.

Nikephoros of Didymoteichon (1989), *Hagios Kyrillos*. Ioannina: n.p.

DB

Cyril VI (2)   Coptic patriarch (1959–71). ʿĀzir Yūsuf ʿAṭā, born in Egypt 1902, entered al-Barāmūs monastery in Wādī al-Naṭrūn as a young man, became a monk there (1928), and was ordained priest (1931), taking the name Mina, in honour of St Menas the Wonderworker, an Egyptian saint to whom he had a lifelong devotion. Elected pope of Alexandria and 116th patriarch of the see of St Mark in 1959, Cyril VI did much to bring the Oriental Orthodox churches together; notably strengthening relations between the Coptic and Ethiopian churches, and also the Coptic and SYRIAN ORTHODOX churches. During his reign the Coptic Orthodox church became a member of various international ecumenical organizations, including the World Council of Churches and the Middle East Council of Churches. As patriarch, Cyril continued to be deeply interested in monastic life, initiating beneficial reforms. Shortly before his death in 1971 he established a monastery of Mar Mina in Mareotis (Maryut), Egypt.

Pope Shenouda III (1984), 'The Alexandrian Papacy: The Saintly Life of Pope Kyrillos VI', *Coptologia* 5, pp. 7–11.
Abdel-Massih, E. T. (1982), *The Life and Miracles of Pope Kirillos VI, Pope of Alexandria and Patriarch of the See of St Mark, 116th Successor of St Mark the Evangelist, Coptic Orthodox Church of Egypt, August 2, 1902–March 9, 1971*. Troy, Mich.: St Mark Coptic Orthodox Church.
Shoucri, M. (1991), 'Cyril VI', *Coptic Encyclopedia* 3, pp. 679–81.

MJB/SHG

Czech and Slovakian Orthodox church   The first Slavonic Byzantine rite church was founded by CYRIL AND METHODIUS in ninth-century Great Moravia, an area the Latin church eventually dominated, though the culture of the region always looked to the Orthodox East. Surviving groups of Byzantine Christians were later augmented by Serbs and Romanians fleeing the OTTOMAN Turks. When Great Moravia fell to the Magyars after 893 the kingdom of Bohemia remained as its true successor state in the West.

The Hussites, opposing Latin practices such as communion in one kind, appealed to their country's older religious traditions. In 1451 a delegation of mainstream Hussites led by the Oxford scholar Peter 'English' travelled to CONSTANTINOPLE and was formally reconciled with the Orthodox church. The fall of Constantinople in 1453 put an end to this promising relationship.

In the nineteenth century Czech political leaders such as Sladkovsky and other intellectuals expressed their commitment to national independence by embracing Orthodoxy. EASTERN CATHOLIC groups seeking to become Orthodox were opposed by the Austro-Hungarian imperial establishment. Orthodox movements received help from Constantinople and St Petersburg and from Greek and South Slav merchants in Vienna.

In 1918 Czechoslovakia became an independent state, making it possible to establish Orthodox parishes freely. Before this date all Orthodox communities were under the

Serbian diocese of Dalmatia. In 1921 GORAZD PAVLIK, elected archbishop of the newly recognized Orthodox church of Czechoslovakia, was consecrated by the Serbian patriarch. Surprisingly, in 1923 the Ecumenical Patriarch was responsible for the consecration of Archbishop Savvatij as a rival candidate. The state recognized Gorazd, who presided over a church of two dioceses, Prague and Mukachevo.

After the Bolshevik revolution the RUSSIAN ORTHODOX CHURCH ABROAD headed by Bishop Sergius also established itself in Czechoslovakia. The state welcomed Russian refugees and soon the Orthodox community had over a million members, including outstanding thinkers such as BULGAKOV. Tragically, in the period after the Second World War most of the Russian community, though by then Czechoslovakian citizens, were deported to the USSR.

The Second World War made unification of the Orthodox jurisdictions imperative. This happened under the aegis of MOSCOW. Only in 1951 did the Czechoslovakian church regain independence, being declared AUTOCEPHALOUS by Moscow, but recognized by the Ecumenical Patriarchate as autonomous under the jurisdiction of Constantinople. Under communist rule state authorities and atheistic organizations forcibly abolished EASTERN CATHOLIC churches across the Soviet bloc, regarding them as virulent opponents of communism. The GREEK CATHOLIC community in Czechoslovakia was forced under the rule of the RUSSIAN ORTHODOX CHURCH, leading to long-standing resentment and suspicion of the Orthodox among the Greek Catholics.

In this period a theological academy was established at Presov and four dioceses were created. Guest-workers, political refugees from Greece and Orthodox Czechs repatriated from Russia swelled the numbers of Orthodox, but from 1948 onwards a militant atheist programme of anti-church propaganda was instituted with state patronage. The crushing of the Prague Spring in 1968 led to a period of oppression.

The fall of the totalitarian regime in November 1989 and the subsequent establishment of independent Czech and Slovak states liberated the Orthodox church and removed restrictions on its social activity. Church property is being restored, though this is problematic given rival claims between Orthodox and Greek Catholics in several areas. In 1990 the theological academy became a faculty of the University of Kosice. Monastic life has been re-established on a modest scale. The Orthodox church is presently organized in four dioceses, the bishop of Prague being also metropolitan. In 1998 the Ecumenical Patriarchate recognized the autocephaly of the Czech and Slovakian Orthodox Church.

Christopher, Bishop and Keogh, M. (1991), 'An End to the Silence', *Sophia* 1. Manchester: Manchester Metropolitan University.

DB

· D ·

Dabra Metmaq, Council of   Major religious controversies involving icon and cross veneration, the observance of Saturday Sabbath, and the unity and trinity of God marked the reign of Ethiopian emperor ZARA YAKUB (1434–68). Dissident movements were monastic in origin, named after their individual founders: the Estifanosites, followers of Abba ESTIFANOS; the Ewostatewosites or Ewostateans, followers of Abba EWOSTATEWOS; and the Zamika'elites, after Abba Zamika'el. Zara Yakub himself presided over the Council of Dabra Metmaq in 1450, which approved the observance of the Saturday Sabbath. It was a crucial step in reconciling the large Ewostatean movement to the Ethiopian church and to its Egyptian leadership, which until then had opposed this custom rooted in the Old Testament.

See also ETHIOPIAN ORTHODOX CHURCH.

Haile, G. (1981). 'The Letters of Archbishops Mika'el and Gabre'el Concerning the Observance of Saturday', *Journal of Semitic Studies* 36, pp. 73–8.
Tamrat, T. (1972), *Church and State in Ethiopia 1250–1527*. Oxford Studies in African Affairs. Oxford: Clarendon Press.

MJB/SHG

daily offices, in the Byzantine rite   Christians have, since apostolic times (see Acts 3: 1), followed Jewish practice in assembling for public prayer at evening and morning, particular importance being given to the day's first office, the evening 'Lighting of the Lamps' (Greek: *lychnikos*; Latin: *lucernarium*). The present form of these daily offices has evolved from elements of the 'sung' (Greek: *asmatike*) or 'cathedral office', and of the monastic office, with its emphasis on the psalter. (*See* ASMATIKE AKOLOUTHIA.)

As in the West, there are theoretically eight hours of prayer distributed at three-hourly intervals, an arrangement reflecting Psalm 118, verses 164, 'seven times a day I praised you', and 62, 'at midnight I arose to give you thanks'. The Byzantine daily cursus is: Vespers, Compline, Midnight, Matins, First, Third, Sixth and Ninth Hours.

The Midnight office has no corresponding office in the Western cursus, since Byzantine Matins corresponds to two Latin offices, Matins and Lauds. The Byzantine rite also includes the Typika, originating, perhaps, as a substitute for the liturgy if the latter was not to be celebrated, but now part of the daily cursus. Elements from it are incorporated into the *enarxis* (opening section) of the Divine Liturgy, except on feasts of the Lord.

The liturgical day begins with Vespers, which, in contemporary Byzantine use follows immediately on the Ninth Hour that ends the preceding day, being read three hours before sunset. The Divine Liturgy stands outside the cursus. Except for the 'Vigil Liturgies' at Christmas, Theophany and Pascha, when it is combined with Vespers, it correctly follows the Sixth Hour. This suggests that originally the liturgy was celebrated quite late in the morning, and there is evidence for this in the writings of Dorotheos of Gaza and in the rubric on certain great feasts to the effect that 'the Liturgy is celebrated earlier, because of the toil of the vigil.'

The lesser hours have a simple structure: three fixed psalms followed by a series of short hymns and two prayers, the first common to all the lesser hours and the second peculiar to each hour, those at the Sixth and Ninth Hours linking them respectively to the moments of Christ's crucifixion and death. At Compline the psalms are followed by the lesser DOXOLOGY and the creed, the final prayers are more elaborated and the office ends with a litany. In many monasteries the AKATHIST is read after the creed, in others the daily canon to the THEOTOKOS. In Lent and on certain other days Great Compline is celebrated: a longer office in three sections, the first including very ancient Christian hymns, the second the Prayer of Mannasse, and the third the daily CANON to the Mother of God.

The Midnight office has two forms, one for weekdays, the other for Sundays. The weekday office has two sections. The first includes Psalm 50, the creed and Psalm 118 – on Saturdays, Psalms 65–9 – short hymns and prayers. The second is a short office for the dead, followed by short hymns and a litany, as at Compline. On Sundays the office consists almost entirely of a canon in the appropriate tone in honour of the Holy Trinity, by Metrophanes of Smyrna.

E

Daniil of Moscow (1261–1303)   The son of Aleksandr Nevskii, Daniil inherited the then minor principality of MOSCOW. He founded churches, extended Moscow's influence and worked for the unity of Rus. Before death he took the great monastic *schema* (habit) and was buried in St Daniil the Stylite monastery, which he had founded. He is commemorated on 4 March and 30 August. The monastery, lavishly restored, houses the offices of the Moscow patriarchate.

DB

David the Dendrite (d. 540)   David 'the tree-dweller' is, along with Demetrios the GREAT MARTYR, patron saint of Thessaloniki. A native of Mesopotamia, he joined the Monastery of SS Merkourios and Theodore near Thessaloniki. To avoid crowds coming for advice and healing he spent three years in an almond tree. David left his tree to visit CONSTANTINOPLE and beg Emperor Justinian to send troops to break the

siege of Thessaloniki. He died on the ship returning to MACEDONIA. He is commemorated on 26 June and 17 July.

Nicolas Velimirovic (1986), *The Prologue from Ochrid*, vol. 2. Birmingham: Lazarica Press.

DB

deacon Greek: *diakonos*, servant, messenger or attendant. The term sometimes designates a temple functionary or official. In the New Testament *diakonos* designates a ministry within the developing church. The Letter to the Philippians opens with a greeting from Paul and Timothy 'to all the holy ones in Christ Jesus' with their *episkopoi* and *diakonoi*. The qualifications for a person who is to become a *diakonos* are laid out in 1 Timothy 3: 8ff immediately after those for an *episkopos*: 'The deacon too, respectable, not duplicitous in speech, not given to excess in wine, not sordidly avaricious, possessing the mystery of the faith with a clear conscience. First let them be tested, and if there is nothing against them, let them serve [*diakoneitosan*]. Women, similarly respectable, not slanderers, but sober and trustworthy in all things. Let deacons be men of one wife, who preside well over their children and households.' While the reference to WOMEN here can be read as a reference to the deacon's wife, it more probably refers to women seeking to be made *diakonos*. In Romans 16: 1 Paul commends to his readers 'Phoebe, *diakonos* of the church at Cenchreae'. But it is unclear whether *diakonos* here designates an office or simply labels Phoebe as a servant of the church.

Acts 6: 1–7 records the Twelve laying hands on seven men selected by the disciples to take over the distribution of food in the Christian community. The seven are not referred to as *diakonoi*, but are traditionally venerated as the first deacons (JOHN CHRYSOSTOM in his Fourteenth Homily on Acts rejects this view).

As the church's institutions developed, a pattern of ministries emerged, based on three orders of clergy ordained by CHEIROTONIA: bishops (*episkopoi*), priests (*presbyteroi*) and deacons (*diakonoi*); and a range of minor clergy ordained by CHEIROTHESIA: door-keepers, exorcists, psalmists, readers and sub-deacons. The survival of the general meaning of the word *diakonia* as ministry and of *diakonos* as minister underlies COPTIC and SYRIAN ORTHODOX terminology, where all these lower ministers are often referred to as deacons, so that a person can be said to have been 'ordained deacon with the rank of reader'.

In Eastern Christian churches, the deacon normally functions as the leader of the people's prayers during services, chanting litanies and certain prayers, as well as assisting the priest at the altar.

The female diaconate ministered to women, keeping order in church and anointing women catechumens with oil at baptism, visiting women in their houses and accompanying them when visiting male clergy. As the baptism of infants became the norm and the baptism of adults rarer, the importance of the female diaconate faded; eventually, probably by the eleventh century, it fell into desuetude.

In the twentieth century, Patriarch MELETIOS METAXAKIS ordained deaconesses, whose status, however, remained uncertain. It is widely believed, but not certain, that Nektarios of Pentapolis ordained two women to the diaconate. By 1988 a consultation organized by the Ecumenical Patriarchate publicly welcomed the proposal to restore the female diaconate.

DM

Dečani The PANTOCRATOR church (1327–35) at Dečani, in the Kosovo region of southern SERBIA, was founded by King Stefan Uroš III Dečanski and his son, later Tsar Dušan. Stefan Dečanski is buried in the church. According to an inscription carved above the south door, the master mason was Vita, a friar from 'the king's city' of Kotor. It is a single-domed, five-aisled basilica with a triple-naved narthex. Architecturally, its design and execution are a blend of Byzantine and Romanesque elements, with its facade of alternate bands of pale coloured marble with mullions and portals. In this, Stefan Dečanski followed his predecessors' example, building a royal mausoleum on the model of STUDENICA, even though Byzantine forms predominated in Serbia. The frescoes, completed in 1350, represent a huge fund of information on theological views, princely ideology and liturgical practices, as well as material culture and everyday life. Aesthetically, in spite of their encyclopedic character, the wall paintings fit admirably into a difficult architectural setting. Some twenty major iconographic programmes are depicted, including rare cycles such as the AKATHISTOS, the Wisdom of Solomon and the Acts of the Apostles. In the narthex, along with an unusual donors' composition, and the family tree of the Nemanjić dynasty, there are illustrations of the church CALENDAR and a cycle of ECUMENICAL COUNCILS. The monastery had an important scriptorium and a rich library and treasury. In the OTTOMAN period the most serious devastation occurred in the eighteenth century. Although impoverished and often unable to pay the tax obligations imposed by the Turks, Dečani remained active and, in periods of comparative peace, its monks produced works of notable literary and artistic quality. Anxious to preserve a venerated shrine, Serbian communities outside the Ottoman empire provided material help whenever possible.

Djurić, V. J., ed. (1995), *Zidno slikarstvo Dečana: Gradja i Studije*. Belgrade: Serbian Academy of Sciences and Arts (English summary).
Gavrilović, Z. (1995), 'Discs Held by Angels in the Anastasis at Dečani', in C. Moss and K. Kiefer, eds, *Byzantine East, Latin West: Art-Historical Studies in Honor of Kurt Weitzmann*. Princeton: Princeton University Press.
Djurić, V. J., ed. (1989), *Dečani et l'art byzantin au milieu du XIVe siècle*. Belgrade: Srpska Akademija Nauka i Umetnosti i NIRO, Priština.
Petković, V. and Bošković, Dj. (1941), *Manastir Decani*, vols 1, 2. Belgrade: Srpska Kraljevska Akademija, Zadužbina M. Pupina.

ZG

Deesis Greek, 'intercession'. Iconographically the Deesis normally shows Christ between the supplicant figures of the Virgin and JOHN THE BAPTIST, great intercessors

158

for humanity since the Forerunner is last and greatest of the prophets, the Virgin the chosen Mother of God's Son, both exercising unique roles in the economy of salvation. The earliest reference to such an image is found in the *Miracles of Cyrus and John*, attributed to Sophronius, bishop of JERUSALEM (634–9).

KP

deification   The doctrine of deification (*theosis*), explicit in 2 Peter 1:4, 'so that through these you might become sharers in the divine nature', was taken up by early Christian theologians. Together with APOPHATICISM, deification became a central pillar of Byzantine theology. For the Greek fathers Christ is the paradigm of human deification, an idea summarized in the dictum: 'God became human that we might become divine.' Christ's humanity is deified humanity. Christians are called to participate in Christ's divinity, not to become disincarnate spirits but to attain a more authentic humanity. This participation (*methexis*) is a gift of grace we are called to accept. In Eastern tradition deification is understood as eucharistic and ecclesial as well as a matter of personal, moral and spiritual life. Ideas of deification are also found in Western theology, not least in the Roman mass.

Mantzaridis, G. I. (1984), *The Deification of Man: St Gregory Palamas and the Orthodox Tradition*. Crestwood, NY: St Vladimir's Seminary Press.
Meyendorff, J. (1979), *Byzantine Theology: Historical Trends and Doctrinal Themes*. New York: Fordam University Press.

KP

Demetrios Gangastathis (d. 1975)   Visionary Greek *gerontas* (elder; *see also* STARETS). Although he was neither monk nor scholar, many people travelled to his remote village to seek the elder's advice. Demetrios, a shepherd from Thessaly, served briefly as a soldier in ASIA MINOR during the collapse of the Greek front in 1922 (*see* IONIA). He married in 1928 and raised nine children. After following a six-month course at the Theological Academy of Tripolis, he was ordained priest in 1931. Demetrios returned to his native village, Platanos in Thessaly, and the church of the Taxiarchs (*see* ANGELS). During the Second World War he interceded with Germans, Italians and partisans on behalf of his fellow villagers and saved the lives of many. He provoked the wrath of the communists by commemorating the Russian NEW MARTYRS by name and narrowly escaped execution himself. He continued to commemorate daily both these and Greeks killed because of their religion during the Second World War and the Greek civil war. Demetrios died of cancer and is commemorated on 29 January.

Kemenzetzidis, N. (1990), *Demetrios Gangastathis: 1902–75*. Thessaloniki: Orthodoxos Kypseli.
Kottadakis, A. (1989), *Synaxari tou Eikostou Aiona*. Athens: Tinos.

DB

Diadochos of Photike   Bishop, ascetic, mystic, theologian; opponent of monophysitism at Chalcedon. He was probably born *c*.400 and died between 446 and 486. Diadochos' principal work, the *Hundred Chapters on Spiritual Perfection*, is a classic of

159

Eastern mysticism. He emphasized the importance of DISCRIMINATION and of awareness of the love of God. He calls his readers to make themselves, especially by 'peace of soul', dwelling-places of the Holy Spirit (ch. 28), which will render their souls silent and 'drunk with God's love'. He speaks of contemplation and of the role of the intellect, but presents the spiritual life as a process of radical transformation based on the awareness of the working of the Spirit. The intellect perceives its own light in the divine light that irradiates it (ch. 40), but Diadochos warns us that anything that appears to the intellect with any shape or form, even light or fire, is the work of the devil. In chapter 59 he recommends occupying the intellect with the continual prayer 'Lord Jesus', so that the name of Jesus can work on us like a refiner's fire, consuming the dross.

Polyzos, T. (1984), 'Life and Writings of Diadochus of Photike', *Theologia* 55.

DM

Diakonikon (1) A Greek liturgical book containing the DEACON's part for ORTHROS, HESPERINOS, the Divine Liturgy and the Liturgy of the Presanctified. (2) Area behind the south door of the ICONOSTASIS where things needed for services can be prepared.

DM

diaspora Greek, 'scattering'. In the Septuagint text of Jeremias 15: 7 God threatens JERUSALEM and its people with dispersion. In Isaias 49: 6 God tells the prophet: 'It is a great thing to be called my servant, to establish the tribes of Jacob and to cause the diaspora of Israel to return...' In Psalm 146/147: 2 the psalmist says: 'The Lord builds up Jerusalem; and he will gather the scattered [diasporas] of Israel.' The BIBLE gives us the image of diaspora as the scattering of God's people from their homeland into foreign and often hostile territory, their scattering sometimes seen as a form of punishment, their return home as a saving act of God. In Jewish history, 'diaspora' came to refer to the Jews living outside the Holy Land. The term came be applied to ethnic communities living outside their homelands, whether because of expulsion, exile or emigration. Exiles, however, share a sense of diaspora identity sharply different from that of voluntary emigrants, who are normally also willing immigrants into a new homeland. Nostalgia for and a commitment to political and economic support for the motherland is common to diaspora communities, but for exiles there is also a sense of loss, deprivation, injustice, frustration and often utter impotence. There exist also exiled communities who after generations are firmly settled in a land where they arrived not as willing immigrants but as refugees. If return becomes possible and is declined, the sense of identity and of diaspora has to be renegotiated, and this can raise tormenting issues of loyalty and commitment.

In EASTERN CHRISTIAN diaspora communities the church has played an important, frequently a crucial, role in maintaining ethnic identity and preserving cultural heritage. In more settled diaspora communities tensions can emerge between the role of the church in the life of the ethnic group and the evangelistic, pastoral and charitable role which the church inherits precisely as the church.

Eastern Christian diaspora communities frequently live in the traditional territory of the Western Patriarchate (*see* ROME) and its daughter churches. A variety of EASTERN ORTHODOX jurisdictions have been established in the West and relations among them are sometimes problematic. Problems of jurisdiction between Latin and EASTERN CATHOLIC hierarchs have also occurred.

The co-existence of different Eastern Orthodox hierarchies in the same territory and of Eastern and Latin Catholic hierarchies have corroded almost completely the ancient canonical principles of the unity of the local episcopate and of the territorial basis of episcopal jurisdiction. Vatican II formally recognized this for Catholic churches in ORIENTALIUM ECCLESIARUM.

The application of the concept of diaspora to the church, as opposed to the ethnic community, is gravely problematic. Historically and culturally it is obvious that there exists an Eastern Christian diaspora, complex networks of groups deriving historically from the movement of individuals, families, whole communities from one geographical location to another. Theologically, however, and especially from the perspective of Eastern Christian tradition, the identity of the individual eucharistic community with the church, and its inheritance of the church's mission in its totality, have to be acknowledged, though it must also be accepted that many factors will affect the ability of any specific church community to carry out that mission.

DM

Diatessaron A harmonized text of the four gospels in a single narrative. It is based mainly on Matthew's Gospel, but also used some non-canonical sources. It was composed by a north Mesopotamian or Syrian Christian, Tatian, in SYRIAC or Greek *c*.160. The only extant fragment, from DURA EUROPOS and dated before 256, is in Greek, but in favour of the theory of a Syriac original stands above all the centrality of the Diatessaron in the SYRIAN church until the fourth century, when a move to replace the Diatessaron with the separate gospels, as in the Western church, gained momentum. In the early fifth century THEODORET OF CYRRHUS and RABBULA of EDESSA destroyed copies of the Diatessaron as a matter of policy. It disappeared so completely that the only surviving evidence of it in Greek and Syriac are the Dura fragment and, very importantly, the Diatessaron citations of EPHREM THE SYRIAN in his *Commentary on the Diatessaron*, a large part of which has been recovered in recent years (manuscripts in the Chester Beatty Library, Dublin: MS 709).

JH

Didymus the Blind (*c*.313–*c*.398) Installed as head of the School of ALEXANDRIA by ATHANASIUS. Although blind from the age of four he was immensely learned, a prolific writer and scriptural commentator. He taught Jerome and Rufinus. Despite his reputation as ascetic and prophet, the Council of Constantinople in 553 condemned him with ORIGEN and EVAGRIUS PONTICUS. Didymus is credited with inventing a system of raised writing for the blind.

DM

Dikaios   Greek: 'just', 'righteous'. (1) Customary title of the saints of the Old Law commemorated in the Byzantine CALENDAR. (2) Title of the officer of a Greek monastery establishment corresponding to the claustral prior of a Benedictine house.

DM

Diodore of Tarsus (d. before 394)   Became bishop of Tarsus *c*.378; anti-Arian theologian and teacher of both JOHN CHRYSOSTOM and Theodore of Mopsuestia. Only fragments of his prolific writings survive, not least since his association with Theodore later made his orthodoxy suspect.

DM

Dionysios of Olympos   Sixteenth-century ascetic and founder of Olympos monastery by Mount Olympos in Pieria; contemporary and friend of NIKANOR. Originally a teacher and calligrapher from Platina in Thessaly, he joined one of the Meteora monasteries, then moved to ATHOS, and travelled widely as a pilgrim. Dionysios was elected abbot of Philotheou but left for Verroia after a dispute with the monastery's Bulgarian monks. Olympos monastery, where he ended his life, was a cultural centre for northern Greeks in the OTTOMAN period; it was destroyed during the Second World War. Dionysios is commemorated on 23/3 January.

See also HOLY MOUNTAINS; MACEDONIA.

Papadopoulos, L. (1988), *Lives of the Monastery Builders*. Buena Vista, Col.: Holy Apostles.

DB

Dionysios the Areopagite   Member of the Areopagite Council; he is mentioned as a follower of Paul in Acts 17: 34. Tradition makes him bishop of Athens, either its first bishop, installed by Paul, or the successor of his teacher Hierotheos. Dionysios is celebrated as a martyr on 3 October. He is sometimes represented, along with Hierotheos, in icons of the DORMITION.

Dionysios' name was assumed by an unknown author of the fifth or sixth century who was probably of Syrian origin and who is known as Pseudo-Dionysios. The first recorded mention of the *Corpus Areopagiticum* is by SEVERUS OF ANTIOCH *c*.513. The authenticity of his writings was first questioned in 532 by Hypatios of Ephesus, at a synod in Constantinople called to discuss differences between CHALCEDONIANS and MONOPHYSITES at which Severus was present.

The Dionysian corpus represents a synthesis of Christian theology and later PLATONISM, especially that of Proclus and his circle. In the *Divine Names* the author discusses the meaning of the divine attributes, while the *Mystical Theology* gives a succinct exposition of APOPHATIC THEOLOGY and DEIFICATION. The *Celestial Hierarchy* offers a description of the angelic orders, while the *Ecclesiastical Hierarchy* offers a symbolic interpretation of the MYSTERIES. Ten *Letters* are attributed to Pseudo-Dionysios; one is addressed to JOHN THE THEOLOGIAN.

John of Scythopolis commented on Pseudo-Dionysios in the sixth century, MAXIMUS THE CONFESSOR in the seventh.

Golitzin, A. (1994), *Et Introibo ad Altare Dei: The Mystogogy of Dionysius Areopagita, with Special Reference to its Predecessors in the Eastern Christian Tradition*. Analecta Vlatadon 59. Thessaloniki: Patriarchal Institute of Patristic Studies.

Rorem, P. (1993), *Pseudo-Dionysius: A Commentary on the Texts and an Introduction to their Influence*. Oxford: Oxford University Press.

Rorem, P. (1984), *Biblical and Liturgical Symbols within the Pseudo-Dionysian Synthesis*. Toronto: Pontifical Institute of Medieval Studies.

Louth, A. (1989), *Denys the Areopagite*. London: Geoffrey Chapman.

Luibheid, C. trans. (1987), *Pseudo-Dionysius: The Complete Works*. London: SPCK.

KP

Dionysius of Tell Maḥrē   SYRIAN ORTHODOX patriarch (818–45). Played a major diplomatic role *vis-à-vis* the Muslim authorities, visiting Egypt (825–7) and Baghdad (829: seeking a concession from Caliph al-Ma'mun; 835: paying repects to al-Mu'ta-ṣim). Within his church he faced a number of disputes.

Dionysius' antiquarian interests are revealed by his visiting the pyramids and other places in Egypt. He is best known as the author of a history, written at the request of John, bishop of Dara, of the time from the accession of the Emperor Maurice in 582 to the death of Theophilus in 842. For the text we depend principally on extensive quotations in later chronicles such as the *Chronicle to* AD *1234* and that of MICHAEL THE SYRIAN (1126–99); a short section survived separately in a Vatican manuscript. The original work had two sections, a church history and a secular history, each consisting of eight books. The author used various sources, including sources in Greek and Arabic.

The *Chronicle of Zuqnīn* written in 775 was mistakenly ascribed by J. Assemani to Dionysius and is sometimes known as the *Chronicle of Pseudo-Dionysius of Tell Maḥrē*.

Chabot, J.-B. (1916–74), *Chronicon ad annum Christi 1234 pertinens*. CSCO 81–2: Scriptores Syri 36–7 (Paris: Gabalda, 1916, 1920); 109: Scriptores Syri 56 (Louvain: L. Durbecq, 1952); 354: Scriptores Syri 154 (Louvain: Sécretariat du CSCO, 1974).

Abramowski, R. (1940), *Dionysius of Tellmahre: Jakobitischer Patriarch von 818–845*. Leipzig: Brockhaus.

For Pseudo-Dionysius, see CSCO 91 (Paris: Typographeum Reipublicae, 1927); 104 (Louvain: L. Durbecq, 1952 [1933]); 121 (Louvain: L. Durbecq, 1949), 507 (Louvain: Peeters, 1989).

JH

discrimination   Greek: *diakrisis*. (1) A spiritual gift enabling its recipient to distinguish the promptings of grace from illusions and delusions and demonically inspired temptations. (2) An exceptional gift enabling one person, usually an elder or teacher, to discern the spiritual state of another.

DM

Divine Wisdom (*Sophia*)   The philosopher Seneca in the first century AD wrote in one of his letters (Epistle 89): 'Wisdom is the human mind's good brought to perfection. Philosophy is the love and pursuit of wisdom; it strives for the goal which wisdom has achieved... Some have so defined Wisdom that they call it scientific knowledge [*scientia*] of the divine and the human. Others have defined it thus: wisdom is knowledge [*nosse*] of the divine and the human and their causes.' The doxographer Aetius, who flourished around the turn of the second century, offers a similar definition. 'The Stoics said that wisdom [*sophia*] is the scientific knowledge [*episteme*] of the divine and the human, and that philosophy is the practice [*askesis*] of expertise [*techne*] in utility. Virtue [*arete*] singly and at its highest is utility...' Such definitions of wisdom and philosophy would be familiar to educated people in the Roman empire in which early Christianity spread. Wisdom as defined here approximates to what later Christian tradition would recognize as theology.

Wisdom, an important concept in, for example, Ecclesiastes 7 and personified in Proverbs 8–9, emerges in the later deutero-canonical books of the BIBLE (e.g. Sirach 1, 14–15, 24; Wisdom 6–10) as a hypostatization of the providence and creative power of the Godhead, both transcendent and immanent. From an early period, Christian thinkers saw the wisdom texts as pointing to the divine Logos.

This is the significance of the dedication of Divine Wisdom (Hagia Sophia) given to the Great Church in CONSTANTINOPLE by Emperor Constantius II in 360. The present building, dedicated in 537, largely the work of Justinian I, represents not only the emperor's humbling himself in worship before Divine Wisdom incarnate, but also his own role as God's vicegerent, agent of the divine providence. The title Divine Wisdom was given to many other churches throughout the Eastern Orthodox world.

The wisdom texts are also sometimes applied to the Holy Spirit and, especially in Russian tradition, to the THEOTOKOS. Traditionally, churches dedicated to Hagia Sophia celebrate their patronal feast at PENTECOST. In the seventeenth century, however, an AKOLOUTHIA (*posledovanie*) was composed in honour of 'Sophia, Wisdom of God' to be celebrated at the cathedral of Divine Wisdom at NOVGOROD on 13

August, the eve of the Dormition of the Virgin, but not officially included in the MENAIA of the Russian church. The complex Russian understanding of *Sophia* fed into the speculative SOPHIOLOGY of late nineteenth- and early twentieth-century Russian thought.

Iconographically Divine Wisdom is depicted in several ways. Sometimes Wisdom is depicted as Christ PANTOCRATOR, sometimes as a female angel or virgin. The use of the Pantocrator image is a reference to Wisdom 7: 25. The female personifications also draw on biblical images, but refer to classical philosophical thought as well. The icon illustrated here is of a type which shows Wisdom as a seated angel, flanked by the Mother of God and John the Baptist, in the manner of a DEESIS, with Christ appearing above. The more elaborate icon of 'Wisdom has built her house' incorporates elements taken from Proverbs 9: 1–6.

Fiene, D. M. (1989), 'What is the Appearance of Divine Sophia?' *Slavic Review* 48, pp. 449–76.

Meyendorff, J. (1988), 'Wisdom-Sophia: Contrasting Approaches to a Complex Theme', *Dumbarton Oaks Papers* 42, pp. 391–401.

KP/DM

Dormition   The feast of the Dormition of the Mother of God (Greek: *Koimesis*) is celebrated on 15 August, making it the last major feast of the liturgical CALENDAR. After becoming fixed in the East in the sixth century, the feast became popular among Byzantine homiletical writers. In the icon of the Dormition Mary's body is depicted lying on a bier surrounded by the twelve apostles. Four bishops are often shown: James the brother of the Lord, bishop of JERUSALEM; Timothy, bishop of Ephesus; DIONYSIOS THE AREOPAGITE; and Hierotheos, bishops of Athens. Chapter 3 of the *Divine Names* of Dionysios the Areopagite is traditionally understood to refer to the Dormition of the Virgin and the Byzantine office of the feast makes use of the text. Circumscribed by a large MANDORLA, Christ holds in his hands the soul of the Virgin wrapped in swaddling clothes, just as she appears in the NATIVITY OF THE MOTHER OF GOD. In some depictions a Jew, Jephonias or Athonius, is shown, an angel cutting off his hands with a sword for trying to touch the body of the Virgin. A lighted candle in front of Mary's bier symbolizes the light she bore.

The KONTAKION of the feast says: 'Nor tomb nor death overpowered the Mother of God,' proclaiming that 'as Mother of Life she has been taken over into life by him

who dwelt in her ever-virgin womb.' The traditional story of the Dormition has the apostles carried on clouds from wherever they were proclaiming the gospel to the place where Mary lay dying. The Virgin's body was buried in Gethsemane. A glorious perfume emanated from her tomb and mysterious voices were heard praising Christ. After three days the voices were heard no more: it was evident her body had been assumed into heaven. The Coptic version of the story is somewhat different: Jesus appears and takes the Virgin's body to heaven in a chariot of fire, 206 days after her death.

Daley, B. E., trans. (1997), *On the Dormition of Mary: Early Patristic Homilies*. Crestwood, NY: St Vladimir's Seminary Press.

Ouspensky, L. and Lossky, V. (1982), *The Meaning of Icons*. Crestwood, NY: St Vladimir's Seminary Press.

Wenger, A. (1955), *L'assomption de la très sainte Vierge dans la tradition byzantine du VIe au Xe siècle*. Paris: Institute Français d'Etudes Byzantines.

KP

Doxastikon   In the Byzantine rite, a hymn normally sung after the short doxology and followed by the verse 'Now and ever and to the ages of ages, Amen' and then a

THEOTOKION in the same tone. On Feasts of the Lord and on some other occasions it is sung after the complete short Doxology with no theotokion.

E

Doxology (1) An ancient hymn of praise, common to both East and West. In the East it has two forms, the Greater and Lesser. The former is used at Matins on Sundays and Feasts, the latter at Matins on ordinary days and at Compline. Like the Latin Te Deum, the hymn itself is followed by a series of verses from the psalter. The Great Doxology ends with the solemn singing of the TRISAGION. The Lesser Doxology ends with the prayer 'Grant Lord this day', which, at both Vespers and non-festal Matins, precedes the Bowing of Heads. (2) The word 'doxology' is also used for other short ascriptions of praise to the Holy Trinity.

E

Dura Europos Archaeologically one of the most important early Christian sites of the Near East, on the Syrian middle Euphrates. Of Seleucid foundation c.300 BC (the title 'Europos' commemorating Seleucus I's home town in Macedonia), it fell under Parthian control c.113 BC and after several incursions was annexed by the Romans c.AD 165. It was destroyed by the Sasanians after a siege c.256 and was in ruins when visited by Emperor Julian in 363 on his way to Ctesiphon. Excavated between 1922 and 1937, Dura appears as a flourishing pagan city, half fortress, half marketplace, notable from a Christian viewpoint for a Greek fragment of TATIAN'S DIATESSARON found there, and for the discovery in the ruins of a Christian church and baptistry, dated c.232, based on the conversion of a domestic building, and holding up to seventy-five people. The Christians may have been Roman soldiers and merchants from the EDESSA region (with which contacts were strong). Another important find was a dated SYRIAC sale document written in Edessa in 243. Most inscriptional finds are in Greek and Latin; architecture too was Hellenistic. Dura has a synagogue dated 245 with well preserved wall paintings depicting Old Testament scenes. There are wall paintings in the church also, including a depiction of the Marys at the tomb of Christ.

Weitzmann, K. and Kessler, H. L. (1990), *The Frescoes of Dura Europus and Christian Art*. Washington, DC: Dumbarton Oaks.

JH

dyophysite One who believes that Christ possesses two natures, divine and human. Both CHALCEDONIAN churches and the CHURCH OF THE EAST are dyophysite. The Christological definition asserted by the Council of Ephesus in 431, recognized by EASTERN ORTHODOX, ROMAN CATHOLICS and Oriental Orthodox as an ECUMEN-ICAL COUNCIL, was rejected by the Church of the East which became separated. The dyophysite definition proclaimed by the Council of CHALCEDON in 451 was the occasion of the separation of the Oriental Orthodox.

DM

◆E◆

Eastern Catholic Generic term used to designate Christians in full communion with ROME who belong to one or other of the Eastern rites. The following are the principal Eastern Catholic churches and communities.

◆Byzantine rite◆

(1) The UKRAINIAN CATHOLIC CHURCH, the largest Eastern Catholic church.

(2) The RUTHENIAN Catholic church, united to Rome since the Union of Uzhorod (1646). Ruthenian or Rusyn communities, who live south of the Carpathians, have a strong sense of ethnic identity, despite living for centuries under Hungarian, Czechoslovak or Soviet rule. Ruthenian Catholics were forcibly united to the Orthodox church under the former communist regime. A Ruthenian hierarchy was re-established by the appointment in 1991 of Bishop Ivan Samedi of Muka-cevo. The Ruthenian church has a close relation with the Ukrainian Catholic church, yet asserts its own traditions and individuality. In the DIASPORA, how-ever, many Ruthenians have joined Ukrainian Catholic jurisdictions. In AMERICA the intransigent opposition of Latin Catholic bishops to married Ruthenian clergy led to over half the Ruthenian Catholic community in the USA returning to the Orthodox church. The Byzantine Catholic metropolia of Pittsburgh, Pennsylva-nia is the organizational base for the Ruthenian Catholic community in the USA.

(3) The MELKITE CATHOLIC CHURCH.

(4) The Romanian Catholic church, whose origins lie in Habsburg-supported Roman Catholic missionary activity after the expulsion of the OTTOMAN Turks from Transylvania in 1687. A metropolitan diocese for Romanian Catholics was estab-lished in 1853, but under the communist regime the Byzantine Catholics of Romania were forced into the Orthodox church or underground. In 1989, with the collapse of the former regime, the Romanian Catholic church re-emerged.

167

The numbers of Romanian Catholics is a matter of controversy; the church claimed about two million by 1990.

(5) The GREEK CATHOLICS of Greece, under the Byzantine Catholic archdiocese of Athens.

(6) The Slovakian diocese of Presov, established in 1937 as an organizational basis for Byzantine rite Catholicism in Slovakia. In 1950 the 300 or more Byzantine Catholic parishes were forced into the RUSSIAN ORTHODOX CHURCH, but most returned to Catholicism under the Prague Spring of 1968, and remained loyal to Rome through the ensuing period of communist oppression. By the late 1990s the community numbered about half a million.

(7) The Diocese of Hajdudorog, founded in 1912 as the organizational base for the Byzantine rite Catholics of Hungary, who number about a third of a million.

(8) The ITALO-GREEKS.

(9) The Russian Catholic church, small but notable for its strict loyalty to Orthodox liturgical tradition, originated in the conversion to Catholicism in 1893 of the Russian Orthodox priest Nikolai Tolstoy and his reception of the eminent theologian Vladimir SOLOVYOV in 1896. The group of Russian converts that gathered around them included OLD BELIEVERS, who retain their traditional rites.

◆ Churches of the East Syrian rite ◆

(1) The CHALDEAN church.
(2) The Syro-Malabar church in South INDIA.

◆ Churches of the West Syrian rite ◆

(1) The MARONITE church.
(2) The SYRIAN CATHOLIC church.
(3) The Syro-Malankara church in South INDIA.

◆ Churches of other rites ◆

(1) The ARMENIAN Catholic church.
(2) The COPTIC Catholic church.
(3) The ETHIOPIAN Catholic church.

There exist in addition to the churches and communities listed here, other Eastern Catholic groups living under the pastoral care of Latin rite bishops.

DM

Eastern Christian   A member of any of the Eastern or Oriental churches. The following groups of Eastern Christians exist.

(1) EASTERN ORTHODOX, the family of churches united by acceptance of seven ECUMENICAL COUNCILS. There are several Eastern Orthodox churches not in communion with the main body of Eastern Orthodox, for example the TRUE ORTHODOX or OLD CALENDARIST churches and the OLD BELIEVERS.

(2) Oriental Orthodox, the family of churches united by acceptance of three ecumenical councils and by the rejection of the ecumenical authority of CHALCEDON. Within this group, the Mar Thoma Church (*see* INDIA) is a special case as a reformed Oriental church which still has a recognizably Oriental Orthodox ethos.

(3) The CHURCH OF THE EAST, which accepts only the Council of Nicea as of ecumenical authority.

(4) The EASTERN CATHOLIC churches, Eastern or Oriental in rite and discipline, but united in dogma and communion with ROME.

(5) Eastern Catholics living under the authority of Latin bishops.

(6) Dissident Eastern communities, e.g. the now extinct dualist PAULICIANS and BOGOMILS, various Judaizing movements and the so-called RUSSIAN SECTS, Khlysty, Doukhobors, Molokans and Skoptsy.

There also exist Protestant churches such as the COPTIC EVANGELICAL CHURCH and the Armenian Evangelical church, which, while more Western in worship and doctrine, retain a particular sense of ethnic and communal identity with the Eastern churches from which their members were originally drawn.

Hinnells, J. ed. (1997), *A New Handbook of Living Religions*. Oxford: Blackwell.
Atiya, S. A. (1991), *A History of Eastern Christianity*. Milwood, NY: Kraus Reprint.
Attwater, D. (1961–2), *The Christian Churches of the East*. Leominster: Thomas More Books.

DM

Eastern Orthodox The family of EASTERN CHRISTIAN churches which acknowledge seven ECUMENICAL COUNCILS and are normally in communion with the ancient PATRIARCHATES of CONSTANTINOPLE, ALEXANDRIA, ANTIOCH and JERUSALEM.

The following churches are recorded as fully independent or autocephalous churches in the official Hemerologion of the ECUMENICAL PATRIARCHATE: Constantinople, Alexandria, Antioch, Jerusalem, Russia, Serbia, Romania, Bulgaria, Georgia, Cyprus, Greece, Poland, Albania. (*See also* SINAI.) The church of the Czech Republic and Slovakia is now also recognized as autocephalous. The church of Finland is recognized as 'autonomous' within the Ecumenical Patriarchate. In 1996 the autocephalous Ukrainian Orthodox church in the DIASPORA was received into the Ecumenical Patriarchate. The ORTHODOX CHURCH IN AMERICA is recognized as autocephalous and the Orthodox Church of JAPAN as autonomous by the patriarchate of Moscow, but not yet by the Ecumenical Patriarchate.

By canon 28 of the Council of Chalcedon (451) the bishop of Constantinople was recognized as second in honour and equal in rank to the pope of ROME. The title Ecumenical Patriarch, which he bears, reflects his status as bishop of the imperial capital and senior bishop of the Eastern Roman empire, and, since the breach with Rome, the most senior hierarch of the Eastern Orthodox church.

There exist churches which, like the RUSSIAN ORTHODOX CHURCH ABROAD, are in communion with some but not all other Eastern Orthodox churches. The OLD BELIEVERS, while divided from the Eastern Orthodox as a result of the liturgical reforms of Patriarch NIKON of Moscow, preserve Orthodox dogmatic tradition and an older form of the Slavonic liturgy. The TRUE ORTHODOX CHURCHES, which broke communion with the Eastern Orthodox mainly over the CALENDAR, are fully Orthodox in dogma and ritual.

Eastern Orthodox churches are defined positively by their adherence to the dogmatic definitions of the seven councils, by a strong sense of being not a sect or denomination but simply the continuing Christian church, and, despite their varied origins, by adherence to the Byzantine rite. Negatively they are distinguished from EASTERN CATHOLIC communities of the Byzantine rite by resolute rejection of papal claims to supremacy and universal immediate jurisdiction.

The Eastern Orthodox are the second largest Christian communion, exceeded in numbers only by the Roman Catholic communion.

Ware, K. T. (1993), *The Orthodox Church*. Harmondsworth: Penguin.
Dunlop, O., trans. (1989), *The Living God, A Catechism for the Christian Faith*. Crestwood, NY: St Vladimir's Seminary Press.
Bulgakov, S. (1988), *The Orthodox Church*. Crestwood, NY: St Vladimir's Seminary Press.
Hussey, J. M. (1986), *The Orthodox Church in the Byzantine Empire*. Oxford: Clarendon Press.
Runciman, S. (1985), *The Great Church in Captivity*. Cambridge: Cambridge University Press.
Meyendorff, J. (1983), *Byzantine Theology*. Crestwood, NY: St Vladimir's Seminary Press.
Pelikan J. (1977), *The Christian Tradition*, vol 2: *The Spirit of Eastern Christendom (600–1700)*. Chicago: University of Chicago Press.
Schmemann, A. (1977), *Historical Road of Eastern Orthodoxy*. Crestwood, NY: St Vladimir's Seminary Press.

DM

echage *Ečagē, eččegē*: the chief administrator of the ETHIOPIAN ORTHODOX CHURCH. The ABOUNA, the spiritual head of the church, was until the mid-twentieth century traditionally an Egyptian Copt, without knowledge of the Ethiopian language and culture. The echage, an Ethiopian monk, was appointed by the Ethiopian emperor from the monastic community of Dabra Libanos and took care of the practical administration of church matters as well as serving as head of the monks and as a channel for liaison between the church and the imperial government. The offices and duties of echage and abouna were merged in 1951 with the advent of autocephaly and the first Ethiopian abouna.

Bairu Tafla (1991), 'Eččagē', *Coptic Encyclopedia* 3, p. 930.
Prouty, C. and Rosenfeld, E. (1981), *Historical Dictionary of Ethiopia*, p. 53. African Historical Dictionaries 32. Metuchen, NJ and London: Scarecrow Press.

MJB/SHG

ecumenical councils There are seven councils acknowledged as ecumenical by the EASTERN ORTHODOX, ROMAN CATHOLIC and EASTERN CATHOLIC churches, but not all are accepted by the CHURCH OF THE EAST and the Oriental Orthodox. The seven councils were all convoked by the emperor and took place in the East; none the less, their decisions were widely received as authoritative in both East and West. The Arians, however, continued to exist as a separate church long after their condemnation at Nicaea I. The Church of the East, already autocephalous before Ephesus, rejected it and consequently later councils. The Oriental Orthodox churches do not accept the authority of Chalcedon and councils thereafter.

The main dogmatic pronouncements of the seven councils are:

(1) NICAEA I (325): that the Son is 'of the substance of the Father'; that is, the Son is consubstantial, *homoousios*, with the Father. This council condemned Arianism.

(2) CONSTANTINOPLE I (381): that the Holy Spirit is fully God. The restatement of the Nicene faith attributed to this council declares the Spirit to be 'Lord and Life-giver, proceeding from the Father, worshipped and glorified together with the Father and the Son'.

(3) EPHESUS (431): that Mary is THEOTOKOS, the one who gave birth to God. This council condemned Nestorius, bishop of Constantinople.

(4) CHALCEDON (451): that Jesus Christ is fully divine and fully human, 'like us in all things apart from sin'. He is acknowledged 'in two natures, without confusion, without change, without division, without separation; the difference of the natures being in no way abolished by the union, but rather the characteristics of each nature being preserved, and concurring into one Person and one hypostasis'. This is known as the hypostatic union (*see* COMMUNICATIO IDIOMATUM). This definition opposes the MONOPHYSITE position of Eutyches. Unfortunately, it proved unacceptable to those who saw it as incompatible with the doctrine and language of CYRIL OF ALEXANDRIA; this eventually led to the establishment of independent Oriental Orthodox churches.

(5) CONSTANTINOPLE II (553): defined the three persons of the Trinity to be consubstantial, and the full hypostatic unity of Christ, born eternally of the Father and in time, as man, of the Theotokos. It rejected every doctrine that makes of Christ two hypostases or two persons. It affirmed the full orthodoxy of the Christological teaching of Cyril of Alexandria and condemned his opponents. It condemned the 'Three Chapters', specific Christological teachings of Theodore of Mopsuestia, THEODORET OF CYRRHUS and IBAS OF EDESSA, who were condemned by name as heretics, as were several others including ORIGEN.

(6) CONSTANTINOPLE III (681): that Jesus Christ has two wills and two energies or operations (*energeiai*), one divine, the other human, inseparably united in the one person. The council condemned MONOTHELETISM and monoenergism. It condemned Pope Honorius I (625–38) as a heretic on account of explicit monothelite statements sent to Ecumenical Patriarch Sergius I (610–38), who was also condemned, together with four other monothelite patriarchs, including Cyrus (630–43) of Alexandria.

(7) NICAEA II (787): that sacred images of Christ, the Theotokos, the angels and saints are to be used in churches and homes and in public. It approves their

veneration. Those who venerate ICONS venerate the person depicted, not the material of the icon. This council marks the end of the first period of imperially promoted ICONOCLASM.

The Synod in Trullo or QUINISEXT COUNCIL of 692 is counted by Eastern Orthodox as sharing the ecumenical authority of Constantinople III. This council, however, was concerned entirely with laying down disciplinary canons, not with definitions of doctrine. The other ecumenical councils also passed disciplinary canons, traditionally accorded an authority in the East far higher than in Western tradition, which distinguishes sharply between the dogmatic authority and infallibility of ecumenical councils and their disciplinary legislation.

In addition to the seven councils listed above, the Roman Catholic communion accepts fourteen further councils as ecumenical, including LYONS II and FLORENCE, at which unsuccessful attempts were made to reunite East and West; the Council of Trent (1545–63), which definitively rejected the doctrines of the Reformation; the First Vatican Council (1869–70), which defined papal infallibility; and the Second Vatican Council, which opened the Roman Catholic church to the modern world and approved the decree ORIENTALIUM ECCLESIARUM.

Davis, L. D. (1987), *The First Seven Ecumenical Councils (325–787)*. Delaware: Michael Glazier.
Mar Aprem (1978), *The Council of Ephesus of 431*. Trichur: Mar Narsai Press.

KP/DM

Ecumenical Patriarch   The word 'ecumenical' seems originally to have emerged into use as an honorific title applied to very senior hierarchs. When JOHN THE FASTER (d. 595) of CONSTANTINOPLE began to use the title 'Ecumenical Patriarch' in official correspondence, Pope Gregory I (590–604), reading the title as a claim to universal authority, sternly rebuked him, pointing out that there was no universal bishop, he himself being no more than the Servant of the Servants of God, a title the pope still bears. Eventually the title 'Ecumenical Patriarch' became the formal title of the PATRIARCH of Constantinople, reflecting his status as bishop of the imperial capital, and his seniority among all the eastern patriarchs. It was never intended to imply any seniority over ROME.

DM

ecumenism, Eastern Orthodox   Despite often claiming that they alone constitute the One, Holy, Catholic and Apostolic Church, the Orthodox have taken a keen interest in Christian unity and have tried to respond to Western Christians in this matter. Since the estrangement (which cannot be precisely dated) from the Roman Catholic church, the Orthodox have held that the breach should be healed by an ECUMENICAL COUNCIL including the hierarchs of both sides; attempts to hold such a council at LYONS in the thirteenth century and at FLORENCE in the fifteenth did not, however, produce the desired result.

Lutherans and Anglicans have sometimes approached the Orthodox; in 1573 a delegation of Lutheran divines from Tübingen presented ECUMENICAL PATRIARCH

172

JEREMIAS II with a Greek translation of the Augsburg Confession. Some correspondence followed, but in 1581 the patriarchate terminated it. Soon afterwards, Patriarch Cyril LUCARIS showed leanings towards Calvinism, but the Orthodox church repudiated Cyril's ideas. The eighteenth-century Non-juring Anglicans initiated correspondence with the Eastern patriarchs and with the RUSSIAN ORTHODOX CHURCH. There were no immediate results, but the contacts were remembered.

The patristic revival has been an essential factor in Orthodox involvement in ecumenism. Orthodoxy above all sees itself as the church of the fathers; when Protestants and Roman Catholics study the fathers, Orthodox are inevitably interested. Beginning with the Roman Catholic John-Paul Migne in the nineteenth century, Western Christians have published critical editions of the fathers, both in the original languages and in translation. The work is done on an ecumenical basis, and its fruits enable the ecumenical process to grow and deepen.

Orthodox have been involved in the ecumenical movement of the twentieth century from its beginnings. In 1902 an encyclical to all the local Orthodox churches from Patriarch Joachim III of CONSTANTINOPLE invited an Orthodox consensus on relations with the Roman Church, Old Catholics and Protestants. In 1920 the Ecumenical Patriarchate issued an encyclical *Unto the Churches of Christ Everywhere*, opening with the significant affirmation that 'Our own church holds that rapprochement between the various Christian Churches and fellowship [*koinonia*] between them is not excluded by the doctrinal differences which exist between them. In our opinion such a rapprochement is highly desirable and necessary.' This was a seminal document for the entire ecumenical movement, and is considered the first proposal in the process that led to the establishment of the World Council of Churches in 1948. In 1952 Patriarch ATHENAGORAS I of Constantinople published another encyclical on the Orthodox understanding of the World Council of Churches. By 1961, almost all local Orthodox churches were participating in the work of the WCC.

The Orthodox DIASPORA plays an important role in Orthodox ecumenical work; some Orthodox theologians even believe this was the purpose of God's sending large groups of Orthodox into exile from their home countries. In consequence of political developments in Eastern Europe and the Near East, millions of Orthodox have moved to Western Europe, the Western hemisphere and AUSTRALIA. Orthodoxy is no longer an 'Eastern' phenomenon, and for Western Christians the Orthodox are no longer far away.

St Sergius' Seminary in Paris and St Vladimir's Seminary in New York have been crucial points of contact with Orthodoxy for many Western Christians; both faculties are heavily involved in ecumenical activities. Holy Cross Greek Orthodox Theological School near Boston, Massachusetts is a full member of the Boston Consortium of Theological Schools, so that many Protestant and Roman Catholic students regularly take theological courses from Greek Orthodox professors. Orthodox literature circulates increasingly in English, French and other Western languages.

'Pan-Orthodox conferences', held first in the inter-war period and then from the 1960s on, have given much attention to Orthodox involvement in the ecumenical movement. Relations between Eastern Orthodoxy and Roman Catholicism, close on matters of doctrine, are strained on ecclesiology, since for several centuries each has claimed to be *the* One Church, at the expense of the other. Catholic ecumenists worked patiently during the first six decades of the twentieth century, cautiously stimulating a greater interest in the Christian East, and Eastern Orthodox leaders such as Patriarch Alexis I of Moscow occasionally spoke of ROME as a 'sister church'. With Pope John XXIII and the Second Vatican Council regular fraternal relations developed between Roman Catholicism and Eastern Orthodoxy. Recognizing the long estrangement between the churches, two sorts of relations are conducted more or less simultaneously and interact: the 'dialogue of love', to bring about a greater and more positive awareness on the part of each towards the other; and the 'dialogue of truth', concerning actual theological questions. In 1965 Patriarch Athenagoras I of Constantinople and Pope Paul VI of Rome simultaneously lifted the excommunications of 1054, which had come to symbolize the schism between Catholicism and Orthodoxy; since then Roman Catholicism has regarded Eastern Orthodoxy as a 'sister church'.

The stated aim of the International Theological Dialogue, the 'dialogue of truth' on the highest level, is to restore full eucharistic communion between Eastern Orthodoxy and Roman Catholicism. To date, the International Theological Dialogue has published four agreed statements. According to the decisions of the Pan-Orthodox conferences, the Orthodox church has entered into this theological dialogue with Roman Catholicism on the strict understanding that the dialogue is conducted 'on equal terms'. Some Orthodox none the less oppose this endeavour, while others remain hesitant. The renascence of the 'Greek-Catholic' Churches in UKRAINE and ROMA-NIA occasioned severe tension between Orthodox and Catholics, and put a strain on the theological dialogue; the 1993 Balamand Statement tried to point the way to a resolution of this problem. A majority of local Orthodox churches appear to favour continuation of the dialogue, and the June 1995 visit of the Ecumenical Patriarch Bartholomew I to Pope John Paul II may well signal the resumption of this work.

Eastern Orthodox relations with the Churches of the Anglican communion have been friendly, even warm. The peak in Anglican–Orthodox relations may have been the inter-war period, marked particularly by the activity of the Fellowship of SS Alban and Sergius; hopes were high that the Anglican churches and Eastern Orthodoxy could establish eucharistic communion. In more recent decades, Orthodox perceive the Anglicans as becoming more distant from Orthodoxy, particularly on such matters as the ordination of women. A dialogue continues, but the Orthodox are generally pessimistic about its prospects.

The most striking success of Orthodox ecumenical activity is with the Oriental Orthodox churches: the Copts, Armenians, Syrians, Ethiopians and Indians. Partly with the assistance of the World Council of Churches, a fruitful theological dialogue, unofficial at first and then fully recognized, began in the 1960s. Participants from both sides have agreed that the differences between them are verbal rather than substantive, and have made proposals for the restoration of eucharistic communion. This restoration has already taken effect in the patriarchate of ANTIOCH; in other places there is still some hesitation, especially in the patriarchates of JERUSALEM and Moscow.

Orthodox consider the mutual celebration of the eucharist as the highest point of church unity and hold that this can be done only when two communities are of one faith and without any canonical impediment (breaches in eucharistic communion among different Orthodox communities have happened with distressing frequency in the nineteenth and twentieth centuries). The movement for frequent reception of Holy

Communion, which has become general in recent decades, has come late to Orthodoxy, and the Orthodox as a rule are puzzled and troubled by the grief of other Christians to whom the Orthodox refuse the eucharist.

The communist governments of the Soviet Union, Romania and Czechoslovakia permitted the local Orthodox churches in those countries to participate in the ecumenical movement through such organizations as the World Council of Churches. There were often accusations that the Orthodox representatives at WCC and other international ecumenical gatherings were *nolentes volentes* the agents of Soviet foreign policy; evidence which has come to light since the collapse of communism in Eastern Europe substantiates this accusation. The new situation of the churches in Eastern Europe requires new modalities for the ecumenical movement, which have yet to develop.

Borelli, J. and Erickson, J. (1996), *The Quest for Unity: Orthodox and Catholics in Dialogue*. Crestwood, NY: St Vladimir's Seminary Press.
McPartlan, P., ed. (1993), *One in 2000? Towards Catholic–Orthodox Unity. Agreed Statements and Parish Papers*. Slough: St Pauls.
Bria, I. (1991), *The Sense of Ecumenical Tradition: The Ecumenical Witness and Vision of the Orthodox*. Geneva: World Council of Churches.
Suttner, E. C. (1991), *Church Unity: Union or Uniatism? Catholic–Orthodox Ecumenical Perspectives*. Rome: Centre for Indian and Inter-religious Studies.
Anglican-Orthodox Dialogue: the Dublin Agreed Statement (1984). London: SPCK.
Patelos, C. G. (1978), *The Orthodox Church in the Ecumenical Movement: Documents and Statements 1902–1975*. Geneva: World Council of Churches.

SK

Edessa Greek name of a city of Seleucid foundation in southern Turkey, which became the centre of an important Christian kingdom (modern Urfa/Şanliurfa; Syriac *'ūrhoy*). We know little about its earliest history, but pagan SYRIAC inscriptions from the city (first to third centuries) and coins indicate that Edessa flourished under Roman domination. Among its more important kings are ABGAR V (4 BC–AD 7 and AD 13–50) and Abgar VIII 'the Great' (177– 212).

Edessa claimed to be the first kingdom to have become Christian. The story survives in Greek (in the works of Eusebius, *c*.260–340) and in the Syriac *Teaching of Addai* (fourth or fifth century). It suggests that King Abgar V of Edessa wrote to Jesus asking him to visit the city. Jesus replied that he would send a disciple after his ASCENSION. The disciple (ADDAI in the Syriac, Thaddaeus in Eusebius) duly arrived and converted Abgar, his court and most of the city's inhabitants from paganism. Abgar's scribe painted a picture of Jesus which became a valued icon. Jesus blessed Edessa and promised it would never be conquered. The text of the blessing may have been placed over the city's gates. Internal evidence in the *Teaching of Addai* suggests we should be suspicious of its claims. PALŪṬ, Addai's second successor, went to ANTIOCH for consecration. This indicates subordination to Antioch. According to the legend, Palūṭ was consecrated by Serapion, bishop of Antioch, *c*.190–211. This is incompatible with first-century conversion. Finally, the authoritative *Chronicle of Edessa* (*c*.540) makes no mention of the Addai story (*see* EDESSA, CHRONICLE OF).

Early evidence of Christianity in the region includes the inscription of Abercius Marcellus, bishop of Hierapolis (Phrygia), dated 192, according to which he visited the trans-Euphrates area and found Christians there; the reference in the *Chronicle of Edessa* (*c*.540) to a flood in Edessa in 201 which destroyed the church of the Christians; the church council which Eusebius says was held in Osrhoene (the Edessa region) during the pontificate of Pope Victor I (189–98); and the fact that BARDAIṢĀN (*c*.154–222) refers to the 'new' sect of the Christians which had appeared in Persia, Media, Edessa, Parthia and Hatra. All of these indications suggest that Christians were present in the area in the late second century. The most likely kings to have presided over the conversion of Edessa are Maʻnu VIII (139–63, 165–77) or Abgar VIII. The Addai story may be dated to *c*. AD 300, and may have arisen as a polemic against the preaching of the Manichaean apostle named Addai (*see* Drijvers 1983).

Edessa subsequently became an important Christian centre, its position boosted by the historical accident of the transfer westwards from 363 of numerous Aramaic-speaking Christians, who fled when Nisibis came under Sasanian control. Many came to Edessa, including the great theologian and poet EPHREM THE SYRIAN (d. 373), and an important theological academy was founded.

Edessa fell to the Arabs in 641 and in the CRUSADES became a Crusader 'County of Edessa' in 1098. In 1144 it was dramatically liberated by Zangi, Atabeg of Mosul. The modern city, Urfa or Şanliurfa, contains few relics of its Christian history, rather more of the earlier pagan period. No significant Christian community survives in Urfa (by contrast with regions further east in the TŪR ʻABDĪN), since most of its Christians have removed themselves to Aleppo in Syria.

Drijvers, H. J. W. (1996), 'Early Syriac Christianity: Some Recent Publications', *Vigiliae Christianae* 50, pp. 159–77.
Drijvers, H. J. W. (1983), 'Addai und Mani. Christentum und Manichäismus im dritten Jahrhundert in Syrien', *Orientalia Christiana Analecta* 221, pp. 171–85.
McCullough, W. S. (1982), *A Short History of Syriac Christianity*. Chico: Scholars Press.
Segal, J. B. (1970), *Edessa, 'The Blessed City'*. Oxford: Clarendon Press.

JH

Edessa, Chronicle of Edited *c*.540, this short chronicle appears to be based on the city archives of EDESSA. It contains entries from 132 BC to AD 540 and is extremely laconic, except in describing in great detail the flood in Edessa in 201, which, we are told in passing, destroyed the church of the Christians. There is no reference to any missionary activity by ADDAI.

Guidi, I. (1903, 1907), *Chronica Minora*. CSCO 1–2: Scriptores Syri 1–2. Louvain: Secrétariat du CSCO.
Cowper, B. H., trans. (1864), 'Chronicle of Edessa', *Journal of Sacred Literature* 5, pp. 28–45.

JH

eiletarion Greek, 'wrapper', 'cover' (cf. EILETON): name given to manuscript scrolls that unroll vertically rather than horizontally, especially those for use during celebration of the Divine Liturgy. Many liturgical *eiletaria* survive; some are still used on ATHOS. The authors of the liturgies and other saints are frequently shown holding *eiletaria*. The word is omitted by Lampe's *Patristic Greek Lexicon*.

E

eileton   Greek, 'folded', 'wrapped': the linen cloth unfolded on the altar at the liturgy after the dismissal of the catechumens and on which the chalice and diskos are placed after the Great Entrance (*see* SACRED UTENSILS); the equivalent of the Western corporal. It is now the custom to use an ANTIMENSION, though the latter is often folded within a silk or linen covering, in effect an *eileton*, which is also unfolded and on which the antimension lies.

Taft, R. (1978), *The Great Entrance. Orientalia Christiana Analecta* 200. Rome: Pontifical Institute of Oriental Studies.

E

ekphonesis   Greek, 'utterance'; in the Byzantine rite, *ekphonesis* has come to be the term used to designate the final doxology of a prayer when it is sung out loud.

E

Ekthesis   Formula promulgated in 638 by Emperor Heraclius (610–41) in response to the rising conflict over the claim of the Ecumenical Patriarch Sergius I (610–38) that in Christ there is one *energeia*, a term often translated as 'energy' but meaning rather 'operation' or 'activity'. Sergius, a loyal supporter of Heraclius, committed like him to the unity of both empire and church, had worked with Cyrus of Phasis, from 631 CHALCEDONIAN patriarch of Alexandria, to develop the monoenergist formula to help reconcile MONOPHYSITES with Chalcedonians. Monoenergism proved both inaccessible and controversial. Sophronios, patriarch of Jerusalem (634–8), and his friend and associate MAXIMUS THE CONFESSOR opposed Sergius, defending the strict Chalcedonian doctrine of the two natures in Christ, seeing nature rather than *hypostasis* as the location of *energeia*.

With the apparent co-operation of Pope Honorius (625–38), later condemned by name as a heretic at the thirteenth session of the Third Council of Constantinople (*see* ECUMENICAL COUNCILS), Sergius drafted the Ekthesis for Heraclius. This imperial edict prohibits all discussion of whether there is one *energeia* in Christ or two and asserts that his humanity and divinity are united by a single will. Its MONOTHELET-ISM raised a new and bitter controversy at precisely the moment the empire most needed unity in the face of the onslaught of Islam. In 638 Sophronios yielded the keys of JERUSALEM to the saintly Khalifa 'Umar: Patriarch Cyrus, hated as a persecutor by the Copts, handed a religiously divided Egypt to the Muslim general 'Amr in 641.

The popes who followed Honorius were firmly opposed to monotheletism. Even Heraclius' successors abandoned his doctrinal policy. In 648 Constans II (641–68) withdrew the Ekthesis and issued the Typos, which forbade all discussion of *energeiai* or wills and returned to the scriptures and the decisions of the five councils recognized by Chalcedonians as ecumenical. The Typos was, not surprisingly, even less successful than its predecessor. In 680–1 the Third Council of Constantinople condemned

177

monotheletism as a heresy and execrated the names and teachings of Sergius, Cyrus and Honorius.

Pelikan, J. (1974), *The Spirit of Eastern Christendom (600–1700)*. Chicago and London: University of Chicago Press.
Meyendorff, J. (1969), *Christ in Eastern Christian Thought*. Washington, DC: Corpus.

DM

Eleousa   Greek, 'compassionate' or 'merciful': iconographic type of the Virgin which shows her and the Christ-child cheek to cheek. Known in Russian as UMILENIE.
   See also GLYKOPHYLOUSA.

KP

Elias   Also called Eliu, Eliyahu, Elijah; Ilya in Russia. This Old Testament prophet ranks among the saints (DIKAIOS) and is honoured along with his pupil and successor Elisaeus on 20 July. Elias (4 Kingdoms; 2 Kings 2: 11ff), like Enoch, is recorded as being taken up to heaven alive. In icons of the TRANSFIGURATION he represents the prophets as Moses represents the Law. He is also depicted as a solitary figure in his cave awaiting the arrival of the raven, or as ascending in the fiery chariot. His sheepskin cloak (Greek: *melote*) is used to divide the waters of Jordan and falls to Elisaeus as the sign of his inheriting a double portion of the spirit of Elias. A similar cloak is worn by JOHN THE BAPTIST (*see* THEOPHANY). Churches dedicated to Elias are often found in high or remote places. Because of his fiery chariot he is known as the protector of forests and woods. He is a type of the monastic life. His feast is celebrated with particular solemnity, with three readings from the Books of Kingdoms at Vespers, a distinction he shares with John the Baptist alone among the prophets.

KP

Elisabeth Feodorovna (1864–1918)   Daughter of Grand Duke Louis of Hesse-Darmstadt and Princess Alice of England, in 1884 Elisabeth married the Grand Duke Sergei Romanov. Her sister, Alexandra, married Tsar Nicholas II of Russia (*see* PASSION BEARERS). Elisabeth embraced EASTERN ORTHODOXY from conviction. When her husband was assassinated in 1905, she visited and forgave his imprisoned assassin, then disposed of her wealth and worked to organize a sisterhood dedicated to the Myrophoroi (myrrh-bearers) Martha and Mary. A convent was founded in Moscow centred on a new hospital, orphanage, facilities for consumptive women and other social services. Elisabeth's attempt to revive the order of deaconesses did not succeed, but the Martha and Mary sisterhood helped to keep social work high on the agenda of the Orthodox church, continuing John of Kronstadt's work after his death in 1908. The foundress and her community enjoyed the public support of Gavrilii Zirianov (d. 1915), a noted elder of Pskov. Under Soviet rule the building became an art restoration centre before being returned to the church. The nuns continued their outreach work among the poor and needy, particularly of the notorious Khitrovo area.

In 1918 under the Bolsheviks Elisabeth was deported to Alapaevsk in Siberia where, with her helper, the nun Barbara, and other Romanovs, she was thrown down a disused mineshaft and left to die. Their relics were recovered during the White Russian advance and removed to Beijing, then to Jerusalem, and were enshrined in the Mary Magdalene church at Gethsemane, which counted the Grand Duchess and her husband among its founders.

The NEW MARTYRS Elisabeth and Barbara were canonized by the RUSSIAN ORTHODOX CHURCH ABROAD in 1981. They are commemorated on 5 June.

Mager, H. (1998), *Elizabeth, Grand Duchess of Russia*. New York: Carroll & Graf.
Millar, L. (1991), *Grand Duchess Elisabeth of Russia*. Redding, Cal.: Nicodemos Orthodox Press.
Koehler, L. (1988), *Saint Elisabeth the New Martyr*. Orthodox Palestine Society, USA.
Kholmogorov, S. (1988), *One of the Ancients*. Platina, Cal.: St Herman of Alaska.

DB

Elisabeth of Thrace The fifth-century wonder-worker, saint and dragon-slayer, like the earlier Eudokia, Marina, Paraskeve and most famously George Tropaiophoros. Elisabeth came from a village near Herakleia-Perinthos, a port on the Propontis; her birth was attributed to the intervention of St Glykeria, patron of the city. According to tradition her parents died when she was fifteen and she disposed of their wealth, moved to CONSTANTINOPLE and joined her aunt in the convent of St George, succeeding her as abbess. Her fame as a visionary, healer and exorcist attracted the attention of the court. Like Daniel the Stylite (d. 493), she predicted to the emperor the fire of 465. Elisabeth is commemorated on 24 April.

See also THRACE.

Cataphygiotou-Topping, E. (1990), *Saints and Sisterhood*. Minneapolis, Minn.: Light and Life.

DB

Entry into Jerusalem The iconographic narrative of this New Testament episode shows Christ outside the city walls sitting side-saddle on an ass (Zechariah 9: 9). He looks back to the apostles following him, while a crowd gathers at the city gate with palm branches to welcome him. Children spread garments and palm branches on the road. The spreading of garments is mentioned in connection with the anointing of a king (4 Kingdoms 9: 13; 2 Kings 9: 13). Christ blesses with his right hand and holds a scroll in his left. Sometimes children appear in the branches of the palm tree. Anachronistically, the Church of the Holy Sepulchre is sometimes shown inside Jerusalem's walls. The icon celebrates Palm Sunday. The first poetic KATHISMA of Matins on the feast identifies Christ as 'spiritually having become the New Adam', and the KONTAKION, proclaiming his divinity, says 'Mounted on the throne in heaven, Christ God, and on the colt on earth... Blessed are you who come to call back Adam.'

Ouspensky, L. and Lossky, V. (1982), *The Meaning of Icons*. Crestwood, NY: St Vladimir's Seminary Press.

KP

Ephrem, 'Greek' EPHREM THE SYRIAN is a key figure in Eastern Christian MONASTICISM. Several Byzantine monasteries have large wall-paintings depicting the death of St Ephrem, surrounded by his brethren and accompanied by scenes from the monks' daily life. The TRIODION prescribes that at weekday ORTHROS in Lent there shall be two readings from his works. The Prayer of St Ephrem is prescribed for all offices on fast days, though in practice this is often limited to Great Lent. Ephrem owes this pre-eminence not to his authentic writings in SYRIAC, which seem to have been unknown to the Byzantine monastic world, but to a large and heterogeneous corpus of texts in Greek, which, with the exception of one sermon on Jonas and the Ninivites, have no equivalents in Syriac. Some of these are in verse, in a Greek form of the Syriac 'metre of St Ephrem' characteristic of his *mēmrē*, or verse sermons: lines of fourteen syllables, each in two half-lines of seven syllables, with no regard to length, as in classical Greek poetry, or to stress, as in later Greek poetry. The impressive poem of the Greek Ephrem on the Binding of Isaac is also found among the *spuria* of JOHN CHRYSOSTOM. Some of these writings influenced the sixth-century ROMANOS THE MELODIST. The Greek corpus also includes many writings addressed to cenobitic monks, notably fifty *Exhortations to the Monks of Egypt*, offering vivid and often pithy guidance for beginners. In the ninth century these were known to Patriarch PHOTIOS THE GREAT, who lists them in his *Bibliotheke*. He remarks that Ephrem was accounted a great stylist in his own language, and can only attribute the low literary quality of the Greek to the incompetence of the translator. The Prayer of St Ephrem catalogues some of the principal temptations of monks in a cenobitic community, of which Ephrem the Syrian had no knowledge. The question of the authorship of these texts is a complicated one. The majority of them are clearly of Greek origin and later than St Ephrem himself, and though some may have a Syriac origin, few if any can be from St Ephrem the Syrian.

This important corpus of texts awaits critical edition and translation into modern languages; we still depend on eighteenth-century editions made in Oxford and Rome. A reprint of these, accompanied by a Modern Greek translation, was completed in 1988.

E

Ephrem the Syrian (*c*.306–73)   The most significant of all the fathers of the Syriac-speaking church tradition. It is a mark of the breadth of his appeal that he was declared a doctor of the church by Pope Benedict XV in 1920. Born in Nisibis, probably of Christian parents (despite erroneous information to the contrary in some SYRIAC sources), at some stage he became a DEACON (never a monk in the later sense, though his ascetic way of life is clear) and may have accompanied James of Nisibis to the Council of Nicea: James is praised by Ephrem in the *Nisibene Hymns*. In 363 Nisibis was ceded to the Sasanians and Ephrem moved to EDESSA. There he remained, though legend reports various travels, including a meeting with St Basil in Caesarea. While in Edessa he was active in famine and plague relief.

Ephrem's writings, most of which belong to his Edessan period (but not the *Nisibene Hymns*) are extensive; many are in the traditional poetic forms of *madrāšā* (hymn) and *mēmrā* (verse homily). There are collections of hymns related to the church's festivals and seasons, and on particular themes (faith, virginity, paradise, against heresies, etc.). Verse homilies include six *mēmrē* on faith. Prose works include polemics attacking the heretics (Bardaisanites, Marcionites, etc.) and his biblical commentaries, including one on Genesis and an important commentary, the Syriac text of which has been redis-covered in recent times, on Tatian's DIATESSARON. Ephrem's *Commentary* is a primary source for the *Diatessaron* itself. Like APHRAHAT, Ephrem shows relatively

little Western influence, and this is reflected not only in his theology but in his way of presenting it: poetry, rather than philosophical language, is his chosen vehicle. Jewish and ancient Mesopotamian traditions are often reflected in his thought. A favourite image is that of the primordial robe of glory, lost at the Fall, recovered by the Incarna-tion and made available through baptism. Ephrem is a little early for major Christological controversy, but was anti-Arian and a supporter of Nicea as well as a devotee of the Virgin Mary. Because he was not involved in later controversies, Ephrem was accepted as orthodox by all later traditions in both East and West, and his work was widely translated: into Greek within twenty years of his death, according to Jerome, and also into other languages including Armenian and Latin.

Mathews, E. G., trans. (1994), *Saint Ephrem the Syrian: Selected Prose Works*. Washington, DC: Catholic University of America Press.
Brock, S. (1992), *The Luminous Eye: The Spiritual World Vision of Saint Ephrem the Syrian*. Kalamazoo: Cistercian Publications.
Brock, S. (1990), *St Ephrem the Syrian: Hymns on Paradise*. Crestwood, NY: St Vladimir's Seminary Press.
McVey, K. (1989), *Ephrem the Syrian: Hymns*. New York: Paulist Press.

JH

Epiphanios of Salamis   Bishop of Salamis and metropolitan of CYPRUS 367–403. Epiphanios was of Jewish origin, an ascetic and a stern defender of Nicene orthodoxy. His *Panarion* is a comprehensive classification and refutation of all heresies. He was a resolute opponent of ORIGEN.

Decow, J. F. (1988), *Dogma and Mysticism in Early Christianity: Epiphanius of Cyprus and the Legacy of Origen*. Patristic Monograph Series 13. Louvain and Macon.

DM

epitrachelion   Greek, 'round the neck': the Eastern priestly stole. It is broader than the Western stole and is always joined down the middle, normally with a series of ornamental studs. It is worn only by bishops and priests. A priest should not celebrate any service unless he is wearing it.

E

era   System of dating. The Roman empire dated events from the foundation of ROME (AUC, *ab urbe condita*). Dionysius Exiguus, a sixth-century monk and canonist, calculated that Jesus was born in 753 AUC. His calculation provided the system of dating events before or after the birth of Christ which is now in common use.

Most EASTERN CHRISTIANS retain the version of this CALENDAR based on the system of year-lengths and dating of leap years originally approved by Julius Caesar in 46 BC; others follow the reformed calendar of Pope Gregory XIII, who in 1582 advanced the date by ten days and altered the rule for determining leap years to maintain a fixed relation between the actual equinoxes and solstices and their calendar dates, or the reformed Julian calendar, slightly different from the Gregorian and more accurate, adopted at a meeting in Constantinople in 1923. Except in Finland, EASTERN ORTHODOX who use the new calendar none the less retain the same system for calculating the Paschal cycle as those who follow the Julian calendar. Some EASTERN CATHOLICS both use the Gregorian calendar and calculate the date of the Paschal cycle in accordance with it.

Other calendrical eras remain in use. Some are based on the supposed date of the creation obtained by analysis of the Old Testament text. The Alexandrian era of the fifth-century monk Panodoros dates the creation at 29 August, 5493 BC. Byzantine dates (AKK, *apo ktiseos kosmou*, from the creation of the world), normally date creation to 1 September, 5509 BC. A Georgian era exists dating the creation to 5604 BC.

At the second Synod of Dvin in 552, the Church of ARMENIA adopted a calendar based on a year of 365 days divided into twelve months of thirty days and one of five, and dating events from 552–3.

The Church of ETHIOPIA often uses the 'Era of Mercy', dating events from the birth of Christ calculated as taking place in year 5501 of the Alexandrian era (i.e. AD 8). A four-yearly cycle is used where every year is named for one of the evangelists, Luke's years being leap years. The Ethiopian year, like the COPTIC, has twelve months of thirty days and a short month of five or, in a leap year, six days. The Coptic calendar dates events from the 'Year of the Martyrs', AD 284, the accession of the Emperor Diocletian (284–305), under whom the Coptic Pope Peter III, the 'Seal of the Martyrs', and huge numbers of his people died. The Seleucid era, calculating dates from 312 BC, was widely used in the Syrian world.

Reconciliation of dates across calendars is complicated by differences in the date of New Year, and also by the use of variants of the eras noted.

See also INDICTION.

DM

Eritrean Orthodox church   The Eritrean Orthodox church was under the authority of the ETHIOPIAN ORTHODOX CHURCH until 1991, when Eritrea gained independence from Ethiopia. Until that point it formed a single diocese of the Ethiopian

Orthodox church. During the thirty-year independence struggle many Eritrean church buildings were destroyed and several priests, nuns and monks were killed by Ethiopian soldiers. The war left several monasteries depopulated. When independence was finally gained from Ethiopia, all the bishops serving in Eritrea who had been appointees of the Ethiopian church during its subjection to the dergue fled the country, leaving it without episcopal oversight.

On 26 May 1991 in Cairo, Pope SHENOUDA III, Coptic patriarch of ALEXANDRIA, at the request of the growing number of Eritrean émigrés, consecrated two bishops for the Eritrean church abroad: Abouna Markos (Menghistu Abebe) for London and Abouna Makarios (Petros Dhere Sellasie) for the USA. This coincided with the liberation of Eritrea in May 1991.

On 1 July 1993 President Isaias Afeworke of Eritrea visited Pope Shenouda in Cairo, followed on 19 July by a delegation from the Eritrean church requesting canonical erection of an independent Eritrean Orthodox church. This approach was accompanied by a letter of support from the former archbishop of Eritrea, Abouna Philipos (Tewolde Berhan), who, as a senior and highly respected churchman uncontaminated by association with Mengistu's Ethiopian regime, had been chosen to head an Eritrean synod.

On Pentecost Sunday, 19 June 1994 Pope Shenouda consecrated five Eritrean abbots, elected by the Eritrean people, as diocesan bishops for their new church: Bishop Antonios of Hamasen-Asmara, Bishop Dioscoros of Serae-Meddefeta, Bishop Kyrillos of Akole Gujay-Adi Qeyeh, Bishop Youannes of Senhit-Keren, Sahil, Barkann and Gashin, and Bishop Salama of Semharn and Dankelnn. With the former archbishop of Northern Gondar, Abouna Jaëqob (Tekle Mariam), consecrated by the Ethiopians before independence, this established nine members of the Holy Synod of the Eritrean church. Following a unanimous vote by the Eritrean synod, Pope Shenouda consecrated Abouna Philipos I as the first patriarch of Eritrea. The consecration took place on 8 May 1998 in Cairo, the enthronement, also by Pope Shenouda III, in Asmara on 29 May 1998. Patriarch Philipos was born in 1905 in Asmara, ordained deacon in 1919, monk of Debre Bizen near Massawa in 1929, ordained priest in Cairo by Pope Yohannes XIX (1928–42) when Eritrea was under Italian occupation, and consecrated bishop with responsibility for Ethiopian monasteries in 1990, then named as archbishop of Eritrea in 1991.

As a result of Coptic support for the Eritrean cause, relations with the Ethiopian church have become very strained, not least since the Ethiopian church spent decades negotiating its own independence while the Eritreans achieved theirs so easily. A protocol governing relations between the Coptic and Eritrean churches was signed in 1998.

St Michael's Eritrean Orthodox parish in London, established in 1989 by Bishop Markos, acquired its own property in Camberwell, south London, becoming the first Eritrean Orthodox church to be consecrated in Europe.

The Eritrean Orthodox church comprises some 1,700,000 faithful, with 1,500 churches and 22 monasteries served by 15,000 priests.

S

Estonian Orthodox church EASTERN ORTHODOX missions were active among the Estonians of the south-east regions of the country, closest to Pskov, in the tenth to twelfth centuries. In 1030 Yuryev, or Tartu, was founded as a Russian trading centre around an Orthodox cathedral dedicated to St George. The Orthodox were later expelled from this city by the Germans, who martyred the priest Isidor and a number of Orthodox faithful in 1472. This group is commemorated on 8 January.

The Estonian Orthodox church emerged as an autonomous body after the 1917 revolution. Plato Kulbusch, the first hierarch of Estonia, was martyred with his deacon, Dorin, and many others by the Bolsheviks in 1919. Bishop Plato and companions are commemorated on 14 January. The Estonian Orthodox church established links with the CONSTANTINOPLE patriarchate and was granted autonomy within the patriarchate in 1923. This provoked a split among the Russian Orthodox of the country. The famous Pechery monastery was the spiritual centre for all the Orthodox of Estonia during the inter-war period. Changes in borders after 1940 transferred the region to Russia. Before 1940 there were around 210,000 Orthodox Christians in Estonia. During the Second World War, the Soviet invasion of 1940 returned the church to the patriarchate of Moscow, but in 1942–4 autonomy under the Constantinople patriarchate was revived. Metropolitan Alexander Paulus led many of his flock to the West when Soviet power was re-established at the end of the war. Before he died in 1953 he had established the Estonian Orthodox Church Abroad as an exarchate under Constantinople. Peeter Pahkel (d. 1948) and most of the other bishops and clergy who remained in Estonia were deported to SIBERIA. A new synod was formed in 1958 and the church was reorganized from Sweden. In the 1990s the Estonian Orthodox church has re-emerged in Estonia. In 1996 difficulties arose as to the church's relations to Constantinople and MOSCOW, but were resolved by an agreement allowing local communities to decide to which patriarchate they would adhere.

See also LATVIAN ORTHODOX CHURCH; LITHUANIAN ORTHODOX CHURCH.

Cherney, A. (1985), *The Latvian Orthodox Church*. Welshpool: Stylite Publishing.

DB

Ethiopian Orthodox church   The largest Oriental Orthodox church. Its official name is *Yä-Ityopya Ortodoks(awit) Täwaḥəya Betä Krəstiyan*: 'Ethiopian Orthodox Tewahedo (i.e. professing the unification of natures in Christ by birth) Church'. Official membership figures are not available: in 1978 they numbered perhaps 20 million, but any such figure is now out of date because of the separation of the ERITREAN ORTHODOX CHURCH.

The legendary origin of Christianity in Ethiopia is connected with the story of the eunuch of the Ethiopian Queen Candace in Acts 8: 26–30. The name Ethiopia, however, in antiquity generally designated NUBIA. Only after the fall of the Nubian kingdom of Meroe did the kings of Axum call their own country Aithiopia, and never exclusively, the name *Ḥabaša* (Abyssinia) also being used. The connection of Queen Candace with Ethiopia was promoted by the identification of the Queen of Sheba (cf. 1 Kings [3 Kingdoms] 10: 1–3: 2 Chronicles [Paralipomena] 9: 1–12: Matthew 16: 42; Luke 16: 31) with the Ethiopian Queen Makeda in an indigenous legend which found its final form in the national epic KEBRA NAGAST.

The historical origin of Christianity in Ethiopia, though handed down in semi-legendary form, goes back to the first half of the fourth century, to the period after the investiture of ATHANASIUS as PATRIARCH of Alexandria and Emperor Constantius' letter to Aizana (Ezana) and Saizana, brothers and co-regents of Axum, seeking alliance with them. According to Rufinus and others, FRUMENTIUS, a Syrian merchant's son, was captured after a shipwreck in the Red Sea and enslaved at Axum, where he managed to preach the gospel. He became teacher of the crown prince. Freed, he went to ALEXANDRIA, where Athanasius made him bishop of the Ethiopians and sent him back to Axum. According to Ethiopian tradition, he converted King Ella Asbeḥa.

The inscriptions and symbols on his coins indicate that Ezana, king of Axum in the fourth century, converted to Christianity. These inscriptions, invoking the Lord of Heaven and Earth, report campaigns to Meroe and various parts of Ethiopia. No further details of the beginnings of Christianity are available. Ezana's successors in the sixth century, Kaleb and Gabra Masqal, led victorious campaigns to Yemen where they dethroned a Judaizing king and established Christianity at San'a and Nağran; perhaps even further north (cf. the story of Abreha and the Elephant in the Qur'an). Quotations from the PSALMS in the inscriptions prove that at least parts of the BIBLE were translated by the sixth century. Ethiopian tradition has the translation of the scriptures completed with the translation of Ecclesiasticus in 678.

Ethiopian tradition says nine saints from Rum (the Byzantine empire), possibly Syria, introduced MONASTICISM in the sixth century, founding several monasteries in the north that are still flourishing today, e.g. Dabra Damo. There is no proof that these nine saints were MONOPHYSITE. Traditions that they 'corrected faith' in a monophysite sense are later adaptations of a different hagiographical tradition.

The political and ecclesiastical history of Ethiopia after the fall of Axum, probably in the ninth century, to the rise of the Solomonic dynasty in 1270 is virtually unknown. The only certain fact is that a metropolitan was traditionally requested from Egypt; but we have no complete lists of metropolitans. (*See* COPTIC CHRISTIANITY.) Christianity and monasteries spread southwards during these centuries. The Zagwe dynasty, although labelled usurpers, founded the rock-hewn churches of LALIBELA, creating a Holy Land in miniature. The restored legitimate dynasty continued the work of expansion and evangelization. The role of monasteries as strongholds of royal power cannot be overestimated. They were not always loyal; we hear of conflicts between monastic reformers and the royal power. Significant issues in the early middle ages were the question of the two Sabbaths (*see* EWOSṬATEWOS) and the question of the veneration of the Holy Virgin Mary and the Holy CROSS. The Emperor Zar'a-Ya'qob (1434–68), reformer and organizer of church and state, resolved most of these conflicts and gave the church its definitive form.

The role of the 'established' church, comparable to the political role of the church in the Western Ottonian empire, was shaken only by the Muslim invasion led by Aḥmad Grañ (1529–43) and the subsequent arrival of the Jesuits, who came with the Portuguese corps to bring military help and union with Europe. The Catholic mission forced the Orthodox to formulate their faith and dogma (cf. the *Confession of Claudius* by Emperor Galāwēwos, 1540–59) and to translate the fundamental catechism into the vernacular, AMHARIC, as the Catholics did. A short-lived union with the Catholic church under Emperor Susneyos (1508–32) ended in civil war. Meanwhile the slow conversion to Christianity as part of the 'Amharic model' of the Oromo (formerly called Galla) tribes continued from their invasion in the sixteenth century through to the twentieth.

The following period was characterized by isolation from Europeans, but Christological dogmatic controversies continued, caused according to tradition by problems raised by the first Protestant missionary, Peter Heyling. Unionists and Unctionists were divided about the interpretation of Acts 10: 38. These disputes also reflected political divisions, north versus south, Tigre versus Shoa. Synods held by the kings at Gondar were both political and religious events. The matter was definitively resolved only after the political reunification under Menilek II, at the Council of Borru Meda (1878). Nowadays it plays a minor role in apologetic literature directed against Catholic Christology.

The established church remained the stronghold of monarchy until the downfall of Haile Selassie I in 1974. Even thereafter links to the state were not loosened. For the traditional Ethiopian Christian the church is part of national identity, influencing everyday life. Autocephaly came with the first Ethiopian patriarch, Abun Baselyos, in 1951. The co-operation and influence of Protestant and Catholic missions helped improve clerical education. Trinity College was founded in the same period as a theological faculty. Dialogue with EASTERN ORTHODOX churches has intensified, with students travelling to GREECE and elsewhere, though prudent reserve marks the church's position in wider ecumenism.

Judaic elements in Ethiopian Christianity – the observance of the Saturday Sabbath, dietary rules of ritual cleanness, circumcision on the eighth day (a custom almost universally observed, but not a religious duty), etc. – often adduced as evidence of Judaizing tendencies, are partly an inheritance from the first Christian communities in the East, partly due to internal developments within the Ethiopian church which go back to its roots and are based on literal interpretation of the Old Testament. This might well be the origin of the Ethiopian Jews, the Falasha. In the early middle ages political and religious dissenters were labelled 'Ayhud' (Jews), which suggests the acquisition of denominational identity by a double process: voluntary Judaizing, and labelling as 'Jews' by others. The whole phenomenon is intrinsically linked to the legend of Israelite origin of the 'Solomonic' dynasty and of Ethiopia as the continuation of ancient Israel.

The label 'monophysite' is rightly rejected by the Ethiopian church. Unionist theology preserves well the Athanasian standpoint; it is 'verbal monophysitism' in modern terminology. Most religious controversies in the Ethiopian church were internally generated; Ethiopia did not stand in the mainstream of Eastern Christianity but developed its own original theology, ways of thought and customs. Besides fundamental theological works, mostly translations from Arabic, the essentials of biblical exegesis and of theology were transmitted and taught orally in the *Amdemta*, a body of commentaries where every phrase of the scriptures in the literary language GE'EZ is followed by a paraphrase starting with the word *andem*, 'as one [says]', and commentary, often freely associated, in the vernacular Amharic. Only part of this theological treasure has recently been written down, mainly at the initiative of European scholars, and the study of it is only beginning. As this traditional mode of church teaching is declining, archival rescue recordings of traditional scholars have been made.

Baptismal vows are renewed annually at Ṭemqat (THEOPHANY). The ritual unity of baptism and chrismation is preserved. Confession is strictly personal; the confessor (*ya-*

nafs abbat: soul-father) plays an important role in family life. Communion is received in both kinds as the body and blood of Christ. Several types of civil matrimony exist and any divorce is normally according to customary law. Only marriages of older couples are usually consecrated by sacramental matrimony, so that most laity are excluded from the eucharist for long periods. Unction of the sick is infrequent. Since autocephaly in 1951 priests are ordained by Ethiopian bishops; before that, priestly status was conferred only by the Abun. Married men may be ordained as priests or deacons. Bishops and monks are celibate. The semi-clerical *dabtara*, a learned class of scribes with an important liturgical role, administer a specific part of the church's intellectual heritage. As they make use of their writing skills for healing and magic (magic scrolls are widespread in Ethiopia) they sometimes enjoy an ambiguous reputation.

In the Divine Liturgy fourteen anaphoras are in use; that of the Twelve Apostles is the most frequently used. The hymnographer and musician Yared is said to have created large collections of hymns (*Deggwa*) under King Gabra Masqal in the Axumite period. A complex system of musical notation exists, dating from the sixteenth century. The *dabtara* chant the hymns and dance during the liturgy, using drums (*kabaro*), systrums (*ṣanaṣel*) and staves (*maqqwamya*). This recalls Old Testament descriptions of liturgical actions, but it is evident that autochthonous African elements of dance and music are also incorporated. The vestments used resemble the RELIGIOUS DRESS of other Oriental churches and similar sacred vessels are used, including ritual bread-baskets. Umbrellas are carried as marks of distinction.

Fetḥa Nagast (Laws of Kings), a translation of the Arabic *Nomocanon* by the Coptic scholar Al-Ṣafī abu l-Fadā'il ibn AL-'ASSĀL (d. before 1260) provides the basis for the regulation of ecclesiastical affairs. Rules of monasteries are partly of Antonian and Pachomian origin, partly Ethiopic. High church dignitaries were at the same time state officials. Highest in rank was the *abun* (Arabic: 'our father'), an Egyptian monk appointed as metropolitan; he was the court of last appeal in questions of dogma, morals and discipline, though his authority was contested by that of synods held under the auspices of the king. Abun ABBĀ SALĀMĀ MATARGWEN (fourteenth century) was a notable translator. The *ečage*, head of the monastic order, was first the prior of Dabra Hayq, then from the fifteenth century that of Dabra Libanos in Shoa. He was formerly appointed by the emperor, and served as a supervisor in ecclesiastical and administrative matters; sending his *Liqa kahnat* (archpriests) to act as supervisors in the provinces. In 1951 the offices of *abun* and *ečage* were merged (*see* ABOUNA; ECHAGE). Bishops (*pappas* or *episkopos*), limited to seven in number by a pseudo-canon of Nicea (to stop Ethiopia consecrating its own patriarch), had a very limited role until Yohannes IV revived the office in the nineteenth century. Haile Selassie I had several Ethiopian bishops consecrated when preparing the church for autocephaly in 1951. Other central offices of the church, such as *Liqa diyaqonat* (archdeacon), are described in medieval state regulations (*ser'ata mangest*). Until 1974 the state legislated for the church. Abbots of larger monasteries and of Axum cathedral (*Nebura Ed*) were often laymen with administrative and nominal functions. Sanctuary played an important historical role, with many monasteries expressly designated as inviolable.

The 'established' church derived its funds from sources including alms, free-will offerings and fees for services, as well as revenues from extensive possessions and land rights, often dating from the early middle ages and constantly augmented by pious donations. The registers and archives of monasteries and churches, often written in the margins of book manuscripts, are important sources for Ethiopia's economic and social history. This situation changed from 1974 with the land reforms of the secular governments.

The traditional literary and liturgical language was Ge'ez, the old Semitic idiom of Ethiopia. Recently vernaculars, mainly Amharic, appear in bilingual editions and increasingly in the liturgy. The BIBLE was translated in antiquity directly from the Greek, the Old Testament from the Septuagint and the New Testament from a version which has not been identified. Some traces of SYRIAC and elements of re-Semitization in respect of Septuagint names need to be investigated. A critical edition of both Testaments is not yet completed. As with many other Eastern Christian churches, there is no definitive canonical text of the Bible. The publications of the British and Foreign Bible Society, and subsequently of certain other presses (e.g. Ras Tafari, the Patriarchate, Asmara), are accepted as equally authoritative as manuscripts of every age. The text was thoroughly revised on the basis of the Coptic–Arabic versions in the thirteenth and fourteenth centuries. ABBĀ SALĀMĀ the Translator played an important role in this. The canon is large, with the New Testament containing thirty-five books and the Old Testament forty-six, and uniquely includes the Shepherd of Hermas, Enoch and Kufale (Deutero-Genesis).

Some theological literature was translated in the Axumite period, including the original *Qerellos* (Cyril), a large patristic collection, as well as secular works such as the *Fisalgo*s (Physiologus). There was a period of reform, with a flourishing Ge'ez literature and translations mostly from Arabic, from the reign of Emperor 'AMDA-SEYON (1314–44) to that of ZAR'A-YA'QOB (1434–68). The numerous writings of the latter are completed by the Ethiopian summa, the *Mashafa Mestir* (The Book of the Holy Mysteries) by Giorgis of Sagla. Another active period of literary production and translations occurred in the sixteenth and seventeenth centuries. The Yemenite convert, and then *ečage*, Enbaqom wrote the anti-Islamic apologetic *Anqaṣa Amin* (The Gate of Faith) and translated the tale of BARLAAM AND IOASAPH (*Barlaam wa-Yosaphat*).

The *Mashafa Qeddase*, nowadays usually bilingual, comprises the fourteen anaphoras. Other liturgical books include the Baptismal Rite (*Mashafa Ṭemqat*), the Rites for the Dead *(Mashafa Genzat)*, the HOROLOGION (*Mashafa Sa'atat*), the Book of the Lamp (*Mashafa Qandil*), i.e. the Rite of the Anointing of the Sick or *euchelaion*, and the *Weddase Amlak*, the Praise of God, containing prayers for every day of the week. Typically Ethiopic is the fine poetry in honour of the Virgin Mary, and hymns to other saints, as well as the hymns called *qene*. These last are based on the principle of *sam-enna warq*, wax and gold: every line has at least two, often totally different meanings. Lives, especially of Ethiopian saints, have value as historical source material.

Churches of ancient Axumite type exist in the north (Axum). There are rock-hewn churches throughout the northern territory, especially the fine complex of LALIBELA. Elsewhere the round church prevails; these are lofty wood constructions with grass roofs and, in the interior, traditionally two cubes one inside the other: *Qeddus* and *Qeddusa Qeddusan*, the Holy and the Holy of Holies. Every church possesses several TABOT, ICONS and wall paintings. Religious painting is influenced by folk art, and book illustrations show traces of European influence already in the fifteenth century. The most original expression of Ethiopian religious art is found in the many crosses – hand crosses for priests, processional crosses with different and very flowery ornamentation – and in other sacred utensils used in liturgy and devotion.

The ecclesiastical calendar is the primitive Alexandrine Computus which must have come very early to Ethiopia. The names of the months are genuinely Ethiopian, most probably in use in pre-Christian Axum. The traditional work on calculating the date of Pascha, *Bahra Ḥesab*, is entitled *Abušaker* from *Abū-Šākir*, a Christian Arabic historian from Egypt, but is not a translation of his work; the great authority of his chronography of world history led to its name. Several ERAS are in use; today *'Amata Meḥrat*, the 'Year of Grace' Ethiopic era, predominates, though the name also designates different eras, seven and eight years behind the date AD. The *'Amata Feṭrat (-a 'Alam)*, 'Year of the Creation (of the World)', is the Alexandrine world era. The *'Amata Sama'tat*, 'Year of the Martyrs', AD 284, served as a starting point for the cycle of 532 years of the most common computus. Several ad hoc eras were used in different monastic traditions.

Major Christian feasts are largely identical with those of the rest of Eastern Christianity, with the feast of the True Cross (Masqal) given particular prominence. The basic datum of the calendar is the Tazkar (commemoration day). Each family has tazkars which are observed with particular devotion because of intimate links to the death of a relative, donations to churches for the respective feasts, local festivals and so forth. Thus Christ, the Virgin Mary and all the saints of the calendar have their yearly tazkar. The SENKESSAR contains commemorations for every day of the year together with short notices on the saints' lives. Besides this the Virgin Mary, the archangels and several others have additional monthly tazkars. Fasting is strictly observed and comprises about 180 days for laity, 250 for clerics. Besides every Wednesday and Friday and Lent, 'Abiy Ṣom or Hudad, there are shorter periods of fasting after Pentecost, before Christmas and Kweskwam, forty days preceding the feast of the flight into Egypt.

Popular belief and devotion has retained and assimilated many traditional African elements. A blue neck-cord, the *mateb*, serves as a distinctive sign of a Christian; sometimes crosses are tattooed on hands or forehead. Amulets are widely used; the Psalms, the most popular book among Ethiopian Christians, are used for daily prayers and, together with other texts, for magic and healing. Icons and relics are venerated. Ethiopia obtained many relics in the middle ages, profiting from a flourishing trade after the fall and sack of CONSTANTINOPLE following the Fourth CRUSADE (1204). For example, a splinter of the true cross and other relics of Christ came to Amba Geshen (Wollo).

Pilgrimages are very popular and take place inside Ethiopia, for example to Mount Zeqwala, south of Addis Ababa, the location of the shrine of St Gabra Manfas Qeddus. The PILGRIMAGE to Jerusalem, mainly via Egypt, played a vital role in Ethiopia's relationship to the rest of the Christian world. Jerusalem pilgrims enjoyed a special status as counsellors and advisers at the Ethiopian royal court, comparable to that in the Islamic world of a Muslim *ḥajjī* to Mecca. Ethiopians were and are present in several monasteries in Upper Egypt and possess a share in the Holy Sepulchre in Jerusalem, besides an Ethiopian monastery, Dayr al-Sulṭān, there.

Grierson, R., ed. (1993), *African Zion: The Sacred Art of Ethiopia*. New Haven and London: Yale University Press.

Munro-Hay, S. (1991), *Axum: An African Civilisation of Late Antiquity*. Edinburgh: Edinburgh University Press.

Cowley, R. (1988), *Ethiopian Biblical Interpretation: A Study in Exegetical Tradition and Hermeneutics*. Cambridge: Cambridge University Press.

Bonk, J. (1984), *An Annotated and Classified Bibliography of English Literature Pertaining to the Ethiopian Orthodox Church*. ATLA Bibliography Series 11. New Jersey: Scarecrow.

Cowley, R. (1983), *The Traditional Interpretation of the Apocalypse of St John in the Ethiopian Orthodox Church*. Cambridge: Cambridge University Press.

Brown, C. F. (1978), *Ethiopian Perspectives: A Bibliographical Guide to the History of Ethiopia*. Westport, Conn.: Greenwood.

Ofosu-Appiah, L. H., ed. (1977), *Dictionary of African Biography*, vol. 1: *Ethiopia–Ghana*. New York.

Assfalg, J. and Krüger, P., eds, (1975), *Kleines Wörterbuch des Christlichen Orients*. Wiesbaden: Harrassowitz.

Matthew, A. F. (1936), *The Teaching of the Abyssinan Church as set forth by the Doctors of the Same*. London: n.p.

Walker, C. H. (1933), *The Abyssinian at Home*. London: Sheldon.

Hyatt, H. M. (1928). *The Church of Abyssinia*. London: Luzac.

MK

Ethiopian liturgy   Since its origins the Ethiopian church has always had close links with the COPTIC CHRISTIANITY of Egypt, though these have at times been more theoretical than real. There is evidence that an early Ethiopic version of the gospels was made from the Codex Alexandrinus, and many of the rites and liturgical texts of the Ethiopian church are translated from Coptic. Indeed, some scholars have assumed the liturgies of the two churches are virtually the same. In fact the Ethiopian church possesses its own distinctive pattern of worship, its own hymnography and euchology. This is in part the result of the isolation of Ethiopia from the rest of Christendom from the fifth century.

The eucharistic liturgy of the Ethiopian church, while it has evident similarities with that of the Coptic church, is distinguished among other things by a very elaborate series of preparatory rites for the vesting of the priest and the preparation of the sacred vessels and the elements. An assistant priest, to whom certain parts of the rite are assigned specifically, and a deacon, are considered necessary for a celebration of the eucharist; indeed, one of the rubrics runs: 'Before he vests himself completely, let him turn to the people and look to see if there is a deacon for service, because it is not fitting for the priest to take off his vestments after having put them on should there be no deacon to help in the service.' As in the Coptic rite there are four New Testament readings: from the Pauline Epistles, the Catholic Epistles, the Acts of the Apostles and the Gospels. The last is preceded, as in the Coptic liturgy, by the Trisagion.

The Ethiopian liturgy is also distinguished by its fourteen anaphoras, which are used on certain specific days. That of St Basil is a translation of the Coptic St Basil; the others are all peculiar to the church of Ethiopia. The basic anaphora, that *Of the*

Apostles, though its present form is much elaborated, is of great interest, since its original is the old Roman anaphora of the *Apostolic Tradition* of Hippolytus, which has had a profound effect on Western liturgical reforms of the late twentieth century. The most complete text of this early Greek work of the old Roman church was preserved, via Sahidic and Arabic versions, in the remote mountains of Ethiopia, and has never fallen into disuse.

Mercer, S. A. B. (1915), *The Ethiopic Liturgy*. London: Mowbray.

E

ethnomartyrs   A title given after the eighteenth century to certain NEW MARTYRS. Ethnomartyrs, usually prominent figures in the wider Christian community, are victims of persecution executed when a particular Christian community or national church is under attack from other groupings. Unlike other national heroes, occasionally also termed 'ethnomartyrs', Christian ethnomartyrs are revered as saints for witness to Christian faith and values. In the OTTOMAN empire the early identification of ethnic groups with a particular faith led to national and religious issues becoming increasingly entangled, particularly in the period of 'national reawakening' during the nineteenth century.

Gregory V (d. 1821), patriarch of Constantinople, executed during the Greek revolution, is the most notable ethnomartyr. Other new martyrs in this category include CYRIL VI, THOMAS PASCHIDIS, ILIA CHAVCHAVADZE, CHRYSOSTOM OF SMYRNA and PLATO JOVANOVIC.

Krikoni, H. (1991), *Orthodoxe Ekklesia, Protagonistes tes Ethnegersias*. Thessaloniki: n.p.

DB

Euchologion   A compendium of texts needed by Byzantine rite clergy for celebration of the liturgy, offices, sacraments and other rites, blessings and prayers. In Slavonic the book is called the *Trebnik*, or Book of Needs. The contents vary from edition to edition, but in Greek it commonly has two forms: the Large Euchologion, which includes a very full series of rites, including those only performed by bishops, such as ordinations, the consecration of churches and the confection of the holy *myron* (the complex process by which the chrism is made from a large number of ingredients), and the Small, which contains only those normally needed by a priest in the performance of his pastoral duties. Texts of the choir offices and the liturgies are also published separately in a volume for priests, the *Hieratikon* or, in Slavonic, *Sluzebnik*.

E

Eulogitaria   A series of short hymns introduced with the refrain 'Blessed [Greek: *eulogitos*] are you, O Lord, teach me your statutes', which are sung at the end of Psalm 118, or the POLYELEOS, at Byzantine rite ORTHROS on Sundays. Another set is sung on Saturdays of the Departed, at funerals and memorial services.

E

Eunomios   Bishop of Cyzicus *c.*366, and a leader of the extreme Arians, the anomoians (Greek: *anomoios*, 'unlike'). Eunomios resigned his see for lack of support from his clergy. He died in exile, banished by Theodosius (379–95). Eunomios was an original theologian, though remote from Nicene orthodoxy. Reworked Platonic and gnostic themes inform his account of the ungenerated but intelligible Creator, who creates the Son and endows him with a creative capacity that makes him the image of the ungenerated. The Holy Spirit he presents as created by the Son for the sanctification of living souls. He denied that the Son ever truly became human. Eunomios seems to have practised baptism, not by triple immersion in the name of the Trinity, but by single immersion into the death of Christ. Eunomios' doctrine left no lasting body of followers, but had a historical impact because of the opposition of the CAPPADO-CIANS; both Basil the Great and Gregory of Nazianzus wrote refutations of Eunomios which are significant theological works.

Kopeck, T. A. (1979), *A History of Neo-Arianism*, 2 vols. Cambridge, Mass.: Philadelphia Patristic Foundation.
Cavalcanti, E. (1976), *Studi Eunomiani*. Orientalia Christiana Analecta, 202. Rome.
Quasten, J. (1960), *Patrology*. Utrecht: Spectrum.

DM

Euphrosyne of Polotsk (d. 1173)   Patron saint of BELARUS, daughter of Prince Vseslav of Polotsk, who fled to a convent rather than accept marriage and later lived as a solitary by the church of Holy Wisdom. Euphrosyne worked at copying books, using most of her income for almsgiving. Disciples gathering around her were moved into newly founded convents (most notably at Selitse). Euphrosyne travelled to CONSTANTINOPLE and the Holy Land, visiting Mar Saba and JERUSALEM, where she died at the monastery of St Theodosios. Euphrosyne is commemorated on 23 May.

Nicolas Velimirovic (1986). *The Prologue From Ochrid*, Vol II. Birmingham: Lazarica.

DB

Eusebius of Caesarea (d. *c*.340)   A pupil of ORIGEN's devoted disciple, the martyr Pamphilios, whose name Eusebius assumed, from respect, as his own surname. In 313 Eusebius became bishop of Caesarea. He sympathized with moderate Arianism; his closeness to Constantine the Great enabled him to influence the deposition of ATHANASIUS in 335. Eusebius's works include the *Ecclesiastical History*, valuable for its account of events but also for the references to his sources; a *Chronicle*, in part a historical apologia for Christian belief; and several theological and apologetic writings, including the *Preparation* which argues the greater antiquity and value of Judaism in comparison with Greek and Roman religions.

Grant, R. M. (1980), *Eusebius as Church Historian*. Oxford: Oxford University Press.

DM

Eusebius of Dorylaeum   In 429, while a layman and lawyer in CONSTANTINOPLE, Eusebius wrote an argued attack on Nestorius, the *Diamartyria* or *Contestatio*. Later, as bishop of Dorylaeum, in 448 he took a leading role in denouncing Eutyches as a heretic before the Standing Synod in Constantinople. Deposed and exiled by the 'Brigandage' of Ephesus (449), he was reinstated under Emperor Marcian (450–7) and took a major role in the formulation of the Christological definition of Chalcedon (451).

DM

Eusebius of Nicomedia Contemporary of EUSEBIUS OF CAESAREA and fellow student of the heresiarch Arius. Eusebius became bishop of Nicomedia about 318. When Alexander of Alexandria (313–28) deposed Arius *c.*321, Eusebius wrote widely in his defence, helping to make Arius and his theology an issue for the universal church. Despite subscribing to the decisions of Nicea (325) he soon became an important leader of the extreme Arian party. He co-operated with Eusebius of Caesarea to bring about the downfall of ATHANASIUS, and like his namesake was favoured by CONSTANTINE THE GREAT (306–37), whom he baptized near the end of his life. In *c.*339 he was made bishop of CONSTANTINOPLE by Constantius II (337–61), and used his high office to oppose Athanasius and the Nicene orthodox. Eusebius probably died in 342.

Quasten, J. (1960), *Patrology*. Utrecht: Spectrum.

DM

Eutychius of Alexandria (877–940) Known in Arabic as Sa'īd ibn Baṭrīq; MELK-ITE Patriarch of ALEXANDRIA from 935 to his death in 940. Ibn Baṭrīq was a practising physician, and information about his life is contained in the collection of biographies of famous physicians by Ibn Abī Uṣaybi'a (d. 1270), which says that Ibn Baṭrīq had a comprehensive knowledge of the sciences of the Christians and of their doctrinal systems. Ibn Abī Uṣaybi'a ascribes three major works to Ibn Baṭrīq: a book on medicine, now lost; a book called *The Debate between the Opponent and the Christian*; and the *Annals*, or *String of Pearls*, under which title the *Annals* circulated in the Arabic-speaking world of his day. Another work, not mentioned by Ibn Abī Uṣaybi'a, has been wrongly attributed to Eutychius of Alexandria: this is the *Kitāb al-burhān*, or *Proof Book*, an apologetic tract of composite character that in its present form was put together in the tenth century by a monk of the Palestinian monastery of St Chariton. The *Annals*, or *String of Pearls*, is Eutychius' most enduring work, albeit considerably enhanced by later hands. In conception, it is a universal chronicle, written in Arabic, beginning with an account of creation. For the portion of the *Annals* covering Islamic times it is clear the compiler drew on Muslim sources. The compiler's confessional allegiance clearly emerges in the account he renders of the succession of bishops and patriarchs, and this confessional profile then serves to commend the orthodoxy of Eutychius' own Melkite Christian community in the Islamic milieu. The text, which survives in two recensions, is a rich repository of much otherwise unobtainable information about the history of Syria, Palestine and Egypt, especially in the periods of the Persian occupation in the seventh century, and in Islamic times up to the early tenth century.

Pirone, B., trans. (1987), *Eutichio, Patriarcha de Alessandria, Gli Annali*. Studia Orientalia Christiana Monographiae 1. Cairo and Jerusalem: Franciscan Centre of Christian Oriental Studies.

Breydy, M., ed. and trans. (1985), *Das Annalenwerk des Eutychios von Alexandrien; ausgewählte Geschichten und Legenden kompiliert von Sa'īd ibn Baṭrīq um 935* AD. CSCO vols 471–2. Louvain: Peeters.
Breydy, M. (1983), *Études sur Sa'īd ibn Baṭrīq et ses sources*. CSCO vol. 450. Louvain: Peeters.
Cachia, P. and Montgomery Watt, W., eds and trans. (1960–61), *Eutychius of Alexandria, the Book of the Demonstration (Kitāb al-burhān)*. CSCO vols 192–3. Louvain: Peeters.

MJB/SHG

Evagrius Ponticus   Evagrios Pontikos, *c.*345–99, associate in his earlier life of the CAPPADOCIANS, ordained reader by Basil the Great and deacon by Gregory of Nyssa, or more probably Gregory of Nazianzus who was his teacher and whom he accompanied to the Second ECUMENICAL COUNCIL, held in CONSTANTINOPLE in 381. A brief career as a popular preacher there was ended by a scandal. Eventually he became a monk in Egypt and an important writer. Evagrius accepted much of ORIGEN's theology, including the doctrine of the pre-existence of souls and of the APOKATAS-TASIS. At the Second Council of Constantinople in 553, Evagrius was condemned as a heretic together with Origen. None the less the monastic tradition continued to hold Evagrius' spiritual teachings in high regard, and his writings on prayer and on temptation were preserved under the name of Neilos the Ascetic. These are contained in the PHILOKALIA; others of his writings have been preserved in translation and some are lost.

Evagrius' spiritual doctrine is rooted in Platonistic psychology with *nous*, intellect, striving to control the appetites and *thymos*, the energy-filled, spirited aspect. He sees the human soul as the battleground of the spiritual war between the divine and the demonic which the apocalyptic writers see as a battle taking place at the end of history. In his texts *On Discrimination* he analyses three different modes of consciousness in terms of which we experience the world: an angelic mode which seeks out the nature of a thing and its spiritual *logos*, its ultimate causal embedding in the structure and pattern of created reality; a demonic mode which has no interest in such knowledge, but seeks to grasp, possess and exploit things; and a merely human mode which is concerned neither with ultimate understanding nor with acquisition, but simply presents to thought the form of the thing without passion or greed.

Evagrius teaches a doctrine of pure prayer, free from words and images. He warns of the danger of visions and advises against any attempt to imagine things in prayer. When we put off the fallen state and attain the state of grace, then the intellect, cleared of all thoughts and passions, is able to perceive its own sapphirine nature, resembling the sky in purity, ready to be filled with the light of God.

Evagrius's writings exercised a great influence on the development of HESYCHASM.

Louth, A. (1981), *The Origins of the Christian Mystical Tradition*. Oxford: Oxford University Press.
Palmer, G. E. H. et al., trans. (1979), *The Philokalia*, vol. 1. London: Faber.
Meyendorff, J. (1971), *St Gregory Palamas and Orthodox Spirituality*. Crestwood, NY: St Vladimir's Seminary Press.

Bamberger, J. E., trans. (1970), *The Praktikos and 153 Chapters on Prayer*. Kalamazoo: Cistercian Publications.
Guillaumont, A. (1962), *Les 'Kephalaia Gnostica' d'Evagre le Pontique et l'histoire de l'origénisme chez les Syriens*. Paris: n.p.

DM

Ewostatewos   Ēwosṭātēwos, Eustathius: Ethiopian monk and saint (*fl.* first part fourteenth century). His birth name was Ma'eqaba Egzi. Ewosṭatewos established an important monastic 'house' in Sära'ē, northern Ethiopia. He advocated various traditional religious practices including observance of the Saturday or Jewish Sabbath. Facing opposition from church leaders, Ewosṭatewos travelled to Egypt, perhaps to present his case to the Coptic patriarch, then to Palestine, Cyprus and Armenia, where he died in exile. After his death, his teachings were spread by disciples, the Ewosṭateans, also attracting interest from the non-Christian Ethiopian Falasha community. The Saturday Sabbath controversy was finally settled a century later by the Ethiopian emperor ZARA YAKUB (1434–68) at the Council of DABRA METMAQ (1450). Both Saturday and Sunday Sabbaths are observed by the Ethiopian Orthodox church.

  See also ETHIOPIAN CHRISTIANITY.

Haile, G. (1991), 'Ethiopian Heresies and Theological Controversies', *Coptic Encyclopedia* 3, pp. 984–7.
Haile, G. (1981), 'The Letter of Archbishops Mika'el and Gabre'el Concerning the Observance of Saturday', *Journal of Semitic Studies* 36, pp. 73–8.
Tamrat, T. (1972), *Church and State in Ethiopia 1250–1527*. Oxford: Clarendon Press.
Budge, E. A. W. (1928), *The Book of the Saints of the Ethiopian Church* (4 vols), vol. 1. Cambridge: Cambridge University Press.

MJB/SHG

exaposteilarion   Troparion sung at the end of Byzantine ORTHROS, immediately before the AINOI. Specific exaposteilaria are provided in the HOROLOGION for each day of the week, in the MENAIA for major feasts and in the PARAKLETIKE for the eleven-week cycle of Sundays through the year. Additional exaposteilaria are provided in the TRIODION for the Sundays of Great Lent and in the PENTEKOSTARION for the period of Pentecost. The Sunday exaposteilaria of the eleven-week cycle are attributed in the Parakletike to Emperor Constantine VII.

E

exarch   An ecclesiastical title deriving from that used to designate the ruler of an exarchate, an administrative region of the Byzantine empire where civil and military command were in the hands of a single person. In ecclesiastical use the title 'exarch' has had a variety of uses, to designate the PATRIARCH, or the senior hierarch of a region, or the patriarch's representative in an area. It came to be used also both of the senior hierarchs of areas under Muslim rule and of bishops whose titles were expanded to include defunct sees and the territory attached to them.

DM

.F.

feast days of saints   Saints' days are an important element of the ecclesiastical year. The Byzantine rite MENAIA contain texts for the feasts generally celebrated on each date in the CALENDAR. The General *Menaia* contains texts for the feasts of various categories of saints: martyrs, women martyrs, priest martyrs, hierarchs, ascetics, etc. Texts for the AKOLOUTHIA of an individual saint not contained in the Menaia are frequently printed as pamphlets (*phyllada*), which often contain texts for the most important celebrations in a particular community.

In communities where a particular saint is specially honoured, Vespers, Matins and the Divine Liturgy will be celebrated, the whole *akolouthia* of the saint may be sung, and bread, wine and KOLLYBA blessed. Processions may be held and the ICON and relics of the saint publicly venerated. A festive meal, often accompanied by dancing, may follow the religious observances. Such celebrations are often preceded by fasts and accompanied by festivals (*panegyria*), which can be of national significance, such as the ancient celebrations in Thessaloniki of GREAT MARTYR Demetrios MYROBLYTES on 26 October.

Every day numerous saints are commemorated. Most feasts have fixed dates; others are associated with the Paschal cycle. There are national and regional variations in the pattern of feasts observed in honour of even the 'universal' saints. It is common for saints to have more than one feast, commemorating separately the death of the saint, the discovery or translation of relics and icons, the founding and dedication of churches and monasteries in honour of the saint, the saint's canonization and the miracles attributed to the saint. Saints are often honoured again on the feast of a group of saints or on national holidays. Eastern Christians often commemorate saints not yet canonized on their name-days, which can give rise to the establishment of yet another feast.

The feasts observed in individual localities are fixed by popular tradition as much as by the local church hierarchy. In DIASPORA communities, and especially those that have lost their churches, shrines and lands, the feast days of what were their local saints can serve to bind scattered communities together and to keep alive a sense of communal, ethnic and religious identity. In many cases relics and icons of local saints have

197

been carried into exile with displaced communities, forming a new religious focus in a new homeland.

See also HEORTOLOGION; MENAIA; NAMES.

DB

filioque   The creed promulgated by the Council of Constantinople in 381, but known as the 'Nicene' or 'Nicene–Constantinopolitan' creed, on the probably erroneous assumption that it is an amplification of the creed approved by the council of Nicea, contains the article: 'and in the holy Spirit, the Lord and Life-giver, who proceeds from the Father...' This creed acquired liturgical importance, both as a baptismal creed and from the fifth century as the creed used in the Divine Liturgy. Canon 2 of the third council of Toledo (589) established its liturgical use, and extant versions of the canons contain the additional word '*filioque*', so that the article reads: 'who proceeds from the Father and the Son...' Whether the original canons of Toledo III contained the *filioque* is doubtful. Soon, however, the doctrine of the double procession of the Spirit from Father and Son came to be widespread in the West, and the modification of the creed spread.

In England the Synod of Hatfield, held in 680 under the presidency of Theodore of Tarsus, archbishop of Canterbury (668–90) to formulate a profession of faith for submission to Pope Agatho (678–81), declared its belief in the double procession. In 796 Paulinus of Aquileia argued in favour of the *filioque* at the Synod of Friuli. In the ninth century the singing of the creed at mass became widespread in the Frankish West, and in 807 Frankish monks of the Mount of Olives brought the *filioque* into use in JERUSALEM, scandalizing the monks of Mar Sabas.

Pope Leo III (798–816) opposed the use of the addition, and had two silver plates engraved with the creed without it and placed in St Peter's. None the less, the addition was adopted in the Roman mass in the eleventh century.

The *filioque* remains an obstacle to East–West unity, for two distinct reasons: the question of the orthodoxy of the addition, and the question as to the legitimacy of altering the 'Nicene' creed. Patriarch PHOTIOS THE GREAT (858–67, 877–86), in an encyclical letter to the other Eastern patriarchs, denounced the *filioque*, which Latin missionaries had recently introduced into BULGARIA, opposing it not merely as an unjustified interpolation into the credal text established on the authority of an ECU-MENICAL COUNCIL, but also as a grave theological error. In his *Mystagogy of the Holy Spirit* he clearly taught that the Holy Spirit proceeds from the Father alone. He rejected both the addition of the *filioque* to the creed and the doctrine it expresses. In doing this he was not, as Latin theologians have often assumed, travelling a lonely theological path, alien to the general tradition of EASTERN ORTHODOX theology. Roman Catholicism adopted the *filioque* doctrine as dogma and uses the interpolated creed. Eastern Orthodox theology rejects the interpolation and generally rejects the *filioque* doctrine.

At the Second Council of LYONS in 1245, and at the Council of FLORENCE in 1439–45, Orthodox delegates accepted the *filioque*. Western theologians faced the Easterns with persuasive collections of patristic texts that used language suggesting that Orthodox doctrine was not incompatible with the *filioque*. The formal definition of Florence is a complex statement taking up the qualifications incorporated at Lyons II into the Constitution on the Sacred Trinity and the Catholic Faith: '. . . proceeds from Father and Son, not, however, as from two principles, but as from one principle, not by two breathings, but by a single breathing . . .'. It even acknowledges a difference between Eastern and Western theologies: *secundum Graecos*, it says, the Son is *quidem causam*, a 'cause of some kind', whereas *secundum Latinos*, according to the Latins, he is *vero principium subsistentiae Spiritus Sancti*, 'truly a principle of the Holy Spirit's subsistence'.

Both Lyons II and Florence resulted in failure, and they left a dangerous heritage: the assumption that the Orthodox, having accepted the *filioque* doctrine at those councils, only oppose the interpolation of the *filioque* into the creed without the sanction of an ecumenical council. That is far from the case. One consequence of the Orthodox rejection of Florence was the emergence of an Eastern dogmatic tradition explicitly opposed to the doctrine of the dual procession. This is evident from that most Western of Orthodox statements of faith, the *Confession* of Peter MOGILA.

An important contribution to the theological understanding of the *filioque* from an Eastern perspective was made by Ecumenical Patriarch Gregory II of Cyprus, who, while rejecting the Western doctrine of the double procession, none the less emphasized the Son's eternal manifestation (*ekphansis*) of the Spirit. This doctrine was formally approved by the Synod of Blachernae in 1285 that repudiated the union of Lyons.

Medieval discussions between Eastern and Latin theologians focused on the legitimacy of specific theological formulae and on specific expression used in the scriptures and by the fathers, to the relative neglect of the way in which Christian doctrine, spirituality and religious life express and are sustained by the lived experience of the mystery of the Holy Spirit. It is such a focus, rather than a return to Florence, that may offer a more fruitful path to ecumenical agreement.

Papadakis, A. (1996), *Crisis in Byzantium: The Filioque Controversy in the Patriarchate of Gregory II of Cyprus (1283–1289)*. Crestwood, NY: St Vladimir's Seminary Press.
Meyendorff, J. (1983), *Byzantine Theology*. Crestwood, NY: St Vladimir's Seminary Press.
Haugh, R. (1975), *Photius and the Carolingians: The Trinitarian Controversy*. Belmont, Mass.: Nordland.
Kelly, J. N. D. (1972), *Early Christian Creeds*, 3rd edn. New York: Longman.
Sherrard, P. (1959), *The Greek East and the Latin West*. Oxford: Oxford University Press.

DM

Finnish Orthodox church   Eastern Christianity reached Finland from NOVGOROD during the eleventh century. The Karelian peoples of the eastern regions became EASTERN ORTHODOX in the next century. It was not until the end of the nineteenth century, however, that Orthodoxy made any significant headway among the Finns themselves, when Finnish was introduced as the language of the liturgy. When the Orthodox diocese of Finland was organized by the RUSSIAN ORTHODOX CHURCH in 1892 its members included numbers of Finns and Swedes. After Finland achieved independence from Russia the autonomy of the Finnish Orthodox church was recognized by the revived Moscow patriarchate in 1918, but the Russian church opposed the adherence of the Finnish Orthodox church to the CONSTANTINOPLE patriarchate in

1923. The Russo-Finnish war and the immediately following Second World War impacted heavily on regions where Orthodox were in the majority, and over 70 per cent of the Orthodox were refugees by the end of hostilities. The church lost 90 per cent of its properties and monasteries like VALAAM were ruined. Support from the Finnish state after the war, however, meant that the refugees were swiftly resettled, a New Valaam was founded at Heinavesi and the church resumed its place in Finnish life. The Finnish Orthodox church is unusual in using not only the new CALENDAR but also the new paschalion, so that its Easter coincides with that of Western churches.

Ramiret, P. (1988), *Eastern Christianity and Politics in the Twentieth Century*. Duke, NC: Duke University Press.
Byzantium and the North (1985). Acta Byzantina Fennica 1. Helsinki.

DB

Flavian   Flabianos, patriarch of CONSTANTINOPLE 446–48, successor of Proclus. Flavian deposed the Archimandrite Eutyches for teaching MONOPHYSITE doctrine. Emperor Theodosius II (408–50) convoked a council, known from Leo the Great's description of it as the Latrocinium, the Brigandage of Ephesus, which deposed and ill-treated Flavian, who died probably on his way into exile. It was to Flavian that the celebrated *Tomos* of Leo the Great was addressed. It was not read at the Latrocinium but was the most influential document presented to the Council of Chalcedon. Flavian's feast in the Byzantine calendar is 16 February.

DM

Florence, Council of (1438–49)   The Second Council of LYONS failed to reunite the Greek and Latin churches, but throughout the thirteenth and fourteenth centuries the Byzantine emperors several times renewed contact with the papacy. The Great Schism (1378–1417), when two, then three rivals competed for the throne of Peter, effectively ended with the election of Martin V (1417–31) at the Council of Constance (1414–18), at which the issue of reunion with the East was also raised. In accordance with the decrees of Constance, Martin summoned another council to meet in Basel, to continue the work of reform, but died before it met in June 1431. His successor Eugene IV (1431–47) dissolved it. Basel, however, refused to be dissolved, and Emperor Sigismund (1410–37) persuaded Eugene to withdraw his bull of dissolution. Basel continued on the path of reform, reunion with the East also on its agenda.

Martin V had already opened discussion of a council with CONSTANTINOPLE. The Council of Basel and Eugene IV now sent separate emissaries to Constantinople. Emperor John VIII (1421–48) accepted the pope's proposals, and in 1437 set out for Italy with the frail Patriarch Joseph II (1416–39) and a substantial entourage, among them GEMISTOS PLETHON, the learned George Scholarios (one of the few Byzantines at home in Latin) and the bishops Mark of Ephesus and BESSARION of Nicea. The other ancient patriarchates were formally represented, and a handful of representatives of other Eastern Orthodox churches travelled separately. The pope had convoked the council in Ferrara. Diehard opponents at Basel refused to move, declared him deposed and elected Antipope Felix V (1439–49).

When the Greeks arrived in Ferrara in March 1438, the pope having formally opened the council in January, delicate concessions accommodated the sharply different Latin and Greek notions of protocol. Weak as he was, Joseph II refused absolutely to kneel to the pope or kiss his foot. None the less, the seating arrangements were papalist: the patriarch was placed opposite the senior cardinals, while the pope's seat was elevated above that of the emperor, whose throne faced that of the conveniently absent Western emperor. John VIII preserved his dignity by ensuring his feet did not touch the floor as he approached the throne.

Business focused on four main issues: purgatory, the FILIOQUE, papal supremacy, and the use of leavened or unleavened bread in the eucharist. For the first four months, preliminary discussions were committed to a small group of delegates; then public sessions took up the issues.

A session in June dealt inconclusively with purgatory. In October the council took up the *filioque*, at first debating the legitimacy of the addition. It soon became evident there was a problem of mutual understanding. Few delegates on either side had a sound working knowledge of the language of the other. By mid-December talk of plague in Ferrara gave Eugene IV the opportunity to reconvene the council in Florence. He was bearing the entire costs of the Greek delegation, and the council was rapidly becoming a financial embarrassment. The Greeks feared an Ottoman attack in Constantinople and were sensitive to living on papal subventions. Despite their grand titles, many of the Greeks were poor. The reconvened council moved more rapidly, the emperor brow-beating his delegates into agreement, the Latins arguing forcefully and convincing some who, like Bessarion and Isidore of Kiev, were sympathetic to their approach. On 5 July 1439 the decree *Laetentur Caeli* was signed by all the Greek hierarchs except Mark of Ephesus, and then by the Latins. On the sixth it was solemnly read in Latin and Greek in the duomo. By the time the degree was promulgated Patriarch Joseph II had died.

The decree proclaims that 'the Holy Spirit is eternally from the Father and the Son', though it adds qualifications to make the decree more accommodating to Greek sensibilities. It confirms that both leavened and unleavened bread can be used in the eucharist and that a priest should follow the custom of his own church in the matter. It teaches the doctrine of the post-mortem purgation by means of *poenis purgatoriis* (purifying punishments) of those who have died 'truly penitent and in the love of God', and teaches the value of prayers, masses and intercessions on their behalf. Using the exact words contained in the profession of faith of Michael VII at Lyons, it affirms that 'the souls of those who die in actual mortal sin or only original sin, forthwith descend to hell, to be punished, however, *poenis...disparibus* [with unequal punishments].'

The decree defines the papal primacy in what appear at first to be unambiguous terms: 'true Vicar of Christ, head of the entire Church, Father and Teacher of all Christians...and that the full power of shepherding, ruling and governing the universal church was handed to him in Blessed Peter'. There follows, however, a clause in the Latin text that makes the definition mean very different things depending on how one reads its first word, *quemadmodum*, and what one assumes the sacred canons are to which it refers: 'in the manner, moreover, that it is contained in the acts of the ecumenical councils and in the sacred canons'; or is it 'just as, furthermore, it is contained...'; and are the sacred canons those acknowledge by the universal church, or the Latin canons?

A further clause of the decree affirms the now traditional order of the patriarchates *salvis videlicet privilegiis omnibus et juribus eorum*. Again, the clause is susceptible of very different interpretations, to refer, for example, to inalienable rights and privileges of the Eastern Patriarchs, or to such rights and privileges as Rome recognized, or even to such rights and privileges as Rome grants them.

The council also received the submission of clergy from the Armenian Apostolic, Syrian Orthodox and Ethiopian churches and from the Cypriot colony of the Church of the East. No actual union with any of the Oriental churches as such took place. The various decrees were, however, to be used at a later date as the basis on which Eastern Christian communities were received into full communion with the Roman Catholic church.

John VIII remained loyal to the union, but it was met in Constantinople and elsewhere with furious opposition. Bessarion, his co-operative attitude rewarded with a cardinal's hat, retired in chagrin from Constantinople. Isidor of Kiev and All Russia, also a cardinal, was thrown into prison by Grand Prince Basil II (1425–34, 1434–6, 1437–42), but managed to escape to Italy. George Scholarios, who had supported union at Florence, was convinced by Mark of Ephesus that he had erred and retired to a monastery. On Mark's death he became the leading anti-unionist. After the fall of Constantinople in 1453, the Ottoman sultan, Mehmet II, was to make him ECUME-NICAL PATRIARCH, as GENNADIOS II.

John VIII and his brother and successor Constantine XI both took steps to make the union a reality. Short of wholesale persecution, however, there was no prospect of success. So clear was this that pro-union Patriarch Gregory III Mammas (1443–50) eventually abandoned his throne and exiled himself. The patriarchs of Alexandria, Antioch and Jerusalem declined to sign the decree.

The pope lived up to his commitment to help John VIII. Eugene worked to organize a crusade with King Ladislas I of Hungary (1439–44) who was also Ladislas III of Poland (1434–44), George Branković of Serbia and John Hunyadi, voyvode of Transylvania. At first the crusaders were successful, and Sultan Murat II (1421–44, 1444–51) signed a ten-year truce offering attractive concessions. The pope was horrified. Cardinal Cesarini, his legate, seems even to have absolved Ladislas of his treaty-oath and pushed the crusaders into action again. George Brankovich refused to join the attack and quietly informed Murat. The sultan, who had abdicated in favour of his son, resumed the throne, rushed to attack the oath-breakers, the defiled treaty fastened to his standard, met them near Varna and defeated them with massive slaughter. Ladislas himself fell in the battle. Hunyadi, however, survived the defeat of Varna to lead yet another crusading army against the Ottomans, only to perish in the battle of Kosovo in 1448 – on the same site where, at the 1389 battle of Kosovo, the Serbian Prince Lazar, Mircea the Great of Wallachia and King Tvrtko of Bosnia were defeated by Murat I, who died in or after the battle, and his son Beyezit I Yilderim (1389–96).

Florence left a poisoned legacy. Eastern Orthodox look back with distrust on a council at which their representatives agreed to a diet of what they see as Latin errors. Roman Catholics, on the other hand, who recognize Florence as the seventeenth ECUMENICAL COUNCIL, have sometimes thought that despite its ultimate failure Florence offers a possible basis for a future reunion.

Nicol, D. M. (1993), *The Last Centuries of Byzantium, 1261–1453*, 2nd edn. Cambridge: Cambridge University Press.

Geanakoplos, D. J. (1989), *Constantinople and the West: Essays on the Late Byzantine (Paleologan) and Italian Renaissances and the Byzantine and Roman Churches*. Madison: University of Wisconsin Press.

Hussey, J. M. (1986), *The Orthodox Church in the Byzantine Empire*. Oxford: Oxford University Press.

Gill, J. (1979), *Collected Studies. Church Union: Rome and Byzantium, 1204–1453*. London: n.p.

Nicol, D. M. (1979), *Church and Society in the Last Centuries of Byzantium, 1261–1453*. Cambridge: Cambridge University Press.

Laurent, V., ed. and trans. (1971), *Les 'mémoirs' du Grand Ecclésiarche de l'Eglise de Constantinople Sylvèstre Syropoulos sur le concile de Florence (1438–1439)*. Concilium Florentinum: Documentes et Scriptores, ser. B9. Rome.

Geanakoplos, D. J. (1966), *Byzantine East and Latin West*. Oxford: Oxford University Press.

Gill, J. (1965), *Constance et Bâle-Florence*. Histoire des conciles oecuméniques 9. Paris.

Gill, J. (1965), *Personalities of the Council of Florence and other essays*. Oxford: Blackwell.

Gill, J. (1959), *The Council of Florence*. Cambridge: Cambridge University Press.

Concilium Florentinum: Documenta et Scriptores. Editum consilio et impensis Pontificii Instituti Orientalium Studiorum (1940–77). Rome: Pontifical Institute of Oriental Studies.

DM

Florensky, Pavel (1882–1937) Spent his schooldays in Tbilisi, GEORGIA, and graduated in mathematics at Moscow University in 1904. He joined the staff at the Moscow Theological Academy in 1908, taking holy orders in 1911. In 1914 he published his most famous work, *The Pillar and Ground of Truth*, subtitled *An Essay on Orthodox Theodicy in Twelve Letters*, in which he drew upon many diverse philosophical and metaphysical themes. In seeking to ground Christian doctrine in religious experience Florensky demonstrated the importance of such things as icon painting and the liturgy as sources of EASTERN ORTHODOX theology. Like other Russian thinkers who renewed their acquaintance with Orthodoxy in the early years of the twentieth century, he shows a predilection for SOPHIOLOGY. He was well respected as a mathematician and a scientist, as well as a theologian and a polyglot. He was imprisoned by the Soviet authorities in 1933 and died in a labour camp some four years later. In recent years his writings have proved an inspiration to a new generation of thinkers in Russia.

Jakim, B., trans. (1997), *Pavel Florensky: The Pillar and Ground of Truth*. Princeton: Princeton University Press.

Florensky, P. (1996), *Iconostasis*. Crestwood, NY: St Vladimir's Seminary Press.

Bychkov, V. (1993), *The Aesthetic Face of Being: Art in the Theology of Pavel Florensky*. Crestwood, NY: St Vladimir's Seminary Press.

Slesinski, R. (1984), *Pavel Florensky: A Metaphysics of Love*. Crestwood, NY: St Vladimir's Seminary Press.

KP

Florovsky, Georges (1893–1979)   Russian philosopher, theologian, patrologist, historian of Russian thought and spiritual culture, ecumenist. Florovsky was born into a clerical family from Odessa. He had a long and distinguished academic career, teaching philosophy at Odessa University before leaving Russia because of the Bolshevik revolution. After that he held a string of academic posts, at St Sergius' Academy in Paris, St Vladimir's Orthodox Seminary in New York, and at Harvard and Princeton universities. He was ordained priest in 1932.

Florovsky was active in the ecumenical movement, in the Orthodox–Anglican Fellowship of SS Alban and Sergius, the Commission on Faith and Order and the World Council of Churches, where he was viewed as an authoritative voice of Eastern Orthodoxy (*see* ECUMENISM). He wrote extensively on what he referred to as the 'challenge of disunity'. In his opinion, every local church can contribute its own particular experience, but the Orthodox church's unique mission is to witness to the common heritage of all Christians, because, he argued, Orthodoxy is the true, though not perfect, manifestation of the living tradition of the universal church.

Florovsky never tried to construct a systematic theology and indeed was very critical of any attempt to do so. Yet his writings give the impression of unity, consistency and coherence. At the centre of his project is a concern to develop what he called a 'neo-patristic synthesis'.

He held the traditional view that the message of Christ and his church is 'eternal and always the same'; the task of the Christian, particularly of the Christian theologian, is to present it creatively as a living reality, to reinterpret it so that it becomes a challenge to each new generation. He thought that the best examples of this reinterpretation of the gospel were to be found in the work of the fathers, especially the Eastern fathers of the fourth to eighth centuries, who completed a process begun in the Septuagint (*see* BIBLE) and in the seminal work of Philo of Alexandria (*c.*20 BC–AD 50), fusing Hebraic biblical tradition, a critical appropriation of all that is best in Hellenic culture and Greek philosophy, resulting in a 'fully scripturalized' Christian Hellenism, in which biblical prophecy finds its true fulfilment. For Florovsky, patristic scholarship was not merely textual study, but a creative dialogue with those 'men of prayer and ascetic achievement', faithful to their spirit and vision, but addressing the problems of the present age. His provocative slogan 'forward to the fathers' proclaims their achievements as alive today, the questions they confront of perennial importance and the answers they provide often more consistent and better grounded philosophically than those of modern theologians and philosophers.

Among his best-known books are *The Eastern Fathers of the Fourth Century* and *The Byzantine Fathers of the Sixth to Eighth Centuries*, but they are only a part of a larger body of work, including many articles and essays. He judged his essays on the doctrines of creation and redemption his most important works.

Florovsky saw the doctrine of creation as the main problem the fathers confronted, and the focus of their greatest achievement. He traced the development of it in his study of ORIGEN, ATHANASIUS and MAXIMUS THE CONFESSOR. Maximus was especially important for Florovsky because of his stress on the salvific significance of the time between *arche* and *telos*, and his stress on the importance of human freedom in the acceptance of redemption.

He worked to clarify the patristic doctrine of the atonement, which he saw in terms of the New Creation, basing himself on the works of Athanasius, the CAPPADOCIANS and Maximus the Confessor. He showed that the patristic understanding both of the atonement and of salvation preserved the importance of both divine grace and human freedom in the process not simply of the restoration of the fallen creation, but of its perfection. He saw Maximus' view of the incarnation as the end and fulfilment of creation as grounding the doctrine of the atonement in the creative will of God, not human sinfulness.

Florovsky's vision of the church makes him the faithful representative of patristic and Russian theology, for it is eschatological, mystical and catholic. The church is firstly the Body of Christ. Christ has conquered the world and his victory is the church, for the church is humanity transfigured and regenerated. In her 'salvation is perfected; the sanctification and transfiguration, the Theosis of the human race is accomplished' (*see* DEIFICATION). The catholicity (Russian: *sobornost*) of the church can be found in the unity in Christ, which exists in the mystery of congregational worship and 'embraces in a mysterious, time-conquering fashion the faithful of all generations ... especially in its Eucharistic experience'. He emphasized that the church, as the Body of Christ, is the source of faith, since Christ ever reveals himself in her. The church 'stands mystically first and is fuller than Scripture'. The tradition of the church is the experience of this unchanging revelation: for Florovsky, tradition is 'a charismatic, not a historical principle'.

Following KHOMIAKOV and Kireevskii he asserted that God's truth is given to humans not in their isolation, but in their catholicity, their union. This *sobornost* entails not only unity, but also freedom, which is why in the true church there is no uniformity, but there is a common mind.

History was Florovsky's great love. Meditation on the meaning of history colours all his work. Early in his career he began a critique of all deterministic theories of history. For him, not necessity but freedom constitutes history; it can be understood only as an ascetic feat, a sequence of free and miraculous encounters with God. History is intelligible only as a tension between creation and *Eschaton*, both of which are categories of metahistory. Florovsky traced the different ways of expressing the essence of the 'ascetic achievement' in the early Christian conception of martyrdom, in the patristic notion of salvation as deification of the creature or participation in the divine nature, and in the teaching of GREGORY PALAMAS on the uncreated divine energies irradiating creation and perceptible in the 'ascetic feat'.

Florovsky combined his knowledge of the scriptural–patristic tradition with a deep and intimate understanding of Russian thought and spiritual culture in his magisterial *Ways of Russian Theology*. Despite its remaining the centre of controversy since its publication in 1937 it is a *tour de force*. Florovsky worked at the problems raised in this book all through his life, using the newest research, and intended to rework radically some of the chapters, but unfortunately had no time to complete this. However, his meditations on Russian intellectual history will long remain an indispensable foundation for all scholars of Russia. Florovsky is undoubtedly the most significant Russian theologian of the twentieth century.

Florovsky, G. V. (1972–87), *Collected Works*, vols 1–14. Belmont, Mass.: Nordland.

Blane, A. (1993), *George Florovsky: Russian Intellectual and Orthodox Churchman.* Crestwood, NY: St Vladimir's Seminary Press.
Chamberas, P. A. (1973), 'Some Aspects of the Ecclesiology of Father Georges Vasilievich Florovsky', in D. Neiman and M. Shatkin, eds, *The Heritage of the Early Church.* Rome: Pontifical Institute of Oriental Studies.
Williams, G. H. (1965), 'George Vasilievich Florovsky: His American Career (1948–1965)', *Greek Orthodox Theological Review* 11.

MV

Franks A term often applied pejoratively by EASTERN CHRISTIANS and Muslims alike to the peoples of Western Europe. This practice can be dated to the period of Charlemagne, although the term's more ambiguous resonances were acquired during the CRUSADES. Since the nineteenth century it has been used most commonly of the local Roman Catholic communities of Greece and the Near East, also known as Franco-Levantines and distinguished from EASTERN CATHOLICS. 'Franks' can also be used, particularly by Muslims, to denote all foreigners.

See also OUTREMER.

DB

Frumentius of Axum Introduced Christianity to Ethiopia in the first half of the fourth century. His story is told in Rufinus' *Ecclesiastical History* 1: 9–10 (*c*.401). Frumentius and Aedesius, brothers from Tyre, were said to have been shipwrecked off the Ethiopian coast. Rescued, they became members of the royal court at Axum. Frumentius is said to have visited patriarch ATHANASIUS in Alexandria to request a bishop for Ethiopia. Himself consecrated bishop by Athanasius, Frumentius returned to Axum as the first in a long line of ABOUNAS sent by the Coptic patriarch to serve as head (metropolitan) of the Ethiopian church. The chronology of Rufinus' account is buttressed by a letter of the emperor Constantius II to the rulers of Axum, written *c*.356 in an unsuccessful attempt to replace Frumentius with an Arian bishop. The text of this letter is preserved in Athanasius' *Apology to the Emperor Constantius II* (*c*.356–7). Frumentius (Abuna Frēmenāṭos) is traditionally associated with ABBĀ SALĀMĀ, named in Ethiopic texts as bishop of Axum in the second half of the fourth century. This identification has been a matter of some scholarly debate.

See also ETHIOPIAN ORTHODOX CHURCH.

Taklahāymānot, A. (1988), 'The Egyptian Metropolitan of the Ethiopian Church: A Study on a Chapter of History of the Ethiopian Church', *Orientalia Christiana Periodica* 54, pp. 175–222.
Dombrowski, B. W. W. and Dombrowski, F. A. (1984), 'Frumentius/Abbā Salāmā: Zu den Nachrichten über die Anfänge des Christentums in Äthiopien', *Oriens Christianus* 68, pp. 114–69.
Haile, G. (1979), 'The Homily in Honour of St Frumentius Bishop of Axum', (EMML' 1763 fos 84^V–86^r), *Analecta Bollandiana* 97, pp. 309–13.
Sauget, J.-M.(1964), 'Frumenzio', *Bibliotheca Sanctorum* 5, cols 1292–4.

MJB/SHG

·G·

Gaza Triad Collective name given to Aeneas of Gaza (d. *c*.518), a Christian Neo-platonist who defended the Christian doctrine of the resurrection of the body against his pagan counterparts (*see* PLATONISM); Procopius of Gaza (d. *c*.528), author of biblical commentaries in catena form; and Zacharius Scholasticus (d. *c*.540), church historian and philosopher. Procopius of Gaza must not be confused with the slightly later Procopius of Caesarea, the Byzantine historian, author of the famous *Secret History* of Justinian and Theodora.

Downey, R. (1963), *Gaza in the Sixth Century*. Norman, Okla: University of Oklahoma Press.

DM

Ge'ez Classical Ethiopic, a member of the Semitic family of languages; the ancient literary and church language of Ethiopia. The Christian Ethiopian literary heritage is largely preserved in Ge'ez.

Haile, G. (1993), 'Ethiopic Literature', in R. Grierson, ed., *African Zion: The Sacred Art of Ethiopia*, pp. 47–55. New Haven and London: Yale University Press in association with InterCultura, Fort Worth, The Walters Art Gallery, Baltimore, The Institute of Ethiopian Studies, Addis Ababa.
Leslau, W. (1988), *Fifty Years of Research: Selection of Articles on Semitic, Ethiopian Semitic and Cushitic*. Wiesbaden: Harrassowitz.
Ullendorff, E. (1955), *The Semitic Languages of Ethiopia: A Comparative Phonology*. London: Taylor's (Foreign) Press.

MJB/SHG

Gelati The monastery complex at Gelati in western GEORGIA contains the Church of the Virgin (1106–25), and the thirteenth-century churches of St George and St Nicholas. The monastery was founded in 1106 by King David the Builder (1106–25), and a chapel houses his tomb. He established an academy at Gelati and invited eminent

207

scholars to teach there, including Ioane PETRITSI who returned from the Georgian monastery of BACHKOVO in BULGARIA to head the academy. The monastery was damaged by fire during Turkish attacks in the sixteenth century. There is an important twelfth-century mosaic of the Virgin and Child flanked by archangels in the apse of the Church of the Virgin.

Mepisashvili, R. and Tsintsadze, V. (1979), *The Arts of Ancient Georgia.* London: Thames & Hudson.

KP

gelbab   Ge'ez: *gelbāb*; Arabic: *ǧilbāb.* A veil, cover or priestly vestment.
See also ETHIOPIAN CHRISTIANITY.

MJB/SHG

Gemistos Plethon (*c.*1360–1452)   Fifteenth-century Byzantine philosopher. Plethon taught at Mistra in the Peloponnese from 1407 and died there in 1452. He attended the Council of FLORENCE (1438–9) and was lionized by Western scholars. His contact with Western thinkers may have inspired his *On the Differences of Aristotle from Plato.* Plethon was more Neoplatonist than Christian philosopher. Many of his writings are lost; they were burned by GENNADIOS II SCHOLARIOS, the first Ecumenical Patriarch under Ottoman rule, and himself a student of Thomism. Plethon's *Book of Laws* survives in a fragmentary form. One of his pupils was BESSARION.

Woodhouse, C. M. (1986), *Gemistos Plethon: The Last of the Hellenes.* Oxford: Clarendon Press.

KP

Gennadios I   PATRIARCH of CONSTANTINOPLE 458–71. As a young man, Gennadios wrote against the theology of CYRIL OF ALEXANDRIA. In 458 he ascended the patriarchal throne, succeeding Anatolios (449–58). The pope of ROME, Leo the Great (440–61) wrote to Gennadios denouncing TIMOTHY AILOUROS, the anti-Chalcedonian patriarch of ALEXANDRIA. Allying himself with the pope, Gennadios helped bring about the deposition and exile of Timothy in 460 by Leo's namesake, Emperor Leo I (457–74). Gennadios wrote an important encyclical against simony, a work in praise of the dogmatic *Tome* of Pope Leo, several biblical commentaries and other theological works, significant fragments of which are preserved. His feast day in the Byzantine rite is 17 November.

Quasten, J. (1960), *Patrology*, vol. 3. Utrecht: Spectrum.

DM

Gennadios II Scholarios   First ECUMENICAL PATRIARCH after the fall of CONSTANTINOPLE to the OTTOMANS in 1453. Originally named George, he was born and educated in Constantinople, studying under Mark Eugenikos (Mark of Ephesus) and following an academic career. His Aristotelian outlook and knowledge of Latin equipped him better to understand Western theology than most contemporaries. At the Council of FLORENCE he supported union with ROME, but was afterwards persuaded by Mark that he was in error, and after Mark's death became the leader of the anti-unionists under the unionist patriarchs Metrophanes II (1440–3) and Gregory III Mammas (1445–51). Under Mammas he was removed from office. George entered monastic life, taking the name Gennadios. Mammas retired to Rome in 1451, finding his bishops lacking enthusiasm for union.

Constantinople fell to the OTTOMANS on Tuesday, 29 May 1543. Sultan Mehmet II Fatih needed a reliable patriarch for the Christian Greeks of his empire, and decided the learned leader of the anti-unionists would make an ideal candidate. A search was instituted. Eventually Gennadios was found: he had been taken prisoner and become the slave of a rich Turk in Adrianople, who, astonished at the learning and culture of his servant, was treating him with awed respect. Sultan Mehmet redeemed and released Gennadios. In January 1454 he was made patriarch, invested with pastoral staff, cross and robes by the sultan, then consecrated and enthroned in the Church of the Twelve Apostles.

Gennadios was now head of the Rum *milet*, holding authority to try cases in his courts in all matters concerning marriage and inheritance, and in many other civil cases where both parties were Christian – an authority inherited by his successors. He worked hard to defend the interests of the Christians under Ottoman rule, but found himself the object of criticism for, among other things, using the principle of economy liberally to regularize marriage problems arising from the conquest, and permitting the marriage of boys under the canonical age to save them from the *devshirme* (the 'blood tax' whereby Christian youths were collected and enrolled in the sultan's service). Gennadios resigned in 1547. After a brief spell on ATHOS he settled at the monastery of St John at Serres. He was twice to be recalled to the throne.

Gennadios was a scholar, an able philosopher and theologian. His defence of Aristotelianism against the PLATONISM of the neo-pagan GEMISTOS PLETHON is important evidence against once fashionable but misguided attempts to identify Eastern Orthodoxy with the Platonic tradition and Aristotelianism with Western theology. He translated and commented on Aquinas. At the request of Sultan Mehmet, with whom he maintained a friendship based on mutual respect, he wrote an eirenic exposition of the Christian faith which was translated into Turkish. His complete works were published in eight volumes edited by Petit, Sideris and Jugie (Paris, 1928–36).

Norwich, J. J. (1995). *Byzantium, the Decline and Fall*. London and New York: Viking.
Nicol, D. (1990), *The Last Centuries of Byzantium*. Cambridge: Cambridge University Press.
Podskalsky, G. (1982), *Theologie und Philosophie in Byzanz: Die Streit um die theologische Methodik in der spätbyzantinischen Geistesgeschichte (14./15. Jh.)*. Munich: Beck.
Turner, C. J. G. (1969), 'The Career of George-Gennadius Scholarius', *Byzantion* 39.
Runciman, S. (1968), *The Great Church in Captivity*. Cambridge: Cambridge University Press.
Gill, J. (1964), *Personalities of the Council of Florence and Other Essays*. Oxford: Oxford University Press.

DM

George of Cappadocia   George, an extreme Arian, took the throne of ALEXANDRIA in 357. He appears to have been a thoroughly unworthy bishop. A mob killed him on Christmas Eve 361. Gibbon is responsible for the chestnut that makes this George the historical figure behind the legend of St George the Great Martyr.

Stevenson, J., ed. (1973), *Creeds, Councils and Controversies*. London: SPCK.

DM

George of Ioannina (d. 1838)   Icons depict the NEW MARTYR in the fez and in  Epirote folk costume. George, a poor Greek of Ioannina, worked grooming horses for wealthy Turks, who nicknamed him Hasan. His association with the Muslim community led to the accusation of having embraced Islam. He was hanged for refusing to abandon Christianity. As a Christian executed at the time of the foundation of an independent Greek state, he represents a confusing interpenetration of religious and national issues. George is the patron of the Greek *evzone* (national) guards; he is commemorated on 17 January and 26 October.

Moutsikou, E. (1995), *Hagios Neomartys Georgios*. Athens: n.p

DB

Georgia, Christian history of   The Georgian Orthodox Apostolic church was established in the 330s, though the gospel was probably preached in East Georgia as early as the second or third century. Christian tombs of this period have been discovered. Further evidence is provided by a Manichaean text fragment, according to which a Manichaean missionary encountered followers of Christ in the Land of *War*, i.e. Iberia (cf. Armenian *Wirk* = Georgia), where they must have co-existed with local paganism, Zoroastrianism and MANICHEANISM. Evidence relating to the early spread of Christianity in Georgia is contained in extant hagiographic works of the sixth to eighth centuries, such as the *Passion of Eustathius of Mtzkheta* and the *Passion of Abo of Tbilisi*.

Acceptance of Christianity as the official religion of the east Georgian kingdom of Kartli, the Iberia of classical writers, is associated in ancient Georgian, Armenian and Greek–Latin sources (EUSEBIUS OF CAESAREA, Rufinus) with the name of the prophetess Nino of Cappadocia, who came to Kartli from JERUSALEM. According to church tradition, King Mirian accepted Christianity in 326, though scholars suggest other dates, the most plausible being 337. The *Life of St Nino* stresses the inherent connection between the Kartli church and Jerusalem, as well as the prominent role of the Georgian Jewish community in the spread of Christianity in eastern Georgia.

The first church erected by Mirian at Mtzkheta, the ancient capital of Georgia, the so-called 'lower church', later the cathedral of Svetitzkhoveli, was known, following the tradition at Jerusalem, as 'the holy of holies'. Later the Georgian church created toponymic foundations in the capital alluding to the life of Christ, e.g. Gethsemane, Golgotha, Bethany, Olivet and Tabor. Connections with Jerusalem can also be traced in the liturgy. During the fifth to tenth centuries, the Georgian liturgy was conducted according to Jerusalem norms. For example, a seven-week cycle was used until the eight-week cycle was introduced in the tenth century by bishop John of Bolnisi. Ancient Georgian lectionaries and hymnographic collections, unlike their Greek equivalents, reflect the Jerusalem practice, which was gradually replaced by the Byzantine only in the tenth to eleventh centuries.

The Feast of the Cross in Mtzkheta, established on the third Sunday following Easter, also reveals connections with the ancient feast of the Holy Cross in Jerusalem. According to the legend, a tree was felled on Friday, 25 March, on 1 May crosses were made from its wood, and on 7 May the cross was erected in Mtzkheta. The first of May coincides approximately with 20 Artemisium and the Feast of the Holy Cross as held in Jerusalem, while 7 May is the Feast of Appearance of the Holy Cross, celebrated in Jerusalem on this day. According to the Greek HOROLOGION this feast commemorates a vision of the cross in glory seen above Golgotha and the Mount of Olives at Pentecost in 346 and related to the Emperor Constantius in a letter from CYRIL OF JERUSALEM. The dates 1 May and the third Sunday following Easter coincided in the year 337, which provides one of the grounds for presuming that this was the year of acceptance of Christianity in Kartli.

One tradition makes Nino the niece of a Jerusalem patriarch called Juvenal (historically he reigned in the fifth century), who blessed Nino and sent her to preach in Mtzkheta, where, according to legend, Christ's robe was kept since the Mtzhketian Jew Elias (Elioz) and his friends, who were present at the Crucifixion, received it by lot.

The first disciples of Nino in Mtzkheta were the Jewish woman Sidonia and her seven women friends; the first person chosen as priest was Abiathar, a *kohen* in the local Jewish community. Sidonia and Abiathar appear as authors of two chapters in *The Life of St Nino*, containing information on the history of the Georgian Jewish community, its ties with Jerusalem and its specialization in the translation of sacred texts. The same source depicts the local, and plausible, Jewish tradition as to when successive waves of Jewish immigrants arrived in Kartli. There is also an indirect indication that the first Jewish migrants had settled in Mtzkheta in 169–166 BC. Aspects of the text in which this tradition is recorded, especially certain linguistic peculiarities, such as SYRIAC grammatical constructions, have led modern scholars to conclude that the earliest variant of the legend of St Nino was created in the community of Mtzkhetian Jewish Christians, perhaps in the Syro-Palestinian Aramaic dialect, and translated into Georgian by the end of the fifth century.

It may be that new details were then added, including mention of the kinship between Nino and the Jerusalem patriarch. This kinship is repeatedly stressed in the received text of *The Life of St Nino*; King Mirian testifies that 'St Nino fulfilled the commandment of her uncle, our blessed father the patriarch of Jerusalem.' Despite further rewritings, the legend's text still evidences the role of the Mtzkheta Jews in the Christianization of Georgia. It is not by chance that the closing phrases of *The Life of St Nino* allude to this tradition: 'And the Jews [in another version, Abiathar] pleaded with the king not to destroy this building [the synagogue], since before the new Divinity was revealed in this country, there had been in it the Name of the Eternal God.' This was the way *The Life of St Nino* was understood in Georgia: a group of Christians was formed among the Georgian Jews by the fourth century.

Official acceptance of Christianity split the Jewish community. In those days, Abiathar says, according to the legend, '*khurii* [the Jews] of Mtzkheta rose against me . . . and felled the tree.' The tree he refers to grew near the synagogue where Nino christened the children of the royal family; once again we have a symbol of the Christianization of Georgia in the bosom of the synagogue. The king resolved the conflict in favour of the Jews who remained faithful to Judaism. Only a small group of fifty people from the Barnaba family finally left the community, 'and they were welcomed by the king and the Christians'. The right of the Jews to follow the faith of their fathers was preserved, 'and the King Mirian favoured the Jews in his days; and relatives of Elioz were the Jewish priests there'. Only much later, when hope for the total Christianization of the Jews was lost, did the eleventh-century author Leonti Mroveli insert in the text of *The Life of St Nino* the motif, absent in early versions, of the Mtzkheta Jews taking blame for Christ's blood. Recollecting the vivid expression of Tertullian, it can be clearly stated that, as in other provinces of the Byzantine empire, the Kartli church also to some extent 'grew out of the synagogue'. By the end of the fourth century small Christian communities were spread throughout Georgia, though when an official Christianity crystallized out as the established church, it conformed to Greek tradition. The tradition that an application to Byzantium resulted in Emperor Constantine sending to Iberia the bishop John and a priest, Jacob (though nothing indicates whether they came from CONSTANTINOPLE, ANTIOCH or JERUSALEM), corresponds to the then political situation of the Kartli kingdom as the ally of the Byzantine emperors.

In western Georgia or Egrisi, the LAZIKA of classical authors, Christianity initially spread directly from Byzantium, and services were held in Greek. Among the participants of the First ECUMENICAL COUNCIL (325) were bishops Domnus Trapezundi and Pythiunda Stratophyl from Roman Pontus. From the sixth century the metropolitan of the Egrisi church was subordinate to Constantinople. During the same period, in 523, King Tzate of Egrisi officially accepted Christianity.

In the fourth and fifth centuries the Kartli church was headed by an archbishop subordinate to the patriarch of Antioch. At the end of the fifth century a reform undertaken by King Vakhtang Gorgasali brought the Kartli church autocephaly under a CATHOLICOS chosen by the king, later from among the Georgian priests; the first catholicos of Kartli was Peter (467–74). At the same time twelve new bishoprics were established. By the sixth century their number had increased to thirty-five. The Kartli church was mainly DYOPHYSITE, while in the two other Christian countries of the East Transcaucasus, ARMENIA and ALBANIA AL'UANK, MONOPHYSITISM prevailed. In 506 the Council of Dvin acknowledged the confessional unity of the three Christian Transcaucasian nations, reflecting, perhaps, the ambiguous Byzantine policy evidenced in the Henotikon of Emperor Zeno. Later, when Byzantium finally adopted dyophysitism, while Persia supported churches condemned by the Byzantine imperial authorities, including monophysites, the confessional contradictions between Iberia on the one hand and Armenia and Albania-Al'uank on the other became acute. Under Catholicos Kyrion (585–610) the Georgian church separated from the Armenian and adhered to Byzantine orthodoxy: by the 720s the split was final. In the ninth century the Mtzkheta cathedral of Svetitzkhoveli received the right to consecrate the *myron* (chrism), formerly received from Jerusalem.

In the ninth and tenth centuries the Kartli church played an important role in the formation of the ideological basis of the unitary Georgian state, integrating religion and language, promoting a Georgian nation-state which thereafter constituted all the Georgian provinces (Egrisi, Kartli, Kakheti, Ereti) where the liturgy was celebrated in Georgian. During the second half of the ninth century the Egrisi church was separated from the Constantinopolitan patriarchate and subordinated to the Mtzkheta catholicos. The West Georgian church, threatened by the growing political, cultural and religious hegemony of Byzantium, had already adopted the Georgian language. In the first half of the eleventh century, East and West Georgia were united under King Bagrat III and the Kartli Catholicos Melchizedech I adopted the title catholicos-patriarch of All Georgia. In 1057 ANTIOCH also re-endorsed the Georgian church's autocephaly.

In 1103 King David the Builder gathered the Synod of Ruis-Urbinis which confirmed widespread reform and reorganization undertaken under the king's authority. The church found itself subordinated to the king's power, a significant step towards a centralized state. But the king remained the secular head of the state, while the patriarch was accepted as the spiritual father of the nation. A great flowering of religious and national culture occurred under Queen Tamar (d. 1213).

The Mongol invasions of the thirteenth century and the onslaught of Timur in the fourteenth brought great disruption. An independent catholicate appears to have emerged in West Georgia in the late fourteenth century; it was eventually suppressed under Russian authority in 1815. In the eighteenth century the learned catholicos Anton I, deposed because of his relations with the Roman Catholic church, fled to Russia, where he functioned as archbishop first in VLADIMIR and then in Yaroslavl. In 1764 his cousin, King Heraclius II, recalled him and he resumed the patriarchal throne. He produced an immense output of translations and original works, and established norms for the transcription of manuscripts. He played a crucial role in bringing about abandonment of Greek and Jerusalemite liturgical traditions in favour of the acceptance of Russian practices.

At the beginning of the nineteenth century, after Georgia had been annexed to Russia in 1801, the autocephaly of the Georgian church was annulled, in 1811 in the East and in 1815 in the West. It now became part of the Russian Orthodox church with the status of exarchate, its exarchs nominated by the hierarchy in Russia. The Georgian church's autocephaly was restored on 12 March 1917, when, as a result of the February 1917 Revolution in Russia, Georgia regained its independence for a short period. Kirion (Sadzaglisvili) became the first catholicos-patriarch of the modern age, though it was only on 23 January 1990 that the Holy Synod of the Constantinople patriarchate officially recognized the church's autocephaly. At present, the Georgian church consists of fifteen bishoprics headed by the catholicos-patriarch Ilias II, who resides in the Zion Church (sixth century) in Tbilisi. In Mtzkheta there is a functioning seminary.

The Georgian Orthodox church did not enter into formal schism with the Roman church after the events of 1054. In the thirteenth century Franciscan missionaries established in Tbilisi a monastery under the leadership of Jacob of Rogsane. The Dominicans were active from 1240 and they also established a monastery. In 1329 Pope John XXII established a Catholic bishopric in Tbilisi. It was abolished in the sixteenth century during the OTTOMAN expansion in the Caucasus. From the seventeenth century, in search for Catholic assistance against Muslim control, Georgian kings sent a number of ambassadorial delegations to Europe, the best known being the missions of Nikolai Cholokashvili-Irbakh (in the 1620s) and of Sulkhan-Saba Orbeliani (1713–16). Though the hopes of the Georgian politicians were not justified, Catholic missionaries again received the right to preach in Georgia. The Vatican sent Theatine missionaries (1628–1700) and Capuchin Franciscans (1661–1845). The Russians put an end to the Franciscans' missionary activities in the 1840s. In the following decade Georgian Catholic monks disassociated themselves from the Mechitarist brotherhood in VENICE and in 1861 they established their own congregation in Istanbul together with one for women, though both are now extinct. At present, one Catholic church is functioning in Tbilisi.

See also ABKHAZIA; ADZHARIA; OSSETIA.

Lerner, K. (1995), *Conversion of Kartli. Parallel Georgian and Hebrew Texts: Translation into Hebrew, Investigation and Comment.* Jerusalem.
Esbroeck, M. van (1975), *Les plus anciens homeliares georgiens.* Louvain-la-Neuve.
Tarchnishwili, M. (1960), 'Die Entstehung und Entwicklung der kirchlischen Autokephalie Georgiens', *Le Muséon* 73.

KL

Georgia, Christian thought in   The gospels and other parts of the New Testament appear to have been translated into Georgian before the mid-fifth century. In the following centuries this text was revised more than once, the style of language going through several changes. Some scholars believe the translation was made from the Greek, but the possibility that it was from Aramaic cannot be excluded. Some archaeological evidence from the second century may support an Aramaic derivation. Many connections have still not been fully investigated, for example, the possible connection with Tatian's DIATESSARON.

Georgian Christian culture has its roots in fourth- and fifth-century JERUSALEM and the desert communities of Palestine. Several scholars have linked the name of PETER THE IBERIAN (*c*.409–88), a bishop in Syria, considered both by CHALCEDO-NIANS and anti-Chalcedonians to be on their side, with the writings of the Pseudo-Dionysios (*see* DIONYSIOS THE AREOPAGITE) and with the Neoplatonic *Book of Causes*. Although this theory has been abandoned by most Western scholars, Georgia is still considered to be the country where the influence of Pseudo-Dionysios was first felt, though lack of sources makes it difficult to give a precise account of his influence on early Christian Georgia. Georgian thought in the sixth century is more clearly visible. Its essential idea is that philosophical wisdom is a means to solve religious questions and to defend the Christian faith. This positive attitude towards the unification of religious faith and philosophical wisdom is thought to be the result of patristic influence. In Georgia, quite a number of the works of the CAPPADOCIANS are preserved and their investigation by Georgian and Western scholars is still going on. Developments in the fifth century included translations of liturgical texts and the use of the Georgian language in worship, both inside the country itself and in areas where Georgian cultural influence was strong. The high standard of the earliest surviving hagiographical work, the *Martyrdom of Shushanik*, composed in the fifth century by Jacob of Tsurtav, is evidence of the maturity of Georgian writing in this early period.

The activity of monasteries in the sixth century and their connection with the arrival of the Thirteen Syrian Fathers raise important questions. Georgian cultural centres abroad, at the monasteries of St Sabas and St Chariton in Palestine, were enlarged during the sixth century and augmented during the ninth and tenth centuries by those at Mount SINAI and the Monastery of the Black Mountain near ANTIOCH in Syria, particularly important for its literary activity. In the eighth and ninth centuries extensive co-operation with other Christians began, notably with Greeks, Copts, Syrians, Armenians and especially Arabs. At that time ARAB CHRISTIAN literature began to emerge in the Near East. From the beginning Georgian scholars were involved in translating and interpreting Arab Christian works. Many lost original Arabic texts can only be reconstructed from Georgian translations.

One example of the close connection between Georgia and the Near East is reflected in the problem of the origin of the story of BARLAAM AND IOASAPH. Some scholars believe that the Georgians were the first to give a Christian slant to the Buddhist legend underlying this story, which reached them in the ninth century through an Arabic recension. It is known in Georgian as *Balavariani* or *The Wisdom of Balahvar*.

From the eighth to the eighteenth century both translated and original polemical works against Islam were written. In the eleventh and twelfth centuries Georgian medicine and astronomy developed under Arab influence. Gradually the changing political and religious situation of the Near East led to a fading of the relation between Arab and Georgian Christian literatures. From the end of the tenth century Georgia turned towards CONSTANTINOPLE, though the Georgians continued to maintain their ancient cultural centres in Palestine, Syria and Egypt. The most important new centre of Georgian culture in this period was undoubtedly the monastery of Iviron on Mount ATHOS. Georgian Christianity embarked upon a period of promoting Byzantine regulations and laws which resulted in the Byzantinizing of Georgian culture as well as the Georgianizing of Byzantine influence.

By the end of the tenth century the Georgian Orthodox church exercised wide jurisdiction over private and public conduct, and had a monopoly in education. Georgian kings, as 'servants of the Messiah', were conscious of their role as defenders of Christendom against the infidel nations. The king and CATHOLICOS-PATRIARCH were considered as heads of the temporal and spiritual orders of the nation respectively. The links between religion, language and state were fully discussed at this time. The influence of Georgian Christianity spread to the north Caucasus, where Georgian inscriptions on architectural monuments have been found. By the close of the tenth century Georgians were participating in the internal affairs of the Byzantine state. The founding of Iviron is one example of Georgian power and prestige at this time. Euthymios (955–1028) and George the Hagiorite (1009–65) were the principal members of the Athonite school, but other monks worked alongside them. St Euthymios translated hagiographical and homiletic works and also biblical books, including the Apocalypse (*see* BIBLE).

Constantinople and Athos became for the Georgians the centres of universal Christian culture. Skills in textual analysis and textual criticism outstanding for the period have been claimed for Georgian scholars of the tenth and eleventh centuries. They translated Greek texts into Georgian and Georgian into Greek. Iviron's rich collection of manuscripts has not yet been thoroughly investigated. Greek sources are often equally important for understanding this new stage in the history of Georgian Christianity. From the eleventh century the works of JOHN OF DAMASCUS and of the Pseudo-Dionysios were translated, and Western scholastic ideas were disseminated in Georgia. The first thinker linked with the introduction of the Neoplatonism of the Pseudo-Dionysian corpus is Ephrem Mtsire (1027–94). Already by the tenth century the term 'outsiders' was used to distinguish philosophers from theologians. Ephrem Mtsire, a prominent translator of philosophical, theological and religious literature, was a notable defender of theology against 'outsiders', while at the same time restoring and preserving the high level of philosophy in Georgia. Greek sources mention an important philosophical school in West Georgia as early as the fourth century, and during the eleventh and twelfth centuries important philosophical-theological schools existed at GELATI and Iqalto in Georgia, and also outside Georgia, for example at Petritsoni monastery at BACHKOVO in BULGARIA. The study of Aristotle is associated with Arsen Iqaltoeli (d. 1125), theologian, philosopher, poet and adviser to King David the Builder who liberated Georgia from Muslim occupation. Iqaltoeli utilized Aristotelian philosophy to strengthen Christian apologetics.

Christian Neoplatonism in twelfth-century Georgia is associated with the name of Ioane PETRITSI (1050–1125), a follower of the Byzantine philosophers Michael Psellos and John Italos. Petritsi tried to prove the existence of God on the basis of Aristotelian logic and Proclus' emanation theory. He identified Aristotelian metaphysics with theology: he does not mention that part of Plotinus' *Enneads* known to the Arabs as the *Theology of Aristotle*. He was sure that only the philosophy of the 'divine Plato' could reach a true understanding of God, Builder of the Universe, the Best Master and Father of Being. Petritsi's ambition was to become the Aristotle of Christian theology and by his philosophical theories to render theology unassailable. He did not, however, attempt to reconcile Aristotle and Plato and put them together into the service of Christian teaching. He translated Proclus' *Elements of Theology* with a commentary, emphasizing Proclus' teaching that God is the One. He criticized those who considered Proclus and certain other Greek philosophers to be polytheists. Petritsi's biblical exegesis greatly influenced Georgian interpretation of the scriptures. His translation of Nemesius of Emesa's *On the Nature of Man* introduced Christian anthropology into Georgian thought. He recognized human love as having two purposes: to rejoin humanity to God and to provide nature with successive generations. During the Golden Age of Georgian culture in the twelfth and thirteenth centuries Shota Rustavelli wrote his famous poem *The Knight in the Panther's Skin*, full of symbols related to Georgian Christian thought despite its non-Christian subject-matter. Significantly, Rustavelli's masterpiece makes no mention of Aristotle, although he is mentioned in other epics of the period. Instead, Rustavelli expressed his admiration for Plato and the Pseudo-Dionysios. Terms and ideas familiar from Petritsi are found in this famous epic. Rustavelli is thought to have died a monk at the Georgian monastery of the Cross in JERUSALEM.

From the Mongol invasion in the third decade of the thirteenth century we detect a decline in Georgian intellectual life. After the fall of Constantinople in 1453 the country was divided between the OTTOMANS and the Persians. An exception was the activity of the Georgian cleric N. Cholaqashvili-Irbaqi (1585–1659). As ambassador in Europe (1626–9) he tried to establish links between the Orthodox and Catholic churches. He supported the establishment of the Georgian printing press in ROME, and was involved with the publication of the first Georgian printed book, a Georgian–Italian dictionary for the use of Catholic missionaries. Not until the seventeenth and eighteenth centuries do we find Georgian Christian culture asserting itself once more. Upper-class Georgians of the eighteenth century, notably the prominent ecclesiastic Sulkhan-Saba Orbeliani (1658–1725), attempted to bring Georgia into contact with Catholic Europe. According to the nineteenth-century thinker ILIA CHAVCHAVADZE (1837–1907), Georgians and Europeans share a common aesthetic appreciation. Yet neither trips to Europe by Georgians nor Catholic missions to Georgia were fruitful. At the same time, King Vacktang VI (1711–24), a pupil of Sulkhan-Saba Orbeliani, was fighting for the cultural independence of Georgia. The printing of the New Testament in Georgian is associated with King Vacktang, who established a printing press in Tbilisi. The Catholicos-Patriarch Anton I (1720–88) strove to Europeanize Georgia. He even became a Catholic for a time, and was dismissed from office, but later returned to Orthodoxy and was restored. He made a notable contribution to the development of Georgian religious literature and fostered relations with Armenia, Russia and Europe.

With the annexation of Georgia by Russia in the early nineteenth century, the country was brought under Russian cultural influence. Situated at the crossroads between East and West, the Georgians held on to their Christian tradition and maintained their identity. Under Russian rule there was no need to defend Christianity, but the state ceased to exist. The link between Christianity and national identity came to the fore again during the struggle for the country's independence in the twentieth century. After regaining its independence in 1991 Georgia is once more seeing the Orthodox church play an important role in society and in the wider Christian world. There are active eparchies, monasteries and seminaries, and efforts are being made to reprint the holy books. The demand for these books has increased significantly, particularly among the younger generation. During the seventy years of Soviet rule the people were deprived of information about Christianity so that several generations grew up ignorant of it.

See also CAUCASUS: CHRISTIANITY SINCE THE COLLAPSE OF THE USSR.

Alexidze, Z. (1995), *The Oldest Recensions of 'Conversion of Georgia' and 'Lives of 13 Syrian Fathers'*. Centro Italiano di Studi Sull'alto Medioevo, XLIII Settimana di Studio.

Murchland, B. (1993), *The Mind of Mamardashvili* (interview). Ohio: Kettering Foundation.

Kiladze, N. V. (1993), *On the Terminology of the Liber De Causis*. Budapest Studies in Arabic 13–14. Budapest.

Lordkipsnidze, M. D. (1987), *Georgia in XI–XII* CC. Tbilisi.

Guaramia, R. V. (1986), 'Versions georgiennes anciennes de la vie de saint Chrysostome', *Le Muséon* 99.

Salia, K. (1983), *History of the Georgian Nation*. Paris: Nino Salia.

Esbroeck, M. van (1982), 'Eglise georgienne des origines au moyen age', *Bedi Kartlisa* (The Fate of Kartli) 40.

Tewsadze, G. (1980), 'Aristoteles in Ioane Petritis Kommentaren', *Wissentliches Zeitschrift* (Friedrich-Schiller University, Jena) 3.

Khintibidze, E. (1978), 'Byzantine–Georgian Literary Contacts', *Bedi Kartlisa* 36.

Lang, D. M. (1976), *Lives and Legends of the Georgian Saints*. London: Mowbrays.
Allen, W. E. D. (1971), *A History of the Georgian People*. London: Barnes & Noble.
Lang, D. M. (1966), *The Georgians*. London: Thames & Hudson.
Tsereteli, G. (1961), 'The Most Ancient Georgian Inscriptions in Palestine', *Bedi Kartlisa* 11–12.
Kekelidze, K., rev. P. M. Tarchnisvili (1955), *Geschichte der kirchlichen georgischen Literatur*. Rome: Vatican.

NK

Germanos I PATRIARCH of CONSTANTINOPLE 715–30. Germanos, probably a eunuch since his father's execution in 669, played an important role in the QUINISEXT COUNCIL (691–2) and became metropolitan of Cyzicus. When General Bardanes usurped the throne as Philippikos (711–13) and executed Justinian II, MONOTHE-LETISM reappeared as the imperial dogma. Germanos seems to have subscribed to the decrees of a monothelite synod convoked in 712, but in 715 became patriarch and soon showed resolute support for CHALCEDONIAN orthodoxy.

In 726 Leo III the Isaurian (717–41) began to attack the worship of images (*see* ICONOCLASM). Because of his opposition to Leo's policy Germanos was forced to resign in 730, but continued to write in defence of orthodoxy. He wrote several CANONS. Various works are attributed to him with varying degrees of certainty; one, the so-called *Ecclesiastical History*, is of outstanding importance. It is a commentary on the BYZANTINE LITURGY, which established a pattern that survives to the present of interpreting the liturgical action as a symbolic and sacramental re-enactment of the life, Passion and Resurrection of Christ. Though a stimulus to popular piety, it tended to overshadow the more realistic and mysteric interpretation later revived by Nicholas CABASILAS.

Meyendorff, P., trans. (1984), *St Germanos of Constantinople on the Divine Liturgy*. Crestwood, NY: St Vladimir's Seminary Press.

DM

Germanos Hatziyiorgis (1906–82) Cypriot abbot. After reading the *Life of John Kalybites* (a monk of CONSTANTINOPLE), Germanos joined Stavrovouni monastery at the age of sixteen. Even before ordination his ascetic lifestyle and wisdom made him one of the foremost elders of CYPRUS. Germanos succeeded Abbot Dionysios in 1952 and established a network of new convents before dying in a road accident.

See also STARETS.

DB

gerontika Parts of the office traditionally read by the Superior, or Elder (Greek: *Geron, Geronta*), or in his absence by the senior monk present. A visiting priest or important visitor is often asked to read them. At festal Matins they include the Six Psalms, Psalm 50 and the concluding prayer of the First Hour when it follows Matins; at Vespers the *gerontika* include the opening psalm, the Phos Hilaron (an ancient hymn for the lighting of the lamps) if it is read and not sung, and the Nunc Dimittis.

E

Glukharev, Mikhail Iakovlevich (1792–1847)   Later Archimandrite Makarii. Born into a Russian clergy family in Vyazma, Smolensk Province. Frail, with poor eyesight, he excelled academically, graduating from St Petersburg Theological Academy. Pietist influence gave him a lifelong conviction of the need for personal rebirth through the power of the Holy Spirit and regular Bible study. While teaching at the Ekaterinoslav Seminary, he clashed with the diocesan authorities for associating with English Quakers and Russian sectarians (*see* RUSSIAN SECTS). A gifted linguist in Latin, French, German, Greek, Hebrew and Altaian, he translated much of the BIBLE, Augustine's *Confessions*, the *Ladder* of JOHN CLIMACUS, the *Discourses* of Gregory the Great and works by Teresa of Avila into Russian, and many scriptural and liturgical texts into Altaian, for which he devised an alphabet.

In 1821 he became rector of Kostroma Seminary and head of a local monastery. Finding the strain too great, he retired to seclusion in the Glinsk *pustynya*. Answering a Holy Synod call to mission he volunteered to go to Siberia, establishing a pioneer mission at Maima in the Altai mountains in 1830 (*see* ALTAI MISSION). Initial proclamations of the gospel led to few responses so he resorted to cleaning houses and minding children. As Altaian confidence in him grew he moved deeper into the territory, in 1834 centring his work on Ulala (Gorno-Altaisk). By his departure in 1844 owing to chest and eye ailments, he had laid a firm foundation, building five settlements for Orthodox Altaians, two churches, three schools and an orphanage. His published letters reveal a deep pastoral concern, evidenced also in a constant stream of visitors during his last years as an abbot in Orel Province. He published *The Widow's Mite* (*Lepta*), a collection of seventeen religious poems set to music, the proceeds to fund the Altai mission. An ascetic whose meagre clothing caused smirks among the Moscow clergy, he was a visionary, but no politician. The hierarchy criticized his translation of the Old Testament from the Hebrew (the Septuagint being canonical), his belief that the scriptures should be read in everyday language and his plan for a joint church in MOSCOW with altars for Catholics, Lutherans and Orthodox. He wrote to Tsar Nicholas I in this vein just as the Russian Bible Society was being closed, receiving a severe rebuke. Glukharev's *Thoughts on the Means for Successful Dissemination of the Christian Faith* (1839, but suppressed until the 1890s) encapsulated his beliefs about mission and the spiritual state of Russia. The Russian church had an apostolic duty: inspired with love towards God and man, empowered with the fire of Pentecost, they were to convert all nations in the empire to Christianity. Yet the Russians were ill-prepared. They needed a Bible in a style which would equal the liveliness of the original. Village clergy and their wives should educate children in a mixture of agricultural pursuits, Bible study and the liturgy to prepare their flock for evangelism. A missionary society should be established with an institute to prepare missionaries, provide medical training, and translate and publish bibles in the empire's languages, with annotated scripture portions for Jews and Muslims. A missionary magazine should publicize testimonies of miracles and missions in other countries. Strategically placed central mission stations scattered throughout the empire, staffed by monks and nuns with a hospital as a focal point, would lead to a network spreading everywhere. The office of deaconess should be revived for work among WOMEN and children. Other-worldly, but profoundly sincere, Glukharev had a prophetic insight which is still of relevance today.

Collins, D. N. (1991), 'The Role of the Orthodox Missionary in the Altai: Archimandrite Makary and V. I. Verbitsky', in G. A. Hosking, ed., *Church, Nation and State in Russia and Ukraine*. London: Macmillan.

Struve, N. (1965), 'Macaire Gloukharev: A Prophet of Orthodox Mission', *International Review of Mission* 54, pp. 308–14.

Stamoolis, J. J. (1986), *Eastern Orthodox Mission Theology Today*. New York: Orbis.

DC

Glykophilousa The icon of the *Glykophilousa*, the Sweetly Kissing, shows the bond of love between the THEOTOKOS and her son and the physical expression of that love in a tender kiss. Often the Mother of God has a sombre, reflective expression, and her infant Son touches her face to comfort her.

This theological icon proclaims the mystery of the Incarnation. It points to the living, human relationship between mother and son. The infant's hand is the hand of the Logos, cherishing the finest fruit of his creative love. Her embrace enfolds the Uncircumscribable whom heaven and earth cannot contain. The Glykophilousa shows Christ as a human child, relating to his mother as any other human child does, but also as a divine person whose every human expression, action, gesture reveals something of the Godhead.

This icon is virtually the obverse of the HODEGETRIA in which the Virgin points to her son as the way, the truth, and the life. Here she gazes at Jesus, not out of the icon at us. She does not point to him, she embraces and kisses him. And the infant is caught in movement as he turns in her arms, returning her embrace, his hand rising up to touch her cheek, drawing our awareness back to her. He does not point to her, he touches her tenderly, with loving trust. As we contemplate the cyclic interplay of divine and human love, of mother and son, our own humanity is interpreted by the relation between them.

See also ELEOUSA.

DM

Golindokht By tradition wife of a sixth-century Zoroastrian arch-magus in Persia, who became a Christian after a series of visions and was exiled to the fortress of Lethe, imprisoned and finally exiled to Byzantium. Golindokht made a pilgrimage to the shrines of the Holy Land, and died either in CONSTANTINOPLE or near Daras in Syria en route there. Her relics were enshrined in the church of St TRYPHON in Constantinople. Golindokht, Golindouch or Maria is commemorated on 12 or 13 July.

Alypy (1990), *Lives of the Saints of the Holy Land and the Sinai Desert*. Buenavista, Col.: Holy Apostles.

DB

Gorazd Pavlik (1879–1942) Founder of the CZECH AND SLOVAK ORTHODOX CHURCH. Originally a Roman Catholic, Gorazd studied theology in Olomouc and was ordained priest in 1902. He was committed to the 'Catholic Reform' movement, which in 1920 became the independent Church of Czechoslovakia and in 1921 was received into communion with the Serbian Orthodox church. Gorazd was consecrated as the first Orthodox bishop of modern Czechoslovakia. He established parishes for the Czech and Slovak DIASPORA in AMERICA. In 1924 a schism depleted the church, but 10,000 believers remained loyal to Gorazd and EASTERN ORTHODOXY.

Gorazd founded churches across the country and sought to unify the various Orthodox jurisdictions. He wrote popular and scholarly tracts and organized pilgrimages to RUTHENIA and SERBIA. Active in the Resistance in the Second World War, he was executed with two priests by the Nazis for giving refuge to partisans after the assassination of Gauleiter Heidrich. In 1987 Gorazd was canonized; he is commemorated on 4 September.

Chaplin, V. (1988), 'St Gorazd', *Journal of the Moscow Patriarchate*.

DB

Gračanica   The Church of the DORMITION (1311–21) at the monastery of Gračanica, near Priština, in the Plain of Kosovo in SERBIA, was built by King Stefan Uroš II Milutin on the site of two earlier churches. Constructed on a cross-in-square plan with narthex, it has five domes and a slightly later open exonarthex. Its svelte, graceful architectural forms and cloisonné facades of unusually large ashlars, framed by slim layers of brick, have earned its reputation as a masterpiece. The frescoes, completed in 1321, show the developed style of Michael and Eutychios and have affinities with those in other of Milutin's churches, especially at STARO NAGORIČINO and St Nikita. The text of the king's charter is painted on a fresco in the DIAKONIKON, under the image of the prophet ELIAS fed by a raven. The programme of wall paintings includes Old Testament typological figures, a symbolic investiture of King Milutin and Queen Simonida, and the earliest preserved genealogical tree of the Nemanjić dynasty, modelled on the Tree of Jesse. Devastated in an Ottoman raid in 1388, the monastery lost its library and much of its treasury. Still active in the 1420s, it was deserted after the fall of Serbia in 1459, but revived by the efforts of Metropolitan Nikanor, who established southern Serbia's first printing press there in 1539. An OKTOECHOS printed that year contains a woodcut with a view of the monastery. According to an inscription dated 1570, Makarije Sokolović, PATRIARCH of PEĆ, and his nephew Andonije, the metropolitan of Herzegovina, commissioned the wall paintings in the exonarthex. After a period of strife in the late seventeenth century, monastic life revived in the eighteenth. It is now a nunnery and serves as a village church.

Ćurčić, S. (1979), *Gračanica: King Milutin's Church and its Place in Late Byzantine Architecture*. Philadelphia: Pennsylvania State University Press.
Ćurčić, S. (1988), *Gračanica, Istorija i Arhitektura*. Belgrade: Prosveta; Priština: Jedinstvo (English summary).
Todić, B. (1988), *Gračanica, Slikarstvo*. Belgrade: Prosveta; Priština: Jedinstvo (French summary).

ZG

Great Martyrs   Greek: *Megalomartyres*; saints venerated by EASTERN CHRISTIANS from early times as outstanding witnesses to Christ, though only legends survive of the lives of many. Male Great Martyrs include MILITARY SAINTS like Demetrios, George, the Theodores and Menas and ANARGYROI like Panteleimon, Orestes, Diomedes and Tryphon. Female Great Martyrs include virgin martyrs PARASKEVI,

Kyriaki, Barbara, Marina and other virgin martyrs, and martyred mothers, including Sophia and PHOTEINE.

DB

Great Week   Great and Holy Week in the Byzantine CALENDAR begins with Vespers of Palm Sunday and ends on Great Sabbath, *Mega Sabbaton*. Throughout Great Week a fast is observed, during the last three days XEROPHAGY. The Saturday before Great Week celebrates the raising of Lazarus as prefiguring the Resurrection of Jesus and the general resurrection. Matins and Divine Liturgy of Palm Sunday commemorate Jesus' ENTRY INTO JERUSALEM to the acclamations of the branch-bearing crowds. On Palm Sunday evening, as on the Monday and Tuesday of Great Week, the Byzantine rite celebrates the Matins of the Bridegroom, the *Nymphios* Christ, the bridegroom of the church, indissolubly wedded to his bride by his Passion and death. Matins of the Bridegroom on Sunday evening, liturgically Matins of Monday, also commemorates Joseph the All-Beautiful and the cursing of the barren fig-tree; Matins of Tuesday, on Monday evening, the wise and foolish virgins of the parable. Matins of Wednesday commemorates the anointing of Jesus by the sinful woman (Matthew 26: 6–16), who in Eastern tradition is not identified with Mary Magdalene; as DOXASTIKON is sung a troparion by the nun Kassiane (*see* KASSIA). Special canons are read at Compline on these days. The Liturgy of the Presanctified is celebrated at Vespers on the mornings of Monday, Tuesday and Wednesday. By tradition the four gospels were read in their entirety during the Hours of these days, up to the end of chapter 12 of John, though in modern use the reading is usually abbreviated or spread through Lent.

On Great Wednesday, the service of the Euchelaion, the Anointing of the Sick, is generally read. On Great Thursday the Mystical Supper, the institution of the eucharist and the betrayal by Judas are commemorated both at Matins and at a Vesper Liturgy of St Basil. Matins also celebrates the washing of the disciples' feet, which may be reenacted in a special ceremony. Matins of Great Friday, normally sung on Great Thursday evening, is structured around twelve gospel readings of the Passion and death of Jesus. In modern Greek use, a crucifix icon is processed around the church and set up for veneration at the singing of the eleventh antiphon, 'Today is stretched out on the wood he who stretched out the earth on the waters...'.

After the ROYAL OFFICE of Great Friday, Vespers celebrates the Descent from the Cross. The evening of the same day matins of Great Sabbath is sung, the burial service of Christ. The Threnoi, poetic lamentations interleaved with the verses of Psalm 118, are sung around the Epitaphios, an image, usually embroidered, of the dead Christ prepared for burial, which is then carried in procession. In Greek use it is normally carried in the KOUBOUKLION, people passing beneath it in reverence.

On Great Sabbath the office of the PROTE ANASTASIS is celebrated, the ancient Paschal liturgy of the harrowing of Hell.

Mary, Mother and Ware, K. (1978), *The Lenten Triodion*. London: Faber.

DM

Greece, church of   The apostle Paul's missionary work laid the foundation of the Christian church in Greece, then under Roman rule. The Acts of the Apostles and the

Pauline Epistles offer vivid glimpses of the first Greek Christian communities. Thessaloniki, Corinth, Philippi and several other cities soon became important centres of Christianity. The spread of Christianity among the Greeks, both in Greece and in the Hellenistic DIASPORA, opened to the church the heritage of Hellenic culture, giving Christianity a new theological and PHILOSOPHICAL VOCABULARY. Athens gave the apologists Athenagoras and Aristeides to the church, as well as CLEMENT OF ALEXANDRIA.

Greece was less affected than the churches of ASIA MINOR by the periods of imperial persecution, and when Christianity became the state religion paganism rapidly lost ground, especially when proscribed by Theodosius I in 394, though it survived beyond the sixth century in the Peleponnese and furnished many elements of folk religion. Illyricum was under the ecclesiastical jurisdiction of ROME until placed under CONSTANTINOPLE in the eighth century, a decision Rome initially did not recognize.

Foreign invasions and economic deterioration resulted in the fading of the Greek cities from the seventh century and the failure of imperial control over many inland areas. Many episcopal sees vanished. During the ninth and tenth centuries, however, Byzantine power was effectively reasserted and once again Thessaloniki and Corinth became major centres of commerce and ecclesiastical life. The foundation of ATHOS in the tenth century provided a major spiritual centre.

The CRUSADES culminated in the fall of Constantinople to the FRANKS in 1204, which was followed by the establishment of Frankish rule over much of Greece. This led to Orthodox resistance to the new Roman Catholic presence, and in the Greek states such as the despotate of Epiros to new ecclesiastical foundations. Arta was the focus of church life until in 1264 Mistra returned from Frankish to Byzantine rule; by the mid-fourteenth century it had become the centre of Orthodox life. METEORA also rose to prominence, almost rivalling Athos as a monastic centre. Church ARCHITECTURE, MUSIC and iconography flourished, and monastic life was stirred by the spread of HESYCHASM.

Byzantine rule in Greece was brief. By the mid-fifteenth century the OTTOMANS ruled all of Greece except for those Ionian islands under Venetian rule. Ottoman rule enhanced the authority of the bishops, who now exercised wide legal jurisdiction over their flocks under the ultimate authority of the ECUMENICAL PATRIARCH. The Greeks proved remarkably resistant to Islamic missionary activity; significant communities of Greek Muslims such as the VALADES came into existence, but the lengthy catalogue of NEW MARTYRS furnishes evidence of the resolute loyalty of most Greeks to their Orthodox faith. Ottoman rule, however, was tolerant of the Christian church provided nothing was done to challenge the supremacy of Islam.

The church struggled to sustain Greek education under Ottoman rule. It maintained close relations with the RUSSIAN ORTHODOX CHURCH and with the Orthodox rulers of ROMANIA, both major sources of financial support and political patronage. In the Ottoman period Greek theologians and iconographers made an important contribution to religious life in the Slav lands. From the eighteenth century church leaders emerged who were committed to the struggle for Greek independence.

The Greek Revolution of 1821 led to the progressive realization of aspirations for an independent Greek state and church. In 1833 the Greek church proclaimed its independence, and in 1850 it was formally recognized by the Ecumenical Patriarchate.

From 1852 the archbishop of Athens has presided over the Holy Synod of an autocephalous church. By 1832, when Otto of Bavaria became king, Greece included only the Cyclades, the Sporades, Peleponnesus and Sterea Ellas. In 1862 the Ionian islands came under Greek rule, followed in 1881 by Thessaly and a portion of Epirus, and in 1905 Crete proclaimed its union (*enosis*) with Greece. The Balkan wars of 1912 and 1913 brought in southern MACEDONIA, another substantial part of Epiros, part of Thrace and many of the Aegean islands. This greatly extended the rule of the Greek church, though eventually arrangements were made to leave Crete and several other islands under the Ecumenical Patriarchate. The failed Greek invasion of Asia Minor (1919–21) resulted in a massive exchange of populations that brought the surviving Greeks of Asia Minor into mainland Greece. As a result of all these changes, the Greek hierarchy grew from ten bishops in 1833 to twenty-four in 1852 and thirty-two by 1899. For a period Greece exercised oversight at the request of the Ecumenical Patriarchate over all Greek Orthodox diaspora communities.

When the Greek church adopted the Reformed Julian calendar a split occurred in 1924 which gave birth to the OLD CALENDARISTS who, despite state persecution, eventually established a number of rival traditionalist churches. The church found itself caught up in the bitter Civil War (1944–8) between royalist and communist groups, and its close involvement in state life led to serious problems with the rise and fall of the Junta (1967–74).

Article 3 of the Greek constitution recognizes the predominant position of the Orthodox Church of Greece, referring to its autocephaly established by the Patriarchal Tome of 29 June 1850 and the Synodical Act of 4 September 1928. The constitution also (Article 13) establishes the inviolability of religious conscience and prohibits proselytism. It refuses, however, to permit any exemption from obligations to the state or from obedience to the law on religious grounds.

The Church of Greece has come to play a progressively important role in supporting new Christian communities in AFRICA and Asia, and in sharing in dialogue with Oriental Orthodox and other churches. The universities have played a crucial role in furnishing theological and pastoral education for clergy and committed laity. The theological brotherhoods Zoe and Soter and the church's official Apostoliki Diakonia have exercised a major educational and spiritual influence on Orthodox life.

See also ATHOS; BYZANTINE CHRISTIANITY AND GREEK ORTHODOXY; MACEDONIA; MANI; ROUMELI; THRACE.

Yiannaras, H. (1992), *Orthodoxia kai Dysi sti Neoteri Ellada*. Athens: Domi.
Frazee, C. A. (1969), *The Orthodox Church and Independent Greece*. Cambridge: Cambridge University Press.

DB/DM

Greek Catholic   A Catholic of the Byzantine rite. Greek Catholics are also known as Byzantine Catholics.

See also EASTERN CATHOLIC.

DM

Greek Orthodox (1) Sometimes, all EASTERN ORTHODOX. (2) More often, Eastern Orthodox of the Byzantine as opposed to the Slav tradition. (3) Sometimes, Eastern Orthodox who are Greeks by culture and identity.

DM

Gregory Palamas (1296–1359) At twenty, together with his two brothers, he became an Athonite monk, but left ATHOS in 1325 because of Turkish attacks on the Holy Mountain and settled in Thessaloniki. He was ordained priest and became part of a spiritual group led by the future Patriarch Isidor, a disciple of the leading exponent of HESYCHASM, Gregory of Sinai (1255–1345). Returning to Athos some six years later, he lived an almost solitary life until elected abbot of Esphigmenou in 1335. His reforming zeal alienated the monks and he returned to solitude in 1336. Soon afterwards he came to the defence of the hesychasts against those who attacked their method of prayer, particularly in letters he exchanged with Barlaam of Calabria (c.1290–1348). He was imprisoned for a while for supporting Emperor John Kantakouzenus during the civil war of 1341–7. He was elected archbishop of Thessaloniki in 1347 and became a prisoner of the Turks in 1354 while on an embassy for Kantakouzenus. After his release the following year he wrote of the tolerant attitude of the Turks towards Christianity. He died in Thessaloniki in 1359 and was canonized in 1368.

Gregory's theological defence of the hesychasts was endorsed by synods held in Constantinople in 1341, 1347 and 1351. The *Hagioritic Tome* (1341), signed by the Athonite community and authored by Palamas himself, became the yardstick of orthodoxy in spiritual theology. Throughout his writings Gregory maintains that APOPHATIC THEOLOGY does not mean that we cannot know God at all, but that we cannot know God in his essence; we can, however, know him in his energies. The distinction he makes between essence and energy, already found in an undeveloped form among the CAPPADOCIANS, does not imply any division in God; rather, it is because God is personal that his existence is not limited to his essence, but is revealed to us through his energies. He supported the claims of the hesychasts to experience God, interpreting that communication in terms of the uncreated light experienced by the disciples at the TRANSFIGURATION of Christ. In the Eastern Orthodox church since 1368 the second Sunday in Lent has become a commemoration of St Gregory. This is also observed by some Byzantine rite Catholics.

Sinkewicz, R. E. (1988), *Saint Gregory Palamas: The One Hundred and Fifty Chapters*. Toronto: Pontifical Institute of Medieval Studies.

Mantzaridis, G. I. (1984), *The Deification of Man: St Gregory Palamas and the Orthodox Tradition*. Crestwood, NY: St Vladimir's Seminary Press.

Meyendorff, J., ed. (1984), *Gregory Palamas: The Triads*. London: SPCK.

Balfour, D., ed. and trans. (1982), *Gregory of Sinai: Discourse on the Transfiguration*. London: Fellowship of SS Alban and Sergius.

Meyendorff, J. (1974), St *Gregory Palamas and Orthodox Spirituality*. Crestwood, NY: St Vladimir's Seminary Press.

Meyendorff, J. (1964), *A Study of Gregory Palamas*. Leighton Buzzard: The Faith Press.

KP

Grottaferrata   Byzantine rite Catholic monastery of St Mary, founded near ROME, in 1004, towards the end of his life, by the ascetic abbot Neilos of Rossano. Grottaferrata became an important outpost of ITALO-GREEK Byzantine Christianity and of Greek learning and culture at the heart of the Roman patriarchate; its library still possesses a rich collection of manuscripts which evidence the learning and the skills of its monks. Cardinal BESSARION was titular abbot 1462–72. Grottaferrata slowly became Latinized until after centuries its Byzantine character was virtually lost. With the active support of Pope Leo XIII (1878–1903) the Byzantine rite was restored and Grottaferrata became once more, and remains, an important centre of Greek Catholic life with a unique role in ecumenical encounter between Catholics and Orthodox.

DM

·H·

Ḥabīb ibn Ḥidmah Abū Rā'iṭah SYRIAN ORTHODOX controversial theologian (*fl.* first half ninth century), who wrote apologetic treatises in his native Syriac and in Arabic directed to the Syrian Orthodox community in response to Muslim challenges to Christian beliefs. Abū Rā'iṭah, along with members of other major Christian confessional groups such as the MELKITE THEODORE ABŪ QURRAH (*c.*750–*c.*825), and the East Syrian ʿAMMĀR AL-BAṢRĪ (d. *c.*845), represents that first generation of Syriac-speaking Christians to answer the challenge of Islam in the Arabic language, making use of the phraseology of contemporary Muslim religious dialecticians.

Suermann, H. (1994). 'Der Begriff ṣifah bei Abū Rā'iṭah', in S. Kh. Samir and J. S. Nielsen, eds, *Christian Arabic Apologetics during the Abbasid Period, 750–1258*, pp. 157–71. Studies in the History of Religions 63. Leiden and New York: Brill.
Griffith, S. H. (1980), 'Ḥabīb ibn Ḥidmah Abū Rā'iṭah, a Christian *mutakallim* of the First Abbasid Century', *Oriens Christianus* 64, pp. 161–201.
Graf, G. (1951), *Die Schriften des Jacobiten Ḥabīb ibn Ḥidma Abū Rā'iṭa*. CSCO vols 130–1. Scriptores Arabici 14–15. Louvain: Imprimerie Orientalist L. Durbecq.

MJB/SHG

haji Also *hatzi, chatzi*; from the Arabic *ḥajjī*, meaning a pilgrim. Title given to those who have visited the Holy Land or have been baptized in the Jordan. Often becomes part of Greek surname, as in Chatzidakis and Hajifanis. The formal Greek term for a pilgrim is, however, *proskynetes*.

KP

Hatay Turkish province which includes ANTIOCH, the Hellenistic capital of Syria. This mainly Arabic-speaking region was joined to Turkey after a controversial referendum in 1938, after which many Christians of the region migrated southwards to Syria. Syria has never recognized the French decision to cede Hatay and other border areas to Turkey; Arab nationalists have claimed that this was an attempt to appease the Turks and ensure their neutrality in the expected conflict (the Second World War).

227

Christian minorities of the Near East have generally opted to live under the rule of Syria or even Iraq rather than Turkey; the various patriarchs of Antioch have all abandoned Antioch (Antakya) for Damascus or Beirut.

DB

Hatherly, Stephen (1827–1905)   First English EASTERN ORTHODOX priest and church musician. Born in Bristol into a devout Anglican family, he graduated from New College, Oxford, later obtaining a doctorate in music from the University of St Andrews. Influenced by the early Tractarians, he nevertheless converted to Orthodoxy and was received at the Russian Embassy chapel in London about 1856. His subsequent career is uncertain, but he was certainly anxious to establish English-speaking Orthodox communities in Britain ministered to by English converts to Orthodoxy. This brought him into conflict with the schemes propounded by J. J. OVERBECK, and the two remained bitterly hostile to each other. Having won the support of the metropolitan of Moscow for his schemes, Hatherly returned to England with sufficient money and furnishings to purchase the freehold of a former Methodist chapel, house and lands in Waterloo Road North, Wolverhampton for £700 and convert it for Orthodox use by 1869.

On 8 October 1871 he was ordained priest by order of Anthimos VI, the ECUMEN-ICAL PATRIARCH. At least four Anglican bishops tried unsuccessfully to exert influence with the Greek church and with the Turkish ambassador to stop the ordination and 'prevent schism'. He gained a following in the Midlands of English Orthodox, who published a number of good translations of liturgical books. Progress was severely curtailed when a letter from the Protosynkellos of the Ecumenical Patriarchate dated 26 February 1873 'invited and ecclesiastically enjoined' Hatherly to adopt the patriarch's ruling that he should not conceive in his mind 'the notion of proselytizing...even one member of the Anglican Church, which has moreover given of late so many proofs of fraternal sympathy towards our Orthodox Church'. This letter put an end to Hatherly's hopes of establishing an English Orthodox mission and in 1874 he let the Wolverhampton church to Wesleyans and moved to Birmingham.

His work now centred on the growing Greek community. In December 1873 he established a Greek Seamen's Church in Cardiff and in 1877 he settled in Bristol, where he established another Greek church. He edited several musical editions of John Mason Neale's *Hymns of the Eastern Church*, and published an important analytical study of neo-Byzantine chant. He died at Bournemouth on 2 November 1905 and was buried by the Church of England.

S

Heirmologion   Or Irmologion: Byzantine rite liturgical book containing the text and sometimes the melodies of the heirmoi which provide the musical and metrical models according to which the troparia of the CANONS are sung. The book may also contain other important AUTOMELA. The Slav Irmologion differs in function in that the troparia of Slavonic canons are sung to standard melodies for the troparia of a specific tone, rather than to the melody of a specific heirmos.

See also MUSIC.

DM

Henotikon   Theological formula promulgated by the Byzantine Emperor Zeno in 482 to reconcile CHALCEDONIANS and MONOPHYSITES. Acacius, patriarch of Constantinople, and PETER MONGOS of Alexandria were probably responsible for its content. The Henotikon condemns both NESTORIUS and Eutyches. It teaches that the orthodox faith is that proclaimed in the Nicene Creed and in the Twelve Anathemas of CYRIL OF ALEXANDRIA. It recognized, that is to say, the Councils of Nicea, Constantinople and Ephesus as authoritative. It also anathematized all who hold or have held any different belief 'whether at Chalcedon or at any other synod whatsoever'. While not a formal repudiation of Chalcedon, the Henotikon tended to undermine its authority. (*See* ECUMENICAL COUNCILS.)

Although the Henotikon won enthusiastic support from some and passive acquiescence from others, the Roman Pope Simplicius (468–83) and his successor Felix II(I) (483–92) protested to the emperor and in 483 Rome proclaimed the excommunication and deposition of Acacius. The ensuing schism between ROME and CONSTANTINOPLE continued until the reign of Pope Hormisdas (514–23), when Patriarch John II (518–20), supported by the new Emperor Justin (518–27), subscribed to a formula drawn up by the pope in 515 which decisively and by name condemned the leaders of the anti-Chalcedonians, TIMOTHY AILOUROS and PETER (THE FULLER) of Antioch and Peter (Mongos) of Alexandria. Monophysite bishops were deposed and Chalcedonians appointed to replace them. The Henotikon had failed.

DM

Heortologion   The EASTERN ORTHODOX churches do not possess the equivalent of the Roman *Martyrology*; there is no pan-Orthodox compendium of FEAST DAYS of saints and commemorations. Instead, each local Orthodox church preserves one or a number of Heortologia (Lists of Feasts). In the GREEK ORTHODOX tradition there are several regional variants (for Aitolia, Eurytania, Lesbos, etc.). The published MENAIA reflect the feasts observed by the patriarchate of CONSTANTINOPLE, but those peculiar to Constantinople itself are listed in the *Byzantinon Heortologion* edited by Manuel Gedeon in 1890. In 1974 the Church of Greece sanctioned its own, general *Heortologion*, edited by Constantine Platanitis. Over the centuries the Eastern Orthodox communities of Syria and Egypt have tended to observe feasts established among the Greeks rather than those of their Coptic and Syrian brethren. In America the Brotherhood of St Herman of Alaska has sought to produce a comprehensive list of Eastern Orthodox saints' commemorations and other feasts in a calendar produced annually. JOHN MAXIMOVITCH and other Orthodox leaders have insisted that Orthodox of the DIASPORA also respect the local saints and traditions of the pre-schism Western church.

DB

heothina   Greek, 'of the dawn'. Used of (1) the eleven Gospels of the Resurrection, read in an eleven-week cycle at Sunday ORTHROS; (2) the eleven IDIOMELA by Emperor Leo the Wise (866–912), sung as DOXASTIKON at the end of Sunday AINOI. There is a *heothinon* corresponding to each of the *heothina* gospels, of which they are poetic summaries. In the old ASMATIKE AKOLOUTHIA as described by Symeon of Thessaloniki (d. 1429), they were sung immediately before the Resurrection Gospel which formed the climax of Sunday Matins.

The practice of reading the Resurrection Gospels in sequence Sunday by Sunday is attested at ANTIOCH in the early sixth century in a sermon by SEVERUS OF ANTIOCH, who describes the practice as 'recently introduced'.

E

Hesperinos   The Byzantine rite office of Vespers, which opens the liturgical day, since the CALENDAR measures the day from sunset to sunset. The day concludes with the Ninth Hour, which is traditionally sung immediately before Vespers.

See also DAILY OFFICES.

Taft, R. (1986), *The Liturgy of the Hours in East and West*. Collegeville, Minn.: Liturgical Press.

E

hesychasm   The Greek term *hesychia* (silence, quiet, leisure) and its derivatives designate the monastic life, or in a narrower sense a specific mystical tradition based on monological prayer (see below), which has been the most influential in EASTERN CHRISTIAN spirituality. It became known in the West, though often in a distorted form, through the fourteenth-century controversy roused by the attacks on hesychast thought and practice by Barlaam the Calabrian and the defence of the hesychasts, especially by GREGORY PALAMAS.

Two major forms of mystical practice existed in the Judaism of the early Christian centuries. One, *merkabah* mysticism, named after Ezekiel's vision by the river Chobar of the chariot in which rode 'something that seemed like a human form' (Ezek. 1: 26), sought angelic guidance to ascend the highest heaven and experience the vision of God's living image, the Lesser Lord, sometimes identified as the ANGEL Metatron, the Enthroned, the transfigured Enoch. The second sought to know the secrets of creation (*ma'aseh bereshit*). Both forms used fasting, concentrated prayer and the invocation of angels.

Paul's brief description of his ascent to 'the third heaven' (2 Cor. 12) and the Apocalypse account of the revelation to John on PATMOS are among the oldest elements in a pattern of Christian writing generally classed as 'apocalyptic', in which visionary ascents to heaven, tours of hell and revelations of various kinds are recorded. Some of these texts are from a very early period. CLEMENT OF ALEXANDRIA (d. *c.*215), for example, cites the Apocalypse of Peter. The content of early Christian apocalyptic texts is evidence for the existence of forms of mystical practice and visionary experience closely similar to that of the *merkabah* and *ma'aseh bereshit* traditions.

Christian mysticism, however, is rooted in the experience of Christ, in the theologies of the New Testament and especially John's Gospel. In addition to the traditions inherited from Judaism, its forms owe much to the impact of philosophical and Egyptian asceticism and Platonic philosophy. Visionary mysticism carries evident dangers of delusion (*plane*), doctrinal deviation and even mental unbalance. Partly in reaction to such dangers, EVAGRIUS PONTICUS taught a spirituality based on an austere Middle PLATONISM, and on the introjection into the spiritual life of the individual of the cosmic battle between angels and demons. He teaches the practice of wordless, imageless prayer, and the purification of the mind until it attains the sapphirine clarity of the sky. Evagrius refers to the ultimate self as *nous*, mind or intellect: Middle Platonism conceived of God as *nous*, so that this term expresses the nature of the image of God in humanity. Later Eastern Christian mystics sometimes speak of *nous*, more often of the heart as the place of pure prayer. The heart image, drawn from the body-rooted thought forms of the Jewish BIBLE, signifies a more incarnational understanding of the human person.

The mystic seeks experience of God. Whether it is possible to attain direct, unmediated knowledge of God is matter for controversy. DIADOCHUS OF PHOTIKE presents the spiritual life as a path of continual transformation under the influence of the fire of God's love, but one which never results in the direct cognition of God. GREGORY PALAMAS speaks of seeing the Uncreated Light that transfigured Christ on Mount Tabor, the immediate experience of God in his energies. For the CAPPA-DOCIAN Gregory of Nyssa, the mystic is led beyond the illuminating knowledge of God to an unknowing of him in darkness, just as Moses encountered God first in the burning bush, then in the cloud, and then (Exod. 33) in thick darkness.

Hesychast practice focuses on the concentration of attention within, and the repetition, first verbally, then in the depth of one's being, of the JESUS PRAYER, one form of which, 'Lord Jesus Christ, have mercy on me', which in Greek is five words, may be inspired by 1 Corinthians 14: 19. A common form is: 'Lord Jesus Christ, Son of God, have mercy on me'; in Slav use, more commonly: 'Lord Jesus Christ, Son of God, have mercy on me a sinner'. Repeated brief prayer is known as monology. Other monological prayers are known in Eastern Christian tradition; certain psalm verses have been used in this way, as has the Kyrie Eleison.

The PHILOKALIA compiled by Nikodemos of the Holy Mountain (*see* NIKODEMOS THE HAGIORITE) and Makarios of Corinth is an encyclopedic collection of mystical and ascetic texts seen by the compilers as embodying the hesychast tradition. A version of the *Philokalia* was produced in Slavonic by PAISSII VELICHKOVSKII and a Russian version by THEOPHAN THE RECLUSE; both with the title *Dobrotolubiye*. The *Philokalia* is an invaluable resource book for hesychasts, but not a replacement of the direct teaching of a spiritual father or mother. Hesychast practice often involves what is best known as *starchestvo*, spiritual eldership exercised by the aspirant's disclosing to the elder all *logismoi* (thoughts), especially those that might be demonically or divinely inspired. The Greek version of the *Philokalia* contains in its latter part detailed directions for the posture to be adopted in prayer, and the control of the breath. The hesychast tradition makes it clear that these practices are inessential and certainly not to be used without the direction of a STARETS or *gerontas* (elder).

Nicodemos of the Holy Mountain (1989), *A Handbook of Spiritual Counsel*, trans. P. A. Chambers. New York: Paulist Press.

Alexander, P. (1983), '3 (Hebrew Apocalypse of) Enoch. A New Translation and Introduction', in J. Charlesworth, ed., *The Old Testament Pseudepigrapha*. London: Darton Longman & Todd.

Palmer, G. et al., trans and eds (1979–95), *The Philokalia*, 5 vols. London: Faber.

Meyendorff, J. (1974), *St Gregory Palamas and Orthodox Spirituality*. Crestwood, NY: St Vladimir's Seminary Press.

Meyendorff, J. (1959), *Introduction à l'étude de Grégoire Palamas*. Paris: Sorbonne.

DM

Hexapsalmos The sequence of six psalms read after the opening prayers of ORTHROS. They are Septuagint Psalms 3, 37, 62, 87, 102 and 142. During the reading of the Six Psalms the officiating priest recites the twelve Matins prayers and the congregation maintains a strict silence.

DM

Hieratikon Greek, 'priest's book'; Slav: *Sluzhebnik*. Byzantine rite liturgical book containing the priest's part of the Divine Liturgy of St John Chrysostom, of St Basil, of the Liturgy of the Presanctified attributed to Pope Gregory the Great, of ORTHROS, and HESPERINOS. It may also contain other services and prayers.

DM

Hilandar Serbian monastery on ATHOS, founded by Simeon and SAVA of SERBIA. By a *chrysobull* issued in 1198, the Byzantine Emperor Alexios III placed the monastery under the founders' direct authority, granting it complete and permanent self-government. Its TYPIKON was drawn up by Sava on the model of the Virgin Evergetis (Benefactress) monastery of CONSTANTINOPLE. In the thirteenth and fourteenth centuries, through the generosity of Byzantine emperors and Serbian rulers and nobility, Hilandar acquired vast lands and revenues. The Mother of God is venerated as abbot of Hilandar. The monks lead a cenobitic life.

ICONS (including the Virgin with Three Hands or Panaghia Tricheirousa), manuscripts, liturgical objects and ecclesiastic embroidery bear witness to the monastery's cultural attainments. The present *katholikon* was built by King Milutin around 1300. Its original wall paintings, later repainted, are now largely restored. The exonarthex was added towards the middle of the fourteenth century, although popular tradition ascribes it to the patronage of Prince Lazar, around 1370. Among Hilandar's fortifications the most prominent is St Sava's *pyrgos*, or fortified tower, with fourteenth-to-seventeenth-century additions. King Milutin's early fourteenth-century tower guards the path from the monastery to the sea. His famous tower in the port, Hrusija, is only partly preserved. Much impoverished during the Ottoman period, Hilandar was helped by the princes of Wallachia, by individual Serbian and Bulgarian donors and by imperial funds from Russia. There was a continuous link with the Serbs in Austro-Hungary and, from 1713, with the Serbian metropolitanate of Sremski Karlovci. In spite of difficulties, Hilandar's monks maintained spiritual and cultural connections with Serbian communities in Herzegovina and Dalmatia, as far as Trieste, as well as with the VLACHS in their communities in the southern Balkans. The monastery played a notable role in preserving the national awareness of the people, leading to the renewal of the Serbian state in the nineteenth century. Today there are around sixty monks at Hilandar.

Nenadović, S. (1997), *Osam Vekova Hilandara: Gradjenje i Gradjevine*. Belgrade: Republički Zavod za Zaštitu Spomenika Kulture (French summary).
Petković, S. (1989), *Hilandar*. Belgrade: Republicki Zavod za Zastitu Spomenika Kulture (in German).

Ćurčić, S., ed. (1987), *Hilandar Monastery: An Archive of Architectural Drawings, Sketches and Photographs*. Princeton: Princeton University Press.

Bogdanović, D., et al. (1978), *Chilandar on the Holy Mountain*. Belgrade: Jugoslovenska Revija.

Matejić, M. and P. (1972), *Hilandar Slavic Manuscripts: A Checklist of the Slavic Manuscripts from the Hilandar Monastery*. Columbus, Ohio: Ohio State University Press.

KP/ZG

Hodegetria   Greek, 'female guide'. Traditionally, this icon-type of the Mother of God is said to have been painted first by St Luke the Evangelist. In CONSTANTIN-

OPLE this icon-type became one of those associated with the church of Blachernai. Christ is depicted seated on the left arm of the Mother of God as she points to him with her right hand. This gesture of indication draws attention to the redeeming significance of the Word made flesh, 'the way, the truth and the life'. Usually there are three stars on the Virgin's *maphorion*, one on each shoulder, one on the brow, representing the miracle of her triple virginity, before, during and after Christ's birth.

Talbot Rice, D. and T. (1974), *Icons and their History*. London: Thames & Hudson.

Lange, R. (1969), *Das Marienbild der frühen Jahrhunderte. Iconographia Ecclesiae Orientalis*. Recklinghausen: Icon Museum.

KP

holy fools   Greek: *saloi*; Russian: *iurodivye*. Fools for Christ, a distinct group of saints venerated by EASTERN CHRISTIANS. They often employ shockingly unconventional behaviour or imitation of insanity to challenge complacently accepted values, to deliver unpalatable prophecies or other teaching and to cloak their own sanctity, so deflecting worldly honour. The phenomenon of Folly for Christ is first recorded with ISIDORA BARANKES of Egypt (d. 369), but only widely popularized by the *salos* Symeon of Emesa (d. 590).

ANDREW THE SCYTHIAN, a Holy Fool in CONSTANTINOPLE (ninth century?), provided the link between the earlier *saloi* and those who emerged in newly evangelized Rus. Andrew, presumed to be of Slav origin, made *saloi* a notable feature of the spiritual life of the Orthodox north. St Basil's cathedral in Red Square is named for a holy fool, Basil of Mangazeia (d. 1552). Isidor of Rostov (d. 1474), XENIA OF ST PETERSBURG (d. 1796), Feofil of Kiev (d. 1853), TERENTII (d. 1886), Pelagia (d. 1884) and Pasha of Sarov (d. 1915) are the best-known of many Russian *saloi*. PANAGIS BASIAS (d. 1888) is a rare example of a Greek *salos* in the modern period.

Krueger, D. (1996), *Symeon the Holy Fool*. Berkeley: University of California Press.

Gorainov, I. (1993), *Oi Dia Christon Saloi*. Athens: Tinos.

Puhalo, L. and Novakshonoff, V. (1990), *God's Fools*. Montreal: Synaxis Press.
Ware, K. (1984), 'The Fool in Christ as Prophet and Apostle', *Sobornost* 6.
Saward, J. (1980), *Perfect Fools*. Oxford: Oxford University Press.

DB

holy mountains Christian tradition inherits from biblical Judaism reverence for a number of holy mountains associated with events in salvation history, e.g. SINAI, the Mount of Revelation, and Carmel, the place of Elias' cave. Events in the life of Christ made Tabor, Mount of the TRANSFIGURATION, a place of PILGRIMAGE. These holy mountains and others appear in ICONS, sometimes portrayed as elements of the landscape which provides the background to an event, sometimes invested with a specific symbolism associated with the mountain itself.

Monastics and hermits were drawn to the holy mountains and also settled on other mountains, often chosen for their remoteness, but which in turn drew pilgrims. The ancient monastery of St Catherine on Sinai and the Syrian monasteries of TUR 'ABDĪN are among the earliest examples. In the fifth century AUXENTIOS established what came to be known as Mount St Auxentios, which served as a holy mountain for northern Bithynia. Holy mountains remain important in the life of contemporary EASTERN CHRISTIANITY. Mount ATHOS, the best-known and most important, is undergoing a notable revival and communities of nuns are seeking to revive the monasteries of the METEORA.

Olympos of Mysia (Ulu Dağ or Keşiş Dağ), on the borders of Mysia and Bithynia south-east of Prousa Theopolis (Bursa), dominated an entire monastic region. From the first monastery, established in the fifth century, Olympos became between the eighth and tenth centuries a monastic republic of about fifty independent monasteries, one female. These included Agauros, Atroa, Medikion, Pelekete, Peristerai, Chenolakkos, Heliou Bomon, Sakkoudion and Symbola. The ICONOPHILE monks of Olympos were targeted by Leo V; the monasteries also suffered from Arab raids in the ninth century. Olympos survived as a holy mountain into the fourteenth century, but Seljuk invasions meant that it was eventually eclipsed by Mount Athos. Mount Olympos of Pieria (*see* MACEDONIA) emerged as a monastic centre in the OTTOMAN period.

Mount Galesios (Turkish: Alamandağ) north of Ephesus near the river Kaystros (Küçük Menderes) was the holy mountain of Lydia. Monasteries here achieved prominence from the eleventh century when a STYLITE saint, Lazaros, was active in the area. Four major monasteries grew around the various columns used by Lazaros. A monastic revival in the thirteenth century was brought to an end in the late fourteenth century when the area was occupied by the Turks. Mount Ganos or Kalonoros in Thrace was another important monastic republic by the late tenth century. Near to the Propontis ports of Ganos (Gaziköy) and Myriophito (Murefte) the area was vulnerable to raids towards CONSTANTINOPLE and was sacked repeatedly from 1199 onwards.

Mount Latros (the ancient Latmos, now Beşparmak) by Lake Herakleia of Caria was settled by monks from the seventh century onwards. According to tradition the founding monastic settlers were refugees from Mount SINAI fleeing the Arabs. The number of monasteries grew from four, when PAUL OF LATROS first came to the region, to eleven in the thirteenth century. By the fourteenth century Mount Latros was controlled by the Turks and eclipsed by PATMOS. Paroria on the borders of

Bulgaria (Strandzha range) was a mountainous region where monasteries flourished in the late thirteenth century and into the fourteenth century, especially when Gregory of Sinai attracted large numbers to the area. Gregory Sinaites founded four *lavras* in the Paroria region from 1330. That of Mount Katakekryomene outshone the others.

Barousis, E. (1988), *Monachismos tes Mikras Asias*. Athens: Tinos.
Menthon, B. (1935), *L'Olympe de Bithynie*. Paris: n.p.

DB

Holy Russia   The vision of the expanding Russian state as heir to the Byzantine empire was espoused by both the Muscovite rulers and the Russian Orthodox hierarchy. Great Russians were portrayed as restorers of ancient Christian glories and the Church of Moscow as the THIRD ROME untainted by heresy. This ideal propelled the Russians towards uniting the eastern Slav lands, carrying Orthodoxy as far as the Pacific Ocean and identifying with the diverse Christian populations of the OTTOMAN empire. The idea bolstered tsarist rule and influence, but was none the less accepted to varying degrees by Eastern and Oriental Orthodox communities in the neighbouring states and beyond. After the 1917 Revolution the idea was maintained both by the Moscow patriarchate and by the RUSSIAN ORTHODOX CHURCH ABROAD. It is now interpreted in a strictly spiritual sense, or as a call for the unity of all northern and DIASPORA Orthodox Christians with the Russian church.

DB

Horaiozele of Byzantium   One of the patrons of CONSTANTINOPLE, the first-century Horaiozele 'the apostle' is venerated as an early Byzantine martyr. Tradition says she was converted by Apostle ANDREW and remained in Byzantion, attached to a church of Michael the Archangel (*see* ANGELS). Horaiozele was beheaded as a Christian and her relics were later moved to a chapel near the church of St Anastasia. She is commemorated on 26 July and is credited with numerous healings, particularly of mothers and children.

Cataphygiotou-Topping, E. (1990), *Saints and Sisterhood*. Minneapolis, Minn.: Light and Life.

DB

Horologion   (Greek; Slav: *Tchasoslov*.) The Book of Hours: Byzantine rite liturgical book. The Great Horologion contains the common of the divine office, and various other liturgical texts, for example the PARAKLESIS, the AKATHIST, APOLYTIKIA and KONTAKIA for the liturgical year. The latter section also includes notices of saints and feasts commemorated. The Small Horologion does not have all the Apolytikia and Kontakia. The texts of the Horologion are mainly for the use of readers and singers.

DM/E

Hovsep Sarajian   Priest of the Armenian Apostolic church sent from Istanbul to AMERICA in 1889 to minister to the Armenian community. His presence stimulated the organization of Armenian parishes, and in 1891 the first Armenian church was dedicated in Worcester, Massachusetts. Catholicos Mugurditch I (1892–1907)

235

established an Armenian diocese in America and Hovsep Sarajian became its first presiding bishop.

Reid, D. G. et al., eds (1990), *Dictionary of Christianity in America*. Downers Grove, Ill.: InterVarsity Press.

DM

Ḥunayn ibn Isḥāq (809–73)   Christian physician, philosopher and prolific translator of Greek scientific works into Arabic and SYRIAC, especially the medical works of Galen. His translations were instrumental in the transmission of Greek scientific literature to Arabic, Islamic science. Ḥunayn was born in Ḥīra, Iraq, to Christian NESTORIAN parents. He served as chief physician to the caliph al-Mutawakkil (847–61) in Baghdad. There he also was appointed head of the *Bayt al-ḥikmah*, House of Wisdom, founded by the caliph al-Ma'mūn (783–833), where Arabic translations of Greek scientific works were made.

Platti, E. (1993), 'Sagesse et révélation: théologiens arabes chrétiens à Bagdad (IXe–Xe siècles)', in R. Lebrun, ed., *Sagesses de l'Orient ancien et chrétien: la voie de vie et la conduite spirituelle chez les peuples et dans les littératures de l'orient chrétien; Conférences IROC 1991–1992*, pp. 169–92. Paris: Beauchesne.
Samir, K. (1981), *Une correspondance islamo-chrétienne entre Ibn al-Munaǧǧim Ḥunayn ibn Isḥāq et Qusṭā ibn Lūqā*. Patrologia Orientalis 40, 4/no.185. Turnhout: Brepols.
Strohmaier, G. (1971), 'Ḥunayn b. Isḥāḳ al-'Ibādī', *Encyclopaedia of Islam*, 3rd edn, pp. 578–81.
O'Leary, L. de (1979 [1949]), *How Greek Science Passed to the Arabs*. London: Routledge & Kegan Paul.

MJB/SHG

Hungarian Orthodox church   Both during their westward migrations across the Pontic steppe and when settled on the Pannonian plains, the Magyars came into contact with EASTERN CHRISTIANS. Certain Hungarian nobles embraced Byzantine Christianity in the tenth century and a bishop, Hierotheos, arrived from CONSTANTINOPLE to organize a mission to Tourkia, as the Byzantines termed Hungary. King Stephen, however, received Roman Catholicism as Hungary's church in 1000. A significant Eastern Orthodox community survived until the seventeenth century, when a movement for union with ROME resulted in a large GREEK CATHOLIC presence. Up to 1868 the remaining Orthodox of Hungary were under the jurisdiction of the Sremski Karlovci Metropolitanate (*see* SERBIAN ORTHODOX CHURCH). Subsequently, the Romanians were granted an independent archdiocese for Transylvania. The Hungarian Greeks seceded to form a separate grouping. Between the sixteenth and eighteenth centuries Greeks had settled throughout Hungary, intermarrying with Hungarians, and were largely assimilated by the nineteenth century, at which time more than thirty-two parishes existed, founded by Greeks but largely Hungarian in character. The 'Greeks' pioneered translation of Orthodox texts into Magyar, which they used liturgically, but were denied official recognition as an independent church. Many Hungarian Greek Catholics were attracted to these Greek parishes by their use of Magyar. This trend halted when Magyar was sanctioned as a liturgical language among

Greek Catholics also. Border changes after the First World War left only 40,000 Orthodox in Hungary. Between the wars the Hungarian Greeks sought links with the Ecumenical Patriarchate. In 1941 all the Orthodox of Hungary were united to Archbishop Sabbatios of Czechoslovakia, representing the Constantinople patriarchate. Following the Second World War the ethnically Hungarian communities were formed into an autonomous grouping linked to the patriarchate of Moscow.

Ramiret, P. (1988), *Eastern Christianity and Politics in the Twentieth Century*. Duke NC: Duke University Press.

DB

hypakoe   Greek; a short hymn, normally read and not sung, that replaces the third poetic KATHISMA at Matins on Sundays and some greater feasts of the Byzantine rite. In Greek use it replaces the KONTAKION at the Hours on Sundays. In strict Athonite use it is sung at the liturgy after the APOLYTIKIA and before the Kontakia.

E

◆ I ◆

Ibas Syriac: *Hībā*. Teacher in the Persian School of EDESSA and bishop of Edessa 435–57 after the great RABBŪLĀ; the translator into SYRIAC of the works of Theodore of Mopsuestia, the teacher of Nestorius (according to 'Abdīšō' of Nisibis' *Catalogue of Books*). Ibas came under theological suspicion and was deposed by the 'Robber Council' of 449, but was reinstated at Chalcedon in 451 after condemning Nestorius and Eutyches, only to be condemned once more at Constantinople II (553) in the condemnation of the Three Chapters. According to the *Chronicle of Edessa*, he built a new church in Edessa.

JH

iconoclasm Conventional term designating any movement against religious images or the veneration of such images and, by extension, movements to overthrow established opinions or practices. In eighth- and ninth-century Byzantium iconoclasm involved destruction of ICONS or their removal from any context where they could be venerated. The term itself derives from the Greek *eikonoklasia* (icon-breaking). Byzantine sources more frequently use the term *eikonomachia* (fighting against icons).

Theological opposition to religious images was not unknown in the early church. Fathers such as EUSEBIUS OF CAESAREA (d. 339/40) and EPIPHANIOS OF SALAMIS (d. 403) were critical of the use of images of Christ, the Virgin and the saints, although their stance also reflected opposition to pagan idolatry. Old Testament passages such as Deuteronomy 4: 16–18 and Exodus 20: 4 were used as evidence for the prohibition of images of the divine and of the saints. Furthermore, Jewish and, later, Muslim criticism of the Christian use of images may have influenced Byzantine iconoclasm. By the early eighth century a group of iconoclast bishops in CONSTANTINOPLE including Theodore of Claudiopolis and Constantine of Nakoleia found support from Emperor Leo III (717–41), who in 726, despite some opposition, removed the icon of Christ over the Chalke gate to the imperial palace and *c.*730 ordered icons to be removed from places of worship. This policy was opposed by Patriarch GERMANOS I (deposed 730), a number of whose letters of protest survive, though some may be spurious.

Leo's son, Constantine V (741–75), persecuted icon venerators, *eikonophiloi*, and initiated widespread destruction of icons, especially following the iconoclast council of Hieria in 754, which claimed ecumenical status. Constantine, whose *Enquiries* contributed to the theological debate, punished the monks, the most tenacious supporters of the icons. Some were executed, others forced into secular life. The ferocity of Constantine V's actions was not imitated by his son, Leo IV (775–80) whose widow, Irene of Athens (780–802), was most likely persuaded by the patriarchs Paul IV (780–4) and Tarasios (784–806) to summon the Seventh ECUMENICAL COUNCIL (Nicea II) in 787, where the icons were restored and the *horos* (definition) of the council of 754 refuted passage by passage.

Political and military setbacks under the iconophile rulers, and a growing tendency to identify icon veneration with military disaster, paved the way for a second period of imperial iconoclasm under Leo V (813–20). Iconoclasm was adopted once more at the Council of Hagia Sophia (815). The policy, officially at least, was now confined to removing icons from places where they could be kissed rather than ordering their destruction. Michael II (820–9) banned all discussion of the issue while maintaining iconoclasm officially. In a letter to the Frankish king Louis the Pious he explained his policy. Michael's son Theophilos, influenced by his mentor the iconoclast John the Grammarian, patriarch 837–43, was responsible for an upsurge in active state iconoclasm between 836 and his death in 842.

The synod of 843 called by Theophilos' widow Theodora, regent for her son Michael III (842–67), finally restored the veneration of icons, its SYNODIKON proclaiming the icon as an imperative in Christian worship. The period following saw intense ICONO-PHILE propaganda in art and letters, aimed at strengthening and disseminating the theological argument for the icon rather than at attacking individual iconoclasts.

Modern historians have associated iconoclasm with political and social as well as religious factors. The disruptive seventh century and the harm done to imperial ideology by Arab invasions may have led the emperors to see in the icon a potential rival to their claimed unique position as thirteenth apostle and living icon of Christ. In general, the intolerance of the seventh-century emperors has been seen as a foretaste of the iconoclast demand for conformity.

In ecclesiological terms the iconoclasts could not point to support from the other four patriarchates (*see* PENTARCHY); their opponents used this to underscore the innovative and heretical nature of their teachings.

There is evidence that, prior to iconoclasm, icons had been exposed to popular use and misuse without the mediation of the secular clergy. Iconoclasm has thus been identified by modern scholars of the Western Christian traditions with an attempt to reform Byzantine attitudes to religious images which deploys a Neoplatonist theory of the image, stressing the need for prototype and image to be alike in essence. Iconoclasts stressed the role of the priest in sanctifying this 'likeness' (since icons were not normally blessed by priests, they regarded them as lacking such sanctity). The iconoclasts saw the eucharist as an 'actual image' (*apseudes eikon* at the Synod of Hieria) and 'type' (*typos* in the *Enquiries* of Constantine V) of Christ, created only after the prayer of epiclesis over the eucharistic elements. The same applied for objects such as the cross, the church building, or the gospel book following the prescribed blessings. This may indicate that the iconoclasts were concerned to deny extra-clerical sources of sanctification to the holy. Iconoclasts also stressed the so-called ethical theory of images where the Christian who had Christ in his heart could be said to be His image.

It has also been maintained that iconoclasm continued the Christological debates of the early church. The iconoclasts were concerned that a graven image of Christ could only represent his circumscribable (*perigraptos*) human form, being unable to depict both natures, human and divine, of his incarnate hypostasis, which because of the divine nature was uncircumscribable (*aperigraptos*). Scholars no longer accept that this represents a MONOPHYSITE or crypto-monophysite line. Monophysites are known to have used icons and religious images. Extant iconoclast definitions and writings are few, but they betray no attempt to tamper with Chalcedonian Christology as then understood. This may explain why iconoclasm initially met with relatively little resistance in ecclesiastical circles. In theological terms, the major problem iconoclasm addressed was whether Christ, the Virgin and the saints could be venerated in a material image.

Iconophile apologists such as JOHN OF DAMASCUS, THEODORE THE STUDITE and Patriarch NIKEPHOROS I had to attack not so much the theological premises of the iconoclasts (in essence, completely Orthodox) as the logical consequences of the rejection of divine images for the place of matter in the salvation of the world. Iconoclast claims that material things such as wood and paint cannot help Christians comprehend the nature of holiness appeared to demote the importance of matter in DEIFICATION. The iconophiles held that Christ's *kenosis* would not be a reality if his visibility, and thus the possibility of his portrayal and of humanity's participation in him, were denied. For the Orthodox, the icon thus came to be seen as a symbol of the faith, and iconoclasm, by extension, associated with the rejection of Christ himself, who was crucified in his image as he was in the flesh. The vehemence of iconophile polemic against iconoclasm should be interpreted in this context. Such ideas found pictorial expression in margins of ninth-century psalters, where iconoclasts are likened to the Jews.

Outside the Byzantine empire, iconoclasm was encountered in seventh-century Armenia. In the West, the eighth-century popes strongly supported the iconophile stance. The Synod of Frankfurt, however, summoned by Charlemagne in 794, was led by a bad interpretation of the decrees of Nicea II to repudiate the cult of images. This act of the Frankfurt synod, though influential in its day, was overturned by the Fourth Council of Constantinople (870) (*see* PHOTIOS THE GREAT) and by the Council of Trent (1563). However, icon theology never attained the same significance in Western theology as in Eastern Orthodoxy. Western Reformation iconoclasm had no effect on the Orthodox church, and though the issue has sometimes been raised, there has been no significant challenge since the 'Triumph of Orthodoxy' in 843.

Corrigan, K. (1992), *Visual Polemics in the Ninth-century Byzantine Psalters*. Cambridge: Cambridge University Press.

Sahas, D. J. (1986), *Icon and Logos*. Toronto: Pontifical Institute.

Grabar, A. (1984), *L'Iconoclasme Byzantin*, 2nd edn. Paris: Flammarion.

Bryer, A. J. M. and Herrin, J., eds (1977), *Iconoclasm*. Birmingham: University of Birmingham Press.

Barnard, L. W. (1974), *The Graeco-Roman and Oriental Background to the Iconoclastic Controversy*. Leiden: Brill.

Hennephof, H., ed. (1969), *Textus Byzantinos ad Iconomachiam Pertinentes*. Leiden: Brill.
Anastos, M. (1954), 'The Argument for Iconoclasm as Presented by the Iconoclastic Council of 754', in K. Weitzmann, ed., *Late Classical and Medieval Studies in Honor of A. M. Friend Jr*. Princeton: Priceton University Press.

DT

iconoclast   In a technical sense, one who favoured the destruction of ICONS during the Byzantine iconoclastic controversy of the eighth and ninth centuries. The most famous iconoclasts were the emperors Leo III and his son Constantine V in the eighth century, and the patriarch of Constantinople, John the Grammarian, in the ninth century.
See also ICONOCLASM.

KP

iconophile   Or iconodule: a defender of the veneration of ICONS during the Byzantine ICONOCLAST controversy of the eighth and ninth centuries. The empresses Irene and Theodora and the theologians JOHN OF DAMASCUS, Patriarch NIKEPHOROS I and THEODORE THE STUDITE were among the most important iconophiles. Iconophiles persecuted by the iconoclast emperors included Stephen the Younger, Theodore and Theophanes Graptoi, 'the inscribed' (the emperor had offensive verses tattooed on their foreheads), and Theodosia, celebrated on 29 May as protomartyr of the icons, executed for casting down from his ladder, and accidentally killing, the soldier removing the icon of Christ from the Chalke Gate. The imperial policy of iconoclasm led to the theological definition of the role and function of the icon in the Byzantine church.
See also THEODORE ABŪ QURRAH.

Parry, K. (1996), *Depicting the Word: Byzantine Iconophile Thought of the Eighth and Ninth Centuries*. Leiden: Brill.
Giakalis, A. (1994), *Images of the Divine: The Theology of Icons at the Seventh Ecumenical Council*. Leiden: Brill.

KP

iconostasis   Screen of ICONS separating the ALTAR from the NAOS in Byzantine rite churches. The *haikal* screen dividing the sanctuary or *haikal* from the nave of a Coptic church may be of carved wood or may take the form of an iconostasis. In Byzantine churches, larger screens usually have three doors: a northern leading to the PROTHESIS, a southern to the DIAKONIKON, and the central holy doors, the gates leading into the sanctuary. Small chapels, as in Athonite monasteries, often have only a central and a north door. Small, low screens may have just the central doors, or a hanging curtain (*see* ROYAL DOORS).
   Icons were being hung on the sanctuary barrier by the sixth century and on the templon by the ninth. It was only in the twelfth to fourteenth centuries that rows of fixed icons began to obscure the sanctuary area, reflecting changes in the BYZANTINE LITURGY and church ARCHITECTURE. In Byzantium two or three rows of icons were the norm, but a five-tiered iconostasis appears in Russia by the fifteenth century. In the

VLADIMIR Dormition cathedral of 1408 Andrei RUBLEV and Daniil Cherny added a tier of prophets. In the seventeenth century another two rows were added.

Only ordained clergy may use the holy doors. In the case of a Byzantine rite priest he must be wearing at least EPITRACHELION and PHELONION, a deacon the STICHARION and ORARION. Coptic Orthodox clergy entering the *haikal* remove their shoes before doing so.

The word *iconostasis* has a second use to describe the domestic icon stand used in many private houses.

Walter, C. (1993), 'A New Look at the Byzantine Sanctuary Barrier', *Revue des études byzantines* 51, pp. 203–28.
Cheremeteff, M. (1990), 'The Transformation of the Russian Sanctuary Barrier and the Role of Theophanes the Greek', in A. Leong, ed., *The Millenium: Christianity and Russia (AD 988–1988)*, pp. 107–24. Crestwood, NY: St Vladimir's Seminary Press.
Epstein, A. W. (1981), 'The Middle Byzantine Sanctuary Barrier: Templon or Iconostasis?', *Journal of the British Archaeological Association* 134, pp. 1–27.

KP

icons, iconography   The Greek word *eikon* means 'image'. Icons can be fashioned in various materials, but the icon most familiar in Eastern Orthodox tradition is painted on a carefully prepared wooden panel.

Tradition declares the first icons of Christ and his mother date from their lifetime. The evangelist Luke is said to have painted the Mother of God from life, she to have approved the likeness. One of the many icons attributed to Luke is the VLADIMIR Mother of God, stylistically of the early twelfth century. Its apostolic ascription implies it is a true descendant from a canonical image attributed to the evangelist. In Eastern Christian thought a copy keeps faith with the original, the artist skilfully interpreting the canonical rules defining his subject, rather as a musician interprets a musical score.

The prototype of all iconography is the icon of Christ's face imprinted on linen, the Acheiropoietos, 'not made by hand'. Its story is in a document attributed to Bishop Addai of Edessa (d. 541) and in liturgical texts of its feast, 16 August. King ABGAR of Edessa, a leper, sent the artist Ananias to Christ with a letter requesting that he come and heal him. Ananias came upon Christ addressing a crowd, and attempted to capture his features, but without success, 'because of the indescribable glory of His face that was changing through grace'. Observing what Ananias was doing, Christ asked for water, washed his face and wiped it with a piece of linen which became mysteriously imprinted with his features. Ananias returned home with this image and Abgar was cured. According to this legend, therefore, the first icon was of Christ and was sanctioned by him.

It took a long time for a genuinely Christian art to evolve to express a new perception of reality and of the spiritual potential in nature. A common theme in early Christian art is the Good Shepherd, which may be derived from images of Hermes Krysophoros. It is not yet a direct image of Christ but a sign expressing Christ's taking upon his shoulders the lamb, fallen human nature.

CONSTANTINE THE GREAT undertook an extensive building programme, including Holy Sepulchre in JERUSALEM and other buildings on sites associated with

Christ's earthly life. The dates of festivals were also established during Constantine's reign and, at some unknown date, iconography of the festivals was set up at these shrines. Pilgrims took home holy oil and water in ampullae of clay and sometimes silver stamped with scenes relating to the sites they visited. One such, the phial of Monza of the Lombard Queen Theodelinda (d. 625), shows festival scenes of a type familiar to us from later iconography evolved and systematized in Palestine and Syria.

The eastern provinces of the Roman empire were heirs of the civilizations of Egypt, Syria and Mesopotamia. The link between early Christian portrait icons and Egyptian funerary portraits is evident. But it is the Syrian physical type which eventually became established in Christian iconography for the portrait of Christ, a bearded figure with full dark hair falling over his forehead, large almond eyes, straight nose and small lips.

The reign of the Roman Emperor Justinian (527–65) marks a turning point in art. His support of the arts was part of his mission to civilize, Christianize and unify God's terrestrial kingdom, of which he was the viceroy. In his capital emerged a synthesis of classical, late antique and hieratic eastern stylistic elements. Justinian's DIVINE WISDOM (532–7) expresses the world view of imperial Christianity. In the sixth century all the essential elements of a truly Christian stylistic system had already been forged and synthesized.

Iconography entered a new phase when canon 82 of the QUINISEXT COUNCIL (692) prohibited symbolic images of Christ, prescribing portrayal of Christ in his human form so that 'we comprehend thereby the humility of God the Word, and are guided to the recollection of his way of life in the flesh'. Although Byzantine ICONOCLASM in the eighth and ninth centuries challenged the validity of the portrayal of Christ and of the cult of icons, the 'Triumph of Orthodoxy' in 843 promoted a creative synthesis of theology and religious art that was of great significance for the subsequent history of European art.

In 988, at a high point of Byzantine cultural achievement, Kievan Rus was converted to Christianity, and clergy, architects, painters and mosaicists were dispatched to the newly Christian capital. The Byzantine artistic and religious heritage attained a new expression in the culture of the Slav nations (BULGARIA, RUSSIA, SERBIA).

From the ninth to the eleventh century, the Middle Byzantine architectural scheme of a cross-in-square church reached its fullest development and most perfect expression with an integrated balance between the architectural volume of the interior and the iconographic cycle of representations in mosaic and paint concisely distributed throughout the church interior. Within the dome Christ, the icon of the Father, appears as PANTOCRATOR. All levels below the dome are perceived to descend from it as a series of images radiating from the supreme archetype like the spokes of a wheel (see ARCHITECTURE; BYZANTINE LITURGY). The essential character of the Byzantine iconographic canon was established during this period.

Thirteenth-century Greek artists found powerful patrons in the kings of Serbia; Serbian wall paintings of the period provide an indication of this stylistic development, a new emphasis on weight and plastic volume as well as on spatial depth so that hieratic abstraction yields to a greater interest in the human body and human emotion. A more corporeal and bulky style is associated with Thessaloniki and MACEDONIA. Historians trace this humanist tendency to one of the periodic revivals of interest in classical and late antique Greek language and culture sponsored by a small circle of courtiers and scholarly elite based primarily in Nicea and Thessaloniki.

In the fourteenth century the controversy over HESYCHASM shook the Byzantine church. The champion of the hesychasts, GREGORY PALAMAS (d. 1359), a monk of ATHOS, affirmed that God, unknowable and inaccessible in his essence, communicates himself to creation through his manifold powers and energies, perceptible above all as light, especially the divine light which manifested Christ's divinity at the TRANSFIG-URATION. The victory of Palamite theology had immense consequences for Orthodox spirituality, art and thought during the second half of the fourteenth century. The earliest dated icon panel displaying hesychast-inspired technique, an image of Christ now in the Hermitage, St Petersburg, is dated 1368, the year of Palamas' canonization: its astonishing treatment creates optical illusion through the distribution of white highlights which flicker and vibrate across the surface of the forms in sure, rhythmic-ally distributed, calligraphic strokes.

Constantinopolitan masters who followed the same path as the anonymous painter of this Christ are Emmanuel Eugenikos (active 1384–96) who worked in GEORGIA, and THEOPHAN THE GREEK (1330–c.1408), who worked in NOVGOROD and MOSCOW. Russian sources call Theophan, one of the most daring representatives of late Paleo-logan painting, a 'sage'. His surviving wall paintings, in the Novgorod Church of the Transfiguration, show statuesque figures, solemn and exalted, executed in almost monochromatic tones. The deep colouring serves as a foil for the impetuous movement of highlights which contrast sharply with the static immobility of the figures.

Associated with Theophan is the development, in Russia, of the extended icon screen (ICONOSTASIS). In the Middle Byzantine period the imagery had been dis-tributed on the walls across the upper reaches of the church building. By the late fourteenth century these scenes are assembled in superimposed rows of panels on a many-tiered screen, showing the unfolding of God's plan through history. The highest tier depicts the Old Testament patriarchs, the next prophets holding texts foretelling the incarnation. Below come the festivals: New Testament scenes, mainly of the life and work of Christ up to Pentecost, showing how, as a consequence of the incarnation, the Holy Spirit enters and sanctifies all human and natural existence and how creation is led to participate in a process of transfiguration through which it may share the divine nature, a process which mirrors and parallels the eucharist. (See MYSTERIES; DEIFICATION.) The next, the DEESIS tier, depicts figures turning in intercession towards the enthroned Christ. The screen's lowest level is dominated by the holy doors, flanked by images of Christ and the Virgin. Other icons at this lowest level include the saint or festival to which the church is dedicated and others of local significance. This extended icon screen represents the last major iconographical devel-opment in Orthodox liturgical art: a major Russian contribution, eventually adopted by Cretan icon painters who interpreted it in their own way.

The greatest figure of fifteenth-century Russian painting is Andrei RUBLEV (c.1360–c.1430). Rublev began his career working alongside Theophan, but his style is quite distinct from the impetuous expressionism practised by Theophan. Rublev's painting represents a trend in the last phase of Byzantine art, reverting to the calm aristocratic neutrality of the early fourteenth century. Specifically Russian in Rublev's manner is the flatness of his imagery and the translucence of pure colour which attests to his hesychast theories of light: not the dramatic lightning flashes of Theophan, but an all-pervasive inner luminosity which has much in common with twelfth-century painting such as the Vladimir Mother of God, with which Rublev was certainly familiar.

There is no reason to assume that icon painting ceased in the capital altogether when it fell to the OTTOMANS in 1453, but the present state of our knowledge does not allow us to identify any icon as having been produced there. On the other hand we have considerable evidence about the icons produced in Crete, under Venetian rule since 1204 (*see* VENICE). The direction taken by Cretan painting is discernible in the panel painting of Angelos Akotantos (mid-fifteenth century), trained, according to Venetian records, as a Constantinopolitan painter, and Andreas Ritsos (active 1451–92). Signed panels ascribed to Akotantos show such discrepancy in technique it is questionable whether we are dealing with a single artist. Some display authentic Byzantine char-acteristics; others point to the emergent system of post-Byzantine painting commonly designated as Cretan. The Cretan tendency is more developed in the panels of Ritsos, who inherited Angelos' preliminary schematic drawings which served him as models. Ritsos' work is less full-bodied, refined, even brittle, exquisitely executed with perfect calligraphic control.

Moscow, by now the only surviving independent Orthodox state and thus the legitimate heir of Byzantium, became during the fifteenth century a great centre of icon painting. This role had been prepared and made possible by the influx of Greeks and Southern Slavs during the preceding century and by the implanting of Byzantine culture and ideology on fertile ground. Rublev's most renowned successor, Dionysii (1440–1503), developed his mentor's artistic system to its logical conclusion, with flatter, even more elongated and ethereal figures, and colours built up of transparent glazes which have a more tender pastel palette.

At the Moscow Council of 1551, the Hundred Chapters (*Stoglav*), iconography was keenly debated, especially the correct way to represent the TRINITY. The council recommended as guides the paintings of Rublev and the Greek masters. It was concerned with iconography, not aesthetics, but paintings in Moscow, especially in the court workshop, were accomplished as befitted an imperial court. Figures are more monumental and sturdy than the weightless, angelic types depicted by Dionysii. The colour grew deeper, with red predominating. Architectural forms in the background display specifically Russian details. The Russian mind was not prone, prior to the nineteenth century, to speculate in theological or philosophical categories, the icon being the natural support for a structure of ideas relating to a theology and a theocratic world view (*see* RUSSIAN RELIGIOUS PHILOSOPHY). It was indeed the free inter-pretation of speculative theology expressed in the icon which caused protests from one of Ivan the Terrible's state secretaries. Among the themes he condemned is a repres-entation of Christ in the garb of a warrior seated on the crossbar of a cross. This image also exists among the sixth-century mosaics of Ravenna.

The most prominent Greek icon painters active *c.*1600 were both named Emmanuel Lombardos. They worked in a similar fashion and, it is believed, in the same workshop, one between 1587 and 1631, the other between 1623 and 1644. Their strict Cretan programme was based on late Paleologan models, in reaction to the failed attempt of painters such as Klontsas and Poulakis to create a synthesis of Byzantine and Western painting.

In Russia, the westward turn of Peter the Great deprived icon painting of imperial patronage. The eighteenth-century Russian court preferred religious paintings by immigrant Western painters, despite the fact that they were inconsistent with the world view which the icon was intended to express. As the ideas of the Western Enlightenment triumphed among the Russian governing class, the traditional iconography came to be seen as 'medieval'. At a popular level icon painting continued, but the rediscovery of the icon both as painting and for its theological content had to wait until the beginning of the twentieth century.

Sendler, E. (1993), *The Icon, Image of the Invisible*. San Francisco: Oakwood Publications.
Ouspensky, L. (1992), *Theology of the Icon*, 2 vols. Crestwood, NY: St Vladimir's Seminary Press.
Evdokimov, P. (1990), *The Art of the Icon: A Theology of Beauty*. San Francisco: Oakwood Publications.
Mango, C. (1986), *The Art of the Byzantine Empire 312–453, Sources and Documents*. Toronto: Toronto University Press.
Ouspensky, L. and Lossky, V. (1982), *The Meaning of Icons*. New York: St Vladimir's Seminary Press.
Maguire, H. (1981), *Art and Eloquence in Byzantium*. Princeton: Princeton University Press.
Popova, O. (1980), *History of Novgorod and Moscow Painting: Links with Byzantium during the First Half of the Fourteenth Century*. Moscow: n.p.
Weitzmann, K. (1978), *The Icon: Holy Images 6th to 14th Centuries*. London: Chatto & Windus.
Heatherington, P. (1974), *The 'Painter's Manual' of Dionysius of Fourna*. London: Sagittarius Press.
Trubetskoy, E. (1973), *Theology in Colour*. Crestwood, NY: St Vladimir's Seminary Press.

JS

idiomelon   Correctly a STICHERON with its own distinctive melody. Paradoxically, new stichera have sometimes been composed to the melodies of existing stichera, beoming *idiomela prosomia*.
   See also AUTOMELON.

DM

Ignatios Agallianos (1492–1566)   Patron saint of Lesbos: an educated copyist and poet, married with children, who entered the priesthood and eventually the monastic life. Ignatios used his wealth to refound Myrsiniotissa Convent and to found the Leimonos monastery complex near Kallone. As abbot of Leimonos, Ignatios presided over an establishment that included schools and a college (closed only in 1923), a library, hospital and other charitable institutions. He was consecrated bishop of Methymne (1531), but ended his life as a monk teacher at Leimonos. He is commemorated on 14 October.

Soteriou, G. (1958), *Lesbiake Hagiologia*. Mytilene: n.p.

DB

Ilarion Little is known about the life of the first non-Greek metropolitan of KIEV (from 1051). His oration *Sermon on Law and Grace* (*c*.1047–50) includes an *encomium* on Prince Vladimir the Baptizer (978–1015), and is considered one of the finest Kievan writings in Church Slavonic.

Obolensky, D. (1994), *Byzantium and the Slavs*. Crestwood, NY: St Vladimir's Seminary Press.
Franklin, S. (1991), *Sermons and Rhetoric of Kievan Rus'*. Harvard: Harvard University Press.

KP

Ilia Chavchavadze (d. 1907)   Poet and leading figure in the late nineteenth-century revival in GEORGIAN civil and religious life who campaigned for return to distinctive Georgian Orthodoxy, suppressed since the establishment of the Russian protectorate. Ilia represented those Georgians who looked to the restoration of Georgian ecclesiastical autocephaly and the general use of Georgian language in their homeland. Ilia, who fearlessly opposed Russian imperialism, was assassinated by the Russian secret police. Already revered as a NEW MARTYR or ETHNOMARTYR and commemorated on 20 July, he was canonized in 1988.

Suny, R.G. (1994), *The Making of the Georgian Nation*. Indianapolis: Indiana University Press.
Allen, W. E. D. (1971), *A History of the Georgian People*. London: Routledge & Kegan Paul.

DB

India, Syrian Christian community   Historical research on the Syrian Christian community of Kerala has concentrated on three main issues: (1) the St Thomas legend in relation to the origins of Christianity in this part of India and its deep Middle Eastern roots; (2) the extensive and sometimes uneasy encounters between Syrian Christians and their European counterparts, notably the Portuguese and the British; and (3) the fragmentation over time of a single community, arising from the difficulties of reconciling its Indian and Middle Eastern heritage with historical demands resulting from European incursions.

A sociological approach would examine the question of origins differently. The arrival of Apostle Thomas at Kodungalur in AD 52 remains an important part of an oral tradition, kept alive by songs and stories about miracles and conversions performed by Thomas during his short sojourn in Kerala. Irrespective of whether it happened or not (and on the existing evidence it could well have happened), the Thomas tradition has shaped the very identity of all Syrian Christians, whatever their ecclesiastical differences.

Associated with this tradition is another legend. It is believed that Thomas converted thirty-two Nambuthri Brahmin families, of which eight were given precedence in Syrian Christian society and two, Pakalamarram and Sankarapuri, traditionally supplied bishops and priests. While their conversion resulted in loss of caste status, they retained certain privileges. An infusion of immigrant Christian traders of east Syrian stock and the granting of further privileges and honours by the Hindu rajahs over many centuries raised the social status of this community. Their high status was, however, conditional on fitting into a totally segmentary caste structure.

A mainly two-tier high-caste system operated in Kerala, with the Nambuthris constituting mainly the Brahmins and the Nairs being given the status of Sudra, the fourth in the conventional caste hierarchy after Brahmin, Kshatriya and Vaisya. In a society divided strictly on caste lines, there is the suggestion that the Syrian Christians may have filled an empty slot in the existing structure: a *jāti* (caste) of Vaisyas or merchants and traders, and later of landlords. All that can be inferred now is that, while the hierarchical relation between Syrian Christian and Brahmin was fairly clear-cut, that between Nair and Christian was more ambiguous.

The retention of caste privileges was ensured in a number of ways. Customs and rituals, heavily influenced by high-caste Hindu practices, relating to food, occupation and rites of passage emerged to define Syrian Christian identity. Strict rules relating to preparation of food and whom one eats with became a part of a complicated system of ritual pollution that the Syrian Christians inherited from other high-caste Hindus. Distance pollution was one of the peculiar facets of traditional Kerala caste structure. The wife of an English missionary, writing in 1860, gave the following description of touch and distance pollution stipulations in descending order of caste hierarchy: 'A Nayar may approach a Brahmin but not touch a Nambuthri Brahmin; a Chogan Ezhava must remain thirty-six paces off, and a Pulayen slave ninety-six steps distant. A Chogan must remain twelve steps away from a Nayar, and a Pulayan sixty-six steps off, a Pariyan some distance further. A Syrian Christian may touch a Nayar but they may not eat with each other. Pulayans and Pariyars, who are the lowest of all, may approach but not touch, much less may they eat with each other.'

Nowhere else in India did such a complex and refined system of ritual pollution exist: a person from the lowest caste was not only untouchable but unapproachable in Kerala. And it had its interesting manifestations in the Syrian Christian community. A custom that still survives among some Orthodox JACOBITES (Yakoba) is that during the Easter service street procession, shouts of '*poyin, poyin*' (go away, go away) are heard, warning members of the lower castes to remove themselves from the path of the higher castes. Further, in the traditional system, the Syrian Christian was frequently called upon to perform a peculiar task set by the Nayars and Brahmins: to purify by touch objects polluted by contact with lower castes. An early campaign to eradicate the severe form of social discrimination exemplified by touch and distance pollution, the Vaikom Satygraha of 1924, was led for a brief but eventful period by a Syrian Christian (cf. AVOIDANCE RITUALS).

In many matters, Syrian Christians had much in common with Hindus. A faith in horoscopes, the tying of a *minnu* (a pendant with a cross replacing the Hindu motif) to solemnize marriage, ceremonial bathing to remove the pollution of death, an insistence on vegetarianism during the period of mourning, and the celebration of *annaprasanam* (the first feeding of a child with rice) are but a few of the customs shared by the two communities.

There are, however, some interesting differences between the majority Hindu community and the SYRIAN CHRISTIANS. Their relative paucity of numbers and vulnerable minority status may explain their over-riding concern to establish genealogical connections between families, a favourite subject of conversation whenever Syrian Christians of Kerala or of the DIASPORA gather together, and their need to keep marriage endogamous and status-driven, or more recently money-driven. Councils such as the church *sabha*, which were formed for corporate action and decision, exerted control over individual members in a manner not dissimilar to caste organizations – disgrace, ostracism and excommunication being its instruments. Strong conformity existed in matters of dress, etiquette, food, occupational choice and leisure pursuits. Interest in intellectual or artistic pursuits was rare, as it was not among the Hindus of like status, and was often seen as mere distraction.

In their reluctance to augment their numbers through evangelization and in their treatment of Christians from other groups, the Syrian Christians show their exclusiveness. Conversion from lower castes and outside groups has long been frowned upon. Even when it took place in the early years of Christianity in Kerala, strict endogamy was practised and commensal restrictions followed rigidly. While these 'old' Christians were allowed to worship in Syrian Christian churches, this privilege was not extended to the 'new' Christians converted by European missionaries.

Indeed, the relationship between European missionaries and Syrian Christians is a complex one that may to some extent betray caste sensibilities. While there is evidence of waves of immigrants from the Middle East during the first millennium of the Christian era being smoothly absorbed into the Syrian Christian community, the arrival of the Portuguese in 1500 led to the first fissure within the community. This resulted from the Portuguese demanding certain fundamental changes: a change in leadership (cutting the umbilical cord joining the Church to the Middle East) and changes in certain practices. A successful rebellion was mounted against Portuguese control in 1653 by Thomas Christians, although a rump had broken away to become Roman Catholics. A root cause of this rebellion was fear that the Portuguese were bent on promoting changes leading to a dilution of the social status of the Christians, with a flood of new converts from the lower castes.

When the British arrived, their original intention was not to interfere with the internal matters of the Syrian church. Despite their attempt to lift the educational standards of the clergy, British missionaries soon found themselves at odds with the Syrian church leadership when they tried to overturn the age-old requirement of celibacy in the clergy and to have a say in the ordination of new priests. The hidden agenda of the British was seen by Syrian Christians as an eventual dilution of the authority of their church and of the social status of the community. While the authority of the Syrian church and its PATRIARCH was reasserted in 1836, it was a Pyrrhic victory, for the fissiparous tendencies resulted in a three-way split of the Syrian church into Anglican Syrian (1840), Mar Thoma (1889) and Orthodox Jacobite (1889), with the last breaking up in 1912 into Malankara Orthodox and Syrian Orthodox Jacobites. The last two groups constitute the Yakoba, numbering about two million, who see themselves as the custodians of the original Syrian church.

Joseph, G. (1996), 'Temple Entry vs Civic Rights: A Leaf from the Vaikkom Satyagraha', in *Kerala Padanengal*, 6, pp. 282–6 (in Malayalam).
Visvanathan, S. (1993), *The Christians of Kerala*. Madras: Oxford University Press.
Brown, L. (1982), *The Indian Christians of St Thomas*, 2nd edn. Cambridge: Cambridge University Press.

GJ

India, Syrian Christianity in South   The Syrian Christian community in South India is a distinctive expression of Eastern Christianity. Originally a single community ecclesiastically and socially, it is today fragmented into a number of jurisdictions, some in communion with ROME, others independent or linked to Middle Eastern patriarchates. The Indian Orthodox churches form the third largest group among the Oriental Orthodox, numbering about two million. The whole Syrian Christian community may number about seven million. It has had a complex history, due largely to the involvement of other churches, European and Middle Eastern. Many issues that led to particular developments or divisions are still contentious today.

The term 'Syrian' is usually applied to the ancient Christian community in South India because its historical links are with those Middle Eastern churches which used SYRIAC either as a vernacular or as a liturgical language. Culturally and ethnically the community has for over a thousand years been fully integrated into Indian society.

'Malabar' and 'Malankara' are ancient names for the region of modern India where the Syrian churches lie. Politically most of the territory was contained in the rajahates of Travancore and Cochin. Today the area lies within the modern state of Kerala.

The Syrian community is united by pride in their church's foundation by the apostle Thomas, hence the description 'Thomas Christians' often applied to them. So firm is this conviction that 1952, the nineteenth centenary of the traditional year of the saint's death, was commemorated by a postage stamp issued by the Indian government. Much scholarly research has gone into trying to prove or disprove the St Thomas tradition. The fourth-century Acts of Thomas tell of Thomas being sold as a slave to the Indian king Gundaphorus, who treated him kindly and commissioned him to build a palace. Thomas, however, used the money to relieve the poor. Gundaphorus discovered this and threw Thomas into prison. The king's brother then died and saw in heaven the palace Thomas had built by his acts of mercy. The brother was returned to life and told what he had seen. Gundaphorus and his brother were baptized. Thomas continued to spread the gospel in India, but was eventually killed with a lance by a Brahmin in Madras.

One difficulty with this legend is knowing whether the India referred to is in fact the south-western region where the Christian community is found today. Other regions, particularly in the north, have been suggested. However, Jewish and Roman trading routes did reach south India and the coastal location of many sites traditionally associated with Thomas lends some support to the traditional story of the community's foundation. Brown's conclusion is perhaps the safest: 'The only certain conclusion which can be drawn from an examination of the St Thomas tradition is that at any rate such a visit was physically possible . . . There were strong Christian and Jewish colonies in these places until the rise of Islam in the seventh century, and it is not unlikely that there would be Persian Christians settling on the Malabar coast . . . and whether or not the Apostle himself ever came to South India, it seems certain that other Christians from East Syria who claimed a connection with him did come to reinforce, if not found, the Malabar Church in the first three centuries.'

Clear historical evidence for the church in south India exists from the sixth century onwards. The traveller Cosmas Indicopleustes describes in his *Christian Topography* (*c.*535) a church with clergy in an area that can be confidently identified as Malabar. From this date references multiply.

The Indian church's earliest links were with the ('NESTORIAN') CHURCH OF THE EAST. There is no clear evidence of native Indian bishops, though local priests and deacons were clearly Indian. Stone crosses, some with Pahlavi inscriptions, surviving in Kerala offer tangible evidence of this EAST SYRIAN connection, the oldest dated to the seventh or eighth century. Copper plates, perhaps dating from the ninth century, apparently recording privileges granted to the Christian community, provide further evidence of the Persian–Syrian connection. In everyday speech East Syrian forms are used – *Mar* rather then *Mor*, *Qurbana* rather than *Qurbono*, etc. – even by those churches which use west Syrian pronunciation in the liturgy.

European involvement, other than via occasional travellers such as Marco Polo, begins with the arrival in Malabar of the Portuguese Admiral Peter Alvarez Cabrol in 1500, followed two years later by Vasco de Gama. The establishment of forts and trading posts quickly followed, bringing increased contact with indigenous Christians. To Portuguese eyes allegiance to an Oriental patriarch, and the stain of 'Nestorianism', were defects to be corrected. Increasingly Portuguese secular and religious authorities interfered with the practices of the Syrian community. Eastern bishops were denied entry or any exercise of authority. By the middle of the century confession, confirmation and extreme unction had been introduced into the Indian church. Eventually in 1599 the Portuguese archbishop of Goa, Alexis de Menezes, arrived in Malabar and began to threaten with eternal fire those who followed their own patriarch rather than the pope of Rome. In June of that year, despite considerable unease in the Syrian community, Menezes obtained the submission of the clergy at a synod held at Diamper, Udayam-perur. The supremacy of the pope as successor of St Peter was affirmed and the liturgical rites modified to remove all suspicion of Nestorianism and to conform in many ways to Latin usage, but the language of worship remained Syriac. Many texts were destroyed. The following year Rome appointed the Jesuit Francis Roz bishop over the Thomas Christians. He was followed by a succession of European bishops who generally dealt with their Indian flock via the Indian archdeacon, traditionally a powerful figure in the community.

Local dissatisfaction came to a head in 1653: receiving a rumour the Portuguese had killed an Eastern bishop trying to reach them, at the stone 'Coonen Cross' in Mattancherry the Thomas Christians swore to expel the Jesuits and to be subject only to their archdeacon, until a bishop could be obtained from their patriarch. The then archdeacon may have been consecrated as Mar Thoma I by the laying on of hands by twelve priests. This did not end the confusion, and eventually the greater part of the Syrian community returned to Roman obedience. Their descendants constitute the Syro-Malabar church today.

The assertion of independence coincided with the decline of Portuguese power and the rise of the Dutch. The control exercised by the Jesuits and other religious orders was severely reduced. Once again, Eastern bishops could gain entry to Kerala. The first to do so was one Mar Gregorios, who arrived in 1665, a bishop of the SYRIAN ORTHODOX patriarchate. Liturgically, he seems to have conformed to local tradition. Though technically MONOPHYSITE, Christologically the antithesis of the community's presumed Nestorianism seems not to have created major problems. Presumably two or more generations of Roman obedience had eroded the community's Christological identity which may never have been strong.

Mar Gregorios was followed by more West Syrian bishops; gradually the non-Roman Syrians seem to have adopted Syrian Orthodox liturgical forms. (*See* SYRIAN LITURGY.) In addition to the usual west Syrian vestments, Indian *metrans* (bishops) also wore on certain occasions a mitre, which seems to have been a combination of Latin mitre and an eastern crown-form mitre, and what seems to be a Latin-derived choir habit. These are now retained only by the Mar Thoma and Malabar Independent Syrian churches.

Throughout the eighteenth century a succession of bishops bore the name of Mar Thoma, though records do not allow confident reconstruction of their consecrations. Much of their energy had to be expended in asserting their authority in the face of an increasing stream of Middle Eastern prelates, and resisting inducements to submit to Rome. At least one, Mar Thoma VI, submitted to reconsecration (as Mar Dionysios I) by Syrian Orthodox bishops.

The arrival of the British in Malabar and gradual improvement in travel and communication brought further influences to bear on the non-Roman Syrian community. In 1795 the British displaced the Dutch from Cochin and soon a British resident was appointed for Travancore and Cochin. Writings of the Revd Claudius Buchanan and others brought the Syrian church to the attention of the British churches. In 1816 three missionaries from the Church of England's Church Missionary Society arrived in Kerala with a brief to assist the ancient church, principally through teaching candidates for ordination. A seminary, known today as the Old Seminary, was established at Kottayam where missionaries taught alongside Indian staff. A new translation of the Bible into the vernacular, Malayalam, had been completed with the assistance of Dr Buchanan in 1811.

The missionaries were not to interfere with the rites, practices and discipline of the Syrian church, but inevitably their influence began to show. It seems, for example, that celibacy had been required of lower clergy as well as bishops, presumably a legacy of the Portuguese period, as both east and west Syrian churches have a married priesthood. The missionaries discussed this with the Syrian metropolitan, and the British resident offered to pay money to priests who married to help with the new cost of maintaining a family. Many clergy did in fact marry, and the Orthodox, Jacobite and Mar Thoma churches still have a married priesthood, though only the Mar Thoma permit marriage after ordination.

Relations between Orthodox Syrians and CMS missionaries eventually began to deteriorate, not least because the missionaries' attempt to veto candidates for ordination was seen as unacceptable interference with the metropolitan's authority, and in 1836 a synod at Mavelikkara presided over by Metropolitan Cheppat Mar Dionysios IV affirmed the Orthodox Syrian church's adherence to the patriarch and the customs received from him. The CMS missionaries then turned their attention to the non-Syrian population, but were joined by a number of Syrians, some of whom were to assume positions of leadership in the new Anglican diocese.

Syrian Orthodox priests and congregations remained, supportive of many of the new insights the British missionaries had introduced but wishing to remain loyal to the Orthodox forms of their church; chief among them was the *malpan* (teacher) Abraham Palakunnathu, parish priest of Maramon, who had taught in the seminary. Abraham Malpan began a reform of the liturgy, comprising chiefly its translation from Syriac into the vernacular and the removal of features such as invocation of saints and prayers for the departed, which he now believed unbiblical. Opposition from the metropolitan led to a desire on the part of the reformers for episcopal support, and in 1842 Abraham Malpan's nephew, Matthew, a deacon, was sent to the Syrian Orthodox patriarch of Antioch, Elias, at ṬŪR ʿABDĪN. Matthew was duly reordained to avoid any doubt about the validity of his previous ordination, then ordained priest, *ramban* and bishop, as Mar Athanasios. After a short period as acting bishop of Mosul he returned to India and sought recognition as metropolitan.

For the next half-century the Orthodox church in South India was dominated by conflict between those professing strict allegiance to Syrian tradition and to the patriarch, and those who supported Matthew Mar Athanasios and a programme which sought to maintain the Syrian rite but reformed to accord with what were seen as biblical norms. The reformers asserted the independence of the Indian church from the patriarch. Patriarchal recognition of Mar Athanasios was withdrawn, but he continued as government-recognized metropolitan until 1876, when Syrian Orthodox Patriarch Peter III visited Kerala, consecrated a number of bishops and divided Kerala into seven dioceses.

The split with the reformers became definitive in 1889 when, by a two to one majority, the judges of the Royal Court of Final Appeal ruled that the Syrian Orthodox patriarch of Antioch was head of the Orthodox church in Malabar and that Thomas Mar Athanasios, Matthew Mar Athanasios' successor, could not be metropolitan as he did not possess consecration or authorization from the patriarch. The reformers lost most of the ancient church buildings and reorganized themselves as the Mar Thoma Syrian church.

The nature of the Orthodox community's relationship with ANTIOCH was to cause further bitter struggles in the twentieth century. A visit to India by Patriarch ʿAbdallah in 1909 precipitated litigation concerning the rights of the patriarch to direct the affairs of the Orthodox church in India and control its assets. Direct patriarchal rule ran contrary to the centuries of local autonomy and was resisted by many who nevertheless remained totally faithful to the church's Orthodox heritage.

The arrival in India of Mar ʿAbdul Massiḥ, Mar ʿAbdallah's predecessor, complicated matters. Claiming his removal from patriarchal office by the OTTOMAN authorities had not deprived him of his spiritual powers, on 14 July 1912 at Niranam, ʿAbdul Massiḥ consecrated Paulose Mar Ivanios as CATHOLICOS, the title in this context to denote an autonomous church, acknowledging the spiritual authority of the patriarch, but not under his rule. Today his successor as catholicos governs the Malankara Orthodox church.

In 1958 a carefully worded constitution brought a temporary cessation of conflict between the catholicos' party and the patriarchal party. The union broke down in 1970 when a letter issued by the patriarch of Antioch, Jacob III, denied that St Thomas had ever established a throne or, on the basis of John 20: 21–4, had even been a priest. The situation rapidly deteriorated and resulted in the creation of the parallel Jacobite Syrian church, with its own catholicos and episcopate loyal to the patriarch.

One result of this prolonged strife was the submission of a number of bishops to Rome. They and their flock constitute the Syro-Malankara church, and follow the west Syrian liturgical tradition.

The following list gives an indication of the fragmentation of the once united Syrian community. Numbers are very approximate; Indian custom counts families, not individuals. Most communities have a DIASPORA, elsewhere in India or overseas, particularly in the Gulf region, Malaysia and North America. The rite followed by each jurisdiction is the basis of the classification presented here.

♦ East Syrian rite ♦

(1) The Syro-Malabar. The largest group, numbering perhaps three million, it descends from the submission of the entire communion to Rome in the sixteenth century. The rite used was a highly Latinized version of the east Syrian, but a 'restored' rite was introduced in 1986 in time for Pope John Paul II's visit to India, though meeting some resistance. In dress and education the clergy and hierarchy appear Western, rather than Orthodox.

(2) The Nestorians. A small group, based around Trichur, owing allegiance to the patriarch of the Church of the East. For some years this community has been led by Mar Aprem. It has suffered schism, reflecting rivalry over the patriarchate. Mar Timotheos currently heads a smaller group, also based in Trichur.

♦ West Syrian rite ♦

(1) The Malankara Orthodox church, often referred to as the Indian Orthodox church. It numbers rather over one million and is headed by a catholicos, who takes the name Basilios, independent of the Syrian Orthodox patriarch. It possesses the Old Seminary at Kottayam and constitutes one of the Oriental Orthodox churches.

(2) The Syrian Orthodox JACOBITES, usually simply known as the Jacobites. They number rather less than a million and have a catholicos who acknowledges the ultimate jurisdiction of the Syrian Orthodox patriarch.

The above two groups have identical liturgical uses and social customs.

(3) The Mar Thoma Syrian church, which claims to represent the original tradition of an independent Indian church, free from what are seen as the doctrinal excesses of both Rome and Antioch. Its liturgical tradition is basically that of the Syrian Orthodox family, though simplified at places. Nowadays Western theological method predominates in sections of the church. The community has probably more than 750,000 members, and is headed by a metropolitan who takes the title Mar Thoma. The Mar Thoma church is in communion with the churches of the Anglican communion.

(4) The Malabar Independent Syrian church, a small, one-diocese church claiming a membership of no more than 25,000. As an independent jurisdiction it came into existence as the result of the consecration of an Indian bishop, probably as a non-Romanizing candidate for the metropolitanate, by Syrian Orthodox prelates in the late eighteenth century. It has a unique place in history as a result of having

consecrated bishops both for the undivided West Syrian community in the early nineteenth century, and for the 'reformers' at the end of that century. It is fully Orthodox in rite and customs.

(5)   The Syro-Malankara church, which descends from those Orthodox who submitted to Rome during the troubles of the first half of the twentieth century. It is headed by an archbishop and has a seminary at Trivandrum. It has over 200,000 adherents.

The history of the Syrian Christian community of south India clearly relates to the question whether the ancient church in India is an Oriental Orthodox church of independent type, as distinct from the others as the Armenians are from the Ethiopians, or merely a sub-division of one or more of the Syrian churches. Whatever the liturgical and jurisdictional affiliations with churches outside India, it is clear that in its general customs and culture the Indian Syrian church is truly indigenous. While the liturgical traditions broadly follow those of the equivalent traditions in the Middle East, these have been interwoven into the Indian context. The architecture and decoration of old churches, for example, often betray both Hindu and Portuguese influence.

Fenwick, J. R. K. (1992), *The Malabar Independent Syrian Church*. Nottingham: Grove Books.

Karaparambil, J. (1992), *The Babylonian Origin of the Southists among the St Thomas Christians. Orientala Christiana Analecta* 241. Rome: Pontifical Institute of Oriental Studies.

Alexander Mar Thoma (1987), *The Mar Thoma Church: Heritage and Mission*. Kottayam: Ashram Press.

Daniel, D. (1986), *The Orthodox Church of India*. New Delhi: Rachel David.

Brown, L. (1982), *The Indian Christians of St Thomas*, 2nd edn. Cambridge: Cambridge University Press.

Podipara, P. S. (1976), *The Hierarchy of the Syro-Malabar Church*. Allepey: Prakasam Press.

Vellian, J., ed. (1970), *The Malabar Church. Orientala Christiana Analecta* 186. Rome: Pontifical Institute of Oriental Studies.

Paul, K. P. (1961), *The Eucharist Service of the Syrian Jacobite Church of Malabar*. India (n.p.).

Cheriyan, P. (1935), *The Malabar Syrians and the Church Missionary Society*. Kottayam: CMS Press.

JF

Indiction   Fifteen-year cycle deriving from Roman imperial fiscal practice. Major taxes and duties were imposed at the start of the Indiction, and renewed annually on 1 September for fourteen further years. The Byzantine church inherited the cycle for financial and especially charitable organization, and as a basis for the CALENDAR. The first of September is Ecclesiastical New Year; 1993, 2008 and 2023 begin new Indictions.

DM

Innokentii Borisov (1800–57)   Scholar, church reformer and monastic founder. Innokentii graduated from the Orel seminary in 1819, then moved to the Kiev

Academy. He was summoned to St Petersburg, ordained priest (1823) and elected to a professorship. Transferred to KIEV (1830), he reorganized the curriculum and introduced the study of canon law. Innokentii was consecrated bishop of Chigirin (1836), translated to Vologda (1840) and Kharkov (1841), and became archbishop of Kherson and Tavrida (1848). From Odessa, he founded a new seminary and revived monasticism in New Russia and the Crimea. During the Crimean War (1853–6) Innokentii travelled along the front line, raising the morale of troops and refugees. He rallied the citizens of Odessa under naval onslaught, joining the defenders of Simferopol and Sevastopol and other besieged outposts. His war experience led to his composition of the *Akathist to the Protecting Veil* (*see* POKROV). He is commemorated on 26 May.

'St Innokenty' (1990), *Journal of the Moscow Patriarchate* 5/6.

DB

Ionia   Recently the term 'Ionia' (Turkish: Yonya) has been applied indiscriminately to the western shores of ASIA MINOR, including the distinct districts of Troad, Aiolia and Doris. Under Ottoman rule the Greek population of the area was stronger in the prosperous coastal areas but significant pockets existed inland. Smyrna was, after CONSTANTINOPLE, the major centre for the Greek bourgeoisie, maintaining links with Athens, ALEXANDRIA and other cities outside the OTTOMAN empire. The region, including districts of Mysia and Lydia, was awarded to Greece by the Treaty of Sèvres (1919) but reannexed by Turkey after the demise of the Greek campaign on the Sangarios (Sakarya). The Greek and Armenian minorities of the region were immediately expelled with much loss of life.
    See also CHRYSOSTOM OF SMYRNA; MEGALE IDEA.

DB

Iosif Semashko (1798–1868)   A GREEK CATHOLIC of Ukrainian priestly extraction. Graduated from the Vilna seminary in 1820 and was ordained priest. In St Petersburg he worked to improve Greek Catholic–Orthodox relations. He became bishop of Mstislav and Belarus, then of Lithuania (1833). In 1839 Iosif presided over the Reunion of Polotsk, leading the LITHUANIA and BELARUS Greek Catholic dioceses into the Orthodox church.

Bulekov, A. (1990), 'Metropolitan Iosif', *Journal of the Moscow Patriarchate* 3.

DB

Irene of Chrysobalanton (d. 991)   Ascetic from Cappadocia. Irene, destined for the bride show of Emperor Michael III, fled to the Chrysobalanton Convent in CONSTANTINOPLE; she became a nun and eventually abbess. She was famous as a seer and a miracle-worker who levitated in prayer. An icon of Irene Chrysobalantine brought from Smyrna by refugees has made the Lykovrysi Convent near Athens a place of pilgrimage.
    See also IONIA.

Rosenquist, J. O. (1986), *The Life of St Irene, Abbess of Chrysobalanton*. Uppsala: n.p.

DB

Isaac of Nineveh   Also known as Isaac the Syrian; lived in the latter part of the seventh century. One of the greatest spiritual writers of the CHURCH OF THE EAST, and regarded as a major spiritual father throughout the EASTERN ORTHODOX world. He was born in Bēt Qaṭrāyē, the area around modern Bahrain and Qaṭar in the Arabian Gulf, which was an important though sometimes troublesome province of the patriarchate in Seleucia-Ctesiphon. Isaac became a monk and may have moved to Khuzistan, though he was eventually taken by the Patriarch George I, who visited Bēt Qaṭrāyē in 676, to be consecrated bishop of Nineveh (Mosul) at the monastery of Bēt 'Ābē. Isaac resigned as bishop after five months for reasons which are obscure. His orthodoxy may have been questioned because of his emphasis on the infinite mercy of God and its extension even to demons. Having retired to Khuzistan and eventually to the monastery of Rabban Shapur, he devoted the later part of his life to the writing of ascetical works. Surviving genuine material in SYRIAC from Isaac's pen includes two collections. The first is well known, and sections were soon translated into Greek, Arabic and Ethiopic. The Syriac text was published in 1909. The second collection is less well known and the Syriac text has only recently been rediscovered.

Brock, S. (1995), *Isaac of Nineveh (Isaac the Syrian): 'The Second Part', Chapters IV–XLI*. CSCO 554–5: Scriptores Syri 224–5. Louvain: Peeters.
Hansbury, M. (1989), *St Isaac of Nineveh: On the Ascetical Life*. Crestwood, NY: St Vladimir's Seminary Press.
Brock, S. (1987), *The Syriac Fathers on Prayer and the Spiritual Life*. Kalamazoo: Cistercian Publications.
Holy Transfiguration Monastery, trans. (1984), *The Ascetical Homilies of Saint Isaac the Syrian*. Boston: Holy Transfiguration Monastery.
Wensinck, A. J. (1923), *A Mystic Treatises by Isaac of Nineveh Translated from Bedjan's Syriac Text*. Amsterdam: Koninklijke Akademie van Wetenschappen.

JH

Ishodad   Īšō'dād of Merv became in 837 CHURCH OF THE EAST bishop of Ḥdattā (in Adiabene, near the confluence of the Great Zab and the Tigris). He wrote extensive biblical commentaries in SYRIAC incorporating quotations from Theodore of Mopsuestia, EPHREM THE SYRIAN and others. While admitting typological exegesis, he, like Theodore, advocated a literal, non-allegorical understanding of the BIBLE in its historical context, with the Old Testament seen on its own terms. He was a candidate for the catholicate in 852 on the death of Abraham II (a former bishop of Ḥdattā), though Theodosius, with support at the court of Al-Mutawakkil, was enthroned in 853.

New Testament: M. D. Gibson (1911–16), *The Commentaries of Isho'dad, bishop of Ḥadatha (c.850 AD)*, Horae Semiticae v–vii (Gospels), x–xi (Acts, Paul, etc.). Cambridge: Cambridge University Press.
Old Testament: C. van den Eynde, *Commentaire d'Išō 'dad de Merv sur l'ancien testament*, vol. 1, CSCO 156 (Louvain: L. Durbecq, 1955); vols 2–5, CSCO 179, 229–30, 303–4, 328–9 (Louvain: Secrétariat du CSCO, 1958–72); vol. 6, CSCO 433–4 (Louvain: Peeters, 1981).

JH

Ishoyab II Īšō'yab (var. Yešū'yahb), CATHOLICOS of Seleucia-Ctesiphon (628–46). A native of Bēt 'Arbāyē, he had studied in Nisibis and been bishop of Balad. Tradition ascribes to him a considerable interest in education, but circumstances forced him into high-level politics. He went on an embassy (perhaps for the Sasanian queen, Boran, but the purpose is unclear) to Emperor Heraclius who was in Aleppo in 630. The emperor accepted the catholicos' orthodoxy and they took communion together. Also in the group visiting Syria was Sahdona, who was persuaded of the correctness of the MONOPHYSITE view by monks in Apamaea. Īšō'yab's reign saw the fall of Seleucia-Ctesiphon to the Arabs (637), and the fall of JERUSALEM and ANTIOCH (638). He appears to have reached some accommodation with the conquerors, as reported by BARHEBRAEUS. According to the twelfth-century 'Nestorian' writer Mārī, Īšō'yab received from Muḥammad a document conferring privileges on the CHURCH OF THE EAST. It is during the time of this same catholicos that NESTORIAN missionaries arrived in China (635 according to the SIAN-FU inscription).

JH

Ishoyab III Īšō'yab III (var. Yešū'yahb), CATHOLICOS of Seleucia-Ctesiphon c.649–59, was born in Kuplānā, the son of a wealthy Adiabenian Christian, and educated at the school of Nisibis. Before becoming catholicos he was bishop of Nineveh–Mosul (620), and c.630 metropolitan of Irbil (Ḥazzā), in which capacity he took part in the embassy to Heraclius headed by Patriarch Īšō'yab II.

Īšō'yab III is credited with the ordering of the *Ḥudrā*, the variable texts for Sundays and major feasts and fasts. The *Chronicle of Se'ert* gives him a major role in the formation of the Eastern liturgy. His main writings are a commentary on the Psalms and 106 letters on ecclesiastical affairs, including lengthy letters concerning a conflict which began c.647 between him and the 'Nestorians' in the Gulf region, which had long been partly Christian. A synod of the bishops of Fars announced their secession. The catholicos sent two bishops from Khuzistan and finally personally visited Rew Ardashīr and succeeded in propitiating its bishop. The revolt then spread to Bēt Qaṭrāyē in north-eastern Arabia. The five letters the catholicos sent to Bēt Qaṭrāyē survive (one to the bishops, two to the people, two to the monks). Īšō'yab decided to visit Bēt Qaṭrāyē, but his death in 659 prevented it.

Fiey, J.-M. (1969–70), 'Īšō'yaw le Grand. Vie du catholicos Īšō'yaw III d'Adiabène (580–659)', *Orientalia Christiana Periodica* 35, pp. 305–33; 36, pp. 5–46.
Duval, R. (1904–5), *Īšō'yahb Patriarchae III, Liber Epistularum*. CSCO 11–12: Scriptores Syri 11–12. Louvain: Typographeum Reipublicae.

JH

Isidora Barankis (d. c.369) A nun of Tabennisi convent in Egypt, generally considered by Eastern Christians to have introduced the notion of the HOLY FOOL into church life. It is believed that she was discovered by the hermit Pitirim, who was informed in a vision of the significance of her lifestyle of absolute humility and feigned lunacy. He travelled to Tabennisi to consult her and to warn the other nuns not to treat her with contempt. After this Isidora fled to the desert to avoid all attention. She is commemorated on 10 May.

DB

Isochristoi   Followers of ORIGEN who taught that in the final APOKATASTASIS all human beings will literally be equal to Christ.

DM

Italo-Greeks   Southern Italy and Sicily contained numerous important Greek cities in ancient times. Greek settlers arrived during the Byzantine period, and ports always drew Greek merchants and sailors. ROME and CONSTANTINOPLE disputed jurisdiction over the area the Italo-Greeks inhabited, the boundary between the patriarchates shifting with changing political circumstances. Indeed, papal action in south Italy was the occasion of the dispute with MICHAEL KEROULARIOS that led to the famous anathemas of 1054.

 When Byzantium and the Balkans fell to OTTOMAN rule in the fifteenth century, Greek and Albanian refugees poured into Italy. Some Greek and Albanian settlers in southern Italy maintained a separate identity as GREEK ORTHODOX, but many melded with the GREEK CATHOLIC population of the region. The Catholic Italo-Greeks or Italo-Albanians have a unique ecclesiastical status as communities of the Byzantine rite which belong to the Roman Catholic communion not as a result of union or conversion, but as communities belonging to the Roman patriarchate.

DM

· J ·

Jacob Baradaeus Born *c.* 490 near Tella (Constantina), the son of a priest called Theophilus bar Ma'anū, Jacob became a monk in the monastery of Psīltā on Mount Izla near Tella. At that time and later he wore as a sign of monastic poverty a horse-cloth, SYRIAC *burda'tā*, from which derived his nickname, *būrd'ānā*, Latinized as *baradaeus*.

About 527–8 Jacob and Sergius, another monk (later patriarch of ANTIOCH), were sent to CONSTANTINOPLE to support the MONOPHYSITE line and remained there for fifteen years under the patronage of the empress Theodora. About 543, at the request of the monophysite Ghassanids, Theodora arranged for the appointment of Jacob as metropolitan, nominally of EDESSA, with authority over a wide area of Syria and Asia. Another bishop, Theodore, was given similar authority in Palestine and Arabia. For thirty-five years Jacob acted as a roving ambassador for monophysitism, travelling with difficulty because of the active persecution of monophysites by the imperial authorities. He visited personally almost every part of his area, ordaining priests and consecrating bishops in large numbers. He visited ALEXANDRIA, Constantinople and Seleucia (seeking toleration for monophysites) and died on the way to see the Patriarch Damian of Alexandria in 578. His remains were later (622) removed to Psīltā.

Although the monophysites experienced serious internal disputes in the later part of his life (Paul of Antioch in conflict with Peter of Alexandria, leading to a council of the Oriental church in 575), Jacob can be regarded as the institutional founder of the SYRIAN ORTHODOX church tradition. He it was who saved it from extinction, organized its hierarchy and laid the foundations for its future development. For this reason the Syrian Orthodox church has commonly been called JACOBITE.

An anaphora is ascribed to Jacob, as are some letters and a few other works extant in Arabic and Ethiopic. A Syriac Life of Jacob Baradaeus is ascribed to John of Ephesus (d. 586).

Land, J. P. N. (1862–75), *Anecdota Syriaca, II*. Leiden: Brill. (The Syriac Life.)

Honigmann, E. (1951), *Evêques et évêchés monophysites d'Asie antérieur au VIe siècle.* CSCO 127, Subsidia 2. Louvain: L. Durbecq.

JH

Jacob of Sarug   (Srūg; modern Suruç) SYRIAC author born *c.* 451 at Kurtam near Batnae/Baṭnān/Sarug, south-west of EDESSA, and educated at Edessa. Already mentioned with approval by the *Chronicle of Joshua the Stylite* while still *periodeutes* or visitor (*c.* 503), in 519 he was appointed bishop of Batnae, but died in 521. Called 'Flute of the Holy Spirit and Harp of the Believing Church', he wrote metrical homilies (760 according to BARHEBRAEUS, of which hundreds survive) and hymns which reveal little of a partisan nature in terms of Christology; however, letters addressed to the monks of Mar Bassus and to Paul of Edessa indicate his support for the MONOPHYSITE party. Many other letters survive, including one to the Christians of Najrān (519–20). A work *On the Fall of Idols* is important for the study of late antique paganism. Several biographies survive, one by Jacob of Edessa (*c.* 640–708).

Alwan, P. (1989), *Jacques de Saroug. Quatre homélies métriques sur la création.* CSCO 508–9, Scr. Syr. 214–15. Louvain: Peeters.
Vööbus, A. (1973), *Handschriftliche Überlieferung der Memre-Dichtung des Ja'aqob von Serug.* CSCO 344–5: Subsidia 39–40. Louvain: Secrétariat du CSCO.
Olinder, O. G. (1952), *Iacobi Sarugensis Epistulae quotquot supersunt.* CSCO 110, Scr. Syr. 57. Louvain: L. Durbecq.
Bedjan, P. (1905–10), *Homiliae Selectae Mar Iacobi Sarugensis.* Paris: Via Dicta; Leipzig: Harrassowitz.
Martin, J. P. (1876), 'Discours de Jacques de Saroug sur la chute des idoles', *Zeitschrift der deutschen morgenländischen Gesellschaft* 29, pp. 107–47.

JH

Jacobite   A name used for the SYRIAN ORTHODOX CHURCH (and occasionally for other Oriental Orthodox). It derives from JACOB BARADAEUS, bishop of EDESSA *c.* 543–78. In early times the name 'Jacobite' was accepted with pride by some in the church, and in later sources it is still found without derogatory meaning; but it is now not used by the Syrian Orthodox themselves, except in India, where it forms part of the official title of one church and is in common use to describe all Syrian Christians of the Orthodox tradition.

See also INDIA, SYRIAN CHRISTIANITY IN SOUTH.

JFC

Japan   The Orthodox church of Japan was founded as a result of the work of NICOLAS KASATKIN (1836–1912), who was made bishop of the Russian Orthodox mission in Tokyo in 1880 and later became archbishop. A persecution of Christians began in 1871 and it was not until 1873 that Christianity was legalized in Japan. A cathedral dedicated to the Resurrection (known as the Nikolai-do) was completed in Tokyo in 1891 and its consecration was attended by the Russian crown prince, later Tsar Nicolas II. During his stay in Japan the crown prince was wounded by one of his police bodyguards, who believed he was surveying for a future military invasion.

During the Russo-Japanese War of 1904–5 Orthodox Christians in Japan were given a hard time and after the Russian Revolution ecclesiastical ties were broken. There were about 30,000 Orthodox in Japan in 1912; about 40,000 in 1931; and there are about 30,000 today. The situation during the Second World War made relations with Moscow difficult and numbers declined. In 1970 the Church of Japan received its autonomy from the Moscow patriarchate and bishop Vladimir (1922–97) of the ORTHODOX CHURCH IN AMERICA became its metropolitan. Vladimir had earlier served as a missionary priest in ALASKA. In 1972 he was succeeded by Theodosius Nagashima. The Orthodox church of Japan awaits full recognition of its autonomy by the Ecumenical Patriarchate.

Mitsuo, N. (1995), 'The Japanese Orthodox Church,' in J. Thomas Rimer, ed., *A Hidden Fire: Russian and Japanese Cultural Encounters 1868–1926*. Stanford, Cal.: Stanford University Press.
Thelle, N. R. (1987), *Buddhism and Christianity in Japan: From Conflict to Dialogue 1854–1899*. Honolulu: University of Hawaii Press.
Drummond, R. H. (1971), *A History of Christianity in Japan*. Grand Rapids, Mich.: Eerdmans.

KP

Jassy, Synod of Synod of the EASTERN ORTHODOX church, held in 1642 in Romania, which both anathematized the Calvinistic heresies attributed to Patriarch Cyril LUCARIS and approved an edited version of the *Orthodox Confession* of Peter MOGILA.

Overbeck, J. J., ed. (1898), *The Orthodox Confession of the Catholic and Apostolic Eastern Church from the Version of Peter Mogila*. London: Thomas Baker.

DM

Jeremias II Patriarch of Constantinople (1572–95) who engaged in correspondence with the Lutheran theologians of Tübingen and whose three *Answers* became one of the symbolic books (compendia of doctrine) of the EASTERN ORTHODOX church. He shows in his response to the Greek translation made of the Augsburg Confession of 1530 that there was no common ground between the Orthodox and the Lutherans over such issues as tradition and the doctrine of justification. He protested to Pope Gregory XIII over the change in the CALENDAR (1582) from the Julian to the Gregorian. It was during his visit to Russia in 1588–9 that he raised the metropolitan of MOSCOW to the rank of PATRIARCH. His purpose in going to Russia was to collect funds to assist the Orthodox communities living in the OTTOMAN empire, but the Russians took the opportunity of his visit to press the case for their own patriarch. This was a decisive moment in the history of the Russian church and a victory for those who saw Moscow as the THIRD ROME.

Mastrantonis, G. (1982), *Augsburg and Constantinople*. Brookline, Mass.: Holy Cross Orthodox Press.
Runciman, S. (1968), *The Great Church in Captivity*. Cambridge: Cambridge University Press.

KP

Jerusalem   The BIBLE identifies Jerusalem, city of Christ's ancestor David, with Salem, city of Melchisedech (Genesis 14: 17), who himself and whose sacrifice of bread and wine prefigure Christ. Having become king of the twelve tribes, David (*c.* 1000–962 BC) took Jerusalem and built his palace and stronghold there. His son and successor Solomon (*c.* 961–922 BC) built its great Temple, placing the Ark of the Covenant in its Holy of Holies. He also built a magnificent palace next to the Temple. Soon, however, Solomon's realm was divided by revolt, Jerusalem becoming the capital of Judah, while Jeroboam (*c.* 922–901 BC) established the secessionist kingdom of Israel, Omri (*c.* 876–869 BC) establishing its capital at Samaria. Israel survived almost exactly two centuries, until the Assyrian Shalmaneser V besieged and overthrew Samaria (724–721 BC). Judah survived a century and a half longer; then, in 587 BC, the Babylonian king the Septuagint calls Nabuchodonosor (Nebuchadnezzar) (4 Kingdoms 24; 2 Kings 24 and 2 Paralipomena 36; 2 Chronicles 36) besieged and destroyed Jerusalem, blinded King Zedekiah and led him and his people to captivity in Babylon. In 539 BC Babylon itself fell to the Achaemenid Cyrus, who returned the Jews from exile and supported the rebuilding of the Temple. The city of the return was a modest and humble place.

Alexander's rise and the break-up of his empire at his death in 323 BC left Jerusalem unhealthily positioned between the Seleucids and the Ptolemies. Throughout the third century BC Ptolemaic pharaohs held Palestine. Then, in 200 BC, the land passed to Seleucid control under Antiochus III the Great (223–187 BC). Under Antiochus IV Epiphanes (175–163 BC) ferocious persecution of observant Jews accompanied a systematic policy of Hellenization. Antiochus had the 'abomination of desolation', an altar dedicated to Zeus, set up in the Temple.

The Maccabean revolt (167–163 BC) eventually established the independence of the Jewish nation and the Hasmonean dynasty ruled, usually, though with dubious legitimacy, as high priests. Between 63 and 37 BC the Romans established themselves in Palestine. The same period saw the collapse of the Hasmonean dynasty and its replacement by the Herodians. Herod the Great (37–4 BC), in the eighteenth year of his reign, began an opulent restoration of the Temple, which was not finished until AD 63: just in time to be destroyed by the Romans seven years later.

The symbolic significance of Jerusalem changed for ever when it became the site of Jesus' later ministry, his challenge to the Temple authority, his mystical supper with the disciples, his arrest, suffering, death and Resurrection. Jerusalem was the birthplace of the church, where James the Lord's brother and then Simeon, his cousin, presided over the oldest Christian community. The oppressive Roman procurator Gessius Florus (AD 64–6) finally drove the Jews to rebellion. In AD 70 the city was besieged from spring to autumn by Vespasian's (69–79) son Titus, reduced to starvation, and finally overwhelmed and sacked. The revolt of Simon Bar Kochba (132–5) led to the Emperor Hadrian (117–38) razing shattered Jerusalem to the ground, filling in the valley that divided it and building on its site a new city to a different plan, Aelia Capitolina, dominated by a great temple to Capitoline Jupiter, and forbidding any Jew to enter the city or even the district around it. The line of Jewish bishops of Jerusalem ended. A new line of gentile bishops of Aelia began, subordinate to the bishops of Caesarea.

Under the rule of CONSTANTINE THE GREAT and his patronage of the church, Bishop Makarios was allowed to pull down the temple of Capitoline Jupiter. The emperor's aged mother Helena came as a pilgrim to patronize an archaeological dig, facilitated by her having the garrison at her disposal, and rejoiced at discoveries identified as the place of the Crucifixion, the tomb and even the CROSS of Christ. PILGRIMAGE now drew Christians in great numbers. Constantine covered the tomb with a rotunda, the Anastasis, and a magnificent basilica, and built the Eleona church on the Mount of Olives and the Nativity basilica in Bethlehem. Soon other churches rose: Holy Apostle on Mount Sion, Ascension and Gethsemane. Imperial patronage, the torrent of pilgrims, the unique festal celebrations of the Holy City, and soon its fame as a centre of MONASTICISM and ASCETICISM made Jerusalem populous and wealthy. In the mid-fifth century the exiled Empress Eudokia poured her immense wealth into a building programme, including churches at many biblical sites, the massive basilica of St Stephen and the restoration of the city's fortifications. Justinian I (527–65) added an even larger church, the Nea Ekklesia of the THEOTOKOS.

Canon 7 of the Council of Nicea (325) recognized Jerusalem as mother of all churches, but left it under the authority of the metropolitan of Caesarea and therefore of ANTIOCH. In the episcopate of Juvenal (c. 442–58) the Council of Chalcedon recognized Jerusalem as patriarchal see, fifth in rank after ROME, CONSTANTINOPLE, ALEXANDRIA and Antioch.

In 614 Jerusalem fell to the Persian Chosroe II Parviz (591– 628), who brought back the Jews and carried off the Cross as a gift for his JACOBITE wife Shirin. About 630, however, Emperor Heraclius (610–41) forced the Persians to return the city and the relic. In 638 Jerusalem was besieged by the Arabs. Patriarch Sophronios (634–8) personally yielded the city to the austere Calif 'Umar. Soon Muslim shrines appeared: the Dome of the Rock, also a monument to Eastern Christian artistry, and al-Aqsa Mosque.

Byzantine warfare in the tenth century compromised Jerusalem's Christians in the eyes of their Muslim rulers. In 969 Patriarch John VII was executed for treason. In 1009 the deranged Calif al-Ḥākim (996–1021) destroyed Holy Sepulchre, declaring the Holy Fire a blasphemous imposture. A treaty between Constantine IX (1042–56) and Calif al-Mustansir (1036–94) allowed the rebuilding of Holy Sepulchre. In 1077 Jerusalem passed under Seljuk rule.

Muslim rule in Jerusalem was overthrown by the crusaders in 1099 (see CRUSADES); the Latin Kingdom of Jerusalem was established and soon a Latin patriarchate followed. The line of Greek patriarchs continued, many living in Constantinople. The 'FRANKS' held Jerusalem until 1187, when Saladin took it, purifying Muslim shrines converted by the crusaders, but returning many churches, including Holy Sepulchre, to the Eastern church, and again from 1229 to 1243. These short periods left their mark on the city's architecture: Holy Sepulchre was largely rebuilt and the Church of St Anne erected. Churches, castles and fortifications rose that still mark the landscape with their Romanesque and Gothic styles.

With the bloody storming of Jerusalem in 1244 by zealot Muslim forces from Mesopotamia, crusader rule finally ended. Until the sixteenth century Jerusalem was ruled, though insecurely, by the caliphate in Egypt. In 1517, however, Sultan Selim I (1515– 20) brought Jerusalem under OTTOMAN rule. On the death of the caliph, a Turkish captive, in 1538 the sultan inherited his title. From the sixteenth century

Jerusalem remained under Ottoman rule, except for the period 1831–40 when the Egyptian army of Ibrahim Pasha held it until dislodged by Britain and Austria.

Throughout this period the patriarchs were Greek. Indeed, into the late twentieth century Greek clergy have held an almost absolute ascendency over Arab Orthodox in the Holy Land. Patriarch Dositheos (1669–1707) reformed monastic institutions, opposed the encroachments of the Latins, wrote important theological works against the Catholics and convened the Synod of Jerusalem in 1672 that condemned the Protestant doctrines supported by Cyril LUCARIS (*see* JERUSALEM, SYNOD OF).

Throughout the Ottoman period, Catholic powers, especially France, sought to enhance the rights of Roman Catholics in the Holy Places. In 1630 this resulted in a *firman* (edict) of Murat IV (1623–40) handing over the main sites to the Latins. In the next seven years they changed hands at least five more times. A Polish treaty with the Sublime Porte in 1676 even sought to exclude 'schismatics' from them. A capitulation of 1740 effectively handed the Holy Places to the Franciscans, traditional Catholic custodians of the Holy Land. A *firman* of Mehmet IV (1748–87) in 1757, however, returned the sites to the Greeks, and in 1774 the Treaty of Kücük Kainarca established Russian presence and influence.

In 1843 Patriarch Cyril II (1845–72) established himself in splendid estate in Jerusalem. In 1847 Pius IX ordered the new Latin patriarch to take up residence in his see to defend Latin interests there.

In 1850 the French ambassador to the Sublime Porte demanded the Holy Places be handed over to the Franciscans. Russia threatened military action if the Greeks were dispossessed, a threat to which France responded in kind. This lamentable confrontation led Sultan Abdul Mecid (1839–61) to set up a commission to investigate rival claims to the Holy Places. The outcome was a *firman* laying down the exact rights of each community represented in Holy Sepulchre. It became known as the 'Status Quo'.

At the end of the First World War the Ottoman empire was falling apart. The League of Nations discussed the Holy Places in the context of the British mandate in Palestine. In 1922 Cardinal Gasparri wrote to record that the Vatican did not oppose the British mandate but proposed that only Catholic representatives should have a vote on any new commission. No new commission was established. A confidential memorandum of 1929 to the government of Palestine on the 'Status Quo' took account of decisions made under the mandate and remains a reference point.

The resolution of the United Nations in 1947 to partition Palestine and establish Jerusalem as a separate body was overtaken by war between Israel and the Arab nations, which left the Old City and the sacred places in the hands of Jordan. The Hashemite Kingdom of Jordan took an active interest in the Holy Places and in the status of the Christian communities. A statute of 1958 required the Greek patriarch and his bishops to be Jordanian citizens and literate in Arabic.

The 1967 Arab–Israeli war, however, placed the Old City of Jerusalem in the hands of the victorious Israelis. The Knesset passed an important law protecting the Holy Places. The process towards peace between Israel and the Palestinians and with the Arab world has raised again the question of the status of Jerusalem and the security of church and community property.

At present many Eastern Christian churches are represented in Jerusalem. The Greek Orthodox patriarchate of Jerusalem has played an important role in Orthodox church life, maintaining links with traditionalist groups. Since the seventeenth century an Armenian patriarchate has existed in Jerusalem. From 1855 to 1867 there was also an ARMENIAN CATHOLIC archbishop in residence. The MELKITE Catholic patriarch of Antioch bears the title of Jerusalem but does not reside there. From the ninth to the thirteenth centuries the CHURCH OF THE EAST had a metropolitan of Jerusalem. Copts and SYRIAN ORTHODOX, like the Greeks, Latins and Armenians, have rights in the sacred places guaranteed by the customary interpretation of the 'Status Quo'. There is an Ethiopian monastery touching Holy Sepulchre. Melkite, MARONITE and SYRIAN CATHOLICS are also present in Jerusalem, but without rights in the Holy Places.

Zander, W. (1971), *Israel and the Holy Places of Christendom*. London: Weidenfeld & Nicolson. (This book contains the 'Status Quo' *firman* of 1852 and the Memorandum of 1929.)

DM

Jerusalem, St   Jerusalem (or Rosalia or Rosa; d. *c.* 276) is the patron saint of Verroia in MACEDONIA, held to intervene against famine. Her Life mirrors those of PARA-SKEVE and Sophia of Rome. Jerusalem, like Paraskeve, travelled around Greece preaching; her three children, like Sophia's, were tortured to death before she died, though Jerusalem was from ALEXANDRIA not ROME and she had sons (Secendus, Secendinus and Kegoros) not daughters. She and they are commemorated on 4 September.
    See also GREAT MARTYRS.

DB

Jerusalem, Synod of (1672)   Sometimes known, not unreasonably, as the Synod of Bethlehem, since it happened in the Church of the Nativity there. A council of the EASTERN ORTHODOX church which defined Orthodox dogma in areas at issue in the Western Reformation. The Synod was not merely an Orthodox rejection of the doctrinal innovations of the Reformers, though it certainly was that; it was also an attempt to articulate the dogmatic heritage of Orthodoxy in face of the disputes between Catholics and Protestants. At first sight the synod seems close to Roman Catholic doctrine, but there are differences of emphasis. The synod asserts the teaching role of the church and therefore of tradition against the Protestant *sola scriptura*, and asserts the role of love and grace, and therefore of deeds, in justification. It affirms seven MYSTERIES and rejects any attempt to make them merely symbolic or expressive, teaching a doctrine of the presence of Christ in the eucharist that even uses the Greek equivalent of the Latin *transubstantiatio*. What is at issue here, however, is not so much a specific metaphysical explanation of Christ's sacramental presence as an affirmation of the objective reality of his active presence. The synod confirmed the canonicity of the deutero-canonical books of the Old Testament, rejecting the Protestant shorter, Hebrew canon.

Robertson, J. N. W. B., trans. (1899), *The Acts and Decrees of the Synod of Jerusalem*. London: T. Baker.

DM

Jesus Prayer   A short prayer composed of phrases drawn from the New Testament. The normal form of the prayer is: 'Lord Jesus Christ, Son of God, have mercy on me', to which may be added 'a sinner'; the form 'have mercy on us' is also used. Other variants exist. In EASTERN ORTHODOX monastic tradition a monk is usually allocated a fixed number of repetitions of the prayer each day as a personal prayer discipline. In HESYCHASM the prayer plays a central role; the consciousness being carried inward with the breath to the region of the heart, the symbolic centre of life and awareness, where the Jesus Prayer is prayed with concentrated and devoted attention. The prayer is at one and the same time a device for excluding thought and images and focusing attention, and an act of acknowledgement, orientation, worship, repentance and devotion, opening up the whole person to the transforming grace of Christ present by his Holy Spirit in the depth of his or her own being.

See also HESYCHASM; MONASTICISM; SPIRITUAL THEOLOGY.

Ware, K. (1986), 'The Origins of the Jesus Prayer', in C. Jones et al., *The Study of Spirituality*. Oxford: Oxford University Press.
Hausherr, I. (1978), *The Name of Jesus*. Kalamazoo: Cistercian Publications.
Brianchaninov, I. (1952), *On the Prayer of Jesus*. London: Faber.
Kadboulovsky, E. and Palmer, G. E. H. (1951), *Writings from the Philokalia on the Prayer of the Heart*. London: Faber.
Gillet, L. (A Monk of the Eastern Church) (1950), *On the Invocation of the Name of Jesus*. London: Fellowship of SS Alban and Sergius.

DM

jizyah Under Islamic law 'people of the book', AHL AL-KITĀB, were permitted to continue to live within Muslim society provided they paid a special poll tax, the *jizya*. Such groups were 'under protection', *dhimmah*, and thus *ahl al-dhimmah*, 'people of protection', *dhimmī*. This status did not confer complete freedom. Apart from special restrictions imposed from time to time (e.g. special rules on clothing), there were regular restrictions, for example on church buildings and public displays of religion, as well as the more obvious legal bans on conversion and restrictions on intermarriage.

JH

John Chrysostom A younger contemporary of the CAPPADOCIANS (d. 407). He came from ANTIOCH, where he trained in rhetoric under the pagan teacher Libanios. When asked who would succeed him as head of his school, Libanios is said to have replied: 'John, if the Christians hadn't got him'. John was ordained priest in Antioch and given the special ministry of preaching. He showed a vigorous commitment to social justice both at the civic level and in family life, defending the dignity of WOMEN in marriage. In Antioch he delivered homilies on Genesis, Matthew and John and on many of the Pauline Epistles. His fame as a preacher won him the name *chrysostomos*, 'golden-mouthed'. In 398 he was appointed archbishop of CONSTANTINOPLE, where his attempts to reform the morals of city and court were taken by Empress Eudoxia, rightly perhaps, as criticism of herself. He was exiled and died from being forced to travel long distances on foot in atrocious weather. His last words were: 'Glory to God for all things'.

The normal eucharistic liturgy of the Orthodox church bears his name, but his connection with it is a matter of debate among experts. Many of the sermons attributed to him are not considered authentic by modern scholars. For convenience these are attributed to Pseudo-Chrysostom. The most notable of these is the Paschal Catechesis read at the Easter Night Liturgy in churches of the Byzantine rite, and quoted in its entirety by THEODORE THE STUDITE in a Paschal sermon.

E

John Climacus (*c.* 579–649) Best known for his guide to the ascetic life, *The Ladder of Divine Ascent*, composed while he was abbot of the monastery of St Catherine on SINAI. Originally written for a monastic community at Raithu on the Gulf of Suez, it was soon translated into many other EASTERN CHRISTIAN languages as well as into Latin. The *Ladder* is divided into thirty steps, each step dealing with a virtue or vice associated with the spiritual life. It offers a penetrating analysis and a psychological profile of each topic. Although the metaphor of the *Ladder* suggests a gradual sequence, the attainment of perfection is not subject to a predetermined pattern of behaviour. We progress in some virtues quicker than in others and slip back into some vices more readily than into others. John suggests that we cannot even take credit for responding to the call to follow the life of virtue, because the initiative comes from God in the first place. Ultimately our own efforts are dependent upon God and the prayers of others. As an ascetic he disparages the capricious nature of the human body while at the same time he recognizes its value as a vehicle for the practice of virtue. This ambivalent attitude is also found in the writings of his contemporary MAXIMUS THE CONFESSOR. Today in many Eastern Orthodox monasteries the *Ladder* is appointed to be read during Lent.

Chryssavgis, J. (1989), *Ascent to Heaven: The Theology of the Human Person According to Saint John of the Ladder*. Brookline, Mass: Holy Cross Orthodox Press.
Luibheid, C. and Russell, N. trans. (1982), *John Climacus: The Ladder of Divine Ascent*. New York: Paulist Press.

KP

John Karastamatis (d. 1985) Greek Orthodox priest of Santa Cruz in California, credited with numerous miracles of healing since his death. He ministered to the unemployed, homeless and drug addicts of the city before being brutally killed by a couple with a history of mental illness. John Karastamatis is widely commemorated on 6 May, though his cult has not won universal support and illustrates the controversy that can arise over the precise boundaries of categories of sanctity.
   See also PASSION BEARERS.

Damascene (1991), 'Passion Bearer John of Santa Cruz', *Orthodox Word* 156.

DB

John Maximovitch (d. 1966) John was born in Adamovka, near Kharkov in Ukraine, in 1896. He studied in Poltava, then graduated in law at Kharkov University. In 1921, during the Russian Civil War, the Maximovitch family moved to Belgrade, where John studied theology and, in 1926, joined the Milkov monastery. Throughout this period he was associated with Antonii Khrapovitskii, metropolitan of the RUSSIAN ORTHODOX CHURCH ABROAD.

John was ordained priest but continued teaching at theological academies, in Belgrade and, after 1929, in Bitola, where he worked with NICOLAS VELIMIROVIC to reconcile the various Orthodox communities of MACEDONIA and to revive church life. John served the Greek community of the region. In 1934 he became bishop of Shanghai, undertaking extensive missionary work, struggling to unite divided Orthodox groups and reorganizing outreach charities. Known as John of Shanghai, he founded a major orphanage and learned Chinese to hold services for the host community.

John held his flock together through the Japanese occupation. After the Second World War he remained loyal to ROCA when the five other Russian bishops in China joined the Moscow patriarchate. In 1946 John became archbishop of China and weathered Chinese and Soviet pressure to resign until 1949, when he organized the evacuation of his entire flock to the Philippines. From here he arranged their immigration to the USA. From 1951 John governed the Western European archdiocese of ROCA. Based in Paris, then in Brussels, he sponsored missions to the host communities and supported establishment of Western rite Orthodoxy. Transferred to San Francisco in 1962, he sought to bring peace to a turbulent archdiocese and worked to root Orthodoxy in modern America. John died in Seattle. He is commemorated on 19 June.

Rose, S. and Herman (1987). *Archbishop John Maximovitch*. Platina, Cal.: St Herman of Alaska.

DB

John of Damascus (*c.* 665–749)   A Syrian or Arab MELKITE, John served in the administration of Caliph 'Abd al-Malik at Damascus before entering Mar Sabas monastery in Judea. In the first period of ICONOCLASM (726–87) he defended the veneration of icons against the iconoclast Emperor Leo III. His *Three Orations* in defence of icons remains the definitive ICONOPHILE statement on the veneration of images. In Syria his work was continued by his Sabaite fellow monk THEODORE ABŪ QURRAH (*c.* 740–820), who defended icon veneration in Arabic against both Muslim and Jewish attacks. John's work helped the iconophile victory at the Second Council of Nicea in 787, and influenced iconophiles of the second period of iconoclasm (815–45) such as THEODORE THE STUDITE and Patriarch NIKEPHOROS.

His three-volume *Fount of Knowledge* (*Pege gnoseos*) is an important work. Book one, the *Dialectica*, offers the most extensive collection of definitions of philosophical (mainly Aristotelian) terminology from his period. Book two is a compendium of heresies based on the works of EPIPHANIOS OF SALAMIS and others. Book three, *De Fide Orthodoxa*, attempts to systematize the Greek patristic tradition, especially on Christology. The book also makes use of contemporary science in its exposition of doctrine.

The situation in Syria/Palestine in the early eighth century was difficult for the MELKITE church. There was no Chalcedonian patriarch in JERUSALEM in the late seventh century, or in ANTIOCH in the early eighth century. Islamic rule sharpened divisions among Christian communities. The independent Syrian churches fared better than the Byzantine communities with their links with the Eastern empire. The *De Fide Orthodoxa* was most likely written to inform MELKITE communities of where they stood on questions of doctrine, supporting them in the face of both Islam and rival churches.

Parts of the *De Fide Orthodoxa* were translated into Arabic in the early tenth century and into Slavonic by John, exarch of BULGARIA, in the late ninth century. A Latin translation was begun by Burgundio of Pisa in 1148, and a further translation, along with the *Dialectica*, by Robert Grosseteste, bishop of Lincoln, in 1235. Thomas Aquinas (1224–74) cites John extensively.

John also wrote homilies and hymns and is credited with the OKTOECHOS. The *Sacra Parallela*, an extensive florilegium, is ascribed to him, and in the medieval period his

name became associated with the story of BARLAAM AND IOASAPH. The earliest refutation of Islam in Greek is attributed to him, and he is thought by some to have influenced the development of Muslim *kalām* (theological dialectic). John shows some knowledge of the Qur'an, although it is unclear in what form he had access to it. Later EASTERN ORTHODOX writers on Islam suffered from inaccuracies in the ninth-century Greek translation of the Qur'an. Niketas Byzantios in the late ninth century offers a systematic refutation quoting from thirty different suras by title and number, but using several of the faulty translations, such as the supposed spherical shape of God (Sura 112) or the leech as the origin of *homo sapiens* (Sura 96 speaks of 'a clot of blood'). These survived throughout the Byzantine era and did nothing to advance Christian–Muslim dialogue.

Parry, K. (1996), *Depicting the Word: Byzantine Iconophile Thought of the Eighth and Ninth Centuries*. Leiden: Brill.
Anderson, D., trans. (1980), *St John of Damascus: On the Divine Images*. Crestwood, NY: St Vladimir's Seminary Press.
Sahas, D. J. (1972), *John of Damascus on Islam: The 'Heresy of the Ishmaelites'*. Leiden: Brill.
Kotter, P. B. ed. (1969–88), *Die Schriften des Johannes von Damaskos*, 5 vols. Berlin: de Gruyter.
Khoury, A.-T. (1969), *Les Théologiens Byzantins et L'Islam: textes et auteurs (VIIIe– XIIIe siècle)*. Louvain: Editions Nauwelaerts.
Chase, F. H., trans. (1958), *Saint John of Damascus, Writings*. Washington, DC: Catholic University of America Press.
Nasrallah, J. (1950), *Saint Jean de Damas. Son époque, sa vie, son oeuvre*. Paris: Office des Editions Universitaires.

KP

John of Damascus, as hymnographer Like his foster brother, Cosmas of Maiuma, John composed canons for most of the principal feasts of the Lord: Nativity,

Theophany, Pentecost, Ascension, Annunciation, Pascha, Thomas Sunday and Transfiguration. The first three of these are composed in classical iambic trimeters, with elaborate acrostics which themselves form elegaic couplets. He also wrote canons for the Nativity and Dormition of the Mother of God and for important saints' days, such as the Nativity of the Baptist and the feast of Peter and Paul. He is often credited with the OKTOECHOS (*see also* PARAKLETIKE), but many other poets also contributed to this and current editions attribute to him by name only the Sunday Resurrection canons.

He also wrote the idiomela in the eight tones of the Byzantine rite funeral service as well as numerous stichera and doxastika for feasts of saints. Many compositions traditionally regarded as his are attributed simply to 'John the Monk'; the iambic canon for Pentecost is attributed to *Kyriou Ioannou tou Arkla*, the meaning of which is unclear (it is discussed by Monk Bartholomew, editor of the current edition of the Greek PENTEKOSTARION), and his authorship has been questioned by, among others, Mark Eugenikos. A number of the compositions attributed to him in the service books may not be authentic.

E

John the Baptist   The Forerunner (Greek: *Prodromos*). In the icon John is depicted wearing a *himation* (cloak) over a fleece (Greek: *melote*) or camel's hair garment (Matthew 3: 4). This is an allusion to 4 Kingdoms 2: 8–13/2 Kings 2: 8–13, where ELIAS divides Jordan with his *melote*, and where the *melote* he drops as he ascends in the fiery chariot is taken up by Elisaeus. The *melote* proclaims John a second Elias, both as prophet and Forerunner of the Messiah and in his ascetic, prayerful life, whereby, like Elias, he is the type of Christian monasticism. The *melote* became part of early monastic attire, just as did the skin or leather belt also mentioned in Matthew 3: 4. (*See also* THEOPHANY.)

The rocky background indicates his life in the wilderness, while his unkempt hair and beard show his asceticism. His head appears in a dish as a sign of his martyrdom.

From about the thirteenth century, icons of the Forerunner begin to represent him with wings. This detail recalls Matthew 11: 10, which speaks of John as a 'messenger' (Greek: *angelos*) preparing the way for the Messiah. It also signifies his ascetic, 'angelic' life. His face is turned towards Christ, who appears out of the open heavens to bless him. John holds a cross and a scroll on which is written: 'Behold the Lamb of God which takes away the sins of the world' (John 1: 29). Canon 82 of the QUINISEXT COUNCIL of 692 specifically forbade the image of the Forerunner pointing to a symbolic lamb, requiring the depiction of Christ in his humanity. The bush and the axe customarily depicted in the icon refer to his preaching of repentance (Matthew 3:10; Luke 3: 9).

The conception of John is celebrated on 23 September, his nativity on 24 June, his beheading on 29 August, the first and second finding of his skull on

24 February and the third finding on 25 May, and the Feast of the Baptist is observed on 7 January.

Corrigan, K. (1988), 'The Witness of John the Baptist on an Early Byzantine icon in Kiev', *Dumbarton Oaks Papers* 42, pp. 1–11.
Sdrakas, E. D. (1943), *Johannes der Täufer in der Kunst des christlichen Ostens*. Munich: n.p.

KP

John the Faster John IV, patriarch of Constantinople (582–95), austere opponent of heretics, whose use of the title ECUMENICAL PATRIARCH was misread by Popes Pelagius II (579–90) and Gregory I (590–604) as a claim to universal jurisdiction, winning from Gregory the famous rebuke that there existed no universal bishop, and that he himself was merely the Servant of the Servants of God, a title still used by the pope of ROME.

Thirty-five canons attributed to John IV are preserved in the *Pedalion* and other EASTERN ORTHODOX books of canon law. They adapt the canonical tradition to the needs of the penitent's spiritual welfare by permitting reductions in the periods of deprivation of the eucharist imposed on penitents guilty of a variety of transgressions. The reduced period involves fasting and many prostrations: refusal to fast or perform the required prostrations invokes the full original penalty.

DM

John the Russian (d. 1730) Patron saint of the KARAMANLIS and other Greeks of Cappadocia. John, a Ukrainian, was enslaved by the OTTOMANS in the wars with Russia. He remained a Christian though serving a prominent Muslim of Ürgüp (Prokopion). John's asceticism won the respect of Turks and Greeks alike: his tomb became a centre for pilgrimage, first in Cappadocia and from 1924, after the exchanges of population and the removal of his relics to Greece, at Neon Prokopion in Euboia. He is commemorated on 27 May.

See also ASIA MINOR.

Vernezis, I. (1988), *Hosios Ioannes o Rossos*. Athens: n.p.

DB

John the Theologian John the Divine (Greek: *ho theologos*), is identified in tradition with the beloved disciple and the author of the fourth gospel and the Apocalypse. He appears with Peter and James in the New Testament as one of an inner triad of the apostles who are the witnesses to the TRANSFIGURATION and to the agony of Christ in Gethsemane. John is often depicted at the foot of the CROSS with Mary, as Jesus makes him her adopted son. He is said to have lived with her in Ephesus, surviving to a great age. His title, Theologian, which he shares with Gregory of Nazianzus (*see* CAPPADOCIANS) and SYMEON THE NEW, reflects the spiritual and mystical content of his gospel, read in the Byzantine rite during the period of PENTECOST, its opening verses at the Divine Liturgy of PASCHA.

In the icon illustrated, the evangelist is shown standing outside a cave on the island of Patmos where its author (Apocalypse 1: 9) says he wrote the work. His disciple Prochoros sits at the cave's mouth, writing at John's dictation. The gesture of discourse he is making towards Prochoros shows that John is passing on to him what the voice from heaven is revealing.

KP

John Vladimir (d. 1015)   Serbian prince of the royal house of Zahumlje, claimed as a patron by Albanians, Greeks, VLACHS and others. John Vladimir was famed for his prayer, fasting and almsgiving. He opposed the BOGOMILS and fought to maintain the unity of his realm. Defeated and imprisoned by Tsar Samuel of BULGARIA, his unworldliness so impressed Samuel that he was released and married to the tsar's daughter, Kosara. He was later captured and killed by Tsar Radislav. John Vladimir was buried in a monastery he had founded near Elbasan (Albanopolis). The incorrupt relics of this PASSION BEARER drew pilgrims from across the Balkans. He is commemorated on 22 May.

Rogich, D. (1995), *Serbian Patericon*, vol. 2. Forestville, Cal.: St Paisius Abbey.

DB

Jonas Pokrovsky (d. 1925)   Jonas, born 1888, was orphaned as a child. He studied in his native Kaluga and in Kazan. While studying theology he joined the OPTINA monastery, but continued to live in Kazan, where he became a popular preacher, and taught as professor of the New Testament. The Bolsheviks exiled Jonas from Kazan; he was rearrested and tortured in Perm but escaped to Omsk and joined a remnant of the White army as military chaplain, trekking across deserts and the Pamirs with the forces of Ataman Dutov, finally crossing into China. The RUSSIAN ORTHODOX CHURCH ABROAD consecrated Jonas bishop of Hankow and sent him to Manchouli in 1922. In Manchuria he worked to help the thousands of Russian refugees, supervising soup kitchens, clinics and schools and running an orphanage. Jonas was respected by both Chinese and Soviets. He taught at Harbin Polytechnic till he died. Revered as a wonder-worker, he is commemorated on 7 October.

See also CHINESE ORTHODOX CHURCH.

'Saint Jonas' (1996), *Orthodox Life* 46/5. Jordanville, NY.

DB

Joseph Gerontoyiannis (1799–1874)   Cretan elder and visionary. A married man with children, Joseph received a number of visions from April 1841 and retired to the Kapsa monastery. Joseph travelled around his native Crete and other islands, preaching and praying, flouting OTTOMAN prohibitions and often opposed by the more privileged clergy. Joseph Gerontoyiannis attracted numerous disciples and refounded the Armenous monastery. He is commemorated on 6 August.

Psilakis, N. (1986), *The Monasteries of Crete*. Athens: Bank of Crete.

DB

Joshua the Stylite   Joshua is traditionally credited with authorship of a SYRIAC Chronicle incorporated into the *Zuqnīn Chronicle* (*see* DIONYSIUS OF TELL MAḤRĒ) and covering 495–507. It was composed as the period ended, and the author appears to have been a monk from EDESSA, who wrote at the request of his abbot, Sergius. It is particularly valuable for its description of the Byzantine–Sasanian war of 502–5 and of the hardships suffered by the people of Edessa and Amida at that time. The ascription of the text to Joshua is the result of confusion.

Palmer, A. (1990), 'Who Wrote the Chronicle of Joshua the Stylite?' in R. Schultz, ed., *Lingua restituta orientale*, pp. 272–84. Wiesbaden: Harrassowitz.

JH

Justiniana Prima   Justinian (d. 565) founded this city close to his home town, Tauresion, in Dardania to replace Dardania (Vranje) as regional capital and to be the centre for the Haimos provinces. The archbishop of the city presided over an autonomous exarchate (from 535), carved from regions previously under ROME. The city was sacked by Avars and Slavs in the early seventh century. Ruins at Caričin Grad near Niš (Naissos) in Serbia have been identified as Justiniana Prima, though speculation continues that Lychnidos (OHRID) may be a possible location.
   See also MACEDONIA.

DB

Justin Popović (1894–1979)   Disciple of NICOLAS VELIMIROVIĆ and his partner in numerous projects. Originally from Vranje, he studied at St Sava Seminary in Belgrade. Justin made his monastic profession in 1916 while working as a nurse during the First World War. Like his mentor, he continued publishing, teaching and further studies, which took him to Russia, Britain and Greece in 1919. Returning to Karlovac in Yugoslavia in 1921 and ordained to the priesthood in 1922, Justin worked with both JOHN MAXIMOVITCH and Antonii Khrapovitskii of the RUSSIAN ORTHODOX CHURCH ABROAD. Justin led an Orthodox mission to RUTHENIA in 1931. Ousted from the university by the communists, he continued to write and translate. Justin moved between several monasteries before settling in Chelije in 1948. He is commemorated on 25 March.

DB

Rogich, D. (1994), *Serbian Patericon*. Forestville, Cal.: St Paisios.

Juvenaly of Alaska (d. 1796)   EASTERN ORTHODOX protomartyr and patron saint of AMERICA. A monk of VALAAM monastery from 1791, Juvenaly joined the Russian Orthodox church mission to ALASKA, working among the native Americans beyond the Russian outposts. He was killed by the Yupik Eskimos near the mouth of the Kuskokwim river at the instigation of a local shaman. Juvenaly is commemorated on 2 July.

DB

· K ·

Kali (Kale)   Manuel Philes (fourteenth century) refers to the relics of St Kali. This may be Kali of Lesbos, commemorated with her daughter Thomais (early tenth century) (*see* MARIA OF BIZYE).

Kyra Kali, the Good Lady, is an important figure in Greek folklore. This Kali, however, represents the unsubdued forces of nature, and seems to derive from the huntress goddess Artemis, one of whose titles was Kalliste, Most Beautiful. Lawson, writing in 1910, records that in Aitolia her name was Kyra Kálo, but that in Athens 'until recently' she was known as Hagia Kali, 'to whom no church was ever dedicated'. St Kore or Korina, revered in northern Greece, may similarly have merged with the folk memory of Persephone or another ancient deity.

Gedeon, M. (1984), *Hagiopoieseis*. Thessaloniki: n.p.
Lawson, J. C. (1910), *Modern Greek Folklore and Ancient Greek Religion: A Study in Survivals*. Cambridge: Cambridge University Press.

DB

kalymauchion   Also in monastic language *skoupho*, or 'bonnet': the familiar 'stove-pipe' hat of Byzantine rite clergy. Those of Greek secular clergy have a brim on top. Monks wear a cowl (Greek: *koukoullion*, from Latin *cucullus*) over their *skoupho*. When worn by celibate secular clergy it is called *epanokalymauchion* or 'over-kalymauchion'. The Russian cowl is permanently attached to the *skoupho*, and the whole is called a *klobuk*; the Greek cowl can be removed separately. Russian, but not Greek, nuns wear a *klobuk* quite similar to that of a monk.

See also RELIGIOUS DRESS.

E

kappa   Ge'ez: *kāppā*. Originally a hooded outer vestment worn by Ethiopian priests. In later times the garment became longer and its hood was discarded.

See also ETHIOPIAN ORTHODOX CHURCH; RELIGIOUS DRESS.

Leslau, W. (1987), *Comparative Dictionary of Ge'ez (Classical Ethiopic) Ge'ez–English/ English–Ge'ez, with an Index of the Semitic Roots*, pp. 288–9. Wiesbaden: Harrassowitz.
Hammerschmidt, E. (1970), 'The Liturgical Vestments of the Ethiopian Church', in Institute of Ethiopian Studies of the Haile Selassie I University, *Proceedings of the Third International Conference of Ethiopian Studies, Addis Ababa, 1966*, 3 vols, vol. 2, pp. 151–6. Addis Ababa: Artistic Printers.

MJB/SHG

Karamanlis   Inhabitants of central and south central ASIA MINOR, regions encompassed by the historical emirate of Karaman established by the Turkmen Karaman-Bey (*c*.1243) in the once Byzantine dioceses or provinces of Lycaonia, Phrygia, Pamphylia, Cappadocia, southern Galatia and western Cilicia. The emirate was allowed political autonomy for a while after the OTTOMAN conquest of these regions in the 1420s. Apart from the important Turkish-speaking Christian population which will be described here, Christian presence continued in this area among speakers of Greek, Armenian, Aramaic and, in southern regions, Arabic.

The Turkish-speaking EASTERN ORTHODOX Karamanlis may originally have been Greeks (Romaioi) who assimilated Turkish language and customs, and/or originally Turkic tribes who settled here before Islamicization and became Christians. Whatever their origins, their substantial presence was an integral part of the patriarchate of Constantinople in Asia Minor during the Ottoman empire. This is evident particularly from their literature, published in many centres including CONSTANTINOPLE, Ioannina, VENICE, Athens, Amsterdam, Basel, Leipzig, Vienna and London.

The Turkish of the Christian Karamanlis is written in the Greek alphabet. In Greek it is called Karamanlidika, in Turkish, Karamanlıca. The first text known to have been composed in Turkish and written in the Greek alphabet is the translation of an exposition of faith by GENNADIOS II SCHOLARIOS for Sultan Mehmet II (1455–6). Although the text's author was not from the Karamanli community, after its publication (1584) and reprint (1816) it evidently became appropriated for their use.

The entire Bible in Karamanlidika was printed in parts by the press of the ECUMENICAL PATRIARCHATE, beginning in 1764, with numerous reprintings. For example, in 1764 the psalter was published in Karamanlidika with intercolumnar Septuagint Greek, and then reprinted in a series of five further editions from 1782 to the turn of the twentieth century. A wide range of liturgical books was published, including the *Paraclisis to the Theotokos* (1756), as well as services for various saints such as that of St JOHN THE RUSSIAN of Prokopion in Cappadocia (1849).

Patristic translations published by the patriarchate include: Clement of Ankara (1776); MAXIMUS THE CONFESSOR (1799); JOHN THE FASTER (1799); ATHANASIUS, EPHREM, SYMEON THE NEW THEOLOGIAN (all 1815); JOHN CHRYSOSTOM (1815, 1820); and the dialogue attributed to Grigentius of 'Greater Arabia' and Ethiopia (1800; 2nd edn 1844). The last was translated initially from Greek in Caesarea, then revised by Metropolitan Seraphim of Ankara for the second edition, published by patronage from a layman of Caesarea. Seraphim had earlier been an ARCHIMANDRITE of the Monastery of Kykkos on CYPRUS, which supported translations of other texts into Karamanlidika.

Numerous expositions of faith were published from 1753, one in the Greek vernacular as well as in Karamanlidika (1817). Other works published include *Neos Thesauros* (1756); *Pilgrimage to Sinai* (1784); *Pilgrimage to Jerusalem* (1799); *Exomologitarion* (1785); *Pilgrimage to Athos* (1806); *Lausaikon* (1806); *Synaxarion* (1st edn 1818).

Other Karamanlidika publications include popular Turkish proverbs compiled with a commentary (mid-eighteenth century); primary school books; Turkish–Greek dictionaries; Turkish grammar books, for instance *Elements of Ottoman Grammar*, as written by Constantine Adosidi, a member of the Bureau of Translators of the Sublime Porte, published by the Ottoman imperial press (1850); a *History of the Ottoman Empire* by N. Th. Sullides (1874); an Ottoman encyclopedia (1876); extracts from foreign philosophies, as permitted by the Sublime Porte's Inspector of the Foreign Press (1846); and even *The Count of Monte Cristo* by Alexandre Dumas, authorized by the Sublime Porte's Ministry of Education in a translation by Stavros D. Teryakoglou (1882). Original novels were also written in Karamanlidika.

From the 1870s American Protestant missionaries, seeking converts among the Christians of Asia Minor, produced in London alternative translations of the Bible into Karamanlidika which competed with the patriarchate's authorized version. Already by 1876, a refutation directed against these missionaries' activities was written and published in Karamanlidika by Hadji Stephanos Ioannou of Ürgüp.

During the first decades of the twentieth century Karamanli emigrants founded at least one Orthodox parish in the USA, in Connecticut. In 1922–3, during the 'exchange of populations', the Christian Karamanlis were expelled wholesale from Asia Minor along with other Orthodox belonging to the patriarchate of Constantinople. Those who survived to reach Greece established Karamanlidika newspapers which lasted among the refugees of the first generation. Their descendants integrated successfully, though they retain their identity and customs to the present day, expressed particularly through fraternal organizations and occasional gatherings in modern Greece.

Kitromilides, P. M. and Alexandris, A. (1984–5), *Ethnic Survival, Nationalism and Forced Migration: Historical Demography of the Greek Community of Asia Minor at the Close of the Ottoman Era.* Athens: Centre for Asia Minor Studies.
Salaville, S. and Dalleggio, E. (1958–74), *Karamanlidika: Bibliographie analytique des ouvrages en langue turque imprimés en caractères grecs*, 3 vols. Athens: Philologikos Syllogos 'Parnassos'.

SM

Karshūnī Var. Garšūnī. When Arabic became the dominant language of the Fertile Crescent, which had been largely a Syriac-/Aramaic-speaking area, scribes sometimes used the SYRIAC script to write Arabic texts. This kind of writing is called Karshūnī. Diacritical points could be added to represent those consonants which occur in Arabic but not in Syriac. There are many parallels to this, including the writing of Arabic with the Hebrew script, and Turkish manuscripts which use the Syriac script. There is no plausible explanation of the origins of the term Karshūnī, which varies considerably in pronunciation and spelling.

JH

Kassia   Or Kassiane: ninth-century noble Byzantine hymnographer and poet. One of her hymns on the penitent woman is sung at HESPERINOS and ORTHROS on Holy Wednesday, another is the DOXASTIKON for Vespers of the Nativity. She wrote secular verses as well as hymns and is considered the most important woman poet of the Byzantine period.

Born about 808 in CONSTANTINOPLE and highly educated, while a teenager she corresponded with THEODORE THE STUDITE and sought his permission to become a nun, but Theodore advised her to wait until the ICONOCLAST persecution ended. In 830 she was selected to appear in the bride show for Emperor Theophilus (829–42), who is reported to have said to her: 'Woman is the source of all evil.' Kassia replied: 'And woman is the fount of the better,' referring to the THEOTOKOS, answering his catch question with a theological rebuke; her impudence led him to reject her. Some time afterwards she became a nun, and in 843 founded her own monastery in Constantinople. She died probably c.865. She is commemorated on 7 September.

Tripolitis, A. (1992), *Kassia the Legend, the Woman and Her Work*. New York: Garland.

KP

katanyxis   Greek, 'compunction'. When a person repents, a spiritual awakening occurs involving a realization both of wrong done, and of God's love and healing forgiveness. Experienced intensely, repentance arouses the feeling of compunction. The music and poetry of the penitential offices express *katanyxis*.

In the PARAKLETIKE for Monday and Tuesday in the eight tones, the first three Prosomia at Vespers, the KATHISMATA at Matins and the first two STICHERA of the APOSTICHA at both Vespers and Matins are described *katanyktika*.

DM/E

katavasia   Greek: *katabasia*. Final troparion of an ODE of a CANON, so called because the singers used to descend (Greek: *katabainein*) from their stalls and unite in the middle of the choir to sing them. Sundays and major feasts have one after every ode. They are often seasonal, anticipating the next great feast. Thus the katavasias of Christmas are sung from 21 November onwards. On non-festal days they occur after the third, sixth, eighth and ninth odes only.

E

Kathisma   Greek, 'seat'. (1) One of the twenty parts into which the psalter is divided for liturgical purposes. Each Kathisma is divided into three sections (Greek: *staseis*). (2) Short hymns sung after the reading of each Kathisma at Matins and after the third ODE of the CANON. (3) A small hermitage.

E/DM

Kebra Nagast   *Kibre Neġeśt* (Glory of the Kings) has been called the masterpiece of GEʿEZ literature. Compiled by one Yeshaq of Axum in the early fourteenth century from Copto-Arabic sources, it uses a variety of Christian biblical and apocryphal literature, as well as Jewish and Islamic sources, to tell the story of Solomon and the Queen of Sheba and Menelik, their son, who took the Ark of the Covenant from

JERUSALEM to Axum in Ethiopia. Thus Axum became the new Jerusalem, and the Ethiopian nation the new chosen people of God. The *Kebra Nagast* helped to legitimize the 1270 restoration of the Solomonic dynasty in Ethiopia.

Johnson, D. W. (1995), 'The Kebra Nagast: Another Look', in T. S. Miller and J. Nesbitt, eds, *Peace and War in Byzantium: Essays in Honor of George T. Dennis*, pp. 197–208. Washington DC: Catholic University of America Press. Shahid, I. (1976), 'The *Kebra Nagast* in the Light of Recent Research', *Le Muséon* 89, pp. 133–78. Budge, E. A. W. (1932), *The Queen of Sheba and her Only Son Menyelek (I), being the 'Book of the Glory of Kings' (Kebra Nagast) . . . Translated from the Ethiopic*, 2nd edn. Oxford: Oxford University Press.

MJB/SHG

Keratea   A number of monasteries, convents and sketes in the Keratea region of Attica form the heart of the OLD CALENDARIST movement in Greece; the most important is the Skepi monastery, founded in 1950 to house the seventeenth-century Unfading Rose icon.

Tsiakos, T. and Sakellaropoulos, S. (1995), *Monasteria tes Attikes*. Athens: n.p.

DB

khatchkar   Armenian name for monumental stone crosses found throughout medieval ARMENIA. Cross-topped stone obelisks are found from the fifth to seventh centuries. From the ninth century stone crosses, *khatchkars*, replace the obelisks. A regular feature of *khatchkars* is the use of the leaved-cross combined with geometrical and botanical patterns, some of which appear to reflect carpet designs. They were used as boundary markers, gravestones, monuments to military victories and foundation-markers of churches. They were also inserted into the exterior fabric of church buildings and carved from living rock.

See also CROSS.

Azarian, L. (1978), *Armenian Khatchkars*. Etchmiadzin: Holy See.

KP

Khomiakov, Alexei (1804–60)   Russian philosopher, theologian and poet. The breadth of his interests may be partly to blame for his never producing a book. Most of his writings, in the form of articles, essays and preliminary drafts, were published after his death; he contracted cholera treating his peasants during an epidemic. Despite the fragmentary nature of his work, his writings manifest the unity of his thought and he rightly shares with Ivan Kireevskii (1806–56) and Petr Chaadaev (1749–1856) the reputation of establishing a tradition of RUSSIAN RELIGIOUS PHILOSOPHY.

Khomiakov was a truly Christian philosopher; the whole of his work centred on the life of the church. He found his main inspiration in the BIBLE and the church fathers. It is difficult to single out a specific influence on him, since he absorbed not simply the letter, but the very spirit of the Christian tradition. He himself always insisted that the authorship of particular texts is less important that the fact that the

Holy Spirit, manifesting itself in the united voice of the church, calls those works its own.

Khomiakov thought philosophy should articulate the real experience of people. He criticized contemporary Western philosophy for excessive rationalism, for refusing to see faith as the fundamental source of humanity's understanding of the world. He expressed deep admiration for Plato: PLATONISM was one of the sources of Christian teaching, Khomiakov's own thought belonging to that tradition. He confronted the view which saw as inevitable the conflict between faith and reason. For him only reason based on faith, what he sometimes calls living knowledge or intuition, is real: reason separated from faith becomes impotent. To talk about these two different kinds of reason Khomiakov uses the distinction which exists in the Russian language between *rasum* and *rassudok*, which can be rendered into English respectively as spirit, divine-like intellect (cf. Greek *nous*), and the calculating, judgmental faculty. (*Rasum* in the Slavonic New Testament translates the Greek *gnosis*.)

Khomiakov established the truly Russian tradition of philosophy, which finds its basis in the concrete and integral life of the spirit, not in abstract logic or alienated intellect, and concerns itself with the search not for propositional truth, but for the Truth which is the life and the way.

It would be very difficult to find a borderline separating Khomiakov's philosophy from his theology: neither is a system of propositions, concerning different subjects; both are part of the same free search for the truth of humanity's existence in God's world. He believed philosophy prepared the Greeks for Christ as the Old Testament prepared the Jews.

The central issue for Khomiakov's understanding of humanity's relation to God is the church. But Khomiakov's teaching on the church is not what is usually referred to as ecclesiology. Just as he criticized talk about religion instead of faith, he was unwilling to talk about Christianity, but spoke rather about the living church, which binds all Christians of the past, the present and the future into one and makes them partakers in the divine life. Though expressed with characteristic simplicity and sobriety, Khomiakov's writings convey a prophetic vision of the church as Body of Christ, neither a doctrine, nor a system of ecclesiastical government, nor an institution. It is for him the one primary reality, leading humankind to its divine source: the experience of the new world to come, in which humanity will be restored to harmony with the creator, and recover mutual fellowship.

The important feature of the church is for Khomiakov a combination of freedom and unity. He salvages the idea of freedom from the programme of secular humanism, proclaiming that only in Christ can human beings find true freedom, only in spiritual unity with their fellows can they find their true nature. He is the faithful heir of MAXIMUS THE CONFESSOR when he asserts that humanity is 'free because it was the desire of God, and because Christ conquered freedom for us by the freedom of his sacrifice'.

Freedom and unity are the two forces deemed worthy of being the guardians of the mystery of man's relation to the God, who saves and justifies his creature through his complete unity with it. The fruit of these forces, by the grace of God, is not the 'knowledge found by analysis, but the perfection and the vision of God, called faith, which is by its very essence not to be penetrated by non-belief'.

The church can combine unity and freedom because it is based on love. In his spiritual, inner and mystical understanding Khomiakov could say that the church is the revelation of the Holy Spirit given to the mutual love of Christians. So love is also the condition of that knowledge which is the 'gift from above which alone can secure the unconditional knowledge of Truth'. He drew attention again and again to the Divine Liturgy, to the words with which the church calls to her people: 'Let us love each other that we may with one accord confess the Father, the Son and the Holy Ghost.'

The vision of the church as a free and selfless unity led Khomiakov to combat all attempts to describe it as 'authority', for, he says, authority is something external to its subjects. The church is not an authority, in the same way as neither God nor Christ is an authority: 'She is truth and life, inner life of a Christian, more intimate than the blood in his veins.'

He also criticized the idea that the church can be divided into two parts: the one that teaches, the clergy, and those taught, the laity. The truth is given in mutual love, and every Christian is a teacher for his or her brothers and sisters. The true church is not a teaching church, but is a witness to the mystery of Christ. The church's true Orthodoxy depends on no other power than the 'willing response of Christians to the guidance of the Holy Spirit'. Infallibility cannot be found in any individual, however saintly, but only in the catholicity of the church, *sobornost* in the Russian translation of the Nicene Creed, its ability to bring all people together in *homonoia*, to unite them in One. The invincible truth of dogma and the immutable certainty of the ritual do not depend on the hierarchs of the church; they are preserved by the 'whole of the people composing the Church which is the Body of Christ'.

Khomiakov could express the experience of the Orthodox church with both freedom and conviction because he was grounded in the spiritual reality of the creative tradition, which for him was not merely texts or rituals, but rather the stream of the life-giving Spirit, the spirit which creates and transfigures life. 'The Church inherits from the Apostles not words, but the treasure of inner life, spiritual treasures, inexpressible, but ever struggling to express themselves'. He expressed disappointment that the fathers are often seen merely as ecclesiastical legislators and not as men of profound and mystical vision. He refused to see the source of faith in the written tradition alone; Christianity can only be properly understood as a unity of scripture, tradition and action, all rooted in faith. These parts are dead if separated from each other and all equally have their origins in the church as a community of believers. The scriptures are not simply the written word, but the inner thought of the community, outward signs of inner faith. It is not possible to understand the Bible in its full significance unless one has direct experience of this inner life.

Catholic tradition is ever growing and rejuvenated, yet constant and unchangeable. He saw the development of doctrine as an expression of the desire to proclaim the divine Truth, constantly contemplated and appropriated. The Truth itself remains unchanging – 'all the mysteries of Faith were revealed to the Church of Christ from the beginning' – but the expression of them is, of its nature, never sufficient, always depending on the language and habits of the period.

Khomiakov belongs to the tradition of APOPHATIC THEOLOGY, claiming that God and the divine are not expressible: the human word cannot define or describe them; reason, at best, deals only with analogies of the divine.

His critique of the Western churches was based on a profound sense of the unity of the church and its ever rejuvenated tradition, not on humanistic individualism. He explained the schism between East and West not as a question of doctrinal difference, though he offers a doctrinal argument as well, nor simply as a consequence of personal ambition or political expediency, though he does not deny their role, but as a moral failure, a violation of the principle of brotherhood and love. The Orthodox church has a mission to preserve the gifts of Christianity not only for itself, but for the whole of Christendom. He does not spare the Orthodox church in his criticism, for, though it is the true church, it does not yet fulfil its mission. He was not afraid to criticize the church: for him, failure to do so is a sign of the sin of not believing in the victory of divine Truth.

In his study of history, Khomiakov presented faith as the most important principle of historical movement in different societies. Modern historical science, he writes, can only present us with a stream of unconnected events, barely sewn together by the thread of determinacy. He insists that history has no meaning unless understood as the spiritual struggle of humanity in its encounter with God. The main idea of his *Essays on World History* is the existence and the mutual struggle of two religious principles: one is the religion of necessity, the power of nature and magic; the other is the religion of freedom, creative spirit. And although all actual religious forms contains a mixture of these elements, they possess them to different degrees. Christianity was for him the culmination of the religion of freedom and creative spirit.

The church alone gives salvation to humanity, but not in a sense that only the person who belongs to the visible church will be saved, for the links of the church to the rest of humanity are too intimate and mysterious for us to judge. If it is only in Christ and in the love of Christ that we can find the way, then surely that is not confined to the historical events of Jesus' life.

O'Leary, P. P. (1982), *The Triune Church: A Study in the Ecclesiology of A. S. Xomjakov*. Dublin: Dominican Publications.
Komiakoff, A. (1969 [1895]), 'The Church is One', repr. in W. J. Birkbeck, ed., *Russia and the English Church during the Last Fifty Years*, vol. 1, *Containing a Correspondence between William Palmer and A. Khomiakoff*. London: Gregg International Publishers.
Komiakov, A. (1965), 'Recent Developments in Philosophy (Letter to Y. Samarin)' repr. in J. M. Edie et al., eds, *Russian Philosophy*, vol. 1. Chicago: Quadrangle Books.
Christoff, P. K. (1961), *An Introduction to Nineteenth Century Slavophilism*, vol. 1: *Xomjakov*. The Hague: Mouton.
Riasanovsky, N. (1955), 'Khomiakov on Sobornost', in E. J. Simmons, ed., *Continuity and Change in Russian and Soviet Thought*. Cambridge, Mass.: Harvard University Press.
Gratieux, A. (1953), *A. S. Khomiakov et le mouvement slavophile*, 2 vols. Paris: Editions du Seuf.
Zenkovsky, V. V. (1953), *History of Russian Philosophy*. London and New York: Routledge & Kegan Paul.
Bolshakoff, S. (1946), *The Doctrine of the Unity of the Church in the Works of Khomiakov and Moehler*. London: SPCK.

Zernov, Nicolas (1944), *Three Russian Prophets: Khomiakov, Dostoevsky, Soloviev.* London: SCM Press.

MV

Kiev, Kyiv Capital of UKRAINE, whose prince Vladimir or Volodymyr was converted to Byzantine Christianity in 988. The centre of Christianity in ancient Rus, it is said to have had over 400 churches in the early eleventh century. The earliest churches were wooden and therefore vulnerable to fire. Vladimir's son Jaroslav, brother of saints Boris and Gleb (*see* PASSION BEARERS), built the cathedral of DIVINE WISDOM (Hagia Sophia) in 1040, and appointed ILARION, the first indigenous metropolitan of Kiev, in 1051. The present church has nine aisles; the original building had five aisles and thirteen cupolas, symbolizing Christ and the apostles. Despite Byzantine architectural influence, no five-aisled churches survive outside the Holy Land, and no thirteen-domed churches anywhere in the Byzantine world. The cathedral was repaired by Peter MOGILA in the seventeenth century, but in the baroque style. The cathedral of the DORMITION in the Monastery of the Caves, Pecherskaya Lavra, was completed in 1078, reconstructed in the eighteenth century and almost totally destroyed in the Second World War. Pecherskaya Lavra, the most prestigious monastery of the pre-Mongol period, adopted the Studite TYPIKON; it produced many leading scholars and clerics. According to its *paterikon* the monastery was founded by Antony and Theodosius *c.*1051. It encompasses a system of caves, connected by tunnels. Many ascetics lived in the caves and are buried there.

North of Kiev lies the town of Chernigov. Its TRANSFIGURATION cathedral, Spaso-Preobrazhenskii Sobor, founded in 1017, was rebuilt in the seventeenth century and almost destroyed in the Second World War. Also in Chernigov is the late twelfth-century church of St Paraskeva Piatnitsa.

Throughout the tsarist period Kiev remained a significant centre of Orthodox learning and culture and developed its own style of ecclesiastical music. Its role has increased in the post-Soviet era, with the independence of Ukraine. It is now the seat of the heads of at least three Orthodox churches.

Franklin, S. and Shepard, J. (1996), *The Emergence of Rus 750–1200.* London: Longman.
Fennell, J. (1995), *A History of the Russian Church to 1448.* London: Longman.
Rappoport, P. (1995), *Building the Churches of Kievan Russia.* Aldershot: Variorum.

KP

kollyba/kollyva A dish prepared for memorial services or celebration of a feast, kollyva originates in pre-Christian Greek rites of Demeter and Persephone. It takes three forms. (1) *Pikrokollyva*, 'bitter' kollyva: plain boiled wheat brought to the grave during the funeral service and cast into or left on the grave. (2) Memorial kollyva, usually a mixture of boiled wheat, pomegranate seeds, raisins, almonds and sometimes sweets of other kinds, often decorated with white icing sugar and silver dragees in the form a CROSS, or with dried fruits or powdered spices. Some places make kollyva from baked flour, and in some memorial kollyva is unsweetened. It is blessed at the memorial service (*mnemosynon*) and distributed, with blessed bread. (3) Festal kollyva, always sweetened, and often elaborately decorated with fruits, nuts or coloured sugar. In monasteries kollyva with ICONS of powdered coloured sugar is blessed at the end of the liturgy, the icon broken by tracing a cross with a wooden spoon, and the kollyva eaten at the end of the festal meal. In Slav churches rice is sometimes used instead of wheat.

In earlier times small loaves or cakes, sometimes in human form, were distributed in memory of the dead. These seem sometimes to have been called kollyva, sometimes kollyris. Idolatrous use of such cakes in worship of the THEOTOKOS was the mark of the heretical Kollyridians, a fourth-century sect of women.

DM/KP/E

Kollyvades   Eighteenth-century monks from ATHOS whose name derives from their insistence that memorial services at which KOLLYBA is blessed should be held on Saturday not Sunday. They led a major spiritual revival, placing particular emphasis on frequent communion. They included Makarios of Corinth and NIKODEMOS THE HAGIORITE, compilers of the PHILOKALIA.

See also KOSMAS PHLAMIATOS.

KP

kontakion   Originally a verse sermon consisting of a proemium followed by a series of longer stanzas, or *oikoi*, all ending with the same phrase, like a refrain. The kontakion is related to the SYRIAC *mēmrā*. The CANON gradually displaced the kontakion; in modern Byzantine rite offices only the proemium, now called the kontakion, and the first oikos survive. In Greek use they are read at Matins, except on great feasts. In Russian use the kontakion is normally sung at Matins on Sundays. The kontakion is also read at the Hours and sung at the liturgy, though in Greek use those at the liturgy are 'seasonal', like the KATAVASIAS.

Lash, E., trans. (1995), *On the Life of Christ, Kontakia by Romanos the Melodist*. London and New York: HarperCollins.

E

Korean Orthodox church   Christian missions were active in Korea from the fourteenth century; an Orthodox presence was established in the late nineteenth century. Russian consuls Shuilskii and Boriaskii acquired land for an Orthodox church in Seoul in 1897 and in Russia an Orthodox mission was organized, though Korean authorities prevented the entry of Russian Orthodox missionaries until 1900, when Chrysanth Shchetkovskii (1869–1906) founded a church for expatriates in Seoul. A graduate of Kazan Theological Academy, Chrysanth had been appointed head of the mission the preceding year. He organized parishes and schools and initiated translation of liturgical texts. Chrysanth oversaw the completion of the missionary centre in 1902; he trained several Korean priests, saving the Korean Orthodox community from annihilation during the 1904 Russo-Japanese war when he was expelled by the Japanese.

Chrysanth's successor, Archimandrite Paul Ivanovskii, founded six new parishes, a college and various charities. After Paul's departure the mission was headed by Russian archimandrites: Irineii from 1913, Vladimir from 1914, Feodosii from 1917 and Polykarp from 1932. In 1945 Polykarp, who was linked with the Orthodox church of JAPAN, was accused of spying and exiled to the Soviet Union. A Korean priest, Alexei Kim, led the Orthodox community until he was imprisoned by the communists in 1950. In 1954 Andreas Halkiopoulos, a chaplain with the Greek forces, revived church structures after the Korean War. Another Korean priest, Boris Moon, headed the community thereafter.

The Greek connection was maintained and in 1976 Archimandrite Soterios Trambas reorganized the Orthodox mission in Korea. Supported by the Ecumenical Patriarchate and linked to the Greek Orthodox archdiocese of New Zealand, this mission is served by priests from Greece, the USA and Korea itself. In 1982 a theological academy was founded and in 1990 the Orthodox Missionary Institute for the Far East was established in Seoul. In the 1990s Orthodox missions from Korea have been active in Hong Kong, Indonesia, the Philippines and Singapore.

Mastroyiannopoulos, I. (1970), *Orthodoxy in the World*. Athens: Zoe.

DB

Kosmas Phlamiatos (1786–1852)   NEW MARTYR of independent Greece. Son of a priest from Kephallonia and named after his father's friend, the martyr Kosmas Aitolos (d. 1786), Kosmas worked as a teacher; he travelled around the Ionian islands, preaching and inspiring an Orthodox revival movement (*see* ZEALOTS). Imprisoned by the British in 1830, exiled from the Ionian islands in 1839 and expelled in 1841, Kosmas denounced British supervision of Orthodox church affairs in the Septinsular Protectorate. He sought refuge in Patras and continued preaching across recently independent Greece. From 1847 Kosmas and another popular preacher, Christopher Papoulakos (1780–1861) became close to the Philorthodox Hetaireia, a pro-Russian spiritual, cultural and political movement dominated by George Kapodistrias, favouring an Orthodox Christian monarchy and the union of the Ionian islands with Greece. King Othon's regime was worried by their growing support, and the Church of Greece was disturbed by Philorthodox agitation for a return to the CONSTANTINOPLE patriarchate and pan-Orthodox reconciliation. Kosmas established a newspaper, *The Voice of Orthodoxy*, which supported Philorthodox positions. Kosmas and Christopher helped to organize of a Philorthodox Congress in May 1851, immediately after which Kosmas was imprisoned for sedition. In prison at Rhio he became a monk before he died of maltreatment in April 1852.

In May 1852 Christopher Papoulakos was condemned by the Holy Synod of the Orthodox Church of Greece for a revolutionary interpretation of the Christian faith. A native of the Kalavryta region, and also known as Christopanagos, Christopher worked as a farmer before becoming a monk of Mega Spelaion. He later founded the neighbouring Dormition monastery. In 1847 Christopher took up pilgrim life, travelling across Greece preaching. Repeatedly imprisoned and severely maltreated, he was eventually exiled to the Panachrantos monastery on Andros, where he died on 18 January 1861. Kosmas and Christopher continued the tradition of Kosmas Aitolos and other preachers. They were linked to the KOLLYVADES and prefigured many of the concerns of the OLD CALENDARISTS. Both are revered as elders (*see also* STARETS).

Bastia, K. (1991), *Papoulakos*. Athens: Ekdotike Athenon.
Sardelis, K. (1988), *Protomartyres tou Hellenikou Kratous*. Athens: Stavros.

DB

Kosovo Established after the Second World War as an autonomous region of Yugoslavia. Since the secession of other Yugoslav republics in the 1990s, clashes have occurred between the majority Albanians, mainly Muslim, and the Orthodox Christian Serbs, who are now, through demographic and political changes, a minority. For the Albanians this region is Illyria, the heart of their ancient homeland; for Serbs it is 'Old Serbia', containing the ancient patriarchal church of PEĆ, the GRAČANICA monastery and numerous shrines. In Kosovo itself in 1389 the OTTOMAN forces crushed Serbian resistance, killing Prince Lazar Hrebeljanović, and embarked on their attempted conquest of Central Europe. This battle, which united Serbians, Albanians and others against the Turks, inspired the Serbs with a vision of their destiny.

    See also ALBANIA; SERBIAN CHRISTIANITY.

Malcolm, N. (1998), *Kosovo*. London: Macmillan.
Vickers, M. (1998), *Between Serb and Albanian*. London: Hurst.
Poulton, H. and Taji-Farouki, S., eds (1997), *Muslim Identity and the Balkan State*. London: Hurst.
Mihaljčić, R. (1989), *The Battle of Kosovo*. Belgrade: n.p.

DB

koubouklion Greek; the bier on which the *epitaphios*, the embroidered icon of Christ laid out for burial, lies during ORTHROS of Holy Saturday in which the burial of Christ is celebrated. Greek *koubouklia* are often canopied, richly carved structures, richly decorated with flowers; Slav churches normally use a simple bier without a canopy. Where possible, the *koubouklion* is used to carry the *epitaphios* in procession through the streets.

DM

koura Greek; 'tonsure'. The Byzantine rite of monastic profession includes a solemn form of tonsure. Scissors are three times offered to the candidate on the gospel book, emphasizing that entry into monastic life is voluntary. This contrasts with CHEIRO- TONIA, where a man is always led before the bishop for ordination, sometimes even compelled to accept the imposition of hands. This can never lawfully occur in monastic profession.

    A simple form of tonsure, not normally referred to as *koura*, is used at baptism. Ordination of a READER or PSALTES involves the clerical tonsure.

DM

Krajina The Serbian minority in Croatia was concentrated in the Krajina marches and in pockets of Slavonia from the OTTOMAN period. The Austrian emperors granted the Orthodox church and the Serbs certain privileges on this military frontier, seeking co-operation to safeguard their southern borders.

Following the collapse of Yugoslavia in the early 1990s, Serbian nationalists sought to secede from Croatia and a short-lived republic was declared in both regions. Reunion of Krajina and Slavonia with Croatia was accompanied by expulsion of most Serbs.

DB

Kritopoulos, Metrophanes (1589–1639)   Greek priest who spent his youth on ATHOS. Cyril LUCARIS, when elected patriarch of ALEXANDRIA, took him as *protosynkellos*, chancellor. Sent to study in England in 1617, he spent seven years in Oxford then travelled to Germany and Switzerland to learn more about Protestantism. Returning to Alexandria in 1631 and consecrated bishop, he became patriarch in 1636, holding the position until his death. In 1638 he attended the Synod of Constantinople, which denounced the Protestant doctrine of Lucaris' *Confession of Faith*. Kritopoulos' own more circumspect *Confession of Faith* (1625) attempted, in the words of Colin Davey, 'to present Orthodox teaching and practice in a way which would be both loyal to the patristic tradition and as acceptable as possible to his Protestant friends'.

Davey, C. (1987), *Pioneer for Unity: Metrophanes Kritopoulos and Relations between the Orthodox, Roman Catholic and Reformed Churches*. London: British Council of Churches.

KP

Kurds   An Indo-European people, closely related to the Persians and other Iranian groups, who have occupied the mountainous region to the north and east of the Fertile Crescent since 1200 BC. To ancient Greeks and Romans this country was known as Gordyene or Kardouchia. Trajan annexed the Kurdish marches in AD 115–17. Christianity penetrated ADIABENE and other Kurdish states by the fourth century. SYRIAN CHRISTIANITY predominated in the area. After the Arab invasions of 641, the Kurds lived under the caliphate. Many followed the Muslim armies to settle towards ARMENIA and ASIA MINOR. The MARDAITES and other tribes remained Christian for some centuries, but Christian Kurds tended to identify with other communities as their compatriots increasingly turned to Islam. Today Christian and other religious minorities still survive among the mainly Muslim Kurds, who have generally been tolerant of them.

For centuries the Kurds retained a degree of autonomy along the OTTOMAN and Persian frontiers. After the First World War their western lands were divided among Turkey, Syria, Iraq and the USSR, Iran retaining the eastern lands. Turkey almost immediately (1925) faced Kurdish revolts that have simmered ever since. A Kurdish republic was briefly established within the USSR as Sor Kurdestan; another was sponsored by the Soviets in Iran (1945). In Iraq the Kurdish struggle for a free homeland finally entered international consciousness during the Gulf War (1991). Conflict in Turkey continues.

See also ALBANIA; NAGORNO KARABAKH.

Izady, M. (1992), *The Kurds*. Washington, DC: Crane Russak.

DB

· L ·

Lalibela *Lālibalā* in Wallo province, north central Ethiopia: site of some twelve monolithic churches, carved out of the local red sandstone below ground level. The rock churches of Lalibela are individually named, and differ in size, form and decoration. The site was once known as Roha, from the Arabic al-Ruha for the city of EDESSA. It took its present name from Lalibela, Ethiopian emperor of the Zagwé dynasty (*c.*1181–*c.*1221) and saint in the ETHIOPIAN ORTHODOX CHURCH, traditionally identified as the builder of these rock-hewn churches. The Ethiopic Life of Lalibela compares his divinely assisted building project to a New Jerusalem, playing on the name Roha and early Christian traditions of Christ's portrait (*mandylion*) at Edessa.

Gerster, G. (1970). *Churches in Rock: Early Christian Art in Ethiopia*, trans. R. Hosking. London: Phaidon.
Jäger, O. A. (1965), *Antiquities of North Ethiopia: A Guide*. Stuttgart: F. A. Brockhaus.
Perruchon, J. (1892), *Vie de Lalibela, roi d'Éthiopie. Texte éthiopien publié d'après un manuscrit du Musée Britannique et traduction française … et la description des églises monolithes de Lalibala*. Publications de l'Ecole des Lettres d'Alger. Paris: Ernest Leroux.

MJB/SHG

lanqa Ge'ez: *lanqā*; Amharic: *lanqa*. A velvet cape worn by Ethiopian ecclesiastical and certain lay dignitaries.
    See also ETHIOPIAN ORTHODOX CHURCH; RELIGIOUS DRESS.

Leslau, W. (1987), *Comparative Dictionary of Ge'ez (Classical Ethiopic): Ge'ez–English/ English–Ge'ez, with an Index of the Semitic Roots*, p. 316. Wiesbaden: Harrassowitz.
Hammerschmidt, E. (1970), 'The Liturgical Vestments of the Ethiopian Church', in Institute of Ethiopian Studies of the Haile Selassie I University, *Proceedings of the Third International Conference of Ethiopian Studies, Addis Ababa, 1966*, 3 vols, vol. 2, pp. 151–6. Addis Ababa: Artistic Printers.

MJB/SHG

Latinization Transformation of certain aspects of Eastern church life to conform to the thought and practices of the Roman Catholic church. (1) Dogma: Eastern Christian communities uniting with the Roman Catholic church are required to accept dogmas defined by the Roman Catholic communion after the schism with the East (e.g. papal infallibility, the immaculate conception and bodily assumption of the Mother of God) and dogmas already a matter of contention between East and West before the schism (e.g the FILIOQUE, purgatory). (2) Theology: the terminology, methods and typical doctrinal positions of Western theology were spread among EASTERN CATHOLIC clergy educated in the scholastic tradition and more recently in the theological fashions of twentieth-century Catholic theology, and among EASTERN ORTHODOX who followed Peter MOGILA in using Western terminology and methods to express Orthodox doctrine, as well as among Eastern Christians educated in Western universities and colleges. (3) Rites and devotions: typically Latin devotions, such as Benediction of the Blessed Sacrament and the Rosary of the Blessed Virgin, were introduced into many Eastern Catholic communities, together with Latin cults such as those of the Sacred Heart or the Immaculate Conception. (4) Feasts: Western feasts such as Corpus Christi and Christ the King appeared in some Eastern Catholic calendars. (5) Vestments and sacred utensils: Latin vestments were widely adopted in the MARONITE and Syro-Malabarese churches. Latin mitres are used in a number of traditions, both Catholic and Orthodox, as are white purificators and the Byzantine rite chalice without the *zeon* (hot water, poured into the chalice). (6) Clerical celibacy: in AMERICA, Eastern Catholic clergy were required to conform to the Latin norm of clerical celibacy: this was a significant element in the reversion to EASTERN ORTHODOXY of many groups of Eastern Catholics. In 1996 a married MELKITE was ordained priest in the USA.

From the reign of Pope Benedict XIV (1740–58), a scholar of Eastern Christianity, there has been significant opposition even on the part of the popes to unnecessary Latinization. Leo XIII (1878–1903) restored the Byzantine rite in GROTTAFERRATA and his encyclical *Orientalium Dignitas* marked a major step in papal support of Eastern tradition. Vatican II (1962–5) inspired a movement to return to Eastern liturgical practice, theology and spirituality in many Eastern Catholic churches. This received strong support in the 1996 *Instruction for the Application of the Code of Canons of the Eastern Churches* of the Congregation for the Oriental Churches, which requires restoration of several liturgical traditions lost in the Latinization process.

DM

Latinophrones Latin-minded: a term used to designate Byzantine theologians who took up the methods and often the doctrinal positions of Western scholasticism. The Latinophrone thinkers opposed GREGORY PALAMAS; some, like the prolific translator Demetrios Kydones (*c.*1324–*c.*1398), eventually converted to Catholicism. The term Latinophrone is also applied as a term of abuse directed at Orthodox Christians favouring union with ROME, especially on terms judged unfavourable to the EASTERN ORTHODOX, or at those bowing to political expediency when Byzantine rulers sought to placate western neighbours or ally with Catholic powers against the Ottomans. The term remains in use among groups suspicious of all dialogue and bridge-building between the Eastern and Western churches.

See also AZYMITE; LATINIZATION.

Papadakis, A. (1994), *The Christian East and the Rise of the Papacy*. Crestwood, NY: St Vladimir's Seminary Press.

DB

Latvian Orthodox church   The Gercike and Koskeinos regions of eastern Latvia were EASTERN ORTHODOX by the twelfth century. Missions from Pskov were active in Latvian and Estonian regions bordering on Russia. The Letgale Latvians were probably mainly Orthodox by the thirteenth century. In 1208, however, Germans sacked Gercike and campaigned against Orthodoxy throughout the Baltic countries. None the less, in 1474 a bishop, Kornily, was sent to Livonia from Russia. Orthodox numbers dwindled over the centuries.

In 1842 Filaret Gumilevskii (d. 1866) became bishop of Riga. He organized an Orthodox mission to the Baltic peoples, supervised translation work and held church services in Latvian and Estonian. Soon twenty permanent and forty temporary churches were established for converts. This success provoked the hostility of the Baltic German aristocracy, and the Russian authorities were obliged to transfer Bishop Philaret elsewhere in 1848. He was succeeded by Plato Gorodetskii (d. 1891), who in 1850 initiated further missionary work. Over 100,000 Latvians may have converted to Orthodoxy between 1845 and 1849. A convent was founded in 1893.

An autonomous Latvian Orthodox church emerged after the 1917 Russian Revolution. Bishop John Pommers (1876–1934), released from Soviet captivity in 1920, became its leader. He reorganized church structures and came to an understanding with the Latvian authorities, who had persecuted the Orthodox for their perceived links with Russia. Over 19 per cent of Orthodox churches in Latvia were destroyed between 1918 and 1925. The situation improved when Bishop John was elected to parliament in 1925. He held together the Latvian and Russian Orthodox of the country, maintaining good relations with both MOSCOW and CONSTANTINOPLE until his death in 1934. Soviet agents appear to have been responsible for his murder. In 1936 the Latvian Orthodox transferred their allegiance from Moscow to the Ecumenical Patriarchate. Augustins Petersons (1873–1955) succeeded as primate. The Soviet invasion of 1940 brought forced subjection to the Moscow patriarchate. Sergii Voskresenskii (1898–1944) was installed as metropolitan of 'Vilnius and All Lithuania, Latvia and Estonia'. After the German invasion Sergii was recognized as exarch of 'Ostland'. The Germans tolerated the revival of the ESTONIAN ORTHODOX CHURCH, but the Latvian Orthodox church remained banned. Sergii was murdered in 1944, possibly by the Germans. Augustins Petersons led many of his flock into exile in 1944 and the Latvian Orthodox Church Abroad was organized from Germany in 1946 as an exarchate of the Ecumenical Patriarchate. In the 1990s the Latvian Orthodox church re-emerged in independent Latvia.

See also LITHUANIAN ORTHODOX CHURCH.

Cherney, A. (1985), *The Latvian Orthodox Church*. Welshpool: Stylite Publishing.

DB

Laurentios of Megara (d. 1707)   A farmer on the Greek isthmus, Laurentios, a married man with children, also worked as a seasonal builder. In later life he became known as a visionary and founded the monastery of PHANEROMENI on Salamis. His family joined him in monastic life and helped run several charitable concerns. He is regarded as the patron saint of Salamis, commemorated on 7 March.

DB

lavra Greek: *laura*. Community of monks living separately, but under a single abbot, and gathering on Sundays and feast days for the liturgy. St Euthymios (d. 473) founded several *lavras* in fifth-century Palestine. In later use, the term *lavra* can simply designate a major monastic house. The Great Lavra founded by Athanasios of Trebizond in 963 is the oldest monastery on ATHOS. KIEV is the site of the Lavra of the Caves.

KP

Lazika By the later Roman period the lands of Colchis at the eastern end of the Black Sea were referred to simply as Lazika, originally the name of a single province at the mouth of the Phasis (Rioni) river. This reflected the domination of the ancient kingdom by the Laz, a Georgian people Christianized before the conversion of CONSTANTINE THE GREAT. Their state included most of the western Caucasus from the fourth century, but succumbed to Arab invaders in the eighth century.

From 788 the Kingdom of Abasgia (ABKHAZIA) was the major Christian power in the Caucasus, and Lazika designated the coastal marches on the southern shores of the Black Sea towards Trebizond. Islam influenced the Laz from an early period, but it was in the OTTOMAN period that majority adherence to Islam was clearly secured.

Fought over by the Russians and Ottomans, Lazika was briefly united to Georgia after the First World War but soon reverted to Turkey. In the 1920s the Christian Laz were expelled together with their Pontic Greek and Armenian neighbours. In Greece all refugees from provinces around Trebizond tend to be called Laz. The Laz-speaking corner of Turkey retains a strong regional identity and has given its name, Lazistan, to a more extensive area. Laz have migrated to every part of Turkey, and are known for their industry and fiery attachment to Islam.

Suny, R. G. (1994), *The Making of the Georgian Nation*. Bloomington: Indiana University Press.

DB

Lesnovo Monastery dedicated to the Archangel Michael near Kratovo in northeastern Macedonia, built 1341–9 by Jovan Oliver, a nobleman at the court of Serbian Tsar Dušan. The site is connected with the cult of Gavrilo of Lesnovo, whose burial is represented in a fresco in the NAOS. In 1347 Lesnovo became the seat of the bishop of Zletovo within the metropolis of Skopje and the patriarchate of PEĆ. The church has a cross-in-square plan and is surmounted by an octagonal dome. A slightly later addition is a domed narthex. On the facades, alternate layers of ashlar and brick are enlivened by patterns of ceramoplastic decoration. Although different in concept and style, wall paintings in the nave and in the narthex show a great diversity of iconographic themes and offer some fine artistic solutions. In addition to an unusual cycle of the Archangel Michael in the nave and a theologically complex programme of frescoes in the narthex, there are several contemporary portraits. The best preserved are those of the donor Jovan Oliver and his wife Ana Maria, Tsar Dušan and his wife Jelena, and bishops of Zletovo, Jovan and Arsenije. An important centre of learning, Lesnovo housed a scriptorium well into the OTTOMAN period. Situated in a region rich in mines, it benefited from comparatively wealthy local citizens and later from donations sent from Russia. Devastated in the seventeenth century, it was restored in 1728–30 on the initiative of the patriarch of Peć, Arsenije, and again in 1805 thanks to the efforts of a monk from DEČANI, Teodosije. People from Kratovo found shelter in the monastery during the plague of 1813–14. The wooden ICONOSTASIS is the work of the craftsman Petar Filipović, dating from 1811–14.

Gavrilović, Z. (1980), 'Divine Wisdom as Part of Byzantine Imperial Ideology: Research into the Artistic Interpretation of the Theme in Medieval Serbia. Narthex Programmes of Lesnovo and Sopoćani', *Zograf* 11.
Radojčić, S. (1971), *Lesnovo*. Belgrade: Izdavački Zavod 'Jugoslavija'.

ZG

Lithuanian Orthodox church   The Yatvyag Lithuanians are believed to have embraced Byzantine Christianity in the period of the evangelization of Rus. Missions from BELARUS won converts among Lithuanian royalty. Prince Gediminas, married into the ruling dynasty of Rus, was a patron of the Orthodox between 1315 and 1340. On 14 April Orthodox Lithuanians commemorate as their patron saints three martyrs, Antony, John and Eustathy, killed by pagans in Vilnius in 1347. The Imud Lithuanians, too, were mainly Orthodox by the fifteenth century. Nevertheless, Roman Catholicism became the majority faith in the reign of Jagailo, who married Jadwiga of Poland and converted to Roman Catholicism before uniting Lithuania to Poland in 1386 (*see* POLISH ORTHODOX CHURCH). Orthodox monasteries founded in the sixteenth century were kept alive mainly among the ethnic minorities. Eleuthery Bogoiavlenskii (1868–1940), Russian Orthodox bishop of Vilnius from 1911, headed the autonomous Lithuanian Orthodox church in the inter-war period. He was deported from Vilnius when the country was annexed to Poland in 1923 and moved to Kaunas. There were 40,000 Orthodox in Lithuania before the Second World War. During the war Metropolitan Eleuthery briefly assumed leadership of the LATVIAN and ESTONIAN ORTHODOX CHURCHES.

Cherney, A. (1985), *The Latvian Orthodox Church*. Welshpool: Stylite Publishing.

DB

Lucaris, Cyril (1572–1638)   The 'Calvinist Patriarch'. Educated in Italy, he spent five years from 1597 teaching in Vilna and Lvov, bolstering Orthodox resistance to the UNIATE movement. At twenty-nine he succeeded his uncle Meletios as patriarch of ALEXANDRIA. In 1620 he was elected ECUMENICAL PATRIARCH, but was deposed and reinstated several times. His contacts with Calvinists had led him to adopt many of their positions on church life and doctrine. The teaching of his *Confession of Faith*, published in Latin in 1629 and in Greek in 1633, on predestination and justification shows Calvinist influence. His teachings were condemned in 1638 by a synod in CONSTANTINOPLE, and in 1642 at JASSY. He was eventually killed by Janissaries who threw his body into the Bosphoros. His life mirrors the struggle of the Ecumenical Patriarchate to come to terms with the Reformation, the Counter-Reformation and OTTOMAN power. Cyril Lucaris gave the Codex Alexandrinus to Charles I in 1628.

Maloney, G. A. (1976), *A History of Orthodox Theology since 1453*. Belmont, Mass.: Nordland Publishing.

Runciman, S. (1968), *The Great Church in Captivity*. Cambridge: Cambridge University Press.

Hadjiantoniou, G. A. (1961), *Protestant Patriarch: The Life of Cyril Lucaris (1572–1638), Patriarch of Constantinople*. London: Epworth Press.

KP

Lyons, Second Council of   For Roman Catholics the fourteenth ECUMENICAL COUNCIL. Convened by Pope Gregory X, it opened in May 1274, a major part of its business being to receive the profession of faith of Byzantine Emperor Michael VIII Palaiologos (1258/9–82).

On 25 July 1261 the Latin Emperor Baldwin II fled and CONSTANTINOPLE was retaken. Very soon after, the Byzantine Emperor Michael VIII approached Pope Urban IV seeking to heal the breach between the Eastern and Western churches. Nothing of substance came of this initiative during Urban's reign, but in 1267 his successor, Clement IV (1265–8), sent a letter, *Magnitudinis tuae Litteras*, to the emperor laying out the profession of faith he would be expected to submit in order to be received into communion with ROME. The letter demanded, inter alia, acceptance of papal primacy and universal appellate jurisdiction. Clement IV died in 1268, and it was almost three years before the cardinals elected Gregory X, an outstandingly able man. Pope and emperor were in contact at once, possibly even before the pope, who was in the Holy Land when elected, reached Rome.

In 1272 Gregory X informed the emperor he intended to convoke a General Council and proposed the terms of reunion. Michael sought to win the support of the Byzantine clergy for reunion, but faced opposition, not least from Patriarch Joseph I. Michael's intimidating severity towards opponents won him a convert, the archivist John Bekkos, whose study of the issues while imprisoned for opposition led him to support the emperor's proposals. Patriarch Joseph led his synod to sign a collective pledge against the union.

The council opened on 1 May 1274 before the three formally accredited Greek representatives arrived. After their arrival, in the fourth session, on 6 July, Michael's letter *Quoniam missi sunt* containing the required profession of faith was read out in the presence of the pope. It contains explicit acceptance of the FILIOQUE – 'We believe too in the Holy Spirit, full, perfect and true God, proceeding from the Father and the Son...' – and of the doctrine of purgatory, the use of unleavened bread in the eucharist (*see* AZYMITE) and the Roman church's 'supreme and full primacy over the entire church'. No effective discussion between Greeks and Latins took place. At a papal mass on 29 June, the former patriarch Germanos III and Bishop Theophanes of Nicaea recited the Nicene Creed with the *filioque*, repeating the *filioque* three times to ensure they were heard. On 6 July the emperor's representative, George Akropolites, formally pledged the end of the schism and the recognition of the pope's primacy.

The emperor's motivations were undoubtedly political. Having just regained Constantinople from the Latins, he needed to defend himself against the aggressive policies of Charles of Anjou. Patriarch Joseph retired and Bekkos replaced him, working with Michael to ensure adherence; but the union was widely and determinedly resisted and eventually failed. Resistence hardened when Pope Nicolas III (1277–80) attempted to impose liturgical use of the *filioque* on the Byzantines. The failure of the union led Pope Martin IV to excommunicate Michael VIII in 1281. In 1282 Michael VIII died, John Bekkos was forced into retirement by the new Emperor Andronicus II, and the aged Joseph I returned to the patriarchal throne. Joseph soon degraded Bekkos and his unionist supporters, including Theophanes of Nicea. In a series of synods, culminating in the Synod of Blachernai in 1285 under Patriarch Gregory II of Cyprus (1283–9), the union was denounced and formally rescinded.

Papadakis, A. (1997), *Crisis in Byzantium: The Filioque Controversy in the Patriarchate of Gregory II of Cyprus (1283–1289)*. Crestwood, NY: St Vladimir's Seminary Press.

Roberg, B. (1990), *Das Zweite Konzil von Lyon (1274)*. Konziliengeschichte, ser. A; Darstellung. Paderborn.

Hussey, J. M. (1986), *The Orthodox Church in the Byzantine Empire*. Oxford: Oxford University Press.

Franchi, A. (1965), *Il Concilio II di Lione*. Studi e Testi Francescane 33. Naples.

Geanakoplos, D. J. (1953), 'Michael VIII Palaeologus and the Union of Lyons', *Harvard Thelogical Review* 46.

DM

· M ·

Macarius Unknown monk of the fourth century whose name is associated with the *Fifty Spiritual Homilies* and the *Great Letter*. Now known as the Pseudo-Macarius to distinguish him from the Coptic desert father, Macarius of Egypt (*c*.345–410). The authorship of the Macarian corpus is attributed in some manuscripts to Symeon of Mesopotamia, a leader of the Messalian movement. Messalianism, which comes from a Syriac word meaning 'those who pray', was a movement that stressed the salvific value of prayer to the exclusion of the sacraments. It spread throughout the monasteries of the Near East and was condemned by several early synods, including the Council of Ephesus in 431. Although written in Greek, the Macarian corpus reflects a Syrian background. The spirituality of the homilies is concerned with unceasing prayer, prayer of the heart, and the idea of progressive perfection as found in the CAPPADO-CIANS. Some scholars of EASTERN CHRISTIAN studies contrast the Macarian spiritual tradition of the 'heart' with the Evagrian one of the 'intellect', viewing the contrast in terms of a Semitic and a Hellenic approach. The Macarian writings may not be as speculative as those of EVAGRIUS PONTICUS, but their influence on later Byzantine fathers such as SYMEON THE NEW THEOLOGIAN and GREGORY PALAMAS is evident.

Maloney, G. A., trans. (1992), *Pseudo-Macarius: The Fifty Spiritual Homilies and the Great Letter*. New York: Paulist Press.
Stewart, C. (1991), *Working the Earth of the Heart: The Messalian Controversy in History, Texts and Language to AD 431*. Oxford: Oxford University Press.
Mason, A. J., trans. (1921), *Fifty Spiritual Homilies of St Macarius the Egyptian*. London: SPCK.

KP

Macedonia Homeland of the ancient Dorian Greeks, and the intermediary between Hellenic and Hellenistic civilizations. The Dorians migrated southwards after 1150 BC, but one branch, the Maketoi or Makednoi, descended from the upper Haliakmon valley and dominated the regions towards the Aegean. Perdikkas I (from 640 BC) formed a Macedonian state, to which Philip II (d. 336 BC) united Upper Macedonia, Strymonitis and Chalkidiki. Alexander the Great (d. 323) consolidated Macedonian influence over Greece before conquering Persia (334 BC). Macedonia dominated Greece until challenged by the Romans. Divided into four states after 167 BC and from 146 BC incorporated into the Roman empire, Macedonia maintained its identity as a Roman province, united from Dyrrhachion to Thessaloniki and Amphipolis by the Via Egnatia.

Barbarian invasions devastated Macedonia and Slavs occupied some regions from the late sixth century AD, though Thessaloniki and other towns remained Byzantine and predominantly Greek. In the tenth century a Byzantine Macedonian theme (province) was created, but this was located around Adrianople in Thrace; Thessaloniki became capital of the Thessalian theme. Basil I, whose Macedonian dynasty ruled Byzantium from 867 to 1056, though from Macedonia, was of Armenian extraction.

The West Bulgarian empire was based on the OHRID–Prespa region, but successive Bulgarian and Serbian states failed to oust the Byzantines from Thessaloniki and their seaward strongholds. Frankish rule, from 1204, ended when Macedonia was united to the despotate of Epirus as the empire of Thessaloniki (1223–46) and later to Palaiologan Byzantium. The OTTOMAN conquest in the fourteenth and fifteenth centuries introduced Muslim elements into the already mixed population. During the Ottoman centuries existing Jewish communities were overwhelmed by brethren fleeing from Spain.

Conflict between Slav and Greek Macedonians in the late nineteenth century sparked off the Balkan Wars of 1912–13. Slav Macedonians generally identified with Bulgaria (independent from 1878) and enjoyed Russian support; Greek Macedonians were aided by volunteers from Greece and Cretan guerrillas. Ottoman authorities played both sides off against each other, while other Balkan states and the great powers championed the remaining minorities. The Balkan Wars fixed disputed borders, paradoxically ending the bloodshed. Greece secured most of 'classical' Macedonia (Aegean or Old Macedonia) while outlying areas were divided among Serbia (Vardar or Greater Macedonia), Bulgaria (Pirin Macedonia) and Albania (the Lakeland). In the 1920s ethnic homogeneity in these regions was pursued by exchanges of populations, resettlement and programmes for assimilation of minorities. The communist parties argued for a united independent Macedonia, but this flew in the face of nationalist sentiment and the changed distribution of ethnic groups during the interwar years. During the Second World War Bulgaria annexed Vardar Macedonia and most of Aegean Macedonia, alienating native Greeks and Slavs by harsh nationalist measures. Under Tito, Yugoslavia capitalized on Slav Macedonian disillusionment with Bulgaria, creating the autonomous republic of Macedonia (Skopje), championing the Slav language and culture of Vardar Macedonia. Claims of this Yugoslav Republic of Macedonia to be the successor of the ancient Macedonian state and to speak for 'all Macedonians' roused fierce opposition from Greek Macedonians, particularly after the secession of the 'Former Yugoslav Republic of Macedonia'. Bulgarians continue to look on their own country as the natural partner and protector of Slav Macedonians, while neither Serbia nor Albania can ignore the existence of kindred minorities in the newly independent Macedonia (Skopje). As in Northern Ireland, the nomenclature adopted and the history held to by each community serve to harden divisions in lands where internecine conflict has been endemic for over a century.

Greek Macedonians deny any other community's claim to the inheritance of ancient Macedonia, arguing that the original Macedonian heartland has since 1913 lain almost entirely within the borders of Greece, and that Greek culture and language always prevailed in Macedonia's undisputed capital, Thessaloniki, founded by Cassander (d. 297 BC) to supersede Pella and Aigai. Slav Macedonians view Macedonia as a larger entity including regions incorporated in the Hellenistic and Roman epochs that have been overwhelmingly Slavic since the sixth century. They identify with the Macedonia-based West Bulgarian empire (up to 1018). Turks are attached to Macedonia as the homeland of Atatürk, while Albanians can see scattered communities of Albanians as evidence of centuries of settlement and incursions across Macedonia. For many reasons, it is probably safer to speak of 'Macedonias' rather than 'Macedonia' in the late twentieth century.

The apostle Paul brought Christianity to Macedonia; it was early established in Thessaloniki. Until 732–3 Greece, Macedonia and Crete were under the pope of ROME; after this CONSTANTINOPLE sponsored missions from Thessaloniki to the pagan tribes beyond Byzantium. The mission of the brothers CYRIL AND METHODIUS to Greater Moravia engendered the Cyrillic alphabet and ensured the entry of the Slav nations into the Christian fold. The creation of the patriarchates of Trnovo (927) and Ohrid or Lychnidos continued this work into the Ottoman period. The Bulgarian exarchate, founded in 1870, extended its hold over populations in the interior (Vardar and Pirin Macedonia) but could not dislodge Constantinople's authority in coastal Macedonia–Thrace, where even communities of SLAVOPHONES remained loyal to Constantinople. From 1913 the Serbian and Greek churches reorganized church life in those areas united to Serbia and Greece respectively. NICOLAS VELIMIROVIĆ (d. 1956), bishop of Ohrid, was influential and popular on both sides of the border. In post-war Yugoslavia the MACEDONIAN ORTHODOX CHURCH seceded from the Serbian Orthodox fold, uniting with Slav DIASPORA communities. In the modern period their common EASTERN ORTHODOX inheritance has failed to unite the Christian peoples of the Macedonias.

Mackridge, P. and Yannakakis, S., eds (1997), *Ourselves and Others*. Oxford: Berg.
Shea, J. (1997), *Macedonia and Greece*. Jefferson, NC: McFarland.
Poulton, H. (1995), *Who Are The Macedonians?* London: Hurst.
Martis, N. (1984), *The Falsification of Macedonian History*. Athens: n.p.
Bozhinov, V. and Panayotov, L. (1978), *Macedonia, Documents and Material*. Sofia: n.p.
Ilievski, D. (1973), *The Macedonian Orthodox Church*. Skopje: n.p.

DB

Macedonian Orthodox church In 1958 Macedonians re-established the archbishopric of OHRID abolished by the OTTOMANS in 1767, electing Dositej as metropolitan. The Serbian Orthodox church protested that his election was uncanonical, but the Serbian Patriarch German travelled to MACEDONIA the following year to consecrate a Macedonian bishop. Macedonians referred to Patriarch German as head of the Serbian and Macedonian Orthodox churches, though the patriarch continued to sign himself patriarch of the Serbian Orthodox church. Relations between the churches were uneasy but not entirely unfriendly, as shown by the joint visit by German with Dositej to Bulgaria in 1964.

In 1967 the Macedonian Orthodox church declared its independence from the Serbian Orthodox church at an assembly of the Macedonian church and people at Ohrid, Metropolitan Dositej becoming archbishop of Ohrid and Macedonia. In spite of its problematic canonical status it has become for many a focal point of national and ethnic pride, both at home and throughout the DIASPORA communities in AUSTRA-LIA, AMERICA and Canada, especially now that Macedonia is an independent republic.

Alexander, S. (1979), *Church and State in Yugoslavia since 1945*. Cambridge: Cambridge University Press.
Ilievski, D. (1973), *The Macedonian Orthodox Church*. Skopje: n.p.

KP

mandorla   Almond-shaped aureole encompassing the figure of Christ in Byzantine iconography. The mandorla is normally an almond of light-rays, but in some TRANS-FIGURATION and ANASTASIS icons it is dark blue, darkest nearest the radiant Christ, as in the sixth-century TRANSFIGURATION apse mosaic at SINAI. This blue mandorla of concentric circles signifies the divine darkness of the inapproachable Godhead. The same colour sequence is used for the cloud from which the hand of God extends in blessing. The origin of the mandorla remains problematic: it is found in Persian and Buddhist art before it appears in Christian iconography.

KP

Mani   The central peninsula extending from the Peloponnese has been known as Mani from the later Byzantine period. This region has been fiercely independent for centuries and, like the Agrapha region of central Greece or Sphakia of Crete, was only loosely controlled by the OTTOMAN Turks. During the *Turkokratia* (Ottoman period) numerous revolts were launched from these regions.

DB

Manicheanism   The religion of Mani entered the Roman empire from Sasanian Persia at the end of the third century. Officially banned from the beginning of the fourth century, it nevertheless enjoyed missionary success in Egypt, North Africa, Italy, Mesopotamia, Syria and Central Asia. Its founder was a gnostic teacher brought up in a Jewish–Christian community in south Babylonia. The religion consists of an elaborate cosmogonic myth which seeks to explain the dualism of body (evil) and spirit (divine), and the consequent impact on the ethics of its followers. The sect was a dyarchy of Elect members, who had to adhere to a strict code of chastity, vegetarianism and quietism, and Hearers, who could follow a more normal way of life. The myth tells of an accidental invasion of the Kingdom of Light by the forces of Darkness. To repel the attack, a redeemer figure called the Primal Man was sent to battle with them, armed with an armour consisting of light elements. The Primal Man fell into a drugged sleep and part of his armour was devoured by the powers of darkness. Another deity, the Living Spirit, was evoked and dispatched to rescue the Primal Man. He called out to him in a piercing voice to which the Primal Man responded and was thereby awakened.

This marks the beginning of a complex process for the redemption of the Light Elements which were held captive in the bodies of the Archons of Darkness. Ten heavens and eight earths were created and the Archons of Darkness were imprisoned in their lower sections. A new evocation, the hermaphroditic (Third) Envoy, then seduced the male and female Archons with his/her good looks and induced them to ejaculate and abort the Light Particles held captive in them. These fell on the earth and brought forth plant and animal life. An elaborate system involving the main planetary and stellar bodies was then set in motion to return the Light Particles to their original abode. However, the chief of the demonic powers then conspired to undermine this redemptive process through the creation of the First Man and First Woman. Through sexual desire and human conception, the Light Elements were perpetually enslaved to bodily flesh. They could be redeemed only through special knowledge (gnosis) provided by the sect and the adherence to its strict code of behaviour and acceptance of a spiritual dyarchy in which the Elect played a direct role in the redemptive process of the enslaved Light Elements. Jesus features as a giver of special knowledge. The suffering of the enslaved Light Elements is also seen as a form of mystical crucifixion. The historical Jesus (i.e. Christ the Messiah) is honoured by the sect as a forerunner of Mani.

The diffusion of the religion into the Roman empire was partly facilitated by the rise of the Sasanian dynasty to dominance in the Near East in the late third century and by the growing Christianization of the empire, which enabled the religion to spread as a an extreme form of ascetical Christianity. Unavowedly anti-Jewish, it also profited from the ambivalent attitude which the church adopted towards the Old Testament.

Lycopolis in the Fayyum in Egypt had become an important centre of Manichaean mission by the end of the third century. From there a group appears to have been driven by persecution into the Dakhleh Oasis, where vestiges of a significant Manichaean community have been found by the excavations at Kellis since 1990. The language of the early missionaries was SYRIAC and the texts were translated into both Coptic and Greek. A library of seven Manichaean codices in Coptic was found by workmen at Medinet Madi. The dialect of the codices was a dialect of Coptic commonly known as Lycopolitan (Sub-Achmimic B) which reveals the original connection of the texts with Lycopolis. In 1970 a small parchment codex (the Cologne Mani-Codex) containing a Greek life of Mani compiled from eyewitness accounts was successfully conserved and deciphered. The text confirms the close links between Manichaeism and Syriac-speaking Christianity.

In the Christian West, the Manichaeans presented themselves as true Christians whose teaching was handed down to them by an apostle of Jesus Christ. They made substantial use of Christian texts, both canonical and apocryphal, to support their dualistic teaching. The extreme ascetical rules governing the daily life of the Elect would certainly have alarmed Christian monastic and ecclesiastical leaders. Severe persecution directed against the sect began towards the end of the fourth century and the sect went into irreversible decline by the early sixth century. Theologians like Augustine, Titus of Bostra, Serapion of Thmuis and SEVERUS OF ANTIOCH, as well as heresiologists like EPIPHANIOS, THEODORET, John of Caesarea and JOHN OF DAMASCUS, also conducted a major literary campaign against the sect. Some of their polemics were later redirected against sects in Byzantium like the BOGOMILS and PAULICIANS which showed distinct gnostic traits and were thus labelled 'Manichaeans' by orthodox churchmen.

The newly discovered material from Kellis, which contains private letters of members of the sect, will undoubtedly revolutionize our knowledge of the history of the sect in Roman Egypt.

Lieu, S. N. C. (1994), *Manichaeism in Mesopotamia and the Roman East*. Leiden: Brill.
Klimkeit, H.-J. (1993), *Gnosis on the Silk Road: Gnostic Texts from Central Asia*. San Francisco: Harper.
Lieu, S. N. C. (1992), *Manichaeism in the Later Roman Empire and Medieval China*, 2nd edn. Tübingen: Mohr-Siebeck.
Klein, W. (1991), *Die Argumentation in den griechisch–christlichen Antimanichaica*. Studies in Oriental Religions 19. Wiesbaden: Harrasouritz.
Tardieu, M. (1981), *Le Manichéisme*. Paris: Presses Universitaires de France.
Decret, F. (1974), *Mani et la tradition manichéenne*. Paris: Senil.
Puech, H.-Ch. (1949), *Le Manichéisme. Son fondateur – sa doctrine*. Paris: Civilisations du Sud.

SL

Maphrian Syriac: *mapryānā*, 'the fructifier'; title of the eastern head of the SYRIAN ORTHODOX church, i.e. in the area of the former Persian empire. The term *qatōlīqā* (CATHOLICOS) was also used at times. Originally independent in the East, the maphrianate came to be purely honorary and the maphrian entirely subject to the patriarch in ANTIOCH. Maphrians resided at different times at Tikrit, Mosul and the monastery of Mar Mattai. The first holder of the title was Marūtā, metropolitan of Tikrit (d. 649); perhaps the most famous was BARHEBRAEUS (1226–86).

JH

Mardaites Tribes on the fringes of ASIA MINOR (Taurasia and Amanos mountains), probably of Kurdish provenance. The Christian Mardaites were employed by the Arabs from 630 to hold the passes towards Antioch, but invariably sided with the Byzantines. Raids as far as Jerusalem after 677 led to Arab insistence that these tribes be removed from the frontier as a condition for peace. Justinian II (d. 711) complied and the Mardaites were evacuated, mainly to Greece. The last Mardaite stronghold fell to the Arabs in 707–8 and the remnants of this warlike people were dispersed throughout Syria.

See also HATAY; KURDS.

Izady, M. (1992), *The Kurds*. London: Crane Russak.

DB

Maria of Bizye (*c*.866–902) Maria, of Armenian extraction, married a Byzantine official, Nikephoros, in CONSTANTINOPLE. He and his family persecuted her for devoting all her time and wealth to charitable works. Eventually Nikephoros beat her to death because he was persuaded she was unfaithful. Her Life tells that miracles occurred at her tomb and even her husband recognized her sanctity. Maria, who is regarded as a PASSION BEARER, is commemorated on 16 February.

The tenth-century Thomais of Lesbos was also killed by her husband for devoting more time to good works than family affairs and for flouting convention. Her mother KALI supported her lifestyle. They are commemorated on 3 January.

Maria and Thomais represent a lesser-known type of Byzantine saint, women martyrs to domestic violence.

Soteriou, G. (1988), *Lesbiake Hagiologia*. Lesbos: Mytilene.

DB

Maronite church   The Maronite church claims to be named after a fourth- or fifth-century hermit called Maron, whose brief life was written by THEODORET OF CYRRHUS in his *Historia Religiosa* XVI. It also believes that the disciples of St Maron formed the great Maronite monastery built in Syria Secunda in 452 by the Roman Emperor Marcian (451–7), according to the Arab historian Abu al-Fida (1273–1331). It was called the monastery of Bet Maroun, and in 532 its superior, Paul, signed the decrees of a synod in Constantinople as the head of the whole monastic community in northern Syria.

The Maronite monks adopted the teaching of the Council of Chalcedon (451) and fought for its implementation in their area of dominion. As a result of their loyalty to the CHALCEDONIAN faith, the Maronites were opposed by the MONOPHYSITES; and, according to a letter which was addressed by the Maronite monks to Pope Hormisdas II in 517, the fratricidal fighting between the two sides was very brutal. Around the beginning of the sixth century the monastery of Bet Maroun was destroyed, either by an earthquake or by the Monophysites, but it was rebuilt by the Emperor Justinian (527–65).

When the Roman Emperor Heraclius came to power in 610, he attempted to unify his empire, and therefore desired to put an end to Christian divisions. After expelling the Persians between 622 and 628 he was attacked by the Arabs, who conquered Syria and Palestine between 635 and 640. After moving against them, Heraclius published the EKTHESIS in 638 in order to unify Christianity in the Eastern Roman empire. The Ekthesis was the formula of MONOTHELETISM which consists in the affirmation of one will in the person of Jesus Christ who is both man and God, and it was considered at that time to be the dogma of the Byzantine patriarch as well as of Pope Honorius I. In 680, the council held at Constantinople nevertheless condemned the Ekthesis and its monothelite teaching, but the Maronite community remained loyal to its tenets.

During the seventh century the Muslim Arab rulers of Syria severely punished all contacts with their main enemy, CONSTANTINOPLE. As a result of their policy, the MELKITE see of ANTIOCH became vacant between 702 and 742, since the Arab rulers were hostile to any Byzantine (Melkite) presence in the city. The Maronite community, which enjoyed good relations with the new Muslim rulers of Damascus, benefited from this vacancy and proclaimed its own bishop, John-Maron, patriarch of Antioch. At this time the Maronite patriarchate was instituted. The Maronite monastic community officially became a church, since it possessed its own patriarch and had ecclesiastical autonomy. Owing to the Maronite–monophysite struggle on the one hand, and the monothelite theology of the Maronites which caused a real conflict with Constantinople on the other, the Maronite church was cut off from other Christian communities and developed independently with its own hierarchy. Its isolation from and hostile relationship with its Christian neighbours made its life more difficult to sustain, and slowly the Maronite community was obliged to move to the isolated and remote mountains of Lebanon. The destruction, for unknown reasons, of the Maronite monastery in Northern Syria during the first half of the tenth century finally compelled the majority of the Maronite community to emigrate to Mount Lebanon in search of peace and freedom.

During the eleventh century the crusaders embarked upon their invasion of the Near East, and, on their arrival in northern Lebanon in 1099, the FRANKS received a warm welcome from the Maronites (see CRUSADES). William of Tyre, a contemporary, wrote in 1182 that 40,000 Maronites joined the crusaders and gave up their monotheletism. Not all Maronites welcomed the Franks, however: some Maronites from the high Lebanese Mountains were quite hostile to the Maronite–Crusader alliance. This Maronite opposition did not stop the Maronite patriarch, Jeremiah al-'Amshītī (1199–1230) from making the first visit of a Maronite to ROME in 1213. He attended the opening sessions of the Fourth Lateran Council (1215), and he also received the pallium of confirmation from the pope as a sign of formal Roman acceptance of his position as the head of the Maronite church. After the death of Jeremiah al-'Amshītī, conflict among the Maronites surfaced again, and there is some evidence from the Maronite historian and poet, Jibrā'īl al-Qilā'i (c.1516) that the opposition group elected its own patriarch, Luke of Bnahran, who, together with his followers, fortified his position in Hadath near Bisharri. Nothing is known about Luke of Bnahran after 1283, but the text of the Arab historian Muḥyi ad-Din Ibn 'Abd az-Zahir (1223–92) strengthens the belief that he was put to death with his followers by the crusaders and their allies in 1283. After the defeat of the crusaders, the Maronites quickly forgot their internal dissensions and gathered themselves around their patriarch who remained in union with Rome and maintained good relations with the Franks. It seems also that the hostile policy of the Mamluks towards those who collaborated with the crusaders contributed greatly both to Maronite unity and to their isolation in the Lebanese mountains.

The alliance with Rome meant that the Maronite church did not escape LATINIZATION, since the Roman church repeatedly tried to transform Maronite spirituality into a Latin form. The influence of Latinization remained marginal until 1580 when Pope Gregory XIII ordered his legate, a Jesuit named John Baptist Eliano, to investigate the Maronite faith. Eliano destroyed many Maronite manuscripts which were not in keeping with Latin dogma and its distinctive ways of worship. Pope Gregory XIII found a more effective way to ensure the submission of the Maronite church to the Latin Roman tradition. In 1584 he founded the Maronite College in Rome in order to educate the elite of the Maronite clergy in the spirit of the Roman Catholic tradition. The pope was very successful in his project, and subsequently Maronite councils merely endorsed decisions by the Roman authorities. Another factor which contributed to the Latinization of the Maronite church was the establishment of Roman Catholic missions, Jesuit and Franciscan, among the Maronites, and the consequent education of the elite of the Maronite community in the spirit of Western European Latin Christianity.

After Vatican II the Maronite church reviewed its own liturgy and spirituality, and in 1992 it published, for the first time since 1763, a complete new version of the Maronite missal. This is believed to be the version closest to the original Maronite mass prior to the onset of Latinization. The Maronite ecclesiastical authority continues to publish new versions of all different aspects of the Maronite liturgy in order to keep the original Maronite tradition of SYRIAN LITURGY alive in the Maronite community. The Maronite patriarch has ordered the clergy of the Maronite church to wear the original Syrian ecclesiastical vestments for the celebration of the Maronite liturgy, and has also ordered that church buildings should adhere to the Antiochian Syrian Christian architectural tradition. Latinization is definitely an influence of the past in the Maronite church. (*See* SYRIAN CHRISTIANITY.)

The full name of the Maronite church is the Antiochian Syrian Maronite Church: the four elements clearly indicate the character of Maronite identity and spirituality. First, the Maronite church derives its existence from the Apostolic see of Antioch, and its patriarch therefore is called 'patriarch of Antioch and all the Levant'. He is elected by the synod of the Maronite bishops, and resides in Lebanon. Before the fourteenth century the Maronite patriarch was elected by bishops, priests, deacons, sub-deacons and representatives of the laity. According to the Maronite Synod of Mount Lebanon (1736), the Maronite patriarch exercises full patriarchal jurisdiction over the Maronites, and he designates the new bishop for a vacant see with the assent of the Maronite bishops by majority vote. Candidates for priesthood are allowed to marry before their ordination to the diaconate, and the majority of secular priests in the Maronite church are now married.

The Maronite patriarchate is divided into the following dioceses: in Lebanon, Tyre, Sidon, Beirut, Antelias, Jounieh, Sarba, Byblos, Batroun, Tripoli, Joubbeh, Baalbak-Dair al-Ahmar, Zahle; in Syria, Aleppo, Damascus, Lattakia; the Holy Lands and Jordan, Egypt and Sudan; Cyprus; in the USA, St Maron, Brooklyn and Our Lady of Lebanon, Los Angeles; Mexico; in Australia, St Maron; in Brazil, Our Lady of Lebanon; in Argentina, St Sharbel; in Canada, St Maron; and Europe.

Second, the original motherland of the Maronites is Syria, where the Maronite church developed from its first nucleus with its Syrian culture and liturgy. Although SYRIAC is the backbone of Maronite spirituality, it is important to note that the term 'Syriac' does not describe the full character of Maronite spirituality, since Syrian writers who wrote in Greek also form part of its background. It is better to use the term 'Syrian', rather than 'Syriac', since this includes the Greek elements of Syrian Antiochian Christianity. Syriac Christianity is nevertheless the closest Christian representative in the world of the cultural background of the BIBLE, and it belongs to the same historical and geographical milieu as did Jesus Christ. Maronite spirituality is thus a strongly biblical one, and it represents, alongside the other Syrian Churches, a genuine Asian Christian spirituality.

Third, the word 'Maronite' points clearly to the monastic origin and identity of the Maronite church, for the monks of Bet Maroun are the real founders of the Maronite church and consequently shaped its personality greatly throughout history. With the emigration of Maronite people to Mount Lebanon, the Maronite monks settled mainly in the Holy Valley (Qadisha), and they retained their Syrian monastic spirituality and discipline at that time. During the seventeenth century the Maronite patriarch Istifān al-Douwaihī decided to reorganize monastic life in the Maronite church by introducing some discipline into its hierarchy as well as into the daily life of the Maronite monks. As a result, monasticism in the Maronite church became institutionalized, and it borrowed some important rules from Western European monastic discipline and structure. At the present time, only a minority still follow the early Maronite rules of the monastic enclosed life; the majority of Maronite monks and nuns are deeply involved in different educational and spiritual activities of their society. The monastic communities of men are: the Lebanese Maronite Order, the Lebanese Mariamite Maronite Order (originally the so-called Aleppine Order), the Maronite Antonine Order, the Lebanese Maronite Missionaries, and the new Maronite Order of the Maronite dioceses in the USA which follows the Maronite rules for enclosed monks. Those of women are: the Lebanese Maronite Nuns, the Maronite Congregation of the Antonine Nuns, the Maronite Visitandines, the Maronite Congregation of the Holy Family, the Maronite Congregation of St Theresa of the Child Jesus, the Missionaries of the Holy Sacrament, the Congregation of the Maronite Nuns of St John of Hrache, and the Enclosed Maronite Nuns.

Fourth, the term 'Church' indicates that The Antiochian Syrian Maronite Church has the full character of a self-governing church with its own apostolic roots and spirituality. At the same time, the Maronite church is united to the Church of Rome and forms a part of the Catholic church, whose head is believed by the Maronites to be the successor of the apostle Peter and the head of the universal church.

Finally, the Maronites believe that their isolation in Mount Lebanon contributed greatly to their independent character as a church and as a society, and their identity is consequently identified strongly with the identity of Lebanon. In fact the Maronite church played the major role in the creation of modern Lebanon, and its followers hold several key positions in the modern Lebanese state.

Abi-Aoun, B. et al. (1994), *Momies du Liban. La découverture archéologique de Asi-l-Hadath*. Beirut: Edifra.
Mahfouz, J. (1987), *Short History of the Maronite Church*. Lebanon.
Moosa, M. (1986), *The Maronites in History*. Syracuse N.Y.: Syracuse University Press.
Dau, B. (1984), *History of the Maronites*. Beirut: Daran-Nahar.
Dib, P. (1971), *History of the Maronite Church*. Beirut: Imprimerie Catholique.
Naaman, P. (1971), *Théodoret de Cyr et le monastère de Saint Maron*. Lebanon: Université Saint-Esprit Kaslik.
Hayek, M. (1965), *La Liturgie maronite*. Paris: Mame.
Salibi, K. (1959), *Maronite Historians of Medieval Lebanon*. Beirut: American University of Beirut.
Salibi, K. (1958), 'The Maronite Church in the Middle Ages and its Union with Rome', *Oriens Christianus* 42, pp. 92–104.

SA

mashafa Or *masehafa*; Ge'ez: *maṣ(e)ḥaf*, pl. *maṣāḥeft*. Classical Ethiopic term for book, scripture, writing, e.g. the *Maṣḥafat Qeddusāt* (*maṣāḥeft qeddusāt*) or 'holy books' of anaphora. Titles of many works from the Christian literature of Ethiopia begin 'The Book of...'. Examples can be found among the works of individual writers such as the fifteenth-century emperor ZARA YAKUB, e.g., his *Maṣḥafa milād* (Book of Nativity), a polemical treatise against the Jews or *ayhud*, as he names his opponents. The term regularly appears in church books, e.g. *Maṣḥafa Qandil* (Book of the Lamp), containing the ritual for unction of the sick, and *Maṣḥafa Genzat* (Book of the Funeral Ritual).

See also ETHIOPIAN ORTHODOX CHURCH.

Haile, G. (1993), 'Ethiopic Literature', in R. Grierson, ed., *African Zion: The Sacred Art of Ethiopia*, pp. 47–55. New Haven and London: Yale University Press, in association with InterCultura, Fort Worth, The Walters Art Gallery, Baltimore, The Institute of Ethiopian Studies, Addis Ababa.
Leslau, W. (1987), *Comparative Dictionary of Ge'ez (Classical Ethiopic): Ge'ez–English/ English–Ge'ez, with an Index of the Semitic Roots*, p. 552. Wiesbaden: Harrassowitz.

MJB/SHG

Matthew the Poor   (1) Coptic fisherman, ascetic and miracle-worker of the early eighth century. He is mentioned in a number of Coptic sources, including the *History of the Patriarchs of Alexandria*, the *History of Churches and Monasteries* once attributed to ABŪ ṢĀLIḤ THE ARMENIAN, and the Copto-Arabic Synaxarion, a collection of brief daily commemorations of the lives and martyrdoms of the saints recognized by the Coptic church according to the calendar of the church.

(2) Matta al-Miskin/Matta el-Meskeen, Coptic Orthodox priest and monk, spiritual director of the Monastery of St Macarius in the Wādī al-Naṭrūn. One of the leaders of the twentieth-century monastic revival in the Coptic church, Father Matta al-Miskin has written prolifically in Arabic about ancient and modern Coptic monasticism, spirituality and theology. Some of his shorter works have been published in English in the North American journals *Coptic Church Review* and *Coptologia*.

Andrawiss, W. (1993), 'Un exemple concret du monachisme copte contemporain: le monastère saint-Macaire du Wadi Natroun', *Le Monde Copte* 21–2, pp. 135–41.
Coquin, R.-G. (1991), 'Matthew the Poor, Saint', *Coptic Encyclopedia* 5, pp. 1571–2.

MJB/SHG

Maxim Sandovich (d. 1914)   Born in Snina in 1886, Maxim studied theology in Zhitomir, Ukraine, and was ordained as a married priest in 1911 by Antonii Khrapovitskii, the future presiding hierarch of the RUSSIAN ORTHODOX CHURCH ABROAD. Maxim returned to Austria-Hungary to work among the mainly GREEK CATHOLIC Lemkos of Galicia. When the entire village of Grybow reverted to EASTERN ORTHODOXY he was invited to become its parish priest. Maxim incurred opposition from the Austro-Hungarian authorities; he was arrested in 1912 and briefly imprisoned in Lviv. On release, Maxim faced harrassment and further arrests; although acquitted of treason in 1914 he was confined to his native Snina. On the outbreak of the First World War Maxim was interned in Gorlice and condemned to death by the military. The entire Sandovich family and other Orthodox activists were sent to the Talerhof prison camp. Maxim is commemorated on 6 September.

'Maxim Sandovich' (1995), *Orthodox Life* (Jordanville) 45/1.

DB

Maximus the Confessor (*c.*580–662)   Probably spent his early years as a monk in Palestine and may have known John Moschus, author of the *Pratum Spirituale* and spiritual father of Sophronius, future patriarch of JERUSALEM. Leaving Palestine in 614 because of the Persian invasion, he stayed in CONSTANTINOPLE, then in 626 moved to North Africa, where he came into contact with Sophronius. In 645 he engaged in debate with Pyrrhus, the deposed patriarch of Constantinople, over the issue of MONOTHELETISM. He was instrumental in persuading Pope Martin to convoke the Lateran synod of 649 which anathematized the monothelites. Arrested in 653, taken to Constantinople, tried and mutilated, he was exiled to the Caucasus. His stand against monotheletism was vindicated at the Third Council of Constantinople (681). His theology carries the CHRISTOLOGY of Chalcedon to its logical conclusion, establishing the DEIFICATION of human nature in Christ as the paradigm of redemption. His writings show a powerful theological mind, from his *Mystagogy*, a symbolic interpretation of the liturgy, to his *Ambigua*, an exposition of the intricacies of the CAPPADOCIANS and the Pseudo-Dionysian corpus. More space is given to his spiritual writings in the PHILOKALIA than to those of any other writer.

Louth, A. (1996), *Maximus the Confessor*. London: Routledge.
Thunberg, L. (1995), *Microcosm and Mediator: The Theological Anthropology of Maximus the Confessor*. Chicago: Open Court.
Berthold, G. (1985), *Maximus the Confessor: Selected Writings*. London: SPCK.

KP

Meeting in the Temple   The Meeting (Greek: *Hypapante*) of Christ in the Temple is known to have been celebrated in JERUSALEM in the fourth century. The feast,

celebrated on 2 February, is known in the West as the Purification of the Blessed Virgin or Candlemas. The icon shows the interior of the Temple with Symeon the Just standing, hands covered, ready to receive the child from Mary. Symeon is called Theodochos, 'receiver of God'. Between them is an altar covered by a baldachin. Following Mary are the prophetess Anna (sometimes also Anna the Lord's grandmother) and Joseph bearing two doves or pigeons (Luke 2: 24), sometimes interpreted as the old and new covenants. Tradition makes Symeon one of the SEVENTY translators of the Septuagint, whom God preserved until that moment. Texts and icons show Symeon as a priest. One of Kosmas' stichera for the APOSTICHA found its way into the Latin office for the feast and the APOLYTIKION into the Dominican breviary.

Ouspensky, L. and Lossky, V. (1982), *The Meaning of Icons*. Crestwood, NY: St Vladimir's Seminary Press.

KP

Megale Idea   Greek, 'Great Idea'. After the creation of the modern Greek state the *Megale Idea* was reformulated by opponents of the political status quo. Nationalists and radicals upheld the ideal of a 'Greater Greece', uniting all GREEK ORTHODOX

Christians, whether Greek-speaking or not, opposing both the conservatism of the new state's establishment, who favoured a small 'Old Greece', and that of the affluent Greeks of the OTTOMAN empire. After the ASIA MINOR debacle of 1922 Great Idea language passed from use, but the same ideal was redeployed to inspire the Enosis movement in CYPRUS and, particularly after 1974, to maintain close links with the wider Greek Orthodox DIASPORA.

See also CHRYSOSTOM OF SMYRNA; ETHNOMARTYRS; IONIA.

DB

Megalynarion Short verse frequently containing the words 'We magnify' (Greek: *megalynomen*). On feasts of the Lord *megalynaria* are sung with the troparia of the ninth ODE of the CANON. In Slav use *megalynaria* are sung with the third part of the POLYELEOS.

E

Meletios Metaxakis (1871–1935) Born in Parsas, Crete, he studied theology in JERUSALEM, where he was ordained in 1894. Elected metropolitan of Kition in CYPRUS, in 1910, then in 1918 metropolitan of Athens and All Greece, in which capacity in 1919 he travelled to AMERICA to organize the GREEK ORTHODOX church there, which had since 1908 been dependent on the Church of Greece. Deposed as Greek primate, Meletios returned to America. Elected ECUMENICAL PATRIARCH in 1921, the following year he brought the Greek Orthodox DIASPORA under his patriarchal jurisdiction. Meletios established the Greek Orthodox archdiocese of North and South America.

Meletios chaired an inter-Orthodox conference which voted to introduce a new CALENDAR, similar to but more accurate than the Gregorian, a decision which proved controversial. In addition to those churches which accepted the decree in 1923, the churches of ROMANIA and BULGARIA later enacted it, but Jerusalem and RUSSIA did not, nor did the monks of ATHOS.

This and other reforms provoked the formation of traditionalist OLD CALENDAR-IST churches. Meletios also issued a decision recognizing Anglican orders as of equal status with those of Roman Catholic and Oriental Orthodox clergy. While this also roused conservative opposition, some (but not all) other Orthodox churches subsequently issued similar statements. In 1923 Meletios was forced to resign the Ecumenical throne, but in 1926 was elected patriarch of Alexandria.

DB

Melkite Also melchite, melkhite; literally 'royalist'. (1) EASTERN CHRISTIANS loyal to the Council of CHALCEDON and to the imperial authority which espoused its decrees. (2) Specifically, CHALCEDONIAN Christians living in areas where their conflict with MONOPHYSITES produced parallel churches no longer in communion. In the modern period the Melkites are predominantly Arabic- or Greek-speaking, but are also heirs to early Syriac and Coptic Christianity. (3) The term now commonly designates Byzantine rite EASTERN CATHOLICS under the jurisdiction of the Melkite Catholic patriarch of Antioch, Alexandria, Jerusalem and All the East. The term is not used to refer to Eastern Catholics of other rites.

Many of the Eastern church's greatest teachers and hymnographers were Melkites, for example ROMANOS THE MELODIST, JOHN CLIMACUS, JOHN OF DAMASCUS and THEODORE ABŪ QURRAH.

Dick, I. (1994), *Les Melkites*. Belgium: Brepols.

DM

Melkite Catholics The name MELKITE designates CHALCEDONIAN Eastern Christians of the ALEXANDRIA, ANTIOCH and JERUSALEM patriarchates. It is now most commonly used to designate the Melkite Greek Catholics.

Despite the popular dating of the schism between EASTERN ORTHODOX and ROME to the mutual excommunications of 1054 (*see* MICHAEL KEROULARIOS), the schism was not accomplished by any single event. Contact with the West through the CRUSADES and under OTTOMAN rule led a minority of Orthodox to forge closer ties with the Western church, though not at the expense of abandoning the ritual, theology and canonical discipline of the East. Latin friars and clerks regular working in Orthodox territory, particularly in the patriarchate of Antioch, based since 1342 in Damascus, fostered better relations with Rome, making secret conversions, whereby clergy especially made submission to Rome while continuing to function as Orthodox, as a means of promoting union in the long term. This policy showed the ambiguity in the minds of both Latins and Orthodox as to the exact nature of the schism between the churches. Where good relations were maintained, some Orthodox clergy became well-disposed to union, or sought pastoral assistance from the better-educated Latins. Throughout the seventeenth century Latin missionary efforts intensified; by 1800 a substantial number of Antiochian bishops were pro-Western or crypto-Catholic.

From 1516 onwards the patriarchate of Antioch was under Ottoman rule, and therefore under the pasha of the *Rum milet*, the Ecumenical Patriarch. None the less, Arab patriarchs continued to occupy St Peter's throne in Antioch. In 1724 the pro-Western Seraphim Tanas was elected patriarch as Cyril VI in succession to Athanasios IV Dabbas (1720–4). Ecumenical Patriarch Jeremias III (1716–26 and 1732–4) responded to what Constantinople saw as a coup by a pro-Catholic cabal by appointing a Cypriot monk from ATHOS as Patriarch Sylvester I (1724–66). Sylvester, however, was unyielding and uncompromising not only to his opponents but even to his supporters and alienated many. Pope Benedict XIII (1724–30) graciously recognized Cyril VI (1724–59) as patriarch of Antioch in communion with Rome.

Since 1724 the ancient Melkite community has been divided between the Eastern Orthodox patriarchate and the Melkite Catholic. The Orthodox patriarchate was in Greek hands from Sylvester I until 1898/9 when Meletios II Doumani (1899–1906) was elected after intense pressure from Russia to return the patriarchate to the Arabs. The Catholic patriarchate remained Arab throughout.

In the 1830s Patriarch Maximos III Mazlum (1833–55) received recognition from the Ottoman authorities as the head of a distinct *milet*. He too established his residence in Damascus. Rome accorded Maximos III the Melkite patriarchal titles of Alexandria and Jerusalem, titles his successors still hold. In 1894 Leo XIII (1878–1903) formally recognized the Melkite patriarch's authority as extending throughout the Ottoman empire.

Patriarch Gregory II Yusuf (1864–97), aware of the disastrous effect its dogmatic definition would have on relations with the Orthodox, was a prominent opponent of the definition of papal infallibility at the Vatican Council (1869–70). The reaction of Pius IX (1846–78) to his opposition was only revealed publicly by the great Patriarch Maximos IV Sayegh (1947–67). After the council an emissary was sent to secure the signatures of the Melkite Holy Synod to the definition. They signed it, but with the qualifying clause used at FLORENCE attached first. When Gregory II next visited the pope, he was cast to the floor at Pius' feet by the guard while the pope placed his foot on the patriarch's head. None the less, he and his successors remained loyal to union with Rome.

The twentieth century has seen patriarchs of exceptional ability. Maximos IV Sayegh, who played a major role at Vatican II, delighted Orthodox observers with his loyalty to Eastern tradition. His successor Maximos V Ḥakīm (1967–) has rivalled his energy and his dedication to improving good relations with the Orthodox.

In the aftermath of Vatican II areas of the Melkite church, such as parishes in America, which had submitted to LATINIZATION, have significantly recovered their Eastern heritage. In some places the Latinization had extended to refusal of communion to baptized infants, use of statues, and even use of Latin rite services. The return to Byzantine tradition has been accompanied by notable spiritual renewal.

Dick, I. (1994), *Les Melkites*. Belgium: Brepols.
Frazee, C. A. (1983), *Catholics and Sultans: The Church and the Ottoman Empire 1453–1923*: Cambridge University Press.
Dick, I. (1965), *Qu'est-ce-que l'orient chrétien?* Tournai.
Maximos IV Sayegh, ed. (1963), *The Eastern Churches and Catholic Unity*. Edinburgh: Nelson.
Attwater, D. (1961–2), *The Christian Churches of the East*, 2 vols. (repr.). Leominster: Thomas More Books.

DM

Men, Aleksandr (1935–1990) Russian Orthodox priest and theologian who sought to present Christianity to an atheistic generation in the Soviet Union. Brought up in a Christian household, though of Jewish descent, he studied theology secretly at home and as a teenager discovered the writings of Vladimir SOLOVYOV and Nicolas BERDIAEV. In 1955 the institute at which he was studying in Moscow was transferred to Irkutsk in Siberia and here he got to know Gleb Iakunin. Both became priests; Iakunin was later to be imprisoned for his involvement with the dissident movement. In the 1960s Father Men began distributing his sermons in *samizdat* form and publishing his books abroad under a pseudonym. In 1970 he embarked upon a seven-volume study of world religions under the title *In Search of the Way, the Truth and the Life*. He believed that the study of ancient religions was necessary for a proper assessment of Christianity's place in the history of human development, whether one accepted or rejected its claims. At the time of his death he had nearly completed a multi-volume dictionary of the Bible. Among those he baptized was Nadezhda Mandelstam, the writer and widow of the poet Osip Mandelstam. Father Men was murdered in September 1990 by unknown assailants on his way to his parish church.

Roberts, E. and Shukman, A. (1996), *Christianity for the Twenty-first Century: The Life and Work of Alexander Men*. London: SCM Press.

KP

Menaia   Greek; Slav: Mineya. Byzantine rite liturgical books, normally twelve monthly volumes, containing texts for the feasts of the daily sanctoral cycle. The General Menaion, found for example in the Anthologion, contains common texts for feasts of categories of saints. The Greek and Slavonic General Menaia are not identical, the Slavonic containing more offices as well as texts for a full vigil for each category of saint, and also for the Lord and the THEOTOKOS. New AKOLOUTHIAI of local saints are also published in the form of individual leaflets.

See also FEAST DAYS OF SAINTS; HEORTOLOGION.

Mother Mary and Ware, K., trans. (1969), *The Festal Menaion*. London: Faber.

E/DM

Mesonyktikon   Greek, 'Midnight': first office of the day in the Byzantine rite, celebrated theoretically at midnight, but in most monasteries immediately before ORTHROS. On ATHOS it begins at around 3 a.m. or earlier. On weekdays it has two distinct parts. The first part is dominated by Septuagint Psalm 118, the Amomos, which contains the verse, 'At midnight I arose to confess you for the judgements of your justice.' This long meditation on God's law is prescribed for Matins every Saturday and most Sundays, and is therefore read daily in the monastic cycle. This is followed by a series of short hymns and prayers, beginning with the troparion 'Behold, the Bridegroom is coming in the middle of the night'. The second part is a short office of supplication for the departed. Sunday Mesonyktikon takes the form of a CANON in honour of the holy Trinity, followed by a series of MEGALYNARIA. The eight canons, one for each tone, are by Metrophanes, bishop of Smyrna, and form a poetic compendium of Orthodox Trinitarian THEOLOGY.

E

metanoia   Greek, 'repentance'. (1) REPENTANCE of an evil act or omission. (2) conversion, the turning around of life away from self and sin and to God. (3) In Greek monastic parlance, 'Where did you make your *metanoia*?' means 'In what monastery were you first enrolled?' (4) A physical gesture of repentance, a *metany*, made either (a) by making the sign of the CROSS while bowing with bent knees until the lowered right hand touches the ground, or (b) by making the sign of the Cross and prostrating oneself in a kneeling posture until the forehead touches the ground. Metanies are prescribed at certain points in services, especially during the Prayer of EPHREM THE SYRIAN during Great Lent, and are imposed in significant numbers as a normal part of daily monastic training.

DM

Meteora   Monasteries in Thessaly constructed around spectacular rocky pinnacles (*see* HOLY MOUNTAINS). The fourteenth-century skete of Doupiani is the earliest recorded monastic settlement in the region. Groups of monks from ATHOS found refuge in Meteora when Turkish and other pirates raided MACEDONIA. The great Meteoron, the major monastery, was founded by Athanasios of Meteora in the late fourteenth century. It achieved fame when the Serbian prince Ioasaph Ouresis became a monk here. Athanasios and Ioasaph, commemorated on 20 April, are the patron saints of Meteora. Other monasteries were founded here into the OTTOMAN period. Varlaam, Rousanou and Prodromos are all post-Byzantine foundations. Indeed, Meteora flourished beyond the sixteenth century, a period when other monastic republics declined as a result of insecurity or Turkish pressure.

The Lives of the Monastery Builders of Meteora (1991), Buena Vista, Cal.: Holy Apostles. Nicol, D. M. (1975), *Meteora: the Rock Monasteries of Thessaly*, rev. edn. London: Variorum.

FB

Michael and Gabriel The principal archangels in Christian tradition are depicted

 winged, their hair tied with ribbons in the manner of Persian kings. In the icon shown here they stand on small carpets. Michael wears a warrior's *chlamys* and holds a sword and spear as Commander of the Angelic Hosts. Gabriel, wearing a deacon's *orarion*, holds an orb and a banner inscribed with the TRISAGION. They appear together as guardians and builders of churches, e.g. in the apse mosaic of Panagia Angeloktistos (sixth century) in CYPRUS. They are celebrated in the Synaxis of the Commanders (*Archestrategoi*), and of the Bodiless Powers, on 8 November (*see* ANGELS). Michael is also celebrated on 6 September, 8 June and 18 June, Gabriel on 26 March.
    See also CHONAI; PANORMITIS.

Tatić-Djurić, M. (1962), *Image of the Angels*. Recklinghausen: Icon Museum.

KP

Michael Keroularios Ecumenical Patriarch 1043–58. Michael received the monastic tonsure (KOURA) when exiled for conspiracy against Michael IV the Paphlagonian (1034–41). Emperor Constantine IX Monomachos (1042–55) appointed him patriarch. Michael I was determined to maintain the dignity of his office and the dogmatic and ritual traditions of the Eastern church against the Latins. Relations between Byzantium and ROME had deteriorated during the pontificate of the bellicose Benedict VIII (1012–24), who had supported rebellion in southern Italy against Byzantine rule and had introduced into the mass in Rome the singing of the Nicene Creed with the FILIOQUE. Hopes of better relations under his brother and successor John XIX (1024–32) proved vaporous, and the pope ceased to be commemorated in Constantinople. Leo IX (1048–54) exacerbated matters by treating areas of southern Italy belonging to the patriarchate of Constantinople as if he himself held jurisdiction over them. When he held a synod on Byzantine territory, appointed Humbert of Silva Candida as archbishop of Sicily, and roused controversy between Greek and Latin clerics, Michael closed the Latin churches in Constantinople and fulminated against a whole diet of Latin practices.

Michael's rejection of Latin customs drew authority from the QUINISEXT COUNCIL (691–2). Some of the 102 disciplinary decrees of this council, regarded in the East as sharing the ecumenical authority of the fifth and sixth councils, were never accepted as normative in the West, and in Western tradition the canonical legislation of ecumenical councils was never accorded the same authority as in the East. The 102 canons prohibited fourth marriages, which Western practice allowed, rejected the symbolic depiction of Christ, forbade Saturday fasting and rejected enforced clerical celibacy. From the point of view of Eastern tradition, Keroularios was opposing anti-canonical practices and, in the case of the FILIOQUE, alteration of the creed forbidden by the ecumenical council which promulgated it.

The Byzantine empire desperately needed to maintain good relations with the West. Emperor Constantine IX, however, was a pleasure-loving man, with nothing like the strength of character to keep his fiery patriarch on the paths of moderation and conciliation. Pope Leo IX became a prisoner of war of the Normans in June 1053 when taking military action against their incursions in southern Italy. He sent Cardinals Frederick of Lorraine, later Stephen IX (1057–8), and Humbert to Constantinople as his legates, facing Michael with the mirror image of his own arrogant intransigence in the person of Humbert. The encounter between the Latin embassy and the Byzantine patriarch and his hierarchs ended with Humbert publicly laying a formal excommunication of Michael on the altar of Hagia Sophia on 16 July 1054. Humbert may well have hoped the emperor would support him and depose Michael. Some five weeks later the patriarch responded with anathemas of his own. Since Leo IX had died two months before Humbert issued the excommunication in his name, the legate's action was probably invalid. The schism between Roman Catholic and Eastern Orthodox churches has conventionally been dated from this event. This is at least misleading. The anathemas were directed against persons, not churches; the pope had not been commemorated in Constantinople for a quarter of a century before the anathemas; and there were bishops in communion with both Rome and Constantinople long after the anathemas were issued. None the less, the anathemas remain a potent symbol of the schism, and the lifting of them by Paul VI and ATHENAGORAS I in 1965 was an important sign; but, just as the original anathemas did not of themselves create the schism, so the lifting of the anathemas did not end it.

Michael had defied the pope, championed Orthodoxy and humiliated the conciliatory emperor. For a while he was unassailable. When, however, Isaac I Komnenos (1057–9) came to the throne, possibly with Michael's active assistance, the emperor put him on trial and the distinguished scholar and philosopher Michael Psellos was designated his prosecutor. Michael died on his way to face his judges.

Hussey, J. M. (1986), *The Orthodox Church in the Byzantine Empire*. Oxford: Oxford University Press.
Smith, M. H. (1978), 'And Taking Bread . . . : Caerularius and the Azyme Controversy of 1054', *Théologie Historique* 47.

DM

Michael Pitkevich (1877–1962)   Latvian STARETS. Michael, orphaned in child-hood, later lived as a pilgrim. In 1902, after military service, he joined VALAAM monastery in Karelia. Ordained priest in 1917, Michael celebrated the Divine Liturgy daily, commemorating long lists of the departed. Like most Valaam monks he opposed the imposition of the New Calendar in 1925 and the persecution of OLD CALENDAR-ISTS by the Finnish authorities. The monks were evacuated to New Valaam in 1939; here Michael lived as a recluse. In 1957 he moved to the Pskov Caves monastery in the USSR with six other elders.

Bolshakoff, S. and Stakhovich, M. (1992), *Interior Silence*. Platina, Cal.: St Herman of Alaska.

DB

Michael I the Syrian   Also known as Michael the Great. A priest's son, born in 1126 at Melitene, he became head of the nearby monastery of Bar Ṣawmā. Elected in 1166 to succeed JACOBITE Patriarch Athanasius VIII, Michael held office until his death in 1199. He was invited to the Third Lateran Council (1187) but did not attend, though he wrote a treatise against the Albigenses, and was received in JERUSALEM by Sultan Kilij Arslan (1172) and Baldwin IV (1178–9). Intrigue involving the Byzantine court resulted in one of his followers, Theodore bar Wahbūn, becoming rival patriarch (1180–93).

Michael's most important work was his *Chronicle*, covering the period from the creation to 1195. The *Chronicle*, in twenty-one books, is partly set out in columns dealing with secular events, religious matters and mixed events. Much material is from sources no longer extant, which Michael acknowledges fully. A manuscript of the SYRIAC text of this enormous work, dated 1598, was discovered in the late nineteenth century at Urfa (*see* EDESSA). This was edited, translated and indexed by J.-B. Chabot in 1899–1924. An eighteenth-century Arabic translation of the *Chronicle* exists, and an abbreviated version in Armenian made in 1248 was known before the publication of the Syriac. Michael also wrote other books (liturgical, dogmatic, prayers, etc.), mostly not extant.

Chabot, J.-B. ed. (1899–1924), *Chronique de Michel le Syrien*. Paris: E. Leroux.

JH

Middle East Council of Churches   Founded in 1974 to encourage Christians to remain in the Middle East and to work for mutual support. The MECC produces several publications in Arabic, French and English, including a quarterly *News Report*. Its headquarters are in Beirut with offices in Limassol, Damascus, Cairo, Amman, Jerusalem and Bahrain. It is composed of Oriental Orthodox, EASTERN ORTHODOX, Catholic, Evangelical and Episcopal churches. In 1995 the CHURCH OF THE EAST became a full member.

KP

Mileševa   Monastery of the Ascension in the Lim valley in western Serbia, founda-tion and mausoleum of King Vladislav, nephew of SAVA of Serbia. Vladislav brought Sava's remains here after his death in 1235 in Trnovo in BULGARIA and his temporary burial in the Forty Martyrs church. Renowned for its wall paintings completed before

1228, Mileševa also possessed an early scriptorium and remained a lively cultural centre well into the OTTOMAN period. Monks learned printing in VENICE and in 1544 installed a Cyrillic printing press at Mileševa. St Sava's relics had given rise to a widespread cult, increasingly important under Turkish rule as both Christian and Islamicized Balkan people made pilgrimages to the shrine. In 1594 the grand vizier Sinan Pasha, quelling a Serbian uprising in Banat, ordered Sava's body removed to Belgrade where it was publicly burnt on 27 April. Life in the monastery continued despite hardship, but by the late eighteenth century it was a deserted ruin. Positioned on a main road from the Adriatic into central Serbia, Mileševa was visited by many Western travellers who left important notes on it. In the 1880s the young British archaeologist Arthur Evans marvelled at the 'classical' qualities of the White Angel from the Resurrection scene above Vladislav's tomb. Renovated in the nineteenth and twentieth centuries, Mileševa retains much of its original frescoes, including a remarkable portrait of St Sava.

Kandić, O., Popović, S. and Zarić, R. (1995), *The Monastery of Mileševa*. Belgrade: Republički Zavod za Zaštitu Spomenika Kulture.
Zivković, B. (1992), *Mileševa. Les dessins des fresques*. Belgrade: Republički Zavod za Zaštitu Spomenika Kulture.
Radojčić, S. (1963), *Mileševa*. Belgrade: Srpska Književna Zadruga i 'Prosveta'.

ZG

military saints   A category of such popular Eastern saints as George, Demetrios MYROBLYTES, Menas, Mercurius, Theodore Stratelates and Theodore the Recruit. Military saints sometimes appear in civil dress, more often, especially in later centuries, in military uniform, frequently mounted. Several are GREAT MARTYRS. The cult of St Menas originated in Egypt, where he remains popular. The cult of St George the Trophy-bearer became popular in Western Europe through the CRUSADES. Mercurius and Demetrios are both credited with returning from heaven, Mercurius to slay Julian the Apostate (361–3), Demetrios to defend Thessaloniki by striking down a Bulgarian invader often identified as Khan Krum (803–14). Nestor, Demetrios' disciple, is also a warrior saint, shown overthrowing the giant gladiator Lyaios. Theodore the Recruit and Theodore Stratelates regularly appear together, Theodore the Recruit sometimes alone, spearing a dragon. In later icons George and Demetrios are often shown riding together, perhaps because George's feast, 23 April, marked the beginning and Demetrios's day, 26 October, the end of the summer pasture period.

Military saints were originally honoured as soldiers who courageously faced martyrdom for confessing Christ and refusing to fight. In later centuries they were venerated precisely as soldiers, fighting the enemies of Christ and of the Christian monarchs ruling in his name. In the OTTOMAN period they inspired Christian youths debarred from military service; some of the NEW MARTYRS were young men who proved their courage and devotion by seeking voluntary martyrdom.

DM/DB

Mogila, Peter (1596–1647)   Metropolitan of KIEV. His writings show strong Western influence, due to the Catholic dominance of UKRAINE as part of the Lithuanian–

Polish state. Peter opposed the UNIATE movement, but made use of Roman Catholic theological language and methods to defend Orthodoxy. This is apparent in his *Orthodox Confession* (1640), in part a rejoinder to the *Confession of Faith* (1633) of Cyril LUCARIS. He also published an important EUCHOLOGION or *Trebnik* (1646). Becoming head of the Kiev monastery of the Caves in 1627, he established a new school run like a Jesuit college and using Latin as the language of instruction. A school already existed in Kiev organized by the Orthodox brotherhoods (*bratstva*). Brotherhoods of lay Orthodox had sprung up in reaction against the movement for union with ROME even before the Brest-Litovsk council in 1596. The brotherhoods of Vilna and Lvov, approved by Ecumenical Patriarch JEREMIAS II in 1586, were among the first to come under Constantinople's direct jurisdiction. Peter's election as metropolitan of Kiev in 1633 was controversial because a metropolitan had already been elected in secret, but he won the backing of Patriarch Cyril Lucaris. An English translation of Mogila's *Orthodox Confession* was edited by J. J. OVERBECK in 1898.

Florovsky, G. (1979), *Ways of Russian Theology*. Belmont, Mass.: Nordland.
Maloney, G. A. (1976), *A History of Orthodox Theology since 1453*. Belmont, Mass.: Nordland.

KP

monasticism   A movement of ASCETICISM and withdrawal, seeking a life of prayer in celibacy and simplicity, monasticism originated in the third-century church, taking several explicit forms in the fourth century, and enduring thereafter as a central part of Eastern Christian life. The word 'monasticism' derives from the Greek *monos*, single or solitary. Even though monasticism soon acquired predominantly a communitarian aspect, at the heart of monastic experience has always been a gravitation to solitude, and the stillness, *hesychia*, or inner concentration it can foster. This movement to a solitary standing before God lies behind the other fundamental characteristics that describe monasticism, primarily its disciplined renunciation and its rich traditions of prayer. The spirituality of the Christian East has been shaped and guided by the monastic experience which has provided for both Eastern and Western churches centres of continuance, endurance and spiritual renewal, through fluctuating political conditions, giving the church innumerable monastic writers and teachers, and many of its greatest missionaries and leaders.

The monastic movement is most clearly seen to develop in the fourth century, when ascetics in Egypt, Syria and Palestine began to assemble and organize into recognizable social groups with distinct patterns of relations to the urban churches and their hierarchies. The movement's roots, however, lie further back in Greco-Roman, Jewish and third-century Christian contexts. Post-exilic biblical literature identified the desert between Egypt and the Promised Land as more than a place of transition where the People of God were condemned to wander. The Pentateuch highlights Israel's disobedience; nevertheless, in the later prophets such as Hosea (Osee 2: 14–17), the desert became also the symbol of a golden age of Israel's simplicity, when God dwelt in a tent in their very midst, and his people heard and responded to his voice. The desert thus became a symbol of covenant renewal. Important elements of this tradition merged with currents of renewal theology implicit in Jewish apocalyptic thought, and Christian exegetes, especially ORIGEN of ALEXANDRIA in the third century, began to develop the themes in a Christological manner, providing, in embryonic form, the first basis for subsequent Christian monastic theology.

Jesus himself is predominantly a figure preaching in an urban landscape. His work, as recorded in the gospels, is rooted in the towns and villages of Palestine; his normal metaphors, drawn from the social archetypes of organized rural communities, presume the standard patterns of social bonding. Villagers sowing, and collectively gathering the harvest, or young men and women marrying, become his data for illustrating the advent of the Kingdom of God. The image of feasting and drinking recurred so often in his teaching, and possibly in his practice, that contemporary opponents dismissed him as 'a glutton and a drunkard' (Matt. 11: 19), starkly contrasting him with the ascetic figure of John the Baptist. The record of the earliest church in the Pauline letters or Acts of the Apostles is one of a missionary movement progressing through an urban nexus. Because of this, many have questioned the legitimacy of the claim of monasticism to have expressed the substance of Jesus's teachings in solitary withdrawal. Indeed, if the 'social gospel' is taken as paradigmatic of Jesus' intent, then the whole monastic impetus appears contradictory and problematic as a form of Christian discipleship.

Early monastic exegetes drew their inspiration from biblical episodes such as Jesus' withdrawing into solitude for prayer, or from biblical 'desert' radicals such as Elias or John the Baptist, who became the patrons of monks; but the more obvious line of continuation from Jesus' teaching to the experience of monasticism was the radical, subversive aspect of Jesus' apocalyptic call to repentance, and the renunciations he demanded to allow this to be expressed – whether involving loss of family, friends or possessions. The demands of the Kingdom, in Jesus' preaching, took such precedence as to marginalize the normal patterns of social behaviour. This attitude, recognized as the spur and impetus of the *kerygma* (proclamation) of Jesus, became for the monks the root of their commitment to poverty, celibacy and disciplined obedience, in a quasi-apocalyptic withdrawal from organized society. In describing themselves as 'living the life of the angels', the early monks evoked their sense that they were anticipating the Age to Come.

The monastic movement thus reappropriated the apocalyptic impetus for the fourth-century church in the Constantinian era, when persecution was largely past, and the church had come into social favour. Several commentators have interpreted monasticism as the recreation of a new age of 'spiritual martyrdom' for a church in danger of losing its fervour (Eusebius, *Ecclesiastical History*, 6: 42). Although the monks did describe themselves as undergoing a 'white martyrdom', this explanation of the movement's origins is too simplistic. There were also political reasons why flight to the desert would be appealing to many at this period. The general collapse of the Roman empire's economy in the third century and the crippling obligations laid upon many smallholders as well as intellectual members of the curial class conspired to make the prospect of private or communal subsistence lifestyles attractive. There was for some a genuine sense of freedom to be gained by living on the fringes of imperial society, away from the excessive demands of sustaining city life in late antiquity. Christian communities labouring together for a common purpose and with a simple lifestyle soon amply demonstrated their economic potential, and although later many monasteries were founded by generous aristocratic or imperial benefaction, from its early origins monasticism proved capable of sustaining itself and generating wealth. For female ascetics, particularly those of an aristocratic background such as Macrina the Great in Cappadocia or the two Melanias in Palestine, monastic life offered possibilities of self-determination not otherwise available (Clark, 1986). This paradox of a simple and poor life dedicated to God, allied with the capability for successful social and economic expansion, has dogged the heels of monasticism throughout its history, threatening its authenticity both in East and West, whenever monasteries came to hold extensive possessions.

The fourth-century movement to the desert may also be seen as an important stage in the development of the notion of personhood, indicating the transition taking place from established *mores* of classical civilisation to the world of late antiquity (Kirschner, 1984), the corporate life of the city beginning to give way to the sense of the individual person as a new focal point for a hermeneutic of human existence. This movement was not simply reducible to the social instability rising out of the third century; it had roots in other philosophical and religious currents occupying Hellenism's intellectuals at the same period (Fowden, 1982). The merging of Platonic metaphysics and Pythagorean ascetic piety dominated Greco-Roman intellectual life by the early third century. Origen demonstrated how such an intellectual ethos could be applied to Christian concerns by using related concepts to elaborate a teaching on the soul's destiny for mystical union with the Logos of God (Crouzel, 1961). Thereafter, the properly Christian notion of ascesis was essentially allied with the idea of the soul's striving for union with God.

The word 'asceticism' derives from the Greek term for physical exercise, such as athletic practice. The idea of training the soul to virtue by disciplining the body is fundamental to monastic theory. Here, Christian monasticism provided a distinct and original anthropology. In many Greco-Roman theories the purpose of 'philosophic' asceticism was to purify the soul of the body's influence. A guiding premise was often the belief that materiality was a fundamental corruption of the true human nature, and that constant suppression of the material passions (*pathemata*) would allow the essential person, conceived as *nous*, or intellective spiritual entity, to go free, permanently liberated from the body and all material forms.

Although some parts of the Christian ascetic tradition came close to such views (especially those in the strongest line of Origenian thought, such as EVAGRIUS PONTICUS), the fundamental impetus of Christian asceticism witnesses to another anthropology altogether, one discernible even in Origen and Evagrius. The biblical and Christological imperatives of the church never allowed monasticism to relegate the body and materiality to the realm of evil. In its purest form the Christian concept of ascesis seeks not the liberation of the soul from the body but the integration of the person, spiritually and materially. Ascesis was thus a manner of disciplining the body and training the mind by prayers, vigils and fasting, until the whole person was attuned to his or her best ability to hear and obey the voice of God. The predominant message of the corpus of monastic literature is the need for a humble remembrance of sin and death, and the spiritual fruitfulness of an attitude of repentant sorrow (*penthos*, KATANYXIS) that this produces in the heart of the monk. The monk is the epitome of one who stands in repentance (METANOIA), like the publican in the parable who finds the favour of God because of his prayer for mercy (Luke 18: 9–14). In later hesychastic monasticism this ancient attitude was summed up in the constant repetition of the JESUS PRAYER: 'Lord Jesus Christ, Son of God, have mercy on me a sinner.'

Monastic literature is largely pedagogical, explaining the nature of ascesis and giving encouragement for the perseverance needed for its practice. There is an urgent desire to liberate the person from the tyrannical demands of the ego. It is, therefore, a neglected but important phase in the emergence of a distinct and fully developed Christian doctrine of the person.

Although scattered groups of Christian hermits were already known by the late third century, Eastern Christian tradition honours Antony the Great as the founding father of monks. His biography, the *Vita Antonii* by ATHANASIUS, which circulated widely in Greek and Latin, did much to popularize his ascetic lifestyle. Antony was born *c.*250 at Coma in Middle Egypt. After hearing in church the gospel text: 'If you would be perfect, sell all you have and give the money to the poor and you will have treasure in heaven; then come follow me' (Matthew 19: 21), he obeyed the prescription literally, leaving at the age of twenty for an ascetic life on the outskirts of the town. Fifteen years later he moved to an abandoned fort at Pispir, the 'Outer Mountain', where colonies of solitary monks grew up around him, attracted by his reputation as exorcist and spiritual master. Other famous colonies were established at Nitria and Scete under Amoun and Macarius. Antony died in 356 at the age of 105 on Mount Colzim near the Red Sea. Throughout his life he had exemplified a form of monasticism based simply on the retreat to solitary life in a cave, abandoned tomb or deserted military outpost. The monk successful in the ascetical struggle was thereby expected to acquire the spiritual wisdom and status as elder, or father, Abba, to allow him to console and strengthen the brethren. So it was that Antony's eremitical or anchoritic monasticism already gave evidence of the other early type of monastic organization that would develop: hermits living together in loosely arranged colonies where practical self-help, emergency food supplies or medical aid could be joined with independent solitary living.

This form of monastic settlement, the LAVRA, later especially vigorous in Byzantine Palestine, allowed for varying degrees of relation among the monks, ranging from occasional meetings for liturgical celebrations, eventually every Saturday and Sunday, to the sporadic consultation of an elder, to a more regularized life in what might almost be described as a monastic village, with individual cells constructed around a common church, the *katholikon*.

A third form of monastic organization, which came to outstrip all others in popularity, was attributed to Pachomius. His was a concept centred on community; accordingly the Pachomian model came to be called cenobitic, i.e. common life. As a conscript in the Roman army Pachomius had been converted by his experience of the charity afforded him by a local Christian community. In 320 he founded an important cenobium by Tabennisi near the Nile in the Thebaid, and he subsequently encouraged eight other foundations for men and two for women, over which he presided as a general authority. Pachomius' innovation was to develop the community into an active spiritual fellowship; he composed the first 'rule' for monks, which had great symbolic influence in the subsequent history of Greek and Latin monastic life. His disciple Theodore, and later the thaumaturge Shenouti (Shenouda) of Atripe, developed his principles in a clearer and more ordered form. Shenouti was the first to demand a written 'profession', an archetype of the monastic profession, or vows, that later became descriptive of entrance into the monastic state.

These three major forms of monastic lifestyle became witnessed across the Christian world. Within a generation Palestine was an important centre, with Euthymios and Sabas the outstanding monastic leaders there, as described by Cyril of Scythopolis. In Syria other types of monastic asceticism soon attracted attention, the most famous exemplified by SYMEON STYLITES (388–460) who spent ten years as an enclosed anchorite before restricting himself, after 423, to the top of a column no more than 3 feet in circumference. He was the first of a series of pillar-dwellers, one of the last living on a column of Hadrian's temple in Athens in the nineteenth century. In the fifth century Symeon's fame attracted pilgrims from all corners of the empire, from simple peasants seeking advice or cure to the emperor himself, who consulted him on matters of state security.

Influential visitors came to the monastic centres in Egypt and Palestine from an early date, and their narratives served to propagate monasticism. Writers such as Palladius (*The Lausiac History*), JOHN CLIMACUS (*The Ladder*) and John Moschus (*The Spiritual Meadow*) helped in the process of gathering together a popular and diffused monastic tradition of oral teachings from the primitive fathers, and that tradition became formalized into collections of spiritual wisdom and edifying biographical tales. An important collection known as the *Sayings of the Desert Fathers* (*Apophthegmata Patrum*) gives an excellent flavour of the often moving, often hilarious, adventures and sayings of the primitive monks.

In the mid-fourth century Eustathios of Sebaste fostered monasticism in Armenia, and influenced Basil the Great (330–79), who was inspired to visit the monasteries in Egypt and returned to recreate monastic life on his estates in Cappadocia. Basil's monastic writings, encouraging and offering guidance for the cenobitic lifestyle, were destined to have a long-lasting influence in Eastern church life. No less important was the paradigm he offered of a vigorous administrator who, in his own person, combined monastic status and hierarchical office.

Comparable to Basil's status in the East was that of Benedict of Nursia (480–547) in the West, whose Rule made him the veritable 'Father of Western Monks'. Basil's friend and contemporary, the learned aristocrat Gregory Nazianzen (*c*.330–91) also theorized about the ascetic life, which he adopted on his father's estates. Gregory's ideas were not popularized in his own lifetime and, lacking the organizational skills of Basil, he attracted no monastic following around his own person; yet his writings became the most widely read texts in Byzantium after the BIBLE. In several of Gregory's poems, orations and letters, we first meet with elements typical of later Byzantine monasticism: the notion of the monastery as a secluded retreat for men of intellect and character to advance the higher affairs of the mind and spirit, and the idea that the seclusion proper to monasticism was an affair of the mind not of geography, so that a true monk could practise his vocation in a city as well as a desert.

From the fifth century onwards CONSTANTINOPLE became significant in the development of monastic lifestyles. At first hermits and cenobites had gathered in the less populated hinterland of the capital, or its neighbouring areas such as Chalcedon. By the time of Theodosius II (408–50) several ascetics exercised considerable influence at court, and attracted royal patronage to their foundations. After barbarian raids devastated the monastic communities at Scete in the early fifth century, and the Empire lost Syria, Palestine and Egypt first to the Persians, then to the Muslim Arabs in the seventh century, Constantinople assumed a leadership role in monastic circles. Many monastic sites were partly or wholly destroyed, although famous foundations such as Antony's fort-monastery Mar Saba, near Jerusalem, and St Catherine at SINAI, continued to flourish beyond the protection of the imperial armies.

In the ninth century THEODORE THE STUDITE incorporated and developed Basil's work by legislating for a cenobitic community in a more regularized and far-reading way than was provided for by Basil's somewhat unsystematic ascetic treatises. After Theodore, the Studite monastery in Constantinople became a standard, and his TYPI-KON gave cenobitic monasticism a settled and assured form throughout the Eastern Orthodox world. In the Eastern church distinct orders never developed as they did in the medieval West; each house developed its own typikon and there was great flexibility around the basic form. A standard daily observance based on Studite principles can be witnessed in the writings of SYMEON THE NEW THEOLOGIAN (d. 1022), especially his twenty-sixth *Catechesis* given to his monks at St Mamas in Constantinople.

Symeon's life, and his theology of God's call to the monk to see the divine light of Christ personally, and while still in the flesh, witnesses to the beginning of a mystical renewal in eleventh-century Byzantine monasticism. At this period monastic foundations began to expand on Mount Athos. In 962 Athanasius the Athonite had founded the Great Lavra there with imperial support, and soon the Holy Mountain became the most important monastic centre for the Eastern Orthodox world. The eleventh-century renewal reached fruition in the fourteenth-century hesychast movement. A controversy surrounding HESYCHASM grew from a conflict between reliance on scholastic method in theology on the one hand, and the appeal to direct mystical experience on the other. GREGORY PALAMAS, defending the Athonite monks, restated the understanding of theology as first and foremost an experience of God. He developed old and typical themes that were henceforth to be constitutive of the spirituality of this school, such as the vision of God as light, the reliance on the Jesus Prayer and the insistence that a direct experience of the unknowable God was possible for a living human being, based on the distinction he drew between God's unknowable essence and his communicated divine energies. Today hesychasm is the dominant spiritual tradition of the monasteries on Mount Athos, and is widely influential in Eastern Orthodoxy as a whole.

McGuckin, J. A. (1996), 'St Symeon the New Theologian and Byzantine Monasticism', in A. Bryer, ed., *Mount Athos and Byzantine Monasticism*. London: Variorum.
Brown, P. (1988), *The Body and Society: Men, Women and Sexual Renunciation in Early Christianity*. New York: Columbia University Press.
Talbot, A. M. (1987), 'An Introduction to Byzantine Monasticism', *Illinois Classical Studies* 12.
Clark, E. A. (1986), *Ascetic Piety and Women's Faith*. New York: E. Mellon Press.
Kirschner, R. (1984), 'The Vocation of Holiness in Late Antiquity', *Vigiliae Christianae* 38.
Fowden, G. (1982), 'The Pagan Holy Man in Late Antique Society', *Journal of Hellenic Studies* 102.
Veilleux, A. (1980–2), *Pachomian Koinonia*, 3 vols. Kalamazoo: Cistercian Publications.

Ward, B. (1975), *The Sayings of the Desert Fathers*. London: Mowbrays.

Charanis, P. (1971), 'The Monk as an Element of Byzantine Society', *Dumbarton Oaks Papers* 25.

Chitty, D. (1966), *The Desert a City*. London: Mowbrays.

Crouzel, H. (1961), *Origène et la connaissance mystique*. Paris: n.p.

JM

monophysite A person who asserts that Christ possesses only one nature. Sometimes the terms 'henophysite' or 'miaphysite' are used with the same connotation. When the aged Archimandrite Eutyches, godfather of the politically influential eunuch Chrysaphios, mounted a vigorous attack on NESTORIANISM after the condemnation of Nestorius at the Council of Ephesus (431) he made considerable use of formulae deployed by CYRIL OF ALEXANDRIA, particularly Cyril's assertion of 'the one incarnate nature of God the Word'. Unfortunately, Eutyches lacked Cyril's subtle intelligence and theological poise, and was understood to have denied that Christ is *homoousios* (consubstantial) with the human race. In November 448 EUSEBIUS OF DORYLAEUM charged him with heresy. Having been summoned before the Standing Synod by FLAVIAN of Constantinople, and excommunicated, he appealed to Pope Leo I. Dioscoros, patriarch of Alexandria, interested himself in the affair, and Chrysaphios influenced Emperor Theodosius II to the end that a retrial was ordered, and a council convened at Ephesus. The pope's legates arrived at Ephesus carrying his *Tome*, formally a letter to Flavian, but had little chance of a hearing. The proceedings were dominated by Dioscoros, the imperial troops and belligerent Egyptian monks armed with staves. The council (449), which Pope Leo was to name the *Latrocinium*, the Brigandage, restored and exonerated Eutyches and deposed Flavian, who was so violently treated that he died of his injuries. This did not end the dispute. In 451 the Emperor Marcian (450–7) convened another council at Chalcedon which anathematized both Nestorius and Eutyches and asserted the existence of two natures in Christ, '…perfect in Godhead, perfect in humanity… consubstantial [*homoousios*] with the Father according to the Godhead, consubstantial with us according to the humanity, like us in everything except sin…'. The council also deposed and excommunicated Dioscoros, who was exiled to Gangra, where he died in 454.

It seemed to some that Chalcedon had condemned not only Eutyches but also, despite its praise of him, Cyril of Alexandria. Many loyal to the theology of Cyril repudiated Chalcedon. In Egypt many remained loyal to their deposed patriarch: his CHALCEDONIAN replacement, Proterius (451–7), installed by military force, won the hatred of much of his flock and was eventually killed by a mob. He faced an impressive anti-Chalcedonian rival, TIMOTHY AILOUROS.

Despite repeated endeavours to heal the breach from Chalcedon on, there have existed in EASTERN CHRISTIANITY two orthodoxies, one accepting the council's ecumenical authority, the other rejecting it. The second tradition, that of the Oriental Orthodox, is often described as monophysite. The uncritical use of the term 'monophysite' is, however, hazardous: a variety of different monophysite positions exist, and to some of them the fathers of the Oriental Orthodox tradition were sternly opposed. Julian, bishop of Halicarnassus, for example, taught that the flesh of Christ was incorruptible from the moment of the Incarnation. This view was condemned by

SEVERUS OF ANTIOCH as a form of docetism; he labelled Julian and his followers 'phantasiasts', but they are more commonly known as aphthartodocetists. The AGNOETAI, led by Severus' pupil the Alexandrian deacon Themistios, emphasized the human attributes of Christ to the point that they attributed ignorance to him. Other pupils of Severus became known as *aktistoi*, uncreated ones, since they denied that Christ's body was ever created.

Severus himself, together with Timothy Ailouros, PETER THE FULLER and PETER MONGOS, represent a tradition loyal to Cyril's doctrine, sternly opposed to all they saw as Nestorianism and to all compromises with it, and in their view the dogma of Chalcedon is just that. Explicitly or implicitly, however, they accept that Christ is indeed *homoousios* with the rest of humanity and *homoousios* with the Father and the Holy Spirit, so that at the crucial point where CHRISTOLOGY intersects with soteriology they and the Chalcedonians are at one. In the modern period the Armenian Archbishop Tiran Nersoyan asserts unambiguously: 'The Lord Jesus Christ is perfect man and perfect God. He is the Logos incarnate, consubstantial with us as to His manhood and consubstantial with the Father as to His Godhood. Both sides, Chalcedonian and non-Chalcedonian alike, agree to this confession of faith fully.'

The recognition that a substantial measure of agreement was possible between moderate Chalcedonians and moderate monophysites underlay several imperially sponsored attempts to generate a compromise doctrinal formula. The attempts were doomed, not because no such formula could be constructed, but because the division was not merely doctrinal. As the emperors imposed dogma by political, judicial and military means, the opposed sides eventually came to represent different ethnic groups, even to think in different languages; they not only expressed their Christological beliefs by means of different formulae, they lived different and opposed histories, revered different martyrs and confessors, and attributed authority to different councils.

Nersessian, V., ed. (1996), *Archbishop Tiran Nersoyan: Armenian Church Historical Studies*. New York: St Vartan Press.
Young, F. (1983), *From Nicea to Chalcedon*. London: SCM Press.
Chesnut, R. C. (1976), *Three Monophysite Christologies*. Oxford: Oxford University Press.
Frend, W. H. C. (1972), *The Rise of the Monophysite Movement*. Cambridge: Cambridge University Press.

DM

monotheletism   The doctrine that Christ possesses a single will, propagated by the EKTHESIS of Emperor Heraclius (610–41) to unite CHALCEDONIAN and MONOPHYSITE Christians. It failed in this object, opposed by monophysites as a worthless compromise, weakening the clarity of their CHRISTOLOGY with a speculative construction, and equally opposed by strict Chalcedonians as denying the perfection of Christ's human nature. MAXIMUS THE CONFESSOR was the most noted opponent of monotheletism, suffering torture and exile in his old age rather than accede to what he saw as a destructive heresy. Monotheletism was condemned as heresy at the Third Council of Constantinople in 680–1.

See also ECUMENICAL COUNCILS.

DM

Montenegro   Serbo-Croat: Crna Gora; Greek: Maurovounion; Turkish: Kara Dağ. Independent for centuries before uniting with Serbia to form Yugoslavia after the First World War, Montenegro was staunchly EASTERN ORTHODOX, even ruled from 1516 to 1815 by the bishops of Cetinje. Its borders fluctuated. The OTTOMANS occupied Cetinje in 1623 and 1687, but Montenegrins clung to the territories of Zeta, a medieval Slavic state, and always opposed Ottoman suzerainty. From 1799 Montenegro expanded at the expense of Turks and Albanians, a process that culminated in the liberation of PEĆ in 1913. The collapse of Yugoslavia in the 1990s has revived memories of former independence and even encouraged a movement to re-establish a separate Orthodox church.

See also SERBIAN CHRISTIANITY.

DB

Morea   A medieval term of uncertain derivation for the Peloponnese, possibly from 'Romaia', the Greek lands, or from an allusion to the mulberry leaf, though other explanations are canvassed. From the tenth century a bishopric of Moreon in Elis is attested, from which 'Morea' may first have been used to name the western half of the peninsula. The Byzantine despotate of Morea flourished 1349–1460, Mistras emerging as Morea's capital until replaced by Tripolis during OTTOMAN rule. Tripolis was taken by the insurgent Greeks in 1821.

Runciman, S. (1980), *Mistra*. London: Thames & Hudson.

DB

Moscow   First mentioned as a small town with wooden ramparts in 1147, the city celebrated its 850th anniversary in 1997. It was destroyed by Tartars in 1238. The Kremlin is first recorded in 1331. Moscow acquired new ecclesiastical importance in 1326, when Metropolitan Peter of KIEV and All Russia took up residence there. Peter began work on the first DORMITION cathedral, Uspenskii Sobor, its foundation bringing secular and ecclesiastical powers together within the Kremlin. The present Dormition cathedral, completed in 1479 by the Italian architect Aristotele Fioravanti, is based on the Dormition church at VLADIMIR. The Annunciation cathedral was built by architects from Pskov in 1489 on the site of an earlier church with murals by THEOPHAN THE GREEK and Andrei RUBLEV. The ICONOSTASIS in the Annunciation cathedral has some panels by Theophanes and Rublev dated to *c*.1405. The Kremlin Cathedral of St Michael the Archangel was constructed between 1505 and 1509 by another Italian architect, again on the site of an earlier church, in which Theophanes had also worked. Renaissance pilasters and scallop shells on its exterior sit oddly with its basically Byzantine conception. The Cathedral of Basil the Blessed in Red Square was built in 1555–60 by Ivan IV the Terrible (1533–84); despite its ornate polychromatic cupolas, it embodies many traditional elements especially of Russian wooden church architecture.

In 1589 Ecumenical Patriarch JEREMIAS II recognized the metropolitan of Moscow as patriarch. The first patriarch, Job, was canonized in 1989, the 400th anniversary of his elevation. The patriarchate, suppressed in the reforms of Peter the Great (1682–1721), was restored in 1917. Moscow, for many the THIRD ROME, remained the spiritual capital of Russia even when St Petersburg became the state capital.

Moscow was a great centre of Russian MONASTICISM up to the Revolution of 1917. In the period of the Revolution and under communist rule many churches were closed, destroyed or converted to museums of atheism. In the post-communist period church property has been returned by the state, churches have been re-opened and monasteries re-established, and the cathedral of the Saviour has been rebuilt.

Like the monasteries, Moscow's cemeteries have played an important role in the cultural and spiritual history of the city. Many famous Russian writers are buried in the cemetery of the Virgin of Smolensk Cathedral at Novodevichii monastery. The Rogozhskii cemetery is the spiritual centre of the OLD BELIEVER church of the Belokrinitsa hierarchy, and the Preobrazhenskii cemetery is the base of a major congregation of the Fedoseevtsy Priestless Old Believers, who, unlike many Old Believers, have no marriage sacrament.

Hamilton, J. H. (1983), *The Art and Architecture of Russia*. Harmondsworth: Penguin.
Burian, J. and Shvidkovsky, O. A. (1977), *The Kremlin of Moscow*. London: Robert Hale.

KP

Moses Putilov (1782–1862)   Moses' parents were merchants of Borisoglebsk. Both his brothers became monks and abbots, Isaias (1842–50) of the Sarov monastery, Antonii (1839–53) of St Nicolas of Maloiaroslavets. At sixteen, after meeting SERAPHIM OF SAROV, Moses became a hermit in the Roslavl forests, joining disciples of PAISSII VELICHKOVSKII. The 1812 war forced Moses to move to Briansk monastery. In 1821, invited by Abbot Daniil (1819–25), he founded a forest skete in the Optina Wilderness, assisted by his younger brother Antonii, whom he left in charge when he became abbot of OPTINA monastery itself. At Optina he was joined in 1829 by STARETS Leonid Nagolkin and his followers. Assisted by a group inspired by the teachings of Paissii Velichkovskii, Moses founded a major library, new churches and other facilities. He welcomed blind and disabled monks, encouraged a unique creative freedom and nurtured respect for independently minded elders like Leonid (d. 1841), Makarii Ivanov (d. 1860) and Amvrosii Grenkov (d. 1891).

Bolshakoff, S. (1976), *Russian Mystics*. Kalamazoo: Cistercian Press.
De Beausobre, I. (1975), *Russian Letters of Direction*. Crestwood, NY: St Vladimir's Seminary Press.
Kontzevich, I. M. (1970), *The Optina Wilderness and its Times*. Platina, Cal.: St Herman of Alaska.

DB

music   Ephesians 5: 19 and Colossians 3: 16 speak of 'psalms and hymns and spiritual songs'. Justin Martyr in the early second century describes the Christians as worshipping God by offering 'solemn prayers and hymns' (Apologia I, 13). Singing was evidently a well-known feature of Christian worship. A letter of Pliny the Younger, governor of Bythinia, seeking advice from Trajan (98–117) on the treatment of Christians, describes them as assembling before dawn 'to recite a song amongst themselves to Christ as to a god'.

Christianity emerged from Judaism, and music, including instrumental music, was an important element in the rites of the Jerusalem Temple. Temple liturgy ended at the Roman conquest of JERUSALEM in AD 70. Many early Christians were Jews or gentiles who attended the synagogue without converting to Judaism. Unfortunately there is no conclusive evidence of the role of music in the synagogue in the early Christian period, so we do not know what their experience of Jewish liturgical music would have been. Scriptural cantillation and chanted psalmody may have been used; certainly memory remained of psalms and doxologies being sung in the Temple. Pagan cults made use of both vocal and instrumental music, and official pagan rites formed part of public civic life. Musicological research into Christian and Jewish chant led to the thesis presented perhaps most fully in Eric Werner's book *The Sacred Bridge*, that Christian chant is fundamentally Jewish in origin. Interestingly, Werner also offers evidence of Jewish liturgical borrowing from Christianity. Diametrically opposed to Werner's thesis is the common belief of those Greek theorists of Byzantine *psalmodia*, who see Byzantine chant as a direct derivative of ancient Greek music, and map the eight tones of ecclesiastical music on to the modal system. It comes as little surprise to find that Coptic chant is claimed to descend from the temple music of ancient Egypt. In reality we lack the evidence to prove any of these claims.

What is clear is that Christian public worship came to make use of unaccompanied monophonic chant, though in Ethiopic tradition the prayer staff and systrum are used, and in Coptic tradition the triangle and cymbal, as rhythmic instruments. All traditions of EASTERN CHRISTIAN music possess simple, recitative melodies for chanting the psalms, and more complex melodies which can be used for solemn psalmody and which are used for the singing of psalm verses used in specific liturgical contexts. This closely parallels the heritage of the synagogue.

Each family of Eastern Christian churches possesses traditional prayer and reading tones; most are based on simple systems of inflection which allow the text to be chanted according to its grammatical structure and provide terminal formulae for the conclusion of the prayer or reading. The Coptic and Ethiopian rites, however, make use of prayer tones of some complexity, the use of which, though not their melodies, is reminiscent of the use of Jewish prayer tones.

The cantillation of scripture serves several functions: chanted text is the ancient world's equivalent of the public address system; simple formulae that indicate division of sentences or clauses inhibit intrusion of personal meanings; the formal rhetoric of chanted text lifts it from the everyday and presents it to the congregation precisely as sacred text. In Byzantine tradition, marks on the scriptural text to aid musical declamation occur from about the eighth century.

It seems probable that Armenian, Byzantine, Roman and Syrian chant of the early medieval period was organized on the basis of a system of eight tones, four considered authentic, four as plagal. The tones differ in the different traditions, but a close relation exists between the Roman tones and the medieval Byzantine tones, and some resemblances elsewhere. Systems deriving from the Byzantine also use eight tones, though sometimes they have changed and sometimes, as in Georgian, Romanian, Russian and Ukrainian traditions, they co-exist with other forms of music, harmonic or polyphonic choral music for example. Tones in modern *psalmodia*, the living tradition of Byzantine chant, are significantly different from those described in the medieval manuals of musical theory. They are, moreover, not eight modes, but eight clusters of modes. The existence of mixed tones and modes outside the system of eight tones is recognized.

The eight tones have a calendrical as well as a musical significance, the offices of each week being sung in the proper tone for that week. In the Byzantine family of rites the offices of a particular tone (*echos*) use texts proper to that tone, so that the text as well as the music of the office varies in an eight-week cycle.

Armenian tradition attributes the eight tones (*dzayn*) to Stephen Siunetsi, an eighth-century musician; his date is interesting, since the traditional organizer of the Byzantine OKTOECHOS is JOHN OF DAMASCUS, also of the eighth century.

The chant of the Coptic rite and that of the Ethiopian rite are not based on a system of eight tones. The Coptic rite has its own system of tones, each a range of melodic elements and patterns used in in liturgical dialogue. There are well-known melodies for many of the hymns and chants used in the Divine Liturgy and the offices. The different tones are used on different days and during different seasons. They require expertise to sing well. Normally they are learned by hearing, but in the modern period some are written down.

The Ethiopian rite has since the sixteenth century possessed a sophisticated and complex system of musical notation. The norm is, however, for the melodies of the three tones (*zema*) to be learned by oral transmission. The three tones are in theory sharply different from each other: *ge'ez* is based on three notes, one pitched low, one middle, one high; *araray* on a pentatonic scale; and *'ezl* on a scale which allows many chromatic variations. Grace-notes, ornaments and tropes can make it difficult to recognize the *zema* being used.

In both Coptic and Ethiopian chant, moments of heightened intensity are marked by the use of rhythmic instruments, and in the case of the *dabtaras*, the skilled chanters and ritual experts of the Ethiopian church, by rhythmic movement and steps. (*See* ETHIOPIAN ORTHODOX CHURCH.)

GEORGIA possesses a unique and ancient system of three-voice polyphony. It may go back as far as the twelfth century. Two of the three voices move to the same rhythm; the third may use more elaborate rhythmic variations. Georgia also developed its own systems of musical notation. A complex early medieval system eventually passed out of use, and its interpretation was lost; another system appears in the seventeenth century and yet another, based on the letters of the alphabet, in the nineteenth.

Armenian chant also possesses its own systems of notation. In the ninth century a system of ekphonetic signs for textual cantillation was already in use. From the same century the *khaz* notation appears, which developed through the medieval period into a system of great complexity, and is still used by the Mekhitarist monks of VENICE in its seventeenth-century form. A new notation, still in use, was created by Baba Hambard-zun Limondjian (d. 1839) in the early nineteenth century

Byzantine notation and chant developed through the middle ages, becoming increasingly complex, until by the fall of the city only experts could master them. In the OTTOMAN period notational reforms were attempted, notably by Peter Lampadarios in the eighteenth century, and in the mid-nineteenth century a simplified notation was derived by the 'Three Teachers' Chrysanthos of Madytusm, Gregorios Protopsaltes and Hourmousios Chartophylax.

Byzantine *psalmodia* is in use in Arabic, Bulgarian and Romanian churches, in the latter two side by side with polyphonic music. In Ukraine and Russia an ancient tradition of chant descending from but not identical with the Byzantine co-exists with a variety of forms of polyphonic music. Ivan IV, the Terrible, was a fine composer of chant.

Eight Syrian tones form the basis of the chant of the SYRIAN ORTHODOX and SYRIAN CATHOLIC churches. In India traditional Syrian chant co-exists with purely Indian styles of music. In the CHURCH OF THE EAST, the CHALDEAN CHURCH and the MARONITE church, the *maqām* system of classical Arabic music forms the basis of most ecclesiastical music. Greek writers of the eighteenth and nineteenth centuries agree that the modes used in modern *psalmodia* are identical with certain Ottoman *maqāms*.

All the Eastern traditions of monophonic chant use techniques of melurgy, which constructs melodies on the basis of formulae typical of a particular mode. This is more than simply combining pre-existent formulae; the elaboration, decoration and extension of subtle variants yields quite new melodies.

While melodic instruments have never been traditional in Eastern Christian public worship, they have been used to accompany sacred chant when sung outside the context of church services.

Foley, E. (1992), *Foundations of Christian Music: The Music of Pre-Constantinian Christianity*. Bramcote, Nottingham: Grove Books.

Tsereteli, E. (1974), 'Le chant traditional de Géorgie, son passé, son présent', *Bedi Kartlisa* 138.

Outtier, B. (1973), 'Recherches sur la genèse de l'octoéchos arménien', *Études grégoriennes* 14.

Hage, L. (1972), *Le chant de l'Église maronite*. Beirut: Imprimerie Catholique.

Strunk, O. (1977), *Essays on Music in the Byzantine World*. New York: Norton.

Hage, L. (1969), 'Le chant maronite', *Encyclopédie des musiques sacrées*, vol. 2. Paris.

Husmann, H. (1969), 'Die Tonarten der chaldäischen Breviergesänge', *Orientalia Christiana Periodica*.

Powne, M. (1968), *Ethiopian Music, an Introduction*. London: Oxford University Press.

Wellesz, E. (1963), *A History of Byzantine Music and Hymnography*. 3rd edn. Oxford: Oxford University Press.

Ingoroqva, P. (1962), 'La musique géorgienne', *Bedi Kartlisa* 56.

DM

myroblytes Greek, 'myrrh-gushing', 'myrrh-flowing': a title of several EASTERN CHRISTIAN saints, whose relics are held to produce or to have produced an aromatic liquid with healing properties. The most famous *myrobletes* is Demetrios of Thessaloniki (d. *c.*306) (*see* GREAT MARTYRS). Barbaros (ninth century) and Neilos of Kynouria (d. 1651) are later examples. Barbaros was, according to tradition, one of a group of Muslim pirates from Libya ambushed by Byzantine troops when raiding the shores of Akarnania and Epirus. Barbaros was captured, but escaped and lived as a lone bandit, preying on travellers. Converted to Christianity by a priest during a liturgy on Mount Nysa, he became a hermit near the village of Trypho. He was killed by a hunter who mistook him for a wild animal; he is commemorated on 15 May and 23 June.

In the KIEV Caves Lavra several myrrh-exuding skulls are preserved. More commonly, icons are held to produce myrrh as a manifestation of divine grace, for example the Myroblytissa icon of the DORMITION treasured in Malevi Convent, Arcadia.

A parallel phenomena is *euodia*, a fragrance experienced as pouring from certain relics, sometimes intermittently, and commonly recorded at the opening of the grave of a saint. Both phenomena are associated with certain Western saints and their relics.

DB

mysteries   The rites the Latin church calls sacraments, Greek Christians call *mysteria*, mysteries.

As Christianity spread, its vocabulary expanded, incorporating something of the terminology of pagan mystery religions, just as its theology took on a PHILOSOPHICAL VOCABULARY drawn from Greek philosophy. The church's central sacramental rites came to be seen as analogous to the initiatory and communion rites of the pagan mysteries and spoken of in somewhat similar terms. Christianity's triumph over paganism laid pagan ideas and cultural forms open to Christian exploitation.

The BIBLE shows the language of the mysteries applied to Wisdom herself, in Wisdom 8: 4 as *mystis* of the knowledge of God. The same book, however, uses the language of the mysteries to refer to the vilest aspects of paganism (e.g. Wisdom 12: 6; 14: 15). The word *mysterion* is also used in the Bible with the non-technical meaning of 'secret'. In Daniel 2: 47 Nabuchodonosor praises the 'God of gods and Lord of kings, who reveals secrets [*mysteria*]', in this case the mysteries hidden in a dream the prophet has interpreted.

In Matthew 13: 11 Jesus says to his disciples: 'To you it is given to know the secrets of the kingdom of the heavens; to those it is not given.' A parallel text, Mark 4: 11–12, makes the contrast even more sharply: 'To you is given the secret of the kingdom of God: to those outside all things happen in parables, so that looking they may look and not see, hearing they may hear and not understand, lest they turn and pardon be granted them.' Christ himself becomes the *mysterion* in the Pauline epistles, for example in Colossians 1: 27: 'How great among the nations are the riches of the glory of this mystery, which is Christ in you, the hope of glory.' There is in the New Testament the basis for a theology of the mystery which sees Christian discipleship as the condition of the disclosure of the mystery of God's kingdom, which becomes concretely present in the life of the believer by the indwelling of Christ, who acquits the repentant sinner and is the living pledge of the fullness of glory to come.

The *Mystagogical Catecheses* preserved under the name of CYRIL OF JERUSALEM show a fourth-century Christian bishop leading believers through the mysteric rites of Christian intitiation, explaining the inner significance of the rites they experience, emphasizing the importance of the *disciplina arcani*. These catechetical lectures, like others attributed to fathers of the fourth and fifth centuries, relate the rites to the life of Christ and to spiritual changes taking place in the initiate. A language is built up which relates the sacramental rite as type, symbol or sign of the reality it signifies.

The description of baptism and eucharist as *mysteria* is common from the fourth century. Exactly how many *mysteria* exist is a question, however, that generally arose for Eastern Christians in contact with the West. Even in the West there was a great variation of view as to the number of sacraments until at least the twelfth century, when the formidable authority of Peter Lombard (d. 1160) asserted a list of seven: baptism, confirmation, eucharist, penance, extreme unction, ordination and matrimony. At the Second Council of LYONS (1274), the profession of faith submitted by Emperor Michael VIII Palaiologos contains an explicit affirmation of the same list of seven sacraments, and the canons of the seventh session of the Council of Trent (3 March 1547) anathematize anyone who says there are more or fewer than these. Besides this list of seven, earlier theologians both Eastern and Western had canvassed the claims of other rites, from the washing of feet and the anointing of a king to the profession of a monk, the consecration of a virgin, the funeral rite and the blessing and use of holy water. JOHN OF DAMASCUS seems to recognize two, DIONYSIUS THE AREOPAGITE six, Bernard of Clairvaux (1090–1153) eleven and Peter Damian (1007–72) twelve, while Hugh of St Victor (d. 1142) lists thirty.

Patriarch Cyril LUCARIS (d. 1638) showed sympathy for the Reformation doctrine of two dominical sacraments, baptism and the eucharist, but his views were condemned at the synods of JASSY in 1642 and Jerusalem in 1672 (*see* JERUSALEM, SYNOD OF). The Roman Catholic doctrine of seven sacraments was more influential, and many Eastern Christians now accept that there are seven mysteries. Baptism, eucharist, matrimony, ordination, the confession of sins, the prayer oil and chrismation are all recognized as mysteries – though whether baptism and chrismation are *distinct* mysteries can be questioned. Moreover, it is possible to argue that the naming of a child, monastic profession, the funeral rites, the breaking of bread and the memorial service, among others, have claims to be recognized as mysteries. Equally, if chrismation is to be accounted a separate mystery from baptism, can we not count ARABONISMOS (betrothal) as a separate mystery from matrimony, and ordination to the diaconate and consecration to the episcopate as mysteries distinct from presbyteral ordination?

Roman Catholic neo-scholastic sacramental theology tended to emphasize (1) the role of the sacraments in personal sanctification, (2) the juridical status of sacramental rites and (3) the status of the sacraments as means of grace. Eastern understanding of the mysteries would tend to emphasize rather (1) the mysteries as divine and ecclesial acts, (2) the theological status of the mysteries and (2) their role in transformation and DEIFICATION. The two approaches are not simply opposed, still less incompatible, but they represent a significant difference of emphasis.

DM

· N ·

Nag Hammadi A modern town in Upper Egypt that has given its name to a collection of some thirteen Coptic codices discovered nearby in 1945. Fifty-one texts, comprising forty-five individual works, originally composed in Greek, survive in Coptic translation in these codices, which date from the later fourth century. Many are extant only in the Nag Hammadi codices, which include gnostic, hermetic and Christian writings from the first four centuries of the Christian era. Best known is a collection of sayings attributed to Jesus, the Gospel of Thomas. A twelve-volume facsimile edition of the Nag Hammadi codices was prepared between 1972 and 1984 under the auspices of the Department of Antiquities of the Arabic Republic of Egypt in conjunction with UNESCO. Publication projects in progress include the Coptic Gnostic Library Project of the Institute for Antiquity and Christianity at Claremont in the USA; the Bibliothèque Copte de Nag Hammadi at the Université de Laval in Canada; and the Berliner Arbeitskreise für koptisch-gnostische Schriften in Germany. Today, excepting a few pieces, the Nag Hammadi codices are in the Cairo Coptic Museum.

Scholer, D. M. (1994), *Nag Hammadi Bibliography 1970–1994*. Nag Hammadi and Manichaean Studies 32. Leiden: Brill.
Robinson, J. R., gen. ed. (1988), *The Nag Hammadi Library in English*, 3rd rev. edn. San Francisco: Harper & Row.
Layton, B. (1987), *The Gnostic Scriptures: A New Translation with Annotations and Introductions*. Garden City, NY: Doubleday.
Scholer, D. M. (1971), *Nag Hammadi Bibliography 1948–1969*. Nag Hammadi Studies 1. Leiden: Brill.

MJB/SHG

Nagorno Karabakh Artsakh or Mountainous Karabakh, formerly an autonomous region of the Soviet Union. The marches of Artsakh and Utik were attached to Armenia in antiquity; in the medieval period they often came under Albanian or Georgian control. Artsakh shared the fate of these three powers, for periods acknowledging Persian, Arab or other suzerainty. From the twelfth century the Armenian Khachen principality dominated the region. In 1216 the Jalalian dynasty founded Gandsazar monastery, which became the seat of the catholicos of Albania, forced from Partav by the steady Islamicization of Caucasian ALBANIA.

The Khamsa or five principalities maintained Armenian autonomy through the Persian–OTTOMAN wars and Turkmen migrations. The Persians established a protectorate over the Khamsa from 1603 and sponsored the emergence of a local Azeri khanate in 1750. Karabakh was occupied by the Russians in 1805. Russian Transcaucasia enjoyed peace until 1905, when confrontations between Armenians and Azeris in Baku led to ethnic conflict throughout the southernmost Russian provinces. The Armenians of Karabakh proclaimed their independence from Russia in August 1918 and sought union with Armenia.

In October 1918 the capital, Shushi, was sacked by the Ottomans. The Armenians resisted and held out elsewhere; nevertheless, after the First World War the occupying British allocated Nagorno Karabakh to Azerbaijan. The Armenians successfully opposed this decision until 1920, when the Azeris invaded and annexed the region. The Soviets initially assigned Nagorno Karabakh to Armenia in 1921, but in 1922 this decision was reversed and the region returned to Azeri control. The overwhelming Armenian majority was, however, acknowledged and Nagorno Karabakh was eventually granted autonomous status within Soviet Azerbaijan. Initially neighbouring Sor Kurdestan also enjoyed autonomy, but Azeri control was tightened and in 1929 autonomy was revoked and the non-Azeri population of the Sor Kurdestan region expelled. (*See* KURDS.)

Nagorno Karabakh similarly was subjected to Azeri assimilation policies, but the issue of separate identity remained and was raised openly in 1987. In 1988 a Karabakh Committee was formed to co-ordinate agitation for union with Armenia. The region was briefly attached to the Russian Federation in 1989, but from 1990 Armenia became directly involved in the conflict. Inevitably, war broke out between Armenia and Azerbaijan. At present Nagorno Karabakh is united to Armenia.

See also ARMENIAN GENOCIDE

Walker, C. J. (1991), *Armenia and Karabagh*. London: Minority Rights Publications.

DB

names In EASTERN CHRISTIAN tradition, children are normally named after saints from the church's CALENDAR, giving the child a name-day and a personal patron saint. Baptism is not of itself a naming service: a separate service to claim the person for Christ and give a new name exists in Byzantine and other service books. The Byzantine rite service of 'Naming' is specified as being held on the 'eighth day', on the analogy of Christ's circumcision under the Old Law (cf. Luke 2: 21). Adult converts normally receive a new Christian name if baptized, frequently even when received by chrismation. Since converts often continue to be known by their original names, many saints are venerated under their pre-baptismal names, e.g. Vladimir and Olga, the PASSION BEARERS Boris and Gleb, Hasan and Ahmet the NEW MARTYRS. Names can be derived from a saint's title, e.g. Chrysostom, Damaskenos, Theologos or Chrysobalantini. Men named may use a masculine derivative of a female saint's name, e.g. Paraskevas for PARASKEVE, just as a woman would be Demetra if Deme-trios of Thessaloniki were her patron saint. A difference in accentuation applied to sacred names, like Stavros, makes them acceptable as personal names. There are names derived from Christian feasts (Natalie, Paschal), sacred places (Gethsemane, Bethlehem), attributes of Christ and the THEOTOKOS, and icons (Odegetriani).

Christians used names derived from those of the pagan gods, and even used the names of the gods where this was not done by their worshippers. CLASSICAL NAMES, folk names (often from flowers) and names from non-Orthodox traditions (Sultana) have been in use among Eastern Christians for centuries. On occasion surnames have been taken as Christian names, often in honour of benefactors or heroes (e.g. Byron).

See also HAJI.

DB

naos   Greek, 'temple'. (1) The Temple in Jerusalem. (2) A church building. (3) The nave area of a church. (4) Mary, hymned as the *naos* in which God makes his dwelling by the incarnation. (5) Every Christian, as a *naos* where God dwells by the indwelling of the Holy Spirit.

DM

Narsai   The theologian Narsai (also Narseh, Narses), formerly a monk at Kpar Mārī, taught at the School of EDESSA from *c*.437. He went with BARSAWMĀ of Nisibis to that city after the death of Bishop IBAS of Edessa in 457 and the imposition of MONOPHYSITE views. Narsai became, and remained until his death, the head of the Persian School of Nisibis, which continued the traditions of the Persian School in Edessa (suppressed in 489), though at one period he became embroiled in an entertain-ing conflict with Barsawmā's wife, who resented his authority, resulting in his tem-porary estrangement from his bishop–patron. Narsai died in 503 and was buried in a church in Nisibis later named after him.

A major figure of the CHURCH OF THE EAST earning the title 'Harp of the Spirit', he was a prolific poet, author of 360 metrical poems in twelve volumes, according to 'Abdīšō' of Nisibis' (d. 1318) *Catalogue of Books*. Several of his hymns survive, some incorporated in liturgical books, and his *Liturgical Homilies* give information about the rituals of baptism and the eucharist. Narsai's statutes for his school do not survive as a separate document, but are probably reflected in a compilation dated 496. He also wrote extensive Old Testament commentaries.

Gero, S. (1981), *Barṣauma of Nisibis and Persian Christianity in the Fifth Century*. CSCO 426, Subsidia 63. Louvain: Peeters.
Gignoux, P. (1968), *Homélies de Narsaï sur la création*. Patrologia Orientalis 34/3–4.
Vööbus, A. (1965), *History of the School of Nisibis*. CSCO 266, Subsidia 26. Louvain: Secrétariat du CSCO.
Mingana, A. (1905), *Narsai Doctoris Syri Homiliae et Carmina*. Mosul: Dominican Fathers.

JH

Nativity of Christ icon   The tradition that Christ was born in a cave is attested as early as the second century. In the Nativity icon overleaf the Christ-child lies in a manger wrapped in swaddling clothes and worshipped by ANGELS and animals. The ox and the ass witness the event, fulfilling the prophecy of Isaias 1: 3 and Ambacum 3: 2

(Habakkuk 3: 2). The star of Bethlehem is represented by a three-pronged symbol associated in iconographic tradition with the TRINITY. The Magi are often represented in early iconography one with a grey beard, one with a black beard and one clean-shaven. Two shepherds approaching from the right look up at the star, listening to the angel (Luke 2: 12). Joseph sits thinking over the birth, knowing he is not the father of the infant. In post-Byzantine tradition, the old shepherd who speaks to him is the devil, who tempts him to disbelieve the Virgin Birth. The THEOTO-KOS reclines on a pallet or bed-roll, her post-natal fatigue indicating the reality of the birth of Christ and of the Incarnation. The two midwives preparing to bathe the Christ-child confirm his humanity. There is a deliberate reference in the manger and swaddling clothes to the tomb and grave-clothes of Christ. Many details are taken from early apocryphal texts, evidence of the importance of non-canonical writings in the development of EASTERN CHRISTIAN iconography.

Kalokyris, C .D. (1969), *The Star of Bethlehem in Byzantine Art*. Thessaloniki: n.p.
Ristow, G. (1963), *Die Geburt Christi in der frühchristlichen und byzantinisch-ostkirchlichen Kunst*. Recklinghausen: Icon Museum.

KP

Nativity of the Mother of God   The feast of the Nativity of the Mother of God on 8 September is the first major feast of the Byzantine liturgical CALENDAR. In some

Oriental Orthodox traditions the feast is celebrated on 1 May. Its icon shows Anna, Mary's mother, lying attended by two servants, while Joachim, her husband, looks out the window of his house. In the lower right of the picture, the infant Mary is shown in the lap of a midwife who is testing the bathwater with her fingers. Mary is wrapped in swaddling clothes, just as her soul appears in Christ's hands in the DORMITION icon. The iconography is based on apocryphal sources. According to the Protevangelium of James the conception of Anna was announced separately to the infertile couple by visiting ANGELS, and in gratitude for her miraculous birth they dedicated Mary to the Temple in JER-USALEM. The piece of scarlet cloth strung between the two towers anticipates one of the duties Mary was to perform in the Temple, that

of vestment-maker to the high priest. It appears again in the icon of the ANNUNCIA-
TION.

The KONTAKION of the feast says: 'Joachim and Anna were set free from the
reproach of childlessness, and Adam and Eve from the corruption of death, by your
holy nativity O Most Pure.' The APOLYTIKION celebrates Mary as her from whom
'there dawned the Sun of Righteousness, Christ our God. He abolished the curse and
gave the blessing; and by making death of no effect, he bestowed on us eternal life.'

Ouspensky, L. and Lossky, V. (1982), *The Meaning of Icons*. Crestwood, NY: St
Vladimir's Seminary Press.

KP

Neophytos-Omar (d. 590)   An Arab commander, credited with a vision of ANGELS
above the Shio-Mgvime monastery in GEORGIA before converting to Christianity. He
became monk, abbot and bishop. By tradition Neophytos-Omar, a great ascetic, was
abducted by pagans, who were incensed by his missionary zeal, and stoned outside
Urbnisi. He is commemorated on 28 October and considered to prefigure later NEW
MARTYRS.

Timotheos (1988), *Hagioi tes Georgias*, vols 1 and 2. Attiki: Moni Parakletou.

DB

Nerezi   The Church of St Panteleimon at Nerezi, near Skopje, was built and
decorated by a member of the Byzantine Komnenos dynasty in 1164. Built to a
inscribed-cross design, it has five domes, the corner domes being square, the central
an octagon. The central dome was damaged by an earthquake in 1555 and new frescoes
painted after its reconstruction in the second half of the sixteenth century. The twelfth-
and sixteenth-century frescoes were painted over in the nineteenth century, but work
to uncover and study them began only in 1926. The twelfth-century Lamentation over
the Dead Christ and the Deposition from the Cross show striking pathos. The
expressive style has affinities with the paintings of 1191 at the church of St George
at Kurbinovo. Fragments of a marble ICONOSTASIS with stucco frames in the church
at Nerezi are from the twelfth century and may well date from 1164.

Balabanov, C. (1975), *St Panetelejmon Nerezi-Skopje*. Zagreb: n.p.

KP

Nestor Anisimov (1885–1962)   Russian hierarch, author of *Memories of Kamchatka*
(1936). Born to a military family of Vyatka, as a child he met John of Kronstadt. He
entered the Kalmyk–Mongol department of Kazan Theological Academy but abandoned his studies, was ordained priest in 1907 and joined the Kamchatka mission.
Travelling widely, Nestor forged links with the nomadic peoples, mastering many
languages of the Russian Far East. Visiting St Petersburg in 1910 he founded an
organization to support the work of the missionaries. Nestor supervised translations
of the Divine Liturgy into Koryak, Tungus and Evenk, presided over a major missionary congress in 1914 where Russian and Koryak had equal status, and set up a
health service for the province.

Nestor returned to St Petersburg at the outbreak of the First World War and organized front-line medical units. He was consecrated bishop of Kamchatka and Petropavlovsk in 1916, war forcing him to return to Kamchatka by way of CONSTAN-TINOPLE, India and China. During the Civil War Nestor joined the many Russian refugees in Manchuria as archbishop of Harbin, first representing the RUSSIAN ORTHODOX CHURCH ABROAD and later (from 1946) the Moscow patriarchate. In Harbin the archbishop remained committed to missionary work, even travelling to India and Ceylon in 1938. Between 1948 and 1956 Nestor was exiled to the Soviet labour camps. When freed he was appointed bishop of Novosibirsk and then metropolitan of Kirovgrad and Nikolayev in 1959.

See also SIBERIA; CHINESE ORTHODOX CHURCH.

Georgievsky, A. (1990), 'Missionary of Kamchatka', *Journal of the Moscow Patriarchate* 11.

DB

Nestorian   A name commonly used for the CHURCH OF THE EAST. Since this church venerates Nestorius (patriarch of Constantinople 428–31) as an orthodox teacher and follows him in his reservations about the use of the title THEOTOKOS for the Virgin Mary, it can be argued that the name is appropriate. Until modern times the Church of the East used the name Nestorian as occasion demanded to distinguish itself from other bodies. However, to preclude any misunderstandings, e.g. that Nestorius was the church's founder, or that it teaches a false Christology, the Church of the East now rejects the name 'Nestorian' and it should be avoided in ordinary use.

See also SYRIAN CHRISTIANITY.

JFC

Newly Revealed Saints   Visions, miracles and discovered remains are all that attest to the existence of a number of saints. Such saints are known in Greek as *Neophaneis*, the Newly Revealed.

The feast of the martyrs of Eugenios (22 February) dates from the reign of Arcadius (395–408) when a visionary priest, Nicolas Calligraphos, uncovered the reputed relics of apostles Andronikos and Junia of the SEVENTY and other martyrs on the outskirts of CONSTANTINOPLE. The cult of Phanourios of Rhodes emerged after an icon was found in a hidden chapel in 1500. Visions also led to the discovery of relics of the Megara Martyrs; the graves of Basil, Demetrios, Dorotheos, Jacob, Sarantis and Seraphim, patron saints of Megara, were discovered from 1798 after a child's visions of the saints. The Megara martyrs (commemorated 16 August) are depicted as soldiers, usually mounted. They grew in popularity after the Greek Revolution: their shrine was rebuilt in 1889.

Relics of a hitherto unknown monk, Eudokimos, were found at Vatopedi on ATHOS in 1841. Tryphon of ALBANIA was recognized as an early Christian martyr after a series of visions led to relics near Berat (Antipatria) in 1848. The tombs of Patapios, Nikon and Hypomone were discovered in a cave chapel at Geraneia in 1904 and soon drew pilgrims, especially those seeking their intercession for the cure of cancer; that of

Abbot Basil of Akarnania, reputedly martyred by pirates in 1006, was discovered in 1923.

The martyrs of THERMI and Ephrem of Amomon are now popular Orthodox saints, but before a series of visions led to the discovery of relics they were not listed in any calendar. The monk Ephrem (commemorated 5 May and 3 January) is believed to have been martyred by Turkish raiders in 1426. After the nun Makaria experienced a number of visions, relics were uncovered in 1950. The revived convent near Nea Makri is an important centre of pilgrimage.

Western parallels to the Newly Revealed Saints exist, notably Gervase and Protase, whose relics were discovered by Ambrose of Milan in 386 as the result of an extraordinary premonition.

The Newly Revealed Saints are to be distinguished from the many locally revered saints of whom no sound historical record exists, but whose cult is often ancient.

Gerasimos of Mikrayiannitis (1990), *Hosios Patapios*. Loutraki: n.p.
Mourtzoukou, D. (1984), *Ton En Megarois Athlesanton Neophanon Martyron*. Megara: n.p.
Hagios Ephraim (1983), Nea Makri. n.p.

DB

New Martyrs   The title originally given to Orthodox martyrs under heretical rulers, then to Christian martyrs under Islam. In the OTTOMAN empire, the Tatar domains and Muslim Persia, Christians were not systematically persecuted; nevertheless, they were vulnerable. In Poland-Lithuania and in Austria-Hungary, Orthodox Christians were equally vulnerable under Roman Catholic rulers.

Muslims viewed all apostates from Islam, whether reverting to their original religion or not, all who sought to convert Muslims and all non-Muslims who insulted Islam as criminals meriting death unless they embraced or reverted to Islam. Orthodox ZEALOTS, like the monk Makarios (d. 1507) and the tailor John of Ioannina (d. 1526), invited martyrdom by proclaiming the Christian message in public. Leaders of Christian revival movements, like PHILOTHEI (d. 1589), Kosmas Aitolos (d. 1779) and THEODORE SLADICH (d. 1788) were martyred for allegedly disturbing the peace. ETHNOMARTYRS, like Patriarchs CYRIL VI (d. 1821) and Gregory V (d. 1821) were victims of reprisals against rebellious groups; others, like THOMAS PASCHIDIS (d. 1890) and CHRYSOSTOM OF SMYRNA (d. 1922), were killed for questioning Muslim hegemony. ANTHIMOS THE GEORGIAN (d. 1716) died as a result of political intrigue.

Demetrios of Philadelphia (d. 1657), like many others, was executed for openly returning to Christianity after having embraced Islam. Up to the exchange of populations in 1923, Philadelphia (Turkish: Alaşehir) in Lydia remained home to a significant Greek community, whose patron saint the New Martyr Demetrios Doukas became. Having converted to Islam at an early age and achieved wealth and status among the Muslims, he none the less, before his wedding, announced his intention to return to his ancestral faith. Demetrios was beaten to death; he is commemorated on 2 June.

Michael Mavroudis (d. 1544), Chrestos the Albanian (d. 1748) and GEORGE OF IOANNINA (d. 1838) died falsely accused of breaking Muslim law. Michael Mavroudis (commemorated 21 March) left the Agrapha region (*see* ROUMELI) for MACEDONIA seeking work, settled in Thessaloniki and opened a bakery; accused of teaching a

Muslim child the tenets of Christianity, he was tortured and burnt alive. Chrestos the Albanian (commemorated 12 February) moved to CONSTANTINOPLE at the age of forty and worked as a gardener until denounced by a Turk who claimed Chrestos had declared his willingness to embrace Islam. He was imprisoned and tortured in dungeons where the scholar Kaisarios Dapontes (d. 1784) was also held. Kaisarios recorded the courageous witness of this illiterate Albanian.

Akylina of Chalkidike (d. 1764), ZLATA OF MOGLENA (d. 1795), Panteleimon Dousa (d. 1848) and others were killed at moments of tension between Christian and Muslim communities. From the nineteenth century onwards such martyrdoms often had national or political aspects. (*See* ILIA CHAVCHAVADZE.) Akylina (commemorated 27 September) came from a village near Thessaloniki. Her father converted to Islam to avoid execution for murder. Akylina and her mother remained Christian. Reaching marriageable age, Akylina refused a Muslim husband, was imprisoned for repudiating Islam and died after repeated beatings.

The child New Martyr Panteleimon Dousa (commemorated 14 November), whose cult is popular especially in his native Crete, was killed by Turkish irregulars in Sitia at the age of twelve. His mother Anna had already entered a convent, but fled to Athens, taking with her the relics of her son. The authorities of the day were disturbed by the attention that a nun and mother was attracting, and the cult has never been officially sanctioned by the church.

The New Martyrs are revered because their deaths, and usually their lives also, openly proclaimed the Christian faith in circumstances when this was otherwise impossible. Most New Martyrs of the Ottoman empire were Christians of the Near East; a few were Muslim converts to Christianity, like Ahmet (d. 1582), Hasan (d. 1814), Constantine the Turk (d. 1819) and Boris the Pomak (d. 1913); others were foreigners, like Paul the Russian (d. 1683). Constantine the Turk (commemorated 2 June) was born on Lesbos, migrated to Magnesia (Manisa), then with his brothers to Smyrna where, through contacts with a *gerontas*, John, he decided to embrace Christianity. Sent to ATHOS, he was baptized by Patriarch Gregory V. Constantine was executed as an apostate from Islam at Kydonia (Ayvalik).

The 1917 Russian Revolution signalled a general assault on religion. Metropolitan Vladimir Bogoiavlenskii of Kiev (*see* UKRAINE) was summarily executed in its early phase, one of the first New Martyrs under communism. Arbitrary killing of clergy and church activists continued to 1922, when the execution of VENIAMIN KAZANSKII signalled the inauguration of a systematic state campaign against Christianity that intensified up to the Second World War and included even pro-Soviet hierarchs like SERAPHIM CHICHAGOV (d. 1937). The RUSSIAN ORTHODOX CHURCH ABROAD canonized many Russian New Martyrs in 1981, including ELISABETH FEODOROVNA (d. 1918) and Tsar Nicolas II and his family, honoured as PASSION BEARERS.

Archbishop GORAZD PAVLIK of Prague, Maria Skobtsova, PLATO JOVANOVIC (d. 1941), the SERBIAN NEW MARTYRS, and others killed by Nazis or by quisling regimes during the Second World War are also recognized as New Martyrs. Less well known are the New Martyrs of CHINA, who suffered together with great numbers of Protestants and Roman Catholics during the Boxer rebellion around 1900.

The designation 'New Martyr' is less commonly applied to the huge numbers of Oriental Orthodox, Roman and EASTERN CATHOLIC and ASSYRIAN martyrs under

Islamic rule or under Nazism or communism. The Armenian church has actively considered the CANONIZATION of the immense number of Armenian Christians killed in the ARMENIAN GENOCIDE. Many Assyrian Christians were massacred by their Muslim Kurdish neighbours in 1845 and thousands of Assyrian refugees by Iraqis and Kurds in 1933. State policy under OTTOMAN RULE contributed significantly to the inter-communal strife that resulted in a massacre of MARONITES by the Druze in 1860. The history of the COPTS AND ISLAMIC FUNDAMENTALISM has led to a considerable number of acts of violence in which Christians have clearly been killed because they were Christian. Specific mention must be made of the many Eastern Catholic victims of oppression and persecution under communist rule in Eastern Europe.

Cavarnos, C. (1992), *The Significance of the New Martyrs*. Etna, Cal.: Centre for Traditionalist Orthodox Studies.

Ikonomou, F. (1991), *Hagiologion Panton ton en Epeirou Hagion*. Athens: n.p.

Millar, L. (1991), *The Grand Duchess Elisabeth of Russia*. Redding: Nikodemos Press.

Paris, E. (1990), *Convert or Die: Catholic Persecution in Yugoslavia During World War II*. Chino: Chick Press.

Dionysiou, G. (1989), *Martyres Tes Katoches*. Athens: Tinos.

Papadopoulos, L. J. and Lizardos, G. (1985), *New Martyrs of the Turkish Yoke*. Seattle: St Nektarios Press.

Theologou, A. (1984), *Hagia Akylina*. Thessaloniki: n.p.

Hackel, S. (1981), *Pearl of Great Price: The Life of Mother Maria Skobtsova*. Crestwood, NY: St Vladimir's Seminary Press.

Gerasimos Mikrayiannanitis (1978), *Eurytanikon Leimonarion*. Athens: n.p.

Polsky, M. (1979), *The New Martyrs of Russia*. Munich: St Job of Pochaev.

DB/DM

Nicolas Kasatkin (1836–1912)   Founder of the Orthodox Church of JAPAN. A Russian from the Smolensk region, Nicolas studied theology in St Petersburg, where he became a monk (1860) and was ordained. Appointed rector of the Russian Consulate church in Hokkaido, he concentrated on mission work among the Japanese. In recognition of his early success, Nicolas was chosen to head the Russian Orthodox Mission in Tokyo (1870). He was consecrated bishop (1880) and after the Russo-Japanese War (1904–5), during which he loyally prayed for the victory of his adopted nation, became archbishop of a virtually autonomous church. Nicolas Kasatkin is commemorated on 3 February.

DB

Nicolas of Sion   Sixth-century abbot of Holy Sion monastery and later bishop of Pinara in Lycia. Unlike his earlier namesake, Nicolas of Myra, reliable historical information survives regarding Nicolas of Sion. By the tenth century hagiographers had begun to absorb episodes from the Life of Nicolas of Sion into the legend of Nicolas of Myra, whose icon is illustrated here. The confusion was compounded by Nicolas of Sion being commemorated on 10 December, Nicolas of Myra on 6 December.

Ševčenko, I. and N. P. (1984), *The Life of St Nicolas of Sion*. Brookline: Hellenic College Press.
Ševčenko Patterson, N. (1983), *The Life of Saint Nicholas in Byzantine Art*. Turin: Bottega d'Erasmo.

DB

Nicolas Velimirović (1880–1956) The major Serbian Orthodox theologian of the modern period, Nicolas was of peasant stock from the village of Lelich. Educated at Chelije monastery and St Sava Seminary in Belgrade, in 1905 he continued further studies in Berne and later in Germany, Britain and Russia. Nicolas became a monk at Ravanica in 1909, but retained a lifelong commitment to teaching and social work. During the First World War he headed a diplomatic mission to Britain (1914) and the USA (1915). He became bishop of the ancient see of ŽIČA in 1919, later transferring to OHRID and in 1921 to Bitola in MACEDONIA. Here Nicolas worked to unite the peoples of Macedonia with the SERBIAN ORTHODOX CHURCH, extended church welfare provision and headed the popular Prayer Movement. As a respected international figure, he travelled to the USA in 1921 and 1927 to organize a network of Serbian Orthodox parishes, and to the Holy Land where he founded centres to care for Yugoslav pilgrims. Nicolas was closely associated with JOHN MAXIMOVITCH; both lectured at the newly established Bitola Seminary and argued for loyalty to Orthodox tradition.

   Nicolas carried this argument to the Pan-Orthodox Conference held at Vatopedi monastery, Mount ATHOS, in 1930, and other gatherings where he united those opposed to the nationalistic narrowing of Orthodoxy in the inter-war years. During the Second World War he was imprisoned in Dachau with Patriarch Gabriel Dozić (1941–5). On release, unable to return to Yugoslavia, he emigrated to the USA, first to St Sava Seminary, Libertyville, in 1946 and finally to St Tikhon monastery, South Canaan, from 1949, where he ended his days. Nicolas is commemorated on 18 March.
   See also JUSTIN POPOVIC.

Rogich, D. (1994), *Serbian Patericon*. Forrestville, Cal.: St Paisios.

DB

Nikanor of Kallistratos (1491–1549) A priest from Thessaloniki who travelled throughout Western Macedonia, preaching and supporting Christian communities under OTTOMAN RULE. Nikanor settled on Mount Kallistratos, other monks joining him, and assisted in founding the Transfiguration monastery, which for centuries worked to counter Ottoman Muslim missions to an area of MACEDONIA where many Greeks, the VALADES, had embraced Islam. Nikanor, commemorated on 7 August, is the patron of Elimeia region.

Lyritzi, G. (1989), *Hosios Nikanor*. Grevena: Mone Zabordas.
Papadopoulos, L. (1988), *Lives of the Monastery Builders*. Buena Vista, Col.: Holy Apostles Convent.

DB

Nikephoros I Patriarch of CONSTANTINOPLE 806–15. Nikephoros soon found himself embroiled with THEODORE THE STUDITE and his brother, Joseph, ecclesiastical poet and archbishop of Thessaloniki, in the aftermath of the Moechian controversy, which arose when another Joseph, Oikonomos of Hagia Sophia, married Emperor Constantine VI to his mistress Theodote after his divorce from his wife Maria. This marriage deeply offended many. Theodore the Studite and his uncle Plato of Sakkoudion were beaten and exiled for their opposition to Constantine. When Nikephoros reinstated Oikonomos Joseph, Archbishop Joseph of Thessaloniki broke communion with him, and in 809 he was removed from office.

The second period of imperial ICONOCLASM instituted by Leo V (813–20) found Nikephoros and Theodore on the same side as opponents of the heretical regime (*see* ICONOPHILE). The patriarch received poor support from the bishops and retired to monastic life, writing several books in defence of the sacred images and their cult, and also historical works. His books are sharply argued despite his mannered, convoluted style.

Nikephoros probably died in 829. In 847 his relics were brought back to Constantinople, though there were still Studite monks unwilling to forgive him his leniency to Oikonomos Joseph.

Parry, K. (1996), *Depicting the Word: Byzantine Iconophile Thought of the Eighth and Ninth Centuries*. Leiden: Brill.
Pelikan, J. (1990), *Imago Dei: The Byzantine Apologia for Icons*. Harvard, Mass.: Yale University Press.
Travis, J. (1984), *In Defense of the Faith: The Theology of Patriarch Nikephoros of Constantinople*. Brookline, Mass.: n.p.
Alexander, P. J. (1958), *The Patriarch Nicephorus of Constantinople*. Oxford: Clarendon Press.

DM

Nikodemos of Emathia A fourteenth-century noble monk from Verroia in Greece, Nikodemos lived as a pilgrim for years, then entered Philokallous monastery in Thessaloniki where he lived as a HOLY FOOL. His brief Life by Ecumenical Patriarch Philotheos Kokkinos (d. 1379), records that Nikodemos enraged many by distributing his monastery's supplies to the poor and working with prostitutes. Opponents of his work with prostitutes knifed him. Miracles were reported and a church was built to hold his relics. He is commemorated on 24 November.

Philotheos Kokkinos (1994), *Hosios Nikodemos ho Neos*. Thessaloniki: n.p.

DB

Nikodemos the Hagiorite (1749–1809) Nikodemos was born on the island of Naxos. Inspired by his meetings with monks of the KOLLYVADES movement, he became a monk on ATHOS in 1775. A bibliophile and prolific author with over one hundred works to his credit, he is best known for his collaboration with Makarios of Corinth in compiling the PHILOKALIA. This compliation of spiritual writings of the fathers reflects the eighteenth-century revival of interest in HESYCHASM on the Holy Mountain, which was part of the wider movement of renewal in the Greek church. He collected information for the hagiographies of the NEW MARTYRS and produced editions of the writings of SYMEON THE NEW THEOLOGIAN and GREGORY PALAMAS. His interest in Roman Catholic spirituality led him to write adapted and expanded Greek versions of the Ignatian *Spiritual Exercises* of the Jesuit Pinamonti and the *Spiritual Combat* of the Theatine Lorenzo Scupoli, enriched in both cases with biblical and patristic quotations. This latter work was translated into Russian and reworked by THEOPHAN THE RECLUSE. Nikodemos was criticized for advocating the reintroduction of the ancient tradition of frequent communion. His compilation of canon law, known as the *Pedalion* or *Rudder*, has become an essential manual throughout the Greek Orthodox world, while his work on the *Interpretation of the Psalms of David* has remained popular since it first appeared in 1821. He is commemorated on 14 July.

Chamberas, R., trans. (1989), *Nikodemos of the Holy Mountain: A Handbook of Spiritual Counsel*. New York: Paulist Press.
Kadloubovsky, E. and Palmer, G. E. H., trans. (1952), *Unseen Warfare: The Spiritual Combat and Path to Paradise of Lorenzo Scupoli edited by Nicodemos of the Holy Mountain and revised by Theophan the Recluse*. London: Faber.

KP

Nikon (1605–81)   Patriarch of MOSCOW whose reform of the liturgical books led to schism. Nikon apparently intended to restore what was in the original Greek sources: however, the new translations in his 1655 *Sluzhebnik* were made from the 1602 VENICE edition of the EUCHOLOGION. But his pro-Greek stance alienated many who looked on Moscow as the THIRD ROME and distrusted a church under OTTOMAN RULE. The Moscow Council of 1666–7, attended by the patriarchs of ANTIOCH and ALEXANDRIA, upheld Nikon's reforms, but deposed him for the way he had enacted them. The same council also denounced the 1551 Council of the Hundred Chapters (*Stoglav*), which had rejected Greek practices in favour of Russian. The OLD BELIEVERS rejected the reforms, and were cruelly persecuted. Nikon himself was eventually canonized.
    See also AVVAKUM.

Meyendorff, P. (1991), *Russia, Ritual and Reform: The Liturgical Reforms of Nikon in the Seventeenth Century*. Crestwood, NY: St Vladimir's Seminary Press.

KP

nipsis   Greek*nēpsis*, 'sobriety': in Eastern SPIRITUAL THEOLOGY a crucially important virtue. It is a state of alert vigilance, of freedom from obsession; not merely the absence of drunkenness but the opposite of drunkenness. Drunkenness narrows attention, dulls self-control, fuddles thought, induces indulgent sentimentality and mawkish self-pity: nipsis involves sharpened attention, resolute self-control, clarity of thought, wakeful awareness and steadiness of judgement.

DM

Non-Possessors   Russian monks of the fifteenth and sixteenth centuries opposed to monasteries' owning land and serfs and accumulating property. The movement was a protest against the Possessors or Josephites led by Iosif of Volotsk (1439–1515) who favoured monastic ownership of land and advocated closer relations between church and state. The Non-Possessors had their centres of support in the monasteries and hermitages of the so-called NORTHERN THEBAID and were known therefore as the Trans-Volga elders. They also received strong support from many of the lay aristocracy. Two notable Non-Possessors were Nil Sorskii (1433–1508) and Maksim the Greek (c.1475–1555). The latter had gone to Russia originally to help revise the liturgical books of the Russian church, but fell foul of the authorities when he supported the Non-Possessors and was banished for twenty-six years as a consequence. Both had spent time on ATHOS and were familiar with the ideals of the HESYCHAST movement. The controversy over ownership of property arose from two different views of the monastic life, the Possessors focusing on the social and evangelical dimension and the Non-Possessors on the ascetic and spiritual. Linked into this was the question of the treatment of heretics. The Possessors believed they were justified in calling in the secular authorities to deal with heretics; the Non-Possessors considered it a matter for the church alone. The victory of the Possessors was also a victory for those who supported the idea of MOSCOW as the THIRD ROME. Both Nil and Joseph were canonized.

Fedotov, G. P. (1975), *The Russian Religious Mind*, vol. 2. Belmont, Mass.: Nordland.
Maloney, G. A. (1973), *Russian Hesychasm: The Spirituality of Nil Sorskij*. The Hague: Mouton.
Haney, J. V. (1973), *From Italy to Muscovy: The Life and Works of Maxim the Greek*. Munich: Wilhelm Fink.

KP

Northern Thebaid   A constellation of monasteries across the northern provinces of Great Russia opened the area to Orthodox missionaries and Slav settlement from the fourteenth century. The region became known as the Russian wilderness, the desert or the Northern Thebaid, taking its name from the early monastic settlement in the Egyptian Thebaid. This last term was favoured by later Russian Orthodox as it reflected a desire to revive the spirit of the ancient desert fathers.

See also MONASTICISM; NON-POSSESSORS; STARETS.

Kontzevich, I. M. (1988), *Acquisition of the Holy Spirit in Ancient Russia*. Platina, Cal.: St Herman of Alaska.
Kontzevich, I. M. (1987), *The Northern Thebaid*. Platina, Cal.: St Herman of Alaska.

DB

Novgorod   One of the few Russian cities not taken by the Mongols, Novgorod lies on the river Volkhov and has many fine medieval churches. On the Kremlin side of the river is the cathedral of DIVINE WISDOM erected 1045–50, and based on KIEV's Divine Wisdom church. Some frescoes survive from the twelfth century. Archbishop Gennadii of Novgorod (1484–1504) established the DORMITION of the Virgin as the cathedral's patronal feast. The city was known as Lord Novgorod the Mighty, powerful and wealthy from its position on the trade route from Scandinavia to CONSTANTINOPLE. It was normally governed by an elected prince and an assembly of the people (*veche*). The Transfiguration church on the market side of the river (built 1374, frescoed 1378) possesses the only surviving paintings by THEOPHAN THE GREEK. Also on the market side are the churches of St Nicolas (1113), St Procopius (1529) and the Myrrh-Bearing Women (1510) in Iaroslav's Court. In the vicinity of Novgorod is the Church of Our Saviour at Nereditsa (built 1198); the present building is largely a reconstruction after the Second World War from old drawings. Nearby is the Dormition Church at VOLOTOVO POLE.

The famous fifteenth-century Novgorod school icon The Virgin of the Sign celebrates a religious interpretation of a secular historical event. It depicts the icon of The Virgin of the Sign being used as palladium to defend Novgorod against the Suzdalian army in the twelfth century, a traditional use of icons in the Byzantine world.

Under Tsar Ivan IV, the Terrible (1533–84), Novgorod, which had lost its independence, became suspected of disaffection and potential rebellion. The tsar twice led his armies against the city. On the first occasion he was turned from violence by a HOLY FOOL clad in chains, a piece of raw meat in his hand. On the second, the tsar presided over a terrible massacre of citizens. Some of the earliest recorded Russian holy fools are from Novgorod.

Brisbane, M., ed. (1992), *The Archaeology of Novgorod, Russia*. Medieval Archaeological Monographs 13.
Likhachov, D. et al. (1980), *Novgorod Icons: 12th–17th Century*. Oxford: Phaidon.
Karger, M. (1973). *Novgorod the Great*. Moscow: Progress.

KP

Nubia In the Hebrew BIBLE Nubia, present-day Sudan, is called Kush, which the Septuagint confusingly renders as Aithiopia. The Ethiopian eunuch (named, by tradition, Agorastos) baptized by Philip in Acts 8: 27 was probably from Nubia, not modern Ethiopia; Candace, his queen, bears the traditional title of Nubian ruling queens.

Nubia had close cultural links with Egypt from at least the third millennium BC. Temples of Egyptian gods are found in Nubia, and the ancient kingdom of Meroë's distinctive Nubian culture had strong Egyptian elements. Recent archeological investigations show a Christian presence in the fifth century and possibly earlier. Nubian monks are found in Egypt, and Egyptian Christians probably travelled into Nubia to spread the gospel there. The thoroughgoing evangelization of Nubia, however, took place in the reign of Justinian I (527–65), COPTIC missions penetrating the northern kingdom of Nobatia and the southern Kingdom of Alodia, while CHALCEDONIAN missionaries converted the Kingdom of Makuria, though eventually all Nubia came under the authority of the Coptic pope in ALEXANDRIA. Greek language, religious literature and art none the less continued to play an important role in Nubian church life.

After the Arab conquest of Egypt in AD 642, despite the fact that Nubia came under attack from the Arabs, notably in 652, and was forced to pay tribute, its Christian culture flourished. Indeed, the Christian Nubian kings felt strong enough to invade Egypt on several occasions to defend the interests of the Coptic pope and his flock. King Merkourios of Makuria (697–710) began the unification of Nubia, annexing Nobatia and moving his capital there. From his reign many churches were built, texts translated into Nubian, native Nubians drawn into the clergy and Byzantine styles of iconography introduced. The clergy appears to have worked closely with the royal court, and it is questionable how deeply Christianity penetrated into rural life.

When the Mamluks assumed power in Egypt in 1172, the Nubians paid dearly for opposing them. In 1272 King David's refusal to pay tribute led to a series of attacks, in which the invaders skilfully played off Nubian factions against each other, so that a Muslim puppet ruler was installed and a severe tribute imposed on the Christians. The church lost royal patronage. Muslim settlers married Nubian wives. Further attacks brought the destruction of many churches and monasteries. Only the southern kingdom of Alodia held out, but Alodia too was under Muslim rule by the early sixteenth century. The distinctive Nubian Christianity passed into history.

Baur J. (1994), *2000 Years of Christianity in Africa*. Nairobi: Pauline Publications Africa.

Plumley, J. M., ed. (1982), *Nubian Studies: Proceedings of the Symposium for Nubian Studies, Selwyn College, Cambridge, 1978*. Warminster: Almquist & Wiksell.

van Moorsel, P., ed. (1982), *New Discoveries in Nubia: Proceedings of the Colloquium on Nubian Studies, The Hague, 1979*. Leiden: Brill.

Vantini, G. (1981), *Christianity in the Sudan*. Bologna: EMI.

Michalowski, K., ed. (1975), *Récentes Recherches. Actes du Colloque Nubiologique international au Musée National de Varsovie 19–22 Juin*. Warsaw: Musée National.

DM

·O·

ode   In the Byzantine rite, (1) one of the nine scriptural odes traditionally sung during ORTHROS, normally omitted in parochial use; (2) a section of a CANON headed by a HEIRMOS to the melody of which, in Byzantine use, the remaining troparia of the ode are sung, and the metrical structure of which they follow. Each ode of a canon is in theory based on the corresponding scriptural ode; sometimes the connection is tenuous.

DM

Odes of Solomon   A pseudepigraphical collection of forty-two early Christian hymns or poems written in SYRIAC and mostly extant in that language, though there are various partial texts in Coptic and Greek. The fullest Syriac manuscript is in the John Rylands University Library, Manchester (Cod. Syr. 9). The estimated date of composition is *c*.125 and the place of origin may be EDESSA or ANTIOCH. The Odes have New Testament, especially Johannine, themes, though with some unusual images, such as the idea of believers receiving milk from the breasts of the Lord in Ode 8: 14. Some scholars have seen a baptismal theme in them, while others emphasize aspects which suggest they have come from an environment in which gnosticism was flourishing.

Charlesworth, J. H., ed. (1985), 'Odes of Solomon', in *The Old Testament Pseud-epigrapha*, vol. 2, pp. 725–71. London: Darton Longman & Todd.

JH

Ohrid   Ancient Lychnidos: town on the north-eastern side of Lake Ohrid in the Republic of Macedonia, an important centre of early Christianity in the Balkans, possibly the seat of an archbishopric in the sixth century (*see* JUSTINIANA PRIMA). Several fifth- or sixth-century churches with mosaic floors have been found in the town and its environs. With the arrival of the Slavs in the seventh century and their conversion to Christianity in the ninth, Ohrid became a major centre of Slavonic culture, largely because of the work of Clement and Naum, disciples of CYRIL AND METHODIUS, who established an academy for the study of Slavonic and clerical education. Made capital of the Bulgarian empire under Tsar Samuel (976–1014), it was briefly a patriarchate, being reduced to an autocephalous archbishopric in 1019 by the conquering Byzantine emperor Basil II. Greeks held the see, among them Theophylact of Ohrid (1090–1108).

The town fell to the OTTOMANS in 1408. The archdiocese remained autocephalous until 1767, when the ECUMENICAL PATRIARCH, supported by the Sublime Porte, abolished it. With the restoration of the Serbian patriarchate in 1919, Ohrid came under the jurisdiction of the Serbian church, though it was transferred to the Bulgarian Orthodox church for a period during the Second World War. Since 1967 the archbishop of Ohrid has been head of the MACEDONIAN ORTHODOX CHURCH.

See also SERBIAN CHRISTIANITY.

KP

Oktoechos   Greek, 'eight tones': either the system of eight tones which are the basis of the liturgical MUSIC of Byzantine, Roman, Syrian and Armenian rites, or a Byzantine rite liturgical book, the PARAKLETIKE, containing the texts for each day's services for all eight tones, or a TROPARION which makes use of all eight tones in the course of its melody.

DM

Old Believers   In 1666 the liturgical books of the Russian Orthodox church were revised on the orders of Patriarch NIKON. He intended to restore ancient uses but actually imported contemporary Greek texts and practices. Nikon was opposed by zealous believers who saw the reforms as a betrayal of true Orthodoxy; many of them believed that the Greek church had compromised itself at the Council of FLORENCE (1439–45). They repudiated the reformed services as implicitly heretical.

Patriarch Nikon seemed prepared to allow the old rites to continue under certain conditions, but when his opponents showed no will to compromise reacted fiercely. Those who rejected and denounced the reforms were excommunicated in 1667, condemned as schismatics. The Old Ritualists or Old Believers abandoned the state church: Archpriest AVVAKUM became their most important leader. A grim persecution of Old Believers (*Staroobriadtsy*) followed, lasting for decades. Avvakum was burned, huge numbers were killed, whole communities immolated themselves. Many austere and respected monastics, however, joined the Old Belief, and Avvakum's extraordinary autobiography stirred support.

The Old Believers had no bishops to ordain new clergy and no unified organization. Some groups accepted clergy seceding from the patriarchal church, whether out of conviction or as runaways. Other groups rejected all the state church's ordinations and relied on lay prayer-leaders to preside over the offices. Old Belief kept alive the ancient tradition of Russian worship: the pre-Nikonian version of the liturgical texts, an austerely beautiful liturgical chant, and a distinctive style of icon painting, of pectoral crosses, even, in more conservative communities, of dress. Many Old Believers rejected use of anything imported into Russian culture after the schism, even potatoes. Prayer mats are often used for the many prostrations made during services. AVOIDANCE RITUALS mark more conservative Old Believer communities, and members of other churches including other Eastern Orthodox are strongly discouraged from joining actively in services, even from venerating icons in Old Believer churches.

Disgust at the westernizing policies of Peter the Great (1682–1725) drove many traditionalist Orthodox into Old Belief, since his policies and what they saw as the state church's supine acquiescence in them seemed concrete evidence confirming the Old Believers' criticism of the 'Nikonian' church. Another period of severe persecution occurred under Nicolas I (1825–55).

In 1846 the deposed Bishop Amvrosy of Bosnia joined the Old Believers and a synod held at Belokrinitsa monastery was able to elect an archbishop and establish the first full Old Believer hierarchy. In 1971 this church, the Old Believer Church of the Belokrinitsa Hierarchy, was officially recognized by the Russian Orthodox church. In 1923 a second priestist (*popovtsy*) church was organized, the Old Believer Church of Ancient Orthodox Christians.

Substantial communities of priestless (*bespopovtsy*) Old Believers continue to exist. Amongst them, the Pomortsy Old Believers have significant groups outside Russia, in Latvia, Lithuania, Estonia and Belarus. The Pomortsy were the first priestless Old Believers to pray for the tsar in their services; more intransigent groups such as the Fedoseevtsy rejected such compromise with what they saw as a Godless authority. The more radical priestless groups have serious problems with the status of priestless matrimony as a MYSTERY.

Both Orthodox and EASTERN CATHOLIC Old Believer 'uniates' exist, the Orthodox Edinovertsy dating back to the eighteenth century.

Ware, K. T. (1993), *The Orthodox Church*. New York: Penguin.
Meyendorff, P. (1991), *Russia, Ritual and Reform*. Crestwood, NY: St Vladimir's Seminary Press.
Lambrechts, A. (1986), 'Les Vieux-Croyants en URSS', *Irénikon* 59.
Lupinin, N. (1984), *Religious Revolt in the XVIIth Century: The Schism of the Russian Church*. Princeton: Kingston Press.
Avvakum (1979), *His Life, Written by Himself*. Ann Arbor, Mich.: Slavic Publications/InterVarsity Press.
Lane, C. (1979), *Christian Religion in the Soviet Union*. London: Allen & Unwin.

DM

Old Calendarists   The bull *Inter Gravissimos* promulgated on 24 February 1582 by Pope Gregory XIII instituted a reform of the traditional Julian CALENDAR. His reform was vigorously opposed by the Orthodox churches. The ECUMENICAL PATRIARCH JEREMIAS II firmly rejected suggestions from Rome that he might adopt the new calendar. He summoned a council which met in Constantinople in 1583 and anathematized those who accepted the new papal calendar. The condemnation was signed by PATRIARCH Jeremias and the patriarchs of Alexandria and Antioch. Until the twentieth century the Orthodox remained opposed to the ecclesiastical use of the Gregorian calendar, and some EASTERN CATHOLIC communities also continued to use the old calendar.

In the early 1920s MELETIOS METAXAKIS, then Ecumenical Patriarch, resolved to reform the Julian calendar. An inter-Orthodox conference under his chairmanship voted in 1923 to adopt for dates and fixed feasts a revised calendar almost though not quite identical to the Gregorian, but in the long run slightly more accurate. This decision proved controversial. The churches of ROMANIA and BULGARIA were slow to enact it; the Russian Orthodox church did not in the event enact it at all. In countries where the new calendar was adopted, it was met with vigorous opposition by some traditionalists.

In Greece the Old Calendarist movement, initially mainly lay but soon attracting numbers of clergy including Athonite monks, was joined in 1935 by three dissenting bishops, Metropolitan Chrysostomos of Florina (d. 1955) assuming a leadership role. Originating from Madytos in Eastern Thrace, Chrysostom Kavourides had already attained fame in CONSTANTINOPLE as a fiery preacher. He was consecrated metropolitan of Imbros in 1908, then transferred in 1911 to Pelagonia-Betolis or Bitola, where he worked to unite the Orthodox split by ethnic strife (*see* MACEDONIA) but was exiled from Serbia after the First World War. Already opposed to reforms being canvassed by the Constantinople patriarchate, Chrysostom sought refuge on ATHOS in 1918 then in Alexandria in 1919; he returned to Greece as metropolitan of Florina (1926–32), emerging from forced retirement to lead the Old Calendarists.

Originally perhaps a million strong, the Greek Old Calendarists weathered severe state persecution, Metropolitan Chrysostom himself being imprisoned on Lesbos in 1951. Internal unity, however, proved elusive. The three bishops who joined the movement in 1935 consecrated four more, but very quickly one of the original three, Chrysostom of Zakynthos, and two of the new bishops returned to the state church, leaving Chrysostom, Germanos of Demetrias, Germanos of the Cyclades and Matthew of Vrestheni to form an Old Calendarist Holy Synod.

In 1937 Matthew led a secession from the synod headed by Chrysostom, when the latter refused to declare the sacraments of the New Calendarists devoid of grace. Matthew Karpoudakis, a Cretan, had joined the Chrysopege monastery in 1872. He studied theology in Egypt and Jerusalem, his fellow students including Meletios Metaxakis, Chrysostom Papadopoulos and others who later introduced the reforms that roused Old Calendarist opposition. He joined an Athonite skete in 1886, was ordained priest in 1893 and became a well-known preacher throughout the Peleponnese, though his uncompromising traditionalism made him controversial. From 1916 he ministered in Athens, but incurring official disapproval was exiled to Sparta in 1922. Allowed back to Athos in 1923, he returned to Athens after the reported apparition of the Cross over Hymettos monastery in which Old Calendarist faithful were besieged by the police in 1925. Matthew denounced church reforms and the repression of traditionalists. In 1927 gendarmes shot his disciple, Catherine Rouka, and wounded others in his presence at a service in Mandra. After his consecration he founded churches, monasteries and charities for the dispossessed Old Calendarists; the KERATEA monastic network was organized covertly as the movement's centre. After his secession from the synod led by Chrysostom of Florina, Matthew of Vrestheni himself eventually consecrated a number of bishops, forming a separate synod under his leadership as archbishop of Athens. He died in 1950.

When Chrysostom of Florina died in 1955 no bishop was left to continue his succession, until in 1960 two bishops of the RUSSIAN ORTHODOX CHURCH ABROAD consecrated Archbishop Akakios, who together with another ROCA bishop then consecrated others to the episcopate.

Under Archbishop Akakios' successor, Archbishop Auxentios, complicated patterns of division and realignment occurred both within his own jurisdiction and among the followers of Archbishop Matthew, as a result of which there presently exist at least five Old Calendarist holy synods headed by an archbishop of Athens as well as the holy synod generally identified as 'Cyprianite' from the strong leadership given by Bishop Cyprian of Oropos and Phyli, founder and abbot of the famous monastery of SS Cyprian and Justina. This is an important focus for PILGRIMAGE. It is dedicated to Cyprian, a sorcerer of Great Antioch who was eventually made bishop of Antioch in Pisidia, and Justina, who converted him to Christianity, both popular third-century martyrs.

In 1924 the reforming Metropolitan Miron Cristea, previously a GREEK CATHOLIC bishop, introduced the Gregorian calendar into the Romanian church, later going further in reform than other new calendar churches and imposing the celebration of Easter on the date used by the Latin church. These and other measures were fiercely resisted by significant groups, especially in Moldavia. Metropolitan Gurias of Bessarabia opposed the decrees emanating from Bucharest, but it was the abbot of Prokof, Glicherie Tanase, who emerged as co-ordinator of the Old Calendarist movement. By 1936 numerous parishes had seceded from patriarchal control and more than forty new churches had been built for dissident communities. However, attempts to have Glicherie Tanase consecrated bishop by sympathetic hierarchs in Greece were thwarted by the Greek government.

From 1935 onwards the Romanian government backed drastic measures intended to eradicate organized opposition to the new (from 1925) patriarchate. True Orthodox Christian churches and monasteries were razed and activists incarcerated. Many, like Abbot Pambo, were killed and Glicherie Tanase was repeatedly imprisoned. This persecution continued until the collapse of the regime at the end of the Second World War.

In 1955 Metropolitan Galaction Cordun joined the True Orthodox Christian Church, and although under house arrest consecrated other bishops. A synod was formally established. In 1977 a formal declaration of intercommunion was signed between the 'Cyprianite' True Orthodox Church of Greece and the True Orthodox Church of Romania. Since the Ceaucescu period the Romanian True Orthodox Church has flourished, establishing a vigorous parochial and monastic life.

The Bulgarian Orthodox church only adopted the new calendar in 1968, under Patriarch Kyrill. The Protection Convent near Sofia, founded by Archbishop Seraphim Sobolev (d. 1950) became a focus of resistance, despite the active opposition of the patriarchal church. Contact with Old Calendarists from Greece brought support, and in 1993 Bishop Photios of Triaditsa was consecrated by the 'Cyprianite' Synod to serve as hierarch of the Bulgarian Old Calendarists.

In 1994 a formal act establishing communion between ROCA and the (Cyprianite) True Orthodox Church of Greece joined these two churches and the True Orthodox churches of Romania and Bulgaria in a single communion.

Old Calendarists frequently describe themselves as 'traditionalist', a description also claimed by many other Orthodox, especially ZEALOTS.

Two distinct trends can be discerned within the Old Calendarist movement; they can be characterized as resistance Old Calendarism and integrist Old Calendarism. The first, most clearly articulated by the 'Cyprianite' True Orthodox, expresses resistance to what it sees as unlawful innovation and walls itself off from churches using the new calendar and compromised by what is seen as the heresy of ecumenism. It refuses, however, to condemn the rites and sacraments of New Calendarists as devoid of grace, and seeks by witness and courteous dialogue to draw the Orthodox majority to its traditionalist outlook. Integrist Old Calendarist churches, by contrast, see themselves as the surviving Orthodox church, maintaining the integrity of Orthodox tradition in the face of massive apostasy. This second trend, typified by the 'Matthewite' succession, rejects all New Calendarist churches, all those in communion with New Calendarists and all who refuse to reject the sacraments of the New Calendarists as outside the Orthodox church and therefore as having sacraments devoid of grace.

The Holy Orthodox Church in North America (1998), *The Struggle against Ecumenism: The History of the True Orthodox Church of Greece from 1924 to 1994*. Boston, Mass.: The Holy Orthodox Church in North America.
Chrysostom (1986), *The Old Calendar Orthodox Church of Greece*. Etna, Cal.: Center for Traditionalist Orthodox Studies.
Cyprian, Metropolitan of Oropos and Fili (1982), 'The True Orthodox Christians of Romania', *Orthodox Word* 102.
Paraskevaidis, C. (1982), *Istorike kai Kanorike Theoresis tou Palaioemerologitikou zetematos*. Athens: n.p.
Kyprianos (1976), *Kyprianos Kai Ioustina*. Athens: n.p.
Tompros, E. (1963), *Matthaios Karpoudakis*. Athens: n.p.

DB/DM

Optina   In the nineteenth century the Russian Optina monastery and skete (*pustyn*) became the spiritual heart of the Orthodox north. Until the monastery was closed and the monks expelled in 1923, many pilgrims came to Optina; even leading intellectuals sought counsel from a series of elders believed to exercise a prophetic ministry. The Optina elders (*see* STARETS) followed the tradition of PAISSII VELICHKOVSKII (d. 1794) and SERAPHIM OF SAROV (d. 1833).

The Optina hermitage, probably established in the fifteenth century, is first mentioned in written sources in the seventeenth century. Although situated in a remote wilderness in the Kaluga region, it was sacked by the Lithuanians. A stone cathedral was constructed in 1680, but the monastery declined and closed between 1724 and 1726.

Feofan the Cossack (d. 1819) reorganized the community in 1800 on the model established by Paissii Velichkovskii. Metropolitan Plato Levshin of Moscow (d. 1812) supported him, approving a cenobitic rule in 1796 and confirming the like-minded Avraamii (d. 1819) as abbot. Metropolitan Filaret Amfiteatrov of Kiev (d. 1857) transferred a group of hermits from the Roslavl Forests to Optina in 1821, including MOSES PUTILOV (d. 1862) and Antony Putilov (d. 1865). Metropolitan Filaret Drozdov of Moscow (d. 1867) helped the Putilov brothers and Isaakii (d. 1894) to expand the library they had assembled as hermits, embark on further translations of patristic texts and publish spiritual classics. Scholarly activities flourished alongside spiritual eldership (*starchestvo*).

In 1829 elder Leonid Nagolkin (d. 1841) moved to Optina, joined in 1834 by his disciple, Makarii Ivanov (d. 1860). Amvrosii Grenkov (d. 1891), best-known of the Optina elders, joined the community in 1839. Anatolii (d. 1894), Osip Litovkin (d. 1911), Varsonofii Plekhankov (d. 1913), Nektarii (d. 1928) and others kept their tradition of spiritual eldership alive into the twentieth century. Linked with the monastery was the Shamordino convent, rather as Diveevo convent was linked with Sarov. Optina monastery was returned to the Orthodox church in 1989. The Optina saints are commemorated on 10 October.

Sederholm, C. (1994), *Elder Antony of Optina*. Platina, Cal.: St Herman of Alaska.
Sederholm, C. (1990), *Elder Leonid of Optina*. Platina, Cal.: St Herman of Alaska.
Meletios of Nikopolis (1987), *Starets Varsanouphios*, vols 1 and 2. Preveza: n.p.
Elder Joseph of Optina (1984). Boston: Holy Transfiguration Monastery.
De Beausobre, I. (1975), *Russian Letters of Direction: Makary*. Crestwood, NY: St Vladimir's Seminary Press.
Dunlop, J. (1972), *Staretz Amvrosy*. London: Mowbrays.

DB

orarion   Greek; deacon's stole, worn on the left shoulder and sometimes taken across diagonally under the right arm and again over the left shoulder. It is also worn crossed on the back by readers and sub-deacons.

E

Orchomenos   Modern Greek icons depict the Miracle of Orchomenos in the manner of the Protecting Veil (*see* POKROV). Many icons (e.g. the NOVGOROD Our Lady of the Sign) depict the THEOTOKOS intervening in moments of crisis, particularly during war. The Orchomenos icon, the best-known modern example, dates from what the people of Orchomenos accounted their miraculous deliverance in the Second World War. The Theotokos, escorted by ANGELS, comes between tanks and soldiers and the town and its people. Many similar miracles of deliverance are represented in iconography: Philiatra attributes its deliverance to CHARALAMPOS in the Second World War, Iraklion to Menas in 1826.

Vassilopoulos, H. (1985), *Vioi Hagion*. Athens: Orthodoxos Typos.

DB

Orientalium Ecclesiarum   Decree of Vatican II promulgated by Paul VI on 21 November 1964, asserting the value of the 'institutions, liturgical rites, ecclesiastical traditions and the established standards of Christian life of the Eastern Churches' and establishing basic principles to promote the flourishing of the EASTERN CATHOLIC churches.

The decree speaks of the faithful of the 'Holy Catholic Church' as 'combining together into various groups which are held together by a hierarchy' and 'from separate Churches or Rites'. It asserts that all the 'individual Churches, whether of the East or of the West . . . are . . . each as much as the others, entrusted to the pastoral government of the Roman Pontiff, the divinely appointed successor of St Peter in primacy over the universal Church'. It then asserts that 'they are consequently of equal dignity'.

The decree supports the establishment of parishes, and where appropriate separate hierarchies, for different rites, and encourages the various hierarchies in an area to co-operate. It instructs that aspirant clerics and the laity in general be taught about the different rites.

Crucially, the decree orders Catholics to retain their own rite and instructs that when baptized members of other churches enter 'the fulness of the Catholic communion' they too are to retain their rite. This rule was intended to stop the seepage of Eastern Catholics and of Orthodox converts into the Latin rite.

Eastern Catholics are exhorted to 'take steps to return to their ancestral traditions'. This aspect of the decree was directed against LATINIZATION. The institution of the patriarchate is recognized, and the patriarch's jurisdiction over the faithful of his rite, wherever they may live, is acknowledged. The decree orders restoration of the rights and privileges patriarchs held in the period of union between East and West, 'adapted somewhat to modern conditions'. The patriarch or major archbishop and his synod are recognized as constituting the 'highest authority for all business of the patriarchate' or church, 'without prejudice to the inalienable right of the Roman Pontiff to intervene in individual cases'.

Paragraphs 24–9 offer what were intended to be conciliatory norms for relations with other Eastern Christians. While pointing out that *communicatio in sacris* which 'harms the unity of the Church or involves formal acceptance of error or the danger of aberration in the faith, of scandal and indifferentism, is forbidden by divine law', permission is given for Eastern Christians 'separated in good faith from the Catholic Church' to be admitted to 'the sacraments of Penance, the Eucharist and the Anointing of the Sick'. Similarly, Catholics are permitted to seek the sacramental ministry of non-Catholic clergy who possess valid orders. These provisions were not based on any formal agreement with the Orthodox and were widely resented. None the less, they represent a landmark attempt at opening up better ecumenical relations.

See also ECUMENISM.

DM

Origen (*c*.185–*c*.254)   Son, according to Eusebius, of a devout Christian family, his father, Leonidas, a martyr. He succeeded Clement as head of the Catechetical School of ALEXANDRIA. He was an ascetic, even castrating himself. Origen visited Palestine several times, and in 230 became a priest there. Patriarch Demetrius of Alexandria (189–*c*.232) deposed him as irregularly ordained. Origen founded a school of his own in Caesarea. Eusebius' statement that Origen studied under the Platonist Ammonius Sakkas, and indeed Porphyry's claim that Ammonius was an apostate, have been challenged, but remain plausible. Origen's writings present a sophisticated Christian PLATONISM, parallel to but not derived from the Neoplatonism of Plotinus.

Soon after his death Origen was under attack. His disciple the martyr Pamphilios of Caesarea (*c*.240–309) wrote an *Apology* in five books to which his pupil EUSEBIUS OF CAESARIA (260–340) added a sixth. EPIPHANIOS OF SALAMIS (*c*.315–403), however, attacked him in his *Panarion*, even claiming, incredibly, that he had apostatized under the persecution of Decius, in which he was actually tortured. Jerome (c.342–420), despite translating some of Origen's writings and despite the support for Origen of his friend Rufinus (c.345–410), became a fierce opponent. When Palestinian monks spread Origen's teachings, Emperor Justinian I condemned him as a heretic in an edict sent to Menas, patriarch of CONSTANTINOPLE (536–52) and published at the Synod of Constantinople in 543. The edict contains nine anathemas condemning a range of doctrines including the following: the pre-existence of human souls and their sending into bodies as a punishment; the pre-existence of the Lord's soul and its union with the Word of God before the Incarnation; the assimilation of the Word of God to each of the heavenly ranks, so that he became a cherub to the cherubim, a seraph to the seraphim, etc.; that in the general resurrection the bodies of human beings will be spherical; that the sun, the moon, the stars and the celestial waters have souls and intelligence; that in the age to come Christ will be crucified for the demons; and the famous doctrine of the APOKATASTASIS. Modern scholars, especially Henri Crouzel, have shown that, while Origen does teach the pre-existence of human souls and that embodiment in the flesh is a consequence of the fall, and does teach some form of *apokatastasis*, most heresies alleged against him depend on misreading, misinterpretation and misrepresentation of Origen's writings.

Origen's greatest scholarly work, the *Hexapla*, probably contained the Hebrew and transliterated Hebrew text of the Old Testament together with four Greek versions. Jerome used Origen's original copy in the library at Caesarea. Origen wrote *scholia* and commentaries on virtually the entire BIBLE. The *De Principiis*, a philosophical and theological treatise, is partly available in translations by Rufinus and Jerome. He wrote many other theological works, almost entirely lost, and ascetical and spiritual works, parts of which survive.

His *Contra Celsum* survives complete. It is a detailed refutation of an attack on Christianity by the Platonist philosopher Celsus, probably published during the reign of Marcus Aurelius (161–80). Origen shows how Christianity can withstand the intellectual assault of philosophically sophisticated paganism, and how fruitfully Christian theology can use the tools of Greek philosophy. Despite the unorthodoxy of aspects of his thought, Origen's influence on Christian THEOLOGY and spirituality was enormous.

Crouzel, H. (1989), *Origen*. Edinburgh: T. & T. Clark.
Trigg, J. W. (1985), *Origen*. London: SCM Press.
Nautin. P. (1977), *Origène: sa vie et son oeuvre*. Paris: n.p.
Armstrong, A. H., ed. (1970), *The Cambridge History of Later Greek and Early Medieval Philosophy*. Cambridge: Cambridge University Press.
Chadwick, H. (1966), *Early Christian Thought and the Classical Tradition: Studies in Justin, Clement and Origen*. New York: n.p.
Chadwick, H., trans. (1965), *Origen, Contra Celsum*. Cambridge: Cambridge University Press.

DM

Orthodox Church in America The OCA was established in 1970 when the Moscow patriarchate granted autocephaly to the Metropolia, the largest Russian

Orthodox jurisdiction in AMERICA. The churches of Bulgaria, Czech Republic and Slovakia, Georgia and Poland have recognized the autocephaly of the OCA; it has yet to be recognized by others, including the patriarchates of CONSTANTINOPLE, ALEXANDRIA and ANTIOCH. The OCA is in communion with the other Orthodox churches, but its involvement in pan-Orthodox activities is limited. Albanian, Bulgarian and Romanian Orthodox jurisdictions in canonical union with the OCA are numbered among its dioceses. In 1995 there were 510 OCA parishes in the USA, 91 in Canada, nine in Mexico, five in South America and three in Australia. Theodosius, archbishop of Washington, metropolitan of All America and Canada is the head of the OCA. Current membership is estimated at 1 million (statistics from Roberson, 1995).

Roberson, P. G. (1995), *The Eastern Christian Churches, a Brief Survey*, 5th edn. Rome: Edizioni Orientalia Christiana.

MJB/SHG

Orthros   Byzantine rite office of Matins.
   See also DAILY OFFICES.

Taft, R. (1986), *The Liturgy of the Hours in East and West*. Collegeville, Minn.: Liturgical Press.

DM

Ossetia   North and South Ossetia are divided geographically by the Caucasus and politically between the Russian Federation and GEORGIA. The Ossetians are an Iranian people descended from the Alans. ALANIA incorporated the entire north Caucasus region during the middle ages, but shrank to the lands on either side of the Darial Pass on the arrival of the Tatars. The mainly Christian Ossetians were influenced by Islam from the seventeenth century; the Digor Ossetians embraced Islam, the dominant Tual and Iron Ossetians remained largely Orthodox, while other tribes reverted to animism. Russian Orthodox missions to Ossetia strengthened Orthodox Christian links. With the collapse of the Soviet Union, South Ossetia sought to secede from Georgia (alongside ABKHAZIA) and unite with North Ossetia. Although the Ossetians have enjoyed Russian support in their conflict with Georgia, their homelands remain divided.

Avtorkhanov, A. (1992), *The North Caucasus Barrier*. London: Hurst.

DB

Ottoman rule and Eastern Christianity   Osman I (1280–1324), founder of the Ottoman dynasty, stretched the borders of his lands on the edges of Seljuk and Byzantine territory to the point where in 1326 his son Orhan was able to take Prousa (Bursa), which thereafter was the capital of the Ottoman domains. When Orhan (1324–59) threatened Nicaea, Andronikos III Palaiologos (1328–41) led a great force to bloody rout at Pelekanos. Soon Nicaea (1331) and Nikomedia (1337) were in Ottoman hands. Civil war in Byzantium (1341–7) served the Ottomans, Orhan offering support to John VI Kantakouzenos (1347–54) while extending his rule east to Ankara and acquiring a fort on the Dardanelles as a thank-offering.

Murat I (1360–89) captured Adrianople, probably in 1361, and defeated a joint Hungarian, Bosnian and Serbian force soon after at Marica river. From 1366 he began a campaign of conquest in Europe. The Western CRUSADE of 1396 against Murat's successor, Beyazit I, collapsed at Nikopolis. In 1400, however, Timur Lenk swept into Anatolia, took Sivas (Sebasteia) and captured Beyazit in 1400 and Ankara in 1402, then in April 1403 withdrew, leaving Beyazit's four sons to scramble for the throne. By 1413 Mehmet I (1413–21) ruled. He removed the Christians his father had welcomed in his court. In 1423 his son, Murat II (1421–51), unsuccessfully laid siege to CONSTANTINOPLE.

In 1443 a crusade led by the Hungarian warrior John Hunyadi defeated the Ottomans and won a truce, whereby the Ottomans withdrew from Serbia and Romania. Murat now handed power to his son, Mehmet. The papal legate persuaded Hunyadi to break the truce and invade Ottoman territory. Enraged, Murat resumed rule, defeated the invaders at Varna in 1444 and then, in 1448, defeated Hunyadi himself at KOSOVO.

Mehmet II (1451–81) returned to the throne on Murat's death in 1451. On Tuesday, 29 May 1453, after a heroic defence, Constantinople itself fell to Mehmet II, who eventually established his rule or suzerainty over Bosnia, Herzegovina, Serbia, Wallachia and Moldavia.

The Christian Byzantine empire was gone. Mehmet allowed his troops only a single day in which to sack the city, then immediately set to redeveloping it as his new capital. New arrivals, many Christian, repopulated depleted Constantinople. Mehmet installed GENNADIOS II SCHOLARIOS as patriarch of Constantinople, granting him also civil authority over his community. The *Rum* were now *dhimmi*, a subordinate nation (*milet*) within the state (*see* AHL AL-KITĀB). *Dhimmi* subjects, unless they converted to Islam, were excluded from military service and from entering the Ottoman ruling class. Legal cases involving a Muslim as well as a *dhimmi* were tried in an Islamic court, and the law privileged the evidence of Muslims. *Dhimmi* purchasers were forbidden to bargain with Muslim shopkeepers, forbidden to ride horses, commanded to step respectfully aside when a Muslim passed and required to pay taxes in a humiliating manner. Physical contact with a *dhimmi* polluted a Muslim. But the rules were often ignored.

Until the seventeenth century the Christians of the countryside were subject to the *devshirme*, the blood-tax that gathered Christian youths for the sultan's service. Some saw this as insensate cruelty, others an opportunity. Boys gathered in the *devshirme* were trained for military service as janissaries, or for other roles; all of them were offered good education, excellent training and a thorough induction into Islam, usually by Bektashi dervishes, whose distinctive brand of Islam made them remarkably successful at proselytizing Christians, especially in the Balkans.

Mehmet II and his successors, particularly Suleiman the Lawgiver (1520–66) had to develop and codify the law to meet the demands of imperial rule. Patriarchal courts dealt with matters of clerical status and jurisdiction, marriage, divorce, wills and inheritance. The patriarch also had jurisdiction in civil cases between Christians and criminal jurisdiction over his clergy, though parties in a case could decide to be heard in an Islamic court, which could also receive appeals. The patriarch became a six-horsetail pasha (horse tails were a symbol of authority, six marking a subject ruler), so long as his enemies lacked the means or the gold to procure his downfall. Monies senior clergy paid on appointment were a major burden on the Christians. The *dhimmi* communities ran their own welfare and educational systems. The patriarch could tax his flock, and could call on state authorities to enforce his rule. Equally, he had to ensure his flock paid their taxes to the state, and was responsible for their order and good conduct. Byzantine law survived in his courts: in mitra and sakkos (*see* RELIGIOUS DRESS) he was a living monument to the fallen Christian empire, but his survival depended on his enforcing loyalty and obedience to the Ottoman power. His vulnerability invited the Catholic and Protestant powers of Western Europe to extend their influence by diplomatic interference and intrigue.

Patriarchal decrees required confirmation by the Holy Synod, now extended to include several of the high officials of the Great Church, in effect the heads of his civil service departments. Episcopal administration was modelled on the patriarchal, but local civil jurisdiction was in lay hands. Lay judges and lawyers were soon to be found among the office-bearers of the Great Church.

The Patriarchal Academy provided a centre for theological study. Talented young men, however, studied in VENICE, Padua and in ROME, many converting, often temporarily, to Catholicism. Venetian Greek presses made a unique contribution to Greek culture. In 1577 Pope Gregory XIII (1572–85) founded the Greek College of St Athanasios in Rome to educate young Greeks and win them for the Catholic church. In 1593 the scholarly Patriarch JEREMIAS II (1572–9, 1580–4, 1587–95) reformed and extended the curriculum of the Patriarchal Academy. A further reform under Cyril LUCARIS made it an important centre of literary and scientific learning. Other schools and academies were founded at different times, the great monasteries remaining centres of learning well into the Ottoman period. The Orthodox princes of Wallachia and Moldavia also offered cultural patronage; academies were established in Bucharest and Jassy. Literacy was common, at least in the towns.

Active persecution of Christians was rare, though it was a capital offence for converts to Islam to return to Christianity or for Christians to insult Islam and its prophet. The right of a Christian to declare his disbelief in Islam was none the less recognized. The lengthy catalogue of NEW MARTYRS is more a testimony to Christian zeal than to Muslim severity. Selim I, the Grim (1512–20), caliph as well as sultan, proposed the forcible conversion of his Christian subjects to Islam. With his vizier's connivance the sultan's intention was forestalled. This rare example of religious fanaticism shows the vulnerability of the *dhimmis*.

The Russian tsars were powerful financial and political patrons of the Eastern Christians under Ottoman rule. They were also the sultan's most formidable opponents. Catherine II (1762–96) concocted a plan to drive the Ottomans out of Europe and place her grandson Constantine on the throne of a new Byzantine empire, while dividing the sultan's western possessions among Austria, Venice and France. Her success was incomplete, but the treaty of Küçük Kaynarca established the tsar as protector of Christians under Ottoman rule, an excuse for future intervention.

The Ottoman system placed all Eastern Orthodox in the empire under the rule of the Ecumenical Patriarch: the ancient patriarchates of ALEXANDRIA, ANTIOCH and JERUSALEM were subordinated to his rule, as were the non-Greek churches of the Balkans. Increasingly the patriarchate found itself with a divided allegiance, identified with the Greek nation and at the same time owing loyalty to Ottoman rule. The grand rabbi and the Armenian patriarch (1461) were early recognized as heads of other *milets*, the Armenian patriarch receiving authority over all non-Muslim groups other than Jews and Eastern Orthodox, including the Gypsies and the MARONITES. The struggle by different Christian communities for recognition as a separate *milet* continued throughout the Ottoman period; the SYRIAN CATHOLICS, for example, won recognition in 1830, the MELKITE CATHOLICS in 1838 and the CHALDEANS in 1845.

The decadence of Ottoman administration through the sixteenth to eighteenth centuries saw the rise of traditional Islamic legal institutions. Local rulers carved out their own states. Conflict with European states in the late eighteenth and nineteenth centuries coincided with the rise of nationalism and a sequence of bloody revolts. A Serbian revolt in 1804 led to a Russian protectorate in 1817 and final independence in 1878. The Greek revolt of 1821 brought independence to much of mainland Greece in 1830. Ottoman authorities reacted to the revolt by executing Patriarch Gregory V (*see* ETHNOMARTYRS) and many other clerical and lay leaders. Romania became independent in 1878; Bulgaria gained autonomy in 1879.

Under Abdul Mecid I (1839–61) the *tanzimat* period, the era of regulations, began with the promulgation in 1839 of the Hatt-i-Sherif. Fundamental human rights for the *milets* were officially guaranteed. Further reforms followed at the end of the Crimean war in the Hatt-i-Humayun of 1856. Universal citizenship was established with a general requirement for military service. The Christians resented and opposed this. Muslim conservatives opposed many of the *tanzimat* as un-Islamic. The rising Young Turk movement opposed them as the product of foreign influence.

Abdul Hamid II (1876–1909) returned to absolutism, based in part on his role as caliph. He became a bizarre figure, lurking in the Star Pavilion with fortune-tellers and favourites, haunted by fear of assassination. The growing sense of nationhood among the Armenian minority was met with a series of appalling massacres in which the sultan's government was implicated. His abdication in 1909 signalled the beginning of the end of Ottoman rule. Mehmet V (1909–18) was ineffective. Initative had passed to the Young Turks. Turkish nationalism and Pan-Turanianism threatened the minorities. Turkey's role in the First World War on the side of the central powers resulted in Mehmet VI (1918–22) seeing Constantinople under allied occupation, deputies exiled to Malta, and the Young Turks establishing a rival government in Ankara. The Treaty of Sèvres (1920) stripped Turkey of its European possessions apart from Constantinople. The Greek army engaged in a fierce invasion that failed before Ankara, and saw the Greeks driven into the sea at Smyrna. British intervention returned Eastern Thrace to the Turks. On 1 November 1922 the last Ottoman sultan was deposed. Turkish nationalism was now to triumph. The Christian minorities had exchanged a clearly defined position of subordination but relative security under the Islamic Ottoman system for the uncertainty of life as non-Turkish communities under a secular regime with a strong commitment to Turkish nationalism.

Bat Ye'or (1996), *The Decline of Eastern Christianity under Islam: From Jihad to Dhimmitude, Seventh–Twentieth Century*. Madison and London: Associated University Presses.
Imber, C. (1990), *The Ottoman Empire, 1300–1481*. Istanbul: Isis.

Bryer, A. A. M. and Lowry, H., eds (1986), *Continuity and Change in Late Byzantine and Early Ottoman Society*. Birmingham and Dumbarton Oaks: Birmingham University.

Shaw, S. J. (1976), *History of the Ottoman Empire and Modern Turkey*. Cambridge: Cambridge University Press.

Inalcik, H. (1973), *The Ottoman Empire: The Classical Age, 1300–1600*. London: Weidenfeld and Nicolson.

Inalcik, H. (1970), 'The Emergence of the Ottomans', *Cambridge History of Islam*, vol. 1. Cambridge: Cambridge University Press.

Runciman, S. (1968), *The Great Church in Captivity*. Cambridge: Cambridge University Press.

DM

Outremer Western Europeans established several client states in the Near East during the CRUSADES: the coastal territories of Syria and Palestine became known in the French of the principal crusading power as Outremer. Conquests by the Venetians and crusading powers in Greece after 1204 were termed New France. The legacy of Outremer can be seen in the constellation of Eastern Catholic churches of the Near/Middle East and in the Francophile tendencies of Arab Orthodox and Oriental Orthodox Christians.

See also FRANKS.

DB

Overbeck, J. J. Joseph Julian Overbeck (1820–1905) was born in Bonn, of rigidly ultramontane parents. At the University of Bonn he distinguished himself as a linguist, specializing in SYRIAC. Ordained a Roman Catholic priest, he studied in the Vatican library, coming to the attention of Pius IX and Cardinal Wiseman, himself a Syriac scholar. Losing faith in Roman claims, he resigned his professorship at Bonn and for a time attended Lutheran worship. He petitioned the Prussian government for a stipend to undertake Syriac studies in the British Museum, but it flatly refused to support 'an apostate'. Friedrich Wilhelm IV finally offered him a stipend from his privy purse.

Overbeck settled in England in 1857, securing a position at Oxford teaching German under Max Müller, and married. In 1863 he became German professor at the Staff College, Camberley.

His translation of works of EPHREM THE SYRIAN from manuscripts in the British Museum and the Bodleian Library led him to examine the history and teaching of the EASTERN ORTHODOX church; he became convinced it was 'the only one that could claim to be the ancient Catholic and Apostolic Church of our creed, and that all the other churches of Christendom were schismatically and heretically cut off from the Catholic and Orthodox Church'. He reasoned that the Orthodox East was the sole means of reviving the Catholic Church of the West which had existed prior to 1054. In 1864 he was chrismated at the Russian Embassy Chapel in London.

In 1866 he published *Catholic Orthodoxy and Anglo-Catholicism*, in which he outlined the scheme on which he was to work for the next twenty years. The following year he published the first issue of the *Orthodox Catholic Review*, which aimed at 'setting forth the truth of Catholic Orthodoxy as opposed to Popery and Protestantism, clearing its way through the heap of rubbish stored up by both parties for centuries past'. Believing both the Church of England and the papacy on the verge of disintegration, he wanted the Orthodox church to revive Western Catholicism by restoring the WESTERN RITE in Orthodoxy.

In March 1867 he circulated a petition to the Russian Holy Synod outlining his scheme and requesting establishment of a Western uniate church in full communion with the Eastern church, for 'we are Westerns . . . and must plead an inalienable right to remain Westerns'. In September 1869 the petition was closed with only 122 signatures, mainly Tractarian clergymen, and sent to Russia. Upon its receipt a synodal commission was formed, comprising seven members under the metropolitan of St Petersburg; Dr Overbeck was invited to attend their deliberations. Accompanied by Father Eugene Popoff, the embassy chaplain in London, he was present in January 1870 when the scheme was approved and he was requested to submit a draft of the Western liturgy for examination.

The liturgy he submitted was based on the 1570 Roman rite of Pius V, but including a brief *epiklesis* and the Hagios O Theos after the Gloria 'in remembrance of our union with the Orthodox Church'. He returned to Russia in January 1871. In two long sessions the commission examined the liturgy and expressed their approval.

Over the next few years Overbeck occupied himself with the growth of the Old Catholic movement in Europe and attended several of the Bonn conferences as an Orthodox observer. Through his magazine he engaged in lively polemics with opponents, sniping at Anglicans and Roman Catholics as well as Orthodox converts who followed the Byzantine rite. In 1876 he issued an *Appeal to the Patriarchs and Holy Synods of the Orthodox Catholic Church* restating his scheme and in August 1879 travelled to Turkey to meet the Ecumenical Patriarch, Ioakeim III, who authorized him to deliver sermons and addresses to defend Orthodoxy. In August 1881 the Holy Synod of CONSTANTINOPLE appointed a commission to consider the scheme and an announcement was made that 'an agreement on certain points has already been reached', which recognized the right of the West to have its Western church and Western rite as it existed before the schism.

Nothing further developed. Overbeck became disillusioned. He had hoped to exercise his priesthood within the Orthodox church, but his marriage after ordination made him ineligible. He saw plots and schemes in every quarter and was sure the Greeks in London were especially hostile towards him. The *Orthodox Catholic Review* ceased publication in 1885, and by 1892 he admitted that his scheme had failed, complaining of 'Hopes entertained with joy by all the truly Orthodox, recommended and pushed forward by the Holy Synods of Russia, Romania and Serbia, approved by the Patriarchs of Constantinople, Alexandria, Jerusalem but finally crushed and destroyed by the veto of the Greek Synod!'

S

·P·

Paisios Eznepidis (1924–94)   Athonite elder, born in Pharasa, Cappadocia weeks before the Greeks were expelled. Arsenios Hatzieffendi (commemorated 10 November) baptized him. In later life he was associated with the Russian elder Tychon Gorainov (d. 1968). In 1949 Paisios settled on ATHOS after active service in the army, staying in various monasteries and sketes. From 1962 to 1964 he lived as a hermit in the desert of SINAI. Seriously ill for most of his life, Paisios emerged from monastic seclusion to visit hospitals and found monastic communities at Souroti. By the time he died of cancer he was reputed the foremost Greek *gerontas* or STARETS and was receiving visitors and letters from across the world.

DB

Paissii Velichkovskii (1722–94)   Paissii was born in Poltava, of Ukrainian and Jewish descent. He was sent to Kiev Theological Academy (1735) but took up the pilgrim life, visiting the monasteries and shrines of UKRAINE. Paissii became a monk at Medvedka monastery (1741) then went on pilgrimage to ROMANIA. He settled on ATHOS (1746) and in 1758, with several disciples, occupied the Prophet Elias skete. Driven out by the Turks, the group moved to Dragomirna in BUCOVINA, then, when that area was ceded to Austria, to Neamt in Moldavia. From this, the largest monastery in the Orthodox East, Paissii supervised several other cloisters. In 1793 he published an abridged, adapted, Slavonic translation of the PHILOKALIA. Paissii is commemorated on 15 November.

Bolshakoff, S. (1980), *Russian Mystics*. Kalamazoo: Cistercian Publications.
Mitrophan (1976), *Blessed Paissy Velichkovsky*. Platina, Cal.: St Herman of Alaska Press.

DB

Palūṭ   The earliest clearly attested bishop of EDESSA, *c*.200, and, according to the *Teaching of Addai*, ADDAI's second successor. The Palūṭians, whom EPHREM

THE SYRIAN regarded as the true Christians at Edessa, were probably named after him.

JH

Panagia Greek, 'all-holy', an epithet of the THEOTOKOS. Two particular uses of the word should be noted, neither of which is listed in Lampe's *Lexicon*: (1) to describe the enkolpion worn by bishops, when it takes the form of an icon of the Mother of God; (2) in 'Raising the Panagia', part of the grace after meals, but now normally limited to monasteries, on Sundays and major feasts. At the commemoration of the Mother of God following the *epiklesis* in the Divine Liturgy, the celebrant raises a small prosphora on a silver dish, saying: 'Great is the name of the Holy Trinity'. He touches the dish to the rim of the chalice. In Greek use, the same is done at this point with the ANTI-DORON. After the liturgy the refectorian cuts a triangular portion from the prosphora. This, the Panagia, is cut in half and laid crumb upwards on the dish on a small table in the refectory. After the meal the refectorian removes his cowl and skoupho, saying: 'Bless me, holy Fathers, and pardon me a sinner.' The community replies: 'May God pardon and have mercy on you.' Taking the Panagia in his fingertips, he raises it, saying: 'Great is the name'; they reply: 'Of the Holy Trinity.' The dialogue continues: 'All-holy Mother of God, help us'; they reply: 'At her prayers, O God, have mercy and save us.' Two troparia are sung while the refectorian, followed by an ecclesiastic carrying a hand-censer (*kapnisterion*), offers the Panagia to the community. Each takes a fragment between finger and thumb, passes it through the incense smoke and eats it.

A footnote in the HOROLOGION recounts the ceremony's legendary origin. After the Resurrection and Pentecost the apostles at first stayed together. At meals they left an empty place with a cushion and on it a piece of bread as Christ's portion. After eating, they would raise the bread, saying: 'Glory to you, our God, glory to you. Glory to the Father, the Son and the Holy Spirit'; from Pascha to Ascension, 'Christ has risen'; after that, 'Great is the name of the Holy Trinity. Lord Jesus, help us.' After separating, each did this wherever he was, until the DORMITION of the Virgin, when clouds bore them to JERUSALEM for her burial. Three days later, after breakfast they rose and lifted the bread fragment named for Christ. When they said, 'Great is the name', Mary appeared accompanied by ANGELS. She said: 'Rejoice! for I am with you all days,' offering this greeting from her Son. The amazed disciples cried out: 'All-holy Mother of God, help us!' Going to the tomb they found it empty, and were persuaded that on the third day, like her Son, she had been raised from the dead and passed over to heaven.

E

Panagis Vasias (1801–88) Greek HOLY FOOL from Kephallonia. A respected teacher and priest, after a long illness he withdrew from worldly affairs and in later life feigned lunacy, but was unable to shed his reputation as a seer whose prayers wrought miracles. He is commemorated on 7 June.

Gelis, K. (1987), *Hagios Panagis Basias*. Athens: n.p.

DB

Panormitis   The Monastery of Archangel Michael at Panormitis on Symi in the Dodecanese. The main church overlooking the bay was built in 1783; the guesthouses surrounding the complex, dating from the turn of the century, are used by numerous pilgrims. Chrysanthos Maroulakis, abbot of Panormitis, was executed by the Italians in 1944 for his work with the Resistance. The restored Byzantine Thari monastery on Rhodes, also dedicated to Archangel Michael, is linked to the Orthodox mission in East Africa.

See also ANGELS; CHONAI.

Hatzifotis, I. (1968), *Iera Moni Panormiti*. Symi: n.p.

DB

Panslavism   Although dominated by Orthodox Christians, the Panslavist movement advocated union of all Slavic peoples regardless of religious allegiance. This ideal was sometimes formulated in a way that seemed to imply Slavic leadership and/or protection of all East Christian communities, but in practice Panslavism promoted solidarity among Slav nations against non-Slav neighbours. The movement was fuelled by conflict between the south and west Slavs and Austria-Hungary, and by the struggle between Bulgarians and Greeks in the OTTOMAN empire.

See also THIRD ROME.

DB

Pantocrator   Greek title meaning omnipotent or all-sovereign, used in the Septuagint to translate the word Sabaoth; in Job it also translates Shaddai. Septuagint Isaias simply transliterates the Hebrew, 'Sabaoth', and the Hebrew word enters Christian Greek, particularly through the Seraphic hymn incorporated into the Anaphora. In patristic and liturgical Greek 'Sabaoth' is usually, like *pantokrator*, treated as a proper noun, in apposition to 'God'. The title *pantokrator* is applied to Christ in Apocalypse 1: 8 and in Christian texts used of the Trinity. In the Creed it is the particular epithet of the Father. According to DIONYSIUS THE AREOPAGITE in *Divine Names*, 10, God is called Pantocrator 'because as the omnipotent foundation of everything he preserves and embraces all the world'.

As an icon type, associated in particular with the image of Christ in the central cupola of many Byzantine churches, the Pantocrator is normally a half-length figure of Christ holding a closed book, his other hand raised in what may be a gesture of blessing. The icon represents Christ's divine transcendence and at the same time his presence in the liturgical assembly. As worshippers face east, the icon is above them, present, but not as object of their gaze. The image reproduced here is based on the Pantocrator in the dome of the monastery church at Daphni in Greece (eleventh century).

Mathews, T. F. (1990), 'The Transformation Symbolism in Byzantine Architecture and the Meaning of the Pantokrator in the Dome' in R. Morris, ed., *Church and People in Byzantium*. Birmingham: University of Birmingham Press.

Kontoglou, F. (1960), *Ekphrasis*, vol. 1. Athens: Astir.

KP

Paraklesis   A service of intercession to the Lord, the Mother of God and the saints. In Greek tradition, evening services are held during the fortnight before the feast of the DORMITION of the THEOTOKOS on 15 August, during which is sung one of the two parakletic CANONS. The small intercessory canon is attributed to Monk Theosteriktos, the great to Emperor Theodoros Doukas Laskaris; both are of high poetical quality. The small Paraklesis is also read in sickness and troubles of every kind, and on ATHOS every weekday before the main meal.

In the Slav service of intercession, or Moleben, the HEIRMOI and refrains of the canon are sung without TROPARIA. Other intercessory canons exist, written to the same heirmoi. The Athonite Docheiariou monastery, for example, uses one composed by NIKODEMOS THE HAGIORITE for the *Gorgoypikoos* icon.

DM/E

Parakletike   Slav: Oktoich. Byzantine rite liturgical book, also known as the OKTOECHOS, containing the texts for the offices in the eight tones. Each tone has its own hymns and antiphons. The ANASTASIMATARION contains the Oktoechos texts for Sundays. Joseph the Hymnographer (ninth century) had a major influence on the final form of the Parakletike.

See also JOHN OF DAMASCUS.

DM

Paraskeve the Roman   Second-century GREAT MARTYR, invoked to cure blindness and other ailments. By tradition Paraskeve was born in ROME to Christian parents, Agatho and Politeia. Arrested and tortured for preaching Christianity, she escaped to Greece to continue her mission. Accounts of her martyrdom differ; one Greek tradition has Paraskeve arrested at Tempe and executed outside Thessaloniki. Acherousia monastery in Thesprotia, Epirus, holds the reputed tomb of the saint; her relics were taken to CONSTANTINOPLE in the Byzantine era. Her feast day is 26 July.

Alongside Paraskeve the Roman are honoured Paraskeve of Ikonion (third century) and Paraskeve of Epibatas (1023–57). The former was martyred in Lykaonia under Diocletian and is commemorated on 28 October; the latter, a hermit, is commemorated on 14 October. Paraskeve of Epibatas is revered throughout the Balkans since her relics were taken to Trnovo in Bulgaria in the thirteenth century, to Romania and then to Serbia in the fourteenth century and finally back to Romania in 1641. Known as Petko, she is claimed by the Serbs to be of Serbian descent. Her tomb in Kallikratia (Catalca) of Eastern THRACE was a pilgrimage centre until 1922; one in Nea Kallikratia in Greece draws pilgrims to this day.

Nicolas Velimirovic (1985), *The Prologue of Ochrid*, vols 3 and 4. Birmingham: Lazarica Press.

DB

Paschal offices, Byzantine rite   The Byzantine offices of the Resurrection begin with the ancient great Paschal vigil, consisting of Vespers followed by the Divine Liturgy (*see* PROTE ANASTASIS). After the liturgy there should be a blessing of bread and wine, but not oil, these being distributed with dried fruit to all who remain in church while the Acts of the Apostles is read continuously until the MESONYKTIKON begins. This reflects an older practice when the vigil took place in the evening. In most places today the Prote Anastasis takes place on Saturday morning and the Mesonykti-kon about an hour before midnight, though in some places some of Acts and the sermon of EPIPHANIOS OF SALAMIS are read before the office.

Towards midnight all the lights are extinguished and the priest comes from the altar with a triple candle, from which all light their candles. The whole assembly then processes around the church, or to a place prepared for the proclamation of the Resurrec-tion. The procession represents the myrrh-bearing women coming to the tomb. In Greek use it is now customary to read one of the Resurrection gospels before the proclamation that 'Christ has risen from the dead', though older editions of the PENTEKOSTARION do not prescribe this; since the people are re-enacting the discovery of the empty tomb and hearing the Resurrection proclaimed, the gospel reading is redundant.

After the proclamation the assembly re-enters the church, now ablaze with light and filled with fragrant clouds of incense burning on a brazier. ORTHROS follows, which consists of the CANON by JOHN OF DAMASCUS, which makes extensive use of the Paschal homilies of Gregory Nazianzen, and the AINOI, which end with the opening verses of Psalm 68 interleaved with special Paschal STICHERA, marked by the trium-phant repetition of the word 'Pascha', and culminate in the call to forgive 'even those who hate us' and to embrace one another in celebration of the Resurrection. This is the signal for all to venerate the Gospel-book, exchanging the Kiss of Peace before hearing the Easter sermon of JOHN CHRYSOSTOM, which invites all to Paschal communion, whether they have kept the Lenten fast or not. Doubts have been raised as to its authenticity, though THEODORE THE STUDITE includes it as John Chrysostom's in one of his own Easter sermons. The Divine Liturgy follows, at which the readings are the opening of Acts (1: 1–8) and John (1: 1–18); these two books have formed the church's paschal lectionary since early times (*see* BIBLE). Vespers on Easter Sunday, the Vespers of Love, are of special solemnity and include the reading of John 20: 19–25. In Greek use this is read in many languages; in Russian use the gospel at the liturgy is read in this way.

The office of each day of Easter week is sung in one of the eight tones in sequence. The first STICHERA and THEOTOKION at Vespers are those the PARAKLETIKE contains for tone 1.

E

Passion Bearers   Boris and Gleb, the first canonized saints of Rus, are the most famous saints in this category; the two sons of Prince Vladimir (d. 1015) were killed, without resisting, by Sviatopolk for political reasons. Pilgrims came from afar to venerate their shrine in Vishgorod. They are often depicted mounted like the two

Theodores (*see* MILITARY SAINTS). They are commemorated six times a year, notably on 2 May and 24 July. According to their Life, all innocent or voluntary suffering undertaken in the name of Christ is sanctified. Self-offering non-resistance became exalted among northern Orthodox to the level of martyrdom. The Serbian JOHN VLADIMIR (d. 1015), murdered in similar circumstances, was also recognized as a saint.

Among the GREEK ORTHODOX Passion Bearers are known, but this category of sanctity is less clearly defined. MARIA OF BIZYE (*c.*866–902) and other saintly women mistreated by their husbands offer the rare example of lay, female passion bearers. John Joasaph IV Laskaris (d. 1305), blinded as a child by Michael VIII Palaiologos and imprisoned until he joined a monastery (*c.*1285), is commemorated with his grandfather, John III Vatatzes, on 4 November. Tsar Nicolas II, and other members of the Romanov family, murdered by the Bolsheviks (1918) for political reasons, won reverence for their fortitude in the face of brutality. The Romanov martyrs were canonized by the RUSSIAN ORTHODOX CHURCH ABROAD (1981) and are commemorated on 17 July. In recent years JOHN KARASTAMATIS (d. 1985), a priest of Santa Cruz in California, is popularly accounted a Passion Bearer.

Lenhoff, G. (1989), *The Martyred Princes Boris and Gleb: A Socio-cultural Study of the Cult and the Texts*. Columbus, Ohio: Ohio University Press.
Hackel, S., ed. (1981), *The Byzantine Saint*. London: Fellowship of SS Alban and Sergius.
Demshuk, V. (1978), *Russian Sainthood and Canonization*. Minneapolis: Light and Life.

DB

Patmos   The holy island of the Dodecanese, united to Greece in 1945. Patmos is associated with JOHN THE THEOLOGIAN, in whose day it was a Roman penal colony, and with the writing of the Apocalypse. The island's major monastery, dedicated to John, was founded in 1088 by Christodoulos, an elder from Mount Latros, to whom Patmos was given by Emperor Alexios I Komnenos. The Theologos monastery enjoyed imperial patronage; from the twelfth century its estates and its wealth increased greatly. Its wealth and privileges were generally preserved through the OTTOMAN period. It attracted monks fleeing from Mount Latros and ASIA MINOR, and replaced Ephesus as principal shrine of the Theologian when Ephesus was devastated by the Turks. The monastery possesses a major collection of manuscripts, relics, icons and liturgical treasures. In recent years the elder Amphilochios of Patmos (d. 1970) has been widely venerated as an outstanding spiritual teacher.

See also TINOS.

DB

patriarch   (1) Title given in Jewish and Christian tradition to the righteous men counted as ancestors of all humanity, including the penitent Adam and Noe (Noah); also to Abraham and his lineage as ancestors of the Hebrews. The matriarchs are also greatly venerated, especially in Jewish tradition. The patriarchs and matriarchs are also celebrated liturgically and iconographically as ancestors of Christ.

(2) With the Christianization of the Roman empire, the bishops of the empire's regional capitals acquired formal recognition of their authority over the churches of their imperial dioceses. ROME, ALEXANDRIA and ANTIOCH became organizational foci of the church, and the bishops of CONSTANTINOPLE and JERUSALEM were later recognized as possessing similar honour and authority, especially in hearing appeals against local bishops and in settling disputes among them. At the councils of Constantinople I (381) and Chalcedon (451) the see of Constantinople was recognized as second in honour to Rome, giving the bishops of the empire's two capitals pre-eminent jurisdiction in East and West respectively. The Roman popes long resisted this decision, actively promoting their rival claim to supreme and universal jurisdiction. The title ECUMENICAL PATRIARCH was first used by the patriarch of Constantinople JOHN THE FASTER in the sixth century.

From the sixth century the hierarchs of these five sees came to be known as patriarchs (see PENTARCHY), though the patriarch of the West and the patriarch of Alexandria both use also the title 'pope'. The title 'patriarch' was probably first used in the patriarchate of Antioch and in the CHURCH OF THE EAST. Christian use of the title may have been inspired by Jewish use of the title to designate the Nasi, the Davidic prince of the Jewish community in the Holy Land, who had a counterpart in the exilarch in Babylon.

With the growth of national churches seeking recognition as independent, the chief hierarchs of RUSSIA, ROMANIA, BULGARIA and SERBIA were all designated patriarchs. Not all heads of autocephalous churches use the title; archbishops head the churches of CYPRUS and SINAI and others, and the chief bishop in the Georgian church uses the title CATHOLICOS or catholicos-patriarch.

The divisions resulting from Christological controversies in the fourth and fifth centuries, and later from the creation of EASTERN CATHOLIC hierarchies, led to the co-existence of parallel hierarchies whose senior hierarchs made use of ancient patriarchal titles. There are presently, for example, not only an EASTERN ORTHODOX and a SYRIAN ORTHODOX patriarch of Antioch, but also a MELKITE CATHOLIC patriarch (who also bears the titles of Alexandria and Jerusalem), a SYRIAN CATHOLIC patriarch and a MARONITE patriarch, who bears the title 'patriarch of Antioch of the Maronites'.

During the CRUSADES Latin Catholic patriarchs were appointed to Constantinople, Alexandria, Antioch and Jerusalem; these titles continued in use into the nineteenth and twentieth centuries, though apart from Jerusalem they became merely honorific titles. In the Latin church the title exists as a mark of honour and distinction, as for example in the patriarch of VENICE.

When patriarchal jurisdiction cannot easily be exercised in a given area, a senior bishop may be appointed as exarch to act on the patriarch's behalf. Many exarchs were appointed to govern churches in Islamic territory.

DM

patriarchate of the East The title CHURCH OF THE EAST has become commonplace in modern times as a more appropriate term for that branch of SYRIAC-speaking Christianity, mostly within the Sasanian Persian sphere (including much of Mesopotamia), which through a series of canonical steps made itself an autocephalous church in the fifth century. It was in the past frequently called the ASSYRIAN church or the NESTORIAN church. This last title, which is polemical, associates the Persian church with the disputes surrounding Nestorius, bishop of Constantinople, his mentor Theodore of Mopsuestia and their DYOPHYSITE christology. Before declaring itself independent of the patriarchate of ANTIOCH in 424, the Church of the East was ruled by a CATHOLICOS, the metropolitan of Seleucia-Ctesiphon (south of Baghdad); by the end of the fifth century the title PATRIARCH came into use.

JH

Paulicians   Although the theology of the sects that developed on the periphery of the Byzantine empire remains obscure, it is clear that they were influenced by earlier dualist movements. The Paulicians, who originated in the Armenian marches in the seventh century, rejected church sacraments, traditions and the Old Testament. During the prolonged Byzantine–Arab struggle they created a state in the Tephrike (Divrigi) region after 843, but existed throughout ASIA MINOR. Whether Paulicians played any significant role in ICONOCLASM is uncertain. In 872 the Byzantines crushed them, resettling them around Philippopolis (Plovdiv) in THRACE.

Nersessian, V. (1988), *The Tondrakian Movement*. Allison Park, Penn.: Pickwick Publications.
Garsoïan, N. G. (1967), *The Paulician Heresy*. The Hague: n.p.

DB

Paul of Latros   (d. *c*.950)   Paul and his brother Basil, natives of Aiolia, became monks, Basil going to Mount Olympos, Paul to Karia monastery on Mount Latros, where he cultivated ASCETICISM. Paul became a hermit near Kellibaron monastery for a time, living like a STYLITE on a rocky pinnacle. Monks joined him and a new monastery was founded, its church dedicated to Archangel Michael. Fleeing fame and disciples, Paul moved to Pythagoras' cave on Samos, but here too others joined him, founding Kerketea Lavra. His last years were spent between Samos and Mount Latros. A famous seer, Byzantine and Bulgarian rulers consulted him. He is commemorated on 15 December; Basil on 26 March.

DB

Paul the Silentiary   Sixth-century author of a lengthy and detailed poem on the church of Hagia Sophia in CONSTANTINOPLE, an important source of information on lost aspects of the church's interior ordering.

DM

Peć   The monastery of the patriarchate of Peć lies on the left bank of the Bistrica in the KOSOVO region. The Holy Apostles church, the oldest in the complex of four, was founded *c*.1230 by Archbishop Arsenije. Its fresco programme, initiated by SAVA of Serbia, evokes the events in the Cenacle in Jerusalem. Seat of the autocephalous archbishop from *c*.1280, and of the PATRIARCH from 1346, it is considered 'the mother of churches' in SERBIA. Archbishop Nikodim founded the church of St Demetrios (1320); the patron of the churches of the Virgin and of St Nicholas

(1330–7) was Archbishop Danilo II, the foremost Serbian scholar of his day. He added a large narthex linking the three larger churches. A bell-tower, now demolished, is seen in a wall painting showing Danilo in prayer before the Virgin, holding the model of his donation. Arsenije, Nikodim, Danilo and many other hierarchs of the see are buried in the churches. The vast fresco decor at Peć, rich in iconographic themes and spanning four centuries, shows a variety of artistic skills, often outstanding. Extinct after the fall of Serbia to the OTTOMANS, the patriarchate of Peć was re-established in 1557, abolished in 1766 and established again, conjoined with the patriarchate of Belgrade, in 1920. Throughout its history the monastery remained a centre of learning and writing. Caves in the surrounding hills sheltered recluses, some distinguished as authors and scribes. Ruined oratories dot the landscape. Although plundered several times, the patriarchal treasury still possesses important manuscripts, icons and other artworks. The monastery, at present run by nuns, serves as a parish church for the Serbian Orthodox of the town of Peć.

Djurić, V. J., Ćirković, S. and Korać, V. (1990), *Pećka Patrijaršija*. Belgrade: Jugoslo-venska Revija.
Gavrilović, Z. (1989), 'Between Latins and Greeks: Some Artistic Trends in Medieval Serbia: 13th–14th centuries', *Nottingham Medieval Studies* 33.
Petković, S. (1982), *The Patriarchate of Peć*. Belgrade: The Serbian Patriarchate.

ZG

Pelagonia martyrs   (d. 303)   Medieval legend makes the Syrian bishop Erasmos the evangelist of Pelagonia in MACEDONIA, recording him as going first to Lychnidos (or OHRID), seeking refuge in Campania, Italy, when 20,000 of his followers were martyred, and finally returning to Chermelia in Pelagonia, where he died a hermit. Known as Elmo or Telmo, he was venerated in the West as the martyred bishop of Formiae in Campania, one of the Fourteen Helpers. When Formiae was sacked by Arabs in 842 his relics were moved to Gaeta. The saint's shrine and cave near Ohrid, like neighbouring St Naum, brought Greek, Slav and Albanian pilgrims together up to the Balkan Wars. Erasmos and the 20,000 are commemorated on 4 May and 2 June.

Nicolas Velimirovic (1986), *Prologue from Ochrid*, vol. 2. Birmingham: Lazarica Press.

DB

Pelagonitissa   An iconographic type of the ELEOUSA named after Pelagonia in the Republic of MACEDONIA. The Pelagonitissa was the palladium of the town of OHRID. It shows the Virgin holding on to the Christ-child as if he is playfully struggling to get out of her arms. One of his hands clutches her cheek. It is an intimate and strikingly modern image.

KP

pentarchy   The theory, supported by Byzantine law, that the supreme government of the church is vested in the five patriarchs of ROME, CONSTANTINOPLE, ALEXAN-DRIA, ANTIOCH and JERUSALEM.

DM

Pentecost icon   Ancient images of Pentecost, for example in the RABBŪLĀ gospels of the sixth century, show the THEOTOKOS standing amid the apostles. In the icon shown here, twelve apostles sit on a synthronon, the empty space in the middle representing Christ, the invisible head of the church (*see* THRONE). At the bottom of the picture is a cavernous dark space, as in icons of the NATIVITY OF CHRIST, the THEOPHANY, the ANASTASIS and the Crucifixion, as well as icons of ELIAS, George and the Dragon, and many hermits and ascetics. Sometimes this represents the realm of death into which Christ descends, as in the Anastasis, or his blood trickles, as in the

Crucifixion, bringing life. Sometimes it is the dragon-infested depths subjected to the Lord's power, or the residue of that spiritual darkness where ascetics do battle with the demonic powers.

In the Pentecost icon a personification of the Cosmos occupies the dark space; he is shown on the threshold of enlightenment. Cosmos wears royal regalia and holds a sheet bearing twelve scrolls representing the divisions of the world, to be the missionary territories of the apostles. Sometimes the prophet Joel appears here, since he foretold the coming of the Holy Spirit on all humankind (Joel 2: 28–9).

Twelve light-rays or tongues of fire descend on the disciples from heaven along with the three-pronged symbol of the TRINITY, representing the sending of the Holy Spirit and the beginning of the DEIFICATION of humanity. For the Jews the festival of Pentecost commemorated the giving of the law to Moses on Mount SINAI.

Ouspensky, L. and Lossky, V. (1982), *The Meaning of Icons*. Crestwood, NY: St Vladimir's Seminary Press.

KP

Pentekostarion   Byzantine rite liturgical book containing the texts proper to the services of the season of Pentecost, i.e. the period between Pascha and the feast of All Saints celebrated on the Sunday after Pentecost.

DM

perichoresis   Greek: encompassing, revolving, interpenetration, co-inherence, permeation, mutual indwelling (Latin: *circumincessio*). The term was used by Christian writers from an early period; its wide range of meanings can lead to its precise significance being unclear. Gregory of Nazianzen, MAXIMUS THE CONFESSOR and JOHN OF DAMASCUS and Byzantine theologians use *perichoresis* to designate and explicate the co-inherence of the divine and human natures of the incarnate Logos; sometimes it expresses the mutual indwelling of the three persons of the divine TRINITY.

See also COMMUNICATIO IDIOMATUM.

Thunberg, L. (1995), *Microcosm and Mediator: The Theological Anthropology of Maximus the Confessor*. Chicago: Open Court.

Wolfson, H. (1970), *The Philosophy of the Church Fathers*. Cambridge, Mass.: Harvard University Press.

KP

Peshitta   The standard Syriac bible came to be known as the *p'sīṭtā*, 'Simple', this being an abbreviation for 'Simple Version'. The title is first used in the ninth century and distinguishes this particular version from various others.

See also RABBŪLĀ; SYRIAC; BIBLE.

JH

Peter Mongos   Anti-Chalcedonian patriarch of ALEXANDRIA, consecrated on the death of TIMOTHY AILOUROS (477). A fugitive during the reign of the CHALCEDO-NIAN patriarch TIMOTHY SALOPHAKIALOS, on the latter's death in 482 he received official recognition from Emperor Zeno since he accepted the HENOTIKON; indeed, he probably influenced its composition. He survived in office until his death in 490, though his support for the Henotikon provoked schism with extreme MONOPHY-SITES, while his anti-Chalcedonian interpretation of the Henotikon provoked opposition from Chalcedonians.

DM

Peter the Fuller   Anti-Chalcedonian patriarch of ANTIOCH, consecrated *c.*469 as rival to the Chalcedonian patriarch Martyrios. Peter displaced him in 471, but was deposed the same year. Returned to office by the usurper Basiliskos, deposed again by Emperor Zeno but later reinstated, he died in office in 488. Peter's famous addition to the TRISAGION, 'crucified for us', rapidly became the watchword of the MONOPHY-SITES and remains in liturgical use among Oriental Orthodox.

DM

Peter the Iberian   (*c.*409–*c.*491)   Son of King Buzmir of Georgia, as a boy Murvan was a hostage in CONSTANTINOPLE. Becoming a monk, Peter, in Palestine, in 452–3 he was consecrated bishop of Maiuma in Gaza, but continued to live the monastic life. Firmly anti-Chalcedonian, he exercised great influence on SEVERUS OF ANTIOCH, who studied in his monastery. A moderate MONOPHYSITE, he accepted the HENOTIKON of Emperor Zeno. He established a Georgian monastery in JERUSALEM and other houses.

See also GEORGIA, CHRISTIAN THOUGHT IN.

DM

Petritsi, Ioane Tchimtchimeli   (1050–1125)   Georgian philosopher educated under Michael Psellos and John Italos at the Mangana academy, CONSTANTINOPLE and associated with the revival of PLATONISM, especially Neoplatonism. He translated into Georgian works of Aristotle, Nemesius of Emesa's *On the Nature of Man* and Proclus' *Elements of Theology*, to which he added a commentary. In 1083 he taught at the Petritsoni monastery at BACHKOVO in Bulgaria, whence his name. He returned to Georgia under David the Builder (1089–1125) to help establish the GELATI academy.

See also GEORGIA, CHRISTIAN THOUGHT IN.

KP

Phaneromene   Greek title of icons, usually of the THEOTOKOS, whose discovery results from visions or dreams and is usually reputedly accompanied by miracles. Phaneromene monastery on Salamis was founded by abbot LAURENTIOS OF MEGARA (d. 1707) to house one such icon; Tatarna monastery in the Agrapha region preserves another, as do Phaneromene monastery on Leukas and the famous TINOS shrine.

Phaneromene icons are a focus of popular piety. A cave near Larnaca in CYPRUS is an example, its church built over the site where a local man, Hatzivassilis, instructed in a dream to bathe his eyes there, was cured of an eye disease; he also found there an icon of the Virgin. Ex-votos are left on the metal grille of the underground chapel of the hagiasma.

Such icons have been the focus of religious and monastic revival; some are pan-Orthodox rallying points. Many are associated with a particular saint, e.g. the Evangelistria-Tiniotissa icon with Pelagia of Kechrovounis. Most are commemorated on the date they were revealed to the faithful.

See also SKOPELOS.

Paraskevopoulou, M. (1982), *Researches into the Traditions of the Popular Religious Feasts of Cyprus*. Nicosia: n.p.

DB

phelonion   Eastern equivalent of the Western chasuble and cope. The phelonion was originally the vestment of both priests and bishops, but in recent times the bishops have replaced it with the sakkos. On the Holy Mountain it is still the custom for bishops, when not celebrating solemnly, to do so vested in the phelonion and little omophorion. This is also usual when a bishop celebrates the Liturgy of St James. The phelonion is worn, together with EPITRACHELION, at the Divine Liturgy, at Great Vespers and parts of festal ORTHROS, as well as at the celebration of the MYSTERIES. The Russian phelon often has a row of buttons across the chest so that the front of the vestment can be raised or lowered.

See also RELIGIOUS DRESS.

E

Pherbutha   (d. 343)   Persian GREAT MARTYR. According to tradition Pherbutha and her widowed sister were Christians accused of poisoning the queen of Persia. With a faithful servant they were sawn asunder, the sick Persian queen passing between their limbs seeking healing in the manner specified by her soothsayers. Simeon Barsabba'e, bishop of Ctesiphon, martyred in 341 with a multitude of Christians, was Pherbutha's brother. His successors Shahdost and Barba'shmin were also martyred in 342 and 346 respectively. Pherbutha is commemorated on 4 April.

Nicolas Velimirovic (1986), *The Prologue from Ochrid*. Birmingham: Lazarica.

DB

Philokalia   A Greek title, meaning 'love of the fine', that came to be used for anthologies. (1) Anthology of ORIGEN's writings published by the CAPPADOCIANS Basil the Great and Gregory of Nazianzus in the fourth century. (2) Anthology of ascetical and mystical texts compiled by NIKODEMOS THE HAGIORITE (1749–1809) and Makarios of Corinth (1731–1805). A Slavonic version of the *Philokalia* by PAISSII

VELICHKOVSKII was published in 1793, but superseded by the enlarged Russian nineteenth-century version of THEOPHAN THE RECLUSE. An English translation of the Greek, edited by Bishop Kallistos Ware, the late G. E. H. Palmer and the late Philip Sherrard, reached the fourth of five volumes by 1995.

DM

Palmer, G. E. H. et al., eds (1979–95), *The Philokalia*. London: Faber.

Philoponos, John   Sixth-century Christian Neoplatonist philosopher and MONO-PHYSITE theologian. His work *On the Trinity*, published probably in 567, so emphasized the distinct reality of the three divine hypostases that it led to his being accused of Tritheism.

Sorabji, R. ed. (1987), *Philoponos and the Rejection of Aristotelian Science*. London: Duckworth.

DM

philosophical vocabulary   The philosophical schools of late antiquity, especially the Stoics, had articulated issues and questions to which Christian theology offered its own distinctive responses. The progressive development of technical philosophical vocabulary provided Christian theologians with an array of terms which could be used to express and to clarify issues arising, for example, in Christology and triadology.

The Stoics played an important role in this since their systematic approach to philosophy shaped a comprehensive curriculum of philosophical studies. Stoic ideas and values were respected in the Roman world not least because of the political stance of Stoic senators, several of whom died for their opposition to the corruption of the imperial rule. The importance of PLATONISM to Christian theology is well recognized. Platonic psychology provided the standard terminology used by the spiritual fathers. Stoic, Platonist and Aristotelian schools existed side by side, but with much mutual influence and cross-fertilization; Middle Platonism is in effect an amalgam of all three.

Stoicism had a strong doctrine of divine providence (*pronoia*). Stoics argued that *pneuma* (understood as a very fine form of matter), is the presence in the cosmos (*kosmos*) of the divine Logos governing and guiding all things. This nexus of terms, *pneuma*, *Logos*, *kosmos*, *pronoia*, links in a significant way concepts important in the Greek BIBLE.

Stoic and peripatetic thinkers discussed the nature of mixture. Alexander of Aphrodisias, a commentator on Aristotle who flourished *c.*AD 200, wrote a monograph *De Mixtione* analysing the terminology underlying the debate between the two schools. This philosophical debate proved crucial for the development of Christian attempts to express clearly and precisely the relation between the human and divine natures of Christ. Philosophical definitions and examples of mixture, especially those canvassed by Stoics, lay behind the Christological models advanced in the disputes among NESTORIAN, CHALCEDONIAN and MONOPHYSITE theologians. Alexander of Aphrodisias presents the following models constructed by the third-century BC Stoic scholarch Chrysippus: (1) *parathesis*, mere juxtaposition where each thing in the mixture retains its own substance (*ousia*) and qualities; (2) *synchysis*, fusion or merging (often translated as 'confusion'), where the original substances and their qualities cease to exist, their fusion giving rise to a new substance with its own qualities (the Council of Chalcedon explicitly denied that Christ's humanity and divinity were fused or merged in this way); (3) *krasis*, blending where different substances permeate or pervade each other, becoming totally co-extensive, but each substance retains its nature (*physis*) and qualities so that in principle they could be separated out again (*krasis* provided the Stoic model of the pervasion of *pneuma* through the *kosmos*). The clear distinctions which Alexander derives from Chrysippus co-existed with a looser set of distinctions made by Aristotle, important because Aristotle sometime uses the term *krasis* to designate a mixture which, like a Stoic fusion, has attributes different from those evident in its elements, but differs from Stoic fusion since the original substances could in principle be separated out. Aristotle also argues that a tiny amount of one substance added to a large amount of another can result in the increase of the latter, not a mixture of the two; for example, a drop of wine added to a huge quantity of water does not produce a mixture or a blend, and the wine does not pervade the water; the wine's attributes disappear, producing a slightly increased quantity of water.

Aristotle's analysis of the wine-drop example was rejected by the Stoics, who argued that, however paradoxically, the wine does pervade the water. In his *Eranistes* THEODORET OF CYRRHUS presents an extreme monophysite as applying Aristotle's analysis to Christology arguing that Christ's humanity is absorbed into his divinity just as a drop of honey would disappear if it were dissolved in the sea.

Greek philosophers had established a set of concepts and definitions useful to Christian theologians, but different philosophers' use of the same term with subtly different senses could create ambiguity and confusion. Examples of this are the ambiguity of *hypostasis*, which led Western theologians initially to reject the assertion of three hypostases in the Godhead, and the differential use of *physis*, sometimes to designate an individuated nature (where it is virtually synonymous with person), a usage common among monophysites, misunderstood by DYOPHYSITE opponents who understood *physis* to designate nature as essence or quiddity.

Zizioulas, J. D. (1985), *Being as Communion*. Crestwood, NY: St Vladimir's Seminary Press.
Wolfson, H. A. (1976), *The Philosophy of the Church Fathers: Faith, Trinity, Incarnation*, 3rd edn. Cambridge. Mass. and London: Harvard University Press.
Sambursky, S. (1959), *The Physics of the Stoics*. London: Routledge & Kegan Paul.

DM/KP

Philothei (d. 1589) Philothei, an educated and wealthy noblewoman of the Athenian Venizelos family, was forced into marriage (1536), but when widowed founded a convent, using her inheritance and influence to organize hospitals, schools and other charitable associations around Attica. She was executed by the local Turks while leading a vigil, but her convent remained a centre of welfare work. Philothei, a patron of Athens and the most popular NEW MARTYR, is commemorated on 19 February.

Pherousis, D. (1982), *Philothei Benizelou*. Athens: Astir.

DB

Philoumenos (d. 1979) A Cypriot monk of Stavrovouni until, after making a PILGRIMAGE to the shrines of the Holy Land, he remained in Israel and became guardian of the Orthodox church at Jacob's Well. Philoumenos was murdered by Zionist extremists determined to remove Christians entirely from this sacred Jewish site. He is commemorated on 16 or 29 November.

Chrysostom of Kition (1988), *Asmatike Akolouthia Ton En Kypro Hagion*. Stavrovouni Monastery.

FB

Philoxenus of Mabbug   Philoxenus or Aksnāyā (*c.*440–523), born in Persia, studied in the Persian School of EDESSA under IBAS, but reacted against its prevailing 'Nestorianism' and became a fervent MONOPHYSITE. In the context of the Christological disputes in Syria, Philoxenus successively was expelled by the CHALCEDONIAN patriarch of ANTIOCH, then appointed bishop of Mabbug (modern Membij, ancient Hierapolis) in 485 by PETER THE FULLER and finally deprived of his see as a result of Justinian's imposition of Chalcedonian doctrine in 519–21. Philoxenus went to Thrace, then Paphlagonia, where he died. As bishop of Mabbug, Philoxenus campaigned for the closure of the 'NESTORIAN' School of Edessa (closed 489) and the removal of Flavian, patriarch of Antioch (498–512), who was replaced by the monophysite SEVERUS.

Philoxenus' extensive writings, many, despite his political activities, completely uncontroversial, include a *Commentary on the Prologue of John* and dogmatic tractates on the Trinity and Incarnation. A series of *Discourses* and various letters giving spiritual advice to new monks display a deep, biblical spirituality with baptism in a pivotal role. His concern with the BIBLE text is also reflected in his sponsoring *c.*508 of a new Syriac translation of the New Testament, the Philoxenian Version.

Brock, S. (1987), *The Syriac Fathers on Prayer and the Spiritual Life*. Kalamazoo: Cistercian Publications.
de Halleux, A. (1977), *Philoxène de Mabbog. Commentaire du prologue johannique (MS Br. Mus. Add. 14,534)*. CSCO 380–1, Scr. Syr. 165–6. Louvain: Secrétariat du CSCO.
Vaschalde, A. (1907), *Philoxeni Mabbugensis Tractatus Tres de Trinitate et Incarnatione*. CSCO 9, Scriptores Syri 9 (Paris: Typographeum Reipublicae); CSCO 10, Scriptores Syri 10 (Rome: de Luigi).
Budge, E. A. W. (1894), *The Discourses of Philoxenus*. London: Asher.

JH

Photeine   Traditional name of the Samaritan woman who met Christ by Jacob's Well. Called Svetlana by the Slavs, she is one of the best-known saints of the Eastern churches. According to later legends she preached in North Africa and Italy and is believed to have died as a martyr in ROME with her five sisters and others in the reign of Nero. Photeine is commemorated on the fifth Sunday after Pentecost and on 26 February (Greeks) or 20 March (Slavs).

DB

Photios the Great   Photios I, patriarch of Constantinople 858–67 and 877–86. His uncle Patriarch Tarasios (784–806), a career administrator in the period of imperial ICONOCLASM, was made PATRIARCH as a capable ally by the ICONOPHILE Empress Irene (780–90 and 792–802), and convened the Second Council of Nicea that condemned iconoclasm as a heresy. Like Tarasios, Photios pursued a secular career and was a layman when elected patriarch. He replaced Ignatios the New (847–58 and 867–77), son of Michael I Rhangabe (811–13), who was castrated and made a monk on his father's deposition. Ignatios, an austere monk, lost favour and was brought to resign. With the support of Michael III (842–67), Photios was elected to replace him. Ignatios' supporters sought the aid of Pope Nicolas I (858–67), a powerful character, convinced he was God's vicegerent on earth. Nicolas hesitated, then declined to accept Photios as legitimate patriarch and sent legates to investigate the matter, but rejected their report in Photios' favour, and in 863 declared Photios deposed and excommunicated. The emperor's protest at this won him a stern papal rebuke and a disquisition on the authority of the Roman see. Photios, also provoked by anti-Byzantine papal action in BULGARIA, convened a synod in CONSTANTINOPLE which in 867 excommunicated Nicholas, declaring him deposed.

Basil I (867–86), co-emperor (since 866) and murderer of Michael III, deposed Photios and reinstated Ignatios. This failed to improve relations with ROME; Ignatios, as resolute as Photios in defence of Constantinople's rights, acted decisively to resolve the conflict between Latin and Greek missions in BULGARIA in favour of the Greeks. Condemned and banished by a council in 869–70, Photios was restored on Ignatios' death and at a council in 879–80 was reconciled with Rome, but when Leo VI became sole emperor in 886, Photios lost favour, was deposed and exiled.

Photios exercised a potent influence on EASTERN ORTHODOX theology, especially through his *Mystagogy of the Holy Spirit*, which both denounces the FILIOQUE as an illegitimate addition to the Creed and teaches that the Holy Spirit proceeds from the Father alone, a doctrine which remains to this day a common doctrinal view among Eastern Orthodox. The *Amphilochia*, a collection of short, mainly theological, essays, shows his interest in philosophy and classical literature. His *Lexicon* is a sign of his interest in language and in poetry. His *Bibliotheke*, a massive collection of critical essays, offers insight into the range of literature available to an educated man in his day, and is a major source of information about many of the books and authors he discusses. His letters and homilies are of considerable historical interest.

Tarasios, Ignatios and Photios are all venerated as saints by Eastern Orthodox; Photios himself was active in promoting Ignatios' cause. In the West, Photios acquired an evil reputation as a schismatic and an unprincipled schemer. The seminal researches of F. Dvornik offered a far more positive and appealing portrait of this great and learned patriarch, established that the traditional belief in a second, 'Photian' schism was based on unreliable evidence, and uncovered the accurate record of the council of 879–80 which reinstated Photios, originally regarded even in the West as the eighth ECUMENICAL COUNCIL, until erroneously, as Dvornik demonstrated, displaced by the anti-Photian council of 869–70, a council with a marked papalist tone.

Hussey, J. M. (1986), *The Orthodox Church in the Byzantine Empire*. Oxford: Oxford University Press.
Lemerle, P. (1986), *Byzantine Humanism: The First Phase*. Canberra.
Wilson, N. G. (1983), *Scholars of Byzantium*. London: Duckworth.
Dvornik, F. (1948), *The Photian Schism: History and Legend*. Cambridge: Cambridge University Press.

DM

pilgrimage   Pilgrimage is a practice common to many religions. Pilgrims travel alone or in groups to a sacred place as a religious duty, a devotional exercise, a profession of faith, a penitential exercise, an act of expiation, a journey of self-discovery, a quest for healing or advice, or an act of spiritual renewal. Pilgrimage is an abiding metaphor of the spiritual life. The place visited may be a holy river (Jordan), mountain (Ararat, SINAI), city or town (JERUSALEM). It may be the birthplace, dwelling-place or tomb of a holy person (Bethlehem, OPTINA) or the site of a sacred event (Cana, Tabor), or may house sacred relics (the *lavra* of KIEV). The pilgrim may visit a sacred ICON (the Virgin at TINOS), a particular church or monastery (Oropos, PATMOS), or a living STARETS or elder for counsel and blessing.

Pilgrimages can have a fixed form all pilgrims are expected to follow or may be a spontaneous matter. A pilgrim site may have its own distinctive liturgical traditions. Accounts written by pilgrims can offer important evidence of this, as, for example, the *Itinerarium Egeriae*. Some pilgrimages involve massive numbers, some places of pilgrimage are visited by few. Many people make pilgrimage to shrines primarily associated with a religion different from their own, and a place of pilgrimage can be sacred to more than one religion (e.g. the Tombs of the PATRIARCHS at Hebron). In INDIA Hindu pilgrims visit the tomb of the apostle Thomas; in the Middle East and the Balkans, Muslim pilgrims visit certain Christian shrines.

Pilgrimage is not an exclusively religious phenomenon: tombs of national heroes, great artists, poets or musicians are also places of pilgrimage, the pilgrimage frequently taking on some of the characteristics of religious pilgrimage.

In EASTERN CHRISTIANITY there is a strong and abiding tradition of pilgrimage, despite reservations about the practice expressed, for example, by Gregory of Nyssa and Jerome. As Eastern Christian communities become established in the West (*see* DIASPORA) there is increasing interest in ancient Christian shrines belonging to the history of the undivided church, or having links with Eastern Christian history. In addition, pre-Christian sacred places have often been resacralized into Christian places of pilgrimage.

The pilgrimage to the Holy Land remains the centrally important form of pilgrimage in Eastern Christian life, and in Greek Orthodox communities the title HAJI is still often given to someone who has completed it.

Among Slavs especially pilgrimage can become a form of spiritual life, individuals or groups moving life-long from shrine to shrine. The WAY OF THE PILGRIM and its less well-known sequel *The Pilgrim Continues His Way* reflect something of this way of life and its spirituality.

See also CHONAI; PANORMITIS.

Hunt, E. D. (1984), *Holy Land Pilgrimage in the Later Roman Empire, AD 312–460*. Oxford: Clarendon Press.
Wilkinson, J. (1977), *Jerusalem Pilgrims before the Crusades*. Warminster: Aris and Phillips.

DM

Plato Jovanović   (1874–1941)   Plato, born in Belgrade to a refugee family from Herzegovina, studied in Belgrade and, from 1896, MOSCOW, where he served as a priest in the Serbian church. On graduation in 1901 Plato returned to Serbia and became abbot of Rainovac monastery. He returned to Belgrade in 1902 before leading a group of monks to DEČANI monastery in KOSOVO, hitherto occupied by Russians from ATHOS. He also taught at various Serbian colleges. During the Balkan Wars he served in ALBANIA and MACEDONIA as military chaplain. In the First World War he was arrested by the Austro-Hungarians and narrowly escaped execution by the Bulgarians. Though officially abbot of Rakovica, Plato administered the affairs of the SERBIAN ORTHODOX CHURCH when leading Serbian hierarchs were exiled. In 1919 he returned to Rakovica and founded a college and press. Plato supervised the church press in Sremski Karlovci from 1932, continuing this work when appointed abbot of Krusedol in 1934. He became bishop of Morava in 1936, of OHRID in 1938 and of Banja Luka in BOSNIA in 1939. Plato was killed by Croatian Ustase when Yugoslavia was occupied by the Axis powers. He is commemorated with the SERBIAN NEW MARTYRS.

Panagopoulos, A. (1996), *Neomartys Episkopos Platon.* Athens: n.p.

DB

Platonism   There can be few more regrettable past generalizations than that, perhaps still current in some quarters, according to which 'traditional' Western Christian thought has been predominantly Aristotelian since the recovery of the corpus of Aristotelian texts in the medieval West, and, by implication and sometimes statement, more 'this-worldly' and 'efficient' for this, while Eastern Christian thought has remained Platonist, and by implication more 'other-worldly' and 'mystical'.

Developing Christian thought was influenced by post-Platonic Greek philosophy from its beginnings in the second century. From the third century the influence was predominantly that of Later Platonism. From the time that the writings of Plotinus, the greatest of the Greek Platonists, became known, their influence was considerable. They were made generally available by his disciple and editor, Porphyry, in 301, and seem to have been fairly widely read by the last quarter of the fourth century. It is strongly probable that Gregory of Nyssa owes something to the thought of Plotinus.

From early in the fourth century the predominant influence in the Later Platonism of the East was that of Iamblichus of Apamaea, a philosopher who adopted and adapted the Platonism of Plotinus. Consequently the main acceptance and determined rejections of ideas from Platonism in this latest stage, which modern scholars call Neoplatonism, by Greek Christian theologians were directed to the Platonism of Iamblichus rather than that of Plotinus. The thought of Aristotle had always been studied and to some extent used by Later Platonists. Aristotle, a member of Plato's circle till Plato's death, was generally regarded as close to the Platonic tradition. There was a vigorous Greek Christian reaction in the sixth and seventh centuries against some aspects of the thought of Iamblichus as they were developed by Athenian Neoplatonists of the fifth century. In their writings much use was made of the study of the works of Aristotle in the form it had taken principally among the Neoplatonists of Alexandria, which passed from ALEXANDRIA to CONSTANTINOPLE in the seventh century.

Christian thought in the most vital stage in its early development, under the Christian Roman empire, which was the age of the fathers and councils, was affected by the thought of its time. This was the thought of a single cultural area, recognized as such, and not divided into East and West. It was primarily a Greek and Greek-speaking thought, at its liveliest in the East, where the Greek texts on which it was based were most read and studied, and which was always the intellectual and religious heart of the empire. With the qualifications already expressed, it was, during the period and in the area with which we are concerned, a Platonic monotheism. As with ancient Platonism in general, the works of Aristotle were always ready to hand and were studied and used as needed and desired. They were much earlier and better understood and used by Christians in the Greek-speaking East than after their to some extent indirect and partial recovery, in Latin translation, in the medieval West. So some historical mis-information lies behind the false generalization with which we started.

It will probably be helpful to the understanding of what is meant by the Platonic or Neoplatonic influence on Christian thought if we briefly consider what is really meant by the influence of a Greek philosophical group, especially a Platonic group. It is better to call the small groups which formed round leading philosophers and sometimes continued after their death 'groups' or 'circles' rather than 'schools' in the medieval or modern sense. When considering Platonists it is apparent that in the most notable Platonic or near-Platonic groups, beginning with Plato's own Academy and Aristotle's Lyceum, the situation we find at the death of the originator is not that of a master handing down dogmas and a system to respectful disciples, but a continuing discussion, or discussions, in which at least the inner circle and those closest to the originator continued to take part. This was probably true in the third century of the group around Ammonius Sakkas, and certainly true, as recent work has shown, of the closest intimates of the group around Plotinus. Philosophers had plenty of dogmas and were very dogmatic about them; indeed, the word 'dogma' is taken from philosophical Greek terminology. But a philosopher spoke, and perhaps wrote, his dogmas, into an always continuing discussion, and that was what made him a philosopher.

The discussion which those attracted by Plotinus have wished to join, from the time of his teaching at Rome to the present day, is that which was going on at his death, and which recent studies have made clearer. It discloses that God simply exceeds our understanding: the best names which Greek philosophy could find, Absolute Being, and Absolute Intellect, are inadequate: even the to some extent privileged names of One or Good do not really help us to understand the Giver of all reality and goodness. How, then, are we to understand that these names, which to some extent correspond to the good diversity of creation, and that diversity itself, spring from That in which no diversity can be discerned, the Giver of All? This too is mysterious, but how best to put it? What shall we say at the end of our understanding when our Creator goes beyond it? This APOPHATIC vision of God and creation is the abiding heart of the philosophy of Neoplatonism, as modern scholars have called the interpretation of Plato after Plotinus, and it is to this, at the deepest level, that all later Platonists, pagan, Christian, Jewish, or Muslim, with their various other commitments, are committed. It is primarily this, the living sense of the mystery of God and creation, which Western Christian Platonists have seen when they have looked at Eastern Christianity and called it 'Platonist'.

As has already been said, the predominant form of Neoplatonism in the East of the empire during the fourth century and after was that inaugurated by Iamblichus. He was in accord with Plotinus on the apophatic vision of God, the First upon whom all things depend for their existence: he and his followers even rejected the names of One or Good for that First, as giving a misleading impression of partial knowability. But he criticized Plotinus severely for what seemed to him vagueness and inaccuracy. He wished to present Platonic philosophy as a rigid intellectual system, highly stratified, with the original members linked by intermediaries in accordance with his own logical principles (basically Aristotelian). This is not in Plotinus, though the beginnings of it can be read back into him. The Greek Christian thinkers were resolutely opposed to this, from the time of their first close contact with Iamblichan Neoplatonism. This was the position of 'Dionysios', the author who decided to write the works of Paul's Athenian convert, DIONYSIOS THE AREOPAGITE, for him, and who studied with the Iamblichan Neoplatonists of Athens, probably in the fifth century. This was by no means only, or principally, because the system of Iamblichus made plenty of room for all the gods of paganism. For 'Dionysios' (often known as Pseudo-Dionysios) and his successors, down to and including GREGORY PALAMAS, God was not to be reached through an ascending hierarchy of logically determined degrees of divinity. God was wholly present and active and creative at every level of the universe. God and divine activities in creation are one. This has seemed to many Christian Platonists a legitimate development of the apophatic awareness of God, the Good, the origin of all and the goal of all desire, which Plotinus thought he had found in Plato, and a development closer to Plotinus himself and earlier than Iamblichus. So the Eastern Christian thinkers and those who study them closely are fully justified in insisting that they have always been most firmly opposed to an essential characteristic feature of the sort of Neoplatonism they knew best, that of Iamblichus and his successors. And other Christian Platonists are equally justified in seeing in the Eastern Christian thinkers an awareness of the mystery of God and creation which they rightly trace back to Plotinus. A recent Western scholar who has taken the trouble to find out what Gregory Palamas actually said, as distinct from what his Western opponents continue to think that he meant, describes his teaching on God and creation as 'a real philosophical development of Neoplatonism on internally necessary lines. It brings to full prominence the antinomy which was already implicit in the Neoplatonic theory of participation. This development was carried out by pseudo-Dionysios, and it is his doctrine that St Gregory reiterates and expounds' (Perl, 1990, p. 130).

Perl, E. D. (1990), 'St Gregory Palamas and the Metaphysics of Creation', *Dionysius* 14.
Corrigan, K. (1987), 'Amelius, Plotinus and Porphyry on Being, Intellect and the One: A Reappraisal', in *Aufsteig und Niedergang der Römischen Welt. Part II. Principate 36/2*. Berlin and New York.
Wallis, R. T. (1972), *Neoplatonism*. London: Duckworth.
Armstrong, A. H., ed. (1970), *The Cambridge History of Later Greek and Early Medieval Philosophy*. Cambridge: Cambridge University Press.

AHA

Platytera   An iconographic type of the Virgin, showing her with arms outstretched, the Christ-child in a medallion encompassed by her bodily form as in the BLACHER-NITISSA. The epithet, which means 'wider than the heavens', occurs in the hymn 'In you rejoices' (Greek: *Epi soi chairei*) in the Divine Liturgy of St Basil, the phrase referring to the incarnation of the Divine Logos in the womb of the THEOTOKOS, who thereby encompasses him the heavens cannot contain. The Platytera is often found in the apse of churches. An icon type In You All Creation Rejoices also exists, portraying all creation celebrating the Mother of God.

KP

Pokrov   The feast of the Holy Protection (Greek: Hagia Skepe; Slavonic: Pokrov) was introduced into RUSSIA by Andrei Bogoliubskii of Vladimir (1157–74). The feast on 1 October commemorates a vision in which the HOLY FOOL Andrew and his disciple

Epiphanios saw the THEOTOKOS in the church at Blachernai, CONSTANTINOPLE, stretching out her veil (*maphorion*) over the congregation. In the top zone of the narrative Pokrov icon the Virgin's veil is held aloft by two ANGELS, usually MICHAEL AND GABRIEL, against a background of cupolas representing the church at Blachernai. In the middle zone the Virgin in prayer (*orans*) stands on a cloud, flanked by apostles and prophets. Below, standing in an AMBO, is ROMANOS THE MELODIST, flanked by ecclesiastical and imperial dignitaries. ANDREW THE SCYTHIAN and Epiphanios watch from the lower zone. Romanos, sometimes credited with the AKATHISTOS hymn, is also celebrated on 1 October. In Greek use the Protecting Veil is now observed on 28 October to coincide with the national holiday celebrating the Greek monosyllabic rejection of Mussolini's ultimatum demanding free passage for his armies.

Rydén, L. (1976), 'The Vision of the Virgin at Blachernae and the Feast of the Pokrov', *Analecta Bollandiana* 94, pp. 63–82.

KP

Polish Orthodox church   After the First World War the revived Polish state had around 4–5 million Orthodox citizens. The Polish Orthodox church needed to establish a national profile without alienating the various ethnic groups which made up the majority of its membership. Russians opposed severing links with the Moscow patriarchate; Belarusians and Ukrainians were apprehensive at perceived moves towards 'Polonization' in church life. The autocephaly of the Polish Orthodox church was proclaimed in 1922. A Russian monk, Smaragd, assassinated Metropolitan Jerzy Jaroszewski in 1923: none the less the church established links with the Ecumenical Patriarchate, which in 1924 confirmed the autocephaly of the Polish Orthodox church, recognizing its new metropolitan, Dionizy Waledynski. To a degree, the Polish authorities supported the creation of a national Orthodox church; hierarchs opposed to its autocephaly were either confined to monasteries or expelled from the country. Only in 1938, however, was the position of the church formally legalized in Poland. Even so, the Orthodox church was officially viewed as linked to secessionist minorities and to Russia. Campaigns were mounted against Orthodoxy and pressure was exerted,

387

particularly on believers in Volhynia and Chelm regions, to abandon Orthodox Christianity. In the 1930s Catholics laid claim to numerous churches, chapels and even monasteries held by the Orthodox; from 1938 over 200 churches in the Lublin region alone passed into Catholic control and 120 Orthodox shrines were destroyed.

Only 350,000 Orthodox Christians remained within the borders of post-Second World War Poland. The church remained strongest in the Bialystok region, bordering on Belarus. In 1948 Metropolitan Dionizy was arrested by the communists and deposed. The Polish Orthodox church was compelled to seek a new grant of autocephaly from the Moscow patriarchate, which in turn confirmed the position of Timoteusz Szretter, the third metropolitan.

Ramet, P. (1988), *Eastern Christianity and Politics in the Twentieth Century*. Duke, NC: Duke University Press.

DB

Polyeleos (1) Septuagint Psalms 134 and 135 sung at the third KATHISMA of the psalter on major feasts; so named from the many (*poly*) repetitions of the word 'mercy' (*eleos*) in Psalm 135. They are followed by selected psalm verses for the feast, in Russian use usually to reduced to one or two, accompanied by a MEGALYNARION. Greek use prescribes Psalm 44 farced with refrains for feasts of the Mother of God. On the Sundays preceding Lent the Polyeleos includes Psalm 136, 'By the rivers of Babylon'.

(2) The chandelier directly beneath the central dome; it symbolizes Christ Most Merciful. When furnished with oil lamps it also uses 'much oil' (Greek: *poly elaion*). On ATHOS the lit Polyeleos is swung, to spectacular effect, at 'Lord, I have cried' and during the Polyeleos at great Vigils. It is also lit at the Great Entrance on major feasts, and at funerals. Around the Polyeleos there often hangs a great metal circle, decorated with icons, normally including the twelve apostles, and surmounted by candles. This is known as a *choros*. The movement of the lights can be seen as representing the turning of the heavens as the whole creation offers glory to God, or the *choros* as the walls of the heavenly Jerusalem with its twelve gates, and the Polyeleos Christ the all-merciful reigning in its midst.

E

Pomaks A people, mainly Muslim and speaking a language related to Bulgarian, found throughout THRACE, though the mountainous Rhodope area is their homeland (Pomakia). The Pomaks, possibly descended from the ancient Bessi, converted to Islam in the OTTOMAN period (seventeenth century). Other Slav Muslims include the Torbeshis or Poturs of MACEDONIA and the Bosniaks (*see* BOSNIA-HERZEGOVINA). Individual Pomaks and entire communities, however, have returned to EASTERN ORTHODOX Christianity, many responding to Greek and Bulgarian missions active in Thrace since 1912, a few, like Boris the Pomak (1913), martyred for embracing Christianity.

DB

Pontus Greek: Pontos. Traditionally Pontus extended from the Halys river (Kızıl Irmak) in the west to Colchis (LAZICA) in the east and inland to Sebasteia (Sivas).

Sinope, founded by Greeks from Miletos, served as a base for founding further colonies, including Trapezous (Trebizond or Trabzon) in 756 BC. After the campaigns of Alexander the Great (d. 323 BC) the Persian satraps of Pontus founded an independent kingdom that, under the Mithridatic dynasty, expanded to include regions across ASIA MINOR and north of the Black Sea. This kingdom was conquered by the Romans and divided into two distinct regions, Pontus Galaticus in the west and Pontus Polemoniacus in the east. The eastern kingdom retained its independence to 63 BC.

Christianity arrived early, and Pontus was largely Christian by the fourth century. Theodoropolis–Euchaneia in the west was named for the GREAT MARTYRS Theodore Stratelates and Theodore Teron, and Diospontus province was renamed Helenopontus for Helen, mother of CONSTANTINE THE GREAT. In the Byzantine era important monastic centres developed (see HOLY MOUNTAINS) including monasteries in Chaldia, like Soumela and Vazelon which survived into the twentieth century. Pontus was open to incursions of the Caucasian peoples, like the Tzanoi (see ADZHARIA), and ravaged by the Persian and Arab invasions from the seventh century.

After the battle of Mantzikert in 1071 the Gabras family established a virtually independent despotate around Chaldia and Gemora in eastern Pontus. Despot Theodore of Atran was defeated by the Seljuks in 1028 and martyred at Theodosiopolis (Erzerum) for refusing to embrace Islam (see NEW MARTYRS). He is commemorated on 2 October. Pontus was reunited to the Byzantine empire in 1140. After the crusaders' sack of CONSTANTINOPLE in 1204 Alexios and David Komnenos re-established an independent state of Pontus, the empire of Trebizond or ROMANIA. This state generally enjoyed Georgian support and held out against Turks, FRANKS and Genoese until 1461 when Trebizond fell to the OTTOMAN Turks.

Pontus retained a significant Greek minority, particularly along the coasts and in the east. Numbers of Greeks and Armenians became Crypto-Christians (see STAVRIOTES), especially in the areas of Kromni and Thoania, in Argyropolis (Gümüşhane). In the late nineteenth century communities felt able to revert openly to Christianity. Many Pontic Greeks migrated to the Russian empire, but here, as in their homeland, they cultivated their specific culture and form of the Greek language. Trebizond remained the cultural capital, and the Soumela–Vazelon– Peristerota monastic region the spiritual heartland of all Pontic Greek people. The Orthodox church was organized around the sees of Amaseia–Amisous, Chaldia–Kerasous, Neokaisareia–Kotyora, Nikopolis–Kolonia, Rodopolis–Karyes and Trebizond. The Trapezuntine Phrontisterion, founded in 1682, served as the regional academy.

In 1916 Russian armies pushed the Ottomans out of eastern Pontus, and were welcomed into Trebizond by metropolitan Chrysanthos. In June–July 1919 a congress of Pontic Greeks in ADZHARIA declared the independence of Pontus and elected Vasilios Ioannidis president. Kemal Atatürk, in Samsun (Amisous) by May of 1919 to assume leadership of the Turkish nationalist movement, organized Turkish opposition to an independent Pontus. In September 1921 the Kemalists tried the leaders of the independence movement in Amasya (Amaseia), the ancient capital of Pontus. Some were executed; others, like Euthymios Agritellis, bishop of Zela, died in prison. Persecution of Pontic Greeks was worst around Paura (Bafra) and in western regions where Topal Osman's irregulars attacked Christian communities indiscriminately. It is claimed that 350,000 Pontic Greeks were killed in this period. In the eastern regions many communities fled to Georgia, Armenia or Russia. Over 500,000 refugees left for Greece through the port of Batum in Adzharia. In the population exchanges of 1923 the remaining Christians of Pontus and Paphlagonia were expelled from Turkey.

Mainly resettled in Greece, the Pontic Greeks remain a distinct community. Cultural and other organizations have maintained links among the Pontic Greek DIA-SPORA worldwide. The refounded Soumela monastery on Mount Vermion in MACEDONIA has served as the major spiritual centre. In Greece alone there are perhaps 1.5 million people of Pontic Greek descent, a further 1 million in the republics of the former Soviet Union and more in AUSTRALIA and elsewhere.

The Lives of the Monastery Builders of Soumela (1991), Buena Vista, Cal.: Holy Apostles.
Ephraimidis, D. N. (1986), *Pontos*. Athens: Pelasgos.
Karzis, T. (1985), *Chamenes Patrides*. Athens: n.p.

DB

prokeimenon A refrain from a psalm, sung together with one or more verses from the psalm, that normally precedes the readings at Vespers, Matins and the Divine Liturgy. It is the equivalent of the Western Gradual. Originally the whole psalm was sung. There is a prokeimenon at daily Vespers, even when there are no readings. Prokeimena for weekdays in Great Lent constitute a *lectio continua* of the Psalter.

E

Prote Anastasis 'First Resurrection', traditional Greek title of the ancient Paschal service of the Byzantine rite now celebrated on Great Sabbath, having been superseded as the main service of the Paschal Office by Matins of the Resurrection, based on the sacred poetry of JOHN OF DAMASCUS, and the Divine Liturgy. The First Resurrection service is a Vesper liturgy, the hymns of which focus on Christ's triumph over Hades and his liberation of the righteous dead, and on the Sabbath of the Old Law as prefiguring Great Sabbath.

A series of fifteen Old Testament readings precedes the apostle and gospel: Genesis 1: 1–13; Isaias 60: 1–16; Exodus 12: 1–11; Jonah; Jesus of Nave 5: 10–15; Exodus 13: 20–2, 14: 1–31, 15: 1–19; Sophonias 3: 8–15; 3 Kingdoms 17: 8–24; Isaias 61:10–11, 62: 1–5; Genesis 22: 1–18; Isaias 61: 1–10; 4 Kingdoms 4: 8–37; Isaias 63: 11–19, 64: 1–5; Jeremias 31: 31–4; Daniel 3 and the Hymn of the Three Children. The apostle (Romans 6: 3–11) is followed by the singing of 'Arise O God and judge the earth, for you shall have inheritance in all the nations' together with its verses. While this is being sung, in many churches clergy put off the sombre vestments they have used so far and vest in Paschal gold or white. In Greek use the priest scatters laurel leaves about the altar and the church, and many congregations make a huge noise by banging the stalls to celebrate the collapse of the Brazen Gates of Hades before the triumphant Christ. Uniquely, there is no ALLELOUIA verse before the resurrection gospel from Matthew 28. The service then follows the order of the Liturgy of St Basil.

At the end of the liturgy bread and wine are blessed but not oil, since this is the only Saturday of the year when oil is forbidden. Dried fruit is often distributed with the ANTIDORON, and eaten with wine in churches where the ancient custom prevails that all remain in church reading the Acts of the Apostles until it is time for the midnight office.

The First Resurrection service is a mystical proclamation of the triumph of Christ over the power of death. It celebrates not so much his physical resurrection from the tomb as the resurrection of humanity by his 'harrowing of Hell', as portrayed in the ANASTASIS icon.

DM/E

Prothesis Greek, 'setting forth' of the bread and wine for the Eucharist; and, by extension, the table or surface on which this occurs and the area of the sanctuary in which it is situated, normally north of the holy table. The rite is also called Proskimidi, 'offering', the word used in the Old Testament for the 'shewbread', called in Greek the 'loaves of presentation', *artoi tis protheseos*. These are given typological significance by ORIGEN, and Isidor of Pelusium writes: 'When we sanctify the bread of proposition on the cloth/winding sheet [ANTIMENSION; EILETON], we undoubtedly find the Body of Christ.' JOHN OF DAMASCUS uses the same expression: 'The bread of proposition, and wine and water, is by the invocation and coming of the Holy Spirit supernaturally changed into the body and blood of Christ.'

The Prothesis is in a sense the equivalent of the Western Offertory, but this does not imply that it originally took place after the dismissal of the catechumens and before the anaphora. Robert Taft has demonstrated that there never was an 'offertory procession' in the Western sense in Eastern rites; the faithful brought their offerings and handed them to the deacons on arrival at church, as they still do. From these the bread and wine for the eucharist, chosen before the service, are brought to the altar by the clergy at the beginning of the Liturgy of the Faithful. In some Eastern churches preparation and selection of the bread is an elaborate ceremony, though the earliest manuscript of the Byzantine liturgy simply has the rubric: 'Prayer which the priest says in the *skeuophylakion* when the bread is placed on the *diskos*.' That this takes place before the liturgy is clear from THEODORE THE STUDITE, who says: 'The complete *proskomidi* takes place at the beginning.' That originally the deacons brought the gifts into the church at the Great Entrance does not exclude the possibility of the priest's being present in the *skeuophylakion* to help select and bless the elements chosen. Inspection and selection of sacrificial victims is a priestly function in ancient Judaism and in other ancient religions.

Two things in particular influenced the development of the Byzantine Prothesis: the increasing use of symbolic understandings of the liturgy, especially those that saw the liturgy as a symbolic re-enactment of the life of Christ (*see* GERMANOS I); and the practice of cutting particles from the eucharistic loaf or loaves to commemorate the living and the dead, documented with certainty from the eleventh century, though recording the names of 'those who offer and those for whom they are offered' in the Prayer of the Prothesis is attested at least from the fifth century.

The number and form of the loaf or loaves have varied, and continue to do so. The present Byzantine rite knows three forms of prosphora: (1) five small loaves recalling the five loaves at the miracle of the multiplication of loaves and fishes recorded in the gospel, three stamped with the words IC. XC. NI–KA, 'Jesus Christ conquers' (*see* BREAD STAMPS), one with a triangular seal, for the THEOTOKOS, and one with nine triangles in three rows for the Nine Ranks (see below); (2) one large loaf stamped with the five seals in the form of a cross; (3) two small loaves, one stamped with the words

IC. XC. NI–KA, for the AMNOS, and one stamped with the other four seals. This last is usual on Mount Athos. The wine is traditionally red and, since many communicants are small children, sweet.

After vesting and washing their hands, priest and DEACON go to the Table of the Prothesis and the priest, raising the prosphora together with the lance (*see* SACRED UTENSILS), says the APOLYTIKION for Holy Friday. Signing the loaf three times 'In memory of our Lord and God and Saviour Jesus Christ', he cuts a cubic piece, the Lamb, from the centre of the loaf with the IC. XC. NI–KA seal, making four incisions, and removes it from the loaf, while reciting Isaias 53: 7–8. To facilitate the fraction he then cuts deeply into the crumb of the Lamb in the form of a CROSS and pierces it in the side, below the letters IC, while saying John 19: 34. Wine and water are poured into the chalice and the priest then begins to cut commemorative particles from the other seals or prosphoras. He first cuts one for the Mother of God, which he places to the north of the Lamb, saying Psalm 44: 10. He then cuts nine particles from the third seal and arranges them in Nine Ranks (Greek: *tagmata*) to the south of the Lamb, to represent the different categories of saint: (i) JOHN THE BAPTIST, (ii) prophets, (iii) apostles, (iv) holy bishops, (v) martyrs, (vi) holy ascetics, (vii) holy ANARGYROI, (viii) Joachim and Anna, the saint of the day and all the saints, (ix) the saint of the liturgy, either JOHN CHRYSOSTOM or Basil of Caesarea. The three rows of three as such symbolize the Nine Orders of the Bodiless Hosts, as the Large EUCHOLOGION makes clear. Modern Greek use, however, gives the first particle to the ANGELS and numbers the Forerunner among the prophets, though one current edition of the HIERATIKON gives the first particle to the angels and the Forerunner. Manuscripts and EILETARIA have many other arrangements, some commemorating the Holy Cross. The other two seals are used to cut commemorative particles for the living and the dead; these always include the bishop of the diocese, the bishop who ordained the celebrating priest, the founders of the church or monastery and the civil rulers, though many priests commemorate the latter only if Orthodox. Finally the priest commemorates himself.

It is customary to bring prosphoras and offer them with lists of names of the living and departed for commemoration. In Russian use small loaves for this purpose are normally sold at the back of the church. Greeks normally bring home baked prosphoras. (In modern practice at a pontifical liturgy the bishop cuts commemorative particles during the singing of the CHERUBIKON, then covers the gifts with the star and veils.) The arrangement of the particles on the circular *diskos* symbolizes the world; at its centre stands Christ, the Lamb of God, surrounded by the members of the church, his mystical body. The priest covers the *diskos* with the star (*asterikos*), and both chalice and *diskos* with three veils. He censes them and says the Prayer of Offering, given in the earliest manuscript for the Liturgy of St Basil, but today used also for that of John Chrysostom. At the end of the liturgy the commemorative particles are placed in the chalice, with the words: 'Wash away, Lord, by your holy Blood the sins of your servants here remembered, through the prayers of the Mother of God and of all your Saints'.

E

Prousiotissa Ancient icon of the HODEGETRIA preserved in Prousa monastery in the Agrapha region of central Greece. It is claimed the icon was brought from Prousa in

Bithynia in the ninth century by a monk fleeing the ICONOCLASTS. In the OTTOMAN period the monastery was a focus for the Greeks of a region that was only rarely penetrated by the Turks. The Prousiotissa is commemorated on 22 August.

DB

Psalterion   (1) The book of Psalms, divided in Byzantine use into *kathismata* (sessions), according to which the psalms are read in the divine office. Psalm 151 is not included in the *kathismata* for liturgical use. (2) The cantors' desk; usually there are two of these, one for the right choir, one for the left.

DM

psaltes   Psalmist or cantor (Syriac: *mzamrono*). Correctly the psaltes is ordained by CHEIROTHESIA, and is expected to know the TYPIKON and to be able to sing all the poeple's sung parts of the services, either singing on their behalf or leading the congregation or singing as part of a liturgical choir.

DM/E

Psychosabbaton   Greek, 'Soul Sabbath'. In the Byzantine rite all Saturdays have an element of commemoration of the dead, and on ATHOS and elsewhere Saturday liturgy is normally celebrated in the cemetery chapel. The Psychosabbata are Saturdays set aside in the Byzantine CALENDAR as days of prayer for all the faithful departed believers throughout the ages. Memorial services are held and KOLLYBA blessed in memory of the dead. Psychosabbata fall on the day before the Sunday of the Last Judgement (Apokreo Sunday) and the eve of Pentecost. The second, third and fourth Saturdays of Lent also commemorate the dead, though with less solemnity.

DM/E

·Q·

Qala'at Sima'ān   The martyrium-church of SYMEON STYLITES in northern Syria, built on the site of the sixty-four-foot pillar on which the saint lived for forty years. The vast church was constructed in 475–91 by Emperor Zeno to a cruciform plan with an octagonal court at the centre enclosing the pillar, the base of which still survives. It is not known whether the octagon supported a dome of some sort. Four basilicas radiate from the central court, but only the eastern one with its three apses was used for liturgical purposes, the others being used as assembly halls for pilgrims. The facade of the main entrance still stands, giving some idea of the magnificence of the original edifice. The construction of this huge building on such difficult terrain was a major engineering feat. There are also remains of an octagonal baptistry and extensive monastic buildings.

Mango, C. (1986), *Byzantine Architecture*. London: Faber.
Krautheimer, R. (1975), *Early Christian and Byzantine Architecture*. Harmondsworth: Penguin.

KP

qene   Ge'ez, *qenē*: the name given to certain religious poems in Ethiopian church services, which, unlike other liturgical chants, are not collected in an official church book; rather, they are brief, often improvised monorhythmic poems composed by individual ecclesiastical cantors or *dabtarā*. Topics include commentary on biblical passages, the praise of Jesus Christ and his saints, and moralizing and edifying themes which may draw on historical, secular events. Some thirteen distinct types of *qenē* poetry are generally recognized.
   See also ETHIOPIAN ORTHODOX CHURCH; MUSIC.

Leslau, W. (1987), *Comparative Dictionary of Ge'ez (Classical Ethiopic): Ge'ez–English/English–Ge'ez, with an Index of the Semitic Roots*, p. 437. Wiesbaden: Harrassowitz.
Godel, E. (1983–4), 'La metrique du *qenē* gueze', *Abbay* 12, pp. 117–203.

Velat, B. (1966), *Etudes sur le Me'eraf. Commun de l'office divin*. Patrologia Orientalis 33. Paris: Firmin-Didot.

MJB/SHG

Quinisext Council   In Greek, Penthekte: the council in Trullo convened under Emperor Justinian II in 691–2 to carry forward the work of the Second (533) and Third (681) Councils of Constantinople, which had passed no disciplinary canons. The Quinisext is held by Eastern Orthodox to have ecumenical status and authority. Its legislation was wide-ranging. Canon 2 ratifies the eighty-five 'apostolic canons' and the canons promulgated by the Councils of Nicea, Ancyra, Neocaesarea, Gangra, Antioch, Laodicaea, Constantinople I, Ephesus, Chalcedon and Sardica, as well as canons propounded by a number of the fathers (*see* ECUMENICAL COUNCILS).

Canon 6 forbids clergy other than a READER or PSALTES to marry, deposing any who do. Canon 9 forbids a cleric to own a tavern; canon 10 forbids a bishop, DEACON or priest to lend money at interest. Canon 11 deposes clergy and excommunicates laity who eat *matzot* sent by Jews, receive medicine from Jews or consort with Jews in the baths. Canon 13 repudiates what it asserts is a Roman practice of making candidates for the diaconate and priesthood undertake to abstain in future from sexual intercourse with their wives. Canon 17 forbids a cleric to move diocese without dismissory letters from his bishop. Canon 19 orders the senior priest of every church to preach daily and especially on Sundays, expounding sacred scripture. Canon 22 deposes those who have been ordained for money. Canon 23 deposes any priest who charges money for Holy Communion. Canon 32 deposes any priest who uses an unmixed chalice (i.e. containing wine only, not mixed with water) in the eucharist. Canon 36 gives the throne of CONSTANTINOPLE equal privileges with that of ROME. Canon 39 places the Hellespontine bishops under the exiled metropolitan of CYPRUS. Canon 50 deposes clergy and excommunicates layfolk who gamble. Canon 55 forbids fasting on Saturday or Sunday. Canon 65 prohibits new-moon bonfires. Canon 68 prohibits eating blood. Canon 69 excludes laity other than the emperor from the sanctuary. Canon 82 rejects symbolic depictions of Christ as a lamb, ordering his portrayal in his humanity (*see* ICONS). Canon 83 forbids giving communion to the dead. Canon 86 condemns pimps and procurers. Canon 90 forbids kneeling on Sunday. Canon 91 subjects women who provide or take abortificient drugs to the penalty laid down for murder. Canon 100 condemns titillating paintings.

The acts of the council were signed by all four Eastern patriarchs and the papal legates. Justinian II had the council's decrees sent to Rome for the pope's signature. Pope Sergius I (687–701) refused to sign, despite the council's explicit claim to ecumenical authority and his aprocrisarii having already signed the decrees, since the canons were at variance with Western tradition. Diplomacy failed to move the pope, and attempted force ended in farce, with the emperor's emissary, in fear of his life, hiding under the pope's bed.

In 695 Justinian II was deposed and mutilated. There seems no sign that Pope John VI (701–5) had dealings with Byzantium over the Quinisext. John VII (705–7), however, son of a Byzantine court official, saw Justinian, complete with golden nose, return to power in 706, conducting himself with great harshness and cruelty. Two metropolitans were sent to Rome to ask John to hold a synod to approve at least those canons acceptable to him. John VII, no doubt bewildered by this, returned the conciliar decrees without amendment or formal approval. John died in October 707. His successor, Sisinnius, survived his enthronement in January 708 by only twenty days. Constantine I (708–15) was invited by Justinian II to visit him, and in October 710 set out on a progress lasting a year, accorded, by Justinian's orders, imperial respect. Constantine met Justinian in Nikomedia, celebrated the liturgy and gave him communion. After bargaining by the pope's clerics, including deacon Gregory (who succeeded as Gregory II, 715–31, and combated imperial ICONOCLASM), an agreed version of the decrees was signed by Constantine I. Whatever this formal approval may have signified to Constantine or his bishops, the canons of the Quinisext remained a reference point for later Eastern polemic against Western customs.

Herrin, J. (1987), *The Formation of Christendom*. Oxford: Blackwell.

Richards, J. (1979), *The Popes and the Papacy in the Early Middle Ages*. London and Boston: Routledge & Kegan Paul.

Sieben, H. J. (1979), *Die Konzilsidee der alten Kirche*. Paderborn: Schöningh.

Laurent, V. (1965). 'L'Oeuvre canonique du Concile in Trullo (691–692), source primaire du droit de l'Église orientale.' *Revue des Études byzantinies.*

DM

qurbānā   SYRIAC, 'offering'; more technically, eucharist and specifically anaphora. Thus at the end of the West Syrian eucharist the priest proclaims: 'The order of the *qurbānā* is complete without defect.' The CHURCH OF THE EAST also uses the term *quddāšā*, 'sanctification': thus the anaphora of Addai and Mari is called the Sanctification of the Apostles.

JH

Quṣṭā ibn Lūqā   (d. 912/13)   Christian physician, scientist, writer and translator of Greek scientific works into Arabic and SYRIAC. His translations, like those of his contemporary HUNAYN IBN ISHĀQ, also fluent in Syriac, Arabic and Greek, were instrumental in the transmission of Greek scientific literature to Arabic, Islamic science. Unlike Ḥunayn and many of the Christian physicians in Baghdad, Quṣṭā was a MELKITE from Baalbek, Lebanon. He worked in Baghdad before moving later in life to Armenia, where he died.

Nasrallah, J. (1988), *Histoire du mouvement littéraire dans l'Eglise melchite du Ve au XXe siècle: contribution à l'étude de la littérature arabe chrétienne*, vol. 2, part 2, *750–Xe siècle*, pp. 67–70. Louvain: Peeters.

Hill, D. (1986), 'Kusṭā ibn Lukā al-Baʿlabakkī', *Encyclopaedia of Islam*, new edn, 5, pp. 529–30.

Samir, K. (1981), *Une correspondance islamo-chrétienne entre Ibn al-Munaǧǧim Ḥunayn ibn Ishāq et Quṣṭā ibn Lūqā*. Patrologia Orientalis 40/4, no.185. Turnhout: Brepols.

MJB/SHG

·R·

Rabbūlā Bishop of EDESSA (412–35), son of a pagan priest and a Christian mother from Chalcis (Qenneshrin), became a Christian under the influence of the bishop of Chalcis, Eusebius. He became a monk in the monastery of Abraham in Chalcis (possibly at Zebed). On the death of Diogenes, bishop of Edessa, Rabbūlā was elected to succeed him in 412.

After some hesitation, he became after the Council of Ephesus (431) a fierce supporter of CYRIL OF ALEXANDRIA and opponent of Nestorius, and publicly burned the works of Theodore of Mopsuestia and Diodorus of Tarsus. According to a surviving biography, he was an austere, scholarly man, devoted to the poor and sick as well as to the administration of his diocese and the regulation of the lives of the monks within his jurisdiction.

Tradition credits Rabbūlā with translating the New Testament from Greek into SYRIAC; certainly he instigated a reform in which the DIATESSARON, of which he is reported to have destroyed 400 copies, was replaced by an improved version of the separate gospels of the Old Syriac and ultimately by the text known today as the PESHITTA.

Drijvers, H. J. W. (1996), 'The Man of God of Edessa, Bishop Rabbula and the Urban Poor: Church and Society in the Fifth Century', *Journal of Early Christian Studies* 4, pp. 235–48.

JH

Rabbūlā Gospels Commonly used title of the oldest dated SYRIAC illuminated manuscript, produced, according to the colophon, in 586 in the monastery of St John of Zagba, in Syria or upper Mesopotamia, under the direction of a master calligrapher called Rabbūlā. There are 292 folios containing the gospels and twenty-six fine illustrations including canon tables gathered at the beginning of the codex. It is not certain whether illustrations and text come from the same date and the same hands. In 1497 the manuscript entered the Laurentian Library, Florence (Cod. Plut. I 56).

Leroy, J. (1964), *Les manuscrits syriaques à peintures*. Paris: Genthner.

JH

Raphael Tuki Coptic: *Rūfā'īl al-Ṭūkhī*, 1701–87. Born into an Orthodox Coptic family in Egypt, as a young adult Tuki converted to Roman Catholicism. He went to study at the Collegio Urbano di Propaganda Fide in ROME, obtaining a doctoral degree in theology in 1735. He served as professor of Coptic Language and Church Rite at the Collegio for more than thirty-five years. Pope Clement XIII consecrated him titular bishop of Arsinoe in 1761. Tuki's greatest contribution to Coptic scholarship lies in his many editions and studies of the Coptic liturgy and the Coptic BIBLE, which remain important scholarly tools today. He also wrote a Coptic–Arabic grammar, *Rudimenta linguae coptae sive aegyptiacae* (Rome, 1778) which introduced Roman Catholic scholars to the Coptic language.

al-Tūkhī, Rushdī (1991), 'Rūfā'īl al-Ṭūkhī', *Coptic Encyclopedia* 7, pp. 2067–8.
Graf, G. (1951), 'Ibrāhīm Rūfā'īl aṭ-Ṭūhī', *Geschichte der christlichen arabischen Literatur*, 5 vols (Studi e Testi, 118, 133, 146–7, 172), vol. 4, pp. 152–3. Città del Vaticano: Biblioteca Apostolica Vaticana, 1944–53.
Detlef, C. and Müller, G. (1975), 'Tuki (aṭ-Ṭūhī), Raphaël', in J. Assfalg and P. Krüger, *Kleines Wörterbuch des Christlichen Orients*, pp. 355–6. Wiesbaden: Harrassowitz.

MJB/SHG

reader EASTERN CHRISTIAN churches have preserved the ancient order of reader, the counterpart of the reader in the synagogue. The reader (Greek: *anagnostes*; Syriac: *qoroyo*) is ordained by CHEIROTHESIA and has the privilege of reading the Old Testament scriptural lessons and the epistle during services.

DM/E

religious dress Five main forms of EASTERN CHRISTIAN religious dress exist: (1) liturgical vestments; (2) choir dress; (3) monastic habits; (4) ceremonial attire of lay participants in the MYSTERIES, e.g. the bride and groom at a marriage, the candidate at baptism; (5) street dress of clergy.

Religious attire has several functions. It identifies the wearer's status. Vestments identify the liturgical role of the wearer and depersonalize that role, presenting the vested minister as priest, deacon, reader, rather than as a particular individual. Vestments differentiate the status and rank of liturgical ministers. In the Latin rites a priest can function liturgically as deacon or sub-deacon, but in Eastern traditions this does not occur: vestments therefore indicate more immediately the clerical status of the wearer than in Western practice.

A cleric or monastic attending service in choir not as a liturgical minister normally wears choir dress, not vestments. In Eastern tradition this means a deep-sleeved outer cassock or rason, together with the appropriate head-covering, a kalimaukion for married clergy, a kalimaukion and veil for monastic clergy. Correctly the black mandyas, a voluminous cloak, is part of the choir dress of monks, just as the coloured silk mandyas, with its 'rivers' (*potamoi*) and velvet tablets representing the two Testaments, is part of the choir dress of a bishop or abbot.

Religious garments frequently carry a symbolic meaning, though this varies in different communities, and may change. The black mandyas represents death to the world, the pastoral staff the role of ruler and shepherd. The symbolism of vestments is made explicit in the prayers recited as ministers vest. A Byzantine priest putting on his stole prays: 'Blessed is God, who pours out his grace on his priests like perfumed oil upon their heads, that flows down on the beard, on Aaron's beard, coming down to the hem of his garment.' This prayer symbolically links the Christian presbyter with the Aaronic priesthood and makes his stole a sign of that link.

Despite many variations in terminology, form, style and use, there is a fundamental unity in the vestments used in Eastern and Oriental traditions and significant links with those of the Latin rite. Eastern vestments almost certainly derive from secular garments in use in the Roman empire in the early Christian centuries, though explicit evidence for the use of vestments is lacking for at least the first four centuries, and precise evidence for the use of specific vestments for a longer period, making it difficult to determine exactly how individual vestments derived from specific secular garments. The problem is exacerbated by the varied form and use a garment could have. For example, the *tunica dalmatica* is in one period a tunic with deep sleeves, at another a tunic with narrow sleeves. There is also the odd custom of Greek artists portraying Roman clients in Greek dress. This warns us that iconography, though the best evidence we have, is not necessarily reliable evidence.

The sleeveless, knee-length tunic of the male Roman citizen was replaced in the imperial period for many purposes by various forms of sleeved, ankle-length tunic. From such tunics developed the sticharion (*stoicharion*), the ankle-length tunic which the Byzantine rite priest wears as an under-vestment when celebrating the Divine Liturgy, normally a simple tunic of coloured fine material. The deacon, sub-deacon, and in Slav use the reader wear a sticharion as outer vestment over an under-cassock. Altar servers usually wear a sticharion. The deacon's sticharion, especially in Greek use, is often made of stiffer, richly patterned material.

Oriental clergy use vestments equivalent to the sticharion, though among CHALDEANS and CHURCH OF THE EAST the *kottina* is often white, as is the sticharion used by Coptic priests, who often wear it with no outer vestment. The West Syrian *kuttino*, Armenian *patmucan* and Ethiopian *qamis* are all similar to the sticharion. A belt of vestment material is commonly used to fasten the sticharion and its equivalents.

The sleeves of the Byzantine priestly sticharion are fastened with a pair of richly ornamented cuffs, *epimanikia* (Armenian: *bazpan*; Syriac: *zendē*; Coptic: *kamasia*; Ethiopian: *akmam*). They may once have been a distinctive mark of clerical rank and ministerial function.

Roman dress in late antiquity knew a variety of cloaks and capes, some a piece of cloth fastened around the shoulders, others a circle or oval of cloth with an opening cut for the head. The typical outer priestly vestment of the Eastern tradition derives from an ornate version of one of these cloaks. The name of the Byzantine or Coptic phelonion or *phanolion*, like that of its Syrian counterpart, *paynā* or *payno*, suggests a derivation from the Roman *paenula*. The vestment may originally have been a full circle cloak of white fabric: it became a splendid vestment of rich material. In Eastern use it acquired a more conic shape, the front cut away to about waist level, giving freedom of arm movement; in Oriental use often divided down the front and clasped at the neck. Functionally, the *phelonion*, the *payno* and their Armenian and Ethiopian counterparts, the *šurdzar* and the *kāppā*, correspond both to the Latin chasuble (*casula*) and to the Latin cope (*pluviale*). In the Byzantine rite the priest wears the phelonion over the sticharion when celebrating the liturgy and officiating at other particularly solemn ceremonies; otherwise it is worn over the rason.

The polystavrion, a phelonion fashioned normally from white material and covered with an all-over pattern of crosses, was used by Byzantine bishops before the adoption of the sakkos, a tunic like a Latin dalmatic, with wide slit sleeves, usually fastened with tiny bells. The episcopal use of the sakkos seems to be a clear case of hierarchical adoption of an element of imperial costume, and became widespread after the Fall of Constantinople in 1453, perhaps to declare to the faithful that the Christian empire lived on in spirit in the Byzantine church.

Various kinds of stole are in use. The Byzantine deacon wears an orarion, a narrow strip of cloth draped over the left shoulder in Slav use; Greek deacons and Slav protodeacons or archdeacons wear a longer stole draped diagonally across the body and hanging down at the side. The sub-deacon wears the orarion wound crosswise across back and chest and beltwise around the waist: the deacon winds his stole about him in this way after the Lord's Prayer in the liturgy. A similar stole is used in Oriental communities.

The Byzantine priestly stole, the epitrakhelion, is buttoned or sewn into a double scarf hanging down to the ankles and usually fringed. Similar stoles are used by priests in Oriental traditions, but some have adopted narrower, unjoined Latin-style stoles.

The SYRIAC word *'ūrārā* or *'ūroro* names both the deacon's and the priest's stole. Virtually the same term, *urār*, is used in Armenian, both Syriac and Armenian clearly deriving from the original Latin *orarium* via the Greek.

In addition to the epitrakhelion, the Byzantine bishop wears an omophorion, a band of rich material fastened about the shoulders and falling down on the chest. The omophorion was originally, like the Latin pallium, made of wool. The Syrian *'uroro rabbo*, or great stole, and the Armenian *emip'oron* correspond to the Byzantine omophorion. A little omophorion, a much smaller stole hanging loose about the neck, is used at certain points in Byzantine worship. The omophorion is a symbol of the bishop's pastoral responsibility.

The origin of the stole is not clear. The omophorion may have been a secular mark of distinction before it attained ecclesiastical use. The diaconal and priestly stoles may originate in such scarves of honour or in the kerchief used by dignitaries to give signals, e.g. in the circus.

A more puzzling vestment is the epigonation, a flat lozenge of stiffened material worn suspended from the girdle by Byzantine ecclesiastical dignitaries. This, symbolically thought of as a sword, may have originated as a kerchief or a purse. A similar vestment, the *konk'er*, is used by Armenian bishops. In Slav use there exists an oblong cousin of the epigonation called the *nebedrennik*, with a similar use.

Shoulder capes of various kinds are used in Oriental traditions, among them the Ethiopian *lanqa*, ornamented with long strips of cloth or crosses. Armenian priests wear a broad, stiff collar, the *vakas*.

Varieties of liturgical head-covering are used. Alexandrian popes, especially ATHA-NASIUS and CYRIL OF ALEXANDRIA, are frequently depicted wearing a cap or hood. Ethiopian clergy make use of cross-embroidered crown-like caps and round caps of plain stuff or rich fabric. The Coptic church has a similar cylindrical cap of vestment material surmounted by a cross which is used by the highest ranks of deacon, and a pointed hood called *taylasan*, worn by priests nowadays, but at its introduction in the eleventh century reserved to bishops. According to local custom a second episcopal headdress, the *ballin*, developed from the omophorion, was worn around the head from at least the fourteenth century; however, it has gradually gone out of fashion. In Syrian use too a priestly head-covering was introduced called *šaddāyā*, in East Syrian *gulltā*. Monastic clergy of the Oriental Orthodox churches wear a close-fitting cap ornamented with twelve crosses, or in the case of the Syrian Catholics a single cross. Syrian bishops may wear over this the *masnapto*, a larger hood usually ornamented with the figure of a dove.

A Byzantine bishop wears a mitre in the form of a crown. This is a late medieval element in episcopal attire. Archbishop Symeon of Thessaloniki (1416/17–29) remarks that Eastern bishops, unlike Latins, do not wear a distinctive head-dress. In Oriental communities Byzantine-style mitres are often used, mitres of Latin style sometimes. Mitres may be given to senior clergy who are not bishops. Armenian priests of high rank wear a mitre of Byzantine style.

The colour of vestments varies; fixed sequences of liturgical colours are usually a sign of Latin influence. In Greek Byzantine use Pascha is normally celebrated in gold, red and gold, or red and white; Christmas in white, silver or gold; feasts of the Mother of God in red. In Slav use, THEOPHANY is frequently celebrated in blue, Pentecost in green and feasts of the THEOTOKOS in blue. Black is the traditional colour for the weekdays of Lent, but white is sometimes used, or mauve. Black is normal for funerals, but white, red and even gold are sometimes preferred.

Eastern monastic dress derives ultimately from the attire of the early Egyptian monks, but has developed into a wide variety of forms, symbolic meaning becoming attached to various elements in the monastic habit. The basic monastic dress is normally a simple tunic with a hood. Items (such as a belt) made of leather are a reminder the monk is dead to the world. The Coptic schema or *iskheem* is now a system of thin leather straps worn around the body to form a diagonal cross on chest and back. Originally it may have served to hold up the tunic during work, but already around 600 symbolized Christ's cross borne on the monk's shoulder. It probably represents a variation on the linen band Cassian calls the *analabos*. The Coptic schema was restored to use in 1996 by Pope Shenouda III. In Syrian use, the term schema now often refers to the cross-covered cap of Oriental monastic clergy, and a part of the Byzantine great habit.

In Byzantine tradition, apart from the aspirant monk or nun, who wears the rason of the monastery, a monk or nun may receive either the little schema or the great schema. The Greek and Slav little schema is a panel embroidered with the cross. The Greek great schema is a larger scapular embroidered with the cross and different inscriptions, worn under the rason; the Slav great schema includes a long scapular and veil embroidered with images of the instruments of the Passion and various texts. Monks wear a soft cap, the skouphos, or the stiff cylindrical kalymaukion (Slavonic *kamilávka*), over which a veil or hood (koukoullion) is worn. The Slav *klobùk* is the *kamilavka* and koukoulion permanently fastened together. Nuns wear similar dress to monks, but with a head covering which completely surrounds the face, and over which the veil, or in Slav tradition the *klobùk*, is worn.

Byzantine monastic choir dress includes the rason and mandyas. Greek monks normally wear the mandyas when actually performing a specific liturgical ministry. An abbot's mandyas and pastoral staff are like those of a bishop.

A square fringed cloth is worn by deacons over the left shoulder when carrying the incense box at great vigils. The monk who censes with the hand censer during the TRISAGION at the liturgy and the second section of the Polyeleos at Matins also wears one tucked in over his right shoulder as he holds the other end together with the handle of the censer.

DM

repentance Greek: METANOIA. Repentance is an essentially theological concept. It signifies the aversion from and repudiation of sin, and conversion to God. In Orthodox use, the whole Christian life, and especially the ascetic and monastic life, is frequently spoken of as repentance: the full fruition of repentance is assimilation to God, DEIFICATION.

DM

Resafa Byzantine Sergiopolis south of Raqqa in Syria; PILGRIMAGE centre of St Sergius, martyred in 303. The basilica church of St Sergius, probably built by Emperor Anastasius (491–518), was originally supported by wide arcades dividing the nave from the outer aisles, but as these arcades proved inadequate they had to be shored up with additional arcades inserted underneath. The massive city walls of Sergiopolis built by Justinian I (527–65) still stand, measuring about 400 metres by 550 metres. The main entrance to the city is through the north gate, one of the best-preserved Byzantine gateways, a triple-arched entrance of blind arcading supported by Corinthian columns with acanthus capitals. In the south-west corner of the complex are extensive brickwork cisterns preserving the city's water supply. An inscription found at Resafa is evidence that episcopal celibacy was by no means universal in the East in the sixth century.

Ball, W. (1994), *Syria: An Historical and Architectural Guide*. Essex: Scorpion Publishing.
Krautheimer, R. (1975), *Early Christian and Byzantine Architecture*. Harmondsworth: Penguin.

KP

rhipidion Liturgical fan, normally made in pairs of metal and mounted on poles. Rhipidia usually bear images of the seraphim and often have small bells attached. Rhipidia are now normally carried at the Great Entrance in the Divine Liturgy. Traditionally the DEACON waved or twirled the rhipidion above the holy table to keep insects away from the sacred elements. On ATHOS their use is rare, but they are twirled above the holy table at certain moments during the PROTE ANASTASIS service.

The *rhipidia*, representing iconographically ANGELS of the presence, both proclaim the presence of God and the heavenly court in the sacred action and identify the Divine Liturgy with the eternal heavenly liturgy.

See also CHERUBIKON; COMMUNION OF THE APOSTLES.

Richardson, H. (1993), 'Remarks on the Liturgical Fan, Flabellum or Rhipidion', in J. Higgitt and M. Spearman, eds, *The Age of Migrating Ideas*. Edinburgh: National Museums of Scotland Publishing.

KP/E

Rila Monastery in the Rhodope mountains of BULGARIA originally founded by John of Rila in the tenth century. The oldest part of the present monastery is the stone tower of 1335 rising to a height of 23 metres in the style of Athonite monastic towers; the TRANSFIGURATION chapel on its top floor has fragments of fourteenth-century frescoes including one of DIVINE WISDOM. The multi-storey monastic complex surrounding the *katholikon* and tower belongs to the period of National Revival (first half of the nineteenth century). The main church of the Virgin, built 1834–7, has a depiction of the Dormition of John of Rila among the murals painted by the brothers Zograph in 1840–8. The elaborate gilded ICONOSTASIS consists of thirty-six panels with individual panels by the Zograph brothers. The treasury holds many artefacts from the history of Bulgarian monasticism, including manuscripts, icons and ecclesiastical vestments, and there is a library of 20,000 volumes. The relics of John of Rila were brought to the monastery from Trnovo in 1469. The monastery had strong connections with the Russian monastery of St Panteleimon on ATHOS in the fifteenth century, and in the sixteenth century groups of monks from Rila travelled to MOSCOW seeking help under OTTOMAN rule. It became a centre of Bulgarian cultural revival in the nineteenth century, and was maintained as a national monument during the communist period.

Chavrukov, G. (1978), *Bulgarian Monasteries: Monuments of History, Culture and Art*. Sofia: Septemvri Publishing.

KP

Romania, in the Byzantine empire In the modern period the name 'Romania' has come to designate the state that arose from the United Danubian Principalities (1858) or Rumania. For centuries, however, 'Romania' referred to the provinces of the Byzantine empire, especially to Greece and ASIA MINOR. This was reflected in the new names given to towns by invading Turks, Franks and others. Nauplion became Napoli Di Romania; Sebasteia or Sivas and its region was entitled Bilad ar-Rum, 'the Roman land'; and Garin-Theodosiopolis on the Armenian frontier was renamed Arz ar Rum, Erzerum or 'Roman Land'. The Byzantines rejoiced in their East Roman inheritance and Romania continued to denote those lands around CONSTANTINOPLE and Propontis centuries after 1453. However, although the Greeks continued to refer to themselves as Romaioi, only the Pontic Greeks (*see* PONTUS) kept the more general term, calling their Black Sea homeland 'Romania' up to the present day. In the early 1990s the nearly 100,000 Pontic Greeks, from a minority 350,000 strong, who applied to migrate to Greece from the former Soviet Union have successfully applied for official funding for an organized settlement called 'Romania' in Western Thrace, in the easternmost corner of mainland Greece and as close as possible to Pontus. Other terms like ROUMELI, Eastern Rumelia and Rum (for Asia Minor) also derive from Romania.

Clogg, R. (1992), *A Concise History of Greece*. Cambridge: Cambridge University Press.

DB

Romanian Christianity   The first Christian communities on the territory of modern Romania were probably in Dobrudja, in Greek colonies established from the seventh century BC along the Black Sea coast of what became known as Scythia Minor, after the Iranian nomads who controlled much of the area from the sixth to the third century BC, and which was incorporated into the Roman province of Moesia in AD 46.

According to Eusebius, the apostle ANDREW was chosen to carry the gospel to Scythia, and the tradition of his activity in Dobrudja is attested in local folk songs and place names. Certainly close trading contacts between these Greek colonies and others in ASIA MINOR would allow for the possibility of a Christian presence there at an early date as well as for some knowledge of the faith to have been communicated to the indigenous Dacian people of the inland region. Archaeological finds support the existence of a Christian community in the third century which, according to tradition, suffered severely in the persecutions of Diocletian. Evangelicus is recorded as bishop in Tomis (Constanta) in 290. In 106 Trajan established a Roman province of Dacia. Modern Romanians claim descent from the Romanized Dacian population which they maintain continued to be the principal ethnic group of the region.

There is some evidence, including gems with orthodox or heretical inscriptions from Transylvania, of Christianity in Dacia prior to the Edict of Milan (313), but the major period of Christianization came with Constantine's reincorporation of the territory between the Danube and the Carpathians into the empire. Finds include a basilica with the tomb of a martyr at Slaveni and an inscription from Biertan recording a gift from a member of the faithful, Zenovius, to the local church, and evidencing the existence of organized Latin-speaking Christianity in Transylvania in the fourth century. The Latin roots of theological and ecclesiastical terminology in the Romanian language demonstrate the origins of Romanian Christianity, although from a jurisdictional point of view the province was, after the division of the empire in 395, part of the Eastern, Byzantine, administration, and the church under the authority of CONSTANTINOPLE.

The migration of the Slavs into the Danubian lands in the sixth and seventh centuries began the process of formation of the modern Romanian language and people as the Daco-Roman population there fused with the immigrants, in contrast to the Slav assimilation of the local population to the south. Byzantine sources from the ninth century refer to the Romanians as a distinctive people, recognizing their Roman roots and using the designation VLACH, a word of obscure origin used to refer to a minority or alien element in the population.

The Bulgars, Asiatic nomads, followed the Slavs, whose language they adopted, and set up a powerful state between Byzantium and Moravia. Following their conversion to Christianity by the disciples of CYRIL AND METHODIUS in the ninth century, the Bulgars used a Slavonic liturgy which was in turn adopted by their Romanian subjects and maintained after the destruction of the first Bulgarian state by Emperor Basil II in

1018. The Bulgarian PATRIARCHATE of OHRID was reduced at the same date to an autocephalous archbishopric, but one which continued to exercise jurisdiction at least over the southern Romanians of Wallachia.

The Magyars established their rule in Pannonia in the ninth century and thereafter occupied Transylvania. What or whom they found there remains the subject of the bitterest historical and political dispute in Central Europe. According to the Hungarians, their ancestors found a loosely organized Slavic population which they turned into a political entity. The presence of Romanian inhabitants is not referred to before 1210. According to the Romanians, the Magyars imposed their rule on a territory organized into Romanian voivodates centred on fortresses which put up a stout resistance to the invaders and impeded the process of Magyarization. Whatever the case, Transylvania was incorporated into the Kingdom of Hungary at the end of the eleventh century.

The Hungarians established a bishopric at Alba Iulia (Gyulafehervar) and intro-duced the Latin religious orders. In the twelfth century they settled Szekler, related to the Magyars, and then Saxon colonists in Transylvania, and continued their expansion beyond its frontiers into Oltenia and Moldavia until catastrophically checked by the Tartar invasion of 1241. Military adventure was combined with religious proselytism, in Moldavia centred on a Catholic bishopric established by Pope Honorius III at Milcov (Odobesti) with the express purpose of challenging EASTERN ORTHODOXY, and which survived until 1336. On the other hand, in 1234 Pope Gregory IX com-plained to the Hungarian Prince Rela about the activities of Greek 'pseudo-bishops' who it seems had had some success in winning Saxons and Hungarians over to Orthodoxy.

Following the establishment of the Romanian principalities of Wallachia and Mol-davia in the fourteenth century, the Ecumenical Patriarch recognized metropolitan sees of Ungaro-Wallachia at Arges, transferred from Vicina in Dobrudja, in 1359 and of Moldavia at Suceava, in 1401. Romanians in Transylvania came under the former jurisdiction. Moldavian and Wallachian delegates attended the Council of Constance (1414–18), and a delegation from Moldavia under Metropolitan Damian accepted the decree of union between East and West at the Council of Ferrara/FLORENCE (1438–9), although this never came into effect.

Throughout this period, and into that of OTTOMAN domination from the fifteenth and sixteenth centuries, Old Church Slavonic remained the language of liturgy, theology and church administration in the Romanian church as well as of locally composed hymns and chronicles. A printing press was set up in Tirgoviste which produced a missal in 1508, a chant book in 1510 and a gospel book in 1512, all in Old Slavonic in the Cyrillic script. A catechism published in Sibiu (Hermannstadt) in 1544 was the first book printed in Romanian. An abridged Romanian-language Bible, the Orastie Bible, was published in 1582. Rituals for funerals and church consecrations first appeared in Romanian in 1650–2, and a complete translation of the BIBLE by Nicolae Milescu, known as the Bible of Bucharest or Serban Cantacuzino's Bible, in 1688. From the beginning of the eighteenth century Moldavia and Wallachia were under Phanariot Greek control in both the political and the religious sphere. The attempted, but not systematic, imposition of Greek as liturgical language led both to a decline in the use of Slavonic and the adoption of Romanian, particularly in less important churches. By the end of the century Romanian was in general use, although it was not made compulsory in Wallachia until 1862.

From the sixteenth century until the Habsburg victory of 1687–8 Transylvania, like Moldavia and Wallachia, enjoyed a semi-autonomous status within the Ottoman empire. The Reformation made rapid progress among its various populations. By the turn of the seventeenth century there were three officially recognized nations: Hungarian, Szekler and Saxon; and four religions: Catholic, Lutheran, Calvinist and Unitarian. The majority Romanian and Orthodox population was completely excluded from participation in the political life of the principality. Its clergy were prevented from levying a tithe and were completely dependent upon fees and donations from their peasant congregations, who were already obliged to pay a tax to the 'accepted' church of the district. Restrictions were placed on Orthodox clergy travelling outside the principality to limit contact with the hierarchy in Wallachia; Calvinist superintendents of the Wallachian churches were appointed; and a pseudo-*sobor* condemned invocation of the saints and other Orthodox customs, and denied the sacrament to those ignorant of the creed and the Lord's Prayer. Despite the harassment of their clergy, and government sponsorship of Protestant preachers, the Romanians were little impressed by a faith which challenged the symbols of their national identity and, because of the three nationalities law, offered them no social or political advantages.

After the end of Ottoman rule, the Habsburg Emperor Leopold I issued a charter maintaining the traditional arrangement in Transylvania. His real intention, however, was to re-establish Catholicism, and on finding Protestantism too firmly entrenched turned his attention to the majority population which his Jesuit agents considered to be strongly attached to the externals of their religion while confused about doctrine as a result of Calvinist proselytism. They therefore proposed that the Romanians should be allowed to preserve the traditional outward forms of Orthodoxy in return for agreeing to the four articles of the Council of Florence: the FILIOQUE, the validity of the use of unleavened bread in the eucharist, the existence of purgatory, and papal primacy and universal authority. The political effect of the union would have been to turn the minority Catholic population into an absolute majority, thus strengthening central government and rendering the constitutional balance obsolete.

A synod of February 1697 accepted the union in principle, subject to the granting of 'accepted' nation status for the Romanian population. The new metropolitan, Atanasie Anghel, despite a solemn promise at his consecration, signed the Act of Union at Alba Iulia in October 1698, though there is a suggestion that the Latin translation omitted the condition that the promises about civil rights be kept. The emperor's confirmation guaranteed the UNIATE clergy the same rights and privileges as the Roman Catholic clergy, but said nothing about the population as a whole. Nevertheless the union was ratified by a general synod of clergy and lay representatives, and Atanasie severed his links with the metropolitan of Ungaro-Wallachia.

The Transylvanian Romanians gained little from the union. The promise of fourth nation status was not kept, and the new GREEK CATHOLIC church was placed under the jurisdiction of the Latin bishop of Esztergom, who appointed a Jesuit supervisor without whose approval the Uniate bishop could not call a synod, make clerical appointments or carry out pastoral visitations. On the other hand, through the union Romanians gained access to the educational resources of Catholicism, and by promising, but not delivering, equality the union became the basis for a Romanian constitutional programme. The chief proponent of this was the third head of the Greek Catholic church, Ioan Inocentiu Micu (also known as Klein or Clain).

Following the establishment of a revolutionary government in Budapest in 1848 the Transylvanians, under the leadership of the Greek Catholic priest and historian Simion Barnutiu and the Orthodox metropolitan Andreiu Saguna, proclaimed, in the Sixteen Points, the equality of the Romanian nation and the two Romanian churches with others in the principality, and demanded Greek Catholic independence from Esztergom and Orthodox independence from the Serbian Orthodox in Carlowitz. Despite this common stand the religious division of the Romanians impeded their national cause and was easily exploited by the authorities. The establishment of a Greek Catholic metropolis of Alba Iulia convinced Saguna of the need for a similar status for the Orthodox, and this was eventually granted in 1861. Saguna's constitution for the Orthodox church provided a system in which the episcopal synod controlled doctrine, ritual and discipline, but all levels of the hierarchy were elected by synods in which there was strong lay representation.

Equality for the Romanian nation and language established at the same date was withdrawn again in 1865, and, with the Ausgleich of 1867, Transylvania was incorporated into Hungary, falling victim to a harsh period of Magyarization which continued down to the First World War. Secret plans of 1907 called for the incorporation of the Greek Catholic into the Roman Catholic church and for 'doing away' with the Orthodox church which was recognized to be the principal vehicle for Romanian aspirations.

Despite Pope Leo XIII's guarantee of the inviolability of the Greek Catholic church in Transylvania in *Praeclara Gratulationis* (1894), the Hungarian government persuaded Pius X to establish by the bull *Christi Fideles* (1912) a Hungarian Uniate diocese at Hajdudorog which, though made up of 83 Romanian Greek Catholic parishes and 382 dependent churches, used Hungarian as the language of liturgy and instruction and was placed under a Hungarian vicar-general.

After the collapse of Austria-Hungary in 1918 Greek Catholics joined with the Orthodox and the Saxon minority at a Grand National Assembly at Alba Iulia and voted to unite with the kingdom of Romania.

As in Transylvania, the church in the Danubian principalities had been a focus of national identity during the period of Ottoman suzerainty. Monasteries served as centres of culture, learning and welfare and were supported by local princes and landowners, and at the end of the eighteenth century owned between a quarter and a third of the total area of the principalities.

Alexandru Ioan Cuza was elected prince of both Moldavia and Wallachia in 1859. Following the political union he declared the Orthodox church autocephalous, and set up a general synod in 1864. Nifon, metropolitan of Wallachia, became primate of the united church in 1865. The following year, after Cuza's forced abdication, Charles Hohenzollern-Sigmaringen was declared Carol I, reigning prince of Romania. A Roman Catholic himself, he married a German Lutheran, but strengthened his position by declaring that his children would be brought up in the Orthodox faith. A constitution, modelled on that of Belgium, was drawn up and remained in force until 1923.

Under the constitution of 1866 Orthodoxy was declared the 'dominant religion', a role clarified in a series of statutes. The Law for the Selection of Metropolitans and Diocesan Bishops and the Composition of the Holy Synod of the Romanian Orthodox Church (1872) opened the way for political interference by laying down that all appointments to the Holy Synod would be made by an electoral college made up of members of the synod and all of the Orthodox senators and deputies in the national legislature. State and political control was extended in 1893 by the Law Governing Clergy and Seminaries, which put clergy stipends and seminaries under the control of the Ministry of Religion and Public Instruction. The central church administration set up by the ministry in 1902 rapidly became the scene of intrigue and favouritism, and after a controversial existence was abolished in 1921.

After 1909 bishops were elected by votes of all members in both houses of parliament, an uncanonical procedure that led to the deprivation of Bishop Gherasim of Roman after he called on the Ecumenical Patriarch to intervene. Bishops were now regularly appointed and removed according to the political climate. The position of Orthodoxy as the 'dominant religion' was challenged when it became known that the heir to the throne planned a Catholic baptism for his son, the future Carol II, and after the incorporation of Transylvania into Romania increased the total Catholic population to about 15 per cent.

The new constitution of 1923 declared the Orthodox church and Greek Catholic church to be 'Romanian churches', the former being described as 'dominant', the latter as having 'precedence' over all other 'cults'. Freedom of religion and conscience was guaranteed. All of the Greek Catholic bishops were given seats in the senate, but relations between the two churches deteriorated as local pressure was put on Greek Catholics to return to Orthodoxy. At the same time tension between the Greek Catholics and the Roman Catholics was encouraged and abetted by the government and the Orthodox church.

The complex relations between the government and the churches in the 1920s are best understood as part of the enlarged nation's need to define its identity and consolidate its authority over its new territories. The elevation of the Romanian Orthodox church to the rank of patriarchate in 1925 and the conclusion of a concordat between Romania and the Holy See in 1927 were important steps towards the attainment of these goals.

The new Law of Cults (1928) was mainly concerned with regulating the 'national' churches, that is, those which could be identified with a particular ethnic group within the state, and protecting them from foreign 'sects' such as Baptists and Adventists. An exception was made for the Catholic church which, under the terms of the concordat, had a privileged position with control of its own schools and institutions.

The growth of Romanian fascism in the 1920s and 1930s suggests that the process of national self-definition remained incomplete. The Legion of the Archangel Michael, after 1930 the Iron Guard, was originally established in 1922–3 by Corneliu Codrianu as the Association of Christian Students and then as the National Christian Defence League. The Legion made free use of Orthodox language and imagery to propagate its anti-Semitic and anti-Western ideology, and attracted a number of priests to its ranks. The hierarchy condemned League-sponsored terrorism, but could never fully dissociate itself from a movement with such claims to patriotic credentials.

The Lord's Army, founded in 1923 by the Transylvanian priest Iosif Trifa, was a highly successful popular movement for moral renewal, an Orthodox response to foreign evangelical proselytism and a protest against government manipulation of the hierarchy. Father Trifa was defrocked in 1935 for failing to curb lay influence in the Army.

Following the communist takeover a new constitution of 1948 guaranteed freedom of worship and the right of the denominations to exist and train their own clergy, but deprived them of a role in public education. In practice the churches were controlled by subsequent legislation which superseded the 1928 Law on Cults. In order to function at all, a religious organization had to be recognized by the state. Clergy and church officials had to take an oath of loyalty, and could be deprived for showing 'anti-democratic attitudes'. Clergy were to be paid by the state and have the same rights and duties as other civil servants. Relations with foreign organizations were to be conducted through the Ministry for Religious Affairs. Article 27 of the 1948 constitution declared the Romanian Orthodox church to be 'autocephalous and unitary in its organization', an apparent echo of the 1923 description of Orthodoxy as the 'dominant' religion and suggesting some continued special status. The declaration was omitted when the constitution was revised in 1952.

The Catholic church received special treatment. Party Secretary Gheorghe Gheorghiu-Dej said it was 'the sole obstacle to democracy in Romania'. Following the repudiation of the concordat in July 1948, a pseudo-*sobor* of the Greek Catholics held at Cluj in October voted for reunion with the Orthodox. The church officially ceased to exist and its assets were taken over by the Orthodox church. The Roman Catholic church might have met a similar fate had not most of its members belonged to the national minorities. An attempt to organize a 'patriotic' church independent of Rome in 1950–1 failed. Greek Catholic communities continued to exist despite persecution. In 1988 the dissident Greek Catholic writer Doina Cornea and others petitioned the pope for support for their restoration and rejected any policy of assimilation into the Latin rite church.

The Orthodox church suffered in the early years of communist rule as the regime attempted to destroy potential centres of resistance. Many clergy were imprisoned and three archbishops, including Patriarch Nicodemus, died in suspicious circumstances. However, persecution was restrained, first because the Orthodox church was already firmly under state control, and secondly because of some close personal relationships between the communist and the ecclesiastical leadership. The first president of the People's Republic, Petru Groza, was the son of a priest and a known Orthodox sympathizer. Justinian Mariana, installed by the new government as patriarch in 1948, had protected Gheorghiu-Dej during the pro-Reich military dictatorship of Ion Antonescu. Furthermore, the pursuit of a 'Romanian road to socialism', which culminated in the withdrawal of Soviet troops in 1958 and the rejection of Khrushchev's plans for economic specialization and integration through Comecon in 1963, gave the Orthodox church some minimal degree of protection and enabled it to retain its traditional role as a focus of national identity.

Western commentators in the 1970s and 1980s sometimes portrayed the situation in Romania as one of the separation of church and state, and praised the integrity of the Orthodox church in comparison with that of BULGARIA which was seen as a mere instrument of the state. The regime attempted to present itself in a favourable light as it sought economic concessions from the West, for example by allowing Billy Graham to make a preaching tour in 1975. Laszlo Tokes, the Transylvanian Hungarian pastor who sparked the Romanian revolution of 1989, on the other hand, has relentlessly criticized the Orthodox church for its collusion with the Ceausescu regime.

Ceausescu's own attitude towards religion was ambiguous and self-contradictory. Under him nationalism degenerated into national chauvinism, with absurd claims being made for Romanian scientific and cultural achievements. Ceausescu was able to employ the Orthodox church as a vehicle for his so-called 'liberal' foreign policy, but had to accept its hold over the people. At the same time he was probably the last communist leader to believe in the possibility of the creation of a 'new socialist man', waged an intense ideological war against religious belief, and ruthlessly destroyed historic churches as part of his 'systematization' policy. Father Gheorghe Calciu-Dumitreasca of the Orthodox Seminary in Bucharest, one of the few to speak out against the destruction of church buildings and renewed anti-religious propaganda, was imprisoned and defrocked. Officially the Orthodox church continued to praise the regime and its head until the moment of its demise.

The situation in contemporary Romania is complex and confusing. After the Christmas revolution of 1989 Patriarch Teoctist resigned following protests from seminary students about his collusion with the 'dictatorship', but was reinstated by the Holy Synod in April 1990. The Greek Catholic church was legalized on the last day of 1989 and fully recognized in April 1990, but quickly fell into dispute with the Orthodox over ownership of 'transferred property'. The new minister of religion, Nicolae Stoicescu, a militant Orthodox believer, raised fears among Evangelical groups when he proposed restoring the 1928 Law on Cults and among Catholics when he criticized the naming of new Catholic bishops by the Vatican, but was quickly replaced by Gheorghe Vladutescu who was more committed to equality among denominations and rejected any special status for the Orthodox.

The government of the National Salvation Front has failed to condemn the Romanian Homeland (Vatra Romaneasca) movement, which exploits traditional xenophobic and anti-Semitic prejudices and which has attracted the support of some Orthodox clerics. The Lord's Army, banned in 1948, has re-emerged and its founder, Iosif Trifa, has been rehabilitated by the church. New movements with an uncertain relationship with the Orthodox church, such as the Pucioasa-based 'New Jerusalem' community led by the sculptor Marian Zidaru, reflect the mystical nationalist tradition. The collapse of the USSR has led to calls for the reincorporation of Bessarabia (from 1940 the Soviet Moldavian Republic) into Romania, and in December 1992 the Romanian Orthodox church announced its intention to recognize Chisinau (Kishinev) diocese as a metropolitan see in response to a request from Bishop Petru Peduraru of Balti. The Russian Orthodox church has responded by granting the 'Moldovan' Church a measure of autonomy.

Mazilu, Dan Horia (1998), 'Roumanians and Christianity (from the Early Times up to the Late 18th Century)', in Dan C. Giurescu and Stephen Fisher-Galati, *Romania: A Historic Perspective*. East European Monographs 457. Boulder, Col.: Westview; New York: Columbia University Press.

Ramet, Sabrina P. (1998), *Nihil Obstat: Religion, Politics and Social Change in East-Central Europe and Russia*. Durham, NC and London: Duke University Press.

Mojzes, Paul (1992), *Religious Liberty in Eastern Europe and the USSR*. East European Monographs 337. Boulder, Col.: Westview; New York: Columbia University Press.

Pacurariu, Mircea (1991), *Pages from the History of the Romanian Church*. Bucharest: Romanian Orthodox Church Bible and Mission Institute Publishing House.

Ramet, P., ed. (1990), *Catholicism and Politics in Communist Societies*. Christianity under Stress, vol. 2. Durham, NC and London: Duke University Press.

Ramet, P., ed. (1988), *Eastern Christianity and Politics in the Twentieth Century*. Christianity under Stress, vol. 1. Durham, NC and London: Duke University Press.

Hitchens, Keith (1977), *Orthodoxy and Nationality: Andreiu Eaguna and the Rumanians of Transylvania, 1846–1873*. Harvard Historical Studies 94. Cambridge, Mass. and London: Harvard University Press.

Bociurkiw, Bohdan and Strong, John W., eds (1975), *Religion and Atheism in the USSR and Eastern Europe*. London and New York: Macmillan.

Hitchens, Keith (1969), *The Rumanian Nationalist Movement in Transylvania, 1780–1849*. Harvard Historical Monographs 61. Cambridge, Mass.: Harvard University Press.

Beza, Marcu (1943), *The Rumanian Church*. London: SPCK.

Seton-Watson, R. W. (1934), *A History of the Roumanians*. Cambridge: Cambridge University Press.

Iorga, N. (1925), *A History of Roumania*. London: T. Fisher Unwin.

AW

Romanos the Melodist   Originally from Emesa (modern Homs) in Syria and of Semitic, very possibly Jewish, ancestry; probably born in the late fifth century. He came to CONSTANTINOPLE in the early sixth century, becoming DEACON at the Church of the Mother of God in the comparatively secluded district of Kyros, later Hexi-Marmara, in the north of the city. He died after 555 and probably before the death of Emperor Justinian in 565. His fame rests on the series of KONTAKIA to which he owes the title *Melodos*. Some have been described as 'among the masterpieces of world literature'. The opening verses of a number of them are still used in the services of the Byzantine churches and are among the best-known and best-loved of hymns. In the manuscripts that have come down to us some eighty-nine kontakia are attributed to him, of which most scholars accept only about sixty as genuine. Romanos is commemorated on 1 October.

Lash, E. trans. (1995), *On the Life of Christ: Kontakia of Saint Romanos the Melodist*. New York: HarperCollins.

E

Rome   Jesus was born in the reign of the first Roman emperor (30 BC–AD 14). Even in the apostolic period, the Roman empire played a crucial role in the spread of the Christian church. The empire's highly effective communication networks had Rome as their hub. When Paul wrote his Epistle to the Romans a significant Christian community already existed there. Rome rose to eminence in the early church not only because of its political and economic importance but equally because the apostles Peter and Paul had preached there and, tradition affirmed, died a martyr's death there, probably when the Great Fire of Rome (AD 64) became for the Emperor Nero (54–68) an excuse to persecute the city's Christians.

Under the rule of the pagan emperors, and despite intermittent persecution, the Roman church managed to grow, to attain a high level of organization, to acquire buildings and assets and to maintain contact with churches in many parts of the Christian world. It became respected as the preserver of a pure and orthodox tradition of doctrine. When disputes arose in or between local churches, Rome's support carried weight. By the last decade of the second century, the bishop of Rome's sense of his own authority had developed to the point where Pope Victor I (189–99) could seriously consider excommunicating the churches of the province of Asia and all their neighbouring churches because of their failure to accept his ruling on the way to calculate the date of Pascha. He was persuaded to milder action, Eastern bishops arguing that his predecessors had lived at peace with those they knew to follow different customs. The assertion in the canons of the Western Council of Sardica (343) of the bishop of Rome's right to general appellate jurisdiction in ecclesiastical disputes shows the clear acceptance at least among the bishops of the West of some form of Roman juridical primacy.

The refounding of Byzantium as CONSTANTINOPLE (324) faced Rome with a rival; it faced Rome's bishop with two. The Christian emperor ruled in Constantinople, and his city had a bishop of its own. The Roman pope had presided over the Western church under the authority of a pagan ruler; he was now under the authority of a Christian ruler. Their relation remained to be negotiated. It is significant that the seven councils accepted by EASTERN ORTHODOX and by Catholics as ECUMENICAL COUNCILS were convoked by the emperor. The relation between the pope and the bishop of Constantinople posed other problems: the Council of Constantinople (381) stated in its canon 3: 'Let the Bishop of Constantinople, however, hold the seniority of honour after the Bishop of Rome, since it is the New Rome.' The title 'New Rome' carried its own claim to equality. How serious that could be was made evident in canon 28 of the Council of Chalcedon: 'We too determine and vote the same as to the seniority of the most holy church of Constantinople, New Rome. For the fathers fittingly accorded seniority to the throne of Elder Rome since that is the imperial city.' It is little surprise that the popes rejected this canon: it seems to imply that the seniority of Rome is something in the council's gift. In Rome the view had already been clearly expressed by Pope Stephen I (254–57) that he sat on the *cathedra Petri* as inheritor of Peter's Christ-given role.

In the Christological controversies that racked the church in the fourth and fifth centuries, Rome cast itself in the role of the defender of orthodoxy, a role exercised most successfully by Leo I (440–61) whose *Tome*, an authoritative dogmatic epistle addressed to Patriarch FLAVIAN of Constantinople (446–9) was read at Chalcedon (451) to acclamations of 'Peter has spoken through Leo!'. The authority of Rome and the dignity of the Western church were exalted by the acceptance of Leo's *Tome*. It became a symbol of the orthodoxy and the authority of the Roman church and its bishops.

The collapse of the Western Roman empire when Odoacer expelled the Emperor Romulus Augustulus (476) faced the papacy with a new problem. The Eastern empire still existed. The pope had to measure with scrupulous care the loyalty he should give to two different rulers, and found that in the midst of warfare and political instability he frequently had to be statesman as well as priest.

In 482 the Byzantine Emperor Zeno (474–91) issued the HENOTIKON, seeking a doctrinal compromise to reunite MONOPHYSITES and CHALCEDONIANS. In 484 Pope Felix II (483–92) broke communion with Zeno's collaborator, Patriarch Acacius, a schism that lasted until 519.

In 493 Theodoric the Great (493–526) and his Arian Ostrogoth forces took control of Italy. He entered Rome and killed Odoacer. Pope John I (523–6) found himself journeying to Constantinople as a virtual ambassador for Theodoric and his Arian followers to Emperor Justin I (518–27), a ruggedly orthodox ruler, determined to resolve the Arian problem by direct action. Pope Agapetus I (535–6) went as advocate for King Theodahad (534–6), expected to dissuade Justinian I (527–65) from invading Italy. None the less, Justinian's general Belisarios arrived before Rome in December 536; Agapetus' successor Silverius opened the gates and let the Byzantine forces in, but Belisarios had him deposed all the same for excessive sympathies for the Goths, sympathies shared by several other popes of the period.

Pope Vigilius (537–55), who had travelled to Constantinople with Agapetus and had been on good terms with Justinian's Empress Theodora, saw the return of Byzantine rule with the Ravenna exarchate, not Rome, as seat of imperial authority. In pursuit of his policies to reintegrate Italy into the empire and to promote unity in the church, he had Vigilius arrested and sent to Constantinople where he vacillated over the issue of the Three Chapters (*see* ECUMENICAL COUNCILS), terrified of the emperor but afraid of offending his own Western bishops, his humiliating treatment showing all too clearly the threat a Christian emperor could constitute to a pope under his political rule.

From the death of Vigilius (555) to the accession of Zachary (741–52) the pope's election required imperial confirmation before his enthronement. Many popes of this period were Greek or Syrian in origin. Gregory I (590–604) was a masterly administrator and a powerful leader, but solidly loyal to the empire. He opposed the use of the title Ecumenical Patriarch by JOHN THE FASTER (585–95), seeing it as a claim to universal jurisdiction: in this he was probably mistaken, since the title had been in use already to designate rather the senior hierarch of a major division of the empire.

Gregory was a contemporary of the prophet Muhammad (d. 632). The Islamic onslaught led the Byzantine emperors to attempt once again to establish reunion with the monophysites, not least because their homelands were in Egypt and Syria. In 524 Emperor Heraclius and the Ecumenical Patriarch Sergius I (610–38) began to seek a formula of union based on the recognition of 'one operation' in Christ. In the MONOTHELETE controversy which followed, Pope Honorius I (625–38) gravely compromised himself, and was personally condemned as a heretic at the Third Council of Constantinople (681).

When Emperor Leo III (717–41) instituted a policy of ICONOCLASM, Pope Gregory II (715–31), though politically loyal, seems to have opposed his religious policy. Significantly, the growing religious tension between Rome and Constantinople coincided with a major, papally supported expansion of missionary activity in Germany, led by the English monk Boniface (680–754). When Gregory II died in 731 he was succeeded by the Syrian Gregory III, who sought confirmation of his election from the imperial exarch at Ravenna, but was the last pope to do so. In November 731

Gregory III excommunicated all iconoclasts. Retaliating, the emperor transferred Illyricum, Calabria and Sicily to the patriarchate of Constantinople. None the less Gregory remained loyal and helped the emperor regain Ravenna from the Lombards, but received no help from the emperor when the Lombards invaded his own domains. Ineffectually on this occasion, the pope appealed to the Franks. His successor, Zachary, won Frankish support by formally recognizing Pepin III's displacement of the Merovingians. Stephen II (752–7) appealed for Pepin's protection and received not only that but also a grant of territory in north Italy. This grant may have been based on the forged *Donation of Constantine*, which recorded a grant by CONSTANTINE THE GREAT of imperial powers and trappings and of land to Pope Sylvester I (314–35). Leo III sealed the bond with the Carolingian house when he crowned Charlemagne emperor on Christmas Day 800.

The close link with the Carolingian Franks faded as the Frankish empire was partitioned in the decades after the death of Charlemagne (768–814). But now the popes looked West, not East, for political and military support; and they had arrogated the right to make, and therefore to unmake, emperors.

The ninth-century papacy came into conflict with the patriarchate of Constantinople in the reign of Pope Nicolas I, an intelligent, energetic partisan of papal supremacy – a supremacy that saw clergy as instruments of papal policy and princes as under papal protection and guidance. He upheld the deposed Patriarch Ignatios against PHOTIOS THE GREAT, ordering his reinstatement and admonishing Emperor Michael III as to the prerogatives of the Roman see. This gave rise to a schism between the two Romes. Another conflict arose over BULGARIA. Both conflicts continued under Hadrian II (867–72). Bulgaria was finally won for Byzantine Christianity but Hadrian could console himself with winning Moravia, evangelized by CYRIL AND METHODIUS, for the West. The schism with Constantinople was ended by a council presided over by Photios in 879. Unfortunately Rome came to accept an earlier pro-Ignatian council as the eighth ecumenical council, rather than this one, the decrees of which, while still asserting papal primacy, were far more acceptable to the East.

The coronation in 962 of the Saxon Emperor Otto I by Pope John XII (951–64) and the designation of his realm as the 'Holy Roman Empire' marked a further political shift. From this point there emerged a sharp division of policy between pope and Holy Roman emperor. Papal ideology saw the emperor as the anointed champion of the church, owing filial obedience in all religious matters to the pope. The Holy Roman Emperor saw himself rather as supreme sovereign, with the right and even the duty to replace unworthy popes. The investitures controversy provided the battleground on which these rival policies were fought out. While the papacy failed to establish the maximalist views of papal authority propounded by Nicolas I (858–67), Gregory VII (1073–85) and Innocent III (1198–1216), and solemnly defined in its most extreme form by Boniface VIII (1294–03) in his Bull *Unam Sanctam* (November 1302), which taught that it is necessary to salvation for any human being to obey the Roman pope, the popes emerged from the conflict with the empire having effectively asserted the independence of their spiritual authority.

When Patriarch MICHAEL I KEROULARIOS closed the Latin churches in Constantinople and opposed many details of Latin practice, such as priests' shaving, Saturday fasting and use of unleavened bread in the eucharist, papal legates were sent to

Constantinople bearing letters rebuking him (*see* AZYMITE; QUINISEXT COUNCIL). Michael, despite the Byzantine emperor's attempts to make peace, treated the legates with such contempt that on 16 July 1054 Cardinal Humbert placed a bull of excommunication on the altar of Hagia Sophia. This date has often been regarded as marking the formal split between Rome and the Eastern Orthodox. This is implausible since the excommunications were personal, Humbert condemning Michael and his associates, Michael anathematizing the bull's authors, and Leo IX (1049–54), whose legate Humbert was, had died before the excommunication. Moreover, the patriarch of ANTIOCH remained on relatively good terms with Rome, and until the final split in 1724 there were often Antiochene bishops in communion with Rome.

Michael I died deposed and disgraced. Relations with Rome had been damaged. None the less, Emperor Alexios I Komnenos (1081–18) appealed to the West for help to defend the Christian East against Islamic military power. Pope Urban II (1088–99) at the Synod of Clermont in 1095 turned this appeal into a call to a CRUSADE, a holy war to liberate JERUSALEM from the Muslims. His rallying cry served also to sideline the imperially sponsored anti-pope Clement III (1080–1100), at that moment reigning in Rome, the greatest of a line of anti-popes thrown up by the conflict between pope and emperor.

The Crusades led to renewed contact between Western Christianity and the churches of the Middle East. The MARONITES came under obedience to Rome in the crusading period, while retaining their SYRIAN rite; Lesser Armenia united with Rome for a time (*see* ARMENIAN CATHOLICS).

The Fourth Crusade, however, bred bitter distrust among Eastern Orthodox: the crusaders took and sacked Constantinople on 12 April 1204, setting up a Latin emperor and Latin patriarch. After an initial expression of outrage, Innocent III accepted the *fait accompli*. The establishment of a rival hierarchy marked a further advance into schism. Titular Latin patriarchs of Constantinople, Antioch and Alexandria were to survive into the nineteenth and twentieth centuries as ornaments of the papal court.

Constantinople was not alone in suffering outrage at the hands of the crusaders. In many cities Orthodox bishops were dispossessed and replaced by Latin clergy. CYPRUS in particular suffered serious persecution at Latin hands.

The restoration of Byzantine rule in Constantinople in 1261 left the Emperor Michael VIII Palaiologos exposed to threats from Western claimants and warlike adversaries. To counter them he sought reunion with Rome, and at the Second Council of LYONS in 1274 a formal reunion was concluded. The emperor could not enforce it and the union failed. A similar attempt was made by John VIII Palaiologos (1421–48) at the Council of FLORENCE. On this occasion, extensive debate preceded the act of reunion celebrated in Eugene IV's Bull *Laetentur Caeli* (1439). Decrees were also passed reuniting groups of Oriental Orthodox with Rome. John VIII had sought reunion to defend himself against the OTTOMAN advance. In 1453 Constantinople fell to the Ottomans, and though the last emperor, Constantine XI (1448–53), never repudiated the union, it died with him.

John Huss was burnt at the stake in 1415. By 1520 Luther had decisively broken with Rome. Both Catholics and Protestants of the now permanently divided West sought to win the Christian East to their cause. Rival diplomats supported or undermined patriarchs they judged sympathetic or hostile. Rome found education an effective bait: Orthodox youths were offered education in Rome and solicited to the cause of union. Jesuits working in the Venetian-ruled Greek islands promoted secret submission to Rome.

The Catholic Reformation fired many clergy, especially Jesuits and friars, with a missionary zeal that saw in the Eastern and Oriental Orthodox schismatics who must be drawn into the Roman communion. The Union of Brest-Litovsk (1596) brought the Orthodox clergy of Polish Ukraine into union with Rome. It also inspired an Orthodox counter-movement on the part of lay brotherhoods and of some clergy, which flowered in the educational work of Peter MOGILA (1597–1646), a noble Wallachian who became metropolitan of KIEV in 1632.

In 1552 part of the CHURCH OF THE EAST opposed to their hereditary patriarch sought union with Rome. In 1662 a SYRIAN CATHOLIC church emerged and was established in a permanent form in 1783 under Patriarch Michael Garweh (1783–1800). The Armenian Catholic church was placed on a permanent foundation between 1635 and 1740. The Franciscans inspired the extraordinary scholar RAPHAEL TUKI (1701–87) to work for reunion of the COPTIC church with Rome, and in 1741 Bishop Athanasios of Jerusalem became the first bishop of the Coptic Catholic church. In 1724 a bishop in communion with Rome was elected as Eastern Orthodox patriarch of Antioch as Cyril VI: the tactless zeal of the Orthodox rival appointed by the Ecumenical Patriarch ensured the survival of a separate Catholic MELKITE patriarchate of Antioch. Portuguese missionary work in INDIA brought the majority of the Thomas Christians of South India into communion with Rome.

The Roman UNIATE policy falls into two fairly distinct phases. In the earlier period, from the failure of the Council of Florence to the early eighteenth century, the Eastern Orthodox were generally treated as wayward provinces of the universal church. Catholic clergy worked to bring them to accept the Roman doctrines of the FILIOQUE, of purgatory, original sin and papal supremacy. They could do this covertly, working with Orthodox clergy, preaching and teaching in their churches when invited, acting as confessors. Pope Gregory XIII (1572–85) created Armenian, Greek and Maronite colleges, and provided scholarships for Eastern Christian students.

In the early eighteenth century *communicatio in sacris* (sharing in prayer, and especially in sacraments) became unacceptable to Rome, and as the ultramontane movement gained ground in the nineteenth century the Orthodox came to be viewed as outside the church. Accordingly, in 1848 Pius IX wrote an encyclical letter to the Christians of the East and had it published to the Orthodox faithful over the heads of their patriarchs and bishops. He then compounded the insult by writing to the Orthodox hierarchs bidding them to reunite with Rome, but allowed his letter to be widely published before the Orthodox patriarchs formally received it. It was not only Orthodox patriarchs he offended. The Catholic Melkite patriarch, Gregory II Yusuf (1864–97) opposed the definition of papal infallibility at the Vatican Council (1869–70); on a subsequent visit to the pope he was cast down at his feet by his guard, while the pope placed his foot on Gregory's head.

Leo XIII (1878–1903) showed a much greater respect for Eastern Christian tradition, and his encyclicals *Praeclara Gratulationis* and *Orientalium Dignitas* (1894) marked a significant warming in the papal attitude to the Eastern churches. Of particular importance to Eastern Catholics was his prohibition of reception of Orthodox converts into the

Latin rite. He restored the Byzantine rite at GROTTAFERRATA. In 1895 he founded a commission, which in 1917 Benedict XV (1914–22) turned into the Congregation for the Oriental Churches, as a focus of information and activity on relations with the East, both Catholic and Orthodox. In 1917 Benedict XV founded the Pontifical Oriental Institute, an institution whose research and publications have been of the first importance in promoting mutual understanding, and in 1919 the Ethiopian College. Pius XI (1922–39) in 1929 published the encyclical *Rerum Orientalium* building on the work of his predecessors, and extended the remit of the Congregation for the Oriental Churches to cover the Latin Catholics of the Middle East.

It was for Popes John XXIII (1958–63) and Paul VI (1963–78), however, to transform Catholic–Orthodox relations. Intimately acquainted with the Orthodox East from his period as papal diplomat in Bulgaria, Turkey and Greece, John invited Orthodox observers to the Second Vatican Council (1962–5), and many came. During its sessions they showed great respect for the intercessions of the Melkite Patriarch Maximos IV Sayegh. Apart from the recognition of the full ecclesial status of the Orthodox churches contained in its documents, the Council worked to create a new friendship between Catholics and Orthodox. This was developed further when Pope Paul VI met Patriarch Athenagoras in the Holy Land in 1964 and when in 1965 the excommunications and anathemas of 1054 were formally lifted by both pope and patriarch. When a delegation from the Phanar visited Paul VI on the tenth anniversary of this event, the pope knelt and kissed the foot of the Metropolitan Meliton, the Ecumenical Patriarch's representative, a gesture that astonished and delighted many Orthodox.

Fruitful theological dialogue between Rome and the Eastern Orthodox ensued. In parallel, the papacy has actively encouraged dialogue with the Oriental Orthodox churches and with the Church of the East. There have, however, been weighty Orthodox voices urging caution in the dialogue with Rome.

Pope John Paul II (enthroned 1978) has made a major contribution to the development of dialogue with his letter *Orientalium Lumen* and his encyclical *Ut Unum Sint*, freely acknowledging that the papacy itself is a great stumbling block on the path to unity, and asking for help in expressing the role of the papacy in the context of Christian ECUMENISM. His pontificate has also been marked by a new closeness with the Church of the East and the Oriental Orthodox. Since Vatican II greetings and visits have regularly been exchanged between Rome and the Orthodox, and recent years have seen warm and friendly meetings between the pope and the principal hierarchs of the Armenian Apostolic, Coptic and Syrian Orthodox churches and the Church of the East.

Meyendorff, J. (1996), *Rome, Constantinople, Moscow*. Crestwood, NY: St Vladimir's Seminary Press.
Papadakis, A. and Meyendorff, J. (1994), *The Christian East and the Rise of the Papacy: The Church 1071–1453*. Crestwood, NY: St Vladimir's Seminary Press.
Herrin, J. (1987), *The Formation of Christendom*. Princeton: Princeton University Press.
Kelly, J. N. D. (1986), *The Oxford Dictionary of the Popes*. Oxford: Oxford University Press.
Krautheimer, R. (1984), *Rome: Profile of a City 312–1308*. Princeton: Princeton University Press.
Tillard, J. M. R. (1983), *The Bishop of Rome*. London: S.P.C.K.

Noble, T. F. X. (1982), *The Republic of Saint Peter*. Philadelphia: University of Pennsylvania Press.
Sherrard, P. (1978), *Church, Papacy and Schism*. London: S.P.C.K.
Gill, J. (1970), *Byzantium and the Papacy*. New Brunswick, NJ: Rutgers University Press.
Dvornik, F. (1966), *Byzantium and Roman Primacy*. New York.
Ullmann, W. (1962), *The Growth of Papal Government in the Middle Ages*. London: Pelican.

DM

Rostislav (d. 870)   Prince of Moravia, honoured as founder of the CZECH AND SLOVAK ORTHODOX CHURCH. Rostislav invited the brothers CYRIL AND METHODIUS to Greater Moravia from CONSTANTINOPLE in 862. The Byzantine mission and its sponsors was opposed by the German clergy who were established along the frontiers of the Holy Roman Empire. In Italy, Cyril and Methodius successfully defended the position of the Byzantine church and its practice of employing the local vernacular when engaging in mission, but in Greater Moravia the Roman church supported those who sought to oust the Byzantine missionaries. Cyril died in ROME in 868 and was canonized by the Roman church; in Greater Moravia his protector, Prince Rostislav, was betrayed to the Germans by his own countrymen, tortured and executed. Methodius was also captured and held by the Germans until 873. The other Byzantine missionaries were enslaved or expelled from Greater Moravia. Rostislav is commemorated on 29 October. Other Czech and Slovak saints of the subsequent period commemorated by the Eastern Orthodox churches include Prince Vyacheslav or Wenceslaus, known to the Greeks as Venizelos, and his grandmother, Ludmilla.

Kantor, M. (1990), *The Origins of Christianity in Bohemia*. Illinois: Northwestern University Press.

DB

Roumeli   Derived from the Turkish term for the Balkan provinces of the OTTOMAN Empire, i.e. as opposed to 'Rum' for ASIA MINOR. For the Greeks, Roumeli became synonymous with Sterea Hellas, mainland Greece below Thessaly and Epirus. Roumeli and the Peloponnese saw the fiercest fighting and the greatest destruction during the Greek War of Independence (from 1821). Up to this period Levadia was the main town of the region and often gave its name to the same provinces.
See also ROMANIA IN THE BYZANTINE EMPIRE.

DB

royal doors   The central doors leading from the narthex into the nave of a Byzantine rite church: in Hagia Sophia in CONSTANTINOPLE the emperor and his retinue made formal entry through these doors. The same name is often misused to designate the holy doors or 'beautiful gates' in the middle of the ICONOSTASIS. Greek use normally denotes the entrance to the church as 'gate' (*pyle*) in the singular and that to the altar as either 'beautiful gate' or 'altar-door' (*bemothyra*, as one word). On ATHOS there are still, except in the tiny katholikon of Stavronikita, two smaller side doors from the narthex or *lite* into the church. At Vigils the abbot vests in the mandyas in the *lite* and makes his solemn entry through the royal doors. The royal door is provided with a heavy curtain, so that the narthex can be cut off from the main church during the Ninth Hour, Compline and the *lite* itself at Vigils.

DM/KP/E

royal office   In the Byzantine rite a short office that precedes the HEXAPSALMOS at Matins. It originated in the monasteries of royal foundation as an intercession for the imperial family.

E

Rublev, Andrei (*c*.1370–1430)   Russian saint and icon- and fresco-painter who may have been a monk at the Trinity–Sergius monastery at Sergiev Posad (Zargorsk) during the time of its founder, SERGIUS OF RADONEZH (1314–92). He seems to have moved to the Andronikov monastery in Moscow about 1400 and worked as an assistant to THEOPHAN THE GREEK on the frescoes and the ICONOSTASIS of the Cathedral of the Annuciation in 1405. He is known to have worked with Daniil Cherny in the Cathedral of the Dormition at VLADIMIR in 1408. His famous icon of the Old Testament Trinity was probably painted at the Trinity–Sergius monastery about 1425–7, for the newly built stone church dedicated to the Holy TRINITY. According to the Life of Nikon, the second hegumen of the monastery (1392–1427), written by Pachomius the Serb in the mid-fifteenth century, Rublev painted his Trinity as a memorial to St Sergius. At the Council of the Hundred Chapters (Stoglav) in 1551 the question of how the Trinity should be represented was answered with direct reference to Rublev's icon. The endorsement of traditional types by the Stoglav was intended to counter increasing decorative and Western elements in Russian icon painting during the sixteenth century. Although Rublev's Trinity departs from earlier models it retains the abstract delineation and spirituality of the authentic icon. Read from left to right, the three angels of the icon conform to a triangle within a circle, with, most probably, the Father and the Holy Spirit on the baseline and the Son at the apex. The heads of the angels corresponding to the Son and the Holy Spirit are inclined towards the angel representing the Father, expressing the monarchy of God the Father. The relations among the angels represent the PERICHORESIS of the persons of the Trinity. Rublev's use of blue in the garments of the angels may reflect the traditional symbolism of blue for the divine presence as seen in the MANDORLA. He was canonized in 1988.

Ouspensky, L. and Lossky, V. (1982), *The Meaning of Icons*. New York: St. Vladimir's Seminary Press.
Vzdornov, G. (1981), *The Trinity by Andrei Rublev: An Anthology*. Moscow: Iskusstvo.

KP

Rufus of Shotep   Sixth-century Coptic bishop of Shotep (Greek: Hypsele) in upper Egypt. Only two sets of Coptic homilies on the Gospels of Matthew and Luke survive from his writings. They are a valuable source of information about Coptic biblical exegesis and Coptic culture more generally in the period immediately before the Arab conquest.

Sheridan, M. J. (1998), Rufus of Shotep, *Homilies on the Gospels of Mathew and Luke: Introduction, Text, Translation, Commentary*. Rome: Centro Italiano Microfiches.

MacCoull, L. S. B. (1989), 'A Note on Rufus of Hypselis in the *History of the Patriarchs*', *Le Muséon* 102, pp. 267–70.

MJB/SHG

Rufina Kokoreva (1872–1937)   Russian monastic founder, revered as a modern worker of miracles. Rufina was from Perm; she followed an ascetic lifestyle from a young age and received visions. Like Thaisia of Leushino (d. 1915) she joined a local convent at the first possible opportunity in 1880. Rufina established connections with the VALAAM *startsy* (*see* STARETS). She briefly moved to MOSCOW before returning to her native region and entering the POKROV convent of Verkhoturie in 1900. In 1911 Rufina was appointed abbess of a convent in Cherdyn, closed since the reign of Catherine II. She gathered a community there, committed the nuns to charitable work and collaborated with Bishop Feofan of Solikamsk, who was martyred by the Bolsheviks on 11 December 1917 (*see* NEW MARTYRS). In 1919 Rufina and her nuns were evacuated with the White Army, accepting care of 150 orphans on the trek eastwards. A new convent and orphanage were organized in Vladivostok, briefly capital of the Far Eastern Republic, but Sovietization of the republic necessitated another move to Manchuria (*see* CHINA) in 1923. With the support of JONAS POKROVSKY, the Convent of the Tikhvin Mother of God in Harbin was founded in 1924 and, from 1927, a daughter house in Shanghai. Here Rufina worked closely with JOHN MAX-IMOVITCH until she died. She is commemorated on 15 August.

Thaisia Salopiv (1989), *Abbess Thaisia: An Autobiography*. Platina, Cal.: St Herman of Alaska.
Ariadna (1984), 'Abbess Ruphina', *The Orthodox Word* 115.

D

Russian Orthodox church   Although the Russian Orthodox church marked the millennium of its foundation in 1988 this was an extended process which began a century or more earlier. Byzantine sources speak of a Russian diocese established by the patriarchate of CONSTANTINOPLE as early as 867. So momentous a development, declared Patriarch PHOTIOS (*c.*810–*c.*895), demonstrated that the warlike Russians could now be considered 'subjects and friends' of the Byzantine empire. By 874, these 'subjects and friends' had clearly gained sufficient status to be accorded an archbishop, although the location of his seat remains unclear.

The evidence of early Russian Christianity is scant; all the more gratifying, then, to learn of Russian Christians acting as co-signatories of a Russo-Byzantine treaty in 944. Some may have acted as supporters for the Kievan princess Ol'ga when she decided to link herself, and therefore, potentially, her subjects, with the Byzantine world by accepting baptism in Constantinople *c.*960. This was the first such symbolic act at her level of society, but it was not to meet with favour among her immediate successors. A determined pagan revival in the Kievan realm over the succeeding twenty-five years is reported in the later chronicles of KIEV and there is some archaeological evidence to support this.

In the event, Ol'ga's policy prevailed. By the end of the tenth century the Kievan elite was driven to accept that the economic, political, cultural and spiritual welfare of the Russian state could no longer be assured unless alliances were made with one of its monotheistic neighbours. These adhered to Islam, to Judaism or to Christianity, in either its Roman or its Byzantine form. According to the stylized account in the *Russian Primary Chronicle* (probably completed by AD 1116) the ruler of the day, Vladimir or Volodimer, sent envoys to each of the relevant religious centres, asking for each to be assessed. Their unqualified preference was for the religion of Constantinople. 'We know only that God abides there among them and their worship is superior to that of any other lands,' they reported after attending Hagia Sophia. 'For we cannot forget that beauty.' Some might think the narrative hardly more than a literary device. Nevertheless it prompted some historians to read into it a predisposition of the Russian people to treat beauty as a path to revelation.

Be that as it may, Vladimir duly accepted baptism (988) as part of a package deal with the Byzantine authorities which involved urgent military support for the latter. More important, it promoted Russia's assimilation to the Byzantine world. Thus the infant Russian church was to receive not only its hierarchy, but also its doctrine, liturgy, canon law, art and music from the Byzantine patriarchate, a dependency of which it remained for six centuries.

The conversion of Vladimir's people was accelerated by use of force. The pace of consequent acculturation was also swift, revealing the recipients' readiness to benefit therefrom. Acculturation and conversion were in turn abetted by the use of Church Slavonic for the translation of scriptural, liturgical, legal and literary texts. Both the new 'Cyrillic' alphabet and an imported corpus of translated work derived ultimately from the ninth-century mission of CYRIL AND METHODIUS to Moravia, with Bulgaria, presumably, as Russia's intermediary for them. Whether Bulgarian clergy made a direct contribution to the Kievan conversion process remains unclear. The contribution may have been of some importance. But the Priselkov hypothesis (1913) that the late tenth-century diocese of Russia was directly administered from OHRID is generally discounted.

A Byzantine metropolitan of all Rus took his seat in Kiev no later than 1037. Initially, the metropolitans were almost invariably Greek by origin and speech, though later Greek and Russian primates appear to have alternated. For almost as long as the Byzantine empire lasted, the metropolitan was to be its agent. He was therefore capable of adopting an independent stance *vis-à-vis* the local rulers when required. There were seven dioceses under his supervision in the early period, rising to fifteen by the mid-thirteenth century. Until the end of that century, Kiev was the actual primatial see, and remained the metropolitan's nominal seat even when displaced by the cities of VLADIMIR (1300) and then MOSCOW (1308). Only when Kiev fell under Polish–Lithuanian rule did the metropolitan adopt the title 'of Moscow and all Rus' (1458). A separate metropolitanate of Kiev was established that same year under Roman auspices, later coming once more under Constantinople (1470), but the coherence of the original metropolitanate was not re-established thereby.

Some monastic foundations date back to the early eleventh century, if not earlier. The most influential, the Kievan Caves monastery, was founded in 1051. Generally the monasteries adhered to the Studite rule, borrowed from Constantinople. By 1240 there were no fewer than sixty-eight monastic foundations. By contrast with foundations of the fourteenth and fifteenth centuries, the early monasteries were almost invariably urban in location, well placed to contribute to the educational, cultural and philan-thropic life of their secular environment. They also produced role models for the spiritual life, several of whom, like Feodosii, abbot of the Kievan Caves monastery itself (1091), were later canonized. But the first saints to gain national recognition (1072) were two young princes, Boris and Gleb, the 'PASSION BEARERS', who chose to die as followers of Christ rather than to resist violence. Many Russian saints were to be canonized over the succeeding centuries; no fewer than thirty-nine were added to the CALENDAR at the church councils of 1547 and 1549. The recognition of the early saints suggested a precocious maturity in the life of the newly founded local church.

The stability of the young church was severely tested by the Mongol invasion. Vladimir was sacked in 1238, Kiev two years later. This was the fate of almost every Russian city except NOVGOROD. More than two centuries were to pass before Mongol suzerainty was brought to an end. In the immediate aftermath of the invasion preach-ers, such as Metropolitan Kirill of Kiev and Bishop Serapion of Vladimir, saw the cataclysm as a punishment from God. Nevertheless, church leaders soon learnt that unsought and unprecedented gains could now accrue to the church. By 1257 it had become evident that the Mongol conquerors were to levy taxes on all and sundry, with exemptions for church property and personnel alone. Such was the Mongols' toleration of religious bodies, however alien to themselves. Thus the period of Mongol rule witnessed a marked increase in the prosperity and status of the church. Not unrelated is the flowering of Russian ICON painting at this time, reaching its apogee in the work of Andrei RUBLEV (c.1360–1430) and his contemporaries. Not unrelated also is the increase in the number and influence of monasteries and monastic land-holdings, much of this involving outreach into virgin lands. No less important were the spiritual achievements of monastic elders like SERGIUS OF RADONEZH (1314–92) and Nil of Sora, inspired by the reception of HESYCHAST teachings from ATHOS and the Byzantine world at large.

Nil is remembered also for his firm opposition to monastic land-holdings of any kind, an opposition which initially found favour with the land-hungry state authorities of the day. Monastic accumulation of tax-exempt properties and economic power was favoured by another and more prominent school of monks, the 'possessors'. Their most effective spokesman was Iosif of Volotsk (1439–1515). Under the auspices of such possessors, ambitious programmes of charitable work could be effectively promoted. For the present, the state decided to align itself with the possessors and to refrain from interference with inherited immunities. Nevertheless, such immunities were to be increasingly challenged, notably at the church councils of 1580 and 1584 (see NON-POSSESSORS).

In the same period, Muscovite diplomacy and duplicity scored a palpable success. In 1589, with the reluctant consent of the patriarch of Constantinople, the Russian metropolitanate was elevated to the dignity of a patriarchate, fifth in seniority among the patriarchates of the East. This confirmed its hitherto self-determined status as an 'autonomous' church (1448). It also compensated for the fall of Constantinople to the OTTOMANS (1453), and the associated diminution of its ecclesial standing from the Russian point of view. Indeed, there were Russians who argued at the turn of the fifteenth and sixteenth centuries that two Romes, Rome proper and Constantinople, the New Rome, had already fallen, while Moscow, the THIRD ROME, had displaced them, and for ever. One thing was sure: Moscow was now alone among the EASTERN ORTHODOX patriarchates in being free of Islamic rule.

Not that the first ROME was to be discounted in determining the status and orientation of the Russian church. The 1448 decision about autonomy had been taken in the aftermath of a crisis brought about by Isidor, metropolitan of Moscow 1436–41. The Moscow establishment, church and state alike, had spurned his initiatives in furthering formal reunion of the Eastern and Western churches at the Council of Ferrara/FLORENCE (1438–9). Isidor had been deposed and the reunion nullified.

By 1458 the southern metropolitanate of Kiev was taking a different view of the matter and accepted the decisions of the Ferrrara/Florence council for a time. In due course, being under Polish–Lithuanian rule, the southern metropolitanate acceded to a further union with Rome, which was signed at Brest (1596). The resulting UNIATE church, even when it was in conflict with the local Orthodox population, was still in a position to exercise an influence on the latter, affecting among other things its theological vocabulary, its iconography and its worship. As Muscovy and Ukraine entered into increasingly close relations during the second half of the seventeenth century and the metropolitanate of Kiev came under Moscow's jurisdiction in the years 1685–7, the influence of Ukrainian clergy in the Russian church tended to increase. Notable as a channel of this influence was a pioneer school of higher education in the Muscovite realm, the Helleno-Greek Academy (1685). Here was the starting point for the later theological academies of Kiev (1701), St Petersburg (1797), Kazan (1797) and Sergiev Posad (1814).

Yet there was also an ingrained reluctance among the Orthodox to accept Western influences in church life, or indeed at all. A spokesman of the Orthodox resistance was Patriarch Filaret of Moscow (c.1554–1634), who had himself been imprisoned by the Catholic Poles for eight years prior to his enthronement in 1618. Opposition to all Western influences was to be most firmly expressed in that conservative milieu which gave rise to the Old Ritualist (OLD BELIEVERS) movement halfway through the century.

Patriarch Filaret, father and mentor of the first Romanov tsar, sought a prominent role in church and state alike. He adopted the title Great Lord. One of his successors, NIKON (1605–81), insisted that the title spoke of the church's pre-eminence in church–state relations. This went further than the Byzantine theory of 'symphony' between the two spheres, reaffirmed at the Moscow church council of 1551. Nikon was opposed by the tsar, deposed (1659) and disgraced (1666). His failure to assert and safeguard the primacy of the church paved the way for the subjugation of the church administration to the bureaucracy of Peter the Great in the eighteenth century.

Nikon is remembered also for the liturgical reforms which he vigorously promoted in an over-ambitious attempt to bring Russian practice into line with Greek. Well-intentioned though they were, these reforms were widely regarded as heretical and alienated large numbers of the faithful, many of whom, like the archpriest AVVAKUM Petrov (1621–82), went to the stake rather than accept their legitimacy. Thus was born that schismatic Old Ritualist movement, which, with its various sub-divisions, has not yet been reintegrated with its parent church.

At the death of Patriarch Adrian (1700), the role of patriarch was consciously allowed to lapse. Peter the Great placed his hopes successively on two church leaders of markedly Protestant orientation, Metropolitan Stefan Iavorskii (1658–1722) and Archbishop Feofan Prokopovich (1681–1736). It was the latter who provided much of the text for Peter's *Ecclesiastical Regulations* (1720) which determined how the Russian church was administered until the fraught summer of 1917. Although it concerned the structure of a church with pronounced conciliar traditions, the text was drawn up in camera at the emperor's behest.

The same emperor nominated his own representative as supervisor of the new governing body of the Russian church, the Holy Synod. No matter how many bishops of that synod subsequently validated them with their signatures, the new regulations accorded the signatories themselves little more than titular status. Appropriately enough, the title of the synod's senior civil servant was given in plain German: *Oberprokuror*; for the Lutheran G. W. Leibnitz (1646–1716) was the ultimate source of much of the regulations' text. The church's administration now took the form of a government department. No longer was there any question of symphony between church and state, still less of state subordination to the church.

In 1762–4, soon after Catherine the Great's accession, the church was deprived of extensive land-holdings and, with them, of over 2 million serfs. The church's economic dependence on the state now matched its administrative subjugation. A symbol of this subjugation was Metropolitan Arsenii Matseevich of Rostov (1696–1776), whose protests against these actions of the state led to his demotion and imprisonment.

Monasteries were among the bodies hardest hit under the new dispensation. But this did not prevent a fresh flowering of the spiritual life in the monastic milieu by the turn of the eighteenth century. Most influential in its promotion was the elder PAISSII VELICHKOVSKII (1722–94). His partial translation into Slavonic (1793) of the recently completed PHILOKALIA provided this revival with its textbook. Paissy is remembered also for his advocacy of the JESUS PRAYER and his validation of the informal institution of the monastic elder or STARETS. For much of his life the Ukrainian Paissii lived on the periphery of the Russian empire, on Athos and in Moldavia. But his influence was to be felt in many Russian monasteries, especially Optina Pustyn'. Among Optina's renowned *startsy* were Leonid Nagolkin (1768–1841), Makarii Ivanov (1788–1860) and Amvrosii Grenkov (1812–91) (*see* OPTINO). No less important was their radiant contemporary at Sarov, SERAPHIM (1759–1833).

Optina's influence was spread also through its publications, including Russian translations of Greek patristic texts. Together with the serial publications initiated by the theological academies, translations such as these paved the way for the work of theologians, something notably lacking in centuries gone by. There were also original writers, such as the Slavophile A. S. KHOMIAKOV (1804–60), who depended less on patristic sources than on early nineteenth-century German and romantic thought. In the process, Khomiakov helped to develop an ecclesiology centred on communality and catholicity, *sobornost*. With Khomiakov began a school of Russian religious thinkers which included P. A. FLORENSKY (1882–1943) and S. N. BULGAKOV (1871–1944). By contrast, a return to patristic tradition was advocated by such theologians as G. V. FLOROVSKY (1893–1979) and V. N. Lossky (1903–58). The Russian Revolution was to stifle the development of theological thought on Soviet soil, and Florensky ended his days in a Soviet forced labour camp. By contrast, the emigration to the West of outstanding theologians, among them Bulgakov, Florovsky and Lossky, acted as a stimulus to Western thinkers, not least in the ecumenical movements.

Until the Revolution of 1917, the Russian state sponsored Orthodox missionary activities in a variety of non-Russian territories linked to the empire by conquest or trade. There were missions in ALASKA (from 1794) and Japan (from 1861), not to mention the Zyrian, Tatar, Chuvash and Votiak areas of the empire's landmass. Religious propaganda was at a discount after 1917, and in 1929 the right to any sort of religious propaganda was formally withdrawn.

In the early part of the twentieth century much thought was given to possible reform – structural, liturgical and social – of the established church. Many churchmen felt that there was room for a plenary council of the Russian church, the like of which had not been seen for two and a half centuries. But the work of an officially sponsored Pre-Conciliar Commission (1907) and a subsequent Pre-Conciliar Consultation (1911–13) came to nothing. By the existing statutes only the tsar could convene such a council. Yet the tsar temporized and delayed its convocation until 'a favourable time shall come'. Paradoxically, the professedly Orthodox monarchy needed to be brought to an end before the council could take place. When it finally assembled in the summer of 1917, its days were numbered and its promise curtailed. Among its decisions was that a patriarch be elected once again to lead and represent the church. But this was carefully qualified: the patriarch, together with his administration, was ultimately answerable to the council itself. Three candidates were elected. The new primate was then chosen by lot. This fell on Tikhon Belavin (1865–1925), only recently elected as metropolitan of Moscow.

A Bolshevik decree of 23 January 1918 which brought about the separation of church from state in no way guaranteed the freedom of the church to act as it deemed fit, or even to survive at all. It was subjected to all kinds of indignities and constraints and simultaneously deprived of the rights of a person-at-law, as were all its clergy. With Tikhon began a remarkable line of martyrs and confessors. Confiscation and destruction of church property brought the secularization programme of Catherine II almost to completion. A distinct programme was organized for the confiscation of church valuables in 1921–2, allegedly to combat famine; its covert aim was to bring the church into disrepute. In its aftermath, Patriarch Tikhon was arrested (1922) and the state sponsored ambitious pro-communist reformers to supplant him. This they proceeded to do at their own council of 1923. However, their schismatic and fragmented movement found increasingly less grassroots support. By the end of the Second World War it had vanished.

When he emerged from prison in 1923, the patriarch was required to affirm that he was 'no longer an enemy of the Soviet government'. He reiterated this statement on the eve of his death. But there was no *quid pro quo*. Tikhon's deputy Petr Polianskii was exiled and eventually shot (1936). The Soviet authorities were to demand a more abject declaration of loyalty than Tikhon's from Metropolitan Sergii Stragorodskii (1861–1944) when they released him from prison and recognized his church administration (1927), a declaration ill received by the body of the church. In any case it brought only formal benefits, if any. Furthermore, it confirmed the suspicions of émigré churchmen, many of whom, under the leadership of Metropolitan Antonii Khrapovitskii (1873–1936), had already formed an independent church administration, the episcopal synod of the RUSSIAN ORTHODOX CHURCH ABROAD, in the early 1920s. Sergii's declaration prompted yet others, led by Metropolitan Evlogii Georgievskii (1866–1946), to join the patriarchate of Constantinople (1931).

New Soviet laws of 1929 confirmed and extended restrictions on church life. The following decade witnessed the dissolution of the few remaining monasteries, the reduction of parish churches to a matter of hundreds and the imprisonment of millions. Anti-religious propaganda presented this 'assault on heaven' as a beneficial piece of social engineering. Yet the census of 1937, at the height of the Stalin terror, elicited so positive a response to the question on belief in God that the result simply had to be suppressed.

The war of 1941–5 proved a turning point in the modern history of the church. Stalin recognized the potential of the church to boost morale at home; he also saw the propaganda value of advertising 'freedom of religion' to his allies. In 1943 he allowed the designation of Metropolitan Sergii as patriarch and, more important, the eventual reopening of theological schools. Overt parish life was resumed, often emerging from the 'catacombs'. At the same time, the revival of church life which the Germans had permitted in occupied regions was not simply nullified once the invaders were expelled.

Continued toleration of the church was conditional on its acceptance of a strictly delimited life, which concerned itself almost entirely with worship. In exchange it was required to offer its services in the diplomatic field and so participated in the World Peace Council (from 1949), the Christian Peace Conference (from 1958) and the World Council of Churches (from 1961). Not that the state honoured its reciprocal, albeit unpublished, obligations; rather, the period of Khrushchev's ascendancy was marked by a return to overt persecution (1958–64) and the closure of something like a half of the Orthodox churches then open. The patriarch of the post-war decades, Aleksii Simanskii (1877–1970) uttered one dignified protest in public (1960), but otherwise maintained a sorrowful silence on the subject. All the more dignified, by contrast, were the dissident statements of Archbishop Ermogen Golubev (1896–1978) and the priests Gleb Iakunin and Nikolai Eshliman. Each in turn was marginalized by the church administration. Iakunin was subsequently imprisoned for his defence of believers' rights (1979–88). Throughout the decades the state sought to ensure that the church continued to be docile, inward-looking, loyal. It imposed its views through the agency of a governmental Council for Religious Affairs, founded in 1943, reorganized and renamed in 1965.

Contrary to expectations, the millennium of the Russian church (1988) helped to bring it out of its prevailing shadows. It was permitted to adopt new statutes, which offered greater freedom to its constituent parts. A new patriarch, Aleksii Ridiger, was elected, rather than appointed by agreement with the state (1989). By the end of communist rule (1991), the church was well placed to proceed with its programmes, which could now concern education, charity and mission. Its members swelled by many millions, since baptism was no longer monitored by the state.

This has had its drawbacks, since not all baptisms were necessarily the result of spiritual zeal. A church which had become profoundly conservative in Soviet times as a defensive measure, has now become no less conservative by choice. Liberal clergy are at a discount. Some have been disciplined and even, as in the case of Iakunin in 1994, unfrocked. Anti-Semitism, an aberration of pre-revolutionary right-wing groupings in the Russian church, has sometimes been propagated. Various kinds of nationalism threaten at least the administrative unity of the Moscow patriarchate, most obviously in the newly independent UKRAINE. Whereas the present Russian constitution makes provision for a free church in a free state, the Moscow patriarchate would clearly prefer a dominant role among the denominations and religions of the new Russia, even the status of an established church, as of old. Positive use has been made of many opportunities, and there is no longer a paucity of churches, monasteries or theological schools. But the hopes which were previously entertained by many an observer for the purgation of the church by the trials of communism have yet to be sustained.

Davis, N. (1995), *A Long Walk to Church: A Contemporary History of Russian Ortho-doxy*. Oxford: Westview.
Fennell, J. (1995), *A History of the Russian Church to 1448*. London: Longman.
Pospielovsky, D. (1984), *The Russian Church under the Soviet Regime 1917–1982*, 2 vols. Crestwood, NY: St Vladimir's Seminary Press.
Freeze, G. L. (1983), *The Parish Clergy in Nineteenth-century Russia: Crisis, Reform, Counter-Reform*. Princeton: Princeton University Press.
Meyendorff, J. (1981), *Byzantium and the Rise of Russia: A Study of Byzantino-Russian Relations in the Fourteenth Century*. Cambridge: Cambridge University Press.
Cracraft, J. (1971), *The Church Reform of Peter the Great*. London: Macmillan.
Zernov, N. (1964), *The Russian Religious Renaissance of the Twentieth Century*. London: Darton, Longman & Todd.
Fedotov, G. P. (1946–66), *The Russian Religious Mind*, 2 vols. Cambridge, Mass.: Harvard University Press.
Curtiss, J. S. (1940), *Church and State in Russia: The Last Years of the Empire 1900–1917*. New York: Columbia University Press.
Frere, W. H. (1918), *Some Links in the Chain of Russian Church History*. London: Faith Press.

SH

Russian Orthodox Church Abroad   Otherwise known as the Russian Church in Exile, the Russian Synod, the Russian Orthodox Church outside Russia (ROCOR) and the Karlovtsians, the ROCA has played a disproportionately important role in the history of the church in the twentieth century for its size, now about 150,000 parishioners, 330 parishes and 24 monasteries in the DIASPORA. Originally formed as a group of south Russian bishops who found themselves in White-held territory and cut off from the patriarch in Moscow during the Russian civil war of 1919–21, ROCA received what it regards as a firm canonical foundation through ukaz no. 362 of the patriarch, the Holy Synod and the Higher Church Council dated 7/20 November 1920, which allowed bishops who found themselves out of communication with the higher church administration in Moscow to form autonomous groups of dioceses led by the eldest hierarch among them. The leader of the ROCA from 1919 to his death in 1936 was Metropolitan Antonii Khrapovitskii of Kiev.

At the end of the civil war, the ROCA emigrated from Russia together with the retreating White troops, eventually setting up headquarters in Karlovtsy, Serbia, as an autonomous administration under the protection of the Serbian church on the basis of canon 39 of the Sixth ECUMENICAL COUNCIL. The headquarters moved to New York after the Second World War. The church's right to form such an administration was recognized in the beginning by all the AUTOCEPHALOUS churches except the Romanian. When, however, ROCA began to rebuke, first the Ecumenical Patriarchate for what it saw as imperialism at the expense of the Russian church and for what were claimed to be uncanonical innovations such as the new CALENDAR, and, from 1928, the Moscow patriarchate for what it condemned as submission to the communists, this recognition was gradually withdrawn by all except two local churches – the Serbian and Jerusalem patriarchates, with which ROCA remains in unofficial communion. In the 1960s ROCA came into communion with the True Orthodox (Old Calendar) Church of Greece; but divisions among the OLD CALENDARISTS meant that by 1995 the ROCA was in communion with only one branch of the Greek Old Calendarists, the 'Cyprianites', and with the Romanian Old Calendarists.

Although not in communion with the Moscow patriarchate, the ROCA always considered itself that part of the Russian Orthodox church which found itself in freedom and able to speak the truth openly about the situation of the church inside Russia. A fierce critic of the Moscow patriarchate, which it claimed had submitted to the communists and was lying about the true situation of believers, ROCA championed the cause of the TRUE ORTHODOX or Catacomb Church of Russia, which broke away from the Moscow patriarchate in 1927–8. Since the 1960s the ROCA has been a vociferous opponent of the World Council of Churches and the participation of Orthodox churches in it.

In 1981 the ROCA canonized the Holy New Martyrs and Confessors of Russia. This act had a significant impact in Russia and provided a stimulus to the revival of Orthodoxy in the Gorbachev years. Then, in 1983, the ROCA anathematized ECU-MENISM, an act which has so far had less of an impact but which may well become more important as the anti-ecumenism movement in the Moscow patriarchate gathers pace.

In 1990 the ROCA decided that the time had come to return to the motherland and open parishes on Russian soil in direct opposition to the Moscow patriarchate. At first, this movement had considerable success, and many parishes from both the Moscow patriarchate and the Catacomb Church joined the ROCA, called in Russia the Free Russian Orthodox Church (FROC). However, a variety of factors, determined opposition from the Moscow patriarchate and local political authorities, a questionable choice of bishops for the FROC and poorly managed relations with the Catacomb Church, most of which remains out of communion with the FROC, have contributed to a slowing in the growth of the movement. In February 1995 five FROC bishops broke away from communion with the ROCA, forming their own autonomous administration. It remains to be seen whether the ROCA can recover from this blow and fulfil its aim of becoming the focus of regeneration in the Russian Orthodox church.

Nazarov, M. (1992), 'Tri Vietvi Zarubezhnogo Pravoslavia', *Posev* 1.
Moss, V. (1991), 'The Free Russian Orthodox Church', *Report on the USSR* 44.

VM

Russian religious philosophy   Reflection upon the religious dimension of human experience became prominent in Russian thought during the nineteenth century, though it had long existed in the form of saints' lives and related writings issuing from the country's strong monastic tradition.

Awareness of the need for a type of reflection which could accommodate the insights of Orthodox spirituality and which promoted the integral nature of the person, 'wholeness', 'integrality' or in Russian *tsel'nost*, was expressed in a celebrated article by the Slavophile thinker Ivan Kireevskii (1806–56) entitled 'On the Necessity and Possibility of New Principles in Philosophy'.

Petr Chaadaev's *Philosophical Letters*, written in 1829 and first published in 1836, had set in motion the increasingly acrimonious dispute that marked Russian polemical writings during the nineteenth century, between advocates of emulation of West European society, the Westernizers or *zapadniki*, and those convinced that Russia possessed social structures and spiritual values, adherence to which would secure the nation's welfare, the Slavophiles or *slavyanofily*. This dispute, still pursued in the post-Soviet era, amounted to a quarrel regarding what form of society, West European or Russian, provides the optimum conditions for the growth of the human personality (*lichnost*). These matters engaged the minds of religious and secular thinkers alike, and the debate extended into areas such as the philosophy of history, which has continued to be a prominent element in Russian thought, both in its religious and secular variants.

Russian religious philosophy came into its own with Vladimir SOLOVYOV (1853–1900), whose writing spanned the last quarter of the nineteenth century. In his person, his work and his preoccupations he exemplified some of the most characteristic positive features of Russian religious thought. These include an abiding concern with those values that honour and secure the growth of the human person in freedom; a keen awareness of the ethical dimension of social relations and organization; and strong measures of idealism and consistency in applying the tenets of Christian belief to problems of the contemporary world.

Solovyov was the first to provide anything in Russian philosophy approaching a coherent system. Highly competent in epistemology and metaphysics and uniquely well versed in the writings of Plato, the Neoplatonists and German idealism, Solovyov wrote numerous works which he intended to serve as the basis for a synthesis of religious and secular thought. He readily acknowledged the achievements of the most far-reaching and inspired pre-Christian philosophers, Plato in particular, but also set out the deficiencies of their systems from the traditional Christian point of view, aiming to present the agnostic and increasingly secularized Russian intelligentsia with sound reasons for re-examining the nature of Christian belief and values with a view to their adopting these, thus healing the serious rift between intelligentsia and people.

Solovyov's reappraisal of Christian values, carried out after a brief but strong adherence to atheism in his youth, proved decisive for the direction taken by many, though not all, subsequent philosophers in Russia. A succession of gifted thinkers explored the common ground between philosophy and theology and wrote extensively, sharing many preoccupations.

Solovyov's writings were the fruit of deep personal religious experience and, consequently, attach importance to experiential aspects of prayer and the sacramental life of the church. As a lay believer with a particularly strong commitment to Christian values, he resembled other religious philosophers in Russia. Sergei BULGAKOV (1871–1944) and Pavel FLORENSKY (1882–1938) were exceptions in being clergy. The Russian Orthodox church regarded some of Solovyov's ideas with suspicion, even animosity. Vasilii Rozanov (1856–1919) and Lev Shestov (1866–1938) were even further removed from the ecclesiastical establishment than was Solovyov, yet they too pursued concerns that were religious and philosophical. The spiritual aspirations of the laity represent a singularly important element in Russian religious philosophy, and the laity's fateful encounter in the mid-nineteenth century with West European secular ideas, radical socialism and utopianism was recorded in fictional form by Fedor Dostoevskii (1821–81), whose contribution to religious thought is likely to endure longer than the influence of some Russian figures usually deemed theologians and philosophers.

Russian religious philosophy is distinctive in its reflections on All-Unity or Pan-Unity (Russian: *vseedinstvo*). Vladimir Solovyov, Sergei Bulgakov, Pavel Florensky, Semyon Frank (1877–1950) and Lev Karsavin (1882–1952) were the philosophers most concerned with this area of speculation. Based on a close reading of a large body of esoteric literature, including the works of the seventeenth-century German mystic Jakob Boehme, the Russian philosophers' purpose was to express the interrelatedness and interdependence of all forms of existence. They recognized this insight as expressed in iconographic form within their own spiritual tradition, and sought means to articulate it in a coherent and organic synthesis of theological, philosophical and scientific speculation. The title of Pavel Florensky's *The Pillar and Ground of Truth* (1914) reveals the spirit and scope of the enterprise.

For Solovyov, Bulgakov and Florensky in particular All-Unity was closely bound up with Sophia, the personification of DIVINE WISDOM, and the attendant symbolism they traced in the mystical literature from which they drew inspiration. Other thinkers in Russia (notably Semyon Frank) were less attracted to the Sophianic motif but nevertheless retained a strong emphasis upon the interrelatedness and interdependence of all forms of life. Their Slavophile precursors, and notably Alexei KHOMIAKOV (1804–60), had underlined the importance in Orthodox spirituality of *sobornost*, that is, the communality-in-freedom of believers in Christ.

Other prominent characteristics of Russian religious philosophy in the nineteenth and twentieth centuries have been its anthropocentric nature and, arising from this, its preoccupation with the application of ethical principles at all levels of the organization of society. This overriding concern has rendered some philosophical schemes particularly susceptible to utopianism, but, on the other hand, Russian philosophers have also proved able to discern the negative aspects of utopian thinking. Nikolai BERDIAEV (1874–1948), whose works in English, French and German translations reached a readership beyond his country and his place of exile, achieved fame largely through his writings on the false nature of secular utopias and of the social experiment then being conducted in the Soviet Union.

A further effect of the Russians' concern with the ethical dimension has been the relative paucity of reflection on legal structures and systems and their role in social organization. That imbalance between the ethical and the legal has been referred to variously as ethical maximalism and legal nihilism, *eticheskiy maximalizm* and *pravovoy nigilizm*. It has numerous variants among religious and secular thinkers, notably among the Slavophiles, and rests upon the notion that ethical imperatives can be understood by the innermost and vital side of the human personality, whereas legal norms are imposed from outside and not infrequently conflict with the individual citizen's intuition of what is morally acceptable. In their own different ways Dostoevskii and Tolstoy subscribed to this understanding of the relationship between ethics and law, and their ideas on this subject could justifiably be cited as instances of ethical maximalism.

Compared to philosophical traditions in other countries, the Russian tradition has placed relatively little emphasis upon epistemology as distinct from other branches of philosophy. In part, this is because Russians tended to value a broader synthesis of knowledge, in which faith also played a role, and worked in the spirit of German philosophers such as Friedrich Schelling. The tendency towards system-building was, however, firmly resisted by Lev Shestov, whose critical articles on Spinoza, Solovyov, Tolstoy and other figures put in question the very nature of the relationship between faith and reason and strongly denied the applicability of reason to the domain of religion. Shestov brought out the contrast by juxtaposing what he called the values of Athens and the values of Jerusalem; he heavily favoured 'the God of Abraham and Isaac' rather than the abstract 'God' of the philosophers and system-builders.

In the 1970s and 1980s, but especially since the demise of the Soviet Union in 1991, there has been a very marked resurgence of interest among Russians in this entire tradition of religious-philosophical speculation. The early 1990s have seen the publication in accessible editions of works by virtually all the noteworthy Russian philosophers of the nineteenth and twentieth centuries. Furthermore, this interest is reflected in scholarly and ecclesiastical journals. It remains to be seen whether this tradition of thought can or will become truly assimilated by a wider public whose education was completed in the years of Soviet rule.

Kornblatt, J. D. and Gustafson, R. F., eds (1996), *Russian Religious Thought*. Madison: University of Wisconsin Press.
Spidlik, T. (1994). *L'Idée russe: Une autre vision de l'homme*. Troyes: Editions Fates.
Copleston, F. C. (1988), *Russian Religious Philosophy: Selected Aspects*. Tunbridge Wells: Search Press.
Zernov, N. (1963), *The Russian Religious Renaissance of the Twentieth Century*. London: DLT.

JNS

Russian sects   Collective name conventionally given to a number of religious movements, the oldest of which, the Khlysty or Khristovoverie, goes back to the seventeenth century, the same period as the origin of the OLD BELIEVERS. Khlysty sought Christ's spirit in the depths of their own souls rather than the rituals of the Orthodox church, whose doctrine, traditions and authority they rejected, following leaders they called 'Christs'. In the early centuries Khlysty and other sectarians sometimes retained a certain degree of contact with the Orthodox church and occasionally attended services. Their worship used song and dance to attain a state of ecstatic, Spirit-filled exaltation for which they prepared by fasting and ASCETICISM.

The Postniki (Fasters), an austere, tightly organized group, separated off under the Christ Kopylov in the eighteenth century, then split in the mid-nineteenth century, producing the Old Israel and then *c*.1885 the New Israel, each following a different Christ. The New Israel practised the re-enactment of events in sacred history, sometimes with great numbers of participants. Many Postniki emigrated to Uruguay in 1911–12.

The Skoptsy (Castrators) emerged from the Khlysty in the late eighteenth century. Led by the Christ Selivanov, who introduced the 'baptism by fire', they practised castration of males, which many women paralleled by cutting away their breasts.

In the late eighteenth century the Orthodox Archbishop Amvrosii of Ekaterinoslav denounced as Dukhobors (Spirit-Wrestlers) a group which had emerged in the mid-century in Ukraine and then come under the leadership in Amvrosii's archdiocese of Silvan Kolesnikov. By the end of the eighteenth century the Dukhobors had become the objects of state persecution and oppression, and when in 1802 Tsar Alexander I offered to resettle Dukhobors in the Tavrida region in Crimea the long saga of Dukhobor migration and resettlement had begun. Other groups were to be resettled in Transcaucasia. Under the leadership of Savelii Kapustin the Tavrida Dukhobors severed all residual involvement in Orthodox religious rites, and practised a life of stern, upright morality. Their emphasis on pacifism, hard work and mutual help was put to a severe test when Nicolas I attempted to force military service and conversion to Orthodoxy on the Dukhobors. The demand for an oath of loyalty from all citizens of the empire in 1894 furnished the occasion for the great Dukhobor leader Peter Verigin (1859–1924) to call for a refusal of the oath, a rejection of the power and authority of the state and of all forms of militarism, and a reformation of life involving vegetarianism and abstention from alcohol and tobacco. In 1895 a mass burning of weapons took place among the Dukhobors of the Caucasus, which led to further acts of repression. Eventually in 1897 the government gave the Dukhobors permission to emigrate and several thousand moved to Canada, where in 1903 Peter Verigin joined them. At first they were granted homesteads mainly in Saskatchewan, but when they refused an oath of allegiance imposed in 1905 were dispossessed, many moving to communally purchased land in British Columbia. The community divided into uncompromisingly traditionalist and more assimilationist groups.

At the heart of Dukhobor religion is a vivid sense of the presence of the Christ-spirit in all things, especially all living things. They refuse to treat the BIBLE as an external authority, emphasizing rather the illuminating presence of God within the individual and the community. Christ is a sinless human being; he and other spiritual leaders they recognize differ from other human beings in the greatness of the divine spark illuminating him. Baptism was abandoned, together with the use of ICONS and all traditional forms of Orthodox worship, the priesthood, hierarchy and ecclesiastical law.

The Molokans (Milk-drinkers) or Spiritual Christians emerged in the same regions as the Dukhobors at a similar period. The formation of the community was strongly influenced by the leadership of Semen Uklein. Molokans, though friendly towards the Dukhobors and often similar in lifestyle, differ sharply from them in centring their religious observance on the authority of the Bible. Molokan communities traditionally attempted to maintain biblical dietary rules and had their own butchers. Several divisions appeared in the community, the most significant between the Postoiannye, the 'Steadfast', who claim to represent the original Molokan tradition, and the Pryguny, the 'Leapers', named from the jumping, dancing movements used in their worship. The Leapers show great respect to the prophets within the community, who have a significant role in worship; *The Spirit and Life* is a collection of prophetic works, which the Leapers use in worship.

A number of Molokans emigrated to America, and there are several Molokan meeting houses on the west coast. The vast majority of Molokans remained in what became the USSR, where their communities withered under state oppression, but have now re-emerged as visible worshipping communities, their known membership now roughly similar to the number of American Molokans. A much smaller community migrated from America to Australia in the 1960s.

Molokan worship is characterized by the recognition of a variety of ministries or functions, elders, singers, readers, and, in some communities, prophets, each of whom has a distinct role to play in the service. Both Molokans and Dukhobors maintain a rich tradition of unaccompanied singing in worship, the Molokans in particular making great use of sung scriptural verses.

The doctrine, lifestyle and worship of the Russian sects often resemble those of religious movements which emerged from the Radical Reformation. They represent, however, distinctly Eastern Christian traditions of reform, and maintain a strong sense of ethnic identity.

Friesen, J. W. and Verigin, M. (1996), *The Community Doukhobors: A People in Transition*. Ottawa: Borealis Press.

Hardwick, S. W. (1993), *Russian Refuge: Religion, Migration and Settlement on the North American Pacific Rim*. Chicago: University of Chicago Press.

Reid, D. G. et al., eds (1990), *Dictionary of Christianity in America*. Downers Grove, Ill.: Inter Varsity Press.

Janzen, W. (1990), *The Experience of Mennonite, Hutterite and Doukhobor Communities in Canada*. Toronto: University of Toronto Press.

Lane, C. (1979), *Christian Religion in the Soviet Union*. London: Allen & Unwin.

Berokoff, J. K., trans. (1966), Rudametkin, M. G., *Selections from the Book of Spirit and Life Including the Book of Prayers and Songs*. Whittier, Cal.

Elkinton, J. S. (1903), *The Doukhobors: Their History in Russia, their Migration to Canada*. Philadelphia: Ferris & Leach.

DM

Ruthenia Ukrainian-speaking regions adjoining Slovakia and long associated with Hungary were united to Czechoslovakia after the First World War, annexed by Hungary in 1938 and incorporated in Soviet Ukraine in 1945. The Ruthenians and neighbouring Lemkos in Poland were mainly GREEK CATHOLIC from the early modern period, but a movement towards Eastern Orthodoxy had gathered momentum in the closing decades of the Austro-Hungarian Empire. Many Ruthenians emigrating to America embraced Eastern Orthodoxy in the same period and formed the basis for the ORTHODOX CHURCH IN AMERICA, the OCA.

See also MAXIM SANDOVITCH.

DB

· S ·

sacred utensils   In the Byzantine rite the principal utensils used in the celebration of the Divine Liturgy are the chalice, paten, star, lance, sponge, spoon and veils. The development of the PROTHESIS rite, with its elaborate arrangement of bread particles on the paten, has affected the form of the vessels. The paten is normally raised on a foot, easily held without disturbing the portions arranged on its surface. The asteriskos or star, two strips of metal, joined at their centres and bent downwards, is intended to prevent the silk veils from disturbing the arrangement on the paten. The lance is used to cut the loaf, or loaves, during the preparation rite and to divide the consecrated bread at the communion. Portions of the consecrated bread are placed in the chalice before the communion of the laity, who are communicated by means of the spoon (in Greek, *labis*, which means not spoon but 'tongs', a name derived from the vision of Isaias, where a seraph takes a burning coal from the altar in tongs and touches the prophet's lips with it). This is taken as a type of the eucharist, which cleanses from sin, and hence the spoon used is named 'tong'. The words of the seraph, 'See, this has touched your lips. It will take away your iniquities and cleanse your sins,' follow the reception of communion.

The increasing use of symbolic explanations of the liturgy influenced the under-standing of the sacred vessels. The lance came to symbolize the lance that pierced the side of Christ, and is so used when the priest at the proskomidi or PROTHESIS pierces the side of the Lamb with the lance in a purely symbolic gesture. The star originally was held to symbolize the firmament of heaven, the paten the round earth. At the centre of earth stands Christ, the Lamb, surrounded by the communion of saints; above, the firmament, or vault of heaven. Originally the placing of the star over the paten was accompanied by the words: 'By the word of the Lord the heavens were made firm.' This text is still used when the bishop covers the relics to be placed in the altar of a new church and the DEACON at the liturgy still says to the priest at the placing of the star: 'Master, make firm'. By the late middle ages, however, the rite of preparation was equated with the birth of Christ in Bethlehem and the star became that which guided the Magi and the words used those from St Matthew's Gospel: 'A star came and stood over the place where the young child lay'. This explanation also influenced iconography. Older schemes have the deposition of Christ from the Cross, or the entombment, behind the table of the Proskomidi; more recent ones tend to have the Nativity.

Traditionally two sponges are used. The larger one is placed in the chalice when not in use. Like the lance this has an obvious symbolic significance, but is also practical, since it helps absorb any moisture left after the chalice has been purified. The smaller sponge is kept in the ANTIMENSION, and is used to help collect crumbs from the paten and antimension. At the ordination of a priest, the bishop, after the invocation of the Holy Spirit, takes the consecrated bread, places it on the sponge and hands it to the new priest with the words: 'Take this pledge and guard it until the Coming of our Lord Jesus Christ, when he is going to require it from you'. The new priest holds it until it is needed for the fraction. Three veils, or covers, made of vestment material, are used; two smaller ones to cover the chalice and paten respectively and a large one, called in Greek *aer*, to cover both. The last is waved over the holy gifts during the recitation of the creed. At a pontifical liturgy, the bishop bows his head on the altar and the concelebrating priests wave the *aer* over him. In some places metal lids replace the two smaller veils.

E

Sava Nemanja (d. 1236)   The 'Enlightener of the Serbians' and a member of the royal Nemanja dynasty, Rastko, son of Stefan Nemanja (d. 1200), fled the Serbian court for Mount ATHOS where he became a monk and took the name Sava. His father, following his example, joined Sava as the monk Symeon; together they founded HILANDAR monastery. From this Athonite base, Sava travelled to CONSTANTINO-PLE and made pilgrimages to the Holy Land and elsewhere. He secured the independence of the SERBIAN Orthodox church; as its first archbishop he founded numerous churches, monasteries and charitable institutions throughout Serbia and the Near East. Sava intervened in the politics of the region, reconciling his warring brothers and the various neighbours of Serbia. This universally respected hierarch died in Trnovo, the guest of the Bulgarian tsar. His relics were translated to MILEŠEVA monastery and with his father, Symeon, he is held to be the patron of the northern Balkan regions. As such, Sava is an example of the ideal of national Orthodox churches interacting harmoniously together and coexisting peacefully with all neighbours. Sava is one of the most popular Orthodox saints; this was acknowledged by the Turks, who felt it necessary to burn his relics publicly (1594). He is commemorated on 14 January and 27 April; Symeon Nemanja is commemorated on 13 February.

DB

Velimirović, Nicolas (1951), *The Life of Saint Sava*. Libertyville, Ill.

Seleucia, Council of (410)   The first synod of the CHURCH OF THE EAST fully documented in the SYNODIKON ORIENTALE, held in SELEUCIA-CTESIPHON south of modern Baghdad, was called on the authority of the Sasanian king Yazdagird I (399–421) at the instigation of Mārūthā of Maiperqaṭ, who had come to Persia as ambassador of Arcadius (395–408) and Theodosius II (408–50). The other central figure was Mar Isaac, bishop of Seleucia from *c.* 399, whose authority as head of the Persian church Yazdagird now recognized.

The synod adopted the Nicene Creed, agreed with the Western church the dates of the principal feasts and adopted twenty-one canons regulating aspects of church life. Isaac is described as 'the great metropolitan, the catholicos of Seleucia and Ctesiphon'. The precedence of the other bishops is established, with metropolitans of Kashkar, Khuzistan, northern Mesopotamia and Mesene (on the Gulf).

JH

Seleucia-Ctesiphon   Seleucia and Ctesiphon, Seleucid Greek and Parthian foundations respectively on opposite sides of the Tigris to the south of modern Baghdad. Seleucia, named after Seleucus I Nicator (*c*.358–281 BC), was the outpost of Greek culture in the East. Even after the fall of the area to the Parthians it retained autonomy and commercial importance until its destruction by Avidius Cassius in AD 164. The Parthians centred their activities on Ctesiphon, the Arsacid winter capital, founded as a military encampment. Impressive Parthian remains include a magnificent arch.

No reliable information on the evangelization of Seleucia-Ctesiphon is available: the Chronicle of ARBELA is suspect and we rely otherwise on the legend of the missions of ADDAI and Mari. The latter is a plausible apostle of the region (Acts of Mari). The first clearly known bishop of Seleucia is Pāpā at the beginning of the fourth century (310–29). It is not, however, until we enter the timescale of the SYNODIKON ORIENTALE (synods from 410) that we are on firm ground. Note may also be made of the eleventh-century Arabic *Chronicle of Se'ert*.

A suburb of Ctesiphon, Kōkē (later Māḥōzā, Veh Ardashīr), was the actual site of the episcopal, later patriarchal, see of Seleucia. Being at the heart of the Parthian and Sasanian empires, it inevitably became the dominant see in the Persian sphere; from the earliest records the bishop of Seleucia-Ctesiphon takes precedence over all others and is called CATHOLICOS (synod of 410) and eventually PATRIARCH (497). With the fall of Seleucia-Ctesiphon to the Arabs in 637, the twin cities came to be known in Arabic as al-Madā'in, 'the cities'. Subsequently, in 762, Caliph al-Manṣūr founded Baghdad nearby and the patriarchs moved to the new capital.

Fiey, J. M. (1970), *Jalons pour une histoire de l'église en Iraq*, CSCO 310, Subsidia 36. Louvain: Secrétariat du CSCO.

JH

semandron   Greek; a long bar of wood or metal which, when struck with a hammer or mallet, gives out a resonant musical sound. The semandron is used in monasteries and sometimes elsewhere to summon the community to church. Intricate rhythmical patterns are traditionally used in striking the semandron. The semandron replaced bells, forbidden in Christian communities under Islamic rule, and may be used instead of bells in penitential and mourning services. The wooden 'hand' semandron is normally called the *talanton*, from the rhythm in which it is struck: to-tá-lan-ton, to-tá-lan-ton, asking the sleepy monk what he is doing about the talents entrusted to him by the Lord. The iron semandron, called 'the iron', has specific uses, in particular to signal moments of the office in the church to those whose duties keep them elsewhere. Large wooden semandra, called 'heavies', anything up to two metres long, and suspended on iron bars, are struck before great vigils, often by two or three monks together. The semandron is mentioned by JOHN CLIMACUS (sixth century) in the *Ladder*, and the TYPIKA and service books often mention both the 'iron' and the 'heavies' in the rubrics, but the opening words of the PENTEKOSTARION are simply: 'Around the time of ORTHROS they sound all the semandra.' The semandron entered the world of Western music in John Tavener's opera *Mary of Egypt*, for which one was specially made by a young North Yorkshire carpenter.

DM/E

Senkessar Geʿez *senkesār* from the Greek *synaxarion* through the Arabic *sinkisār*. The Senkessar or Synaxarion is a collection of brief daily commemorations of the lives and martyrdoms of the saints recognized by the Ethiopian church, arranged according to the calendar of the church. The Ethiopic *Senkessar* seems to have originated as a GEʿEZ translation, perhaps from the fourteenth century, of the Copto-Arabic Synaxarion. During the fifteenth and sixteenth centuries many commemorations of Ethiopian monks, saints and martyrs were added to the *Senkessar*.

See also ETHIOPIAN ORTHODOX CHURCH.

Colin, G. (1988), 'Le synaxaire éthiopien, état actuel de la question', *Analecta Bollandiana* 106, pp. 273–317.
Budge, E. A. W. (1928), *The Book of the Saints of the Ethiopian Church: A Translation of the Ethiopic Synaxarium*... 4 vols. Cambridge: Cambridge University Press.
I. Guidi, S. Grebaut, G. Nollet, G. Colin, eds and trans. (1905–97), *Le Synaxaire Éthiopien*. Patrologia Orientalis 1, 7, 9, 15, 26, 43–7. Paris: Firmin-Didot; Turnhout: Brepols.

MJB/SHG

September events In 1955 intercommunal strife in CYPRUS and mounting tension between Greece and Turkey led to anti-Greek rioting in Istanbul (CONSTANTINOPLE). The situation worsened: from 6 September demonstrations developed into a pogrom against Greeks across the city. The Orthodox church in particular was targeted, and of forty-five churches and thirty chapels only five remained unscathed after a few days of rioting. Greek business premises, homes, libraries, colleges and schools were gutted. Inestimable damage was inflicted on historic buildings, large numbers of icons were destroyed and cemeteries were vandalized. A famous icon, Our Lady of the Mongols, disappeared and the ZOODOCHOS Pege monastery was sacked. The September events represent the final act in the decline of the Constantinopolitan Greek community. Only fifteen churches were fully restored over the next decade or so. The last Greek printing houses were closed in the early 1960s, the Megale tou Genous Schole of the Phanar and the celebrated Halki Theological Academy (Heybeliada) in 1971. By 1980 it was calculated that there were more Constantinopolitan Greeks in Glyphada, a single suburb of Athens, than in the ancient Byzantine capital. Nevertheless, in 1987, the Orthodox church was permitted to rebuild a wing of the patriarchate complex that was destroyed in 1941.

Psarakis, T. (1991), *Anthologio tes Konstantinoupolis*. Athens: Nea Synora.

AK

Seraphim Chichagov (1853–1937)   Russian author and NEW MARTYR. A prominent aristocrat, Seraphim served in the military during the 1877–8 war against Turkey. He was promoted colonel in the artillery and entrusted with the organization of medical care and other charities for veterans, orphans of war and families connected to the forces. Influenced by John of Kronstadt (d. 1908), Seraphim took his family to Moscow in 1891 and was ordained. After he was widowed in 1895 he joined the Holy Trinity monastery but continued writing. Seraphim was responsible for supervising the celebrations to mark the canonization of SERAPHIM OF SAROV in 1903. He was consecrated bishop in 1905, transferred to Kishinev in 1908 and became archbishop of Tver in 1912. In 1918 Seraphim was elected metropolitan of Warsaw but was refused permission to enter Poland. First arrested in 1922, he was only released in 1927 when he expressed support for Metropolitan Sergii Starogorodskii (d. 1944). Between 1928 and 1933 Seraphim was metropolitan of Leningrad; he was rearrested and executed during the purges. Seraphim is commemorated on 11 December.

Chernaya, V. (1989), 'Seraphim Chichagov', *Journal of the Moscow Patriarchate* 2.

DB

Seraphim of Boiotia (1527–1602)   Founder of the Saviour monastery near Levadeia, Seraphim was a renowned elder (STARETS) who lived as a hermit before joining the Mount Sagmation monastery. He later moved back to a hermitage (Domvous) close to Mount Helikon; this grew into a new monastery as disciples came to join him. Seraphim travelled to Piraeus and elsewhere, preaching and praying for the oppressed Christians living under OTTOMAN rule. His life's work, like that of Kosmas of Aitolia, can be viewed as mission among the Orthodox Christians of the Ottoman empire. Seraphim is commemorated on 6 May.
   See also DIONYSIOS OF OLYMPOS.

DB

Seraphim of Sarov (1759–1833)   Russian monk and STARETS who for many years lived the life of a hermit in the forests around Sarov. From 1825, after spending seventeen years in seclusion, he began to give spiritual direction to the many thousands of visitors who came to him. His spiritual life was marked by experience of the divine light as witnessed by the disciples at the TRANSFIGURATION of Christ and which in the Orthodox tradition is associated with HESYCHAST prayer. A vivid account of the effect of this effulgent light is given by one of his spiritual children. In it he describes a conversation he had with the *starets* in the forest and how he could not look into his face because of the light radiating from him; and how, in spite of the snow falling around them, he felt a great warmth enter his heart. For Seraphim this light and warmth was a gift of the Holy Spirit. He was canonized by the Russian church in 1903.

Zander, V. (1975), *St Seraphim of Sarov*. London: SPCK.

KP

Serbian Christianity   One of the groups of South Slavs, Serbs settled in the Balkans in the sixth and seventh centuries. In *De Administrando Imperio*, Byzantine Emperor Constantine VII Porphyrogennetos (945–59) states that the first Christian mission among them was sponsored by Emperor Heraclius (610–41). A second phase of conversion occurred under Basil I (867–86). The earliest recorded Christian names among local Serbian *archontes* (local princes) are those of Stefan son of Mutimir and Peter son of Gojnik, both born around 870.

After the disintegration of the Moravian mission in 886, disciples of CYRIL AND METHODIUS started work among the South Slavs. The best known were Clement and Naum. From centres at Preslav and OHRID, they spread Christianity and literacy over the south-eastern Balkans, including lands inhabited by Serbs. A new script, based on the Greek alphabet, was created; it became known as Cyrillic. It replaced the Glagolitic, in which the earliest Old Church Slavonic translations of liturgical and biblical books were written. The whole process played a decisive role in the orientation of the larger part of South Slav converts, Bulgarian and Serb, towards Byzantine Orthodoxy.

Few Old Church Slavonic manuscripts of the tenth and eleventh centuries, whether in Glagolitic or Cyrillic, are preserved. Two illuminated lectionaries, those of Miroslav (*c.*1185) and Vukan (*c.*1200), both Cyrillic, in Serbian recension, throw light on earlier liturgical, linguistic and artistic developments and open a better-documented period of medieval book writing. Miroslav and Vukan were respectively the elder brother and eldest son of grand zupan Stefan Nemanja (1169–96), who united the Serbian lands, founding a dynasty which reigned over 200 years. Nemanja's state stretched from the southern Adriatic to the valley of Morava in the north-east, including KOSOVO and Metohija in the south.

In his efforts to secure political independence for Serbia, Nemanja spent much time at war with Byzantium. However, he provided his state with stable institutions in which, as in Byzantium, the Christian church played a major part; and Byzantium, once the enemy, became an admired model. Nemanja and his successors wisely accepted the Byzantine cultural influence and adapted it to local traditions and practices. Thus the ancient Serbian institution of councils of elders (*sabori*), combined with the Byzantine institution of regional church synods, assumed from Nemanja's time onwards a new constitutional role as an assembly of both secular and ecclesiastical representatives, presided over by the head of state. Rooted in the people's consciousness, the *sabori* had a prolonged career throughout the period of OTTOMAN domination, organized, in the absence of a monarch, by church leaders, but comprising large numbers of people's representatives.

On Stefan Nemanja's initiative, many churches and monasteries were built. His mausoleum, the monastery of the Virgin at STUDENICA, its ARCHITECTURE an original combination of Romanesque and Byzantine, gained a particular place in the spiritual tradition of later generations: royal mausolea of his descendants were modelled on it, and the LAVRA of Studenica became one of the holiest shrines in the land.

Towards the end of his life, Nemanja left the throne to his second son Stefan, later known as Stefan the First Crowned, and became a monk at Studenica. His wife Ana took the veil at the monastery of the Virgin in Toplica. Soon, however, Nemanja, now Monk Symeon, went to ATHOS where his youngest son SAVA of Serbia (1175–1235) had been a monk since around 1190. They founded the monastery of HILANDAR, to which 'independent and self-governing' status was granted by Emperor Alexios III. This outpost on Athos established a permanent link between Byzantine and Serbian monasticism; relations were opened with other non-Greek monastic communities already represented there. Hilandar rapidly developed into an important centre of Orthodox spirituality and learning.

Stefan Nemanja's piety and patronage of the church are prominent components in the formation of Serbian Christianity. Sava enhanced these achievements, laying down new guidelines which thoroughly involved Serbia in the spiritual and cultural trends of the time.

Although he started his career on Mount Athos, and kept in touch with it all his life, Sava later spent much time in Serbia. In his multiple roles as monk, head of the church, author, statesman and diplomat, he also travelled to Nicea and Constantinople, and then, under Latin rule, to Thessaloniki, BULGARIA and the Holy Land. In 1219, at Nicea, he was appointed first autocephalous archbishop of Serbia by Emperor Theodore I Lascaris and PATRIARCH Manuel Sarantinos. The autocephalous status of the Serbian church allowed Serbian clergy to elect and consecrate their own archbishop, whose seat was first at ŽIČA and later moved to PEĆ.

Sava's organizational and legislative work opened a new era for the Serbian church. Sava's Nomocanon (*Krmcija*), his selection of Byzantine canons, served as the principal ecclesiastical and civil constitution in medieval Serbia. Rules were provided for monastic communities, encouraging, in addition to the ideal of a life of work and prayer motivated by humility and obedience, care for the sick and infirm. Monastic hospices were opened. Monasteries created their own scriptoria, providing means for icon painting and book illumination. Rather than being remote, they often maintained close contact with surrounding villages. Sava twice travelled to the Holy Land, visiting some of the oldest Christian monastic communities; he studied their customs and liturgical practices, extended his patronage to them and provided means for organizing Serbian monastic colonies there. This led to a relationship between the monasteries of Serbia and Palestine that lasted well into the Ottoman period.

Sava wrote the Life of Stefan Nemanja, initiating a tradition of princely, royal and archiepiscopal biographies in Serbian medieval literature. In these *Vitae* (*Žitija*), accounts of true events and information on family history are combined with hagiographical details, theology and political ideology, skilfully interwoven in the story. Other well-known authors of such Lives were Sava's brother Stefan; the monks Domentijan and Teodosije in the thirteenth century; Archbishop Danilo II in the fourteenth; Konstantine of Kostenec and Gregory Camblak in the fifteenth; and Patriarch Pajsije in the sixteenth and seventeenth centuries. Many whose Lives had been written, Nemanja and Sava first among them, were proclaimed saints, liturgical offices with appropriate hymnography being written. The influence of HESYCHASM, already felt in some earlier works, became prominent from the time of Archbishop Danilo II.

In 1217 Sava's brother Stefan was crowned king, receiving the crown from Pope Honorius III. This apparent political anomaly is explained by the intricacies of contemporary diplomacy, but also reflects the policy of a ruler whose land lay at the crossroads of East and West. Sava and Stefan, both devout Orthodox, remained in touch with their Western neighbours, dealing realistically with the kingdom's two dioceses under Roman ecclesiastical jurisdiction with suffragans in Dubrovnik and Bar. Openness towards the West remained a characteristic policy of the Nemanjic dynasty. Later in the thirteenth century, Roman Catholic Saxon miners settling in Serbia were granted confessional privileges by the king and entitled to build their own churches. French-born Queen Helen, wife of Stefan Uroš I (1243–76), helped both Orthodox and Catholic monasteries in the land.

Visual arts are important to Serbian Christianity. Sava, in complete accord with Byzantine Orthodox tradition, saw icons of Christ, the Virgin and the saints as confirming the dogma of the Incarnation, and fostered devotion towards saintly pictures, contributing to their immense popularity. Magnificent wallpaintings at Studenica (1208), Žiča (1220) and MILEŠEVA (1228), executed in Sava's lifetime and followed by those of Moraca (1251), SOPOĆANI (1260), Peć (1260) and Arilje (1296), characterize the artistic scene in thirteenth-century Serbia. Serbian popular ballads which sing of the shimmering beauty of these pious foundations (*zaduzbine*) are evidence of the esteem in which people held their churches.

In addition to churches founded by princes and prelates, there were sanctuaries where the memory of local holy men and women was celebrated. Many became renowned places of PILGRIMAGE. The cults of early Christian martyrs and other saints, already widespread in Byzantium, became firmly implanted in Serbia: they included those of Stephen, Nicholas, George and Demetrius, the Forty Martyrs of Sebaste and other MILITARY SAINTS. Among women saints one should mention Paraskeve, Kyriake (Nedelja), Anastasia, Barbara and Catherine. There was, naturally, a profound devotion to the Mother of God and John the Baptist. As in Byzantine THEOLOGY, the value of Christian baptism as an illumination of humanity and as the first step towards salvation was underlined by Sava and other Serbian church authors, sometimes emphasized, perhaps, to counteract dualistic heresies opposed to baptism, such as BOGOMILISM, spreading west from Bulgaria in the twelfth century.

Sava's impact on Serbian Christianity can also be judged from certain specifics of uncertain origin, but attributable to his influence. The most remarkable among them is the importance in Serbian culture of the celebration known as *Slava* (Glory), or *Krsno Ime* (the Name of the Cross), when each family expresses its devotion to its patron saint at the annual celebration of his or her feast. The feast is celebrated liturgically, as normally in Byzantine churches, with the burning of a candle and of incense, the priest's blessing of water, wine, cooked wheat (*see* KOLLYBA) and bread bearing Christian symbols (*see* BREAD STAMPS), these actions accompanied by hymns glorifying the Incarnation, and by prayers and troparia to the saint (*see* SLAVA).

By the early fourteenth century the borders of Serbia had expanded to include other Slav-populated areas formerly under Byzantine administration. They encompassed the river basins of Morava, Ibar, Drim, Morača, Neretva and Drina, a stretch of the Adriatic coast (without Dubrovnik) and parts of MACEDONIA. During the reigns of King Milutin (1282–1321) and his successors, religious art continued to flourish.

Heading a long list of fourteenth-century churches are Bogorodica Ljeviška at Prizren (1308), St Nikita (1316), STARO NAGORIČINO (1317), GRAČANICA (1321), DEĆANI (1330–50), Peć (1337, 1345) and LESNOVO (1341–9).

In 1346, before King Stefan Dušan (1331–55) was crowned emperor, the Serbian archbishopric was raised to a patriarchate, as the patriarchate of Peć. This caused a temporary rift with CONSTANTINOPLE, settled by Constantinopolitan recognition of the Serbian patriarchate in 1375. Dušan was a capable statesman and his reorganization of Serbian and Greek lands could have prevented the conquest of the Balkans by the Ottoman Turks, had he not died prematurely.

In 1389 the Serbian army, led by Prince Lazar, was defeated by Sultan Murat at Kosovo Polje. Soon after the battle, Lazar was canonized and literary and liturgical works written interpreting his military defeat as a moral victory: renouncing worldly fame, Lazar had chosen the Kingdom of Heaven. Linked to the previous tradition of Sava's teaching, and seen as a symbol of Christian sacrifice leading to salvation, the memory of Kosovo made a lasting impression, inspiring one of the finest cycles of epic poems.

A reduced state, the despotate of Serbia, survived until it succumbed to the Turks in 1459. In this last phase, under the patronage of despots Stefan Lazarević (1389–1427) and Djuradj Branković (1427–56), important monastic centres of writing and book illumination were active in the regions of Morava and Branicevo in north-eastern Serbia. Monasteries with outstanding frescoes are Ravanica (1387), Ljubostinja (1402), Kalenić (1413) and Manasija (Resava) (1417).

The Patriarchate of Peć, extinct since 1459, was re-established in 1557, following an agreement with the Ottoman authorities. Having obtained a degree of autonomy, the Serbian church assumed the role of mediator in ecclesiastical and secular matters between the Serbian Orthodox people and their Ottoman rulers. Its jurisdiction was not restricted to the lands of the former Serbian state and BOSNIA-HERZEGOVINA, but reached the peripheral regions conquered by the Turks north of the Sava and the Danube and west into Dalmatia, where, following migrations from the eastern parts, the Orthodox population had increased. On the part of the Ottomans, this was a pragmatic move ensuring that large sections of Christians under their rule would pay regular dues and be kept fairly content on a territory whose strategic position was crucial.

Through this tortuous period, characterized by considerable demographic changes, the role of the church in preserving national and confessional identity was crucial. As far as Serbian Christianity is concerned, claims representing the Ottoman domination as an era of total darkness are as unfounded as those disregarding its negative sides. In periods of comparative peace, churches were renovated and much new adornment produced. Book copying continued in many modest scriptoria. However, the institution of *devshirme*, by which the healthiest Christian male children were taken and, in general, Islamicized and recruited as janissaries, the destruction of scores of churches or their conversion into mosques and the general humiliation of the non-Muslim population (*rayah*) were already features of the Ottoman conquest in the fifteenth and sixteenth centuries, not merely of the Ottoman empire's later decadence when the suffering of Christians reached its peak.

As Roman Catholic countries fought against the Turks over the possession of the Balkans, Serbs were also under pressure from the pro-UNIATE zeal of the Roman Congregation of Propaganda, causing renewed migrations and hardship. In these difficult circumstances, a reorganization of the Serbian church took place in 1713 with the creation of the metropoly at Sremski Karlovci, then on Austro-Hungarian territory, with the consent of the Austro-Hungarian emperor. Under this metropoly's jurisdiction were Serbian Orthodox communities in the 'military cordon' on the southern and south-eastern flank of the Habsburg empire, where Serbs were engaged in defending the borders from Turkish attacks. Many Orthodox churches and monasteries in that area, especially those around Sremski Karlovci, on the slopes of Fruška Gora and between Sava, Drava and the Danube, had already become depositories of relics, icons and other sacred objects brought by monks fleeing persecution in parts still under Ottoman rule. The reorganized church assisted the liberation movements, leading to the creation of the modern Serbian state in 1878. Dissolved once more in 1766, the patriarchate of Peć was re-established in Belgrade and Peć in 1920, after the creation of Yugoslavia.

During the Second World War Serbian Christianity faced another challenge, caused by the invasion of the German Nazis and their satellites from countries bordering Yugoslavia. Patriarch Gavrilo Dozić was sent to the concentration camp at Dachau and the hierarchy decimated. Most devastating were persecutions of Serb Orthodox in the independent state of Croatia, then including Bosnia-Herzegovina. The post-war communist regime retarded the healing process and left all vital problems unresolved.

See also KOSOVO; KRAJINA; MONTENEGRO; SERBIAN NEW MARTYRS.

Maksimović, Lj. (1992), 'The Christianization of the Serbs and the Croats', in Tachiaos, A.-E. N., ed., *The Legacy of Saints Cyril and Methodius to Kiev and Moscow* (Proceedings of the International Congress on the Millennium of the Conversion of Rus to Christianity, Thessaloniki, 26–8 November 1988). Thessaloniki: Hellenic Association for Slavic Studies.

Samardzić, R., Ćirković, S., Zirojević, O., Tricković, R., Bataković, D., Djurdjević, V., Čavoški, K. and Jevtić, A. (1990), *Le Kosovo-Metohija dans l'histoire serbe*. Lausanne: L'Age d'Homme.

Obolensky, D. (1988), *Six Byzantine Portraits*. Oxford: Clarendon Press.

Weitzmann, K. et al. (1987), *The Icon*. London: Bracken Books.

Čanak-Medić, M. and Bošković, D. (1986), *L'Architecture de l'époque de Nemanja*, vol. 1, and Čanak-Medić, M. (1989), vol. 2, Belgrade: Institut pour la protection des monuments historiques de la RS de Serbie et Institut archéologique.

Ćurčić, S. (1984), *Art and Architecture in the Balkans: An Annotated Bibliography*. Boston, Mass.: G. K. Hall & Co.

Radojčić, S. (1969), *Geschichte der Serbischen Kunst von Anfangen bis zum Ende des Mittelalters*. Berlin: De Gruyter.

Hussey, J. M., ed. (1966), *Cambridge Medieval History*, vol. 4. Cambridge: Cambridge University Press.

Hafner, S. (1964), *Studien zur altserbischen dynastischen Historiographie*. Munich: Oldenbourg.

ZG

Serbian New Martyrs The Serbian Orthodox church commemorates 800,000 Serbian New Martyrs of the Second World War period. From April 1941 to 1945

Yugoslavia was divided into German and Italian zones of occupation and also among neighbouring Hungary, BULGARIA, ALBANIA and the new Croatian state. It was in the provinces assigned to Croatia, under the nationalist regime of Ante Pavelić, that the Serbian Orthodox population was systematically uprooted or massacred, but throughout Yugoslavia the Serbian Orthodox church was targeted: bishops were put to death and the patriarch of Serbia, Gavrilo, along with bishop NICOLAS VELIMIROVIĆ and others, was incarcerated in the Nazi concentration camp at Dachau. Many Orthodox Christians were put to death in Ustase concentration camps such as that at Jasenovac, usually for refusing to convert to Roman Catholicism.

See also ETHNOMARTYRS; PLATO JOVANOVIĆ.

DB

Sergius of Radonezh (1314–92)   Sergius, born in Rostov, moved with his family to Radonezh where he and his elder brother Stephen established a hermitage in nearby forest and built a chapel dedicated to the Holy Trinity. When Stephen moved to a monastery, Sergius stayed on alone until his reputation attracted a community about him. The metropolitan of MOSCOW, impressed by his humility, wanted to make him his successor, but Sergius preferred to remain in his hermitage, although he carried out several peace missions for the metropolitan. Dmitrii Donskoi consulted him before defeating the Tartars in the battle of Kulikovo (1380). Some thirty-five monasteries were founded by his disciples during his lifetime. The upsurge in Russian monasticism in the fourteenth and fifteenth centuries owes much to his promotion of HESYCHASM. The Life of Sergius was written about twenty-five years after his death by his former pupil Epiphanios the Wise. The Trinity-Sergius Monastery at Sergiev Posad (Zargorsk) is a monument to his work. Holy Trinity church at Sergiev Posad was completed in 1425; Andrei RUBLEV probably painted his famous Trinity icon at the monastery around this time. Sergius was canonized in 1422.

Fedotov, G. P. (1977), *A Treasury of Russian Spirituality*. London: Sheed & Ward.
Kovalevsky, P. (1976), *Saint Sergius and Russian Spirituality*. Crestwood, NY: St Vladimir's Seminary Press.

KP

Seventy   (1) In addition to the twelve apostles, EASTERN CHRISTIAN tradition honours the seventy apostles Jesus commissioned to spread the gospel (Luke 10: 1, 17). Many are commemorated by name in the Synaxarion and MENAIA, their names often derived from people mentioned in the epistles. On 17 May, for example, the Byzantine rite celebrates the apostles Andronicus and Junia: Junia is, like Priscilla in EASTERN ORTHODOX tradition, both a woman and an apostle (*see* WOMEN).

(2) 'The Seventy' also designates the Jewish fathers who translated the Septuagint (*see* BIBLE), regarded in Eastern Christian tradition as an authoritative and inspired translation. Tradition identifies one of the Seventy, Symeon the Just, with the Symeon of Luke's Gospel, who held the infant Jesus in his arms. Symeon, doubting whether it was right to translate the Hebrew *'almāh* as *parthenos*, virgin, in Isaias, was told by an angel to write *parthenos* and to wait to see the fulfilment of the prophecy. The Nunc

Dimittis declares he has now seen the promised salvation: 'a light to enlighten the gentiles and the glory of your people Israel'.

DM

Severian Severianos, bishop of Gabala: early fifth-century orator, exegete, narrow-minded and vitriolic upholder of Nicene orthodoxy. His interpretation of biblical texts is so literal that he sometimes turns what is clearly poetic imagery into pseudo-scientific fact. A celebrated preacher in CONSTANTINOPLE, he supported Empress Eudoxia against JOHN CHRYSOSTOM. Paradoxically, a number of his writings, marked by a bitter anti-Jewish tone, seem to have been handed down as works of Chrysostom.

DM

Severus ibn al-Muqaffaʿ (*c*.905–after 987) Sawīrus is the earliest Coptic Christian author regularly to write Christian theology in Arabic. Since the early eighteenth century his name has wrongly been associated with the *Historia Patriarchorum Alexandrinorum*, a reference work indispensable to historians of medieval Egypt, for which credit should go to Mawhūb ibn Mufarrij of Alexandria (*c*.1025–1100). After a period in government service, Severus underwent a religious conversion and entered the monastic life. He was consecrated bishop of al-Ashmūnayn by Patriarch Theophane (953–56). It was as bishop that Severus achieved his fame, not only as a writer but as a Christian controversialist in Arabic, arguing the cause of the Christians even in the court of the Fatimid caliph al-Muʿizz (969–75). More than twenty works in Arabic are credited to Severus, but only a few have been edited and published in modern times. Among them is a presentation of the principal Christian doctrines called *Kitāb al-durr al-thamīn fīḍah al-dīn*, a *History of the Councils*, and an intriguing book entitled by its modern editors *Affliction's Physic and the Cure of Sorrows*. Severus' main contribution to Coptic church life was the adoption of Arabic as a medium for the publication of Christian doctrines.

Ebied, R. Y. and Young, M. J. L., eds and trans (1978), *Severus ibn al-Muqaffaʿ, Affliction's Physic and the Cure of Sorrow*. CSCO, vols 396–7. Louvain.

Ebied, R. Y. and Young, M. J. L., eds and trans (1975), *The Lamp of the Intellect of Severus ibn al-Muqaffaʿ, Bishop of al-Ashmunain*. CSCO, vols 365–6. Louvain.

Maiberger, P. (1972), *'Das Buch der kostbaren Perle', von Severus ibn al-Muqaffaʾ; Einleitung und arabischer Text (Kapitel 1–5)*. Wiesbaden.

Jirjis, M. (1925), *Kitāb al-durr al-thamīn fīḍah al-dīn*. Cairo: n.p.

Leroy, L. (1911), *Sévère ibn al-Moqaffaʿ, évêque d'Aschmounaïn, Histoire des Conciles (second livre)*. Patrologia Orientalis 6. Paris.

Chébli, R. (1905), *Réfutation d'Eutychius par Sévère, (le livre des conciles)*. Patrologia Orientalis 3. Paris.

MJB/SHG

Severus of Antioch PATRIARCH of ANTIOCH (512–18) and leading anti-CHAL-CEDONIAN theologian. After studying law in ALEXANDRIA and Beirut, he was converted and baptized at martyr Leontios' shrine in Tripoli in 488. Having become a monk, on the deposition of the Chalcedonian Flavian he was consecrated patriarch of Antioch in 512. His consecrators included Dionysios of Tarsus and PHILOXENUS OF

MABBUG. He was present at the notorious battle of the Trisagion in Hagia Sophia, vividly described by Gibbon. Deposed under Justin I (518–27), he fled to Egypt. Empress Theodora befriended him, though he complained she did not understand his theology. After the failed attempt to reconcile the opposing parties under Justinian I (527–65), Severus was condemned by a synod in CONSTANTINOPLE in 536. His writings were ordered destroyed. Severus died in exile in Egypt in 536.

Apart from a single homily, his numerous writings have perished in the original Greek, but many exist in SYRIAC translations, some contemporary or almost so, including works defending a moderate 'MONOPHYSITE' position against both Chalcedonian and extreme monophysite opponents. He saw himself as the defender of the Christology of ATHANASIUS and CYRIL OF ALEXANDRIA as propounded at Ephesus, opposing what he regarded as the Nestorianism of Chalcedon and the *Tome* of Leo. This position is clearly set out in the first of his 125 Cathedral Homilies, preached at his consecration and repeated two days later by popular demand because of 'the noise and tumult' on the first occasion. This homily survives only in Coptic, the rest in an almost complete seventh-century Syriac version by Jacob of EDESSA. Some 400 letters survive, translated by Jacob, and a large collection of hymns, or OKTOECHOS. One homily survived in Greek under the name of Gregory of Nyssa (*see* CAPPADOCIANS) or Hesychios of Jerusalem; it helps date the introduction of the HEOTHINON gospel at Sunday ORTHROS in Antioch. Greek fragments survive in Old and New Testament catenae, whence some reached the West and were used in Aquinas' *Catena Aurea* and *Summa Theologiae*. A Coptic catena on the Gospel of Mark consists almost entirely of passages from Severus. He is honoured as a great doctor of the Oriental Orthodox churches, but vilified by name in Byzantine rite hymnography.

See also HEOTHINA.

E

Shenouda III Coptic Patriarch (1971–). Naẓir Ǧayyid became a monk in 1954 at the monastery of the Syrians in the Wādī al-Naṭrūn. Elected pope of ALEXANDRIA and 117th PATRIARCH of the see of St Mark in 1971, he took the name Shenouda III. Escalating tensions and conflicts between Muslims and Copts in Egypt culminated in bloody incidents in Alexandria in 1980 and Cairo in 1981. Coptic protests in the United States exacerbated already difficult relations between the Egyptian government and the Coptic Orthodox church. In September 1981 Shenouda III was exiled by President Anwar Sadat to the monastery of Saint Bishoi. He was released from house arrest in January 1985 by President Hosni Moubarak. Shenouda III has travelled extensively on behalf of the Coptic Orthodox church, visiting Coptic immigrant communities throughout North AMERICA, Europe, Africa and AUSTRALIA. He has sought to foster ecumenical dialogue, meeting with church leaders around the world. Shenouda III is a prolific writer and poet.

See also COPTIC CHRISTIANITY.

Abdelsayyed, G. (1991), 'Shenouda III', *Coptic Encyclopedia* 7, p. 213.
'Chronique: Egypte', *Proche-Orient Chrétien* 32 (1982), pp. 125–69; 33 (1983), pp. 236–44; 34 (1984), pp. 289–90; 35 (1985), pp. 87–93.

MJB/SHG

Sian-Fu stele In 1625 Jesuit misssionaries discovered a nine-foot-high stele erected in 781 to commemorate the initial preaching and subsequent establishment of Christianity in T'ang China by missionary monks of the CHURCH OF THE EAST (*c*.635). The main text is in Chinese, with a briefer SYRIAC dedication containing names of many priests and monks. According to the stele, the first missionary to visit China carrying the scriptures of the 'luminous religion' was one Alopen. The name appears only in the Chinese text, A-lo-pên, and is probably a Chinese approximation to a Syrian name: Alopen is described as coming from the Kingdom of Ta-ch'in (Syria). The scriptures were translated into Chinese and widely distributed. The stele was erected, according to the text, during the time of the Patriarch Ḥanan-īshūʻ II: news of his death in 779 had not yet reached the Christians of China.

Parry, K. (1996), 'Images in the Church of the East: The Evidence from Central Asia and China', in J. F. Coakley and K. Parry, eds, *The Church of the East: Life and Thought*, *Bulletin of the John Rylands University Library of Manchester*, 78/3, pp. 143–62.
Saeki, P. Y. (1916), *The Nestorian Monument in China*. London: SPCK.

JH

Siberia Though EASTERN ORTHODOX missions existed beyond the Ural mountains from the sixteenth century, reaching the Russian Far East and the Pacific shores in the seventeenth, Orthodoxy was often brought to Siberian peoples through trading links and intermarriage. Russian settlers organized a network of parishes, and major expeditions invariably included clergy and monks. Monasteries were established in both the new urban centres and outlying regions.

Patriarch Filaret of Moscow (d. 1633) created the Tobolsk diocese to co-ordinate the Christianization of Siberia. Metropolitan Filofei Leshchinskii (d. 1727) sponsored thirty-seven monastic missionary outposts and supervised the conversion of over 40,000 Siberians. He sought to organize a mission in CHINA. This process culminated in 1793, when Russian missionaries were invited to ALASKA. The first group from VALAAM included the monk Herman (d. 1837), Orthodox patron saint of America.

From Siberia, missions penetrated the Kamchatka peninsula in the eighteenth century, reaching the Altai regions, Kazakhstan, Kirghizstan and Central Asia more widely during the nineteenth century. Innokentii Popov organized a network of missions that constituted the diocese of YAKUTIA in 1868. Innokentii Veniaminov (d. 1879) continued this work among native peoples of both Siberia and Alaska, translating or editing translations of Christian tracts into native languages that had previously lacked any script. A widower when consecrated, Innokentii was assigned the Kamchatka, Kuril and Aleutian Isles diocese, and travelled across this vast region until he was transferred to the see of MOSCOW in 1868; here, in 1870, he founded the Orthodox Missionary Society to co-ordinate existing missions and sponsor further work. One of the society's first successes was the organization of the Biisk diocese, supervised by Peter Ekaterinovskii (d. 1889).

An important work of Orthodox missions in Siberia was the creation of written languages for the native peoples and the translation of Christian and secular texts, and the creation of original works in these languages. John of Tobolsk (d. 1715), Grigorii Novitskii (d. 1725), Makarii GLUKHAREV (d. 1847), Innokentii Veniaminov (d. 1879),

Vassilii Verbitskii (d. 1890), Dionisii Khitrov (d. 1896), Makarii Nevskii (d. 1926) and NESTOR ANISIMOV (d. 1962) all contributed to this process.

Gedeon of Stavropol (1990), 'Orthodoxy in Siberia and America', *Journal of the Moscow Patriarchate* 11.
Verkhovsky, V. (1990), *Elder Zosima of Siberia*. Platina, Cal.: St Herman of Alaska Press.

DB

Sinai Mount Sinai is the traditional site of Moses' vision of the Burning Bush and his receiving the Law. The story of Catherine of Alexandria told that after her martyrdom angels carried her body to Mount Sinai. From an early period Christian hermits settled there, and under Emperor Justinian I (527–65) an important monastery was established which still survives. The monastery, originally 'of the Bush' but renamed for St Catherine in the medieval period, is a major repository of ancient icons and manuscripts as well as a living monastic community.

The abbot of Mount Sinai is an archbishop and head of an autonomous church. Though consecrated by the PATRIARCH of JERUSALEM, he is not his subject. The Church of Sinai, consisting of the monastery and a handful of dependencies, is the smallest EASTERN ORTHODOX church.

The monastery's collection of ICONS includes the famous dyophysite image of Christ in which the icon-maker has attempted to show the serene, eternal divinity and the afflicted humanity united in the single person whose portrait the icon is. Two uniquely important pre-ICONOCLAST icons are preserved, one the Mother of God enthroned between two saints, the other a remarkable portrait icon of the apostle Peter. The monastery's library was the source of the Codex Sinaiticus (*see* BIBLE) and a Syriac codex containing the Gospel text. It still possesses an important collection of manuscripts and printed texts.

The monastic church dates from the reign of Justinian I. Its architect, Stephen of Aila, built a three-aisled, wood-roofed, basalt basilica, the nave columns having a variety of carved capitals derived from the Corinthian order. The varied capitals and columns here seem a matter of deliberate choice, not the result as elsewhere of the re-use of columns taken from other buildings. The basilica possesses five side chapels. Towers flank the west end of the church, and the sacred bush was left growing in the open beyond the east end of the building.

Galey, J. (1979), *Sinai and the Monastery of St Catherine*. London: Chatto and Windaus.
Weitzmann, K. (1976), *The Monastery of St Catherine at Mt Sinai: The Icons. 1, from the Sixth to the Tenth Centuries*. Princeton, NJ: Princeton University Press.
Forsyth, G. H. and Weitzmann, K. (1973), *The Monastery of St Catherine at Mt Sinai: The Church and Fortress of Justinian*. Ann Arbor, Mich.
Skroboucha, H. (1966), *Sinai*. Oxford: Oxford University Press.

DM

Skopelos Village on the island of Lesbos, where the discovery in 1898 of an ICON of Mary Magdalene in catacombs under the village followed visionary experiences of local people, similar to those of THERMI. In 1919 a church dedicated to Mary Magdalene was built above the now extended underground passages. This is now a centre of PILGRIMAGE.

See also NEWLY REVEALED SAINTS; PHANEROMENE.

Hatzistylianos, G. (1990), *Hagia Myrophoros Magdalene Skopelou*. Mytilene, Lesbos: n.p.

DB

Slava   Celebration of the family patron saint's feast among Serbian Orthodox. *Slava* and *Krsno Ime* are names for the same celebration. *Slava* means literally 'glory', referring to the glorification of the patron saint of the family. *Krsno Ime* means literally 'name of the Cross': it refers to the sign of the CROSS, *znamenje* in Slavonic languages, *semeion* in Greek, with which a Christian is marked in the ceremony in which he or she receives a Christian name. The importance of the symbolism of the cross in the celebration of *Slava* is emphasized by the fact that the round loaf of bread which the family brings to the church for blessing is decorated with five BREAD STAMPS placed in a cross-shaped pattern, each bearing the letters IC.XC.NI-KA. This is often called *Krsnik*, 'Cross-loaf'. The large candle which burns all day in the house, bearing a small picture of the saint attached to its lower end, is called *Krsna sveća*, 'Cross-candle'. During the liturgical celebration of *Slava*, the priest makes a cross-wise incision in the bottom of the loaf and pours a few drops of red wine into it. Then, supported by the priest and by all members of the family, the bread is 'turned' three times; one of the hymns sung during the turning of the bread is the heirmos of the ninth ODE of the CANON of the THEOTOKOS from Sunday ORTHROS in Tone 5, which mentions Isaias, Emmanuel and the Incarnation (Isaias 7: 14). The priest then breaks the loaf along the lines of the incised cross and offers it to all members of the family to kiss, saying 'Christ is among us now and always, Amen.'

The celebration of *Slava* also includes the blessing of a dish of cooked wheat mixed with sugar and ground walnuts (*see* KOLLYBA). In addition to the hymns sung in honour of the Virgin and the Incarnation and the TROPARIA to the saint, prayers are said for the living members of the family, each mentioned by name. All this is preceded by the Lord's Prayer. The family group and the priest stand before a small table bearing the Cross-loaf, kollyba, incense, holy water and Cross-candle and placed in front of the main icon of the saint, before which an oil lamp is burning. In towns the priest normally comes to the family home, except on the feasts of popular saints, e.g. St Nicolas, when the families take the Cross-loaf etc. to the church for the ceremony.

Slava is distinct from the *Imendan*, the name-day of an individual celebrated in Greece and Russia: *Slava* is a family's saint's day, observed from generation to generation, from father to son. (Greek families whose surname derives from a saint will also celebrate that saint's feast as a family name's day, *onomasteirion*.) When a woman marries, she adopts her husband's patron saint for the *Slava*. Each church also celebrates its *Slava*. Before the communist regime was established in Yugoslavia, all Serbian schools celebrated *Slava* on St Sava's day, 14/27 January (see SAVA).

Velmar-Janković, S. and Kovačević, I. eds (1985), *O Krsnom Imenu*. Belgrade: Prosveta.
Bogdanović, D. (1961), 'Krsna Slava kao svetosavski kult', *Glasnik srpske pravoslavne crkve* 42, pp. 200–7.

Grujić, R. M. (1930), 'Crkveni elementi krsne slave', *Glasnik Skopskog Naučnog Društva* 7–8, pp. 35–77.

KP/ZG

Slavophones Communities who have generally considered themselves, or been considered by the Greeks, to be ethnic Greeks, but now speak a Slav language. 'Slavophone' is often treated as synonymous with 'Grekoman', a perjorative epithet used by the Bulgarians for Slav speakers enamoured of Greek culture or who chose to remain under the CONSTANTINOPLE patriarchate after the foundation of an independent Bulgarian exarchate. The Tosks, the VLACHS and the KARAMANLIS of Cappadocia are other non-Greek-speaking peoples that have contributed to mainstream Greek life and culture and can be identified as specifically GREEK ORTHODOX.

See also ALBANIA; MACEDONIA.

DB

Sofrony Vladislavov (d. 1813) A widowed priest of Kotel in BULGARIA who became a monk of ARBANASSI in 1794. Sofrony visited Paissy of HILANDAR in 1764 and was inspired by his ideas and his *History of the Slavic Bulgars*. Consecrated bishop of Vraca, he devoted himself to the spiritual awakening of Bulgaria and spent many years translating and improving existing translations of Christian texts into Bulgarian. Persecuted by the OTTOMAN authorities, he was exiled to Vidin and in 1803 fled to ROMANIA. In Bucharest, Sofrony wrote *The Life of the Sinful Sofrony* and published the first printed book in Bulgarian, *Nedelnik*. He is commemorated on 22 September.

Stoikov, V. (1989), 'The Works of St Sofrony', *Journal of the Moscow Patriarchate* 11.

DB

Solovyov (Solov'ev), Vladimir (1853–1900) Russian philosopher, theologian, poet and mystic; born in Moscow into the family of the historian Sergei Solovyov. At different stages of his life he underwent three mystical experiences that were highly significant to him.

Solovyov worked at interpreting Christian belief in terms clear to the modern world to combat the view that there is an inevitable contradiction between faith and reason. He summarized this in two phrases: 'justification of the ancient faith of our forefathers' and 'justification of the Good'. He followed KHOMIAKOV and Kireevskii in his careful study of Western philosophy and his study supported their fundamental analysis. He asserted that the only possible way out of the impasse of modern thought between empiricism and rationalism is a mystical philosophy.

He also explored the different religions of the world, trying to avoid the oversimplification of standard nineteenth-century European accounts, and cited Schelling and Khomiakov as his predecessors. Though his views on Chinese and Indian religions now appear rather narrow, his understanding of Judaic faith and the meaning of biblical history was very deep. He underlined the unique place of the Jews in human history and the continuity between the Jewish Old Testament and Christian spirituality.

The main part of his work concerns Christianity, which he saw as the most complete religious revelation. In his early work he criticized religious forms of deism and pantheism, as exclusive affirmations of divine transcendence or immanence, and complete dualism, which separates the empirical from the spiritual. He saw all material reality as grounded in the spiritual and having its true being in it. In his *Lectures on Godmanhood* he sought to show that in Christianity the opposition between divine and human is reconciled by distinguishing between God as He is in Himself and God as He is in relation to the world, allowing for both the radical transcendence of God and His active creative presence in the world. His views are Christocentric; he raises the CHALCEDONIAN dogma of the union of two natures, divine and human, in Jesus Christ, 'without division or confusion', to the level of a philosophical principle embracing the whole of existence. His interpretation of traditional teaching is based upon a strong sense of the TRANSFIGURATION of creation. The Incarnation is an essential part of the divine plan of the universe, providing for the possibility of salvation, or, in patristic terms, for the DEIFICATION of the world. The whole of the cosmogonic process, centred on the history of humanity, is a process of the deification of creation. Deification, however, is a matter of potentiality not certainty; each person has the freedom to accept the redemptive possibility and actively work towards it by virtuous conduct, fighting evil and surrendering to the will of God, or to reject all this. On this view is based his understanding of the importance of asceticism, which he defined not as mortification of the flesh, but as a strengthening of the spirit with a view to a transfiguration of the flesh.

A vital feature of Solovyov's understanding of Christianity is its social character. The problem of Christian culture is connected for him with the idea of theocracy, a community ordered by the search for God, as can be seen in Jewish biblical history. In the course of his life he moved from various concrete political plans for a theocratic state to an eschatological and mystical understanding of this community. He never doubted that Christians have responsibilities for the practical betterment of society. He saw this view reflected in Platonic philosophy as well, arguing that the word philosophy meant the love of wisdom and wisdom referred not simply to 'theoretical knowledge', but also to practical and moral conduct.

An important element in Solovyov's teaching was his idea of the pan-unity (*vseedinstvo*) of the created world, of the cosmos and humanity, in its intimate connection with the creator. Initially this intuition was a parallel to Plato's 'world soul', but Solovyov's subsequent attempts to theorize it as DIVINE WISDOM (*see* SOPHIOLOGY) met with criticism as not in accordance with traditional Orthodox theology.

Solovyov was one of the first in the nineteenth century to advance ecumenical work, because, like Khomiakov, he could see the mystical unity and eschatological significance of the one church as the body of Christ, and regarded the schism of the churches as one of the gravest sins committed by Christians.

Sutton, J. (1988), *The Religious Philosophy of Vladimir Solovyov*. London: Macmillan.
Soloviov, V. (1982), *The Antichrist*. Edinburgh: Floris Books.
Soloviov, V. (1980), *The Drama of Plato's Life*. Edinburgh: Helios Fountain.
Stremoukhov, D. (1980), *Vladimir Soloviev and His Messianic Work*. Belmont, Mass.: Nordland.
Frank, S. L., ed. (1974), *A Solovyov Anthology*. Westport, Conn.: Greenwood.
Soloviov, V. (1973), *God, Man and the Church*. Cambridge: James Clarke and Co.

Lossky, N. (1952), *A History of Russian Philosophy*. London: Allen & Unwin.
Soloviov, V. (1948), *Lectures on Godmanhood*. London: Denis Dobson.

MV

Sophiology Theosophical speculation centred on 'Sophia', DIVINE WISDOM, developed by certain late nineteenth- and early twentieth-century Russian thinkers including Vladimir SOLOVYOV, Sergius BULGAKOV and Pavel FLORENSKY. One influence on the development of Sophiology was the seventeenth-century German Lutheran mystic Jakob Boehme. Sophiologists perceived Sophia as a living, creative presence which links God and creation. For Solovyov, Sophia is part of the divine essence and is identified with the Platonic world soul. Sophia is also associated with the THEOTOKOS, an association strengthened by the feminine gender of the name Sophia. This is also why Sophiology has been taken up in recent years by some feminist theologians. Christ himself bears the title 'Divine Wisdom' on some Byzantine icons. Sophiology in general, however, represents a development in speculative thought not easily squared with traditional Orthodox theology.

KP

Kornblatt, J. D. and Gustafson, R. F., eds (1996), *Russian Religious Thought*. Madison: University of Wisconsin Press.
Zernov, N. (1963), *The Russian Religious Renaissance of the Twentieth Century*. London: Darton, Longman & Todd.
Bulgakov, S. (1937), *The Wisdom of God: A Brief Summary of Sophiology*. New York and London: n.p.

Sopoćani The Holy Trinity church at Sopoćani lies at the source of the Raška, near Novi Pazar, in south-western SERBIA. Founded *c*.1256 as his mausoleum by King Uroš I (1242–76), the church is single-naved, surmounted by a dome, with a large apse and a narthex. An open exonarthex and a bell tower were added to the west wall *c*.1340. Monastic buildings and strong walls encircled the church. As in some other thirteenth-century Serbian churches, the earliest wall paintings (*c*.1263) covering large surfaces of the church's interior had a golden background imitating mosaic. Painted by anonymous artists whose brilliant style shows a great sensibility for the beauty of the human figure and its central position in the splendour of God's creation, these frescoes are in harmony with the views expressed through Serbian literary works of the period. A historical composition of the funeral of the founder's mother Queen Anne is preserved in the narthex, as well as portraits of King Uroš I, his wife Helen of Anjou, and their two sons, in a donor's composition, approaching Christ and the Virgin. As in STUDENICA, scenes of Stefan Nemanja's life and the translation of his relics from HILANDAR decorate one of the side chapels. In the OTTOMAN period, the monastic buildings were demolished soon after 1389, but rebuilt during the despotate in the early fifteenth century. Quite prosperous in the late sixteenth and early seventeenth centuries, the monastery was ruined in 1689 when the Ottomans removed the lead roof of the church, causing gradual decay of the building's upper parts. Deserted for over two centuries, but visited by occasional travellers, the church was restored in 1926. Excavation of the entire complex and modern restoration started in 1975.

Kandić, O. and Milošević, D. (1986), *The Monastery of Sopoćani*. Belgrade: Institute for the Protection of Cultural Monuments of the Socialist Republic of Serbia.

ZG

Soterichos Panteugenos   Ecumenical Patriarch elect, condemned for heresy at the Council of Constantinople of 1156 for refusing to acknowledge that the sacrifice of Christ on the Cross, as also his mysterically identical sacrifice as unbloody victim in the Divine Liturgy, is offered to all three persons of the Holy TRINITY.

DM

spiritual relationships   Created by the MYSTERIES of baptism, chrismation and matrimony, in EASTERN CHRISTIAN tradition and canon law such relationships are treated seriously. The most important relationships are those between godparent (*anadochos*) and godchild, established at baptism, and between the best man (*koumbaros*) and the bride and bridegroom, established by matrimony. The *koumbaros* is, by tradition, godparent to the first child of the marriage.

Spiritual relationships traditionally limit choice of marriage partner. If A is godparent of B, then Eastern Orthodox canonical tradition prohibits the following marriages: A with B; A's child with B; A with B's parent; A with B's child; A's child with B's parent; A's child with B's child; B with any other godchild of A; B with the widowed partner of any other godchild of A; A's godchild with the godchild of A's husband or wife; B with A's son- or daughter-in-law.

Spiritual relationships of a different kind exist between a spiritual father or mother and their spiritual children; among those spiritual children; and among the monks or nuns of a monastic house, and between them and the abbot or abbess.

DM

spiritual theology   The very term, formed from three words sacred to Christians, *theos*, *logos*, *spiritus*, contains a juxtaposition to be reflected upon. From the earliest centuries, the Christian East has understood the practice of theology as primarily a personal communion with Ho Theos, the Father, through the Logos, Christ, in the Holy Spirit, an experience lived in the state of prayer. The tradition of the Eastern and Oriental churches cannot be separated from their devotional and liturgical life. Eastern Christendom came to be characterized by features that early distinguished it from the Latin West; and within the East, ethnic, geographical or historical areas developed their own unique characters.

Eastern writers' esteem for the common tradition of the fathers is well known. It bestows a certain unity underlying the many differences among the various churches. The analogy with sacred iconography is striking. ICONS show a surprisingly rich combination of colours, and the register of feelings which they evoke varies greatly, while the lines and forms of individual icon types are almost unchanging. Writing a book on the spiritual life is not entirely different from writing a work on painting. Such a book offers a set of common 'rules', which are the result of long experience. Here we outline some of these common traditions.

'For it was for this end that the Word of God was made man and he who was the Son of God became the Son of Man, that man, having been taken into the Word, and receiving adoption, might become son of God.' This summary of sacred history, presented by Irenaeus in the third book of his *Adversus Haereses* and borrowed with variations in every period, lies at the base of the spiritual teaching of the East. The aim of this instruction is the DEIFICATION of humanity.

Eastern spirituality is seen not only as moral, but more as ontological. The decisive characteristic of the concept of spirit in the BIBLE, as distinguished from that found in philosophical reflection, lies in this immediate personal association with God, in the New Testament with the spirit of Christ, the Holy Spirit. Christian faith in the Spirit became more explicit later: the human being is qualified as *pneumatikos*, spiritual, through the operation of the spirit. According to Irenaeus, 'the perfect man consists of three elements: flesh, soul and spirit.' This the famous trichotomy of the East. Spirit is the soul of the human soul. Summarizing this traditional teaching, the Russian author THEOPHAN THE RECLUSE (d. 1894) stated that 'the essence of the spiritual life, the life in Christ, consists in the transformation of soul and body and their introduction into the sphere of Spirit, that is, in the spiritualization of soul and body.' Placed in the visible world, the human being achieves the spiritual goal through 'cosmic spiritualization'.

The God of Christianity is the Father who reveals himself through the Son in the Holy Spirit. The royal road of sanctification is the ascending movement which goes in the Spirit through the Son to the Father. The contemplation of the TRINITY is the summit of theology.

Eastern spirituality starts with the image of God according to which the human being was created and arrives at the likeness to the Creator (Genesis 1: 26). Although the attempt of Augustine to discern within the human mind a replica of the life of the Trinity is not entirely alien to Eastern Christian tradition, the Eastern tradition came to emphasize rather that the human being is 'after' the image of God through the mediation of Christ, the true archetype. The Christian is therefore 'an image of the Image'. This image is always present. According to ORIGEN's well-known idea, our sins superimpose on us images of the worldly, of the bestial, of Caesar. The image of God is obscured. Once the evil is removed, the qualities of the original image reappear, veiled only by a sort of 'ugly mask'. Hence, to know oneself signifies one's capacity to grow in imitation of Christ and in the contemplation of God.

The *tserkovnost*, the 'sense of church' so familiar to the Russians, amounts to the consciousness that salvation is universal and that no one is to believe he is saved unless he is saved together with others. The unity of human nature, presupposed in the reflections of the ancients, is seen and lived to a surprising degree by Christians. Because humanity's true nature includes the Holy Spirit, it is 'like a soul' common to all human beings; the spirituality of one person can progress only in a deified human *pleroma*, the church.

The Jews found God in history; the Greeks searched for him in the beauty and harmony of the cosmos. Having become Christians, Hellenized peoples were deeply conscious of their cosmic vocation – not a matter of inserting oneself into a universal harmony, but rather of actively co-operating to re-establish this beauty, spoiled by sin. By vocation, the Christian must work at the perfection and the deification of the world, through ascetic purification which precedes cosmic joy.

Monks and monasteries have played a decisive role in shaping Eastern ways of thinking the Christian life. From the beginning, MONASTICISM was the image of the authentic Christian life. Monastics strove to observe the commandments – all the commandments.

Their determined flight from the world, their rigorous asceticism and their hard work were all aimed at attaining the very goal of baptism: to purify the image of God in humanity, which has been tarnished, and to return it to its full splendour.

The West has been compared to Martha and the East to Mary. The entire spiritual life in the East has often been structured as a means to contemplation, which according to Emperor Justinian's legislation is the only aim of monastic life. With the spiritual masters, the term's meaning crystallized in a definition: contemplation (*theoria*) meant *theon horan*, to see God in all things. The word *theoria* is supposed to be derived from *thea* (sight). But its object is not the surface of things. In the search for the truth, Greek wisdom, in the person of Plato and his followers, came to discern that the senses and through them the physical sciences only yield opinion (*doxa*). The truth (*aletheia*) is perceived through a non-bodily sense, the intelligence; it is a 'meta-physical' knowledge, its object the *logos*, the idea of the reality. Greek antiquity stressed the excellence of the mind (*nous*).

Christian writers, however, were convinced that even such knowledge was not true gnosis. There is a double knowledge of the world: the pragmatic, which even the impious obtain, and the spiritual, reserved for saints. Spiritual contemplation must understand beings in their ultimate truth. Its object is not the Platonic idea, but the *theoteles logos*. Things must be seen as they relate to God, in their providential function. Its organ is not the senses, nor the abstract intelligence, but the pure heart (Matthew 5: 8).

Eastern spiritual writers speak frequently of the heart: the custody of the heart, attentiveness to the heart, purity of heart, prayer of the heart, the divine presence in the heart. The concept can appear elusive. Attempts have been made to locate the heart in a psychological framework, and only subsequently ask what function such a 'heart' can have in the spiritual life. This procedure needs to be reversed. The use of the term 'heart' in Eastern Christian literature poses religious questions. Once these have been clarified, we can ask how they are reflected in human psychological structure. As the pupil of the eye is the point of intersection between two worlds, the outer and inner, so there must be in the human being a mysterious point through which God enters the human being with all his riches. We know that for Plato the *nous*, the mind, is the faculty or organ which is in contact with the divine. But this would be only one of the many relationships to God. The Eastern mystics no longer speak of an 'organ' or a 'faculty' but look for the point where all human powers are concentrated. In biblical and popular parlance, this focal point is the heart, seen as the principle of human integration. 'The heart sustains the energy of all the forces of soul and body,' wrote Theophan the Recluse. It is my 'I', the source of human acts.

The heart, the principle of unity within a person, gives stability to the multiplicity of moments in life. For the Eastern Christian, the ideal has always been the state of prayer, an habitual disposition which somehow in itself deserves the name of prayer, aside from the specific acts it produces with greater or lesser frequency. This state of prayer is at the same time the state of entirely spiritual life, a steadfast disposition of the heart.

But how can one know the heart? Eastern authors reply: to the degree that it is pure, the heart has a direct intuition of itself. Therefore attention to the heart is a well-known expression in Eastern spirituality. It assumes, first, a negative aspect: keeping away all evil coming from outside. Its positive aspect is attentiveness to the voice of God, a readiness to perceive the divine mysteries as they exist within us. The heart then becomes a wellspring of revelation.

The Eastern rites abound with insistent repetitions of the Kyrie eleison, with requests for the remission of sins. REPENTANCE is called a second baptism. The desert fathers firmly believed in the rapid effect of repentance, METANOIA. And yet, among the ascetics, forgiveness never made the fountain of tears run dry. 'Once purified from sins we must yet have the same faults before our eyes', wrote JOHN CHRYSOSTOM. How is the promptness of remission reconciled with perpetual compunction? This lasting compunction (*penthos*) is also a joyous faith: sin is the only evil, but it can always be wiped out by repentance. According to JOHN CLIMACUS it is a 'joy-making mourning' (Matthew 5: 4). The doctrine of *penthos* was so deeply ingrained in the Syriac-speaking Christians that monks became known as *'abīlē* ('mourners').

The term 'JESUS PRAYER' is a literal transcription of the Greek *euche Iesou*, in Russian *molitva Jisusova*. For centuries it has taken the following form: 'Lord Jesus Christ, Son of God, have mercy upon me, a sinner,' or 'Lord Jesus Christ, Son of God, have mercy on us.' This prayer has been called the 'heart of Orthodoxy'. Byzantine and Russian monks associate the Jesus Prayer with use of a prayer rope similar to a Western rosary (*komboskoinon, lestovka, vervitsa, tchotki*), which helps to count the invocations and the bows that may accompany them. Through the WAY OF THE PILGRIM, now translated into several languages, and more recently from the PHILOKALIA, readers in the West have become acquainted with the Jesus Prayer. According to the story of the *Way of the Pilgrim*, the pilgrim, a simple peasant, is seeking an answer to the traditional question: how to pray without ceasing? The STARETS, the spiritual father, suggests a simplified method to him. He begins with the repeated invocation of Jesus and goes from 3,000 to 6,000 and then to 12,000 aspirations a day. After that he no longer counts them because his lips and tongue pronounce the words by themselves, even during sleep. After some time the movement is transferred from his tongue to his heart. The pilgrim is aware that his prayer is now recited within the beating of his heart, as if the heart somehow began to say, one, 'Lord', two, 'Jesus', three, 'Christ', and so on.

The aim of the Jesus Prayer is to reinforce a certain state of heart. Athonite HESYCHASM wanted to help this process of interior assimilation by mean of a 'psychosomatic method'. Its best-known theoretician was Nikephoros the Monk of the later thirteenth century. The exercise contained a regulated slowing down of the breathing, a mental exploration of the visceral 'me' in search of the place of the heart, and the unceasing invocation of the name of Jesus. The unification of the mind joined to prayer soon led to joy, a growing love of God and a great light, called 'Taboric' (*see* TRANSFIGURATION).

By the richness of their ceremonies and their chants, but also by the contemplation of the cosmos, the Eastern churches seek to unveil the presence of God within creation. 'To him, the God who did appear and did descend into this world, to him who transfigured creation, be glory and praise for ever' (Byzantine Matins of the feast of EPIPHANY).

Špidlík, T. (1994), *L'idée russe. Une autre vision de l'homme*. Troyes: n.p.
Špidlík, T. (1986), *The Spirituality of the Christian East: A Systematic Handbook*. Kalamazoo: Cistercian Publications.

Špidlík, T. (1979), *Les grands mystiques russes*. Paris.
Špidlík, T. (1967), 'Moral Theology and Spirituality, Greek Orthodox', *The New Catholic Encyclopedia*, vol. 9, cols 1126–8.

TŠ

starets Russian equivalent of Greek *gerontas* (elder). *Starchestvo* (eldership) may be exercised by charismatic priests, monks, nuns and even laypeople, either in a general way, in a relationship between a spiritual father or mother and a lay person or cleric living in the world, or in a structured spiritual discipline, normally lived in a monastery or skete, where thoughts (*logismoi*) are disclosed, usually daily, to the elder and counsel given; the counsel may be given in the form of silence, a repeated scriptural phrase or even what seem riddles. DISCRIMINATION is essential for eldership. *Starchestvo* is a fundamental element in the central tradition of HESYCHASM.

This tradition of spiritual eldership can be traced to the desert fathers and mothers of Egypt and Syria. It received new impetus in the eighteenth century. The subjection of Orthodox church structures to state control from this period, in the Russian empire and the Balkans, led Christians to seek spiritual guidance from hermits, pilgrims and others outside the established order.

Returning from ATHOS, PAISSII VELICHKOVSKII (d. 1794) inspired a general rebirth of traditional spirituality in monasteries and society at large. SERAPHIM OF SAROV (d. 1833) provided an example of sanctity that fired the imagination of Orthodox throughout Russia and, later, worldwide. *Starchestvo* was practised at OPTINA and VALAAM. Russian elders include John of Kronstadt (d. 1908), Isidor of Gethsemane (d. 1908) and Gabriel of Eleazar (d. 1915), the spiritual father of ELISABETH FEODOROVNA (d. 1918), Silouan Antonov (d. 1938) and MICHAEL PITKEVICH (d. 1962). SYMEON POPOVIĆ and JUSTIN POPOVIĆ (d. 1979) were their Serbian Orthodox equivalents. George Karslidis (d. 1959), Porphyrios of Oropos (d. 1991), Jacob Tsalikis of Euboia (d. 1991) and PAISIOS EZNEPIDIS of Athos (d. 1994) are among the successors of the KOLLYVADES, whose leader, NIKODEMOS THE HAGIORITE (d. 1809) was a Greek counterpart of Paissii Velichkovskii. The tradition of Greek *gerontes* has continued to the present, Amphilochios of PATMOS (d. 1970) being a well-known example. In the West, elders like Gerasim of Alaska (d. 1969), Maria Gysi of Whitby in England (d. 1977), Seraphim Rose of Platina in California (d. 1982) and Sophrony Sakharov of Tolleshunt Knights in England (d. 1993) have provided a contact point enabling Western Christians, Orthodox and others, to draw on this ancient tradition.

Christensen, D. (1993), *Not of this World: The Life and Teaching of Seraphim Rose*. Forestville, Cal.: Seraphim Rose Foundation.
Cherubim (1992), *Contemporary Ascetics of Mount Athos*, vols 1 and 2. Platina, Cal.: St Herman of Alaska Press.
Vlachos, H. (1991), *A Night in the Desert of the Holy Mountain*. Levadia: Theotokos Monastery.
Kholmogorov, S. (1988), *One of the Ancients*. Platina, Cal.: St Herman of Alaska Press.
Florensky, P. (1987), *Salt of the Earth*. Platina, Cal.: St Herman of Alaska Press.
Balan, I. (1985), *Roumaniko Gerontiko*. Thessaloniki: Orthodoxos Kypseli.

Jardine Grisbrook, W. (1981), *The Spiritual Counsels of Father John of Kronstadt*. Crestwood, NY: St Vladimir's Seminary Press.

Martha (1981), *Papa Nicolas Planas*. Boston: Holy Transfiguration Press.

Zervakos, P. (1980), *Geron Philotheos Zervakos, 1884–1980*. Thessaloniki: Orthodoxos Kypseli.

Alekseyev, J. (1979), *Christ is in Our Midst*. London: Darton, Longman & Todd.

Thekla (1979), *Mother Maria, Her Life in Letters*. London: Darton, Longman & Todd.

Metrophanes (1976), *St Paisius Velichkovsky*. Platina, Cal.: St Herman of Alaska Press.

de Beausobre, I. (1975), *Russian Letters of Direction, 1834–1860*. Crestwood, NY: St Vladimir's Seminary Press.

Sophrony (1975), *The Monk of Mount Athos, Staretz Silouan*. Crestwood, NY: St Vladimir's Seminary Press.

Sophrony (1975), *Wisdom from Mount Athos*. Crestwood, NY: St Vladimir's Seminary Press.

Dunlop, J. B. (1972), *Staretz Amvrosy*. London: Mowbrays.

Zander, V. (1970), *St Seraphim of Sarov*. London: SPCK.

DB

Staro Nagoričino The Church of St George near Kumanovo in the Republic of Macedonia was built in 1313 by King Stefan Uroš II Milutin (1282–1321), replacing a ruined eleventh-century basilica whose dressed stone walls form the base of the new building, a cross-in-square structure, surmounted by one large and four small domes. An extensive programme of wall paintings by Michael and Eutychios, completed 1317–18, includes detailed illustrations of Great Feasts, Miracles and Parables of Christ, the life of the Virgin Mary, cycles of St Nicolas and St George and 365 scenes from the church CALENDAR, the earliest representation in Serbian art. Busts and standing figures of the fathers wearing the *polystavrion* are represented in the altar area. A place of honour is reserved for the first Serbian archbishop, SAVA. The donor's panel with King Milutin, holding the model of his church, and Queen Simonida, approaching St George and the Virgin, is in the narthex. Two large fresco-icons, also dating from 1317–18, built into the stone ICONOSTASIS, represent the Mother of God (PELAGONITISSA) and St George. In the sixteenth century, during the OTTOMAN period, extensive repair work on the church was done and the monastery was active until the nineteenth century. Apart from the church itself, no visible traces of the monastic buildings remain, but the site awaits archaeological investigation.

Todić, B. (1993), *Staro Nagoričino*. Belgrade: Republički Zavod za Zaštitu Spomenika Kulture, Prosveta, Srpska Akademija Nauka i Umetnosti.

ZG

Stavriotes Orthodox crypto-Christians of the OTTOMAN empire. Their name derived from that of a village in PONTUS, but was widely applied to EASTERN ORTHODOX outwardly conforming to Islam while secretly remaining Christian. As early as 1339 and 1340, letters from Patriarch John Kalekas to Nicea acknowledge the existence of such groups in areas under Islamic rule. The Roman Catholic church regarded any formal conversion to Islam as apostasy. The Orthodox hierarchy, however, tolerated crypto-Christianity while encouraging communities to declare their Christianity when circumstances were favourable. Catholic crypto-Christians none the less existed under Ottoman rule.

Crypto-Christians existed throughout the Ottoman empire but particularly in Pontus (Stavrin, Kromni, etc.), Crete and CYPRUS. In the nineteenth century certain groups publicly acknowledged their Christianity, notably in Crete (1821), ALBANIA (1832), Albania again and Pontus (1846), around Ankara (1876) and Cyprus (1878, when British administration began). Such communities faced reprisals when they rejected Islam; Catholic crypto-Christians of Skopje who publicly declared their Christianity in 1846 were massacred or deported to ASIA MINOR. There is evidence that crypto-Christians still exist in Turkey and elsewhere in the Middle East.

Nikolaidou, E. I. (1988), 'KryptoChristianismos', *Praktika Theologikou Synedriou eis Timen kai Mnemen ton Neomartyron-1986*. Thessaloniki.

DB

Stephen ad-Duwaihi   Iṣṭifān al-Duwaihī, Stephanus Aldoensis, Stephanus Edenensis (1630–1704): MARONITE scholar and churchman. Educated at the Maronite College in ROME, ad-Duwaihi was consecrated Maronite bishop of CYPRUS in 1668 and elected patriarch in 1670. He helped establish the Order of St Anthony and other religious orders in Lebanon. He compiled and composed many important liturgical and historical works. He is credited with the first major history of the Maronites, and with making the first scientific study of the origins of the Maronite church.

Dau, B. (1984), *History of the Maronites: Religious, Cultural and Political*. Lebanon: B. Dau.
Raphael, P. (1950), *Le rôle du Collège Maronite Romain dans l'orientalisme aux XVIIe et XVIIIe siècles*. Beyrouth: Université Saint Joseph de Beyrouth.

MJB/SHG

Stephen of Perm (1340–96)   Apostle to the Zyrians, a Finnish people living in the region of Perm; began his missionary work in 1378–9 and invented the Zyrian alphabet in order to translate the scriptures and liturgical books. His life was written by his friend Epiphanios the Wise, who also wrote the life of SERGIUS OF RADONEZH. Stephen studied at the monastery of St Gregory in Rostov where he learned Greek and became a leading scholar of his times. He visited NOVGOROD on several occasions, attending the council of 1390, but died in MOSCOW where he was buried in a monastery inside the Kremlin. The Permian liturgy was replaced by the Slavonic in the sixteenth century.

Fedotov, G. P. (1975), *The Russian Religious Mind*, vol. 2: *The Middle Ages: The Thirteenth to the Fifteenth Centuries*. Belmont, Mass.: Norland.

KP

sticheron   A hymn that follows a verse (Greek: *stichos*) from the Psalms. At Vespers there are always stichera at 'Lord, I have cried', but at Lauds at 'Let everything that has breath' only on Sundays and feasts. At the Aposticha one sticheron is sung before the first psalm verse. The Aposticha at Vespers on Sundays form an alphabetical acrostic, three letters each week, but the first sticheron in each tone does not form part of the series.

E

Strigol'niki Russian sect (lit. 'Shearers') appearing around NOVGOROD and Pskov in the later fourteenth century, opposed to the church's owning property. An attack on their ideas by STEPHEN OF PERM dated 1386 claims the sect originated as a protest against clerical simony because of which they refused to accept the sacraments from priests. Their stand against simony seems to have led to their rejection of liturgical services in churches and to the practice of calling on earth and sky to witness their confession. This latter practice is attested among later groups, such as the priestless (*bezpopovtsy*) OLD BELIEVERS and the Orthodox alike, but appears first among the Strigol'niki. There is no hard evidence of any connection with later groups such as the NON-POSSESSORS, but the influence of the BOGOMILS on them has been asserted by some.

Fedotov, G. P. (1975), *The Russian Religious Mind*, vol. 2: *The Middle Ages: The Thirteenth to the Fifteenth Centuries*. Belmont, Mass.: Norland.

KP

Studenica Lying in a hilly region above the Ibar valley in south-western SERBIA, the monastery of Studenica was built between 1186 and 1196 by Stefan Nemanja, founder of the Serbian medieval state. In the middle of a circular fortified compound, typical of Serbian monastic architecture, stands the church of the Virgin, where in 1196, having left his grand-zupan's throne to his son Stefan, Nemanja took his monastic vows. As the monk Symeon, he soon joined his youngest son SAVA on ATHOS where in 1198 they founded the monastery of HILANDAR. Simeon died there in 1199 and in 1206–7 Sava brought his relics to Studenica. Studenica's status as mausoleum of the founder of the Nemanjic dynasty was enhanced by Sava's presence and activity between 1207 and 1215–16, when as abbot he prepared the ground for the Serbian church's autocephaly, attained in 1219, two years after Serbia became a kingdom. Within Studenica's TYPIKON, for which, as for Hilandar, he adapted the Evergetis model, Sava included a biography of Nemanja, thus initiating a particular genre in Serbian medieval literature.

Renowned for its white marble architecture on whose facades Romanesque influences from the Adriatic coast are fused with Byzantine forms, Studenica's interior displays a solemn programme of wall paintings of a highest stylistic quality. A Serbian Church Slavonic inscription in gold lettering in the dome, mentioning Sava's care, records their completion in 1208. A large exonarthex with two side chapels, one with frescoes depicting Nemanja's death and the translation of his relics, was added in 1233–4 by Nemanja's grandson King Radoslav. At the beginning of OTTOMAN rule the monastery was badly damaged, but from 1568 a number of frescoes were restored, including the donor's composition above Nemanja's tomb. Since his tomb was plundered during later devastations, the most venerated relics came to be those of Stefan the First Crowned, the 'Holy King'. In the course of the seventeenth to twentieth centuries they were several times carried to safety by the fleeing monks and returned when circumstances permitted. In the periods of strife, Studenica's monks travelled to

RUSSIA and other EASTERN ORTHODOX lands outside the Ottoman empire, seeking and receiving help in money as well as in books and liturgical objects. Of some twelve other churches and chapels within the monastery's walls only two survive: St Nicolas (thirteenth century) and King Milutin's church of SS Joachim and Anna, known as Kraljeva Crkva, dating from 1314, with remarkable frescoes, including the portraits of the royal donors and those of the king's holy ancestors, Symeon Nemanja and Sava.

Gavrilović, Z. (1989), 'Between Latins and Greeks. Some Artistic Trends in Medieval Serbia (13th–14th centuries)', *Nottingham Medieval Studies* 33.
Babić, G. (1987), *Kraljeva Crkva u Studenici*. Belgrade: Prosveta.
Šakota, M. (1986), *Monastery of Studenica*. Belgrade: Institute for the Protection of Cultural Monuments of the Socialist Republic of Serbia.
Babić, G., Korać, V. and Ćirković, S. (1986), *Studenica*. Belgrade: Jugoslovenska Revija.

ZG

stylite   Stylite ascetics followed the example of SYMEON STYLITES in living on the top of a pillar (*stylos*). Their basic motive was physical separation from worldly affairs, but stylites were often surrounded by followers and supplicants, so that they were far from solitary. Depictions of stylite pillars suggest they sometimes had quite elaborate roofed structures for shelter.

JH

Symeon Popović (1855–1941)   Montenegrin STARETS and theologian of noble descent. He studied in KIEV and then, from 1878, Paris and Geneva. Returning to UKRAINE, Symeon joined the Pecherskaya Lavra brotherhood and was priested in 1887. Sent back to MONTENEGRO, he worked to revive monasteries and opened a theological academy in Ostrog. Symeon visited JERUSALEM and ATHOS before taking up eremitical life in 1896 in caves near Podgorica. Here he celebrated the eucharist daily, wrote and preached. Disciples gathered and helped found the Dormition monastery.

Ivosevic, V. (1987), 'Starets Simeon', *Journal of the Moscow Patriarchate* 3.

DB

Symeon Stylites (*c*.390–459)   The first great STYLITE ascetic. Both during his life and after his death Symeon attracted an enormous following. Several lives of the saint exist, including one in THEODORET OF CYRRHUS' *Historia Religiosa* and one in SYRIAC. Born in Cilicia, he spent a decade in a monastery and then the remaining fifty years of his life in Telanissos in northern Syria, where he eventually installed himself on a pillar, increased in height from time to time until it reached *c*.60 feet. He became famous for his sanctity and for practical advice, as well as through miracles. During Symeon's lifetime

Telanissos became the focus of PILGRIMAGE and Theodoret even reports that Britons came to the saint. After his death there was rivalry over his body, which was taken to ANTIOCH. A great cruciform basilica was built *c*.476–91 around the site of his pillar, QALA'AT SIMA'ĀN. The saint's cult was encouraged by the Byzantine authorities, since Symeon seems to have steered clear of the Christological controversies of his time.

Doran, R. (1992). *The Lives of Simeon Stylites*. Kalamazoo: Cistercian Publications.

JH

Symeon the New Theologian (949–1022)   Byzantine monastic reformer, mystic and hymnographer. His political career in CONSTANTINOPLE led to high rank in the imperial service. At fourteen he stayed for a while in the Studios monastery, where he first met the elder Symeon Eulabes, but was twenty-eight before he finally entered the monastery and devoted himself to the elder Symeon. After a year with his spiritual father he moved to the monastery of St Mamas where he was to serve as abbot for twenty-five years. A group of monks rebelled against his abbatial authority and the austere discipline he maintained. Around 1003 he began to clash with church authorities on several points, notably the saintly cult he had established for the elder Symeon, and he was obliged to resign as abbot. Forced to leave Constantinople in 1009, he spent the rest of his life in exile, writing and meeting the many disciples who came to see him.

Symeon criticized those who claimed that no one now could observe the gospel commandments and become like the great Christians of the past. This for him was the mother of heresies: not to believe that the Christian life is a living encounter with Christ. He proclaimed all Christians capable of knowing God directly. Though it was unusual in Byzantine tradition for spiritual writers to talk openly of their own religious experiences, Symeon's writings contain many references to his; he declares himself unworthy of the grace to write about his experiences and asserts he does so to encourage others in their quest for spiritual perfection. His openness did not endear him to some of his contemporaries who considered he was setting himself up as equal to the apostles.

Turner, H. J. M. (1990), *St Symeon the New Theologian and Spiritual Fatherhood*. Leiden: Brill.
Krivocheine, B. (1986), St *Symeon the New Theologian: Life, Sprituality, Doctrine*. Crestwood, NY: St Vladimir's Seminary Press.
McGuckin, P. (1982), *Symeon the New Theologian: The Practical and Theological Chapters and the Three Theological Discourses*. Kalamazoo: Cistercian Publications.
DeCatanzaro, C. J. (1980), *Symeon the New Theologian: The Discourses*. London: SPCK.

KP

Synodikon Orientale   Name given to a late eighth-century collection in which are preserved the acts of thirteen 'NESTORIAN' synods from 410 to 775. This is a fundamental source for the study of the history of the church in Persia. J.-B. Chabot edited and translated the collection in 1902.

Chabot, J.-B. (1902), *Synodicon Orientale, ou Recueil de synodes nestoriens.* Paris: Klincksieck.

JH

Syriac One of the late Aramaic dialects which developed after the unity imposed on Aramaic by its administrative use in the Achaemenid empire, Syriac is specifically the dialect of the city and region of EDESSA. It is first known in pagan inscriptions of the first three centuries AD, especially inscriptions from Sumatar Harabesi east of Edessa and texts in mosaics. There are important parchment texts from the mid-third century from the Middle Euphrates. Syriac has its classical form as the language of the Christian tradition of the area, and because of the translation of the BIBLE into Syriac it became an important theological and liturgical language over a wide area. As the Eastern and Western Syriac regions went their separate ways theologically and liturgically, Syriac underwent a gradual dialectal bifurcation, most obviously with regard to pronunciation of vowels. Eastern and Western versions of the old Syriac script developed, resulting in three styles, the traditional *estrangelā*, from the Greek *strongulē*, 'rounded'; *sertā*, 'line', Western Syriac, used especially by the SYRIAN ORTHODOX; and a distinctive Eastern script usually called NESTORIAN, though the term is less than satisfactory. *Estrangelā* has never fallen out of use and enjoys a scholarly revival since it is used for most modern printed academic publications, such as the Leiden edition of the PESHITTA.

Syriac survives as a liturgical and scholarly language in the traditional Syriac-using churches, principally the Syrian Orthodox and SYRIAN CATHOLIC, the CHURCH OF THE EAST, the CHALDEANS and the MARONITES, but its use is rather restricted in those traditions which have embraced the use of Arabic, or in INDIA Malayalam. As spoken vernacular a much-modified survival of classical Syriac is still used, mostly in the domestic context, in south-east Turkey, northern Iraq and north-east Syria. The language is also undergoing revival in DIASPORA communities, especially in AMERICA.

It may be noted that the form of Aramaic still spoken in the area around Ma'lūlā north of Damascus is of a completely different Aramaic tradition, more akin to the Jewish Palestinian Aramaic spoken in first-century Palestine. This Jewish Palestinian Aramaic was one of the other post-Achaemenid Aramaic dialects which developed alongside Syriac, as did also Nabataean, Palmyrene and Mandaic.

Beyer, K. (1986), *The Aramaic Language.* Göttingen: Vandenhoeck & Ruprecht.
Nöldeke, T. (1904 [1898]), *Compendious Syriac Grammar.* London: Williams & Norgate. (German repr. 1977, Darmstadt: Wissenschaftliche Buchgesellschaft.)

JH

Syrian Catholic church One of the Syrian churches in communion with the Roman Catholic church, and one of the two Catholic bodies using the West Syrian rite, the other being the Syro-Malankara church in INDIA. Initiatives to unite the SYRIAN ORTHODOX to the Roman church began in crusader times. Declarations of common faith in the thirteenth century under the Patriarch Ignatius IX Bahnām and in the sixteenth century under Patriarch Ignatius XVII Ni'matallāh came to nothing. It was under the influence of the Franciscans that most of Aleppo's Syrian Orthodox accepted a 'Catholic' bishop, Andreas Aḥījān, in 1656, and in 1662 he became the first 'Syrian Catholic' patriarch of ANTIOCH, though the succession was interrupted in 1702 then re-established under Michael Ǧarweh only in 1783. In the nineteenth century most Syrian Catholics lived in western Syria and around Mosul. The independence of the Syrian Catholics from the Syrian Orthodox was officially recognized by the Ottoman government in 1830, when their existence as a separate community was recognized by a *firman*, and in 1843 when their patriarch was given full authority.

Syrian Catholic clergy, supported by ROME, were better educated than their Old Church counterparts. A synod at Sharfeh in Lebanon in 1888 enacted the rule of celibacy for the clergy. Patriarch Ignatius Ephrem Rahmani (1898–1929), an eminent SYRIAC scholar, moved the patriarchal residence from Mardin to Beirut, where it remains. Patriarch Ignatius Antony II Hayyek was elected in 1968. His faithful (reckoned at 107,279 in 1994) are organized into seven dioceses in Lebanon, Iraq, Egypt and Syria.

JFC/JH

Syrian Christianity   The term refers to the various Middle Eastern and Indian churches of SYRIAC liturgical tradition, namely: the Syrian Orthodox and its Eastern Rite Catholic counterparts, Syrian Catholic and, in INDIA, Syro-Malankara churches; the Maronite church; and the Assyrian CHURCH OF THE EAST and its Eastern Rite Catholic counterparts, the Chaldean and, in India, Syro-Malabar churches. Up until about the sixteenth century the term also applied to parts of the 'Rum' Greek Orthodox patriarchate of ANTIOCH. The term 'Syrian' is thus much broader than the geographical area of modern Syria; indeed, members of these churches are spread now over all five continents, with sizable DIASPORA communities in western Europe, North and South AMERICA and AUSTRALIA.

Syrian Christianity split into three main doctrinal groups as a result of the Christological controversies of the fifth century. The SYRIAN ORTHODOX, who, along with the ARMENIAN, COPTIC and ETHIOPIAN Orthodox, constitute the Oriental Orthodox churches, follow the 'Alexandrine' Christological tradition, which emphasizes the oneness of the humanity and the divinity in the incarnate Christ; they reject the doctrinal definition of the Council of Chalcedon (451), with its phrase 'in two natures'. The Church of the East adheres to the opposite Christological tradition, the 'Antiochene', where emphasis is laid on the distinction between the divinity and the humanity in the incarnate Christ; they reject the Council of Ephesus (431). The MARONITES, along with the former Syriac-speaking parts of the Rum Orthodox patriarchate of Antioch, or MELKITES, accept the CHALCEDONIAN definition of faith, which had aimed at a middle way between the Alexandrine and Antiochene positions; since the time of the CRUSADES the Maronite church has also been in communion with ROME.

In theological polemics the true positions of both the Syrian Orthodox and the Church of the East have frequently been seriously misrepresented, and the misleading nicknames of 'MONOPHYSITE' or 'JACOBITE' have been applied to the former, and 'NESTORIAN' to the latter. Since 'monophysite' is also used to describe the position of Eutyches, whom the Syrian Orthodox have from the beginning condemned, and since the Church of the East's connections with Nestorius are very tenuous, these terms invite confusion and should be avoided. The addition of 'ASSYRIAN' as part of the official name of the Church of the East was made in the twentieth century.

In South India, where tradition takes Christianity back to the apostle Thomas, the church was originally subject to the CATHOLICOS (PATRIARCH) of the Church of the East, but from the sixteenth century onwards, after the arrival of European missionaries, this branch of Syrian Christianity has been fragmented, and there are now eight different churches in India of Syriac liturgical tradition.

The confusing nomenclature is best clarified by means of a table.

CHURCHES OF THE SYRIAC LITURGICAL TRADITION

Non-Chalcedonian	Chalcedonian
	Maronite (Catholic: former Syriac-rite Melkite)
Assyrian Church of the East (*Nestorians**)	Chaldean Catholic
	Syro-Malabar Catholic
Syrian Orthodox (*Monophysites**, *Jacobites**)	Syrian Catholic
	Syro-Malankara Catholic
	Mar Thoma (reformed Syrian church in India)

The terms marked with an asterisk are inaccurate and best avoided.

Very little is known for certain about Syrian Christianity prior to the fourth century. Although credence cannot be given to the tradition, already known to Eusebius (*Ecclesiastical History*, 1: 13), that King ABGAR the Black of EDESSA corresponded with Jesus, it is likely that Edessa was an important Christian centre from an early date, since its local dialect of Aramaic, today known as Syriac, became the literary language of all Aramaic-speaking Christians in the Near East. By the fourth century Syriac Christianity was well established both in the Eastern Roman empire and in the Persian Sasanian empire to the east (approximately modern Iraq and Iran).

Within the Roman empire Syrian Christianity was directly involved in the theological controversies of the fourth to seventh centuries; the resulting divisions which emerged in the course of the sixth century became effectively fossilized when Arab rule was established in the mid-seventh century. In Syria the division was mainly between those who rejected Chalcedon (the Syrian Orthodox) and those who accepted it, usually referred to as Melkites, i.e. followers of the *malkā* or emperor. Adherents of the Antiochene Christological tradition had been particularly strong at the 'Persian School' in Edessa, but when this was closed by Emperor Zeno in 489 the school transferred to Nisibis in the Persian empire, and it was through this channel that the Church of the East, in the Persian empire, came to adopt a strictly Antiochene position on Christology.

From an early date the church in the Persian empire had developed independently from the church in the Roman empire, and so was not directly involved in any of the great councils; the Council of Nicaea (325), however, was eventually officially accepted at a synod in 410. In the course of the fourth century the bishopric of

SELEUCIA-CTESIPHON (south of Baghdad) emerged as the senior see, and its holder acquired the title 'catholicos', then 'patriarch'. Long after it ceased in the Roman empire, periodic persecution occurred under the Sasanians, with serious outbreaks in the 340s, 420s and 440s, usually at times of war with the Roman empire; isolated martyrdoms continued until the end of the Sasanian dynasty (651). For the most part, however, the church in Persia acquired a recognized status in the eyes of the government, and several of the main elements of the later OTTOMAN *milet* system can be traced back to this period.

The advent of Islam and the end of both Roman and Persian empires in the Near East meant that Syrian Christianity became effectively cut off from the Byzantine world, though it remained strongly imbued with the Greek culture of the time and so was in a position to transmit this over the next few centuries to the Arab world. As AHL AL-KITĀB, 'people of the book', Christians had a recognized, albeit subordinate, position under Islam. At first there was no pressure to convert, and where conversions did occur, as, for example, in the Qaṭar region, this was largely for economic or social reasons; only later, especially from the tenth century onwards, were there outbreaks of forced conversions. The Crusades had a particularly bad effect on relationships between Christians and Muslims in the Near East, and though Mongol rule, from the mid-thirteenth century, was at first advantageous to Christian communities, this soon changed when the Mongol khans adopted Islam.

In the early Arab period (seventh to eighth centuries) Syrian Christianity actually continued to expand eastwards, spreading along trade routes, in particular the Silk Road, leaving scattered archaeological traces. It had reached China before 635, as is recorded in a Syriac–Chinese inscription from Xian (*see* SIAN-FU STELE) dated 781, and was present there until the end of the Yuan dynasty (1368); in the late thirteenth century a monk from near Beijing, who went on combined embassy and PILGRIMAGE to JERUSALEM, ended up as catholicos of the Church of the East (Yahballaha III, 1281–1317; the diary of his travelling companion, Rabban Ṣauma, survives).

The history of the Syriac churches from the fourteenth century onwards has been little studied, and much remains obscure. Their main location lay in what is today south-west Turkey, Syria, Lebanon, northern Iraq and north-west Iran. European missionary activity first made itself felt in 1551, when the patriarchal line in the Church of the East divided, with a separate Eastern Rite Catholic line, known under the name 'Chaldeans'. Subsequently two new starts were made in the Chaldean Catholic line, first from 1681 to 1828 at Amid (Diarbekir) and then, from 1830 onwards, 'of Babylon'. The separate Syrian Catholic line finally emerged in 1782–3. Protestant missions arrived in the nineteenth century, and the American Presbyterian Mission at Urmi set up a printing press and translated the BIBLE and other texts, including Bunyan's *Pilgrim's Progress*, into modern Syriac. Another printing press in Urmi was established by the archbishop of Canterbury's educational mission, printing works in both classical and modern Syriac. Printing in Syriac had been established much earlier, in 1610, by the Maronites in Lebanon.

The First World War, and especially the 'year of the sword' (1915), was a disastrous period for the Church of the East and the Syriac Orthodox, with large-scale massacres and forced flight. With subsequent political and economic developments in the Middle East, emigration has become a major factor in the life of all Middle Eastern churches, and most Syrian churches now have archdioceses in North and South America, Australia and Europe; one of the two patriarchs of the Assyrian Church of the East (there has been a schism since 1968 over the calendar) now lives in America.

The literary heritage of Syriac Christianity is extremely rich; this applies primarily to the first two of the three periods into which Syriac literature can be conveniently divided, namely, up to the seventh century; seventh to thirteenth centuries; and fourteenth century to the present day. During this first period the most distinctive feature of Syriac Christianity lay in its use of poetry to convey profound religious insights.

With the exception of BARDAIṢĀN (d. 222), the great early Syriac writers like APHRAHAṬ (fl. mid-fourth century) and EPHREM (d. 373) were comparatively little Hellenized, and Ephrem in particular represents an outstanding example of a theologian whose prime medium is not prose but poetry. Ephrem's theological concerns are very close to those of his Greek contemporaries, especially the CAPPADOCIANS, but his mode of expression is totally different. This tradition of using poetry as the vehicle for theological reflection continues in the fifth century, adapted then above all to the field of biblical exegesis, where NARSAI (d. c.500), JACOB OF SARUG (d. 521) and various anonymous authors provide highly imaginative explorations of particular episodes. Indeed, poetry has remained a prominent element in this tradition to the present day.

The sixth and seventh centuries witnessed a marked increase in the influence of Greek on Syriac literary culture, on the choice of genres and on style, as well as on the theological agenda. This period also saw the production of a vast number of translations from Greek into Syriac (far fewer texts travelled the opposite way, though some were very influential). Most translations were of Greek patristic writings, usually post-Nicene. In some cases the Syriac translation survives today: this applies to writers such as Evagrius, Theodore of Mopsuestia and Severus, who fell out of favour in the Greek-speaking church. Secular Greek texts were also included, notably in philosophy, especially logic and ethics, and medicine. As a result many of the same Greek texts available to Latin readers in the West at the end of late antiquity were also available to Syriac readers in the East.

The Arab invasions did not put an end to the translation activity, and famous Syrian Orthodox scholars such as Jacob of Edessa (d. 708) continued to translate or revise both patristic and philosophical texts. Scholars of the Syriac churches were thus in an excellent position to act as transmitters of Greek philosophy to the Arab world in ninth-century Baghdad when Muslim scholars, including several caliphs, became receptive to this tradition; indeed, virtually all the early translators of Aristotle and other Greek authors into Arabic belonged to one or other of the Syriac churches; the famous ḤUNAYN IBN ISḤĀQ, for example, belonged to the Church of the East. In this way the Syriac churches provided an essential link in the chain of tradition lying behind the birth of scholasticism in the medieval West that resulted from the translation into Latin of Arabic versions of Aristotelian writings, often via Hebrew.

The seventh to thirteenth centuries can be seen as a period of consolidation in Syriac as well as in Byzantine Greek tradition, with prominence given to the commentary and the encyclopaedia. Commentaries covering the entire Bible now appear, produced for example by ISHODAD of Merv (ninth century) in the Church of the East, and Dionysius bar Ṣalibi (d. 1171), among the Syrian Orthodox. This process saw its culmination in the encyclopedic writings of the Syrian Orthodox Gregory abū'l-Faraj, better known as BARHEBRAEUS (d. 1286), covering theology, philosophy, history, canon law, grammar, medicine and astronomy, and many other fields. His counterpart in the Church of the East is 'Abdīshō' of Nisibis (d. 1318); significantly, both men also held high ecclesiastical office.

From the late eighth century many scholars of all Syrian churches chose to write in Arabic, rather than Syriac, though a few wrote in both; in the Maronite and Melkite churches, indeed, Arabic soon took over entirely as the literary language, though Syriac remained the normal liturgical language in the former up to the 1960s and in the latter up to about the sixteenth century. As a result, only a small amount of Syriac literature from these communities has been preserved, apart from liturgical texts (see ARAB CHRISTIANITY).

In the Church of the East the early Arab period witnessed a remarkable flowering of literature in Syriac on the monastic life. ISAAC OF NINEVEH, or Isaac the Syrian (late seventh century), is the best-known name, since part of his writings were translated into Greek at the monastery of Mar Saba in the eighth and ninth centuries; he has exerted a great influence on Greek and Russian spirituality, and today continues to exert an even wider influence. Writings of several other fine authors, especially from the seventh and eighth centuries, such as Martyrius (Sahdona), Dadīshō', Simeon the Graceful, Joseph the Seer and John the Elder (or John of Dalyatha) also survive.

Although a few of the numerous surviving liturgical texts of the Syriac churches go back to earlier times, notably the anaphora 'of Addai and Mari', most of them are likely to have been composed or compiled during the periods of Arab and Mongol rule. Especially in the tenth and eleventh centuries, with the Byzantine reconquest of Syria, there was considerable Constantinopolitan influence on Syrian Orthodox liturgy in western Syria. The Syrian Orthodox tradition of writing anaphoras continued till the end of the middle ages; nearly seventy survive (see SYRIAN LITURGY).

Very little literature from c.1300 onwards has been printed, and the impression has sometimes been given that Syriac literature ended at this time. This is completely wrong. The fourteenth and fifteenth centuries were times of great difficulties for all the churches in the Middle East, but in the sixteenth century it was Syrian Orthodox and Maronite scholars who played an essential role in the birth of Syriac scholarship in Europe. Thanks to his calendrical knowledge, the Syrian Orthodox patriarch Ni'ma-tallāh was appointed by Pope Gregory XIII as a member of the commission that produced the Gregorian calendar (1582).

The seventeenth to nineteenth centuries saw a number of translations into Syriac and Arabic of European spiritual literature, both Catholic and, later, Protestant. Classical Syriac still continues as a literary vehicle in the twentieth century, although largely confined today to the Syrian Orthodox; at the influential monastery of Mar Gabriel at ṬUR 'ABDĪN in south-east Turkey it also serves as the language of communication, and in the eastern Netherlands the monastery of St Ephrem, consecrated in 1984, has a remarkable record of publications in Syriac. In this century, for the first time, a few European secular literary texts, chiefly French, have also been translated into Syriac. Many writers, however, like the great Syrian Orthodox scholar-patriarch Ephrem Barsaum (1887–1957), have written primarily in Arabic.

Large-scale emigration has brought problems to all the Syriac churches; it has nevertheless led to greater awareness among other Christian churches both of their existence and of the richness of their tradition. While the difficulties that the Syriac churches face at the end of the twentieth century are numerous and formidable, new opportunities are nevertheless also present.

Coakley, J. F. and Parry, K., eds (1996), *The Church of the East: Life and Thought.* *Bulletin of the John Rylands University Library of Manchester* 78, 3.
Albert, M. et al. (1993), *Christianismes Orientaux*. Paris: Cerf.
Fiey, J.-M. (1993), *Pour un Oriens Christianus Novus. Repertoire des dioceses syriaques orientaux et occidentaux*. Beiruter Texte und Studien 49. Beirut and Stuttgart: Franz Steiner.
Moffett, S. H. (1992), *A History of Christianity in Asia*, vol. 1: *Beginnings to 1500*. San Francisco: Harper.
Geerts, A. (1992), *Le christianisme syrien*. Antwerp: n.p.
Beggiani, S. (1991), *Introduction to Eastern Christian Spirituality: The Syriac Tradition*. Scranton: University of Scranton Press; London and Toronto: Associated University Presses.
Selis, C. (1988), *Les Syriens Orthodoxes et Catholiques*. Turnhout: Brepols.
Brock, S. P. (1987), *The Syriac Fathers on Prayer and the Spiritual Life*. Kalamazoo: Cistercian Publications.
Yonan, G. (1978), *Assyrer Heute. Kultur, Sprache, Nationalbewegung der aramaischspre-chenden Christen im Nahen Osten*. Hamburg: Gesellschaft fur bedrohte Völker.
Murray, R. (1975), *Symbols of Church and Kingdom: A Study in Early Syriac Tradition*. Cambridge: Cambridge University Press.
Atiya, A. S. (1968), *A History of Eastern Christianity*. London: Methuen.

SB

Syrian liturgy Today at least ten churches exist which, whatever the doctrinal and jurisdictional divisions among them, share to varying degrees a common cultural, theological and liturgical heritage, SYRIAC being the linguistic medium. The Syrian churches fall into three groups: (1) those of the East Syrian tradition, the CHURCH OF THE EAST, the CHALDEAN Catholics and the Syro-Malabar church; (2) those of the West Syrian tradition, the SYRIAN ORTHODOX, SYRIAN CATHOLIC, Malankara Orthodox, Syrian Jacobite (in South India) and Mar Thoma churches: and (3) the MARONITE church. Withdrawal from ecclesial communion has never precluded borrowing liturgical ideas and materials, and communities periodically enriched their respective inheritance by cross-fertilization and, in some cases, wholesale borrowings.

Older scholarship was content to characterize the East and West Syrian rites as two branches descended from a common Antiochene liturgical tradition, with the Maronite rite a minor variant of the West Syrian. The Maronite rite has, in the course of its history, assimilated and adopted material of Syrian Orthodox origin. Other elements suggest, however, an earlier independent development. Furthermore, the East Syrian rite seems to have derived from EDESSA, not ANTIOCH.

Most liturgical scholars are agreed that the East Syrians, by virtue of living eventually beyond the Roman empire, isolated politically, doctrinally and linguistically, have preserved some very early and primitive liturgical material. The anaphora of ADDAI and Mari is an original Syriac composition, probably of the late third century. However, this prayer has a twin, being almost identical to the Third Anaphora of St Peter, or

'Sharar', found in older Maronite missals. The relationship between the two anaphoras is such that they represent independent developments of a common tradition rather than a subsequent borrowing by one or the other. Other features common to the East Syrian and Maronite rites include the sacerdotal prayer of the Trisagion, the prayer of the fraction, and the Sancta Sanctis. Although rather later in date, the Syrian Orthodox baptismal rite attributed to Timothy of Alexandria, used alongside that of SEVERUS OF ANTIOCH, is clearly related to the Maronite baptismal rite attributed to JACOB OF SARUG. An early Syriac commentary on the liturgy (British Library Additional MS 14496) was used by subsequent East and West Syrian commentators; and the baptismal rites of all three groups echo the features and ethos of the baptismal rites outlined in the third-century Acts of Judas Thomas. Again, all three groups ascribe prayers and hymns to EPHREM, the great Syrian theologian to whom they give the title 'Harp of the Spirit'. All these point to the earlier common heritage and cross-fertilization.

Antioch was a Greek-speaking city, its extensive hinterland mainly Syriac-speaking. Edessa and Nisibis seem to have developed as centres for Syriac-speaking Christianity, and may well have influenced the Syriac-speaking area of Antioch more than the metropolitan Greek rite. Furthermore, the eucharistic model adopted by Syrian Orthodox was not the Byzantine, but the Jerusalem rite, particularly the anaphora of St James. The vast number of West Syrian anaphoras use St James as their main inspiration. There is also some similarity between GEORGIAN ordination rites (which have a Jerusalem origin) and East Syrian. According to W. F. Macomber, the Syrian Orthodox rite is basically that of Antioch, but with the anaphoral structure borrowed from the rite of Jerusalem and metrical hymns either borrowed from or inspired by those of Edessa. The Maronite and East Syrian rites, on the other hand, are, in origin, independent developments of the ancient Edessene rite. The common denominator is the Syriac language, which accounts for the affinity with parts of Palestine. The type of Christianity represented in the earlier Syriac sources reflected what Daniélou has termed 'Jewish Christianity', where the Targums played an important part in scriptural exegesis and theological method. The Edessene rite was later conserved in the Orontes valley and in the community which later removed to Lebanon, though the latter also absorbed Syrian Orthodox usages.

◆ The East Syrian rite ◆

Centred at Edessa and Nisibis, the East Syrian church was safe from Imperial presence, being inside the Persian empire. Much of its Christology was simply conservative Antiochene and 'primitive' rather than blatantly and self-consciously NESTORIAN. Indeed, immediately after CHALCEDON, East Syrian commentators preferred to appeal to Theodore of Mopsuestia, who was not pronounced heretical until 553. On gaining independence the successors of the archbishop of SELEUCIA-CTESIPHON took the title 'CATHOLICOS of the East'. The East Syrian liturgical rites are collected in a number of books. The *Taksā dRāzē* contains the three anaphoras used by that church, also often found with the baptismal rite in the *Taksā dKāhnē*, the ritual, and the *Ḥudrā*, which contains the texts proper to specific festivals. The *Šamāšūtā* provides the texts for the deacons. The *Gazā* has variable hymns and collects, and is needed together with the *Dawīdā* (the psalter), the *Qdām wa-dbātar* ('Before and After') and the *Kaskul* (chants) for the daily office. The *Taksā dSyamdā* is the ordination rite, the *Taksā Ḥūssāyā* the rite of penance, and *Ktābā dkurrāstā 'annīdē* contains the funeral rites.

Of the three anaphoras, that of Addai and Mari is the oldest. It has no institution narrative. Older scholarship, for Western doctrinal reasons, tried to argue that it once contained one; the present consensus is that it dates from a time when a reference to 'the example which is from you' was sufficient. The anaphoras attributed to Nestorius and Theodore are later, and tradition attributes them to Mar Abbas and Mar Thomas at the beginning of the sixth century. That of Nestorius is based on the Byzantine anaphoras of St Basil and St John Chrysostom, and indigenized; that of Theodore is based on Nestorius, Addai and Mari, and, probably, the *Catechetical Homilies* of Theodore of Mopsuestia. Others may have existed, but a liturgical reform is attributed to the seventh-century patriarch ISHOYAB III (Īšō'yab), who was also responsible for giving most rites a common structure based on the first part of the eucharistic rite. Private prayers called *kūššāpē* are interspersed in the eucharistic rite; although the written texts of these enter the manuscript tradition late, the genre can be traced back to the fourth century. The baptismal rite, reformed by Īšō'yab as a rite for infants, still echoes the older order of anointing–baptism–communion, with no post-baptismal anointing. The marriage rite is particularly rich in imagery, preserving many Semitic customs including the construction and blessing of the bridal chamber.

Little is known of the earlier forms of the daily office, though it contains hymns attributed to Ephrem, his contemporary Jacob, bishop of Nisibis, Catholicos Simeon bar Sabba'e, Marutha of Maiperqat, NARSAI and BABAI the Great, the latter having explicit Nestorian phraseology. Modern research on the daily office identifies an original core of praise with selected psalms, canticles and intercession. Like the daily office everywhere, the East Syrian was influenced by the monastic office; none the less it has preserved many primitive features, including the lack of scripture reading other than at Easter.

Vespers, *Ramšā*, once contained the lighting of the evening lamp, as attested by Gabriel Qatrāyā (*c*.615), but this fell into desuetude.

A rite of penance was known prior to the Synod of Mar Yahbalāhā, 420. This rite is explicitly modelled on the Liturgy of the Word, and according to Jacques Isaac, the manuscript Mardin-Diabekir 31.47 represents the earlier stage of this rite. The Chaldeans have abandoned this rite, replacing it with the Roman rite of confession. The Church of the East retains it as a general confession in preparation for communion. The manuscripts containing the ordination rites are late, and it is disputed as to whether the first or second ordination prayer is the original. Different funeral rites are provided for clergy and laity. Only in the case of clerics does the body enter the church; for laity the Jewish sequence of preparing the body, procession to the grave, and burial is retained.

◆ The West Syrian rite ◆

The origins of the Syrian Orthodox church lie in part in the vacillation of the patriarchate of Antioch between Chalcedonian Orthodoxy and monophysitism, though the fact that it later took the form of a Syriac-speaking community distinct from the imperial Chalcedonian Greek-speaking community suggests that political alignments were not totally irrelevant.

The main liturgical books of the West Syrian rite are the *Ktobo dQurbono* (the missal), *Ktobo dtešmešto* (the diaconal), the *Evangelion* (the Gospel book) and the *Egroto dašlīḥē* (the Epistles), together with the *Phenqīto* and *Šḥīmo*.

A major feature of this liturgical family is the number of anaphoras: well over eighty are known, though never all contained in one book. That attributed to the twelve apostles has much in common with the Byzantine anaphora of St John Chrysostom, both perhaps having a common ancestor. The Syriac version of St James is very close to the Greek version, and they continued to influence each other after the Christological split. These two anaphoras have inspired many of the others which represent variations, permutations and independent inspiration.

The baptismal rites share a common Syriac origin with an underlying anointing–baptism pattern, but probably Antioch followed Jerusalem and adapted its pre-baptismal anointing to symbolize exorcism or preparation for spiritual combat, and adopted a post-baptismal anointing with myron. The tradition developed several baptismal ordos, perhaps suggesting regional differences, attributed to Severus of Antioch, Philoxenus of Mabbug and Timothy of Alexandria. As in all traditions the daily office has been affected by the monastic office. One particular feature of the office is the use of *boʿūto* and *qolo*, strophic chants and ecclesiastical poetry, and in *Ramšo*, Vespers, there is a highly developed ceremony of offering incense. The marriage rite has the traditional joining of hands as betrothal, blessing of the rings, originally one ring, and crowning of bride and groom. There was once a blessing of the bridal robes, as in the East Syrian rite. The ordination rites show Byzantine influence, though both may indicate a common Antiochene source.

♦ The Maronite rite ♦

This community traces its origins to St Maro, a hermit living near Cyrrus on the banks of the Orontes, who died *c*.410. Its origins in the Orontes valley account for the Edessene origin of its liturgical tradition. It also uses anaphoras in common with the Syrian Orthodox, and under Roman influence even adopted the Roman Canon Missae. Its baptismal rites show a similar variety to that of the Syrian Orthodox, its main rite being similar to one of those of the West Syrians, but the manuscript tradition gives considerable variation, and a particular concern with pre-baptismal exorcisms. Likewise its daily office is very similar to the West Syrian office. The oldest marriage manuscripts contain an anointing of bride and groom, elsewhere only found in the COPTIC rite, and apparently used quite independently of other Syriac churches. Later marriage rites use many of the prayers of the West Syrian rite. Eclecticism is also found in the ordination rites, with parallels indicating borrowing from the West Syrian, but in places also sharing material with the MELKITE and Byzantine rites, and even from the fourth-century *Apostolic Constitutions*. Since the CRUSADES, when the Maronites were rediscovered by the West and accepted communion with ROME, a process of Latinization occurred, with some surrender of liturgical heritage. For example, the text of the epiclesis was altered, the Roman rite of penance was introduced, the Roman form of vows was incorporated into the marriage rite, and in 1716 its oldest anaphora, 'Sharar', was reduced to a liturgy of the presanctified. In recent years, under the leadership of the Lebanese Maronite Order, this process is being reversed, and newer liturgical books represent a restoration of some of the earlier authentic Maronite usages.

Spinks, B. D. (1993), *Worship: Prayers from the East*. Washington: Pastoral Press.

Gelston, A. (1992), *The Eucharistic Prayer of Addai and Mari*. Oxford: Clarendon Press.

Spinks, B. D. (1992), *Western Use and Abuse of Eastern Liturgical Traditions*. Rome: Centre for Indian-religious Studies.

Varghese, B. (1989), *Les Onctions baptismales dans la tradition Syrienne*. Louvain: Peeters.

Taft, R. (1986), *The Liturgy of the Hours in East and West*. Collegeville: Liturgical Press.

Mouhanna, A. (1980), *Les Rites de l'initiation dans l'église Maronite*. Rome: Pontifical Institute of Oriental Studies.

Jammo, S. Y .H. (1979), *La Structure de la Messe Chaldéenne*. Rome: Pontifical Institute of Oriental Studies.

Macomber, W. F. (1973), 'A Theory of the Origins of the Syrian, Maronite and Chaldean Rites', *Orientalia Christiana Periodica* 39.

Brock, S. P. (1972), 'Studies in the Early History of the Syrian Orthodox Baptismal Liturgy', *Journal of Theological Studies*, n.s. 23.

Tabet, J. (1972), *L'Office commun Maronite*. Kaslik: Bibliothèque de l'Université Saint-Esprit.

BS

Syrian Orthodox church   The Syrian church which is the descendant of the anti-CHALCEDONIAN party in Syria and Mesopotamia in the fifth century. It is usual to call this party, and hence the present-day church, along with the other Oriental Orthodox churches, MONOPHYSITE; but some consider that this name should be avoided. The other name commonly, but often pejoratively, used for the Syrian Orthodox is JACOBITES.

Membership of the church was reckoned in 1988 at 340,000, excluding the much larger community in INDIA. This figure reflects a recovery from the mere 80,000 estimated on the eve of the First World War, the result of centuries of losses to Islam, isolation, poverty and persecution. Just over half the faithful now live in the Middle East, and the church's former stronghold, the region of ṬUR 'ABDĪN between Diyar-bekr and Mardin in south-east Turkey, is depopulated. The monastery of Mar Gabriel at Ṭur 'Abdīn survives as an important spiritual centre. The patriarch, styled 'patriarch of Antioch and all the East', has his residence in Damascus. The present patriarch is Mar Ignatius Zakka (1980–). The hierarchy outside India consists of about fifteen metropolitans, including two in Europe and one in Brazil. Mar Athanasius Y. Samuel, who led the church in AMERICA and Canada from 1948, died in 1995. In India there are about 2 million more Syrian Orthodox, but since the present schism began in 1975, somewhat less than half this number, with about twelve metropolitans under their CATHOLICOS, belong to the patriarchal obedience.

JFC

· T ·

tablitho (ṭablīto)   Wooden tablet consecrated by the bishop or PATRIARCH for use as a liturgical ALTAR: it is placed on the holy table and the paten and chalice stand on it during the Divine Liturgy. Used in SYRIAN ORTHODOX, SYRIAN CATHOLIC and MARONITE churches and formerly in East Syrian rites also. The tablitho is functionally equivalent to the Byzantine rite ANTIMENSION and the Ethiopian TABOT.

DM

tabot   Ge'ez, *tābot*: chest, case, coffer, slab. The Ark of the Covenant is referred to as tabot in the GE'EZ version of the BIBLE. This word is also used for the tablets on which the ten commandments were inscribed. In Ethiopian churches a wooden coffer, *manbara tābōt*, throne or seat of the tabot, containing a consecrated altar tablet, which has also come to be called tabot, rests on the ALTAR proper and is used in the Divine Liturgy. The tabot evokes a rich typology, e.g. the Ark of the Covenant as a type of the Christian altar.

See also ETHIOPIAN ORTHODOX CHURCH; TABLITHO.

Grossmann, P. (1991), 'Altar', *Coptic Encyclopedia* 1, pp. 105ff.
Leslau, W. (1987), *Comparative Dictionary of Ge'ez (Classical Ethiopic): Ge'ez–English/ English–Ge'ez, with an Index of the Semitic Roots*. Wiesbaden: Harrassowitz.

MJB/SHG

Tana, Lake   An important centre of monastic life in Ethiopia, bordering the provinces of Gojjam and Bagemder in the western highlands; it is the source of the Blue Nile. The lake contains thirty-eight islands, some of which include important monastic sites. Today these Monastery Islands preserve many examples of religious painting from the seventeenth to nineteenth centuries. One of the better known islands is Ṭānā Čerqos, legendary resting place of the Holy Family during their flight to Egypt. Here too the Ark of the Covenant was supposed to have been taken from JERUSALEM,

477

before being deposited in Axum. Various Ethiopian emperors of the thirteenth to seventeenth centuries are buried on the island of Dāgā Esṭifānos. Some of the Lake Tana areas are restricted to male visitors.

See also ETHIOPIAN ORTHODOX CHURCH.

Abbebe, B. (1977), 'Painted Churches of Lake Tana', *Unesco Courier* 30 (February), pp. 13–17.
Jäger, O. A. (1965), *Antiquities of North Ethiopia: A Guide*. Stuttgart: Brockhaus.
Cheesman, R. E. (1936), *Lake Tana and the Blue Nile, An Abyssinian Quest*. London: Macmillan.

MJB/SHG

Tatian Born *c*.110–20 in Mesopotamia or Syria. Eusebius says he travelled to ROME, where he converted to Christianity and witnessed the martyrdom of Justin Martyr (165). His only surviving work is a strongly worded polemic against the Greek culture which he had grown up to admire. He became associated with an extreme ascetic encratism (i.e. rejection of wine, meat and even marriage), for which he was condemned as a heretic. About 172 he returned to Mesopotamia.

Tatian's major contribution was to compose the DIATESSARON, a harmonized text of the four gospels in a single narrative. It is not known exactly when this was done and there is doubt about its original language: SYRIAC or Greek. The only extant fragment, from DURA EUROPOS and dated before 256, is in Greek, but in favour of a Syriac original stands above all the centrality of the Diatessaron in the Syrian church until the fourth century, when a move to replace the Diatessaron with the separate gospels gained momentum. The Old Syriac gospels began to be used alongside the Diatessaron until the early fifth century when THEODORET OF CYRRHUS and RABBŪLĀ of EDESSA acted more decisively, destroying copies of the Diatessaron as a matter of policy. It quickly disappeared so completely that the only surviving evidence of it in Greek and Syriac is the Dura fragment and, very importantly, the Diatessaron citations of EPHREM THE SYRIAN in his *Commentary on the Diatessaron*, a large part of which has been recovered in recent years (Chester Beatty Library, Dublin: MS 709, amounting to *c*.80 per cent of the original).

JH

Tbilisi martyrs Jelaluddin Mango-berti, last shah of Khwarezm, fled before the Mongol hordes to Armenia in 1227. His Khwarezmis sacked ANI and other cities, then moved on to defeat the Georgian armies in the Akhaltsikhe area and march, unopposed, to Tbilisi. Queen Rusudan (d. 1237), ruling from Kutaisi in Imeretia, withdrew her forces from the ancient capital which surrendered. Thousands of Christians were slain by the shah between the Martyrs' Bridge over the Kura and the Sion Cathedral. The entire population of Tbilisi was exterminated or expelled; tradition numbers the martyrs between 10,000 and 100,000. To the Tbilisi martyrs are attributed all Georgian names not found in lists of saints, similar to Greek practice regarding the martyrs of Nicomedia.

See also CLASSICAL NAMES; GEORGIA; NEW MARTYRS.

Gerasim (1992), 'The Holy Martyrs of Tbilisi', *Orthodox Word*, no. 164.

DB

Telemachos   Greek monk and martyr; also known as Almachius. Gladiatorial combat to the death continued under the Christian emperors of the fourth century. The monk Telemachos, sickened by the bloodshed, eventually entered the arena in Rome and separated two fighting gladiators, who killed him in the process. His death fuelled Christian opposition to mortal combat as a public spectacle. Emperor Honorius (393–423) eventually banned it. Telemachos is commemorated on 1 January.

DB

Vassilopoulos, H. (1985), *Bioi Hagion*. Athens: n.p.

Terentii (d. 1886)   Konstantin Dobronravin, priest of a village in Orlov, Russia, wrote the life and miracles of this modern HOLY FOOL. Terentii's feigned madness evoked persecution; ultimately he was burnt. Like other holy fools he is held to have been a seer and worker of miracles. He is commemorated on 28 October.

DB

Tewodros II   Born Kasa Haylu, emperor of Ethiopia 1855–68, he is accounted Ethiopia's first modern and modernizing ruler. Tewodros II did much to unify Ethiopia politically. His unification efforts with regard to the ETHIOPIAN ORTHODOX CHURCH were less successful. These efforts began with his agreement with the Ethiopian Metropolitan Abba Salama III to promote the Ethiopian Orthodox doctrine of *Täwaḥǝdo* or union and to support church opposition to Roman Catholic missionaries. Tewodros II made various attempts to limit the Ethiopian Orthodox church's prerogatives, including state appropriations of church lands. Distrust of the Egyptian government led him to arrest the visiting Coptic Patriarch CYRIL IV and Abbā Salāmā III in 1857. Tewodros II's interest in the new technologies introduced by Protestant missions to Ethiopia was a significant factor in his encouragement of their evangelistic work.

Zewde, B. (1991), *A History of Modern Ethiopia, 1855–1974*. Eastern African Studies. London: James Currey; Athens, Ohio: Ohio University Press; Addis Ababa: Addis Ababa University Press.
Rubenson, S. (1966), *King of Kings, Tewodros of Ethiopia*. Historical Studies 2. Addis Ababa: Haile Selassie University.

MJB/HG

Theochares Douias (d. 1829)   Lay ascetic. He and his brother Apostolos Douias (d. 1846), sons of a priest of ARTA in Epirus, lived a life of prayer and charity. Despite the disruptions of the Greek revolution, they are recorded as leaving home only to visit the sick or those poorer than themselves. They are both venerated as examples of lay sanctity. They are commemorated on 23 March.

Provataki, T. (1988), *Theochares Kai Apostolos Douias*. Athens: n.p.

DB

Theodora of Arkadia   By tradition a tenth-century Peloponnesian woman who entered a monastery disguised as a man. Accused of raping a woman, Theodora was beheaded near Megalopolis, and her true identity then revealed. Her story echoes that of the fifth-century Theodora of Alexandria and others.

DB

Theodora of Pontus (d. 748)   One of several Byzantine saints who fled marriage. Theodora, an aristocrat from Helenopontos, was taken to CONSTANTINOPLE to marry a royal prince, but as an ICONOPHILE she fell foul of the ICONOCLAST court and PATRIARCH. She escaped to Cappadocia to the Rigidion convent and ended her life as a nun. Like KASSIA (d. 865), her life has been romantically reworked in novels. She is commemorated on 30 December.

Magdalini of Analipsi (1985), *Hagioi tou Pontou*. Kozani: n.p.

DB

Theodore Abū Qurrah (*c*.750–*c*.825)   The earliest Christian Arabic writer known by name. A monk of Mar Sabas monastery in the Judean desert, for a time he served as MELKITE bishop of Harran in Mesopotamia. He travelled to Egypt and Armenia and back to Mesopotamia as an itinerant religious controversialist, defending the CHALCE-DONIAN faith in Arabic against the challenges of Islam and Judaism, and commending his own Melkite orthodoxy to other Christian communities. Apologetic treatises comprise a large part of his extant Arabic writings. Other surviving works include defences of ICON veneration and of the church councils (*see* ECUMENICAL COUNCILS). Abū Qurrah spoke and wrote in SYRIAC, his native language; in Greek, the language of his religious patrimony; and in Arabic, by then the language of the Melkites. No Syriac writings survive, but some forty-three Greek works attributed to him exist. Works in Georgian attributed to him are also preserved (*see* GEORGIA, CHRISTIAN THOUGHT IN). Theodore Abū Qurrah, along with the SYRIAN ORTHODOX (Jacobite) ḤABĪB IBN ḤIDMAH ABŪ RĀ'IṬAH (*fl*. first half ninth century) and 'AMMĀR AL-BAṢRĪ (d. *c*.845) of the CHURCH OF THE EAST, represent that first generation of Syriac-speaking Christians to answer the challenge of Islam in the Arabic language, making use of the phraseology of contemporary Muslim religious dialecticians.

Griffith, S. H. (1993), 'Reflections on the Biography of Theodore Abu Qurrah', *Parole de l'Orient* 18, pp. 143–70.
Griffith, S. H. (1992), *Theodore Abū Qurrah: The Intellectual Profile of an Arab Christian Writer of the First Abbasid Century*. The Dr Irene Halmos Chair of Arabic Literature Annual Lecture, Tel Aviv University, 1992.

MJB/SHG

Theodore Sladich (d. 1788)   Serbian Orthodox NEW MARTYR, born in the mid-eighteenth century in BOSNIA, who became a fiery preacher and a zealous opponent of both the GREEK CATHOLIC movement and those Serbs who sought to secularize church and community structures. Arrested and condemned as an agitator by the OTTOMAN authorities, he was burnt at Moshtanica monastery with 150 followers.

Rogich, D. (1994), *Serbian Patericon*, vol. 1. Forestville, Cal.: St Paisius Press.

DB

Theodore the Studite (759–826)   Byzantine ICONOPHILE, hymnographer and monastic reformer. He began monastic life at Saccudion monastery near Mount Olympos in ASIA MINOR, later succeeding his uncle Plato as abbot, but attacks by Arab raiders led to the removal of the Saccudion monks to the abandoned Studios monastery in CONSTANTINOPLE. Under Theodore the monastery grew to around 600 monks, its many scholars promoting the ninth-century cultural revival and developing the Greek minuscule script. Theodore was several times exiled, twice during the later ICONOCLASM (815–43) as an uncompromising iconophile. His treatise *On the Holy Images*, his nearly 500 surviving letters, his hymns and his *Catecheses* continue to play an important role in Eastern thought and worship.

See also NIKEPHOROS I.

Roth, C. P., trans. (1981), *St Theodore the Studite: On the Holy Icons*. Crestwood, NY: St Vladimir's Seminary Press.
Speck, P. (1968), *Theodoros Studites, Jamben auf verschiedene Gegenstände, Einleitung, kritischer Text, Übersetzung und Kommentar*. Berlin: de Gruyter.

KP

Theodoret of Cyrrhus (*c*.393–*c*.458)   Born in ANTIOCH, entered the monastery of Nicerte and was appointed bishop of Cyrrhus in Syria in 423. Influenced by Theodore of Mopsuestia, he supported Nestorius against CYRIL OF ALEXANDRIA, even after the Council of Ephesus (431). Condemned and deposed by the 'Robber Council' of 449, he attended the Council of Chalcedon (451), was persuaded to condemn Nestorius and was reinstated. In a written attack on Cyril he had accepted the term THEOTOKOS; none the less, at the Council of Constantinople (553) he was again condemned. Particularly important for the history of the Syrian church is his *Historia Religiosa*, containing biographies of thirty Syrian ascetics.

Theodoret of Cyrrhus (1985), *A History of the Monks of Syria*, trans. R. M. Price. Kalamazoo: Cistercian Publications.

JH

theology, Eastern Christian   The vast and vigorous productivity of Christian theologians in the East throughout the centuries makes it clear that although the characteristic Eastern emphasis upon dogma and insistence upon orthodoxy have tended to preclude the sort of dichotomy between 'official' and 'private' teaching found above all in modern Liberal Protestantism but to some degree also in many other Western traditions, these characteristics of the EASTERN CHRISTIAN tradition have not, as critics and caricaturists have supposed, stifled the intellectual creativity of individual theologians and communities, who have tended to find it possible to express that creativity within the confines of church doctrine, although sometimes at or near its fringes.

It may be useful to specify at least some of the principal meanings of the word 'theology' (Greek: *theologia*; Russian: *bogoslovie*) in Eastern usage. In a strict and narrow sense it refers to the doctrine of the nature and attributes of God; hence the designation of John the Evangelist, or Gregory of Nazianzus, as *ho theologos*, 'the divine', 'the theologian', because of their importance for the doctrine of the Trinity; and therefore, especially when in contrast with 'economy', the term applies specifically to the inner mystery of the divine Being as distinguished from the activities of the divine Being in relation to the universe, to history and to humanity, especially through the Incarnation. The Greek fathers use *theologia* and its related verb, *theologein*, to mean 'praise', which comports well with the typically, though not uniquely, Eastern emphasis on the doxological–liturgical context of theologizing. None of this has, however, precluded the application of the term to ordered intellectual reflection on the mysteries of divine revelation, including the relation of those mysteries to truth that may be apprehended without the aid of specific historical revelation.

Eastern thinkers, especially those who wrote in Greek or SYRIAC, predominate, both quantitatively and qualitatively, within the total corpus of patristic theology. Most heretics of the patristic period were also Eastern, with the major exception of Pelagius, who did, however, seek (and obtain) Eastern approval in 415, only to have his teachings condemned, without being specified in detail, at the Council of Ephesus in 431. All seven councils recognized by EASTERN ORTHODOX as ECUMENICAL COUNCILS of the 'undivided church' were held in the East, all except Ephesus in, or in the environs of, CONSTANTINOPLE. A full account of 'Eastern Christian theology' in the first millennium of Christian history would be virtually coextensive with the history of Christian doctrine during that period, especially if it included, as it should, the major Eastern contributions to the thought of such Western figures as Hilary of Poitiers, Ambrose of Milan and even Augustine of Hippo. To avoid this account becoming little more than an onomasticon or patristic telephone directory, it will itemize only a few of the most indispensable figures. Most spoke and wrote in Greek, but those who wrote in Syriac, such as APHRAHAṬ and EPHREM THE SYRIAN, and those whose works though written in Greek are preserved in Syriac, such as, on opposite sides of the Christological argument, Theodore of Mopsuestia and SEVERUS OF ANTIOCH, have places of honour in the catalogue, as do those who later wrote in Arabic, such as THEODORE ABŪ QURRAH.

Because of his blending of learned scholarship, where he may be regarded a peer of Jerome, with speculative philosophical theology, where he may be regarded a peer of Augustine, ORIGEN of Alexandria is, arguably, the most influential theological thinker in the history of Eastern Christianity: from ATHANASIUS to SOLOVYOV and BUL-GAKOV his questions, if not his answers, have shaped the agenda of widely divergent systems of thought, and the condemnation of some of his teachings by the Second Council of Constantinople (553), at the instance of the Emperor Justinian, did not eradicate the influence of his writings, especially if one includes, as one must, his biblical commentaries. There is a direct line from Origen to the orthodox dogma of the Councils of Nicea I (325) and Constantinople I (381), as there is to the heresies of Arius and Eunomios. As the implacable opponents of Eunomius, the CAPPADOCIANS were nevertheless dependent on Origen both for their biblical learning in the succession of his *Hexapla* and for their speculative thought; that becomes evident above all in the formulation of the doctrine of APOKATASTASIS put forward by Gregory of Nyssa, which was spared the official condemnation visited upon Origen's doctrines.

Clarification of the doctrine of the Trinity, to which Western theology from Tertullian to Ossius to Augustine also contributed much, was the major task of those fourth-century Eastern theologians. That required them to develop a conceptual framework and vocabulary for formulating in an intellectually consistent manner the fundamental mystery of theology in the first sense of the term specified above. With the introduction and gradual elucidation of the *homoousion* and of such technical terms as *ousia* and *hypostasis*, the formula of Nicaea, as expanded at Constantinople and as defended and recast by the Cappadocians, became such a framework. But the clarification of the relation of the second hypostasis of the Trinity to the first, and of the third to both, helped precipitate conflict over the relation, within that second hypostasis, of the nature he shared with the Father and the Spirit to the nature he shared with the human race. Once again, the principal alternative positions carried Eastern labels. The identification of Antiochene and Alexandrian styles of dealing with the relation of divine and human in Christ, though an oversimplification, does involve a genuine difference. The former, of which JOHN CHRYSOSTOM was a spokesman acknowledged to be orthodox and Nestorius an exponent condemned at Ephesus, strove to read scripture in such a way as to do justice to the true and complete humanity of Jesus Christ; and therefore, as in its insisting that the Blessed Virgin Mary should be called only 'Christotokos', it distinguished sharply between the divine and the human, incurring the accusation of separating them. The latter, of which Apollinaris was among the first to arouse sharp criticism and Cyril of Alexandria, implacable foe of Nestorius, the most prominent, saw in such a distinction a threat to the oneness of the incarnate Logos and therefore to the reality of salvation, and made THEOTOKOS as title for the Virgin its slogan.

The condemnation at Ephesus of the Nestorian extreme of Antiochene theology, and then at Chalcedon of the Eutychian extreme of Alexandrian theology, did not accomplish the desired reconciliation, leaving particularly unsatisfied the need to locate the unity of the hypostasis of Christ – in one nature (MONOPHYSITISM), in one action or *energeia* (monenergism), in one will (MONOTHELETISM). As Severus of Antioch formulated the persistent differences, 'The term "union" is affirmed both by our opponents and by us. It is also acknowledged that a conjunction of two natures has taken place. But that which was accomplished by the union...is the basis of the opposition between the doctrines.' It was apparently during the time of these Christological controversies and councils that the pseudonymous writings bearing the name of DIONYSIOS THE AREOPAGITE arose, probably at the beginning of the sixth century and in Syria, gaining almost immediate acceptance as authentic in the East and going on through successive Latin translations to authoritative standing in the theology of the West. Although both the Council of Chalcedon, at which Pope Leo I's *Tome*, coming from the West, played a determinative role, and the career and the thought of MAXIMUS THE CONFESSOR a century and a half later, certainly belong to the West as well as the East, the Christological issues with which the Second (553) and Third (681) Councils of Constantinople dealt and the dogmatic decisions to which they came, while qualifying in the Chalcedonian tradition as 'ecumenical', pertained most directly to Eastern developments.

As repeated Western misunderstandings of its formulas have demonstrated, the same must be said of Nicaea II, the 'ecumenical' synod which addressed the challenge of ICONOCLASM. Leading defenders of the use of images were JOHN OF DAMASCUS, NIKEPHOROS I, patriarch of Constantinople, and THEODORE THE STUDITE. In their writings the legitimacy of icons was asserted not only on the pedagogical grounds that images could serve as 'the bible of the illiterate', but as a necessary implication of the

Incarnation: when the divine Logos assumed flesh and therefore visible form, God provided humanity for the first time with an infallible image of himself, which it was therefore permissible, indeed, obligatory, to image in representational form. Both the substance of this theological position and the methodology for arguing it bear the identifying marks of Eastern theology.

The theological dispute with Islam, which likewise eventually became an ecumenical task and, through the CRUSADES as well as in the work of such theologians as Peter the Venerable, a Western concern, claimed the attention of Eastern theologians earlier and more insistently. The high estimate placed by the Qur'an on Jesus as prophet and on his mother Mary, together with other parallels, prompted some Eastern theologians to classify Islam as a Christian heresy. The rapid spread of the religion of the Prophet, initially through Eastern Christian territory, represented a strong challenge to the Eastern theological belief in the divine providence that had established the Christian empire. From Byzantine and Arabic responses it is evident that the uncompromising monotheism of the Qur'an posed a challenge to the distinction among the divine hypostases as a special emphasis of Eastern Trinitarianism, which nevertheless continued to insist, as it had already in the title of a treatise by Gregory of Nyssa, '*That It Is Not Correct to Say "Three Gods"*'.

In the Byzantine period the principal theological differences between Eastern and Western Christianity were identified and debated. In the realm of dogma, the most prominent of these was the FILIOQUE, the addition of 'and from the Son' to the words, referring to the Holy Spirit, 'who proceeds from the Father' in the text of the Niceno-Constantinopolitan Creed. Eastern theology protested against this on procedural grounds, as a violation of the *paradosis* (tradition) and an unwarranted innovation interpolated into the only truly ecumenical creed by one section of the church, but even more on substantive doctrinal grounds, as a threat to the very unity of the Godhead: it appeared to be confusing the distinction clearly made in John 15: 26 between the eternal proceeding, *ekporeusis*, of the Holy Spirit only from the Father and the temporal sending, *pempsis*, of the Spirit by the Son as well as by the Father into the world and history, and thus to be positing two sources or grounds (*archai*) within the Trinity.

As the dispute over the mission of CYRIL AND METHODIUS in the ninth century made clear, the evolution of a monarchical papacy in the West represented not merely a jurisdictional dispute over the Eastern theory of PENTARCHY as a system of ecclesiastical governance and over the special position of CONSTANTINOPLE as the 'New Rome' as defined by the First Council of Constantinople and the Council of Chalcedon, but a theological disagreement over the very nature of the church, as well as over the lawfulness of liturgical languages other than Hebrew, Greek and Latin, the three languages in the superscription on the Cross of Christ (John 19: 20). Even the conflict over *azymoi*, the use of unleavened bread in the eucharist, seemingly no more than a problem of ritual, acquired in Eastern theology a more far-reaching significance. Carrying still further both the devotion and the speculation of SYMEON THE NEW THEOLOGIAN, the theological reflection on 'uncreated light' and on the divine energies in the thought of Nicolas CABASILAS, and even more sharply that of GREGORY PALAMAS, expressed distinctively Eastern ideas growing out of HESYCHASM, but hesychast theology became a target of Western polemics at the hands of Barlaam, and its condemnation created another barrier between the two traditions.

The condemnation of John Italus and the vicissitudes of Michael Psellus are evidence that, no less than in Western scholasticism but in a different modality, the relation of Christian theology to Greek philosophy was an enduring preoccupation of Byzantine thought. Nor was it only with Plato and Neoplatonism (*see* PLATONISM) that this preoccupation was concerned, as some superficial Western interpretations have supposed; for example, John of Damascus, whose influence was great in the East and perhaps even greater in the West, dealt with Aristotelian metaphysics at a time when the West still regarded Aristotle as primarily a logician. Because Byzantine scholars could read Plato and Aristotle in the original, their manuscripts and their erudition repeatedly contributed to Western revivals of the knowledge of the Greek classical and the Greek Christian tradition, notably in connection with the reunion efforts at the Western Council of FLORENCE. Even before the Fall of Constantinople (1453), other centres of Eastern Christianity had begun to develop their own theological traditions. The conversion of KIEVAN Rus precipitated the translation of Greek writings and the gradual evolution of an Eastern theology within the Slavic cultures. Its most abiding product was the *Orthodox Confession* usually associated with the name of the metropolitan of Kiev, Petro Mohyla (Peter MOGILA). Written originally in Latin, then translated into Greek, then revised and translated into Ukrainian as well as into Polish, the *Confession* thus symbolizes the predicament of Eastern theology during the seventeenth and eighteenth centuries, as, in the words of Georges FLOROVSKY, 'Latin influences on religious thought and practice were to intensify and expand in a more systematic manner'.

Thus, as Florovsky's magisterial history indicates, it was finally in the nineteenth and twentieth centuries that Russian theology came of age, developing in interaction not only with philosophy, as theology has always done, but with literature and political thought. For example, the Raskol (schism of the OLD BELIEVERS), though precipitated by reform of the liturgical books, had thrust the doctrine of the church into the centre of theological attention. Once again, it is possible to refer only to a few important figures. A. S. KHOMIAKOV, lay theologian and man of letters, articulated a vision of the church, its unity and *sobornost*, that eventually was to make a major contribution to ecumenical thought. Fedor Dostoevskii utilized narrative and characterization as vehicles for theological insight especially into the doctrines of sin and of grace, while Leo Tolstoy went his own way, setting forth a radical interpretation of the teachings of the gospels as an alternative to Orthodoxy. Best known in the West for his efforts to find a *via media* between Orthodoxy and Roman Catholicism, V. S. SOLOVYOV approached that issue from the perspective of far-ranging speculations that his followers saw as necessary implications of Orthodox Christology but his critics attacked as a 'seductive path' (Florovsky). During the twentieth century, in the aftermath of the Bolshevik Revolution, theological study and theological thought became all but impossible within Russia, although P. A. FLORENSKY, above all in his *Pillar and Ground of Truth*, published in 1914, had presented the traditional dogmas of Trinity and Incarnation as the foundation of a theological–philosophical world view, and in his later works, suppressed by the authorities, continued his theological work under great difficulties.

The centre of Russian Orthodox theology shifted to the West. Writing chiefly in French, Nicholas BERDIAEV clearly manifested his Eastern Orthodox roots, but his philosophy took him beyond those roots into speculations that more traditional thinkers attacked as 'gnosticism' and 'theosophy'. Although he did not escape criticism either, especially for some of his bolder speculations about the divine Sophia (*see* SOPHIOL-OGY), the thought of Sergei BULGAKOV pulled together many of the major themes of Eastern theology. As an interpretation of distinctively Eastern ways of speaking about the doctrine of the image of God and about mystical theology, the theology of Vladimir Lossky, especially in French and in English, introduced many readers to the Eastern tradition for the first time. And in a lifetime of research and writing about the Eastern and Byzantine church fathers and about the *Ways of Russian Theology* which was combined with vigorous participation in ecumenical discussion, Georges Florovsky became almost certainly the most influential Eastern Christian theologian of the modern period.

Although often overshadowed by their Russian Orthodox *confrères*, Greek Orthodox theologians in the modern period, especially since independence from the OTTOMAN empire, have continued to make significant contributions, which have, however, exerted less influence in the West because they have not been translated as often. On the border between those two Orthodox communities was such a work as the *Enchiridion of the Orthodox Christian* by Alexander Sturza, which was published, at St Petersburg but in Greek, in 1828. In that same period Athanasius of Paros published an *Epitome* of church doctrine, which appeared in the West. Biblical exegesis provided the basis for the theological presentations of Metropoulos Hierotheos and Apostolos Makrakis, in works that went on being reprinted in the twentieth century. Early in the twentieth century, sacramental theology was the object of a summary interpretation by K. Dyobouniotes. Chrestos Androutsos contributed to the comparative study of Orthodox theology in relation to other traditions and to a systematization of its teachings, and Nicolas Bulgaris prepared a new catechetical exposition of those teachings.

It involves very little risk to predict that in the twenty-first century anyone with an interest in Christian theology will be obliged to pay more attention to its Eastern development than most Western students have done.

Florovsky, G. V. (1979–87), *Collected Works*. Vaduz: Büchervertriebsanstalt; Belmont, Mass.: Notable and Academic Books.

Meyendorff, J. (1974), *Byzantine Theology: Historical Trends and Doctrinal Themes*. New York: Fordham University Press.

Pelikan, J. (1974), *The Spirit of Eastern Christendom (600–1700)*. Chicago: University of Chicago Press.

Meyendorff, J. (1969), *Christ in Eastern Christian Thought*. Washington, DC: Corpus Books.

Schmemann, A. (1963), *The Historical Road of Eastern Orthodoxy*. New York: Holt, Rinehart & Winston.

Beck, H.-G. (1959), *Kirche und theologische Literatur im byzantinischen Reich*. Munich: Beck.

Gordillo, M. (1950), *Compendium Theologiae Orientalis*. Rome: Pontifical Institute of Oriental Studies.

Fedotov, G. P. (1946), *The Russian Religious Mind*. Cambridge, Mass.: Harvard University Press.

Vacant, A., Mangenot, E. and Amann, E., eds (1930–50). *Dictionnaire de théologie catholique*: S. Vailhé, 'Constantinople (Eglise de)', 3–II: 1307–1519; J. Ledit and M. Gordillo, 'Russie (Pensée religieuse)', 14–I: 207–371. Paris: Libraire Letouzey et Ané.

JP

Theopaschite formula In 519 controversy arose in CONSTANTINOPLE when 'Scythian' (i.e. Gothic) monks led by John Maxentius proclaimed their opposition to NESTORIANISM by use of the Theopaschite formula, 'One of the Trinity suffered.' Despite the hostility of the *akoimetoi* ('unsleeping', since the divine office was recited continuously in their monasteries by relays of choirs), Emperor Justinian was convinced the formula was orthodox. Through the good offices of Bishop Hypatios of Ephesus, who visited ROME in 533, Justinian won the support of Pope John II in his letter *Olim Quidem* to the Constantinopolitan Senate.

The Theopaschite formula can be read in a heretical sense to assert that one of the Trinity suffered *as God*, but also in a perfectly orthodox sense as asserting that Jesus who suffered is the same person as the Logos, the second hypostasis of the TRINITY. The doctrine of COMMUNICATIO IDIOMATUM provides the theological basis for the formula's orthodox sense, attributing all acts of Jesus Christ to one and the same divine person.

The term 'Theopaschite' has a confusing use: it designates the orthodox doctrine that the divine Logos is the person who suffered as man on the cross of Calvary, but also designates an extreme MONOPHYSITE position regarded by CHALCEDONIAN Christians as heretical.

DM

Theophan the Greek (Theophanes/Feofan) (1330–1408) Fresco- and icon-painter who worked in northern Russia. His wall paintings survive only in the Transfiguration Church of NOVGOROD, completed 1378. Theophan's expressionistic style is distinguished by white highlighting, restricted use of colour (red and brown) and a disregard for detail. His paintings have great pyschological intensity, capturing the spiritual essence of individual figures. His style resembles that of the unknown painter of VOLOTOVO POLE, but his is a firmer hand and his orientation Byzantine. His treatment of light has affinities with Domenikos Theotokopoulos (1541–1614), El Greco. Epiphanios the Wise, biographer of SERGIUS OF RADONEZH and STEPHEN OF PERM, who was also a painter, praised his architectural draughtsmanship and portraiture skills in a letter (1415). We learn that he painted from inspiration rather than copying prototypes and that he had worked in Constantinople and the Crimea. Andrei RUBLEV worked with him in MOSCOW in 1405 on the interior of the Kremlin cathedral of the Annunciation. Unfortunately these paintings were destroyed when the Kremlin cathedrals were rebuilt in the late fifteenth century.

Hamilton, G. H. (1983), *The Art and Architecture of Russia*. Harmondsworth: Penguin. Meyendorff, J. (1981), *Byzantium and the Rise of Russia: A Study of Byzantino-Russian Relations in the Fourteenth Century*. Cambridge: Cambridge University Press.

KP

Theophan the Recluse (Feofan) (1815–94) Having studied at the KIEV Theological Academy and spent several years abroad, seven in JERUSALEM, he was made rector of the St Petersburg Theological Academy. In 1859 he was elected bishop of Tambov, then of VLADIMIR, but in 1866 he became a recluse at Vichenskii monastery, appearing only to attend the liturgical services. In 1872 he built a small chapel where he celebrated the liturgy daily, confining himself to contact with his confessor and abbot. He corresponded with many who sought spiritual guidance. Between 1876 and 1890 he produced the *Dobrotolubiye*, a Russian version of the PHILOKALIA, including works not in the original. He also translated the *Spiritual Combat* (1589) of Lorenzo Scupoli from the Greek version of Nikodemos of the Holy Mountain (NIKODEMOS THE HAGIORITE), adapting this Counter-Reformation classic for Orthodox use.

Kadloubovsky, E. and Palmer, G. E. H., trans (1978), *Unseen Warfare: The Spiritual Combat and Path to Paradise of Lorenzo Scupoli edited by Nicodemus of the Holy Mountain and revised by Theophan the Recluse*. Oxford: Mowbray.
Bolshakoff, S. (1977), *Russian Mystics*. London: Mowbray.

KP

Theophany Epiphany, feast of the baptism of Christ. In the icon of the feast, the Holy Spirit is shown as a dove in a roundel between the vault of heaven and the three-pronged

ray of light symbolizing the Holy Trinity. Similar rays appear in the PENTECOST icon and in the icon of the NATIVITY OF CHRIST. In the Old Testament the dove flew over the waters of the flood carrying an olive branch as a symbol of reconciliation and renewal. Likewise the dove hovers over the waters of baptism. JOHN THE BAPTIST is shown wearing his garment of hair or fleece (Greek: *melote*), laying his hand on the nimbate head of Christ. John's *melote* recalls ELIAS' dividing the waters of Jordan with his *melote*, the divided river becoming the pathway to the fiery chariot that takes him up into heaven; here this is clearly a reference to Christian baptism as the road to salvation. The division of the Jordan by Elias recalls the division of the Red Sea in Exodus 14–15, which is in turn a prefiguration both of Christ's triumph over death (ANASTASIS) and of Christian baptism as a means of sharing in that triumph.

Near to John appear a bush and axe, identifying the one he baptizes as the one who comes to lay an axe to the tree. The figure of Christ is often portrayed naked. ANGELS wait with their hands covered: covering the hands to avoid direct contact with holy things and persons is an ancient and widespread gesture of reverence.

488

In the icon illustrated here, as in icons of the Anastasis, Christ stands on the gates of Hades, a detail drawn from the dragons of Septuagint Psalm 73: 13, who appear several times in the texts of the feast, not least those of the Great Hagiasmos, the Blessing of Waters. Christ blesses the waters of the Jordan with his right hand. The trampled gates of Hades, and the dark cave-like representation of the river Jordan, indicate that baptism is a symbol of death and rebirth (Col. 2: 12). The descent of Christ into the Jordan and the driving out of the dragons represent the deliverance of the material world from the powers of darkness. Jordan itself appears as an old man; a female figure riding on a sea-horse represents the crossing of the Red Sea.

The icon of the Theophany is regarded as an icon of the TRINITY. The feast of the baptism of Christ is celebrated on 6 January.

Ristow, G. (1967), *The Baptism of Christ*. Recklinghausen: Icon Museum.

KP

Theotokion   Most series of hymns in Byzantine rite offices end with one to the THEOTOKOS, which commonly follows the second part of the short doxology, 'both now and for ever, and to the ages of ages. Amen', and is normally in the same tone (*see* MUSIC) as the preceding DOXASTIKON. On Saturday evening, however, the Theotokion at the Entrance is usually that of the tone of the week, whatever the tone of the Doxastikon. It is sung again at Vespers on the following Friday. In Slav usage this Theotokion is called the Dogmatic, because it contains a succinct summary of the doctrine of the Incarnation. In Greek the name Dogmatikon is used for the corresponding Theotokion at Small Vespers. On Wednesdays and Fridays and in offices connected with the CROSS and Passion a Stavrotheotokion is used, which normally depicts the lamentation of the Mother of God at the foot of the Cross.

E

Theotokos   'The one who gave birth to God', principal title of Mary the Mother of Jesus for all EASTERN CHRISTIAN traditions except the CHURCH OF THE EAST, and in liturgical use as early as the third century in ALEXANDRIA.

When Patriarch Nestorius of CONSTANTINOPLE (428–31) supported his subordinate, Anastasius, who denounced the use of the title, a major split ensued. Nestorius argued that the title Theotokos could be misunderstood to imply that Mary was the Mother of God in the heretical sense of Mother of the Godhead. Without absolutely forbidding use of the title, he recommended the less problematic Christotokos, 'the one who gave birth to Christ'. Cyril of Alexandria accused Nestorius of heresy and in 431 he was condemned and deposed at the Council of Ephesus.

The title Theotokos remains a crucially important symbol of Christological orthodoxy among most Eastern Christians, and is a common title of Mary in Eastern worship; the corresponding Latin titles Deipara and Dei Genetrix are less used and the title Mater Dei, Mother of God, is far more common. The title Theotokos proclaims that Jesus, the divine Logos, as God, born eternally from the Father, is born in time as the human child of a human mother. Mary is not mother of the Godhead, but she is mother of a divine person. The title Theotokos is used by COMMUNICATIO IDIOMATUM.

489

In Eastern Christian worship Mary is venerated as ever-virgin and as sinless, as 'more honoured than the Cherubim, more glorious than the Seraphim'. If Jesus represents the ultimate descent of God into human life, Mary is the supreme moment in the ascent of humanity to meet God, the conception of Christ the fruit of her free decision in humble submission to God's will.

Pelikan, J (1996), *Mary through the Ages: Her Place in History and Culture*. London and New Haven: Yale University Press.

DM

Thermi   Convent on Lesbos and major centre for PILGRIMAGE. It preserves RELICS of numerous martyrs believed to have been killed in two groups by Turkish marauders: a group of nuns, including Olympia and her helper Euphrosyne (1235); and the monks Raphael and Nicolas, the child Irene and many villagers (1463). From 1959 people across Lesbos, and later more widely, claimed to have seen visions of these and other saints (*see* NEWLY REVEALED SAINTS). Devout Christians began to excavate the Thermi site, traditionally associated with the martyrs, uncovering the ruins of a monastery. Miracles were soon being linked to the relics found.

The iconographer Photis Kontoglou compiled a book entitled *The Great Sign*, chronicling the unfolding revelations. The current abbess, Eugenia Kleidara, has transformed Thermi monastery into a pan-Orthodox centre and major shrine ranking with nearby Mantamados (*see* ANGELS) and TINOS. Olympia and her companions are commemorated on 11 May, Raphael and his companions on 9 April and Tuesday of Renewal Week. Other feasts exist, including a synaxis (general commemoration) on 5 July.

Cavarnos, C. (1990), *Saints Raphael, Nicolas and Irene of Lesbos*. Belmont, Mass.: Institute for Byzantine and Modern Greek Studies.

DB

Third Rome   Title given to Moscow by the monk Philotheos, writing to Basil III of Moscow (1505–33), claiming that two Romes have fallen and MOSCOW is the third which will never fall. The two fallen are ROME itself and CONSTANTINOPLE, the New Rome. The title 'Third Rome' is controversial, since it can imply a claim to the primacy held by the pope, then, after the schism with the West, by the PATRIARCH of Constantinople. The claim to inherit the mantle of Constantinople was enhanced by the marriage of Princess Sophia (Zoe) Palaiologina, niece of Constantine XI, the last emperor, with Ivan III. At the time of her betrothal in 1472 Zoe, a convert to Catholicism, was living under papal protection with BESSARION as her guardian; once in Moscow she reverted to Orthodoxy, taking the name Sophia. After the fall of Constantinople the Russian tsar, the only EASTERN ORTHODOX emperor, gave financial and political support to Orthodox communities under OTTOMAN rule. The splendour and majesty of the architecture, iconography and liturgy of the great centres of the Russian church lent experiential credibility to the Third Rome claim.

DM

Thomas of Margā   Writer of the CHURCH OF THE EAST, possibly of Persian origin, who produced an important monastic history, *The Book of Governors*. Thomas entered the Bēt ʻĀbē monastery east of Mosul in 832 and, having been secretary to the PATRIARCH CATHOLICOS Abraham, later became bishop of Margā and metropolitan of Bēt Garmai near Seleucia-Ctesiphon. *The Book of Governors*, written *c*.840, while it focused on the history of his own monastery, Bēt ʻĀbē, also contains much information on the history of East Syrian monasticism.

Budge, E. A. W. (1893), *The Book of Governors: The Historia Monastica of Thomas Bishop of Margā*. London: Kegan Paul, Trench, Trübner.

JH

Thomas Paschidis (d. 1890)   Greek nationalist. Originally from Ioannina, Thomas represented the Epirote rebels in various negotiations, arguing their case in his own newspaper and other publications. OTTOMAN authorities exiled him with other journalists to the Fezzan desert in Libya, where he was brutally killed for refusing to embrace Islam. The circumstances of his death led to his being counted among the NEW MARTYRS. Thomas is commemorated on 5 July.

See also ETHNOMARTYRS.

Hatzifotis, I. M. (1988), 'Thomas Paschides', *Praktika Theologikou Synedriou eis Timen kai Mnemen ton Neomartyron – 1986*. Thessaloniki: n.p.

DB

Thrace   The ancient Thracians were an Indo-European nation related to the Phrygians and other peoples of ASIA MINOR. In the classical period Thrace was considered to extend from the Aegean Sea up to the steppes and Scythia. Thracian kingdoms (for example Odrysia) established south of the Danube in the Hellenistic period were overwhelmed by the Romans in AD 46. Though Thrace was under Hellenizing influences from Aegean and Black Sea Greek colonies, the Bessi and other tribes kept their language alive into the sixth century. The Byzantine theme (province) of Thrace was confined to the Black Sea coast; another theme, Thrakesion, centred on Lydia. Philippopolis (Plovdiv), the metropolitan see of Thrace, was outshone by Adrianople (Edirne) after the barbarian invasions from the fourth century onwards. Thrace (Thrake/Trakya) is a term in continuous use to the present for regions in Greece, Bulgaria and Turkey (western, northern and eastern in sequence).

The Bulgarians briefly united most of Thrace in 1912 but ceded Eastern Thrace to Turkey in 1913 and Western Thrace to Greece after the First World War. The Greeks controlled both Western and Eastern Thrace for a few years before 1922 when the Turks again retrieved Eastern Thrace and expelled the substantial Greek population of the region.

See also POMAKS.

DB

Three Hierarchs   Traditional title of JOHN CHRYSOSTOM (*c*.347–407), bishop of Constantinople, Basil the Great (330–79), bishop of Caesarea, and Gregory the Theologian (*c*.329–90), bishop of Constantinople (*see* CAPPADOCIANS). According to the HOROLOGION, the feast of the Three Hierarchs was instituted around 1100 under Alexios Komnenos (1081–1118) because of disputes among the devotees of the three

saints over their respective merits. The office was composed by John Mavropous, later bishop of Euchaita. In the icon illustrated here, each is shown wearing the ancient episcopal vestments including the polystavrion and omophorion (though John often wears the sakkos), and holding a gospel book (*see* RELIGIOUS DRESS). The liturgies of Basil the Great and John Chrysostom are the most frequently celebrated in the Byzantine tradition. The feast day of the Three Hierarchs is 30 January, in Greek churches also the feast of Greek Letters, celebrating the culture, art and learning of the ancient world, to which, as Basil asserted against Emperor Julian the Apostate, Christians too are heirs, and the Christian Hellenism which flowered as a result of the church's acceptance of this heritage (*see also* THEOLOGY, EASTERN CHRISTIAN).

The CHURCH OF THE EAST has a parallel feast of the Three Greek Doctors, but this celebrates Nestorius, Theodore of Mopsuestia and Diodore of Tarsus.

KP/DM

throne (1) The holy table. (2) The bishop's seat in the centre of the apse. The bishop should go up into his throne during the TRISAGION and the subsequent *pheme.* (3) In Greek use there is an episcopal throne at the west end of the choir, but this is really the stall of the (monastic) superior, as on ATHOS (an Athonite abbot uses it only when presiding solemnly at a vigil). The senior stall in Western monasteries is in the equivalent place. (4) An iconographic symbol of the godhead of Christ in the Byzantine ICON known as the Hetoimasia, which shows the empty throne prepared for the triumphant Christ. (5) In hymnography a title of the THEOTOKOS, 'Throne of the King of All', as 'greater in honour than the Cherubim' who in Ezekiel's vision form the throne of God.

DM/E

Tigré (1) Tigré or Tegré, a Semitic Ethiopian language, spoken today in northern Ethiopia, parts of Sudan, and in Eritrea (*see* ERITREAN ORTHODOX CHURCH). A majority of Tigré speakers are Muslim. (2) Tigré or Tegray, a northern highland province of Ethiopia that encloses the ancient kingdom of Axum. It has been called 'the birthplace of Ethiopia'.

Ullendorff, E. (1955), *The Semitic Languages of Ethiopia: A Comparative Phonology.* London: Taylor's (Foreign) Press.
Prouty, C. and Rosenfeld, E. (1981), *Historical Dictionary of Ethiopia*. African Historical Dictionaries 32, pp. 167–8. Metuchen, NJ and London: Scarecrow Press.

MJB/SHG

Tikhon of Zadonsk (1724–83) Russian monk and spiritual writer. He studied at the Latin seminary in NOVGOROD, following the curriculum type adopted by Peter

MOGILA at KIEV, then became rector of the Tver seminary and head of the Otroch monastery in 1760. Elected bishop of Voronezh in 1763, he retired four years later to a life of seclusion in the Zadonsk region. He admired two books by Protestant authors, Joseph Hall's *Occasional Meditations* (1695) and Johann Arndt's *True Christianity* (1605). His own *True Christianity* became a standard work in Russian seminaries. Under Western influence he stresses the personal relationship with Christ and dwells upon Jesus' sufferings. He considered translating the New Testament into colloquial Russian, and the Old Testament from the Hebrew rather than the Septuagint (*see* BIBLE) but decided against the project in view of the controversy it would cause.

Bolshakoff, S. (1977), *Russian Mystics*. London: Mowbray.
Gorodetzky, N. (1976), *Saint Tikhon of Zadonsk: Inspirer of Dostoevsky*. Crestwood, NY: St Vladimir's Seminary Press.

KP

Timothy Ailouros Timothy 'the Weasel', anti-CHALCEDONIAN patriarch of Alexandria, elected by the clergy to replace Proterius, who was killed by a rioting mob. Timothy opposed the dogmatic decree of Chalcedon and the *Tome* of Pope Leo I, but equally opposed the doctrine of Eutyches, condemned at Chalcedon, and like the Chalcedonians taught that the incarnate Christ is fully one with the human race just as, being the eternal Logos, he is consubstantial with the Father. Like SEVERUS OF ANTIOCH, PETER THE FULLER, PETER THE IBERIAN and PETER MONGOS, Timothy represents a MONOPHYSITE position loyal to the doctrine of CYRIL OF ALEXANDRIA's teaching of 'the one nature of the Word incarnate'.

Timothy was deposed and exiled by Emperor Leo I *c*.459, but recalled by the usurper Basiliskos in 475. He died in office in 477, just before receipt of an order from Emperor Zeno deposing him once again. Timothy's nickname is often attributed to his size and figure, but may refer to his theological subtlety.

DM

Timothy Salophakialos Timothy 'Wobble-Cap', CHALCEDONIAN patriarch of ALEXANDRIA 460–75 and 477–82. He replaced TIMOTHY AILOUROS when the latter was exiled by Emperor Leo I; on Timothy's restoration by Basiliskos, he withdrew to the monastery at Canopus, but returned to the throne on Ailouros' death in 477. He was now faced by an anti-Chalcedonian rival, PETER MONGOS, who won imperial recognition as patriarch on the death of Salophakialos in 482.

DM

Tinos Island of the Cyclades with a large Catholic community coexisting with the Orthodox population. Tinos became a centre of Orthodox PILGRIMAGE from 1823 when the visionary nun Pelagia successfully directed the search for a buried ICON of the ANNUNCIATION (*see* PHANEROMENI). The Evangelistria church erected on the spot became the major shrine of the new Greek state. This church and the older Mantamados monastery of Archangel Michael on Lesbos, where a relief commemorates a miracle against Saracen raiders, draw pilgrims from across the Orthodox world. Before the 1923 population exchanges both shrines were focal points for the scattered Greek communities of ASIA MINOR and PONTUS.

See also CHONAI; PANORMITIS; PATMOS; SKOPELOS.

Dubisch, J. (1995), *In a Different Place: Pilgrimage, Gender and Politics of a Greek Island Shrine*. Princeton: Princeton University Press.

DB

Transfiguration icon   The icon of the Transfiguration (Greek: Metamorphosis) of Christ on Tabor is based on Matthew 17: 1–9. The earliest Transfiguration icon is the sixth-century apse mosaic in the monastery church of St Catherine at SINAI. An almost contemporary symbolic representation exists in the apse of Sant'Apollinare in Classe at Ravenna. The colour symbolism of the MANDORLA is especially significant in the icon of the Transfiguration. The dark blue at the centre of the mandorla reminds us that the divine nature remains unknowable, despite the divine light emanating from the transfigured Christ. In the cross in Christ's halo appear the Greek letters *ho on*, from Exodus 3: 14, emphasizing the deity of Christ.

On separate peaks stand two Old Testament prophets, Moses, holding the tablets of the Law, and ELIAS, to both of whom God revealed himself on HOLY MOUNTAINS. Beneath them sprawl the disciples Peter, James and JOHN THE THEOLOGIAN, pinpointed by three divine rays from Christ's mandorla, which hint at the mystery of the TRINITY. Divine glory illuminates the entire foreground, signifying the enlightenment of the created world.

During the fourteenth-century controversy surrounding HESYCHASM the Transfiguration icon acquired new importance owing to discussions on the uncreated light. The transfiguring light of Tabor, associated with hesychast spirituality to a degree not encountered before, became a crucial representation of the EASTERN ORTHODOX vision of God. The feast of the Transfiguration falls on 6 August.

McGuckin, J. A. (1987), *The Transfiguration of Christ in Scripture and Tradition*. New York: Edward Mellon.
Farandy, R. de (1978), *L'icône de la Transfiguration*. Abbaye de Bellefontaine.

KP

Trinity   The basis of the Christian doctrine of the Trinity was laid down at the Councils of Nicaea (325) and Constantinople I (381) in response to the heresy of the Alexandrian presbyter Arius, who taught that the Son of God was created. The Council of Constantinople II, held under the Emperor Justinian in 553, proclaimed the dogma of the Trinity thus: 'If anyone does not confess the one nature [*physis*] or substance [*ousia*] and the one potency [*dynamis*] and power [*exousia*] of the Father and the Son and the Holy Spirit, the consubstantial [*homoousion*] Trinity, one Godhead worshipped in three hypostases or persons, let such a one be anathema. For there is one God and Father, from whom are all things, and one Lord, Jesus Christ, through whom are all things, and one Holy Spirit, in which are all things' (*see* ECUMENICAL COUNCILS). This definition defends the church's absolute commitment to monotheism while at the same time developing the use of existing Greek PHILOSOPHICAL VOCABULARY to express the church's awareness of the deity of the Logos and of the Holy Spirit, read from the testimony of the scripture, communicated in the lived theological experience of the Christian community and disclosed in its liturgical language. The dogma of the Trinity as promulgated in the *horos* of Constantinople II was the result of a process of theological development enabled by accessing contemporary philosophical thought as well as scriptural, liturgical and patristic writings.

Although by the time the definition was promulgated the CHURCH OF THE EAST and the Oriental Orthodox were already separated from the Byzantine and Roman churches, the dogmatic definition of Constantinople II expresses the trinitarian doctrinal tradition of those churches also.

The doctrine of the Trinity was formulated to avoid all forms of polytheism, especially tritheism, all forms of subordinationism and all attempts to deny the true deity of the Son or the Holy Spirit. Equally it excludes any doctrine that presents the Father, the Son and the Spirit as merely modes or manifestations of the unique Godhead. The doctrine of the Trinity found clear dogmatic expression only after a lengthy process of theological and doctrinal development, the earlier stages of which were dominated by disputed questions of CHRISTOLOGY. The initial expression of the doctrine at Nicea and Constantinople I was a response to the heresy of the Alexandrian presbyter Arius who had taught that the Son of God is a created being and has an origin in time. Constantinople I also condemned the Christological doctrine of Apollinarios and extreme Arian bishop Eunomios of Cyzicus (d. 394) who taught that God, whom he calls Birthlessness (*agennesia*), is a simple eternal reality, totally intelligible, devoid of all multiplicity or distinctions.

Some of the fathers saw the Trinity as manifested sequentially in revelation; Gregory Nazianzen, for example (*see* CAPPADOCIANS), argued that the Old Testament clearly proclaims God the Father, but more obscurely hints at the Son, whereas the New Testament clearly proclaims the Son but merely hints at the deity of the Spirit, who now abides in the church, which therefore receives from the abiding Spirit a fuller awareness of his nature.

For EASTERN CHRISTIANS the doctrine of the Trinity belongs to THEOLOGY in the strict sense. Liturgical prayer is rich with trinitarian formulae; doxologies especially are strongly trinitarian. Sacramental rites and all forms of blessing are understood in relation to the theology of the Trinity and their language is explicitly trinitarian. The ancient baptismal creeds and the forms of the creed used in the eucharistic liturgy are also trinitarian. Eastern theology identifies the monarchy of the Father as the ground of unity in the Godhead, where Western theologians tend to see the divine nature as the ground of unity. This distinction became particularly clear in the controversy over the Western addition of the FILIOQUE to the liturgical creed. It also became evident that Western theology was more ready than Eastern to infer the eternal relations among the persons of the Trinity from the economy as disclosed in scripture. Both traditions accepted the authority of the fathers of the church, but differed in the interpretations placed on specific formulae used in their writings. The statement that the Spirit proceeds 'through the Son' (Greek: *dia ton uion*; Latin: *per filium*) caused the greatest problems, Western theologians and controversialists asserting that this referred both to the sending of the Spirit by the Son and to the eternal procession, which it implied to be from both Father and Son, Eastern writers either, like PHOTIOS the Great, limiting the reference of the phrase to the sending in time or, like Nikephoros Blemmydes (1197–*c*.1269) and Patriarch Gregory II (1283–9), whose teaching received approval at the Council of Blachernai in 1285, seeing that sending as reflecting the eternal manifestation of the Spirit by the Son. Gregory taught that the Father is the sole source of the Spirit's being as one of the three divine hypostases, but it is through the Son that the Spirit's graces and gifts are both manifested eternally and sent forth in time. In Byzantine tradition, Pentecost is the feast of the Trinity, and the texts of THEOPHANY and TRANSFIGURA-TION show that these too disclose and celebrate the Trinity.

In the fourteenth century the HESYCHAST theology of GREGORY PALAMAS emphasized the distinction, already adumbrated in the thought of the Cappadocians, between the unknowable divine essence and the eternal energies of God, which suffuse and sustain the created universe, and which are ultimately knowable to some degree. The essence is absolutely one, the energies many and diverse. The 'uncreated light' is a divine energy the hesychasts seek to perceive, preparing themselves by discipline and prayer, especially by use of the JESUS PRAYER.

More recently, the SOPHIOLOGY associated particularly with the Russian thinkers SOLOVYOV, BULGAKOV and FLORENSKY appears sometimes to give the DIVINE WISDOM a problematic status, generally rejected as compromising the orthodox doctrine of the Trinity.

Burgess, S. M. (1989), *The Holy Spirit: Eastern Christian Traditions*. Peabody, Mass.: Hendrickson.

Zizioulas, J. D. (1985), *Being as Communion*. Crestwood, NY: St Vladimir's Seminary Press.

Young, F. (1983), *From Nicea to Chalcedon*. London: SCM Press.

Meyendorff, J. (1978), *Byzantine Theology*. Crestwood, NY: St Vladimir's Seminary Press.

Pelikan, J. (1977), *The Spirit of Eastern Christendom (600–1700)*. Chicago: University of Chicago Press.

Pelikan, J. (1971), *The Emergence of the Catholic Tradition*. Chicago: University of Chicago Press.

DM/KP

Trinity icons   The Trinity is traditionally represented by Abraham's three vistors at Mamre (Genesis, 18: 1–15) in the icon of the Hospitality of Abraham, or the Old Testament Trinity. (An alternative and patristically well-grounded tradition sees in Genesis 18 an appearance of the Word, accompanied by two angels.) The earliest Hospitality of Abraham, a mid-fourth-century painting in the Via Latina New Cata-comb in ROME, shows three angels appearing before a seated Abraham. The mid-fifth-century mosaic in St Mary Major in Rome shows the angels seated at a table, as does the mid-sixth-century mosaic in San Vitale, Ravenna. The basic elements of the iconography of the Trinity were therefore established relatively early, but only attained their apogee in RUBLEV's famous Trinity.

An icon known as the Paternity appears in eleventh-century Byzantium. In fifteenth-century Russia, Paternity icons show the Father enthroned, the Son on his lap holding a disc within which hovers the Holy Spirit as a dove. A third development, the New Testament Trinity, shows Father and Son enthroned with the dove between them. THEOPHANY and TRANSFIGURATION icons are also considered icons of the Trinity, a point made explicitly in the Slavonic Trebnik rite for blessing icons.

The MOSCOW Council of 1553–4 justified images of the Father in human form on the basis of prophetic visions of the Lord Sabaoth (Isaias 6: 5) and the Ancient of Days (Daniel 7: 9). This was repudiated by the Moscow Council of 1666–7, and a ruling of the Russian Holy Synod in 1722 directed that the image of the Father be removed from the ANTIMENSION.

The Paternity icon may have developed as a pictorial expression of the Orthodox doctrine of the procession of the Holy Spirit. It can be read as rejecting the FILOQUE, as can Rublev's Trinity.

Ouspensky, L. (1992) *Theology of the Icon*, 2 vols. Crestwood, NY: St Vladimir's Seminary Press.
Papadopoulos, M. (1968). 'Essais d'interprétation de thème iconographique de la Paternité dans l'art byzantin', *Cahiers archéologiques*, 18, pp. 121–36.

KP

Triodion   One of three Byzantine rite service books that contain the offices for the cycle of movable feasts (*see also* PARAKLETIKE; PENTEKOSTARION). It contains texts for offices for Great Lent and GREAT WEEK, ending with the PROTE ANASTASIS, and preceded by those for the four Sundays and the last two Saturdays before Lent. The Triodion is so named because the CANON at weekday Matins contains only three ODES (on Saturdays four), not the usual eight. The modern Triodion is largely the work of the Constantinopolitan Studite monastery in the ninth century, particularly of THEODORE THE STUDITE and his brother Joseph, though many texts are earlier or later. Notable among the former are the daily IDIOMELA for Vespers and AINOI by two monks of the Lavra of St Sabas, Andrew and Stephen; among the latter the Enkomia sung Matins of Holy Saturday and the office for GREGORY PALAMAS, composed by Patriarch Philotheos of Constantinople, both of which appear in the fourteenth century. The Triodion also contains two celebrated texts not originally composed for Lent, the Great Canon of ANDREW OF CRETE, sung on the fifth Thursday, and the sixth-century AKATHIST to the Mother of God, sung on the fifth Saturday. In Slav use the Triodion is known as the 'fasting Triodion', as opposed to the 'flowery Triodion', the name given in Slavonic to the Pentekostarion.

Mother Mary and Ware, K., trans. (1978), *The Lenten Triodion*. London: Faber.

E

Troparion   Greek, in present use a hymn verse. A hymn may consist of a single troparion, or a number of troparia may form a sequence, e.g. to form an ODE of a CANON. An AUTOMELON troparion provides the model for both the metrical structure and the melody of its PROSOMIA.

DM

Trisagion   Greek, 'thrice holy'; the name given to the invocation 'Holy God, Holy Mighty, Holy Immortal, have mercy on us', presently sung before the PROKEIMENON that precedes the reading of the APOSTLE in the BYZANTINE LITURGY, and used in the sequence of prayers that open many services and mark off discrete sections of services. It is also sung at the entry of the coffin into the church at a funeral and when the coffin is carried to the grave. In Oriental Orthodox use the trisagion has been used in a modified form since an addition to the text was made by PETER THE FULLER. In the current Coptic Liturgy of St Basil the trisagion, sung, usually in Greek, immediately before the prayers which precede the reading of the Gospel, has an additional Greek phrase added to each repetition: 'born from the Virgin, have mercy on us', 'crucified for us, have mercy on us', 'risen from the dead and ascended into Heaven, have mercy on us'. The Oriental Orthodox address the trisagion to the second person of the Trinity; in Byzantine tradition, which vigorously rejects the added phrases, 'Holy God' is addressed to the Father, 'Holy Mighty' to the Son and 'Holy Immortal' to the Holy Spirit. The Sanctus is also sometimes referred to as the trisagion.

DM

True Orthodox church   Or 'True Orthodox Christians': terms denoting those Orthodox Christians who, since the 1920s, have broken communion with the official Orthodox churches for various reasons and united in their traditionalist Orthodoxy and in their opposition to the submission of most local Orthodox churches to communism and/or their involvement in ECUMENISM. In the former Soviet Union the True Orthodox church was also called the 'Catacomb Church'; in ROMANIA, BULGARIA, GREECE and CYPRUS they are generally known as OLD CALENDARISTS.

The True Orthodox church of Russia broke communion with the MOSCOW patriarchate in 1927–8, and was led initially by senior and respected bishops, including Metropolitans Peter of Krutitsa, Joseph of Petrograd, Kyrill of Kazan and Agathangel of Iaroslavl, who refused to submit to Metropolitan Sergius of Nizhnii-Novgorod, as deputy to the locum tenens of the Patriarchal Throne of Moscow. Metropolitan Peter declared him to have uncanonically usurped authority over the other bishops and, by his declaration of 16/29 July 1927, to have subjected the Russian church to the communists. Christians who refused to recognize Metropolitan Sergius and his declaration were persecuted by the KGB. By 1940 all the True Orthodox bishops either had been shot or were in hiding. Successors were secretly consecrated in the catacombs, and apostolic succession preserved in the four or five major surviving branches of the Catacomb Church. From 1990, when the RUSSIAN ORTHODOX

CHURCH ABROAD opened its first parishes on Russian soil, many Catacomb Christians joined the ROCA.

In Greece and Romania, the True Orthodox movement dates from 1924, when the reformed calendar was introduced by the official churches of those countries. The movement involved only priests and laypeople, including several hundred monks from ATHOS, until in 1935 three Church of Greece bishops joined the movement in Greece, and in 1955 one Church of Romania bishop joined the movement in Romania. Since 1937, the movement in Greece has divided over the validity of New Calendarists' sacraments. An attempt by the ROCA in 1971 to unite the factions failed. Greek Old Calendarists have split into a number of groups, the most important being the Chrysostomites, Matthewites and Cyprianites. A more recent cause of division, especially among Matthewites, is the icon of the Holy TRINITY: some Old Calendarists reject the icon, others reject the rejecters as ICONOCLASTS. In Romania the movement remains united, and since the fall of Ceausescu has grown notably. There are probably over one million Old Calendarists in Romania, somewhat fewer in Greece, and considerably fewer in Bulgaria, Cyprus and the DIASPORA.

In 1994 the ROCA united with the Romanian Old Calendarists and the Cyprianite Greek Old Calendarists; but most True Orthodox Christians of Russia, Greece, Cyprus and Mount Athos remain outside this unity. In the early 1990s, it seemed Patriarch Diodorus of JERUSALEM, who had broken ties with the World Council of Churches and is sympathetic towards Old Calendarists, might provide a focus of unity; but these hopes evaporated when Diodorus returned to communion with CONSTANTINOPLE. Despite disunity and other problems, the True Orthodox church remains a magnet for the many Orthodox unhappy with the ecumenical movement. In the Moscow patriarchate a growing movement opposed to ecumenism looks with sympathy on the struggle of the True Orthodox Christians.

Moss, V. (1991), 'The True Orthodox Church of Russia', *Religion in Communist Lands.* n.p.
Kalliopios, Metropolitan of Pentapolis (n.d), *Nobles et Saints Combats des Vrais Chretiens Orthodoxes de Grèce.* Lavardac: Orthodox Monastery of St Michael.

VM

Tryphon   Third-century GREAT MARTYR of Lampsakos (Hellespontine Phrygia). By tradition, Tryphon worked on a farm tending geese. He acquired fame as a healer, especially of animals, and is considered one of the ANARGYROI, particularly invoked on farms. Prayers attributed to him are used against infestations of rodents and locusts. One such prayer appears in the Great EUCHOLOGION.

Vassilopoulos, H. (1985), *Vioi Hagion.* Athens: Orthodoxos Typos.
Velimirović, N. (1985), *Prologue From Ochrid*, vol. 1. Birmingham: Lazarica Press.

DB

Ṭūr ʿAbdīn   'Mountain of the Servants (of God)': an area of south-east Turkey, centred on Midyat between Mardin and Cizre, which became the focus of SYRIAN ORTHODOX monasticism (also with some CHURCH OF THE EAST presence: the so-called ASSYRIANS call the area Kashiari). Dozens of monasteries with thousands of monks flourished in the middle ages; today, only a few monastery-schools remain, such as Dayr az-Za'aferān (near Mardin) and Dayr Mār Gabriel (near Midyat). The traditional Syrian Orthodox population of the area has been greatly depleted through migration, with an attendant decline in the modern SYRIAC vernacular tongue of the area, Ṭūrōyō.

JH

Typikon (1) Document prescribing the rule of life of a monastic community; (2) book (Slav: Ustav) prescribing the order of services for the liturgical year; consequently, (3) the order (AKOLOUTHIA) followed in the celebration of a service or services. The main examples of Typikon (2) currently used in EASTERN ORTHODOX churches derive from the ancient Typikon of St Sabas, and the modern Constantinopolitan Typikon published by Protopsaltes George Biolakis. The Archon Protopsaltes is custodian of the Typikon of the Great Church, the Cathedral of the ECUMENICAL PATRIARCH.

DM

·U·

Ukraine   *Ukraina*, literally 'on the edge' or 'borderland': the second largest country in Europe, bordering on the Black Sea, Romania, Hungary, Slovakia, Poland, Belarus and Russia, traces its national and religious identity from the history of Kievan Rus, the work of Volodymyr the Great (980–1015) and his son Iaroslav the Wise and the role of Kyiv (KIEV) in the Christianization of the Eastern Slavic lands.

Tradition has St Andrew Protoclete travelling up the Dnieper from Korsun to CONSTANTINOPLE and predicting the future emergence of a city on the Dnieper that would offer a foothold for the Christian gospel. Grand Duchess Ol'ga (946–50) visited Constantinople and was later baptized; her grandson, Volodymyr, baptized in 988, played a crucial role in Christianizing the Kievan state.

Kyiv was destroyed in 1240 by the Mongol Golden Horde. In 1299 the Metropolitan of Kyiv and All Rus moved his residence to VLADIMIR and in 1326 to MOSCOW. Soon Poland and Lithuania were competing for dominance over Ukraine. The Ecumenical Patriarch appointed a metropolitan of Galicia in 1371, and in 1375, although there was a metropolitan ruling from Moscow, consecrated the Bulgarian monk Cyprian as Metropolitan of Kiev, Russia and Lithuania. Dynastic union of Poland and Lithuania in 1386 and again in 1569 brought discrimination against the Orthodox and Polonization of the Ukrainian elite. Political independence returned briefly with the successful rebellion of 1648, only to vanish with the partition of Ukraine between Poland and Russia in 1667.

The OTTOMAN conquest of 1453 weakened the status of Constantinople in Polish territories, as did rival claims of Moscow to jurisdiction over Ukraine. Lay brotherhoods formed to defend Orthodoxy found themselves in tension with hierarchs to whom the Poles offered promises of equal status with the Latin hierarchy if they united with Rome. This eventually happened in the Union of Brest-Litovsk in 1596. The Union roused bitter interconfessional struggle in Ukraine. The UNIATE Greek Catholic Church flourished in Austrian-annexed Galicia, while in 1686 Russia annexed the Metropolitan See of Kyiv from the Ecumerical Patriarchate to the Russian Orthodox Church. Unity with Russia disguised cultural and linguistic differences which gave birth to the movement of Ukrainian nationalism. This in turn gave birth to the movement for Ukrainian ecclesiastical independence that appeared in strength after the fall of the Russian empire in 1917. Three times in the twentieth century (1917–30, 1941–5 and since 1989) the success of movements for national independence was paralleled by the establishment of an autocephalous church. The October 1921 founding council of the Ukrainian Autocephalous Orthodox Church (UAOC) created its own hierarchy by laying on of hands. The UAOC was wiped out by Stalin in 1930.

During the Second World War the UAOC was re-established, this time with a canonically consecrated episcopate. After the war Stalin ensured that the remnants of the wartime UAOC were absorbed into the Russian Orthodox Church (ROC). In 1946 the pseudo-Council of Lviv abolished the 1596 Union of Brest and voted to 'return' to the ROC. This provoked the creation of the catacomb Ukrainian Greek Catholic Church in western Ukraine.

In August 1987 a group Greek Catholic clergy, led by the Committee for the defence of the Ukrainian Catholic Church, emerged from the underground and appealed to the Pope for help in the restoration of the church's rights. By 1989 it was clear that the process of disintegration of the ROC in Galicia had begun, as individual priests departed from the ROC to the UAOC or the Ukrainian Greek Catholic Church. The UAOC now announced the formation of the Initiative Committee of the Revival of the Ukrainian Autocephalous Orthodox Church headed by Bohdan Mikhailechho. By August 1989 SS Peter and Paul ROC Parish in Lviv with its rector Volodymyr Yarema announced its transfer to the UAOC. On 10 October the UAOC held a *sobor*, the first since its forced liquidation, at which Ioann Bodnarchuk of Zhytomyr withdrew from the ROC (which later excommunicated him) and became leader of the UAOC. The UAOC was officially registered in 1990. Headed by the outspoken, fiercely patriotic and anti-communist Metropolitan Mstyslav Skrypnyk, the UAOC grew at the expense of the ROC. At its All-Ukrainian Council in Kyiv in June 1990, the UAOC proclaimed itself a patriarchate and elected (in absentia) its first patriarch, Mstyslav Skrypnyk, then primate of the UOC in the USA and UAOC in the diaspora, the only surviving hierarch of the wartime UAOC.

Filaret Denysenko, ROC Metropolitan of Kiev, fearful for his position after over 90 per cent of the population voted in December 1991 for Ukrainian independence, began to campaign for his metropolitanate's ecclesiastical independence from Moscow. The ROC synod of May 1992 rejected this appeal. Patriarch Aleksii II denounced Filaret and replaced him with Volodymyr Sabodan, Metropolitan of Rostov and Novocherkassk, an ethnic Ukrainian. The Kharkiv Council of May 1992 deposed Filaret from his see and suspended him as bishop. The Kyiv Metropolitanate of the ROC became the Ukrainian Orthodox Church of the Moscow Patriarchate (UOC-MP), with Metropolitan Sabodan as its head.

Filaret was still supported by a portion of the clergy and faithful and was close to Ukrainian President Kravchuk. He now approached the UAOC which agreed to a merger on condition that the UAOC charter be adopted by the united church and Ukrainian be used in services. The Council of Unification of 26 June 1992 established the Ukrainian Orthodox Church of the Kyiv Patriarchate (UOC-KP), electing (in absentia) Patriarch Mstyslav as its head. Initially Mstyslav accepted the union, but soon rejected it an uncanonical and illegal, reasserting his authority as head of the UAOC, but failing initially to draw much support.

Patriarch Mstyslav, the outstanding personality in Ukrainian Orthodoxy, died on 11 June 1993 in Canada, and is buried in South Bound Brook, NJ, the centre of diaspora Ukrainian Orthodoxy. He died recognized as patriarch by both the UAOC and UOC-KP. Each elected a *locum tenens*: Archbishop Petro of Lviv and Halych and Metropolitan Volodymyr Romaniuk of Chernihiv and Sumy. On 7 September 1993 the UAOC elected Dmytrii Yarema, bishop of Pereiaslav and Sicheslav, as patriarch. In 1989 he had been the first ROC priest to bring his parish into the restored UAOC. The UOC-KP *sobor* of 20–1 October 1993 appointed Volodymyr Romaniuk as Patriarch of Kyiv and All Ukraine, with Metropolitan Filaret as his deputy. The new Patriarch had served nineteen years in Soviet labour camps and been exiled for promoting religious freedom and human rights.

In 1994 five hierarchs defected from the UOC-KP to the UOC-MP, led by Metropolitan Antonii Masendych, first *locum tenens* of the UAOC and initiator of the merger with the pro-Filaret UOC, who expressed deep disillusionment with Filaret, claiming abuse of power and failure to obtain canonical recognition for the church.

A year later Patriarch Volodymyr of the UOC-KP died at the aged of sixty-nine. On what became known as Black Tuesday, riot police beat Kyivan faithful when they attempted to bury Patriarch Volodymyr in St Sophia Cathedral. He is presently buried in a makeshift grave outside the cathedral walls and gates.

Delegates at the UOC-KP *sobor* on 20 October 1995 elected Filaret as patriarch. Alternative candidates stood down at the last moment leaving Filaret unopposed. This prompted four hierarchs and twenty lay delegates from central and western Ukraine to abandon the *sobor* and join the UAOC.

Thus Ukraine now has two patriarchs of Kyiv and three Orthodox churches: the UAOC, ethnic and predominantly Galician (1,063 parishes in 1998); the UOC-KP (1,901 parishes), a quasi-state church, with mostly Ukrainian and partly Russian membership; and the largest of the three, the territorial UOC-MP (6,300 parishes in 1998).

In the westermost regions of Ukraine, the Greek Catholic Church, another ethnic church (3,151 parishes in 1998) and now the second largest religious organization in Ukraine, represents a national church with a regional base and a slowly expanding diaspora in the rest of Ukraine and beyond.

Since Ukrainian independence the Ukrainian Orthodox Churches in the DIASPORA have returned under the *omophorion* of the Ecumenical Patriarchate.

Dawisha, K. and Parrott, B. (1994), *Russia and the New States of Eurasia*. Cambridge: Cambridge University Press.
Keleher, S. (1993), *Passion and Resurrection: The Greek Catholic Church in Soviet Ukraine 1939–1989*. L'viv: Stauropegion.

BM

Ukrainian Catholic church   The Christianity of the ancient Kievan state was Byzantine. Prince St Volodymyr (980–1015) and his son Iaroslav (1019–54) forged close links with the Byzantine empire and the church of CONSTANTINOPLE. This occurred in a period when relations between ROME and Constantinople were slowly crystallizing out into schism. The Mongol destruction of Kiev in 1240 left Ukraine partly or wholly under successive foreign rulers. In 1340 Galicia was annexed by Casimir III of Poland, while Volhynia fell under Lithuanian rule.

In 1569 the Union of Lublin united Poland and Lithuania. The Eastern Orthodox subjects of the new state found themselves socially disadvantaged and facing the active presence of the Roman Catholic church, which enjoyed a privileged position and possessed highly educated and disciplined clergy, especially in some of the religious orders. Poland viewed all contact between the Orthodox hierarchs and their mother church in Ottoman-ruled Constantinople, and all contact with Russia, with equal suspicion. Eventually the hierarchs of the Kievan church, after considerable deliberation, formulated a carefully considered document laying down thirty-three conditions under which they would be prepared to enter into union with the Roman church. The Union of Brest-Litovsk was concluded at a synod in 1596, on the basis of the conditions set out by the Orthodox hierarchs. These include the retention of their traditional creed and rites, including communion under both kinds, the retention of typically Eastern feasts, the retention of a married clergy, freedom to have bishops consecrated without mandate from Rome, and the assurance the church's hierarchs would always be 'of our religion'. Monasteries were to remain under episcopal control, Eastern clergy to have parity of esteem and privilege with the Roman clergy.

The union won the support of most of the hierarchy, but was opposed by many of the Orthodox nobility. It was also rejected by the fiercely independent Cossacks, whose opposition to Polish rule broke into open rebellion in 1648, when Bohdan Khmelnytsky won freedom from Polish rule, but at the price of an oath of loyalty to the tsar. From 1667, when a Cossack state was recognized east of the Dnieper, Russia absorbed progressively more of the eastern Polish domains until Ukraine became a province of Russia and subject both under tsarist rule and under Soviet rule to a deliberate policy of Russification. In 1839 an imperial decree suppressed the Eastern rite Catholic church throughout the Russian empire.

The Ukrainian Catholic church was able to defend its position not least because of the reorganization of the monastic order under the powerful influence of Josaphat Kuntsevych, an austere monk who became bishop of Vitebsk in 1617 and archbishop of Pskov in 1618. The monastic houses were brought into a single structure with clear lines of authority, independent of the bishops. Monastic education and formation were improved, and the new Basilian order became a major force in religious education and pastoral work. Josaphat himself was a resolute supporter of the union, ready to use state law to fight his Orthodox opponents. In 1623 he was murdered in Vitebsk. He was beatified in 1643 and canonized in 1867.

After the Second World War western Ukraine too fell under Soviet rule. In 1946 a pseudo-synod was organized in Lviv to dismantle the Greek Catholic church and incorporate clergy and faithful into the RUSSIAN ORTHODOX CHURCH. Recusants were persecuted. Most of the hierarchy resisted forcible conversion and died in prison camps. An underground church complete with monastic institutions and even seminaries coexisted with groups who followed the Latin rite or formally adhered to the Orthodox church, while remaining secretly loyal to their Ukrainian Catholic tradition.

In 1963, however, Metropolitan Joseph Slipy was released and travelled to Rome, where he proposed the creation of a Ukrainian Catholic patriarchate, and from 1975, despite absence of papal approval, assumed the title patriarch of Kiev and Halych and

All Rus. From 1987 groups of clergy and laity began to announce openly their adherence to the Ukrainian Catholic church, and demands for the legalization of the church were made. In 1989 a meeting of the hierarchs of Ukraine undertook the re-establishment of the church's traditional eparchies. In December 1989 official permission was received to register Ukrainian Catholic parishes, and by 1993 over 1,350 were registered with over 1,000 priests, about a third of them formerly Russian Orthodox clergy. In 1990 the Cathedral of Saint George in Lviv was returned to the Ukrainian Catholic church and the next year Cardinal Liubachivsky came from Rome to assume leadership of the church. In 1992 a synod under his presidency condemned the Lviv synod of 1946 and took significant steps to re-establish the organizational base of the church.

Substantial Ukrainian Catholic communities exist in the DIASPORA, in the USA, Canada, Western Europe and South America, and smaller communities elsewhere, most under the jurisdiction of the Ukrainian Catholic church, some under Latin bishops, others under a variety of other Eastern jurisdictions, such as the diocese of Presov in Slovakia or the Pittsburgh Metropoly in the USA. The opening up of freer contact and movement between Ukraine and the Ukrainian diaspora offers a means to further the unity and common purpose of the entire Ukrainian Catholic community.

Bourdeaux, M. (1991), *Gorbachev, Glasnost and the Gospel*. London.
Subtelny, O. (1988), *Ukraine: A History*. Toronto: University of Toronto Press.
Blazejovskyi, D. (1980), *Byzantine Kyivan Rite Metropolitanates, Eparchies and Exarchates, Nomenclature and Statistics*. Rome.
Szporluk, R. (1979), *Ukraine*. Toronto: University of Toronto Press.

DM

Umilenie   Russian term for the iconographic type ELEOUSA; an example is the Virgin 'of VLADIMIR', painted in Byzantium and taken to Russia in 1131.

KP

Uniate   A term used to designate EASTERN CATHOLIC churches, communities and individuals, but usually perceived by Eastern Catholics as abusive, and sometimes so used by Orthodox. It is, however, a term used in formal papal documents, e.g. in the bull *Ex Quo* of Benedict XIV (1740–68).

DM

· V ·

Valaam monastery By tradition Valaam's founders in the period of the Christian-ization of Rus were the Greek monks Sergei and German. Sacked by the Swedes in the mid-twelfth century, but soon restored and rededicated to the Transfiguration, the monastery was rebuilt in stone in the fourteenth century after a fire. It was razed by the Swedes in 1581 and again in 1611, then refounded in 1717 when Russia regained western Karelia. After another fire in 1754, Abbot Nazarii (d. 1801) constructed a new monastic complex and initiated a major spiritual revival. Valaam was abandoned during Soviet–Finnish conflict on the eve of the Second World War. A 'New Valaam' was founded in Finland by monks evacuated from the war zone; another has been organized at Ouzinkie in Alaska. Valaam was in ruins until 1988 when it was returned to the Orthodox church.

Stakhovich, M. and Bolshakoff, S. (1992), *Interior Silence*. New Valaam, Alaska: St Herman of Alaska.
Seide, G. (1990), *Monasteries and Convents of the Russian Orthodox Church Abroad*. Munich: St Job of Pochaev.
Kontzevitch, I. M. (1988), *The Acquisition of the Holy Spirit in Ancient Russia*. Platina, Cal.: St Herman of Alaska.
Kontzevitch, I. M. (1988), *The Northern Thebaid*. Platina, Cal.: St Herman of Alaska.
John of Valaam (1980), *Christ is in Our Midst*. London: Darton, Longman & Todd.

DB

Valades Muslim Greeks of western MACEDONIA, the largest Greek community to have embraced Islam under OTTOMAN rule and yet maintained their ethnic identity. The Greek Orthodox church argued that those who apostatized were also abandoning their nation and culture and 'turning Turk'. However, the Valades remained Greek-speaking up to the population exchanges of the early 1920s when they were resettled in Turkey.
    See also DIONYSIOS OF OLYMPOS; NIKANOR OF KALLISTRATOS.

DB

Veniamin Kazanskii (1874–1922) Russian NEW MARTYR. From the northern province of Olenets, Veniamin was consecrated bishop of Gdov in 1910. He worked throughout the St Petersburg region, reviving parish life, founding schools and preaching. Elected metropolitan of Petrograd during the 1917 Revolution, Veniamin fearlessly opposed arrest and execution of clergy and church activists. Arrested in 1922 for non-cooperation with the Soviet authorities' campaign to expropriate church valuables, he stood trial with eighty-six priests and was executed with Archimandrite Sergeii and Professors N. Kovsharov and Y. Novitskii. They are commemorated on 1 August.

Vostryshev, M. (1993), 'Saint Veniamin'. *Journal of the Moscow Patriarchate* 3.

DB

Venice The cathedral (since 1991) of San Giorgio dei Greci, completed in 1573, an important architectural work and a treasurehouse of ICONS and wall paintings, became the focus for a Greek community with a vigorous religious and intellectual life. From 1577 onwards the Venetian authorities permitted the church of St George the unique privilege of being directly under the authority of the Ecumenical Throne, rather than of ROME, its rector being also a titular metropolitan. The Venetian Greek publishing houses printed many liturgical and religious books for the EASTERN ORTHODOX church. From 1662 to 1905 the Flaginean College educated clergy and teachers for a church languishing under OTTOMAN rule. Its buildings now house the Hellenic Institute of Byzantine and Post-Byzantine Studies. In 1991 the Ecumenical Patriarch erected the Greek Orthodox archdiocese of Italy and exarchate of Southern Europe, with San Giorgio dei Greci as cathedral.

As early as 1512 Jacob 'the Sinner' published an Armenian CALENDAR in Venice. In 1717 San Lazzaro island, a former leper colony, was granted to the Armenian Catholic Mechitarists, many in flight from the Turkish attack on their monastery in the Morea (1715). Their communities in Trieste and Vienna are daughter houses of Venice. All three houses have sustained a remarkable level of cultural and scholarly life, supporting both Orthodox and Catholic Armenian communities with their liturgical and religious publications. (*See* ARMENIAN CHRISTIANITY.)

Runciman, S. (1968), *The Great Church in Captivity*. Cambridge: Cambridge University Press.

DM

Vlachs Known by themselves generally as Aroumanians, in GREECE as Koutzov-lachs, in ALBANIA as Ciobans, in the former Yugoslavia as Cincars, in ROMANIA as Macedo-Romanians and by many other local names, the Vlachs pose many problems besides nomenclature. The name 'Vlach' is generally recognized, although it too presents difficulties, as it can just mean a shepherd or be used as a term of abuse. Vlachs are sometimes confused with Saracatsans, sharing the same nomadic habits, but the two ethnic groups are distinct from and sometimes hostile to each other. The term Vlach seems to derive from the Germanic word for stranger which gives us 'Welsh' and 'Walloon'. One certainty about the Vlachs is their firm GREEK ORTHODOX faith; another, that their language derives from Latin.

The origin of the Vlachs is disputed. Greeks maintain that they descend either from Roman legionaries set to guard the mountain passes, who married Greek girls, or from Byzantine inhabitants of the Balkans who were, like Emperor Justinian, bilingual. Neither theory is convincing. We learn languages from our mothers, not our fathers, while early references show the Vlachs fighting against the Byzantine empire rather than being part of it. Romanians like to think of the Vlachs as honorary Romanians, pointing to the close resemblance between their languages, but are unable to explain why, when or how the Vlachs left the Danube to settle in the inaccessible mountains of the central Balkans.

It seems more likely that at least some Vlachs were autochthonous inhabitants of the Balkan peninsula, Illyrians and Thracians, who learned a rudimentary Latin before the collapse of the Danube frontier in AD 602. People in northern and western parts of the Eastern Roman empire spoke some Latin and would have learned Christianity in a Latin form. In the Vlach language, though detailed words of Christian ritual are Greek, the basic words of Christian faith are Latin. Thus *basearica* is a church. Slav invasions of the sixth and seventh centuries swept away or assimilated many such Latin-speakers, but Latin was the language of religion and civilization, and Latin in the central Balkans may have been strengthened by refugees from further north. The resilience of Vlach in the modern period owes much to Vlachs from one part of the world making their homes near Vlachs in another part; flourishing Vlach communities in AUSTRALIA and AMERICA settled along these lines.

Byzantine references to Vlachs are neither precise nor complimentary, but show us features of Vlach life which have lasted until the present. In 976 we hear of Vlach *hoditai* or travellers: the Vlachs gained great wealth in the eighteenth and nineteenth centuries as controllers of trade and traffic along the primitive routes of the Balkans. Other medieval discussions of Vlachs point to their close connection with sheep: many modern Vlachs still work as shepherds and dealers in wool and cheese. Finally, medieval records show Vlachs practising transhumance, flocks and families moving from high summer pastures to the plains in winter. These features of Vlach life gave them a certain strength in dealing with central authorities. They were hard to tie down, and good at extracting tax concessions. The Vlach way of life, dangerous and demanding, strengthened family loyalty and firm commitment to religion.

The OTTOMAN invasion made little practical difference to the Vlach way of life: similar control was exercised and similar concessions were extracted. Permanent settlements and church building in the mountain villages seem to have begun in the seventeenth century. With Ottoman power extending beyond the Danube, Vlach merchants carried their wares all over Eastern Europe. Vlachs settled and prospered in the Austro-Hungarian empire. They played a prominent part in the affairs of Romania, where the church leader Saguna (*see* ROMANIAN CHRISTIANITY) was of Vlach origin. Merchants and churchmen conversed in Vlach, but Greek was the language of commerce, religion and education. Hence it was difficult for Vlachs to establish a separate identity. The great Vlach city of Moschopolis in southern Albania, with its wealth of churches, its academy and its printing press, is hailed as a monument to Vlach culture, yet the Albanians claim it as their own and the Greeks, not without reason, think of Moschopolis as Greek: the language used in the churches, the academy and the printing press.

Greek churchmen like Kosmas Aetolos are said to have taught that Vlach, like Albanian, is the devil's language. Not until the later nineteenth century was there any attempt to foster the language in schools, inspired, rather artificially, with help from distant Romania. Attempts to found a separate Vlach church were largely unsuccessful, although Apostol Margarit made valiant attempts. In general most Vlachs threw themselves behind the movement for Greek independence. The early Greek patriot Rigas Pheraios and the first Greek prime minister John Kolettis were both of Vlach origin. Some Vlachs opposed independence from the Turks, seeing the break-up of the Ottoman empire as a threat to their freedom of movement across boundaries. In 1905 the Vlachs were recognized as a separate *milet*. There was also a small pro-Romanian element. The English scholars Wace and Thompson give an excellent picture of Vlach society just before the First World War.

That war, and the Balkan wars that preceded it, saw the Vlachs divided among various nation states, most of which had very little time for them. Romanian schools continued in Greece until the Second World War, but there was considerable emigration from Greece, Albania and Bulgaria to Romania and America. In Greece Vlachs tended to become assimilated to the Greeks, in Romania to the Romanians. In many villages only the old now speak Vlach, though emigrant associations try to keep the Vlach culture alive. In Albania, where religion was suppressed under Enver Hoxha, there is a large Vlach population, and the revival of religion may result in Vlach services being held there, though there are formidable obstacles to this. There is as yet no standard Vlach alphabet, and Greek speakers in Albania face political difficulties.

Winnifrith, T. J. (1987), *The Vlachs: The History of a Balkan People*. London: Duckworth.
Peyfuss, M. (1974), *Die Aromunische Frage*. Vienna: Hermann Bohlhaus.
Wace, A. J. B. and Thompson, M. (1914), *The Nomads of the Balkans*. London: Methuen.

TW

Vladimir   The city of Vladimir in north-eastern Russia was sacked by the Mongols in 1238; by 1300 it had become the metropolitan see. It has two outstanding twelfth-century churches, of the Dormition and St Dmitrii. The Dormition cathedral was built by Andrei Bogoliubskii in 1158–61, and rebuilt by his brother Vsevolod III in 1185–9 after a fire. Andrei RUBLEV and Daniil Cherny undertook some repainting of the frescoes in 1408. Andrei Bogoliubskii was also responsible for the POKROV church on the Nerl, built in 1166. This church is used in the opening sequence of Tarkovskii's *Andrei Rublev* (1966). The church of St Dmitrii, built by Vsevolod III in 1194–7, was consecrated with relics from its namesake at Thessaloniki. Small but majestic, it has a central dome like the Pokrov church, and also, like the Pokrov, it has unusual bas-reliefs, possibly inspired by Armenian examples, such as the AGHTAMAR church of the Holy Cross. Alternatively, they may owe something to Romanesque influence.

Brumfield, W. C. (1993), *A Hisoty of Russian Architecture*. Cambridge: Cambridge University Press.
Hamilton, G. H. (1983), *The Art and Architecture of Russia*. Harmondsworth: Penguin.

KP

Volotovo Pole   The Dormition Church at Volotovo Pole near NOVGOROD, built in 1352, partly frescoed in 1363 and completed in 1380, was destroyed in the Second World War. Fortunately, photographs and copies of the frescoes were made in the early twentieth century. Their style is akin to that of THEOPHAN THE GREEK, and they were once thought to be by him, but this has been disproved. Outstanding in a programme of dynamic images are those of JOHN OF DAMASCUS and the TRANSFIGURATION. It has been suggested that the depiction of DIVINE WISDOM is directed against the heresy of the STRIGOL'NIKI. The preoccupation of the unknown master of the Volotovo frescoes with the spiritual presence of his subjects, at the expense of detailed locality, may reflect the fourteenth-century interest in HESYCHASM.

Alpatov, M. V. (1977), *Frescoes of the Church of the Assumption at Volotovo Polye*. Moscow: Iskusstvo.

KP

· W ·

Way of the Pilgrim Nineteenth-century Russian story of a wandering pilgrim who had learned the JESUS PRAYER from a STARETS. He carries the abridged *Dobrotolubiye* (PHILOKALIA). It is an edifying story with episodes reminiscent of hagiographical accounts of HOLY FOOLS. The book shows considerable insight into the practice of HESYCHASM. The manuscript is said to have been found on Mount ATHOS by the abbot of a monastery in Kazan. The letters of Amurosii of OPTINA are evidence that copies were known in Russian monasteries before its publication in 1884. It has been translated into many languages; an English translation appeared in 1930. Mention of it in J. D. Salinger's novel *Franny and Zooey* aroused wider interest in the book. A sequel, *The Pilgrim Continues his Way*, is also published in English.

French, R. M., trans. (1975), *The Way of the Pilgrim*. London: SPCK.

KP

Weddase Maryam Weddāsē Māryām or 'Praise of Mary' is an important collection of seven prayers, one for each day of the week, in honour of the Virgin Mary, often found in Ethiopic manuscripts alongside the Psalms and Canticles. Traditionally attributed to EPHREM THE SYRIAN, it seems in fact to have been translated at least in part from the Copto-Arabic Theotokia, hymns to the Virgin Mary which are part of the Psalmodia, a choral service (and service-book) of the Coptic church. The Wēddasē Māryām is part of an enormous collection of Marian literature in Ge'ez.

See also ETHIOPIAN ORTHODOX CHURCH.

Cerulli, E. (1943), *Il Libro Etiopico dei Miracoli di Maria e le sue fonti nelle letterature del medio evo latino*, vol. 1. Studi Orientali Pubblicati a cura della Scuola Orientale. Rome: University of Rome.

Budge, E. A. W. (1933), *Legends of Our Lady Mary the Perpetual Virgin and her Mother Hanna*. Oxford: Oxford University Press.

Euringer, S. (1911), 'Der mutmassliche Verfasser der koptischen Theotokien und des äthiopischen Weddâsê Mârjâm', *Oriens Christianus*, n.s., vol. 1, pp. 215–16.

MJB/SHG

Western rite Orthodoxy The issue of 'restoring' the Western rite in Orthodoxy provokes strong feelings, supporters regarding it as an inalienable right for Orthodox Christians in the West, opponents viewing it as UNIATISM in reverse. Building on the principle established by the Russian Holy Synod's approval of the scheme put forward by Dr J. J. OVERBECK, there have been two significant movements.

In 1937 the patriarchate of Moscow received a small group under the former Liberal Catholic bishop, Louis-Charles (Irénée) Winnaert (1880–1937), as l'Eglise Orthodoxe Occidentale. His work was carried on (though not always in complete unity) by Evgraph Kovalevsky (1905–70) and Lucien Chambault (1900–65), who as Père Denis presided over a small Orthodox Benedictine community in the rue d'Alleray, Paris. Associated with them was the former Benedictine monk Archimandrite Alexis van der Mensbrugghe (1899–1980), who favoured the restoration of the Roman rite purged of medieval accretions and supplemented by Gallican and Byzantine interpolations. In 1948 he published his Liturgie Orthodoxe de Rite Occidental and in 1962 the Missel Orthodoxe Rite Occidental.

After 1946 Kovalevsky developed the Eglise Orthodoxe de France with a specific commitment to reconstruct the pre-Carolingian Gallican rite based on the letters of Germanus of Paris. These were troubled times for the Orthodox community in Paris which involved several changes of jurisdiction, but van der Mensbrugghe eventually returned to the Moscow patriarchate and was consecrated bishop in 1960. After some years of independence Kovalevsky's following came under the Synod of the RUSSIAN ORTHODOX CHURCH ABROAD between 1959 and 1966, and Kovalevsky was consecrated as Bishop Jean de Saint-Denis (1964). The group received considerable encouragement and support from Archbishop JOHN MAXIMOVITCH (1896–1966), the synod's representative in Western Europe, and his death deprived them of a prestigious advocate. Between 1966 and 1972 when they were again independent of any oversight Kovalevsky died, but in 1972 they were received into the Romanian Orthodox church and Gilles Bertrand-Hardy (b. 1930) was consecrated as Bishop Germain de Saint-Denis. The Western rite under Moscow soon withered and perished. The restored Gallican rite became the liturgy used by the many small French Orthodox parishes established throughout France and can be seen in all its splendour in the Cathedral of St Irénée in Boulevard Auguste-Blanqui in Paris. In 1994, following protracted problems with the Romanian authorities over a number of canonical irregularities, they were once more outside canonical Orthodoxy. The Romanian patriarchate established a deanery under Bishop Germain's brother, Archpriest Gregoire, to minister to those parishes that wished to stay with Romania.

In 1961 members of the Society of Clerks Secular of St Basil, centred on Mount Vernon, New York, were received into the Antiochian Orthodox diocese of New York. Headed by the hitherto uncanonical but much respected Bishop Alexander (Paul Tyler Turner, 1905–71), they became the basis for a Western rite vicariate. Numbers have never been large, but with the upheavals following the Episcopal Church of the USA's ordination of women to the priesthood, there has been steady growth. There are two permitted rites: one based on the Roman rite of 1570 ('St Gregory'), one on the Book of Common Prayer ('St Tikhon'), both with minor but very significant amendments to conform more closely to EASTERN ORTHODOX tradition. The complete Roman rite of Benediction is also permitted. In 1995 the Antiochians also established a British deanery to absorb Anglican converts.

The principle of Western rite Orthodoxy having been established, other small groups were accepted into Orthodoxy, but had little impact and often declared their independence. Western rite parishes were established in Poland in 1926 when six parishes of the Polish National Catholic church were received into Orthodoxy, but the movement dwindled away during the Second World War.

Western rite Orthodoxy has not been the sole preserve of the Byzantine patriarch-ates, but received early support from Oriental Orthodox. The Syrian 'JACOBITE' patriarchate of Antioch authorized the erection of a Roman rite diocese with the consecration of Antonio Francisco Xavier Alvarez (1837–1923) as archbishop of Cey-lon, Goa and India in 1889, and again in 1891 with the consecration of Joseph René Vilatte (1854–1929) as archbishop for the American Old Catholics.

Kovalevsky, M. (1990), *Orthodoxie et Occident Renaissance d'une Eglise Locale*. Paris: Carbonnel Editeur.
Bunnen, A. van (1981), 'L'Orthodoxie de rite occidentale en Europe et aux Etats-Unis', *Irénikon* 54.
Newman-Norton, S. (1980), 'New Light on Ferrette's Consecration', *Glastonbury Bulletin* 58.

S

women 'O strange Orthodox Church... Church of contrasts, at once so traditional and so free, so ritualistic... and so living. Church where the biblical pearl of great price is carefully treasured up, sometimes under a layer of dust... but it can sing as no other the joy of Easter.' The contrasts here invoked by ARCHIMANDRITE Lev Gillet are strikingly illustrated in the status of Christian Orthodox women. The liberating message of the gospel is mingled with archaic taboos, a spiritualistic and personalist theological anthropology and misogynistic stereotypes inherited from patriarchal soci-eties. A grave and tender femininity radiates from the icons of the Mother of God which are found everywhere, but women are forbidden access to the ALTAR. Those women who first proclaimed Christ's Resurrection, the Myrophoroi, are honoured as 'apostles to the apostles', but reading the Gospel in public worship is reserved to male ministers. In all sorts of ways, however, now as in the past, women are playing an active role in Orthodox church life. Contact with modernity is etching out a new realization. A sign of the times is the call for a balanced view of the place of women between a living tradition and a rigid traditionalism.

The common calling of all baptized persons, men and women alike, is prophetically proclaimed in the Christian initiation MYSTERIES, conferred without distinction of sex. Baptism by immersion signifies the passage, the birth to a new life by communion in the death and Resurrection of Christ. The marking with the seal of the Holy Spirit on different parts of the body, chrismation, makes each man and woman one of the Lord's anointed, a second Christ by communion through the Spirit with the Anointed par excellence, Jesus Christ: 'As many as have been baptised in Christ have put on Christ' (Galatians 3: 27), sing the choir when, clothed in a baptismal robe, the newly baptized, whether female or male, is led into the eucharistic congregation, Christ's visible body, of which both she and he have become fully members. And yet, at the very moment when all separation seems to have been abolished, there occurs a traditional rite which contrasts with that proclamation: the baptized male is taken into the sanctuary behind the ICONOSTASIS, but its doors remain closed to a woman or a little girl. Growing numbers of Orthodox Christian women resent this rite as discriminatory.

The charge of misogyny has been brought against the fathers of the church chiefly by Western feminists with reference to the Latin tradition from Augustine to Thomas Aquinas and Bonaventure. A number of Orthodox voices have joined this chorus, for example those of the Greek American Byzantine scholar E. Katafygiotu-Topping and the Romanian theologian A. Manolache. On the Orthodox side a more detailed study of this aspect of the teaching of the Greek fathers was initiated in an article entitled 'Femininity and Masculinity in the Theology of the Cappadocian Fathers' by the theologian Verna Harrison. The founding fathers of Orthodox theological anthropology, the three CAPPADOCIANS Basil the Great, Gregory of Nyssa and Gregory of Nazianzus, and similarly, after them, MAXIMUS THE CONFESSOR, vigorously asserted the ontological unity of humanity, of man and woman, in the order of creation, an order disrupted by sin, which is essentially separation, but restored in Christ according to the order of redemption. At the heart of their anthropological meditation are Genesis 1: 27–8 and Galatians 3: 27–8; 'The wife, like the husband, has the privilege of having been created in the image of God. Both their natures are equally honourable,' asserts Basil, answering a woman questioner who seems to doubt it ('On the origin of man', *Homily* 1: 18). Commenting on the baptismal hymn in the Epistle to the Galatians, he evokes the image of Christ present in all the baptized. It eclipses differences of race, social status and sex: 'Just as in the emperor's portrait the beauty of the face renders unimportant, transfigures the material used by the artist, whether wood or gold' (*Treatise on Baptism*, quoted by Verna Harrison). Gregory of Nazianzus summed up the theological anthropology of the Cappadocian fathers with the words: 'One and the same Creator for man and for woman, for both the same clay, the same image, the same death, the same resurrection' (Oration 37: 6).

Behind these words emerge the images of the real women who inspired them: the martyr Julitta, whose example Basil exhorts Christian men and women to follow, as, in his eulogy of her, he puts into her mouth an exegesis of Genesis 21–2 which today would be considered 'feminist'; Macrina the Elder, confessor of the faith, grandmother of Basil and Gregory of Nyssa; Nonna, mother of Gregory of Nazianzus, who led her husband to the Orthodox faith; Gorgonia, his sister, described as a woman educated in the scriptures, assiduous in prayer and generous to the poor, 'instructing the women and men around her in private while refraining from speaking in church or in public'. The figure who best illustrates the position of Christian women in the Cappadocian milieu is Macrina the Younger, elder sister of Basil and Gregory of Nyssa. The brothers talk of her as their teacher, *didaskalos*. In the *Dialogue on the Soul and the Resurrection*, Gregory wrote up the conversation which he had with his sister on her deathbed, a text which has been compared to Plato's *Phaedo*. The fathers, far from regarding woman solely as sexual object, looked upon her as the opposite, the 'other', with whom they are in dialogue, their companion and sometimes their teacher in the spiritual battle. Their egalitarianism is located in the eschatological perspective of the plenitude at the end of time when sexuality, having become redundant, is surpassed or rather transcended. MONASTICISM aims to anticipate that eschatological plenitude. Within the framework this alternative society represents, the fundamental equality of women and men, expressed in the Cappadocians' anthropology, is most easily, though not exclusively, realized.

This patristic era coincided with the development of the female diaconate: a ministry orientated to the service of women, meeting specific needs within a given society, but theologically grounded and remarkably complete, with liturgical, catechetical and philanthropic aspects, and conferred by true ordination (*see* DEACON).

In the patriarchal agrarian societies of the Mediterranean and of Eastern Europe, which became Orthodoxy's homeland as a consequence of the missionary expansion of Byzantine Christianity, above all after the fall of Byzantium, the luminous anthropology of the gospels and the fathers survives in the deepest levels of ecclesial consciousness. But, like the 'treasure hidden in a field' of the parable, it is buried under a welter of archaic taboos: the idea of the periodic ritual impurity of women derived from a misogynistic reading of Leviticus, and truisms about their 'weakness' and 'inferiority'. Yet the seed of the gospel never ceased to bear fruit. The flame of female sanctity was never put out. The church canonized NEW MARTYRS: great women monastics, princesses like Olga of KIEV, venerated with her grandson Vladimir as 'equal to the apostles', and ordinary lay women like Julia Lazarevakaya in RUSSIA, at the dawn of the modern era, whose Life, edited by her own son, exalts heroic charity. Mention must also be made of the images of women believers in the Russian literature of the nineteenth century, whether simple peasants or aristocrats, virtuous women or prostitutes, the Princess Mary of *War and Peace* or the Sophia of *Crime and Punishment*; and of the influence of particular cultured Christian women, such as the wife of the slavophile philosopher Ivan Kireevskii (*see* RUSSIAN RELIGIOUS PHILOSOPHY).

If we turn to the present day, the question arises as to the place of women in an Orthodox church which has ceased to be monolithically 'Eastern' either geographically or culturally. Emigration has resulted in sizeable Orthodox communities establishing and inculturating themselves in Western Europe, AMERICA and AUSTRALIA. Western modernity is invading traditionally Orthodox countries. It may be asked how far the telescoping of different cultures has affected the status and way of life of Orthodox Christian women. The limits of space and context here allow only a few observations.

In the course of the recent and often dramatic history of the Orthodox churches, women have assumed significant responsibilities, particularly in Russia under the Soviet regime. It was women, often the famous *babushkas*, who preserved parish structures from the total destruction planned by the atheistic state. These same grandmothers would secretly have their grandchildren baptized. There were Orthodox Christian women among the dissidents. Today, in the new climate of freedom, younger women are taking over from those intrepid matrons, sometimes tending towards excessive ritualism, taking on much of the church's *diakonia* (ministry) towards the victims of chaotic social and economic change. The militancy of some brands of Western feminism, however, remains alien to them. Far from contesting the principle, inherited from monasticism, of obedience to the 'spiritual father', who is a priest or monk, many new converts fervently support it. Paradoxically, however, it is these 'submissive' women who are often the dynamic, even dominant, element in the new parishes or lay 'fraternities'.

In traditionally Orthodox countries like Greece or Romania and in the DIASPORA, Orthodox women are taking an active part in church life. Religious education and the catechesis of children and young people is almost entirely in their hands. Orthodox women theologians are beginning to teach in theological faculties and seminaries. They take part in ecumenical dialogue at the highest level, notably in the World Council of Churches (see ECUMENISM), yet within the Orthodox Church are rarely to be found in those places where decisions are taken. These contrasts provide the context within which the question of women's access to sacramental ministry is beginning to be raised in Orthodox churches, not just as an issue arising from without, but as an internal problem. During the international meetings of Orthodox women in Agapia (Romania) in 1976 and in Crete in 1984, the wish was expressed that the matter be given serious examination, in a spirit of serenity. At the Rhodes Inter-Orthodox Consultation Meeting (1988) on 'The Ordination of Women and the Place of Women in the Church', organized by the Ecumenical Patriarchate, the restoration of the female diaconate was positively envisaged and unanimously welcomed.

For reasons of liturgical symbolism the ordination of women to the priesthood is still unacceptable to most Orthodox. The question rises, however, as to whether such ordinations would actually be heretical. It is a question to which Orthodox theologians, both men and women, offer a range of different and subtly nuanced answers. None the less, ever-increasing numbers of Orthodox aspire to a fuller participation of women in all aspects of church life, in accordance with the spirit of conciliarity or *sobornost* in the image of the *koinonia* (communion, community) of the TRINITY which characterizes Orthodox ecclesiology.

Evdomikov, P. (1994), *Woman and the Salvation of the World: A Christian Anthropology on the Charisms of Women*. Crestwood, NY: St Vladimir's Seminary Press.

Harrison, V. (1992), 'Orthodox Arguments against the Ordination of Women', *Sobornost* 14/1.

Manolache, A. (1991), 'Orthodoxy and Women, a Romanian Perspective', in J. Becher, ed., *Women, Religion and Sexuality*. Geneva: World Council of Churches.

Behr-Sigel, E. (1991), 'The Ordination of Women, an Ecumenical Problem', *Sobornost* 13/2.

Gvosdev, M. E. (1991), *The Female Diaconate: An Historical Perspective*. Minneapolis: Light and Life Publishing.

Harrison, V. (1990), 'Male and Female in Cappadocian Theology', *Journal of Theological Studies* 41.

'La Consultation de Rhodes 1988' (1989), special edition of *Contacts*.

Behr-Sigel, E. (1987), *The Ministry of Women in the Church*. Oakwood, Cal.: Oakwood Publications.

Katafygiotu-Topping, E. (1987), *Holy Mothers of Orthodoxy: Women and the Church*. Minneapolis: Light and Life Publishing.

Albrecht, R. (1986), *Das Leben der heiligen Makrinna auf dem Hintergrund der Thekla-Traditionen*. Göttingen: n.p.

Hopko T., ed. (1983), *Women and the Priesthood*. Crestwood, NY: St Vladimir's Seminary Press.

'La Femme, vision orthodoxe' (1979), special edition of *Contacts*.

Tarasar, C. and Kirillova, I., eds (1977), *Orthodox Women, their Role and Participation in the Church*. Geneva: World Council of Churches.

EB-S

Xenia of St Petersburg (d. 1806)   When Kseniia Grigor'evna, aristocratic wife of a Russian colonel, was widowed at twenty-six, she disposed of her possessions, adopted her husband's name and went to live among the capital's homeless. Although she feigned madness, her self-sacrificing care for the poor and unemployed established her as a saint in her own lifetime. People travelled from afar to seek her prayers or healing. Her grave in the Smolenskoe cemetery draws pilgrims from across the world. Xenia the HOLY FOOL is commemorated on 11 September and again with Xenia-Eusebia the Roman, a nun of Mylasa (d. 450), on 24 January. With Xenia of Messenia, a third-century Greek martyr (commemorated on 3 May), they form a group especially loved by EASTERN ORTHODOX of the DIASPORA.

Blessed Xenia (1986), Jordanville, NY: St Job of Pochaev Press.

DB

xerophagy   Greek, 'dry eating'. Fasting plays a significant role in EASTERN CHRISTIAN religious discipline. In addition to observance in some measure or other of the traditional seasons of fasting (*see* CALENDAR) – Lent, the pre-Christmas fast of forty days days, the Fast of the Apostles preceding 29 June, the Fast of the THEOTOKOS from 1 to 14 August, and in some churches the Fast of Nineveh – eves of great feasts are commonly observed as days of fasting, as are Wednesday and Friday, unless they fall in Paschal week or on a great feast. It is normal to prepare for participation in the MYSTERIES or setting out on a PILGRIMAGE by fasting. In the early church a fast was commonly observed by abstaining from food until early evening, and then eating a single austere meal, often bread and water. In later periods a distinction was made of various degrees of austerity in fasting diet, the most austere involving total abstinence from food and drink, observed by many Oriental Orthodox at the three-day Fast of Nineveh. In Eastern Christian tradition, fasting diet involves abstinence from all meat and dairy products and fish, though Byzantine churches allow the eating of shellfish. Wine and olive oil are also prohibited. If a feast day falls on a fast, fish, wine and oil may be permitted. Xerophagy is a more severe fast which nowadays permits eating of dry bread and fruits or vegetables prepared raw or sometimes with water, vinegar and salt.

DM

· Y ·

Yaḥyā ibn 'Adī (893–974)   Abū Zakariyyā Yaḥyā ibn 'Adī al-Takrītī al-Manṭiqī was a JACOBITE Christian, born in the city of Takrit in Iraq. As a young man he moved to Baghdad, and studied with the NESTORIAN philosopher Abū Bishr Mattā ibn Yūnus (*c*.870–*c*.940) and the famous Muslim philosopher Abū Naṣr al-Farabi (*c*.870–950). By the mid-940s Yaḥyā had become a major figure in a new generation of philosophers in the world of Islam. While working as a professional scribe, he was also the leading exponent of Aristotelianism in Baghdad. Several of his numerous disciples, both Christian and Muslim, became eminent scholars in their own right. Yaḥyā wrote prolifically on philosophy and Christian theology and apologetics. He translated many Greek works of Aristotle and his commentators from Syriac into Arabic. His remarkable text *Tahdhīb al-aḥlāq*, a treatise on the improvement of morals, in which he teaches that virtue itself suffices to attain the happiness of which human nature is capable, has circulated for centuries in the Islamic world, taken by many as one of the earliest books on Islamic ethical philosophy.

Kraemer, J. L. (1986), *Humanism in the Renaissance of Islam: The Cultural Revival during the Buyid Age*. Leiden: Brill.
Platti, E. (1983), *Yaḥyā ibn 'Adī, théologien chrétien et philosophe arabe*. Orientalia Lovaniensia Analecta, 14. Leuven. Departement Oriëntalistiek.
Endress, G. (1977), *The Works of Yaḥyā ibn 'Adī: An Analytical Inventory*. Wiesbaden: Reichert.

SHG/MJB

Yakutia   Christianization of the native peoples of Yakutia, the Sakha (Yakuts), Evenks, Evens, and Yukaghirs, began as an integral part of tsarist policy in northeast Asia during the mid-seventeenth century soon after Yakutia was joined to RUSSIA. Conversion to EASTERN ORTHODOXY was considered an effective way of consolidating the various peoples of the Lena region politically, economically and spiritually. At first, voluntary baptism only was state policy; however, in the eighteenth century and

523

sporadically thereafter some conversions were coerced or politically induced. An effective means for this was a system of tax relief granted from time to time to the converted. Intermarriage, economic partnerships and other social and cultural interactions with the newly arrived Orthodox population contributed significantly to conversions.

The conversion process was substantially completed by the mid-nineteenth century. The consolidation of the new religion now began. Churches were built in the *ulusi* (administrative regions), and parish schools and other ecclesiastical institutions were established. Measures were taken to prepare Yakut clergy and to translate and publish the service books in the Yakut language.

The first book in the Yakut language, printed in 1812, was *Prayers, the Creed, and Commandments*; the second, printed in 1819 (2nd edn 1821), was *The Brief Catechism*; and the third, in 1844, the bilingual *Concise Catechism*. Archbishop Innokentii's efforts intensified translation and publication in the Yakut language during the 1850s. Eight books were published in the Yakut language in 1857 and 1858, including *The Holy Gospels*; *The Concise Grammar* by D. Khitrov; *Indication of the Way into the Kingdom of Heaven*, by I. Veniaminov; and *The Didactic Discourse of Revd Innokentii and Other Sermons*. On 19 July 1859, in the Yakutsk Cathedral of the Holy Trinity, the Divine Liturgy was celebrated for the first time in the Yakut language, and Yakut leaders petitioned that this date be designated as a festival in posterity.

In 1853, at the urgent request of Innokentii Veniaminov, archbishop of Kamchatka, the Kurile Islands and the Aleutian Islands, the Yakut region with a population of 280,000 was separated from the Irkutsk diocese and incorporated into the Kamchatka diocese. Yakutia had belonged to the Irkutsk diocese from 1731, earlier to the Tobolsk metropolis (Siberia). The seat of the archdiocese and the ecclesiastical seminary at Novo Arkhangel'sk (ALASKA) were now transferred to Yakutsk, where Archbishop Innokentii established his residency in the Spasskii monastery from September 1853 to 1860. From 1860 the vicar-bishops in Yakutsk were: Pavel (Popov), 1860–8; Petr (Yekaterinskii), 1861–7; and Dionysii (Dmitrii Khitrov), 1867–70.

On 29 March 1870 the independent diocese of Yakutsk and Viluisk was inaugurated, after years of effort by Innokentii Veniaminov. The Ecclesiastical Consistory and Diocesan Committee of the Orthodox Missionary Society also opened. Committee members studied the ways of life, customs and traditions in the *ulusi*, and helped establish churches, chapels and schools. The 165 churches and chapels in the region in 1865 increased to 196 by 1889, to 249 by 1895 and to 333 by 1917. Parish schools numbered 8 in 1860, 21 in 1880 and 178 in 1917.

The bishops of the diocese of Yakutsk and Viluisk were: Dionysii (Dmitrii Khitrov), 1870–84, Innokentii's recommendation; Iakov (Domskii), 1884–9; Meletii (Yakimov), 1889–96; Nikodim (Preobrazhenskii), 1896–8, Nikandor (Nadazhdin), 1898–1905; Makarii (Pustynskii), 1905–9; Innokentii (Pustynskii), 1909–12; Meletii (Zaborovskii), 1912–15; Evfimii (Lagin), from 1915 and after 1917.

The Soviet period undermined the position of the Orthodox church in Yakutia; even the religious outlook was condemned as atheist propaganda took over. The diocese and its churches, chapels, schools and monasteries were closed down. The Yakutsk Regional Committee of the Communist Party of the Soviet Union in 1970 recorded about 200 believers in the Yakut Autonomous Soviet Socialist Republic. In 1976 thirteen churches and chapels were listed as historical and cultural monuments of the Yakut ASSR to be protected by the state. Several were put to use for civic purposes: the Cathedral of the Holy Trinity, Yakutsk, became the quarters of the state theatre, then of the state philharmonic society with a café; the main Church of St Nicholas became the distribution centre for the state library; the Bishop's Palace became the Em. Yaroslavskii State Museum. By 1993 only one church and one chapel were functioning in Yakutia: in Yakutsk, the little wooden Church of St Nicholas, and in Nerungri, the Chapel of the Kazan Icon of the Mother of God.

On 23 February 1993 an independent diocese was recreated for the Republic of Sakha (Yakutia) by decision of Alexei II, patriarch of Moscow and All Russia, and the Holy Synod. Archimandrite German Moralin, appointed bishop of Yakutsk and Viluisk, arrived there on 10 April 1993 to take up a permanent ministry. Patriarch Alexei also visited, by invitation of the Republic's President M. E. Nikolaev. Churches and chapels are currently being rededicated or rebuilt, and religious education is being reintroduced throughout the republic for natives and settlers alike: for instance, in Aldan, Cherski, Chulman, Lensk, Mirny, Nerungri, Udachny and Zyrianka, as well as Yakutsk. The publication of the *Yakut Diocese News* has been recommenced.

The work of the diocese builds on the efforts of the outstanding missionaries and fellow workers still remembered today: Bishop Dionisii Khitrov, first Yakut bishop and compiler of the Yakut grammar; Archpriest Grigorii Sleptsov, itinerant preacher; Dmitrii Popov, churchman and compiler of the *Dictionary of the Yakut Language*; and many others, including Innokentii Veniaminov himself.

See also SIBERIA.

Shishigin, E. S. (1991), *Rasprostranenie Khristianstva v Iakutii*. Yakutsk: Yakut State Museum of the Histories and Cultures of the Peoples of Siberia.

ES

·Z·

Zara Yakub Zar'a Yā'qob, Zera Yaiqob (b. 1399); emperor of Ethiopia 1434–68. His reign was marked by major religious controversies introduced by dissident monastic movements led by followers of Abba Estifanos, Abba EWOSṬATEWOS, Abba Zamika'el and others, which had grown steadily before the emperor's reign. Zar'a Yā'qob did much to quell the controversies and to unify and reform the Ethiopian church. In 1450 he presided over the Council of DABRA METMAQ, which successfully reconciled the Ewosṭateans with the Ethiopian church. The unification and preservation of the Ethiopian church was a major theme in the large collection of GE'EZ religious literature written or commissioned by Zar'a Yā'qob, such as the *Maṣḥafa Berhan* (Book of Light), which includes among its wide range of topics a defence of the Trinity and a condemnation of divination and magical practice; the *Maṣḥafa Milād* (Book of the Nativity), which contains an attack on the *ayhud* or Jews for their denial of the Incarnation; and a series of works in honour of the Mother of God. Zar'a Yā'qob also took the initiative in representing the Ethiopian church outside Ethiopia. He sent delegates to the Council of FLORENCE (1431–45). In 1443 he sent a delegation to Cairo to protest against Muslim persecution of Christians in Egypt.

See also ETHIOPIAN ORTHODOX CHURCH.

Haile, G. (1992), *The Mariology of Emperor Zara Ya'eqob of Ethiopia: Texts and Translations*. Orientalia Christiana Analecta 242. Rome: Pontifical Institute of Oriental Studies.
Haile, G. (1981), 'Religious Controversies and the Growth of Ethiopic Literature in the Fourteenth and Fifteenth Centuries', *Oriens Christianus* 65, pp. 102–36.
Tamrat, T. (1972), *Church and State in Ethiopia, 1270–1527*. Oxford Studies in African Affairs. Oxford: Clarendon Press.

MJB/SHG

zealots Zealots, fervently traditionalist EASTERN ORTHODOX who see MONASTICISM and ASCETICISM at the heart of church life, exist in both Old and New Calendar

527

jurisdictions (*see* OLD CALENDARISTS). No single organization expresses this anarchic movement in its entirety. In secular politics zealots have taken up widely divergent positions, some staunchly monarchist, others allied with radical groupings to oppose any state attempts to attain a stranglehold over church life. Pilgrimage to the Phyli monastery of SS Cyprian and Justina provides a meeting place for zealots and zealot sympathizers.

On Mount ATHOS zealots are characterized by opposition to ECUMENISM. Esphigmenou monastery is a centre for the most committed zealotism, taking no part in the general life of ATHOS; the meetings of the Epistasia of the Holy Mountain usually record 'Esphigmenou, absent, for the usual reasons'. Zealots are well represented among small kellia and hermitages of the 'desert' at the southern tip of the peninsula. Athonite zealots are frequently on bad terms with their bishop, the ECUMENICAL PATRIARCH.

DB

Žiča The monastery of the Saviour at Žiča, near Kraljevo in SERBIA, is the foundation of Stefan the First Crowned (1196–1228), son of Nemanja and elder brother of SAVA. Stefan was crowned there in 1217. In 1219, returning from Nicea where he was consecrated first archbishop of the Serbian autocephalous church, Sava chose Žiča as the seat of the archbishopric (moved to PEĆ in the late thirteenth century following attacks by Cumans). Sava, like Stefan, took a personal interest in the building and decorating of Žiča's katholikon, a spacious single-naved and single-domed building with a low transept, a narthex flanked by two side-chapels surmounted by small domes, and an exonarthex and tower at its west end. Only a fine Crucifixion and some individual figures of apostles remain of the original wall paintings, but the church was renovated in the fourteenth century. Among the better-preserved frescoes from that period which follow the previous choice of themes are a DORMITION in the nave and scenes from the life of Stephen the protomartyr in the south side-chapel. Of particular interest is the programme of frescoes dating from 1309–16 in the vestibule under the tower, including royal portraits, an unusual illustration of the Christmas stichera, the Forty Martyrs on the frozen lake of Sebaste, monumental figures of Peter and Paul and two large panels with the text of the royal charter. Žiča's most venerated relic, the right arm of John the Baptist in a silver mount with an inscription mentioning Sava, is now in the treasury of Sienna Cathedral. Because of its exposed position, Žiča suffered numerous devastations, including major damage from bombing in the Second World War. Restoration works were carried out in 1855, in 1925–35 and in 1953–76.

Živković, B. (1985), *Žiča. Les dessins des fresques*. Belgrade: Republički Zavod za Zaštitu Spomenika Kulture.
Gavrilović, Z. (1982), 'The Forty Martyrs of Sebaste in the Painted Programme of Žiča Vestibule: Further Research into the Artistic Interpretations of the Divine Wisdom-Baptism-Kingship Ideology', *Jahrbuch der Österreichischen Byzantinistik* 32/5: *XVI Internationaler Byzantinistenkongress, Akten II/5*, pp. 185–93.
Subotić, G. (1978). *Žiča*. Belgrade: Turistička Štampa.

ZG

Zichia Regions in the northern Caucasus, roughly corresponding to Circassia and Adyge, evangelized from Byzantium from the tenth century. The church of Zichia was also linked to the Orthodox churches of GEORGIA and ALANIA. Zichia came under Islamic influence during the period of Tatar domination. The Abazas initially vacillated between Christianity and Islam; the Janey group embraced Islam in the 1560s, other tribes reverting to animism. After the sixteenth century the Circassians were almost entirely Muslim.

Dunlop, J. (1998), *Russia Confronts Chechnya*. Cambridge: Cambridge University Press.
Chenciner, R. (1997), *Daghestan*. Richmond, Surrey: Curzon Press.
Gall, C. (1997), *Chechnya*. London: Pan.
Avtorkhanov, A. (1992), *The North Caucasus Barrier*. London: Hurst.

DB

Žitomislić Monastery on the river Neretva between Mostar and Medjugorje in Herzegovina, built 1566–1602/3 on the site of an earlier Orthodox church by Milisav Hrabren-Miloradović, descendant of the regional *voivods* whose lands are listed in fifteenth-century Turkish documents. The family's cemetery at nearby Radimlja contains the best examples of fourteenth- and fifteenth-century *stecak* type tombs. Although a Christian, Milisav held the OTTOMAN military title of *sipahi*. Dedicated to the ANNUNCIATION, the church was a simple stone building with an apse, a narthex and a later bell-tower. It had wall paintings dated to 1609, but since the nineteenth century only the Annunciation in the lunette above the entrance survived. In the nave, capitals with reliefs combining Christian and Islamic motifs and including unusual scenes of animal hunting, as on *stecak* tombs, were the work of the stonemason Vukašin (inscription dated 1602–3). Of particular interest is a seventeenth-century wood-carved gilt templon surmounted by a large crucifix. The DEESIS of the templon beam, harmoniously composed of a central panel and eight *dypticha*, includes the icons of Symeon Nemanja and SAVA of Serbia. Dating from around 1618–19, the templon icons are attributed to the painter Georgije Mitrofanović, while the Annunciation on the intricately carved ICONOSTASIS door was painted by Radul in 1676. The fine wood-carved main entrance door was made in the eighteenth century. The monastic scriptorium was active until the beginning of the eighteenth century. An illuminated liturgical book written in Serbian Church Slavonic at Žitomislić in 1706 is preserved at the British Library (Add. MS 16373). The first Orthodox theological school in Herzegovina was opened at the monastery in 1858. Žitomislić possessed an important library and treasury housing fine examples of regional goldsmiths' work and gifts received from Russia where a part of the Hrabren-Miloradović family had emigrated in the seventeenth century. In 1941 the entire community of monks were killed by the Croat Ustase; the monastery's living quarters and museum were burnt down. Restoration works started in the 1960s. In June 1992 the church was completely destroyed when Croat forces took the village. Parts of the templon, however, were taken to safety and the nuns escaped to the monastery of Dokmir in Serbia.

Petković, S. (1984), 'Rukopis Manastira Žitomislića iz Britanske Biblioteke u Londonu', *Naše Starine* 16–17.
Kojić, Lj. (1983), *Manastir Žitomislić*. Sarajevo: Veselin Masleša.

LJK

Zlata of Moglena (d. 1795)   Known to Greeks as 'Chryse the Bulgarian'; a devout Christian young woman, seized by a group of Muslims who pressed her to embrace Islam and marry one of them. Zlata refused, even under torture, despite her family's pleas that she compromise to save her life. Her martyrdom near Aridaia in MACEDO-NIA is commemorated on 13 October.

Nicolas Velimirovic (1986), *The Prologue from Ochrid*, vol. 4. Birmingham: Lazarica Press.

DB

Zographou martyrs   Troops sent by Michael VIII Palaiologos (1260–81) to eliminate opposition on ATHOS to union with ROME incarcerated Abbot Thomas and twenty-five monks and laymen in a tower of the Zographou monastery and burnt them to death in 1282. Commemorated on 10 October these martyrs are particularly revered in Bulgaria, Zographou being a Bulgarian monastery, but also in Greece where girls are named Zographia in their honour. Monks of Karyes, the Athonite capital, martyred in the same period, are commemorated on 5 December.

See also NEW MARTYRS.

DB

Zoodochos   Greek, 'life-receiving': an attribute of the tomb of Christ, the Zoodochos Taphos, which received Life itself, Christ. The tomb of Christ is the great symbol of his Resurrection and it is in this sense that the word is also used of the Zoodochos Pege shrine and monastery outside Constantinople. This title is also given to the THEOTO-KOS, particularly with reference to the Zoodochos Pege. Miracles at the shrine are associated with several feasts, notably that celebrated on the Friday of Renewal Week. This shrine also figures in Greek folklore. Known as Balıklı, it survives as a pilgrimage centre and is the burial place of the more recent Ecumenical Patriarchs.

   The title applies to the Theotokos first because she receives Life himself into her womb, and second because, by tradition, she receives into her arms the body of the Crucified who is Life, when he is taken down from the Cross. In her DORMITION, as the Mother of Life, she passes over into life.

DB/DM/E

Zuart'noc'   The seventh-century rotunda church of the guardian angels near Ejmia-cin is one of the great achievements of early medieval Armenian architecture. Built 643–52 by Catholicos Nerses III, the Builder, a Byzantine sympathizer, it was in ruins by the tenth century, probably because of an earthquake, but its fame inspired later developments in Armenian church building. Its influence is seen in the eleventh-century church of St Gregory at ANI. It was constructed in three tiers to a height of 45 metres and was 33.75 metres in diameter, with richly ornamented capitals and reliefs, including depictions of the masons working on it, with an inscription in Greek. According to one Armenian chronicler, Emperor Constans II attended the cathedral's consecration in 652.

der Nersessian, S. (1978), *Armenian Art*. London: Thames & Hudson.

KP

◆ Index ◆

531

◆ Index ◆

◆ Index ◆

♦ Index ♦

◆ Index ◆

◆ Index ◆

◆ Index ◆

557